Publication Number 29

Duke University Commonwealth-Studies Center

Canada and "Imperial Defense"

Duke University Commonwealth-Studies Center Publications

1. *The British Commonwealth,* by Frank H. Underhill   2. *South Africa,* by Hector Menteith Robertson   3. *Some Comparative Aspects of Irish Law,* by Alfred Gaston Donaldson   4. *Economic Analysis and Policy in Underdeveloped Countries,* by P. T. Bauer   5. *The Higher Public Service of the Commonwealth of Australia,* by Howard A. Scarrow   6. *Economic Opinion and Policy in Ceylon,* by Henry M. Oliver, Jr.   7. *Problems of the New Commonwealth,* by Sir Ivor Jennings   8. *Commonwealth Perspectives,* by Nicholas Mansergh *et al.*   9. *Evolving Canadian Federalism,* by A. R. M. Lower, F. R. Scott *et al.*   10. *The Commonwealth Economy in Southeast Asia,* by T. H. Silcock   11. *Public Expenditures in Australia,* by B. U. Ratchford   12. *The American Economic Impact on Canada,* by Hugh G. J. Aitken, John J. Deutsch, W. A. Mackintosh *et al.*   13. *Tradition, Values, and Socio-Economic Development,* edited by Ralph Braibanti and Joseph J. Spengler   14. *The Growth of Canadian Policies in External Affairs,* by Hugh L. Keenleyside *et al.*   15. *Canadian Economic Thought,* by Craufurd D. W. Goodwin   16. *Economic Systems of the Commonwealth,* edited by Calvin B. Hoover   17. *The Nigerian Political Scene,* edited by Robert O. Tilman and Taylor Cole   18. *Administration and Economic Development in India,* edited by Ralph Braibanti and Joseph J. Spengler   19. *Canada–United States Treaty Relations,* edited by David R. Deener   20. *Post-primary Education and Political and Economic Development,* edited by Don C. Piper and Taylor Cole   21. *Bureaucratic Transition in Malaya,* by Robert O. Tilman   22. *The West African Commonwealth,* by C. W. Newbury   23. *The Transfer of Institutions,* edited by William B. Hamilton   24. *Economic Enquiry in Australia,* by Craufurd D. W. Goodwin   25. *A Decade of the Commonwealth, 1955–1964,* edited by W. B. Hamilton, Kenneth Robinson, and C. D. W. Goodwin   26. *Research on the Bureaucracy of Pakistan,*° by Ralph Braibanti   27. *The International Law Standard and Commonwealth Developments,* by Robert R. Wilson *et al.*   28. *Asian Bureaucratic Systems Emergent from the British Imperial Tradition,* by Ralph Braibanti and associates

° Program in Comparative Studies on Southern Asia publication.

Canada and "Imperial Defense"

*A study of the origins of
the British Commonwealth's defense
organization, 1867–1919*

Richard A. Preston

Published for the
Duke University Commonwealth-Studies Center
Duke University Press, Durham, N.C.
1967

Printed in the United States of America
by Kingsport Press, Inc., Kingsport, Tenn.

To Marjorie whose contribution
is greater than she realizes.

Preface

This book developed from an investigation into officer education in Canada and Britain which showed the importance of a common system of organization and training, rather than of political agreements, in the great achievement of effective co-operation between British Empire and Commonwealth armies and navies in the two world wars of this century. That study also suggested that the British Commonwealth military system was not a vestige of the earlier system of Empire defense but was created as a result of *ad hoc* decisions which resulted from the natural aspirations and needs of colonial peoples.

Subsequent search for the origins of Commonwealth defense co-operation led to the conclusion that in the past too much attention has been given to imperial defense planning and too little to military and naval developments in the colonies themselves. The lack of adequate studies of colonial military and naval history based on original research made it necessary to resort to defense files in dominion military archives which (although more work has been done from them in Canada than elsewhere) have in many cases not previously been used. Much work on defense history remains to be done in all the dominions; and definitive conclusions about the origins of Commonwealth defense co-operation must therefore await the appearance of many monographs. But extensive research has suggested the need for a reinterpretation of the history of what has been called "imperial defense."

Tentatively, this reinterpretation is to the effect that in view of the nature of the British Empire at the end of the century, imperial defense was unsound and inadequate for military as well as political reasons. Colonial rejection of imperial defense was not a mere result of local political opposition but came because history, geography, and constitutional development made voluntary military and naval co-operation more effective.

This book was made possible only by the generosity of several foundations and institutions: e.g., the Nuffield Foundation, the Duke University Commonwealth-Studies Center, the United States Social Science Research Council, and, last but not least, the Canada Council, each of which made travel grants. The Royal Military College of Canada gave me a sabbatical in which to visit the dominions and to write. The Warden and Fellows of Nuffield College kindly provided a room in which to work, and with it their good fellowship. The Oxford University Institute of Commonwealth Studies received me warmly into its community for discussions.

Like all other historians I owe tribute to the unflagging zeal of library staffs. In first place I wish to mention my friends Mr. John Spurr and Mr. Cliff Watt of the Royal Military College of Canada's Massey Library and Mr. H. P. Gundy of Queens University's Douglas Library. I am, however, also indebted to the staffs of many other libraries: of Duke University, of the War Office (especially Mr. David King), of the Admiralty, of the Royal United Service Institution, of the Commonwealth Relations and Colonial Offices, of the Johannesburg Public Library, of the Transvaal State Library in Pretoria, of the State Library of Victoria in Melbourne, of Melbourne University Library, of the Auckland Institute, of the Australian War Memorial, the National Library of Australia (especially Mr. H. L. White), the Turnbull Library, Wellington, the New Zealand General Assembly Library, the Nuffield College Library, Rhodes House Library, and the Bodley Library.

My thanks are also due to the staffs of many archives: the Public Archives of Canada (especially Dr. K. Lamb, Mr. W. G. Ormsby, and Miss Barbara Wilson), the Public Record Office, the Australian Commonwealth Archives Office (Mr. J. J. Maclean and Mr. Gilbey), the New Zealand Archives (especially Miss Judith S. Hornabrook), the Defense Department Library in Canberra, the Australian War Memorial (Mr. J. J. McGrath and Mr. K. R. Lancaster), and the Royal Australian Navy Archives Branch, Melbourne (Mr. Minnear, Registrar). By gracious permission of Her Majesty the Queen, I was allowed to use papers in the Royal Archives at Windsor Castle.

Many people interested in Empire, Commonwealth, and dominions' defense history have discussed this book with me, but special mention must be made of the following: my former colleague and friend at the Royal Military College of Canada, Dr. D. M. Schurman, whose insistence upon the effects of pernicious departmentalism in British defense planning did much to guide my early steps; Professor Norman Gibbs and Mr. John Ehrman who advised me at an early stage in the search for material; Professor Fred Gibson of Queens University who shared with me his conclusions about the Canadian naval problem; Leon Atkinson, then at the Australian National University, who helped me locate material in the Australian Archives; Professor J. A. La Nauze, who discussed his work on Deakin and showed me parts of his manuscript; Sir Frederick Shedden, former secretary of defense, who explained much about Australian defense history, on which he is now writing; Mr. Sam Landau, the secretary of the Australian Defense Department, who gave me access to papers in the department library; Mr. Robert Hyslop and Mr. Peter Heyden of Canberra who told me about biographical work on which they were engaged; the late Honorable J. J. Hurley, Canadian ambassador in South Africa, the Honorable Evan Gill, high commissioner in Canberra, the Honorable Kenneth Burbridge, high commissioner in Wellington, and Miss Vivienne Allen, first secretary, who unlocked many doors; Major Heinrich Du Toit, chief of the Historical Section of the General Staff of the South African Army, who was a most courteous guide to archives; Mr. Ian Hancox and Miss Meredith Rooney of Nuffield College who discussed my ideas in common coffee room breaks; and the members of the Oxford Seminar on Commonwealth History led by Professor Jack Gallagher, Dr. F. Madden, Dr. David Fieldhouse, and others, who received a paper presenting my views and were charitable in their comments.

My special thanks are also due to Colonel Charles P. Stacey of the Canadian Army Historical Section for many years of encouragement and for reading an early draft of the whole manuscript; to two good friends made as a result of the inquiry, namely, Major Warren Perry of Melbourne and Mr. Ian Wards of the Historical Publications Branch, New Zealand Department of Internal Affairs; to an old friend, Dr. "Mac" Hitsman of the Canadian Army Historical Section, and to Mr. Brian Tunstall of the London School of Economics, all of whom read all the manuscript; to Gerald S. Graham, the Rhodes Professor of Imperial History at London University, who read the chapter on naval imperialism; and to the dean of all military historians, Sir Basil Liddell Hart, who read the last chapter. Each of these people pointed out errors, made helpful suggestions, and generously shared his great knowledge of the subject. Needless to say, I accept sole responsibility for the finished product.

Finally, I must record my debt to the Duke University Commonwealth-Studies Center for sponsoring the publication of this volume and especially to Professor Alan Manchester for his encouragement and his patience during a long period of gestation.

RICHARD A. PRESTON

Durham, North Carolina
December 25, 1965

Contents

Introduction

The importance of Canada's influence upon the development of the British Empire and Commonwealth has been generally recognized. Canada played a greater part than any other dependency if only because more than a generation before other colonies attained a similar stature, the Dominion was organized as a federal nation equal in potential strength to some contemporary states and with a large degree of autonomy. Canadian concern with, and interest in, the evolution of the Empire's defense planning has, however, been overshadowed by that of the Australasian colonies because these made direct contributions to imperial naval defense. Refusal to follow a similar policy has led to a commonly accepted assumption that Canada's influence in the defense field was largely destructive and negative.

Because of her vulnerable position in relation to a potentially great land power, Canada's defense problem was, of course, very different from that of any other portion of the British Empire. Every other part could be defended by Britain against a major attack by the direct use of sea power. Canada could not. Canada's peculiar strategic problem thus set her apart and suggested that although her influence might be great, it was inevitably at the opposite pole from that of the other colonies and must be antagonistic to the development of an effective system of imperial security.

Certain other circumstances have been used to explain this traditional Canadian reaction of indifference or hostility to British defense proposals. These were the great influence of a minority ethnic group, the reluctance of voters (who had turned their backs on European militarism) to pay for expenditures they thought unnecessary, and the failure of politicians to instruct voters in the realities of the international scene lest they lose elections. The considerable attention given by historians to these not unimportant aspects of the Canadian scene has served to make more difficult a correct estimate of the effect of Canada's influence upon the defensive system of the British Empire and Commonwealth which, before the significance of other factors can be assessed, must be based on a study of British defense policy and a comparison of Canadian policy with the policies of other dominions.

The evolution of the British Empire's defensive organization during the last quarter of the nineteenth and the first decade of the twentieth centuries was the result of an attempt to prepare the Empire to face increasing external dangers. Those who pointed to the need to foster preparedness usually called the remedy which they prescribed "imperial defense." Although "imperial defense" was sometimes used loosely and generally, it normally meant something more precise and positive than merely "the defense of the Empire." "Imperial defense" began with the strategic withdrawal of land forces from scattered colonial garrisons in 1870–1871 and their concentration in the United Kingdom and in a few imperial bases. It signified principally a proposed development and deployment of naval strength to make the fullest use of sea power, a quest for more effective command and control and co-ordinated planning, and the support of self-governing colonies for British efforts to make the Empire secure.

It was a basic assumption in the arguments in favor of imperial defense that the colonies had the same overriding degree of interest in the continued existence of the Empire as Britain had herself. But in contemporary literature, and also in later accounts of the history of imperial defense, the future dominions, and particularly Canada, are usually seen conforming reluctantly and irregularly to the imperial defense program. Colonial leaders have therefore been criticized, implicitly or explicitly, for their slowness to recognize an obligation to contribute to the general security. Colonies excused this reluctance by saying that public works were far more onerous and expensive in a new country than in an old one and were a long-term contribution to colonial, and therefore to imperial, strength. Furthermore, some colonial leaders alleged they feared that imperial defense arrangements might permanently jeopardize hard-won colonial autonomy. Others, who were prepared to participate in the imperial defense program, would do so only with the expectation that it would bring a voice in British foreign policy. One source of difficulty was that the details of British intentions were never fully spelled out, especially in the political sphere, and British strategic ideas tended to alter radically from time to time. Hence, it was not until war came that dominion governments at last realized their duty and supplied men and money on an adequate scale for the defense of the Empire.

Victory in World War I resulted in part from the successful preparatory work of imperial defense strategists and administrators, and particularly that of Sir Maurice (later Lord) Hankey, the able secretary of the Committee of Imperial Defence. It is usually taken for granted, therefore, that although organization for the defense of the Empire had had to be modified by British statesmen like Arthur Balfour and Lord Haldane, and by soldiers like General Sir William Nicholson, one-time chief of the Imperial General Staff, to make it acceptable to colonial idiosyncracies, the system that existed in 1914 was nevertheless a system of "imperial defense." The phrase was so deeply imbedded in British military language that it continued to be used long after World War I to describe the defense organization of the British Commonwealth, an entirely different kind of political structure from the Second British Empire.[1]

Soldiers often wrote as if imperial defense in the sense of a particular policy was a fact rather than an aspiration, a reality rather than a hope, and historians have followed them in this belief. Furthermore, some historians continue to make understanding difficult by talking of "imperial defense" without explaining whether they mean the defense of the Empire or that particular system of defense which imperial defense advocates peddled so

---

1. E.g., in General K. Stuart, "Canada and Imperial Defence," *Canadian Defence Quarterly*, XII (1934–1935), 40–46, 183–188.

energetically and so long. It is, however, very questionable whether a system of imperial defense in the narrow sense of the word ever existed at any time. Full co-ordination of land and sea planning, a principal aim of the imperial defense strategists, had not been achieved in Britain when the war began in 1914; [2] and it will be shown in this book that the dominions had firmly rejected a centrally controlled peacetime defense organization. A spate of imperial defense propaganda hid the fact that imperial defense had not passed from planning to achievement, especially insofar as it concerned the dominions, and that what had actually been produced (a system of co-operation with voluntary commitment to a central command only when war was imminent) was something very different from the blueprints of the imperial defense school. Although the word "Commonwealth" was not yet in vogue, the military organization of the Empire in 1914 was already based on a Commonwealth system of co-operation.[3] To call this "imperial defense" makes discussion about its origins meaningless.

Although a system based on the principles of imperial defense might possibly have been more successful in forestalling war in the 1930's, it is hard to believe that dominion refusal to accept imperial defense before 1914 brought on, or made inevitable, the earlier conflict. Furthermore, the Commonwealth showed itself in the first half of the twentieth century to be a remarkably effective and successful military organization in time of war. In both major wars the dominions, on a basis of co-operation that was voluntary even though under a central command, made important contributions to victory, perhaps even decisive ones. For instance, the Canadian and Anzac Corps on the Western Front played a leading role at the crucial time when the Allies passed over to the offensive in 1918. Then in 1940, when Britain stood alone against Hitler, her only allies were her dominions. Modern wars are won by nations rather than by armies alone. Imperial sentiment had been a useful rallying cry that brought some

2. John P. Mackintosh, "The Role of the Committee of Imperial Defence before 1914," *English Historical Review*, LXXVII (July, 1962), 490–503.
   3. Richard A. Preston, "The Military Structure of the Old Commonwealth," *International Journal*, XVII (Spring, 1962), 98–121.

colonials to aid the mother country, but national sentiment in the dominions was in the long run the more potent and the more lasting force. It affected even dyed-in-the-wool colonial imperialists when, under stress of adversity, imperial ties wore thin and dominion criticism of British policy had to be voiced. The "ifs" of history are always an unsatisfactory basis for argument, yet it is tempting to suggest that if the imperial defense planners had had their way, and if dominion contributions had been automatic, obligatory, or subject to a British direction that could not be questioned or criticized, the resulting dominion efforts would have been smaller and the two wars might have taken very different turns.

Much of the confusion about the condition, nature, and terminology of Britain's defense organization in the years before, and even after, World War I derives from Hankey's lectures and publications in which he, not surprisingly, showed his tremendous achievements in their most favorable light.[4] Historians of imperial defense have invariably tended to follow him and to assume that institutions that were called "imperial" in the sense of being concerned with Britain's imperial interests were also imperial in the sense of involving the participation of the self-governing colonies, even when in fact they were merely British institutions given an imperial label. Misinterpretation has also stemmed from the fact that the history of imperial defense has inevitably been written from the vantage point of the center of the imperial defense organization, looking outward, rather than from the outer circle of dominions, looking inward. It could hardly have been written otherwise without loss of coherence, but the result has been a bias toward an imperialist point of view and an assumption that, as a result of the urging of the publicists and by the strenuous efforts of soldiers and statesmen, an effective, although still too weak, imperial defense organization had actually been created.

Another cause of prejudgment is that historians of imperial

4. E.g., Maurice P. A. Hankey, *Government Control in War: Lee Knowles Lecture* (Cambridge: Cambridge University Press, 1945); Hankey, "Origin and Development of the Committee of Imperial Defence," *Army Quarterly,* XIV (1927), 254–273.

defense have mainly used British sources, particularly those files of the Cabinet, the Colonial Office, the Admiralty, and the War Office now preserved in the Public Record Office. These records in London, and especially those of the first two groups, are not only more complete than any that are extant in the dominions, but they are also much better organized and today more easily accessible than the records of some dominions. Although British sources do not exclude colonial opinions and policies, they have a natural tendency to be unsympathetic toward them. Furthermore, colonial authorities sometimes omitted from dispatches and from published memoranda those more extreme statements that showed the extent of their dislike for imperial measures or policies. Some printed papers on defense relations were not bound with volumes of published parliamentary papers and are now little known. Significantly, they may be found in defense department archives in some colonies.

Many writers on imperial defense have thus tended to use evidence which presented British aims favorably. They have been inclined to believe that the contemporary danger to the Empire was invariably as great as British leaders said it was; they have assumed that colonial preparation was as essential as imperialists asserted; they have concluded that unification of command was as imperative as was claimed; and they have accepted uncritically the thesis that colonial neglect endangered the Empire. Greater use of dominion sources, and an attempt to look at the problem through dominion eyes, is necessary to give a more balanced picture.

The successful British Commonwealth co-operative military system had roots deep in the past. The First British Empire had faced problems similar to those of the Second and had produced precedents that affected later development. A study of the origins of the system must therefore go back to the beginnings of British colonization. But responsible government and the creation of the first dominion by the confederation of the British North American provinces was what made the Commonwealth military system possible. These great political events must therefore be the real starting point for an account of its evolution.

The Commonwealth military system can be understood only by examining British policy in relation to military developments in the various British dependencies. But the preliminary studies of dominion military and defense history upon which such a study can be based do not yet exist. Canada has fared better in this respect than other dominions. Yet, when this investigation began, the only available Canadian military history based on documentary sources that went deeply into the subject was Charles P. Stacey's *Canada and the British Army, 1846–1871: A Study in the Practice of Responsible Government,*[5] which ends before imperial defense planning started. J. Eayrs's *In Defence of Canada: From the Great War to the Great Depression,*[6] which appeared while this book was in progress, begins at the time when the imperial defense concept was dying. Norman Penlington's *Canada and Imperialism, 1896–1899* [7] deals with a very short but crucial period; however, the book was published too late for use here except for minor additions to the manuscript.[8] Apart from these monographs the student of the development of Canadian defense can turn only to general accounts not based on deep research; and the position is even less satisfactory in the case of the other dominions. For this reason it has been found necessary in preparing this study to go to primary sources for information about dominion military history. This whole area is one in which much work remains to be done.

The influence of the Indian Army and its problems upon the development of the British Army and defense system, which was probably profound, has also not yet been adequately investigated; but it is safe to assume that since India was as yet a long

5. London: Longmans, Green, 1936; rev. ed., Toronto: University of Toronto Press, 1963.
6. Toronto: University of Toronto Press, 1964.
7. Toronto: University of Toronto Press, 1965.
8. After the manuscript was complete except for the Introduction and some editorial revision, three important manuscripts on related subjects which had been produced contemporaneously were seen by the courtesy of their authors. They are J. Mackay Hitsman, "The Defence of Canada: To the Withdrawal of the Garrison"; Desmond Morton, "The Canadian Militia, 1867–1900: A Political and Social Institution"; and C. S. Mackinnon, "The Imperial Fortresses in Canada: Halifax and Esquimalt, 1871–1906" (2 vols.; unpublished Ph.D. dissertation, University of Toronto, 1965). The publication of these excellent works will fill a great void in Canadian military history.

way from responsible government, it contributed little if anything to the development of the British Commonwealth co-
operative defense system. The Bantu and South African wars
prevented the development in the South African colonies of that
degree of independence upon which the normal dominion peacetime military relationship could be based. Therefore, South Africa
also added little to the Commonwealth system except by providing an arena in which one of the first examples of dominion
support for an imperial military effort could take place. This
study is thus restricted to the influence of development of the
defense system in Canada, Australia, and, to a lesser extent, New
Zealand.

The early history of Canadian defense policy shows the development of the Dominion's determination to be master in its
own military house. Although the Canadian Militia was for a
long time of doubtful military value, its creation established an
interest, a tradition, and a certain degree of expertise among a
small group of enthusiastic part-time soldiers that was to serve
as a useful foundation for wartime expansion. The relation of
this development to the imperial military system depended on
many technical and personal problems. The study of command
systems, of training techniques, and of personalities is therefore
necessary in order to understand the evolution of the Commonwealth system. These things must be set beside the better-known
Australasian and Canadian naval developments and disputes
which must, however, be re-examined, not merely to give a
balanced picture of the whole problem, but also to show that
they too were affected by the same force that fashioned Canadian
militia policy—a desire to retain colonial control and to co-
operate with Britain rather than to enter into a tight imperial
defense organization.

The question of retention of dominion control was deeply
intermingled with the problem of the political developments of
the Empire as a whole. Imperial federation, though never a
practical possibility in the foreseeable future, seemed the ultimate objective for all imperial defense planning. To offset the
fact that it was not immediately attainable, proposals for im-

perial defense federation on a non-political level were advanced. Failure to appreciate the fact that such proposals were always alternatives for political co-operation that must inevitably follow has been responsible for much misunderstanding about the imperial defense story and about the origins of the Commonwealth defense system.

Finally, a study of the origins of the Commonwealth system, or of "imperial defense," must not stop short in 1914. This is not merely because the dominions matured in war to become military powers in their own right. What is more important for this study is that from the outset of the war the relations of dominion forces with British forces were on a Commonwealth basis of co-operation rather than as part of a system of imperial defense. Imperial defense had been rejected as a result of Canada's reaction, which had eventually, despite their different circumstances, been followed by the other dominions. It follows, therefore, that the Commonwealth military system of defense co-operation was a dominion, rather than a British, invention. Like the Commonwealth as a whole, it was fashioned by the people of the dominions, especially by Canadians.

Canada and "Imperial Defense"

Colonial Defense

The military relationships within the Commonwealth, although different in kind from the military relationships within the earlier British Empire before the development of responsible colonial government, grew out of past experience. With representative institutions established almost everywhere in the colonies of the old Empire, organization for defense posed many problems that had much in common with those of later days and set precedents and attitudes that were to affect the development of the military structure of the British Commonwealth. The history of attempts to share the defense burden in the old Empire and, later in the nineteenth century, to fashion an imperial strategy is therefore important for a study of British Commonwealth defense relations, not only by way of contrast, but also because it throws light on their early origins.

The Old Colonial System

The safety of the First British Empire, scattered as it was over the seas, depended primarily on sea power; and the cost of the Royal Navy, and of naval expeditions, fell on Britain. Though the colonies were not expected to assist in bearing the chief continuing burden and the overhead expenses of naval defense, they did provide irregular aid during time of war in the form of privateers operating with letters of marque issued by colonial governors, and their experienced seamen served, though not always voluntarily, in the fleet.[1] Furthermore, at times the colonies

1. Dora Mae Clark, "The Impressment of Seamen in the American Colonies," *Essays in Colonial History Presented to Charles McLean Andrews by His Students* (New Haven: Yale University Press, 1931), pp. 198–224.

provided the greater part of the land forces for particular naval enterprises like the reconquest of the Leeward Islands in 1666 by Barbados and Massachusetts, and the capture of Louisbourg by New Englanders in 1745.

In the early years of the First Empire, England's expenses for naval defense were not especially heavy. By the eighteenth century, however, improvements in naval architecture and navigation, and in the methods of preserving food and protecting health, had greatly increased the effectiveness of naval operations generally, had made French attacks upon the colonies and raids on ports and commerce more possible, and had, therefore, made naval defense more costly. By that time it had become the practice to retain single warships in particular colonial ports to supplement the protection provided by the navy on the high seas. Known as "stationed" vessels, such ships were normally provided and maintained by the Admiralty in the West Indies and Nova Scotia; but sloops and schooners used for this same purpose in the other mainland colonies were often provided and maintained by the colonial assemblies. A squadron of the Royal Navy had been stationed in the West Indies under the commonwealth, and from the time of Queen Anne's War one was permanently based in Jamaica. In 1743 it was supplemented by a squadron stationed in the Leeward Islands and from 1745 by a North American Squadron first at Louisbourg and later at Halifax.[2]

Toward the end of the seventeenth century there had been a distinct possibility that local naval vessels would come under the colonial governors. While these governors were, of course, royal appointees in all the royal colonies (including Massachusetts from 1688), control by governors would have opened the way for the subjection of naval forces in the colonies to the pressures of the elected colonial legislatures. But by the end of Queen Anne's War, the Admiralty had asserted its control over all the King's ships doing station duty except for a few small ships raised and

2. Gerald S. Graham, "The Naval Defence of British North America, 1739–1763," *Transactions of the Royal Historical Society*, 4th Ser., XXX (1948), 96–98.

maintained locally.[3] From 1745 even these locally maintained vessels served at times under the commander in chief of the North American Squadron.[4] Central control of naval strategy, thus assured, made possible a strategy based on the realization of the principle that although completely adequate naval protection could not be guaranteed to each individual colony, the ultimate security of the colonies rested on retention of control over sea routes that were important to them, on the prevention of an invasion of Britain, and on an effective blockade (or at least a "close watch") of the enemy fleets in their home ports to deny them the use of the seas.[5]

The defense of the island colonies in the West Indies depended on sea power even more clearly than was the case on the mainland. As their white populations were small, the islands could be defended only by the presence in the area of a superior naval force, which incidentally also provided security against Negro insurrection. The wars of the seventeenth century had shown that much damage could be caused in the sugar islands by a very small enemy naval force. Because of prevailing winds, a squadron stationed at the largest British island, Jamaica, was no deterrent to an attack on St. Lucia or Barbados. Therefore, the planters and sugar interests continually made extravagant demands for yet more naval protection. French naval policy differed from British in that squadrons were not permanently based in the Caribbean but were sent out for a season's campaign. Whenever a French squadron appeared, the British planters and merchants shrieked to the Admiralty for more protection.[6] They were not much comforted by the "close watch" being maintained in Europe, where blockade could, indeed, never be completely infallible. The planters of each sugar island were far more concerned with the defense of their own island than with a wider strategy.

3. *Ibid.*, p. 101.
4. *Ibid.*, p. 97; Gerald S. Graham, *Empire of the North Atlantic: The Maritime Struggle for North America* (Toronto: University of Toronto Press, 1958), pp. 161–162.
5. Graham, "Naval Defence of British North America," pp. 104–105.
6. Richard Pares, *War and Trade in the West Indies, 1739–1763* (Oxford: Clarendon Press, 1936), pp. 227, 265–288.

They were not even attracted to a strategy embracing the West Indies as a whole; for not only were West Indian concepts of strategy defensive, they were also local in scope. Each island legislature was reluctant to allow its militia to leave the island to aid another or to take part in offensive campaigns against enemy islands. Each wanted its own fortifications and demanded gifts of ordnance from the British government. But when an island had fortifications that were tenable (and often they were not), the militiamen sometimes refused to be shut up in them lest their estates be devastated in their absence. Some islands were without any militia at all; and where a locally raised defense force did exist, it was usually of poor quality. But as fortification, the militia, and the enlistment of Negroes (which was sometimes resorted to) were insufficient to make the planters feel entirely secure, they often turned to the British government for garrisons of regulars.[7]

Regiments raised in England were stationed in various islands at intervals from 1689 to 1739 and continually thereafter. The British government acted on the general principle that an island had no right to a garrison unless it contributed to its upkeep. Usually, the colonial legislature was expected to provide barracks, hospitals, and also a supplement to the soldiers' pay to make up for the higher cost of living in the West Indies. It was only this obligation to contribute that prevented the sugar colonies from calling on the government for unlimited military support. But the garrisons were "not very actively useful," especially since fever invariably decimated troops not seasoned to a tropical climate. "No doubt," as Richard Pares has written, "they frightened the Negroes into obedience, but there is little evidence that they deterred the French from attacking the islands."[8]

Increasing losses at sea during the Seven Years' War led to a greater readiness of West Indian legislatures to assist in expeditions against the French sugar islands. In the previous conflagration, because of their reluctance to see the acquisition of rival sugar plantations, they had been willing only to distress the

7. *Ibid.*, pp. 232–234, 240–252, 257–264.
8. *Ibid.*, pp. 257–258, 262.

French and to clean out privateers' nests; they were now prepared to give active support to Pitt's campaigns of conquest. Although they were still not eager for the annexation of French islands which would compete with them in the production of sugar, they and the sugar interests in London came to accept Pitt's idea of conquest as a means of acquiring pawns that could be exchanged at the peace for more valuable places like Minorca. Yet it was through British rather than colonial effort that by the end of the war all the French sugar islands had been captured.[9]

Thus, it can be seen that Britain assumed responsibility for the direction, and even for the cost, of operations against a European power in war; but she continually strove to press the colonists to bear some part of that burden. And she usually expected them to provide for, or contribute to, their own internal security and for their own protection against non-European peoples. For these purposes, universal obligation of military service had been carried over from England to the colonies and was continued there long after it had become a dead letter at home. In the West Indies the militia of European settlers was usually much too small to cope with the dangers threatened by the larger Negro and Carib populations, especially when many of the available men had flocked to the more lucrative profession of privateering.[10] In the mainland colonies the militia was theoretically more formidable. There, however, it tended to become a paper force, rarely drilled, almost without arms, and liable only for home service in desperate emergencies. The militia in the early days, and later on the frontier, was indeed useful for protection against sporadic raids; but a more permanent military force was obviously necessary for more onerous tasks and duties.

Some experienced servants of the crown believed that the colonies could be made really secure only by garrisons of British regulars.[11] But permanent garrisons in the First British Empire

9. *Ibid.*, pp. 179, 185, 221.
10. Richard Pares, "The Manning of the Navy in the West Indies, 1702–1763," *Transactions of the Royal Historical Society*, 4th Ser., XX (1937), 31–60.
11. E.g., Archibald Cummings, the collector of Boston; Sir William Keith, a former governor of Pennsylvania; and Governor Samuel Ogle of Maryland. See Stanley McCrory Pargellis, *Lord Loudoun in North America* (New Haven: Yale University Press, 1933), p. 12; Richard A. Preston, "Sir William Keith's Justi-

were always small. Most such garrisons were found in the West Indies, where the Negro and slave populations presented a serious threat to public order and where secure bases were needed for the exercise of naval power. In this context it should be noticed that the West Indies were more highly regarded for their economic value by the mercantilists who influenced British policy. However, a practice of stationing small garrisons also had been begun on the mainland after the seizure of New York from the Dutch. Four independent companies remained there as a garrison.[12] Garrisons were also to be found at times in Georgia, Virginia, South Carolina, and Nova Scotia. These were all too small to meet any really serious threat, and indeed they were frequently shamefully neglected by the home government. In the West Indies, part of the 4½ per cent export duty was eventually applied to the costs of defense,[13] but there was no comparable source of revenue to pay for defense needs elsewhere. Further expansion of the garrison system was ruled out on the grounds that the colonies ought to bear the costs of their own defense. It was argued that regular troops could be moved from island to island by sea either for attack or defense. In fact, as George Louis Beer has shown:

Great Britain was willing to spend large sums upon the defense of the outlying frontiers of the Empire, and . . . she was likewise willing when necessary to establish garrisons in the most exposed colonies, [but] the cost of the permanent garrisons in all the colonies was unimportant, and in the case of those that ultimately formed the United States it was trifling.[14]

In the mainland colonies several different plans for producing forces to supplement the militia and the garrisons were tried at one time and another as required. At first, everything except the supply of small quantities of military stores and ordnance was left to the colonial assemblies, which were expected to raise pro-

fication of a Stamp Duty in the Colonies," *Canadian Historical Review*, XXIX (June, 1948), 168–182.

12. Stanley McCrory Pargellis, "The Four Independent Companies of New York," *Essays in Colonial History* . . . , pp. 96–123.

13. Ruth Bourne, *Queen Anne's Navy in the West Indies* (New Haven: Yale University Press, 1939), pp. 46, 52; John William Fortescue, *A History of the British Army* (13 vols.; London: Macmillan, 1910), II, 42–43, 257; IV, 379, 384.

14. George Louis Beer, *British Colonial Policy, 1754–1765* (New York: Macmillan, 1922), p. 14.

vincial volunteer regiments and to combine with neighboring colonies for mutual security. Jealousy among the colonies made this plan unworkable; the capture of Louisbourg in 1745 by a force representing several colonies was an outstanding exception to the general rule that they could not combine for military purposes. The attempt of the Albany Congress to create a voluntary military union of the mainland colonies in 1754 was wrecked on the rock of colonial separatism.

The French menace at the beginning of the century, and again in the 1740's and 1750's, brought the need for the creation of larger expeditionary and defensive forces, and various expedients were adopted. For some campaigns regiments were raised in the colonies by British recruiting parties, and the colonies were requested to bear the initial costs on the understanding that most of the expense of such regiments would eventually be borne by the British government. These regiments were officered by Americans, but they served in conjunction with British regular regiments and the higher command was British. The dismal failure of campaigns in which the new American regiments took part served to destroy American confidence in British leadership. At the same time, senior British officers complained continually of the inefficiency of the American officers and also of the greed of colonial assemblies which tried to place the whole cost upon the British government.

To provide for closer supervision of the building of forces in America, and to decrease their cost, the practice of raising new American regiments locally was ended, and instead Americans were recruited into old established British regiments presently serving in the colonies. Enlistment in British regiments was for longer periods of service than the annual engagement of provincial regiments, and the officers were strangers whom the Americans often disliked and mistrusted. After some success in the early years of the Seven Years' War, this new expedient failed to produce enough men, and Pitt was forced to resort to the practice of sending more regiments out from Europe.[15]

Meanwhile, attempts to impose a military union on the North American colonies had also failed. As early as 1686 the Dominion

15. Pargellis, *Lord Loudoun in North America,* pp. 6–44.

of New England seemed a big step toward a union of the mainland colonies organized by higher authority. It had quickly come to grief with the Revolution of 1689 and the parallel upset in America. Attempts by Lord Loudoun to build a new compulsory union for defense in 1757 produced a centralized command in the field, but nothing more than that. Pitt, seeking to obtain provincial regiments to reinforce the British regulars he was sending out to execute his great plan for the reduction of New France, abandoned Loudoun's plan for a military union in North America. His statesmanship and qualities of personal leadership overcame not only the disunity of the colonies and the lack of an effective relationship between the colonies and the home government but even the internal conflicts between soldier, sailor, and civilian at home. As a result, New France was conquered; the British Empire in America, however, still remained militarily disorganized and disunited.[16]

Although the French threat was apparently removed, a lesser one from the Indians remained. All the best available land in the British mainland colonies was rapidly filling up, and the movement of population was obviously about to spill over into the lands occupied by those Indians to the west of the Alleghenies who had recently been allied with the French. French influence was believed still to exist. The American colonists were inclined to ignore the land titles of the Indians and at the same time to underrate their military power. The British government, on the other hand, believed that hasty encroachment on Indian territory ought to be restrained and that fortified posts must be manned to protect the established settlements. Their opinion was confirmed by the Indian war that came to be called "Pontiac's Conspiracy." Once again, as during the French war, the British found that the colonies would not co-operate willingly for their own safety: in 1764 colonial failure to supply the troops requisitioned for duty against the Indians led the British to retain a large force of regulars on the continent and to become convinced of the need for a permanent standing army in America.

The heavy cost of a permanent military establishment might

16. *Ibid.*, pp. 211–227, 253–278.

possibly have been borne entirely by the British government, but this would have constituted a radical departure from earlier practice. Moreover, the national debt had been doubled by the war, and naval defense still remained a British commitment. The commercial and landed interests in Britain who paid the taxes were therefore in no mood to accept further expenditures for colonial defense, especially as these defense forces had every appearance of becoming permanent. It seemed reasonable to British statesmen that the colonies should pay for their own defense and that, since they could probably not be brought to pay by agreement through their legislatures, they should be taxed by the imperial Parliament. Taxation without consent to pay for defense was just as revolutionary a departure from the principles upon which the Empire had hitherto been run as would have been an arrangement for Britain to bear the whole cost. But it was preferred to the latter policy, which might have bankrupted the British government. It need not be elaborated that it was the adoption of this new imperial defense policy to replace the long-established practices of the old colonial system that broke the back of the First British Empire.[17]

Although the revenue-raising Stamp Act, when withdrawn, was followed by a Declaratory Act that affirmed the right of the British Parliament to tax the colonies, the failure of the succeeding attempt at "indirect" taxation by the Townshend duties led in 1778 to a specific renunciation of this claim, except in regard to taxation to regulate trade. Too late to save the thirteen mainland colonies which were already in open revolt, the abandonment of the claim to tax was to have a profound effect on future British imperial defense policy. Although not fundamental law, for the act could have been revoked by any succeeding Parliament, it was intended as a binding pledge; indeed, it became an accepted constitutional principle of British colonial policy, applicable to all colonies and not merely to those American colonies to which this act had specifically referred. There should be no

17. David Fieldhouse, "British Imperialism in the Late Eighteenth Century," Kenneth Robinson and Frederick Madden, eds., *Essays in Imperial Government Presented to Marjorie Perham* (Oxford: Blackwell, 1963), pp. 28–29.

British taxation of the colonies except for "the regulation of commerce." [18]

The Second British Empire

During the peace negotiations in 1782, when Shelburne hoped that some kind of union for defense and other purposes might be worked out to forestall the complete loss of the American colonies, he came to realize that this might be on the lines of a federal union in which the Americans would possess an adequate voice. "My private opinion," he wrote, "would lead me to go a great way for Federal Union. But is either Country ripe for it? If not, means must be left to advance it." [19] Actually, it was already too late for a federal solution of any kind, if, indeed, one had ever been possible. The United States was determined upon independence.

Within two years of the permanent loss of the American colonies, Britain had another opportunity to redefine the principles of imperial defense, this time much nearer to home, in respect to relations with Ireland. Irish merchants were restless at being excluded from British markets and from trade with the colonies, and the Irish Parliament had no control over the Irish ministry, which was controlled by Westminster. In attempting to work out a solution that would eliminate Irish unrest, the younger Pitt approached the problem as an imperial question similar to the relationship of Britain with her overseas colonies. He offered a compromise by which Ireland would receive free trade with Britain in return for the permanent guarantee of an Irish monetary contribution to imperial naval defense. However, implicit in this arrangement was to be the principle that control of naval policy would remain with the British Admiralty. On this matter Pitt commented, "There can be but *one navy* for the Empire at large, it must be administered by the executive power in this

18. Robert Livingston Schuyler, "The Recall of the Legions: A Phase in Decentralization of the British Empire," *American Historical Review*, XXVI (Oct., 1920), 21.
19. Quoted by Vincent T. Harlow, *The Founding of the Second British Empire*, 1763–1793 (London: Longmans, 1952), I, 232.

country. . . . Nothing else can also prevent the supreme executive power . . . being distracted into different channels." [20] He was thus not prepared to offer to Ireland as favorable terms as Shelburne seems to have contemplated for the American settlements; and other members of the British Parliament were even less liberal on this matter than Pitt.

When the scheme for a guaranteed naval appropriation was seen to be unlikely to obtain Irish approval, despite the fact that the Irish Commons was filled with normally obedient placemen, the lord lieutenant of Ireland suggested that the Irish Parliament perhaps might be willing to equip and supply a squadron for service in Irish waters only. The British Cabinet, however, rejected the idea of an Irish navy as "utterly inadmissible." [21]

Writing about the failure of this attempt to work out what might have been a new basis for the organization of imperial defense, Professor Harlow said, "Pitt and his colleagues conceived of the Empire as closely knit together by a mutual interest in privileges and burdens, its policy co-ordinated by the acceptance of British supremacy." [22] It was that supremacy which an Irish Parliament, even one filled with placemen, could not be induced to accept. Having refused to accept an inferior status, Ireland disappeared for a century from the imperial scene.

It was Professor Harlow's belief that if the younger Pitt's Irish proposals had been accepted, Ireland would have become the first dominion and Britain would have gained valuable experience and precedents for her future dealings with her daughter states. Ireland's proximity to England, however, made centralized control of defense even more necessary than was to be the case in the Second British Empire, and the Irish were asked to make substantial contributions for naval defense but were offered no voice in the navy's disposal and employment. Pitt's offer to Ireland was, therefore, not really a forerunner of the kind of autonomy eventually claimed by all the dominions. An Ireland

20. Quoted by Vincent T. Harlow, in "The New Imperial System, 1783–1815," *The Cambridge History of the British Empire* (Cambridge: Cambridge University Press, 1940), II, 133.
21. *Ibid.*, pp. 133–134.
22. *Ibid.*, pp. 134–135.

without control of its defense policy could not be properly described as a dominion in the fullest sense. If Pitt's offer had been accepted by Ireland, and if it could have been applied later to the dominions overseas, the Second British Empire would have evolved on lines very different from the present Commonwealth. But it is inconceivable that an Irish precedent could have worked for more distant daughter nations where the defense problems were less closely akin to those of the mother country.

Although it was now acknowledged that Parliament could not legislate on the subject, British policy after the American Revolution showed that hope of obtaining aid from colonies for their own defense had not been abandoned. A need still existed for greater defenses than the colonies were likely to provide on their own initiative. However, in the mainland colonies this need for defense, including the cost of presents to appease the Indians, was so much beyond the resources of the colonies that no attempt was made to induce them to make substantial contributions. William Grenville personally believed that colonists ought to bear their fair share of defense expenditures. But when he drafted the Constitutional Act for Canada in 1791 he considered it impossible to impose this upon them because it would be contrary to former practice. Hence, his Canada Act limited taxation by the imperial Parliament to taxes for the regulation of commerce. The cost of the garrisons that remained in North America, and the cost of Indian presents, remained a charge upon the British budget.[23]

The situation was different in the West Indies. The West Indian colonies were more prosperous, as yet, than those colonies on the mainland that had remained British; the islands were much more exposed to a renewed French or Spanish attack; and,

23. Helen Taft Manning, *British Colonial Government After the American Revolution, 1782–1820* (New Haven: Yale University Press, 1933), pp. 213–217; J. Holland Rose, "The Conflict with Revolutionary France," *CHBE,* II, 23; George Burton Adams, "The Influence of the American Revolution on England's Government of Her Colonies," *Annual Report of the American Historical Association,* 1896, I, 375–376; Robert Livingston Schuyler, *Parliament and the British Empire: Some Constitutional Controversies Concerning Imperial Legislative Jurisdiction* (New York: Columbia University Press, 1929), p. 198.

more important, their large Negro population made the planters favor British garrisons rather than reject them as the Americans had done. When British ministers in the years after the Revolution sought to insure that the defenses of the West Indies were adequate for all contingencies, they tried to persuade West Indian assemblies to assume at least a part of the cost.[24]

After a few sporadic attempts had been made to reduce the cost of West Indian defenses in the immediate postwar years, Britain was obliged by fear of France to build extensive fortifications and to increase the garrisons. The planters were persuaded, with some difficulty, to provide Negro labor to work on the fixed defenses. However, the beginnings of the French Revolution led Pitt to believe that the danger from France had decreased. He therefore proposed that the garrisons should be reduced or that, henceforward, the colonies should pay for garrisons over and above a single regiment provided by Britain. Various colonial assemblies promptly claimed that their payment of the 4½ per cent duty and their expenditures on labor for fortifications or for subsistence for troops entitled them to British protection.

Before this dispute could come to a head, the outbreak of a new war with France and of bloody Negro insurrections in the French sugar islands forced the government once again to abandon its plans for economies. As the war went on, in consequence of the frightful mortality in British regiments in those tropical islands, Britain began to recruit regiments of Negro slaves, an expedient that Jamaica found so distasteful that at last the island's assembly agreed to pay for extra white troops. Thus, it came about that in the closing years of the eighteenth century the revenues of this one colony supported a British garrison larger than the total military establishment in the West Indies prior to 1783. But the immediate result of this revolutionary development was that the Jamaican assembly virtually took over control of the military forces from the lieutenant governor because the planters who were represented in it were anxious to see that the forces which they had provided were used for their own

24. Manning, *British Colonial Government . . .*, pp. 217–224.

protection and not for wider imperial strategy. The British government, therefore, broke the "contract" by which Jamaica had assumed responsibility for its own defense and resumed the policy of paying for white and Negro regiments. As in the early days, the Jamaican assembly came to pay only for the extra tropical subsistence of the white troops and not for their "British pay." [25]

Thus, during the great struggle with Napoleon, the British government retained central strategic control of all overseas land forces, even though this usually necessitated bearing most of the cost. One notable attempt to derive the fullest benefit from a centralized strategy can be seen in the plans made to expel Napoleon's troops from Egypt in 1801. Troops were dispatched to the Nile Delta from both Bombay and the Cape. Although they arrived too late to share in the honor of this important victory, this concentration of forces from remote parts of the British Empire was an indication of the value of a coherent, co-ordinated strategy. Britain became, once again, a formidable military and naval power. The defeats of the period of the American Revolution were avenged, and all the overseas possessions of France and her satellites were captured. Britain's dominion of the world outside Europe was almost as complete in 1815 as it had been in 1763. [26]

Seeking no territorial acquisitions in Europe, the British secured at the Vienna Congress in 1815 the naval bases all over the globe from which their enemies had previously threatened their maritime position. More than half of the British Army was then stationed overseas, and a third of the total was in India. By 1826 most of those troops in the United Kingdom were in Ireland. In each colony the primary reason for a military garrison was different. In Gibraltar it was for imperial defense, in Canada

25. *Ibid.*, pp. 224–249.
26. Rose, "Conflict with Revolutionary France," pp. 75–76. Rose argues that the events of 1801 pointed the way to the participation of the dominions in World War I. But Baird's and Popham's forces were under direct British control and in 1914 those of the dominions were not, at least in regard to numbers provided. A better parallel might be the Indian contribution in two world wars in France and the Middle East which was quite different from the voluntary co-operation of the Commonwealth; but even this was subject to considerable negotiation between the British and Indian governments.

for protection against the United States, at the Cape for protection against dangerous native tribes, and in Jamaica for internal security because of the large black population.[27] Everywhere, as civil police forces had not yet been developed, troops were needed to assist the civil power in keeping order. Garrisoning the Empire (including India and the British Isles) for these various purposes cost about £3 million per annum; naval expenditures for all purposes from 1818 to 1840 cost annually little more than half as much again as the garrisons. To justify the expense, much of which had to be borne by the British government, it was argued that an empire won at such great cost was worth defending and that colonial garrisons were an outward sign of imperial unity. There was also need to hide troops in the colonies because of the opposition at home to the maintenance of a standing army. Some defenders of the principle of British financial responsibility added that British control of military affairs served to protect the indigenous inhabitants against arbitrary acts of white settlers, and others declared that as the government at Westminster controlled the foreign policy which might involve the colonies in war, Britain was obliged to protect the colonists from the consequences of her policies.[28]

The colonies in North America and the newly acquired possessions at the Cape could not pay for their own defense, let alone for a wider imperial defense policy. In the Australian convict settlements internal security was a British responsibility, and the small imperial naval stations were obviously also an imperial charge. But there seemed reasonable grounds for transferring some of the expense of the West Indian garrisons to the planters of islands whose wealth had become a byword in the eighteenth century. Another attempt was therefore made in 1816 to obtain colonial support for defense. It met with stubborn resistance. The sugar islands, now freed from the French menace and already starting down the slippery road to economic ruin, vigorously refused to pay. Hence, the new Empire, which had been built up soon after

27. Schuyler, "Recall of the Legions," pp. 22–23.
28. Manning, *British Colonial Government . . .*, pp. 500–501; Brian W. C. Tunstall, "Imperial Defence, 1815–1870," *CHBE*, II, 808–810.

the old one had been lost as a consequence of a dispute about taxation for imperial defense, came to be defended almost entirely by the British government and at the expense of the British taxpayer. In the decade following Waterloo, the West Indian colonists paid only about one-tenth of 1 per cent of the total cost of garrisons; they contributed nothing to the cost of the navy. The metropolitan government shouldered practically the whole burden.

But British control and financial responsibility did not necessarily mean a defense policy based on a sound imperial strategy. For more than a generation there was no threat or danger to the Empire. A period of profound peace was broken only by the 1837 rebellion in the Canadas and the ensuing fear of American filibustering, and by the Kaffir wars that went on from 1832 to 1852; each of these, however, was only of local concern and could be isolated by British naval strength. In the past, a major threat to the Empire had usually forced the formulation of a grand strategic plan. Now, a long period of peace led to the negation of strategic planning on an Empire-wide scale. Lacking a global stimulus, the machinery of colonial defense, never tested in these years, was never looked at from a grand strategic point of view. Constitutional, administrative, and, even more, financial problems outweighed military considerations. The result was that Empire defense was treated as if it consisted of a collection of separate and purely local problems which had no clear relation to the defense problems of Britain itself or of the Empire as a whole. Control and financial responsibility by the metropolitan government thus led not, as one might have expected, to an imperial defense policy, but to what was aptly called by contemporaries "colonial defense," "as if the defense of each separate part of the Empire was a problem entirely self-contained." [29] After the removal of war pressures, the metropolitan government

29. *Ibid.*, p. 806. The phrases "colonial defense" and "imperial defense" as used in relation to the organization of the defense of the Empire in the early nineteenth century and to the plans for an over-all strategy in the last quarter of that century are peculiarly unapt. The earlier "colonial defense" system was actually an imperial system maintained by the imperial government without colonial aid. The later "imperial defense" concept was in part an attempt to get autonomous colonies to pay toward a general system of defense under imperial control.

began to administer a defense policy which was more like the localism that one would have expected from each separate colony.

In Britain the chief interest shown in colonial defense in the early nineteenth century was merely in possible economies. During the fifteen years that Tory rule outlasted the war against Revolutionary and Napoleonic France, the government whittled away at the defense budget and succeeded in reducing it to about £2.5 million.[30] Some items formerly charged to the military budget were placed on the civil list,[31] but there was undoubtedly an over-all reduction of military costs even before the Whigs came to power in 1830 with a program of retrenchment as well as reform.

By 1832 colonial military expenditures had been reduced to £2 million, of which the colonies paid about £240,000.[32] Two years later a parliamentary committee appointed to inquire into military establishments and expenditures in the colonies was able to make a few further recommendations for reductions of garrisons in specific colonies, and especially of staffs, but it emphasized that the government was responsible for defense and that the size of garrisons must vary according to particular circumstances. It urged that there should be the strictest economy and that "any surplus revenue that may remain after defraying their [the colonies] civil expenses should, in accordance with the Regulations which had been adopted by the Ordnance and Colonial Departments, be applied to the payment of their military charges." In 1835 another committee continued the work of investigation, but as far as North America was concerned it could

30. *Ibid.,* p. 809.
31. E.g., Great Britain, "Estimates for 1826, Upper and Lower Canada," Colonial Office Library, now amalgamated with Commonwealth Relations Office Library. (Colonial Office will hereinafter be abbreviated as C.O.) Some £5,000 for the Rideau Canal was accounted a civil expense, as was also the salary of the commander at James Fort in Sierra Leone in 1827. In 1828, civil and military establishments on the Gold Coast were lumped as a civil expense, and in the same year "Certain colonial services (formerly part of the Extraordinaries of the Army) and including the salaries of the Superintendent of Honduras, the salaries of the Private Secretary of the Governor of Barbados, Dominica, etc., and the supply of stationery" were transferred to the civil list ("Military Expenses on the Civil List, 1828," Commonwealth Relations Office Library).
32. Schuyler, "Recall of the Legions," p. 23.

advise no further reduction except in the expenses of the Indian Department and in commissariat, ordnance, and barrack establishments.[33]

The year 1834 had, indeed, seen garrisons reach their lowest point. The Canadian rebellions and the native wars in South Africa soon reversed the trend. To meet these dangers, troops had to be rushed from Britain to colonies in which defenses had been stripped to the bone. Thus, despite the efforts of the Whigs, the cost to Britain of the military defense of the colonies tended to grow rather than decrease. This tendency was strengthened by humanitarian factors. Victorian England was less disposed to leave British troops for interminable tours of duty in unhealthy tropical garrisons.[34] The provision of more frequent reliefs was more expensive. In the 1830's and 1840's the cost of colonial defense began to climb.

Thus, throughout the years before the development of responsible government, British colonies were not always able to provide even for the first requirement of the old defense system—local defense against petty native aggression and internal upheaval. Threats to the Empire as a whole invariably led to the creation of imperial defense forces at British expense and under British control. Attempts to obtain colonial contributions to such defense forces had had a very limited success. They had destroyed the First British Empire in North America, and it has been seen that on occasions colonial legislatures, if jockeyed into the position of bearing a large proportion of the defense costs, would seek to exercise a control over strategy and military affairs for which they were ill-equipped. While great crises usually produced an effective centralized imperial strategy, colonial authorities were inclined to urge local interests. And when the Empire was at peace and in no danger, the British government itself took a myopic view of imperial strategy and developed a series of local colonial policies rather than a sound disposition of force.

33. Great Britain, *Parliamentary Papers*, 1834, *Report from Select Committee on the Colonial Military Expenditure, 1834*, VI, Pt. II, 3 (570); *ibid.*, 1835, *Report from the Select Committee on Colonial Military Expenditure, 1835*, VI, 3 (473). *Parliamentary Papers* will hereinafter be cited as *P.P.*

34. Charles P. Stacey, *Canada and the British Army, 1846–1871: A Study in the Practice of Responsible Government* (rev. ed.; Toronto: University of Toronto Press, 1963), p. 52.

On top of all this, while in some colonies white populations were growing rapidly and might be expected to bear a greater share of defense costs, the drain on British resources was also growing and seemed likely to continue to increase.

Responsible Government

The historian of the collapse of the colonial defense system in Canada, Colonel C. P. Stacey, has shown that in the middle of the nineteenth century desire for economy, more than anything else, initiated a revision of policy.[35] Logical arguments about a new constitutional relationship and about the responsibility of free peoples to defend themselves merely made the economy drive respectable. A new disposition of imperial forces, with a search for a more effective imperial defense strategy, was a byproduct of the search for a means of cutting costs. By the third quarter of the nineteenth century it no longer seemed obligatory, as it had been ever since the American and French Revolutionary wars, for Britain to bear most of the burden of colonial defense. Several British colonies were now, like the colonies of the eighteenth century, big enough and rich enough to carry a greater share.[36]

But the new Empire was not merely a repetition of the old. Responsible government, a new element in the imperial system, was recommended for Canada, though not clearly introduced, by Lord Durham in 1839. It was achieved in Nova Scotia in 1848 and confirmed in Canada a year later. In the ensuing years it was introduced into New Brunswick, Prince Edward Island, and Newfoundland. The North American colonies smoothed the way for its introduction within a decade into the colonies in Australia and New Zealand. After an interval it was established in Cape Colony in 1872. There the movement stopped for a time. Western Australia did not get responsible government until 1890, and economic and social conditions long prevented its develop-

35. *Ibid.*, pp. 37–63.
36. The need for a new policy was set in its historical context by its initiator, Lord Grey, in a letter to Elgin, dated March 14, 1851 (G.B., *P.P.*, 1851, *Canada Correspondence Relating to the Civil List and Military Expenditure* . . ., XXXVI, 253–257 [1334]).

ment in the older West Indian colonies where, indeed, there was a retrogressive withdrawal of some long-established rights of representative government. However, by 1872 most of the British colonies in North America, Australasia, and South Africa (but only those) had already been equipped to take up a new role in government and defense.

The British assumed that the introduction into colonial dependencies of the principle of responsible government, a revolutionary departure from the practices of the first Empire, included control of local defense forces and carried with it a greater colonial obligation to assume a reasonable part of their defense costs. What was, perhaps, more important was that it provided governmental machinery by means of which a colony could initiate and conduct its defense more effectively. As Canadian historians have been fond of saying, in so doing it created an entirely new situation in which the imperial constitutional conflicts that had proved so frustrating during the wars with France and had eventually broken the first Empire might be avoided. Clashes of interest between metropolitan and colonial governments were no longer staged in the cockpit of colonial executive-legislative relations where they had always become enormously magnified. Instead, they could be decently hidden from publicity in official dispatches. But one big question remained to be answered. Would the result be a harmonious parting of the ways or the achievement of harmonious co-operation? In particular, how would it be possible, under the new system, to provide for the defense of the Empire?

Before these questions can be answered, the way in which contemporary thought about colonial defense had developed must be examined. The fashioning of a defense policy for the new Empire, or more particularly for the newly autonomous parts of it, had first been brought up in debates over what were actually only incidental problems. Long before a re-examination of defenses was made imperative by the darkening international scene in the 1850's, two groups had combined for an assault upon the prevailing system of colonial defense. The Radical Imperialists were the chief proponents of the new form of empire in which colonies would have liberty, in which self-government would bring colonial responsibility for defense, and in which free colonies would be linked to the mother country by bonds of sentiment and affection that would be stronger than ties based on force. Their efforts were seconded by the Manchester Radicals who, however, did not look forward with them to the future continuance of an imperial association.

Both groups had found common ground in attacks upon the increasing expense of overseas defense. In 1846–1847 the cost to the British Treasury of colonial garrisons was one-third of the total cost of the army, and the army and navy accounted for roughly 73 per cent of the national expenditure excluding debt services.[37] Such figures made the garrison system vulnerable to criticism. Faced with Maori wars, Lord Grey reduced the imperial garrison in New South Wales between 1846 and 1852, and that colony was made responsible for the accommodation of those British troops remaining and for the cost of any others above a certain minimum if they were desired.[38] The absence of danger to Australia had, in fact, made Grey's economies possible there and suggested a means of reducing the over-all military budget. Grey made a minor reduction in Canada in 1849.

But fear of the United States postponed an immediate implementation of his ideas and policies.[39] For a time, current defense and security problems in New Zealand and South Africa were an impediment to the withdrawal of their garrisons. In 1851, however, Grey told the governor general of Canada, Lord Elgin, that as a result of the growth of Canada, the British people could now be relieved of a large proportion of the charge "for the protection of a colony now well able to do much towards protecting itself." He said that this new policy would have been extended to Canada in 1846 had it not been for the commercial uncertainty caused by the repeal of the Corn Laws, but that the depression had now been overcome by the effects of the repeal of the Navigation Acts and the building of the St. Lawrence

37. These estimates are made in Stacey, *Canada and the British Army*, p. 43.
38. Schuyler, "Recall of the Legions," p. 28. Grey was secretary of state for war and the colonies.
39. Stacey, *Canada and the British Army*, pp. 73–76.

canals. The importance of the Oregon crisis with the United States was thus played down. Grey announced in this letter that certain reductions were to be carried out. The garrison in Canada would in due course be restricted to two or three posts, probably Kingston and Quebec.[40] A year later a parliamentary committee investigating the possibility of reducing colonial naval and military expenditures by the consolidation of various departments and services pointed out that military outposts in the colonies had frequently been established in the past at the expense of the colonies, only to become within a short time charges upon the imperial government. Stricter control should therefore be exerted. This same committee, among other recommendations, stated that in view of the construction of certain military defense works in Canada, the naval establishment on the Great Lakes should be terminated.[41]

These reductions, aimed at economy, were soon jeopardized by increasing dangers. During the 1850's the peace that had marked the nineteenth century since the defeat of Napoleon was shattered. By 1852 England was already anxiously watching the meteoric career of a new Napoleon. A year later came the war with Russia. At the peace conference in 1856 the allied French, by their posturing, renewed apprehension of danger from that direction. There followed the Indian Mutiny (1857–1858) and the Second China War (1856–1860). At the end of the decade deteriorating relations with France led to competition in the building of new types of armored war vessels, and soon afterward the American Civil War gave rise to friction with the United States and also caused speculative men to wonder whether a victorious Union Army would turn north if it conquered the South. Not one of these conflicts and crises compared with the global wars of the past in the threat that it presented to the Empire as a whole. For this and other reasons the troubles of the fifties did not lead to strategic thinking on a

40. G.B., P.P., 1851, XXXVI, 255–256.
41. G.B., P.P., 1852, *Reports of the Committee Approved by the Treasury Board to Inquire into the Naval, Ordnance, and Commissariat Establishments in the Colonies; with Treasury Minutes and Correspondence Relating Thereto,* XXX, 376–547 (1515). It had been reduced by the Whigs in the 1830's but had been revived as a result of the rebellion of 1837.

global scale. But they had the effect of forcing attention upon the Empire's defense problems.

Queen Victoria, in 1856, commenting severely to her minister of war upon the lack of defense planning, expressed a feeling that was widespread in England.

The Queen . . . is glad to hear the Military and the Defense Committees of the Cabinet are to be reassembled. The absence of all plans for our defenses is a great evil, and hardly credible. There should exist a well-considered scheme for each place supported by a detailed argument; this, when approved by the Government, should be sanctioned and signed by the Sovereign, and not deviated from except upon resubmission and full explanation of the causes which render such deviation necessary; no special work should be undertaken which does not realize part of this general scheme. The Queen trusts that Lord Panmure will succeed in effecting this.[42]

Three weeks later, General Sir John Fox Burgoyne, a distinguished military engineer who had been recalled a year earlier from the Crimea to resume his duties as inspector general of fortifications, completed a memorandum on defense. Burgoyne proposed a complete scheme for the fortification of home naval bases at a cost of £4 million.[43] With regard to overseas bases, he divided the imperial fortresses of Gibraltar, Malta, Corfu, Bermuda, and Mauritius, that must be maintained by the British government, from all the rest, which, he said, were

so numerous that the task of endeavouring much protection to all is hopeless . . . . [They] have dropped their attributes of Colonies, and, having constitutions and self-government, have entered into a species of Federal Union, and will henceforward have to rely, it is understood, upon their own exertions for their defence, receiving a varying degree of support or co-operation from Great Britain, chiefly it is presumed, in warlike implements and reinforcements of troops.

Burgoyne also noted that the Fleet Stations, i.e., the places designated as essential to the navy, St. Helena, Ascension, and the

42. Queen Victoria to Lord Panmure, Nov. 9, 1856, in Arthur C. Benson and Viscount Esher, eds., *The Letters of Queen Victoria: A Selection from Her Majesty's Correspondence between the years 1837 and 1861* (London: John Murray, 1907), III, 269–270.
43. Wrottesley, *Life and Correspondence of Field Marshal Sir John Burgoyne, Bart* (London: Bentley, 1873), II, 363.

Falkland Islands, were "worthy of attention." [44] Burgoyne thus reflected the contemporary emphasis on fortification for defense. But fortifications are not merely local and static; they are also expensive. This new technical element therefore served to exaggerate the effect of the simultaneous tendency to think of colonial defense in terms of finance rather than of strategy.

Dealing with those dependencies with independent legislatures that must now rely upon themselves for their own protection, Burgoyne commented that large military reserves of land had been handed over to Canada. Much of the proceeds, he wrote, had been

naturally applied by the Provincial Government to profit and civil improvements, [but] it is yet to be seen what measures are to be adopted for defence, which appears to be very tardy; so that it may be apprehended that when the evil day of a state of warfare with its neighbour shall arrive, this Province will probably be found in a very unprovided state. . . . The British government maintain a division of Regulars in Canada, and the stations of Quebec, Montreal, and Kingston, as the reserve and nucleus of defence, but they will be of little value without the active co-operation of the Province, in the establishment or improvement of certain ports, and, above all, in the organization of a large and effective Militia.[45]

After surveying the other colonies in similar fashion, and with almost equal pessimism, Burgoyne concluded,

At all foreign [i.e., overseas] stations, it is of the greatest importance to obtain the utmost amount of cordial local co-operation in assisting to repel foreign aggression, which can only be done by conciliation and by political and commercial advantages that the population would lose, without any compensating benefits, if subjected to another power. This is peculiarly necessary where the people are not British, or may perhaps even be of the same origin, and socially connected with the very enemy with whom we may be contending at the time.[46]

Burgoyne's use of the word "foreign" as applied to the colonial possessions of the crown was typical of an age which had not yet begun to think imperially. His belief that self-government

44. J. F. Burgoyne, "Memorandum on Defences for the Foreign Possessions of Great Britain, 28th November, 1856," in G.B., [War Office], *Collected Papers and Memoranda on Foreign Defences, 1856–59* (London, 1859), p. 410. War Office hereinafter will be cited as W.O.

45. Burgoyne, "Memorandum . . . 1856," p. 43.

46. *Ibid.*, p. 45.

had brought a form of federal union between the colonies and the mother country was far from their actual relationship. But he fully understood the solution for the new imperial defense problem—that colonial co-operation now depended more than ever before upon colonial goodwill.

Burgoyne's reference to colonial co-operation may have been inspired by what had happened in the colonies during the Crimean War. The withdrawal of the regulars initiated by Grey had been hastened by the need to call veterans home for service in the Crimea. To provide for local defense, rudimentary volunteer militia had been raised in Nova Scotia, New South Wales, and Victoria in 1854, and in Natal, Canada, and South Australia in 1855. Furthermore, the colonies all rushed to send loyal messages of support for Britain and backed them by contributions to the Patriotic Fund. Individuals volunteered personally for service against Russia,[47] often in the hope of getting a commission in the British Army and half-pay upon the termination of hostilities. Thus, although Burgoyne's reference to the use that had been made of the military land reserves in Canada reveals he had some doubts about the policy a colonial government might pursue, he had reason to believe the spirit of the colonists themselves was sound and would assert itself.

As part of the reforms introduced as a result of the Crimean War, the Department of War and Colonies had been divided in 1854 and a secretary of state provided for each. Although this reorganization had the advantage that one minister could give his undivided attention to military problems, it had the unfortunate effect that, in colonial defense, the secretary of state for war, who had to find the men and money, no longer had official knowledge of conditions in the colonies and no longer had the means of communicating directly with the colonial governments. This weakness was pointed out by the assistant undersecretary for war, J. R. Godley, an intimate friend of Gibbon Wakefield and a member of the Colonial Reform League, who had been

47. Brian Tunstall says that Canada sent volunteers to the Crimea and that this was a "new step" in imperial history ("Imperial Defence, 1815–1870," p. 818). However, if any volunteers went from Canada (and there may not have been any), they acted on their own initiative and went at their own expense, which gives their action much less significance than if they had been sent by the Canadian government.

active in politics in New Zealand and had learned there to dislike Colonial Office rule.

In a memorandum prepared in 1858, Godley declared that the present mode of providing for the military expenditures of the colonies was anomalous and caused confusion in the War Office. Every year, he said, disputes arose about the respective liabilities of the imperial and colonial governments. These were never settled on principle but were adjourned with the British government "almost invariably yielding the points at issue." He blamed the lack of "recognized principles of mutual relation to which appeal can be made, or upon which a permanent settlement can be founded." He claimed that arrangements already in force in certain colonies showed that such principles could be established more generally. Malta, Mauritius, the Ionian Islands, and Ceylon paid a pecuniary contribution into the Exchequer. The Australian colonies paid for military buildings and for troops beyond a specified number. He proposed that the principles underlying these arrangements should be extended to other colonies as far as circumstances would permit.

Distinguishing between the requirements for defense against foreign aggression and those for internal security, Godley asserted that while England's exclusive control of foreign policy carried with it an obligation to defend the colonies against the effects of her actions,

the connexion between the Colony and the mother Country is generally maintained more for the advantage of the former than for the latter; indeed there are comparatively few cases in which the latter has any but quite subordinate and secondary interest in the defence of the colonies; and for the protection of a powerful state, admittedly a great advantage to the weak one, it is right that the protected state should in its proportion pay.

Reflecting the views of the colonial reformers, he went on,

the habit of self defence, rightly considered, is a privilege, not a burden. It constitutes, in fact, a most important part of the national training of a free people, and for the sake of the colonies themselves, even more than for that of the mother country, they should be called upon not to neglect it.

The principle which Godley proposed for the sharing of defense costs was that Britain should assist in defense against foreign civilized nations and (in a lesser proportion) against formidable native tribes; but except where colonies were garrisons maintained for imperial purposes, she should never bear the whole charge. The proportion in each case must be set down. The cost of internal security was, he believed, a colonial responsibility except where the population was composed of district and semi-hostile races and where the bulk of the property was in the hands of the less numerous race. But even in these cases the whole expense should be thrown on the community, employing forces provided by the imperial government. Godley said that if the government accepted these principles, a committee should be established to apply them to each colony and upon its recommendations the Executive could act, "of course after communication with the Governments of the Colonies concerned." [48]

It had already been implied in another instance, however, that communication with a colony about the proportion of its defense which it would assume would not necessarily mean consultation on that subject. In 1856 Sir William Denison, the governor of New South Wales, had proposed to London that the United Kingdom and the colony should bear the cost of garrisons in equal proportions and that the colonial government should determine the amount required both in peace and in war. But this proposal had been rejected in London on the grounds that it might compromise the independent action of the central government and the security of the Empire. [49] Central direction of defense policy must remain with the government in Britain. Though colonies were now to be told that they must bear a greater share of their own defense costs, they were not to be given the opportunity to say how much.

To attempt to find a way out of the embarrassment caused him by the lack of principles upon which to divide colonial de-

48. G.B., W.O., [J. Godley], "Military Expenditures in the Colonies," Oct. 2, 1858, W.O. Library, A Papers 50/1858, pp. 1–5.
49. Schuyler, "Recall of the Legions," pp. 29–30; Sir William Denison's dispatch (Aug. 14, 1856) on the military expenditure in New South Wales, and Lord Stanley's reply, in New South Wales *P.P.*, in Australian National University Library.

fense costs, the secretary of state for war, General Peel, on March 14, 1859, initiated the erection of an interdepartmental committee representing the War Office and Colonial Office under the presidency of Mr. George A. Hamilton, secretary of the treasury. Godley represented the War Office. He obtained support from Hamilton for proposals which formed the substance of the committee's report in 1860. They recommended that military posts maintained for purely imperial purposes should not be included in any general scheme of colonial contribution, but that the remaining colonies in which "the garrison is maintained for merely colonial defense [ought] to be defended under colonial management" with the costs borne by the home and colonial governments in a settled proportion that would be "uniform everywhere." The amount of the imperial force was to be decided by colonial demand "as to maximum" and by imperial convenience. It was hinted in the report that the imperial government's share, as Sir William Denison had suggested earlier, might be one-half.

The Colonial Office representative, T. Frederick Elliot, dissented vigorously from the majority proposal. He rejected Godley's premise that the only reason for the imperial government to aid colonial defense was that it controlled matters of peace and war; he argued that the imperial government had a material interest in the colonies;[50] he also denied that a uniform system could be introduced without reference to local circumstances. The War Office and Colonial Office were thus unable to come to an agreement or to establish a principle upon which the proportion of contribution could be divided. The incidental effect of this stalemate was that the committee's suggestion that colonies should be invited to take the initiative for their defense under "colonial management" (whatever that meant) was not

50. G.B., *P.P.*, 1860, *Report of the Committee on the Expense of Military Defences in the Colonies*, (282) XLI, 573–591. A summary of the conclusions of the committee and of action taken upon them is in G.B., W.O., "List of Committees," No. 60 of 1860, W.O. Library. See also Schuyler, "Recall of the Legions," pp. 24, 30–32. Godley's reply to Elliott was that Britain had an interest in Belgium but did not propose to garrison and fortify Antwerp; see James Edward FitzGerald (ed.), *A Selection from the Writings and Speeches of John Robert Godley* (Christchurch: Press Office, 1863), p. 301.

realized. The committee's report is sufficiently different from Godley's proposals to suggest that the Treasury representative, seeking a "uniform" contribution, had introduced the rigidity that had frustrated this possibility of achieving an arrangement for colonial co-operation in defense measures.

Failure to reach a solution on colonial defense at the departmental level led to reference of the problem to a parliamentary committee chaired by Arthur Mills, a member of Parliament who had been insistent on the need for an investigation of the problem. Palmerston, conceiving it to be a surrender of executive functions, did not like the idea; but Gladstone agreed. This committee, after examining a large number of expert witnesses, rejected the idea of colonial financial contributions on a uniform scale, proposed some minor adjustments of various colony contributions, rejected Burgoyne's proposals for a vast extension of fortification in distant places like Mauritius, and declared that the responsibility and cost of military defense in colonies proper ("not being military dependencies") should "mainly devolve upon themselves." The parliamentary committee restated the important proviso that the proportion of cost to be borne by the colony should not be the subject of negotiation.

When the Mills Committee reported its findings on March 4, 1862, the British House of Commons unanimously passed the famous resolution which purported to set down principles for the sharing of the defense burden between the mother country and her colonies:

That this House (while fully recognizing the claims of all portions of the British Empire to Imperial aid in their protection against perils arising from the consequences of Imperial policy) is of opinion that Colonies exercising the rights of self-government ought to undertake the main responsibility for providing for their own internal order and security, and ought to assist in their own external defense.[51]

It is of interest to note that the important last clause, "and ought to assist in their own external defense," without which the reso-

51. G.B., *Hansard,* 3rd Ser., CLXV, 1060. The background of the resolution is presented by Stacey, *Canada and the British Army,* pp. 123–130.

lution would have had little meaning, was added by the House and was not in the committee's original proposal.[52]

This resolution, bringing to a head more than a decade of discussion on the theme "self-government begets self-defense" and aimed mainly at justifying the Whig policy of retrenchment and economy by the recall of troops from the colonies, was the enunciation of an abstract principle that did not, of course, have the force of law. It was, in fact, also only a reversion to concepts of long standing that had at one time been generally applied. From the beginning English colonies had been expected, if they were able, to provide their own protection against local dangers and to co-operate with the mother country against major dangers. What was significant about this resolution was not so much that the basic principles of British imperial defense were again changing, but that the nature of the Empire, and therefore the way in which the old principles could be applied, was now different. Responsible government could provide a more effective means for putting this ancient principle into effect.

At the end of its report, the Mills Committee stated the basic principles of the strategy of imperial defense in a way which needs further examination.

The tendency of modern warfare [it said] is to strike blows at the heart of a hostile power; and it is, therefore, desirable to concentrate the troops required for the defense of the United Kingdom as much as possible, and to trust mainly to naval supremacy for securing against foreign aggression the distant dependencies of the Empire.[53]

This emphasis on the defense of the United Kingdom was in accord with contemporary professional military theory; but the reference to naval supremacy for the defense of the Empire is interesting. It is easy to show that the committee's questions to witnesses had been slanted to produce answers in favor of reliance upon cheap naval defense instead of expensive fortifications in the colonies. Nevertheless, although as Brian Tunstall has

52. G.B., *P.P.*, 1861, *Report from the Select Committee Appointed on Colonial Military Expenditures, to Enquire and Report Whether Any Alterations May Be Advantageously Adopted . . .*, (423) XIII, 75. The Mills Committee recommendations, with a note of action taken, are in W.O., "List of Committees," No. 60 of 1860, W.O. Library.

53. *Ibid.*

pointed out the Mills Committee scarcely considered the problems of combined defense for the Empire as a whole,[54] it still remains true that it came nearer to a sound statement on the nature of imperial strategy than many soldiers, who at this very time, in a seeming panic, were planning vast fortresses to protect London and the British Isles and were ignoring the navy altogether.[55]

The politicians were, perhaps, chiefly interested in discovering a military excuse for cutting down expenditure in the colonies; Gladstone may have agreed to refer the question of colonial defense to a parliamentary committee merely because he saw that economy would be its recommendation; the radicals who urged the withdrawal of the colonial garrisons may have been guilty of a willingness to let the Empire disintegrate; a reference to the navy may have been inserted only because, when the soldiers were withdrawn, there was no other defense force available; but whatever its motives, the Mills Committee had suggested the lines on which the later structure of Commonwealth defense was to evolve. However, its proposed solution, the transference of responsibility for defense to the self-governing colonies, automatically created difficult obstacles. How could an effective plan of concerted action for imperial defense be worked out between autonomous units? How would a workable strategy of naval defense, the need for which the Mills Committee had reasserted in its report in general terms, be attained? And how could the cost of naval defenses be shared? More important and more immediate, how would the colonial governments accept their new burden of defense? The Mills Committee's statement of the principle that the proportion of the cost of defense to be borne by a colony should not be the subject of negotiation with it was obviously unlikely to be accepted by colonies with responsible government. Self-government might beget self-defense, but would the child survive?

54. Tunstall, "Imperial Defence, 1815–1870," pp. 829–832.
55. See the pamphlet attack on the defense commissioners of 1861 by Sir S. Morton Peto, a civilian contractor and M.P., *Observations on the Report of the Defence Commissioners* (London: James Ridgway, 1862); and Walter Bagehot, *Count Your Enemies and Economize Your Expenditures* (London: James Ridgway, 1862), p. 16.

The Withdrawal of the Garrisons

No sooner had the policy of withdrawing colonial garrisons been decided upon in Britain than the American Civil War threatened the security of British North America. At the same time, in New Zealand, the attitude of the Maoris threatened the expansion of the British colony. The two situations were distinctly different. In North America the danger was an external menace from a white power, British provocation might be claimed as cause of war if it should come, and a serious dislocation of the British strategic position and prestige in the North Atlantic, and therefore in the world, could ensue. In New Zealand the menace was internal, from a primitive race, provoked largely by the land-grabbing policy of the colonial government, and, even if the worst came to pass, was hardly a threat to the Empire as a whole or to British security and status. The immediate effect of both crises was to postpone, and then reverse, the policy of withdrawal.

But as a result of the different situations which pertained, colonial reactions and the policy of the home government revealed characteristic differences. Britain showed no hesitation in rushing troops to Canada, and the successive governments of Canada during and after the Civil War made no secret of their belief that Britain should protect them because they were exposed to dangers which would only be provoked by British policy. On the other hand, regulars were sent only reluctantly to New Zealand, and in view of the prospect of the withdrawal of the Royal Navy to cope with the American danger the New Zealanders for a time talked of "self-reliance." By the time the Civil War ended, however, limitations upon British financial responsibility in peacetime in North America had been established. These, although too high for the comfort of the British taxpayer, nevertheless made it clear that future military preparation in Canada was a Canadian responsibility. In New Zealand no similar simple formula for dividing the responsibility and the expense could be found. Ultimately, frustrated in its efforts to discover a formula for sharing defense expenditures and motivated as always by the desire to reduce expenses, Gladstone's Liberal government decided to cut its cloth everywhere, to resume its policy of withdrawal, and to carry it through to its logical conclusion, the recall of the garrisons from all self-governing colonies.

So, despite colonial disapproval, the Commons' resolution on the theme of self-government begetting self-defense was put into effect by the precipitate "recall of the legions" from all colonies except where it was prevented by local difficulties. The process was, of course, only plausible because the introduction of responsible government had made possible the transfer of responsibility for defense. Furthermore, concentration of the army in the United Kingdom had been carried out more readily because tension in Europe and danger to the British Isles themselves were increasing. At the end of the 1850's the French bogey had produced the Volunteer Movement, which the professional soldiers disparaged, and an unsound reliance on fortifications, to which reference has been made. During the Danish crises of 1862 and 1864, the discovery that Britain's voice was small in international politics because of her lack of an adequate professional army in Europe had furthered the process of withdrawal. The American Civil War had reversed the process in North America for a time, but the subsequent spectacular rise of Prussia saw the completion of the withdrawal of British regiments which might have been disgraced by the annihilation of all the small garrisons west of Quebec in the event of an American attack. In 1870–1871, as part of the Cardwell program of army reform, the last British troops in Canada outside the naval base at Halifax sailed away. The regulars also returned from Australia where some colonies at that time would have been willing to pay for their retention if they could obtain a guarantee that the troops would not be removed for emergencies elsewhere. The garrisons also came home from New Zealand where the Maoris were still unquelled. "By 1873," writes Colonel Stacey, "the Colonial Office could boast that in the colonies possessing responsible government there was no Imperial expenditure except for Imperial purposes." [56] Only in South Africa where responsible government was just being intro-

56. Stacey, *Canada and the British Army*, pp. 247–253, 255–256.

duced at the Cape was the reduction not as complete as Cardwell had planned. There the natives were too dangerous.

The "recall of the legions," which had been brought about for the sake of economy as a result of the agitation of the radicals, colonial reformers, and "Little Englanders," was sometimes rationalized on the grounds that strategic requirements had been altered by developments in technology. The new "fortress England" concept had, indeed, also been produced for similar technical reasons on the basis of the unsound premise that "steam bridged the channel." It was argued, though in fact it was not yet true because of the limited range of the new ships, that steam power could provide a more effective reinforcement of colonial outposts in emergency than in the days of sail and that scattered garrisons were, therefore, no longer necessary. Cardwell also needed a larger home force to provide reliefs for the garrisons that remained in imperial fortresses and in those colonies still without responsible government. Furthermore, growing humanitarianism was demanding yet more forcibly that British soldiers should not be left for unduly long tours in unhealthy tropical stations. And the need to build up a reserve in England by short-service enlistment made the colonial defense system inconvenient.

Nevertheless, although there was much truth in all these military arguments, this regrouping of forces for imperial defense was not militarily sound in itself. As there was a complete lack of cooperation between the departments of the home government, the withdrawal was not accompanied by a plan for imperial defense on effective strategic lines. While the Colonial Office and the War Office had tried, though with no great success, to agree on a pattern of colonial defense, the Admiralty had stood aloof. Much good work was being done by the sailors in the technical field in an effort to keep up with the French in warship development, but their lordships acted at times as if they thought that steam power had destroyed the navy's role as the main bulwark of imperial defense. The new defense policy of "fortress England" was, therefore, in some ways actually worse than the policy of scattered garrisons for colonial defense which it was replacing;

and the government and the soldiers, in their haste to economize and at the same time provide a larger military capability in the United Kingdom, had made little effort to insure that there would be adequate protection for the colonies that were being evacuated and had negotiated no defense agreements with them. The colonists were discouraged by evident signs that some of the Queen's ministers would be glad to see the Empire disintegrate. In the case of Canada, the first of the self-governing dominions, although imperial sentiment was as strong as in other colonies, defense against the United States seemed to be either impossible or unnecessary and to be needed only for imperial considerations. Military and naval concentration in Britain coupled with responsible government in the colonies posed a threat to the continued existence of the British Empire.

2

The American Civil War and the
Defense of Canada

The Origins of the Canadian Militia

The militia organization of Canada can be traced back to the *habitant*'s obligation of military service in New France, to early eighteenth-century militia companies in Nova Scotia, to the location of disbanded Loyalists by military companies in townships in Canada where the settlers were reissued their small arms "to shoot pigeons," to Simcoe's organization of a militia of Upper Canada in 1808 copied from the current English law, and to the "flank companies" which fought alongside the regulars in the War of 1812. But by the middle of the nineteenth century, all that remained of these precedents was an unused law requiring universal service for defense, and a false tradition that the militia had saved Canada in 1812. A more direct link can be established with the organization of volunteers in Upper and Lower Canada at the time of the Crimean War (partly modeled on volunteer movements in New York and New England) and with companies raised spontaneously in the Maritime Colonies in 1859 in anticipation of a visit by the Prince of Wales. In both instances, recruits were organized in a fashion similar to, but not copied from, the British Volunteer Movement. But these volunteers were ill-organized and amateur, little more effective from a military point of view than the rifle associations that flourished in Canada and other colonies. The real beginning of the organized Canadian Militia dates from the time of the American Civil War. With the rise of the military strength of the North, there was fear that the lust of conquest might lead the Union to want to round out

victory by overrunning the rest of North America; more especially, the *Trent* and *Alabama* incidents that brought Britain and
the United States close to war aroused concern for the security of
Canada.[1]

The story of British response to the *Trent* crisis is well known.
Despite the fact that a House of Commons committee had just
reported that self-governing colonies should protect themselves,
regulars were rushed to Canada in large numbers in winter to
warn off a feared American attack.[2] But when the first crisis
passed with the surrender of the Confederate delegates who had
been taken by the Union navy from the *Trent*, feeling in Britain
against colonial garrisons reasserted itself and Mills's famous
resolution was passed. At the same time the War Office, thinking
of its European worries, breathed a sigh of relief. The inspector
general of fortifications, General Sir John Burgoyne, drafted a
memorandum in which he stated his belief that the United States
would be disunited and weak for a long time, whatever the outcome of the war. Looking at the defenses of the Empire, he
argued that although the navy could not give adequate protection to any of the colonies, and although only the colonies in
Australia by reason of their purely British population and their
remoteness from danger could hope to protect themselves, the
principle that had now been adopted meant that in Canada the
colonial government must provide for defense by giving training
to the inhabitants, "to which the home government would add
a powerful assistance in case of attack, as it has done most liberally in the late threatening of hostilities." Fortifications, he went
on, and permanent standing defenses, though attractive to con-

1. For the history of the Canadian Militia, see C. F. Hamilton, "Defence,
1812–1912," in Adam Shortt and A. G. Doughty, eds., *Canada and its Provinces:
A History of the Canadian People and Their Institutions* . . . (Toronto: Glasgow, Brook, 1914), VII, 379–468; George F. G. Stanley, *Canada's Soldiers: The
Military History of an Unmilitary People* (rev. ed.; Toronto: Macmillan, 1960);
and Stacey, *Canada and the British Army*. For extra details on the militia before
1812, see Richard A. Preston, *Kingston before the War of 1812: A Collection of
Documents* . . . (Toronto: Champlain Society, 1959), pp. 69, 152, 230, 241,
244, 256, 280.
2. Full details of the British reinforcement of the Canadian garrison can be
found in Stacey, *Canada and the British Army*, pp. 117–178, and in J. Mackay
Hitsman, "Winter Troop Movements to Canada, 1862," *Canadian Historical Review*, XLIII (1962), 127–135.

template, were "out of the question." Neither the home government nor the colony could afford them.[3]

The rising might of the North's armies and a steady deterioration of relations between Britain and the United States soon renewed concern. To make proposals for the future security of
Canada, a military commission set up by the governor general,
Lord Monck, to advise the provincial government spent several
months going over the ground. Its military members and a Canadian engineer were appointed by the lieutenant general commanding in British North America, Sir W. Fenwick Williams;
and the Admiralty sent a naval captain from Washington, with
the appropriate name of Bythesea, to advise on naval matters.
These "professional gentlemen," as they were described, said the
defense of Canada would require 150,000 men, extensive fortifications of both a permanent and a temporary nature at nine
places from Quebec to Sarnia, and ironclads on the Great Lakes
armed with 550 guns and manned by 9,350 men. The cost of the
fortifications and dockyards alone would be £1,611,000.[4]

Following upon this report, the Horse Guards also recommended fortification in Canada. A Select Committee on Colonial
Defence, listing twenty-three colonial fortifications to be constructed, decided that Quebec should be made into a first-class
fortress.[5] Both recommendations, influenced by the contemporary
"fortress mentality," had ignored the significance of sea power,
had not faced up to the question of who would pay for the
elaborate works they proposed, and had not followed up Burgoyne's suggestion that the Canadian Militia should provide a
substantial part of the men.

Shortly afterward, Lieutenant Colonel W. F. D. Jervois, R.E.,

3. G.B., W.O., "Memorandum by Sir John Burgoyne on the Defence of Canada," Feb. 15, 1862, Confidential Papers, A 0165.
4. *Report of the Commissioners Appointed to Consider the Defences of Canada, 1862* (London, 1862), P.A.C., R.G. 8, Ser. 2, Vol. 18. The commissioners
were Col. John William Gordon, R.E., C.B., A.D.C. to the Queen; Lt. Col.
Henry Lynedoch Gardiner, R.A.; Hon. Hamilton Hartley Killaly, a distinguished
Canadian engineer; Capt. William Crossmann, R.E., Sec.; Col. Edward R.
Wetherall, C.B., chief of staff in Canada; and Capt. John Bythesea, V.C., C.B.,
R.N., naval attaché at Washington.
5. G.B., W.O., Duke of Cambridge, chairman, "Special Committee on Colonial Defence," 1863, Confidential Papers, 0172.

was sent to give his expert advice. He was a man with considerable experience during a period of extensive fortification in the British Isles. He had been an assistant to Burgoyne since 1856, the secretary of the Royal Commission on the Defences of the United Kingdom in 1859–1860, and from September 5, 1862, special adviser on fortifications to the secretary of state as deputy director of works for fortifications.

After a brief three weeks' stay in the Province of Canada (he spent a considerable part of his time on this trip in the West Indies), Jervois came to conclusions that were somewhat different from those of the commission of 1862. He had received a copy of its report which he annotated thus: "What is the good of these little posts. They can delay the enemy but a very short time, must eventually fall—why waste troops to defend them or money to build them." Noting that the Americans were erecting temporary, rather than permanent, defense works along their Atlantic coast, he argued that they must be expecting an early war with Britain. In that case Canada would be invaded. He said that the Canadians had not hitherto provided for their own defense because no "distinct systems of defence" had as yet been suggested to them. But the time had now come "to bring the matter to a point." To compel the province to contribute to its own defense, it should be threatened with the deprivation of the investments and credits which were an advantage of the British connection. The Western districts could not, however, be defended without naval superiority on the Great Lakes; and not even Lake Ontario could be held unless the Ottawa and Rideau canals were enlarged. Fortifications should be built at Montreal. Without them the army must retire to Quebec. The improvement of the defenses at Kingston, which Jervois preferred as the location of the naval base on Lake Ontario to a Bay-of-Quinte base recommended in 1862, was "contingent on measures being taken by the Province for the enlargement of the Ottawa and Rideau canals." In his first report Jervois thus virtually advocated the abandoning of Upper Canada in the event of war with the United States.[6]

6. G.B., [C.O.], *Report on the Defence of Canada by Lt.-Col. Jervois, February, 1864* (London, 1864).

When he received Jervois's report, W. E. Gladstone, who was chancellor of the exchequer, seized upon it to support his own "Little Englander" position. He pointed out that there were serious discrepancies between the proposals made by the 1862 commission and those now made by the inspector of fortifications. Both had recommended fortifications—but in very different places. Gladstone doubted whether even the lower St. Lawrence River could be held now that the Americans had steam warships; and he therefore questioned whether Quebec itself was really worth fortifying. He declared that Britain's responsibilities terminated at the end of the sea lanes and that British North America ought to unite in order to defend itself. He showed that the commissioners of 1862 and Colonel Jervois alike had based their proposals on an estimate of American capabilities rather than on American intentions. He obviously thought it very unlikely that after its present traumatic experience the Republic would want to embark upon new adventures.[7] Palmerston, the prime minister, did not act on these lines. But allowing for Gladstone's known prejudices, his assessment was a fair indication of the real problem. Future Canadian defense policy must be based on a sound judgment of American intentions, for these would govern any British and Canadian measures made to meet a potentially overwhelming attack.

Meanwhile, British efforts exerted through the governor general to attempt to bring John A. Macdonald's government to face the cost of the defense of Upper Canada had led to stalemate. In 1861 a government of the Province of Canada had asked for arms to encourage the development of the militia, and some had been sent. But the province had not offered to pay for transportation.[8] On the other hand, the British government had decided in 1860 that whereas since 1854 it had been the practice for the War Office to provide small arms, ordnance, ammunition, and

7. William E. Gladstone, "Confidential Memorandum on the Defence of Canada," July 12, 1864, in Paul Knaplund, *Gladstone and Britain's Imperial Policy* (New York: Macmillan, 1927), pp. 228–242.

8. Stacey, *Canada and the British Army*, p. 119. See also an account of Prince Edward Island's difficulty in obtaining arms in J. MacKay Hitsman, "Military Defenders of Prince Edward Island, 1775–1864," *Annual Report of the Canadian Historical Association*, 1964, pp. 25–36.

other military stores to the colonies either as gifts or as loans on repayment according to circumstances, rifles and ammunition for volunteers were now to be issued only against payment or loan subject to withdrawal. On May 14, 1862, the government applied this principle to "arms of any description" issued to colonies.[9] Both countries were now beginning to look more closely at the reckoning.

The bill for the defense of British North America was bound to be immense. While the cost of reinforcements to the Maritime Provinces and Canada increased Britain's annual appropriation for this area (excluding that for the naval base at Halifax) from about £250,000 to about £850,000, with an extra non-recurring charge for transportation costs of £274,000, Macdonald's Militia Bill would have added over $1,000,000, or a little more than one-tenth of the annual revenue of the province, to a militia appropriation that was less than $100,000.[10] Unable to put through so great a levy, Macdonald's government, which had become corrupt and unpopular, fell without making provision for the militia. Fifteen of his French-Canadian supporters deserted him over his proposals to introduce conscription, but it was clear that dislike for the bill was not restricted to Quebec. So, partly because of Canadian public opinion on this matter, the Province of Canada did little in 1862 to help to ward off an American invasion, which, in fact, then seemed hardly credible. In view of the very different spirit previously shown in the province during the brief *Trent* crisis, it is clear—now that the British government had temporarily patched up its more serious differences with the Union—that the Canadian people and also Sandfield Macdonald's government, which followed that of his more illustrious namesake, were no longer convinced there was urgent danger. The Canadians had begun to question the extent of their obligation to back British policy. In these circumstances it was obviously unlikely that Canada could be brought to assume a charge for more

9. "Regulations Concerning the Despatch of Arms to the Colonies," Lugard to Rogers, March 27, 1862, and Newcastle to Monck, May 14, 1862, P.A.C., R.G. 7, G. 26, No. 165, Vol. 1.
10. These figures are adapted from those given in Stacey, *Canada and the British Army*, pp. 128, 131–132, 143.

than £1.5 million for permanent fortifications on the American border. Hence, at a time when Britain had just sent vast help without a moment's hesitation, Canadian indifference in their own defense aroused intense ill-feeling in the mother country. At no other time have Canadians been in so low esteem in Britain as they were in 1862.[11]

In 1863, however, after Vicksburg and Gettysburg made a Northern victory likely, and as friction over the blockade continued, the province began to awaken to a sense of its responsibilities. The Militia Act and Volunteer Militia Act of that year produced a thorough reorganization of the system of enrolment, paid for schools of instruction (to be manned by British regulars and conducted in the barracks of the garrison), but replaced the compulsion of Macdonald's bill by a renewed emphasis on the voluntary principle. In this form, and in the circumstances of the obviously growing military might of the North demonstrated at Gettysburg, the act was passed. The province now spent $500,-000 a year on defense where eight years before it had reluctantly spent $10,000.[12]

Jervois was sent back to Canada at Canadian request in 1864 to make a more detailed report and to advise the provincial government about the defense of the province. He now modified his earlier recommendations. He said he found that the provincial ministers were "ready to meet the mother country in a fair and becoming spirit in carrying out the measures which are requisite for the defence of Canada," and he dropped his earlier proposals for using financial pressure on them. Without again insisting upon the improvement of the Ottawa and Rideau canals, he stated that he understood Lake Ontario could be held because the province would make provision for a fortified harbor and naval establishment at Kingston; and he proposed a scheme for the defense of the west of the province, either until reinforcements arrived from other parts of the country, or until the winter season obliged the enemy to retire. He estimated the total cost

11. *Ibid.*, pp. 137–142.
12. *Ibid.*, pp. 148–152.

of the necessary fortifications, mainly at Quebec and Montreal, at £1,754,000.

Jervois advised the provincial government to convert its militia into a trained force that could wage a delaying campaign in the event of an American attack. He believed that if Canada had 140,000 men, they might be able to hold the country as far west as Lake Huron against the largest invasion the Americans could mount, if at the same time the Americans were being forced by the Royal Navy to disperse their manpower to protect their whole Atlantic coast. But his reference to successive lines of defense in Upper Canada suggests that he was still not completely confident on this score. In the covering letter to the secretary of state for war when his report was forwarded to the War Office, Jervois said he hoped British regulars would be left in the west of the province to train the militia.[13]

Jervois's second report was thus significantly different from his first. The difference was influenced by a growing expectation that Canada would organize her manpower for self-defense. Despite the fact that the freezing of the St. Lawrence would prevent British reinforcements and supplies from reaching Quebec by water, he stressed reliance on winter for the protection of Upper Canada. He thus repeated a point which had been forwarded earlier by Dorchester and Simcoe and which Burgoyne had made in his instructions to the commissioners of 1862. In fact, Jervois's proposals for the defense of Canada, which were described soon afterward as being a new approach to the problem, largely followed Burgoyne's first thoughts in 1862.[14]

By 1865 Canada was frightened again. The war was obviously coming to an end, and no one knew what the American armies might do next. Canadian commissioners went to England to negotiate—according to Gladstone in "feverish impatience"—for aid against a threat which they were now convinced would come

13. G.B., [C.O.], *Report on the Defence of Canada, 10 November, 1864* [Col. Jervois] (London, 1865), *passim*.
14. *Report of the Commission of 1862*, Memorandum of Instructions, Gen. J. F. Burgoyne, Feb. 24, 1862, P.A.C., R.G. 8, II, 18; "Colonel Jervois's Memorandum" [1873?], P.A.C., Dufferin Papers, Canadian Letters, Vol. 2, No. 48.

the following spring. But they still argued that danger to Canada would come only from "an Imperial War on Imperial grounds." For this reason they claimed that Britain ought to give them special and generous consideration. All that they could obtain was a promise that the imperial government would complete the defenses at Quebec. The Canadians could secure no promise of the maintenance of British ships on the Great Lakes and no loan to build fortifications west of Quebec. They accepted instead a proposal to the effect that Britain would guarantee the interest on money which the province would borrow to fortify Montreal.[15] Because the commissioners were unable to obtain satisfaction over the return of the gunboats to the Great Lakes (which would have involved repudiation of the Rush-Bagot Agreement), Quebec was in fact to be fortified in accordance with the plans originated by Burgoyne without any reciprocal action by Canada.

Thus, the defense of Canada in 1865 continued to depend on British regulars, and there were no border fortifications for their use. However, the young men of the province showed great enthusiasm for the new militia training they received in schools of instruction, and great strides were made. To foster the militia, the War Office had sent Colonel Sir Patrick L. MacDougall, whose text on *The Theory of War* was regarded as the foremost work on military theory in English at that time. As a former superintendent of studies at the Royal Military College at Sandhurst and as first commandant of the Staff College, he was one of the army's leading thinkers. MacDougall had gone to Canada in 1862, and around that time he had written memoranda on the possibility of war with the United States and the defense of Canada which may have influenced those who had reported on defense during the Civil War years. MacDougall was appointed adjutant general of the Canadian Militia in 1865. A year later,

15. [Province of Canada, Legislative Assembly], *Papers Relating to the Conferences Which Have Taken Place Between Her Majesty's Government and a Deputation from the Executive Council of Canada Appointed to Confer with Her Majesty's Government on the Subject of the Defence of the Province* (Ottawa: [Queen's Printer?], 1865), pp. 1–5.

Colonel Garnet Wolseley, who had become deputy quartermaster general of the British garrison, acted as commandant of a camp of instruction on the Niagara peninsula. Wolseley was to gain a great reputation in the colonial wars of the late nineteenth century as one of the British army's fighting soldiers and military organizers. The combination of MacDougall, the academic theorist, and Wolseley, the vigorous practical leader, was a rare one which rapidly showed results in the improvement of the Canadian Militia. Wolseley's work has attracted the greater attention, and MacDougall's has been largely overlooked. But Wolseley himself and Governor General Lord Monck, who were in a position to know, attributed to MacDougall the rapid creation of an efficient militia force which eventually numbered 25,000 men.[16]

The Reassessment of Defense Responsibilities

During the Civil War, in anticipation of the danger of an American attack, Britain had had to shoulder almost the whole burden of Canadian defense measures. Despite the efforts of Cardwell at the Colonial Office, the old principle of sharing defense responsibilities had not been effectively re-established; only in the years that followed the war had Canada moved hesitantly to provide for resistance to raids or to the first wave of an invasion. During the same years the Maoris had rudely demonstrated in New Zealand that the reaction of a primitive people to colonial invasion or an internal security problem, whichever the troubles in that colony can be labeled, could be enough

16. Monck, Testimonial to MacDougall, Oct. 3, 1868, P.R.O., C.O. 42/611, Monck 186; Field Marshal Garnet Viscount Wolseley, *The Story of a Soldier's Life* (New York: Scribners, 1904), I, 145–151; Jay Luvaas, "General Sir Patrick MacDougall, the American Civil War, and the Defence of Canada," *Annual Report of the Canadian Historical Association*, 1962, pp. 44–54. MacDougall's writings on Canada were "On the the Prospect of War with the United States" (National Library of Wales, Aberystwyth, Lewis Papers, 2943); By an Officer, *Forts versus Ships: Also Defence of the Canadian Lakes* (London: James Ridgway, 1862), which included *The Defence of the Canadian Lakes and Its Influence on the General Defence of Canada;* and Anon., "Canada: The Fenian Raid and the Colonial Office," *Blackwood's Edinburgh Magazine*, CVIII (Oct., 1870), 493–508. MacDougall seems to have had a passion for anonymity. His biography of Napier was published in 1864 under the name of its editor, H. A. Bruce, later Lord Aberdare, who was also a son-in-law of the historian.

to render quite impossible a rational apportionment of the responsibilities of a mother country and colony.[17] Nevertheless, in 1865, Canadian and British ministers, negotiating about defense, exchanged mutual promises which revised the old formula by suggesting something more than the traditional willingness to supply untrained militia units as an administrative tail to a British regular force. As the Canadian minister of militia was to state on a later occasion, this change was to the effect that "the Imperial government will defend every portion of the Empire with all its resources at its command, on the reciprocal assurances given by the Canadian ministers then in London that Canada was ready to devote all her resources both in men and money to the maintenance of her connection with the mother country." [18] The last part of the statement could only mean that Canada would prepare to defend herself until help should come; and it had been expected, though not actually agreed, that this would be done by building fortifications at Montreal and further west and by the development of the Canadian Militia.

This new attempt to restate and redefine the apportionment of the defense burden, however, was subject to considerable strain. Before the negotiations had begun, a Canadian Cabinet committee had reported the following:

> On the one hand there is the accumulated wealth of centuries, nourishing and stimulating the national industry to the highest point and drawing yearly into the national coffers vast tribute from the industry of colonies and foreign countries, all over the world, mortgaged to the Capitalists of England. On the other hand there is a Country of yesterday, vast in extent, sparsely populated without accumulated wealth, almost entirely agricultural, and the profits of its annual industry to be found, not in floating wealth but in lands cleared, new woods opened, new mineral resources discovered, new barns, new orchards, improved stock and gradually increasing ca-

---

17. Angus John Harrop, *England and the Maori Wars* (London: New Zealand News, 1937), pp. 241–242. Gerald C. Hensley, "The Withdrawal of British Troops from New Zealand, 1864–1870" (unpublished M.A. thesis, University of Canterbury, 1957), gives a stimulating account of the difficulties of "self-reliance" on the one hand and of a sharing of defense burdens on the other.

18. Department of Militia and Defence, Memorandum, "Withdrawal of the Garrisons," March 16, 1870, P.A.C., Macdonald Papers, M.G. 26, A 1 (a), Vol. 100, p. 102.

pacity of production. . . . The capacity for taxation for defence [is] necessarily limited for years to come.[19]

This argument, of course, was prepared to strengthen the resolution of the negotiators going to London; but Canadians undoubtedly believed that there was much truth in it.

Furthermore, there was room for divergence of opinion about whose interests defensive measures were designed to protect, and therefore who should pay for such measures. At first sight it might seem that Canadians, being exposed to danger and loss, should provide the greater part of the defenses in North America. But quite apart from their capacity to do so, there was a question whether the British, rather than the Canadians, were greater beneficiaries of the freedom of Canada from American conquest. Lieutenant General Sir John Michel, leaving his command in North America in 1867, wrote to urge the development of the Canadian Militia. "The worst that could happen to Canada," he said, "would be annexation to a free and prosperous country. To England, pecuniary ruin and loss of prestige." [20] The existence of several printed copies of this letter among Sir John A. Macdonald's papers suggested that someone thought it important, perhaps as a stimulus for the Militia Bill. But the sentence quoted may have had the opposite effect from that which the writer obviously intended. Two or three years earlier, the colony of Victoria had produced figures which showed the trade and shipping that needed protection in Australian waters was almost all British-owned.[21] The belief that the interests in jeopardy were British rather than colonial was everywhere, to a greater or lesser degree, always a deterrent to the assumption by the colonies of a heavier share of the general burden of defense. To assert that a colony should be prepared to protect itself was not suffi-

19. *Report of the Committee of the . . . Executive Council . . . Approved by His Excellency*, March 27, 1865, P.A.C., R.G. 7, G. 21, No. 165, Vol. 2.
20. Michel to Macdonald, Aug. 14, 1867, P.A.C., Macdonald Papers, M.G. 26, A 1 (a), Vol. 100.
21. Victoria, *Report of Select Committee on National Defences*, July, 1865, (n.p., n.d.), in Australian National War Memorial Library; *Report of Mr. Verdon's Proceedings as the Delegate of Victoria to H.M. Govt. Upon the Subject of the Colonial Defences* (Melbourne, 1867), in Victoria, Department of Defence, *Printed Papers*, I, 1862–1901, No. 3, Department of Defence Library, Canberra.

ciently precise. In Canada the result was that although the fortifications at Quebec—described by the Defence Committee in
1865 as the "Torres Vedras" of Canada—were substantially developed by the British in the two or three years following the
Civil War, there was no agreement that other fortresses were
necessary, and no sod was turned by Canada at Montreal or
further west.

Canadian reaction to the American Civil War was indicative
of future developments. Slowness to arm was due not merely to
objection to expenditure on arms, or to objection to conscription,
but also to the unsatisfactory nature of imperial defense relations.
When the danger was great, the government and people of Canada were ready to defend their homeland, even though, as they
realized on reflection, the emergency had been created by British
policy in which they had had no voice. When crises passed, and
there was only the need to prepare for a future attack based
on the potential military strength of the United States, military
ardor waned. Furthermore, as a result of frequent British intimations that Britain could not protect Canada fully against a major
invasion, "whatever the cause," Canadian confidence in the British connection was shaken. The experience of the Civil War
seemed to show that Canada would only be likely to experience
American aggression as a result of a British clash with the United
States about matters that were not of direct Canadian concern.
And Britain, even when the St. Lawrence was unobstructed by
ice, could guarantee Canadian security only by the deterrent
power of her naval guns. Nevertheless, this did not signify a spirit
of defeatism on the part of Canadians. On the contrary, if war
must come, whatever its origin, Canadians would resist the invader. Although not very willing to make defense preparations
in time of peace, they would play their part in time of war.
Richard Cartwright, political opponent of Sir John A. Macdonald
from his own hometown of Kingston, analyzed this dichotomy
of the Canadian mind in an attempt to promote development of
the militia; and he was not merely whistling to keep up his courage. He believed that American exhaustion at the end of the
war, and American obligations in event of war, would mean that

only 250,000 men could be sent against Canada. When they were defending their homes, 100,000 Canadians would be sufficient to meet such a threat with the aid of half as many British regulars.[22] But in the years immediately following the war, few more than one-tenth of that number were being trained annually. Canada's security, even by Cartwright's reckoning, was therefore problematical. It rested on the fact that the Americans had rapidly reduced their wartime military strength.

The significant strategic consideration was that in a war between Britain and the United States, Canada would not be the decisive theater. The province was not a vital part of the Empire, and the British could not launch a war-winning drive from Quebec or Ontario, although some professional strategists were actually still thinking forty years later on the lines of Major General Sir James Carmichael-Smyth's plan of 1825.[23] In the event of war with the United States, Britain's plans were built upon the capacity of sea power to launch attacks on American trade and the American coast.[24] In these attacks, Halifax would be useful, which is one reason why it was maintained so long as a British naval base.[25] As the coast defenses built by the United States in the next twenty years clearly show, a threat to the American seaboard would be Canada's best defense. But Canada would be merely expendable, something to divert the Americans while the Royal Navy got to work. The prospect of being a sacrifice was unattractive. Hence, Canadian interest in building up military strength to make the sacrifice useful was sluggish. At the same time, the argument that Canadian independence ultimately rested on the effectiveness of the Royal Navy and on its power to deter the United States from aggression did not encourage Canada to build up land forces that were merely secondary

22. Richard Cartwright, *Remarks on the Militia of Canada* (Kingston: Daily News Office, 1864), p. 27.
23. See below, pp. 329–332; James R. Talman, "A Secret Military Document," *American Historical Review*, XXXVIII (Jan., 1933), 295–300.
24. Kenneth Bourne, "British Preparations for War with the North, 1861–1862," *English Historical Review*, LXXVI (1961), 621.
25. Halifax's strategic significance is described in Charles P. Stacey, "Halifax as an International Strategic Factor, 1749–1909," *Annual Report of the Canadian Historical Association*, 1949, pp. 46–56. A full account is in Mackinnon, "The Imperial Fortresses in Canada."

weapons. The Canadian defense dilemma was that which inevitably faces the small power closely allied to a greater one. The small power does not make the policies which lead to war, and it does not decide the nature of the over-all strategy. It may well find itself sacrificed as a pawn for the common good, with its only consolation a promise that it would be recovered with the eventual victory which would come more surely if it pulled its full weight. In these circumstances a small power often finds it difficult to do its duty and to maintain its honor. The problem of the British Empire in the future was to find a formula that would spur colonials to greater defense efforts.

3

The Origins of Canadian Control
of Military Affairs

"The crown of the edifice is military force." These words, used
by George Etienne Cartier in the debate on his Canadian Militia
Bill in 1868, suggest an awareness of the relation between armed
strength and the Dominion's autonomy that at first sight appears
extremely misleading. In view of Canada's continued dependence upon Britain, which had been so spectacularly demonstrated during the recent Civil War, and also in view of the fact
that it was not yet known that within three years the transports
carrying the last of the British garrison would loose their moor-
ings and slip quietly down the St. Lawrence to the sentimental
strains of "Auld Lang Syne," Cartier cannot have meant that he
was preparing for a military capability to give full protection to
the new Dominion. Nor did he intend to imply that he would
complete the process of political separation by giving Canada
absolute command of its own forces and therefore of its destiny.
He was not attempting to suggest that Canada should be able to
defend herself against all comers, even the mother country. What
he meant was merely that in accordance with the liberal doctrine
by virtue of which the new Dominion had been conceived, political autonomy was not enough: Canada must also contribute
to her own defense. It is true that like politicians everywhere,
Cartier had a quick eye for immediate political advantage, and
the militia could provide a cheap form of patronage. But if he
had an ulterior purpose, the natural result was nevertheless
Dominion control of military affairs. Cartier's Militia Act, it will
be shown, suggests a realization of the desirability for the new

state to have as complete control over its own forces as it possessed in the political and economic fields. If its political development as a self-governing colony were to be effective, the Dominion could not tolerate external interference in military matters. Most Canadian statesmen since that time have seen the force of this argument which some critics, who have spoken of "excessive Canadian sensitivity" on the point, have missed.

This assertion of Canada's control of its own military strength came at a time when the threatening shadow of the might of the neighbor to the south had not yet entirely lifted. With this the fact, it is all the more remarkable that Cartier and his colleagues in the Cabinet should have insisted upon their right to decide what they would add to the British military force protecting Canada and how the force would be organized. The explanation for their position may be either that they were confident that effective British help would come to reinforce the garrison and militia, or that they believed defense against the United States would be hopeless, or, what is more likely, that they felt such defense would never be required. In all probability, all these ideas were interwoven in the minds of Canadians. Furthermore, after the British garrison had left, from the time the shadow seemed to lift in 1871 until the first Russian scare in 1878, there was little thought that specific preparations were needed against any other enemy. This fact would make it appear that such steps as were taken in military organization in Canada in the next seven years, even if they also had a political motive, were designed to put into practice the abstract doctrine that Cartier had enunciated in 1868: that a state, if it wished to claim mastery in the conduct of its own affairs, must possess armed strength and control it. These early years in the history of the Dominion were, then, an important formative period in the defense structure of the future British Commonwealth. During this period must be sought the origins of the principle of mastery of the dominions' own military resources that was to enable them to contribute so effectively to the defense of the Commonwealth and the free world in the twentieth century.

The Dominion Reaches for the Sword

Despite the apparent reluctance of the new Dominion to shoulder its military responsibilities, there was evidence that it was dimly aware of the relation between armed force and nationhood. When Cartier, introducing his Militia Bill in 1868, uttered the sentiment quoted at the beginning of this chapter, he told the Canadian House of Commons, "three indispensable elements constitute a nation—population, territory, and the sea. But the crown of the edifice—also indispensable—is military force. No people can lay claim to the title of a nation if it does not possess a military element—the means of defence."[1] A similar need for the development of the military strength of the self-governing colonies was seen by British soldiers and Colonial Office officials. Thus, for instance, Colonel Garnet Wolseley, deputy quartermaster general in Canada from 1867, urged the Canadian government to "adopt some line of military policy that would at least make those who ruled in 'the Old Country' anxious to help them effectively in case of need."[2] But these two statements on the same theme show that although British and Canadians had the same end in mind, they looked at the problem of the military relations between the mother country and colony from different points of view. Wolseley regarded the growth of Canadian military strength merely as an auxiliary to British power. Cartier, although soon to protest against the withdrawal of British garrison troops and so to admit tacitly that Canada depended on Britain, already had a fleeting vision of a Canada of the future that would be strong in its own right.

Canadian politicians had long been aware of the need to keep control of military expenditure in their own hands. In 1862, when Governor General Monck had suggested cyclical five-year budgeting to offset the dangers that might result from a political crisis like the defeat of Macdonald's Militia Bill, Canadian ministers

1. John Boyd, *Sir George Etienne Cartier: His Life and Times: A Political History of Canada from 1814 to 1873* (Toronto: Macmillan, 1914), p. 291.
2. Wolseley, *Story of a Soldier's Life*, II, 145–151.

had been shocked. His proposal, they had said, "will never and ought never to be entertained by a People inheriting the freedom guaranteed by British institutions." If there were reasons in its favor, this device would have been applicable in England as well as in Canada. "Popular liberties are safe against military despotism wielded by a corrupt government only when they [the people] have in their hands the means of controlling the supplies required for the maintenance of a military organization." The awkward fact, pointed out by the colonial secretary when quoting these statements, namely that the Canadians saw no threat to their liberties in continued reliance upon British regulars, did not deny this argument.[3] It was by dislike of British control, rather than of corrupt government, that the Canadians were actually motivated, and five years might well have been long enough to destroy their effective control of the sword and with it of their own destiny. The foundations for "self-reliance," although not made into a shibboleth as in contemporary New Zealand, were thus effectively established in Canada in the 1860's. They may have survived in both countries simply because they were not subject to heavier pressure than was then experienced.

The federation of the North American provinces was an important stage in the evolution of Canadian military strength. During the British-Canadian defense discussions in 1865, when experiencing difficulty in securing a guarantee of British naval protection on the Great Lakes, the Canadian representatives realized confederation might bring some of the security which they sought.[4] Actually, the union of the British North American colonies brought no immediate military advantage; indeed, when it was followed quickly by westward expansion, confederation seemed actually to increase the vulnerability of Canada. But the instinct of the "Fathers of Confederation" was sound. The ultimate significance of confederation in the military field was that

3. Newcastle to Monck, Dec. 20, 1862, P.A.C., R.G. 7, G. 21, Vol. 74, No. 165, Vol. 1.
4. Gabrielle J. Sellars, "Edward Cardwell at the Colonial Office, 1864–66; Some Aspects of His Policy and Ideas" (unpublished B. Litt. thesis, Oxford University, 1958), pp. 96–102.

it made responsible government potentially more effective for the organization of defense. Furthermore, it at once laid the foundations for a Canada that would remain independent of the United States. Whether Canada would have so remained had it not been for the silent pressure of the Royal Navy is a question that cannot be answered with certainty, for it was never put to the test. Even without a test, it is safe to assume that it was not British sea power but the creation of the Dominion that ultimately forestalled manifest destiny in the Middle West. Therefore, confederation is a landmark in the history of Canadian defense. It and responsible government, taken together, are far more important events on the road toward the assumption of Canadian responsibility for defense than is the more obvious military measure, the withdrawal of the British regulars. For once the foundations of a nation were laid, the days of the garrisons must surely have been numbered.

The Control of the Canadian Militia

The framers of the British North America Act were careful to assert more specifically the Canadian control of Canadian military power that had been implicit since the introduction of responsible government in the 1840's. In the old Province of Canada, in many contemporary colonies including Prince Edward Island (of which Lord Monck was "Governor and Commander-in-Chief" while "Governor General" of the Dominion of Canada), and indeed in Canada itself in the twentieth century, command of the armed forces was lodged in the governor, or governor general, by virtue of his royal commission; but in 1867, Section 15 of the British North America Act declared that the commander in chief of the armed forces continued to be the Queen. Although Monck's commission for the Province of Canada had been as "Captain General and Governor-in-Chief," he became simply "Governor-General of the Dominion of Canada," and neither his commission nor his instructions made reference to a military command. With the Queen as commander in chief, the way might seem to have been opened for British influence through the general officer commanding the regulars.

However, Cartier's Militia Act of 1868 authorized the Queen "personally," or the governor general as her representative, to act as commander in chief to Canada. In so enacting, the statute declared that it was repeating Section 15 of the British North America Act; but that section makes no reference to the governor general. It seems very likely then that here there was a premeditated assertion of the Canadian Parliament's control of the militia.[5] It was a retort to the recent position taken by the Colonial Office in 1863 when it had advised the governor of Victoria that the governor of a colony ought to be the commander in chief "as was the case already in Canada" and elsewhere.[6] It also was a retort to the implication in the British North America Act which, by giving "Her Majesty" vast powers in relation to the command and calling out of the militia, appeared to empower the British government. The governor general was commander in chief in the Dominion of Canada from 1868, but he held that position only by virtue of an act of the Canadian Parliament and not by the authority either of the Queen or of the British Parliament.

Like the Queen, the governor general, of course, was intended to be only a titular commander of the forces. What is more, he was usually a civilian with little knowledge of military matters. Even so, he was still in some degree the agent of the British government, and the War Office provided him with a lieutenant colonel as military secretary to advise him and help him administer his military functions. As the Canadian ministers were also inexperienced in military matters, it was still possible for the governor to have influence and to exert pressure in military af-

5. Vict. c. 40. Monck's commission for the Dominion is in Canada, *Sessional Papers, I, 1867–1868*, Vol. 7, No. 22. He had been "Governor-General of British North America" before 1867, but this was an unimportant office. The title "commander in chief" was reintroduced into the governor general's commission in 1905 after the Militia Act of 1904 had set up a Militia Council and had transferred the emergency power to call out the militia from the sovereign to the governor in council (Canada, *Sessional Papers, XLVI, 1912*, Vol. 24, No. 83, p. 2; Charles P. Stacey, "John A. Macdonald on Raising Troops in Canada for Imperial Service, 1885," *Canadian Historical Review*, XXXVIII [March, 1957], 39). By that time the governer general's military functions were clearly nominal.

6. Newcastle to Barkly, April 6, 1863, Victoria, *P.P.*, 1862–1863, IV, No. 82.

fairs, even though the source of his command powers was Canadian legislation. His actions could affect both the regular forces in Canada (insofar as the general officer who commanded them would permit) and also the Canadian Militia.

The use of the governor general's influence, or even something more, was believed likely by British soldiers and perhaps by the British government as well. Sir John Michel, the lieutenant general commanding the British forces in North America, when acting as administrator of the Dominion during the absence of Lord Monck in 1867, proposed that the governor general's authority in time of peace should be extended over the naval forces on the Great Lakes. He added that in time of war those forces, being secondary, should come under the general officer commanding. His knuckles were rapped by the colonial secretary, not for claiming too much for the governor general in military matters, but for making a suggestion that might upset the Admiralty.[7] The governor general's potential influence in military matters was thus taken for granted. Hence, the fact that he held his authority by virtue of a Canadian act had considerable importance. It was equally significant that the clause in the Militia Act (para. 61) arranging for the militia to be handed over by "Her Majesty" in emergency to the commander of the regular forces in Canada was permissive and not obligatory, and that it was never made clear who was to advise the sovereign when action was to be taken. British soldiers (and later historians) were often to talk as if the handing over of the militia would be automatic in an emergency. But the use of the phrases "Her Majesty" and "Her Majesty personally" in connection with the command, discipline, and calling out of the Canadian Militia cannot be taken to mean that either Queen Victoria or the British government had unrestricted power or untrammeled authority. The Canadian Parliament's control of the purse was a restriction on that power. In fact, the act had been so framed that when the need arose the government of Canada would decide.

Cartier, who was responsible for the Militia Bill, being Mac-

7. Michel to C.O., March 25, 1867, P.R.O., C.O., 42/662, Monck 36.

donald's chief French-Canadian colleague, had had his choice
of ministerial offices. IIis biographer says that he selected the
Militia Department because it was a challenge.[8] It gave him control of a considerable amount of patronage. But is it too much
to believe he realized that it also gave him the opportunity to
supervise completion of the structure of confederation in what
was probably the most important remaining sphere—the grasp
of the sword? Cartier's Militia Act followed largely the lines of
the militia acts of the Province of Canada, but it differed in some
very important details. It greatly strengthened the position of the
minister by comparison with his position in the Province of Canada. In a new clause placed prominently at the beginning of the
text, the minister was made responsible for administration of the
militia and for initiating all militia matters involving the expenditure of money, under the supervision of the governor in council,
i.e., the Cabinet.

With regard to the actual military command, the act made
provision only for an adjutant general who was required to be a
professional soldier who had reached field rank in the regular
army and who was charged "under the orders of Her Majesty
with the Military command and discipline of the Militia." At
this time an adjutant general was merely an administrative staff
officer. In the administration of the militia the adjutant general
was given great responsibility. It had been laid down in supplementary regulations before confederation that he was "solely
responsible" to the government for all expenditure on militia
account, and that he alone "under the minister" had power to
authorize expenditure.[9]

However, less than a year after the bill was passed, Cartier
showed where power of command actually lay. Colonel Mac-
Dougall, whose work had strengthened the Canadian Militia,
resigned. Officially, to save Cartier's face, MacDougall was said
to have left because the rates of pay and allowance provided
under the bill were too low. Actually, he informed Cartier that

8. Boyd, *Sir George Etienne Cartier*, p. 293.
9. Report of Col. P. L. MacDougall, Ottawa, March, 1868, Appendix No. 10,
"Regulations Respecting the Volunteer Militia," Sept. 6, 1866, in Canada, *Sessional Papers, I, 1867–1868*, Vol. 7, No. 35, p. 129.

he would resign as adjutant general unless penalties were included in the act to compel men who had volunteered to complete their terms of engagement. MacDougall had also protested against political interference with his attempts to discipline two militia officers, Lieutenant Colonel Shaw and Major Bowell. Shaw had been convicted by a Court of Enquiry for conduct unbecoming an officer and gentleman by making false statements about the performance of his duties. Bowell had criticized a senior officer and had claimed impunity as a member of Parliament and a newspaper editor. Cartier, although expressing great appreciation of the work MacDougall had done, made no effort to keep him.[10]

Constitutionally, Cartier may perhaps have been correct in overriding the adjutant general's action; but this form of assertion of the supremacy of the civil power carried with it the serious danger of political interference with the standards of professional competence in the armed forces. Although MacDougall's successor, Colonel P. Robertson-Ross, was allowed to call himself "the Chief Executive Officer . . . charged under the orders of Her Majesty with the Military Command and Discipline of the Militia," [11] it was now unlikely that the authority of the minister would again be challenged by an adjutant general. Executive command in this case was very far from supreme command.

Nevertheless, by 1870 the Canadian Militia had progressed a long way toward fulfilling the ideas of British soldiers as well as Canadian statesmen. Cartier's Militia Act had reaffirmed the voluntary principle which the electorate had indorsed in 1863, and the militia had been expanded by a few more than the 40,000 contemplated by the act. But those who served voluntarily often thought their neighbors ought to be compelled to share the burden, and recruits were not always plentiful, even

10. MacDougall to Cartier, May 13 and 18, 1868, R.A.C., R.G. 9, I.C. 1/290; "Return to an Address of the House of Commons, 10 May, 1869 . . . ," Canada, *Sessional Papers, II, 1869,* Vol. 5, No. 31; D. P. Morton, "The Canadian Militia, 1867–1900" (Canadian Army Historical Section MS, 1964), pp. 15–16.

11. "Militia Report for 1869," Canada, *Sessional Papers, III, 1870,* Vol. 4, No. 8, p. 3. Robertson-Ross had commanded irregular cavalry in the Kaffir wars and had served in the Crimea, earning distinction on both occasions (*Army and Navy Gazette,* July 28, 1883).

in the English-speaking areas.[12] The Canadian part-time soldiers
had shown themselves able to muster quickly against the Fenians
and to accompany the regulars on a remarkable long march into
the interior against Riel. In the West they had not been called
upon to fight great battles, but in a crisis the system had worked
well until fighting was necessary at Ridgeway. The militia was
not yet ready for operations, and training and discipline left
much to be desired, but the foundations of a Canadian army had
been laid.[13] MacDougall, in an article which he published after
his resignation, defended Canada's military effort by describing
the volunteer militia as "a force which, in proportion to the
wealth and population of the two countries respectively, is much
larger than the English army and militia, and even exceeds that
army with all its reserves taken together." [14] Robertson-Ross reported that the militia administration under the minister "was
simple and effective" and "worked with ease and smoothness." [15]
The organization of individual rifle companies into battalions,
instituted for urban units in 1859, was extended to rural units on
a territorial basis in 1866.[16] However, the Canadian Militia had
as yet no operational staff and no supporting units. It was not
an army capable of taking the field on its own. It depended
upon the British regulars for stores, services, and instruction,
and as long as the garrisons remained, further development in
these respects was not needed.

The Effect of British Withdrawal

Early in 1869 Granville and Cardwell resumed the policy of
bringing home British troops from self-governing colonies. Cartier had been warned of this action in London in December,
1868. The instructions came to Canada first in a letter from the
Horse Guards dated February 18, 1869, and the Canadian Parlia-

    12. Canada, *Sessional Papers, I, 1867–1868,* Vol. 7, No. 35, p. 1; *II, 1869,*
Vol. 4, No. 10, p. 3; *III, 1870,* Vol. 4, No. 8, p. 25.
    13. Stanley, *Canada's Soldiers,* pp. 223–232, 236–240.
    14. [MacDougall], "Canada: The Fenian Raid and the Colonial Office," p. 497.
    15. Canada, *Sessional Papers, III, 1870,* Vol. 4, No. 8, p. 3.
    16. *Ibid., I, 1867,* Vol. 7, No. 35, pp. 1, 12.

ment was told officially in July.[17] For over a year thereafter colonials everywhere fought against the policy, and they were often aided by British soldiers in colonial service. There were many reasons why colonials disliked the policy. Not merely did it threaten to impose a financial burden on the colonial taxpayer which he thought unnecessary, but it would also remove a social and economic asset, for the regiments brought with them a flavor of the sophisticated society of the Old World and also money to stimulate trade. Undoubtedly, an underlying reason for colonial resistance to the withdrawal was a refusal to face the full responsibilities of a new community. Colonel Stacey has noted this reaction in his study of the withdrawal from Newfoundland; [18] and it must have been an even stronger factor in Canada where Cartier's political triumph in getting the Militia Act passed was jeopardized almost as soon as it was won. The departure of the regulars would mean the removal of the staff, the auxiliary services, and the instructors upon whom his new militia system depended.

Moreover, the going of the regulars seemed likely to destroy a necessary bond of Empire, so much so that it was difficult to believe that the British government was serious. Almost a year after the withdrawal was announced, Cartier expressed dismay at its suddenness; [19] when it was barely completed, William Fox, premier of New Zealand, told the colonial secretary that if Britain did not provide defenses, the result would be that in a war of British making his colony might be neutral. In a later memorandum Fox admitted that he was bluffing; but the very next day rumors of a Russian cruiser in Australian waters led him to repeat the statement.[20] Fox's real aim was to obtain the pres-

17. *Fortification, and Defence, Arms, etc., Laid Before Parliament by Command of His Excellency the Governor-General,* 11 June, 1869 (n.p., n.d.), in P.A.C., R.G. 7, G. 21, Vol. 168, No. 295a, Vol. 1, 1869–1870. Subsequent correspondence was published in a Return to Parliament, Canada, *Sessional Papers,* IV, A, *1871,* Vol. 5, No. 46.
18. Charles P. Stacey, "The Withdrawal of the Imperial Garrison from Newfoundland," *Canadian Historical Review,* XVII (1936), 147.
19. Cartier to Young, May 19, 1870, in Canada, *Sessional Papers,* IV, *1871,* Vol. 5, No. 46, p. 66.
20. Bowen to Kimberley, Jan. 5, 1871, July 6, 1871, in New Zealand, *Appendix to the Journals of the House of Representatives,* 1871, A-1, Nos. 78, 109.

ence of a British warship to impress the Maoris; and one reason behind the Canadian maneuvers was a desire to strengthen the Canadian position in current treaty negotiations at Washington by a warning to the United States that "to attack Canada was to attack Britain." [21] The colonials thus again revealed their understanding of the fact that there was a relation between armed strength and political influence, even though they had not yet seen that it also applied in their own case to the maintenance of the autonomy which they had so recently won. They wanted to eat their cake and keep it: to be free of British influence, but to have the backing of British strength.

Canadians thought the continued possibility of Fenian raids on the border gave Canada a powerful argument for retention of British troops. Sir Alexander Campbell, the postmaster general who negotiated with the government in London, told Lord Kimberley, the colonial secretary, that the trouble was not of Canadian making but arose from imperial causes, and that the British government should either protect Canada or indemnify the Dominion for expenses incurred.[22] Although he was willing to concede the logic of Kimberley's reply, that "the present generation of Canadians were as responsible for the alleged wrongs of Ireland as the present generation of their fellow subjects residing in Great Britain," this irrelevant argument could hardly be expected to carry much weight in Canada. Kimberley failed to halt withdrawal, which went ahead according to plan.

To arrange the military handover the Duke of Cambridge, commander in chief, sent to Canada Lieutenant General James M. Lindsay, son of the Earl of Crawford and Balcarres, and a Conservative M.P. for many years. His wife had an appointment at court. Lindsay had had no operational experience, but he had served with the Grenadier Guards in Canada, where he had commanded the brigade. He had become inspecting general of the Foot Guards and in 1868 was made inspector general of the

---

21. Stacey, *Canada and the British Army*, p. 206; Kimberley to Cardwell, Dec. 2, 1870, Kimberley to Gladstone, Dec. 9, 1870, P.R.O., Cardwell Papers, Microfilm, Box 5/31.
22. Campbell to Young, Sept. 10, 1870, Canada, *Sessional Papers*, IV, 1871, Vol. 5, No. 46, p. 26.

Reserve Forces.[23] He may have been selected for this special service in Canada because of his political experience and knowledge of the country as well as because of his social eminence. He was instructed to afford the Dominion government all possible assistance in organizing such military and naval forces as befitted a country of 3,500,000, and he was empowered to facilitate the formation of a regular Canadian regiment from the British troops then in the Dominion.

Lindsay offered the services of the men of the Royal Canadian Rifles, but not of their officers, and he pointed to the need to man certain military posts which were to be handed over to Canada on condition that they be maintained. He also urged that

the Canadian military system should be to some extent affiliated with the Imperial, in the same manner as it is in Civil policy, . . . that a General Officer of the rank of Major-General should be selected with the concurrence of the Dominion government for the command of the military forces who should serve the period of five years and whose pay and allowances should be defrayed by the Colonial Revenues.

The present adjutant general should act as his chief staff officer. He suggested that a lieutenant general commanding British North America and the Dominion of Canada, located in what he called the "Imperial station at Halifax," should occasionally visit and inspect the military arrangements in Ontario and Quebec. "In this manner," he said, "the military connection between the colony and the mother country will be maintained, the latter being prepared to defend the country in conjunction with the local forces, in the event of attack from a foreign enemy." [24]

Receiving no answer at all to these proposals—except for an intimation that Canada would not take over the Royal Canadian Rifles, and until they had been discharged would not even recruit them as individuals for service in the Manitoba expedition then

23. Williams to Cambridge, June 13, 1864, R.A.W.; *Army and Navy Gazette*, Aug. 22, 1874; Capt. C.R.B. Knight, *Historical Records of the Buffs* (London: Medici Society, 1935), pp. 644–645. A close connection with the Duke of Cambridge is suggested by the fact that Lindsay later became the Duke's military secretary.

24. Lindsay to Young, April 14, 1870, P.A.C., R.G. 7, G. 21, Vol. 168, No. 295A, Vol. 1, 1869–1870.

being prepared—Lindsay again urged conformity of the "affiliated" military systems of the two countries, adequate garrisons,
and the creation of a supply staff.[25] When he finally came to
realize that Canada would not set up a regular force, he made
new proposals based on the existing militia. To provide for a feeling of security for the Canadian people he recommended the
establishment of a Canadian naval force of three gunboats on the
Great Lakes; he also urged that a young but experienced major
general should be appointed as chief military adviser to the
government to inspect, and when necessary command, the militia. The post of adjutant general could then be filled by a retired
officer.[26] He pointed out that with the departure of the British
forces there would be need for a "control system" (that is to say,
provision for commissariat and transport) for the Canadian Militia.[27] At the same time, he told the Horse Guards that the withdrawal of the regular garrisons would necessitate measures "to
prevent the possibility of incompatible differences of system,
organization, armament, etc., etc. growing up in the military and
defensive arrangements of the Empire," and he hoped that the
Duke of Cambridge would approve his recommendations and
recognize that they were of high imperial concern.[28] He also
urged the War Office to adopt throughout the Empire the system
he had recommended for Canada.[29]

Lindsay was told that Cardwell was willing to approve everything except an earlier suggestion by Lindsay that Britain should
retain and pay the expenses of one or more regiments of the line.
But Cardwell had emphatically warned against any continuance
of divided responsibility. "It should be distinctly understood
that in all arrangements for the command of troops, an undivided

25. Lindsay to Young, May 27, 1870, *ibid.*
26. Lindsay to Young, July 26, 1870, *ibid.*
27. Lindsay to Young, Aug. 19, 1870, *ibid.* About this time the War Office
was also trying to persuade the Treasury of the need for a "control system"
for the British forces in England (G.B., W.O., Confidential Papers, A 0419).
28. Lindsay to Military Secretary, Horse Guards, Aug. 19, 1870, Canada,
*Returns to Addresses of the Senate and House of Commons Relative to the
Withdrawal of the Troops from the Dominion and in the Defence of the Country
and Honorable Mr. Campbell's Report* (Ottawa: I. B. Taylor, 1871), p. 58.
29. Lindsay to W.O., Aug. 19, 1870, *ibid.*

responsibility must rest upon the Government of the Dominion without any of those causes of confusion which in other colonies have given rise to disputes" between the commanders of the forces and the local governments.[30] The Canadian ministers must have had the same idea in mind, though they looked at it from a different point of view.

When Lindsay arrived in the country, trouble on the Red River had led to the need for an expeditionary force and a request for the use of regulars. There was some confusion because Lindsay and the Militia Department both had a hand in preparing the force.[31] In his reports Lindsay wrote as if he were in sole charge of the whole operation. But the Canadian government got its way about the appointment of a commander, namely Colonel Garnet Wolseley, who had won Canadian approval because he had trained the militia. No doubt Cartier overlooked Lindsay's high pretensions because he needed the loan of troops; and fortunately the expedition, under Wolseley's vigorous leadership, went so well that it did not lead to recrimination.[32] Wolseley came to the conclusion that the Canadians had great military potential. "What is it that a large army of such men under some great leader might not achieve?" [33]

There was plenty of evidence in contemporary New Zealand that when things went ill, divided control could lead to disaster; and Australian experience had shown that even where there was no war, and even when the colonials were willing to pay for troops, dual control could cause difficulties. Commandants there had claimed powers which have been described as much greater

30. Lugard to Lindsay, Sept. 24, 1870, P.A.C., R.G. 7, G. 21, Vol. 168, No. 295A, Vol. 1, 1869–1870.
31. Stanley, *Canada's Soldiers*, p. 236.
32. The *Army List* for June, 1870, shows Doyle as commander in chief and Lindsay as on "Special Mission." Lindsay's correspondence about the organization of the expedition, which is in G.B., W.O., Confidential Papers, A 0418, shows that he usually signed himself "Lieutenant-General Commanding in Ontario and Quebec," and only on one occasion "Lieutenant-General Commanding British Troops in North America," presumably when Hastings Doyle, normally holding that appointment, was temporarily absent from the command. The Manitoba expedition was an occurrence incidental to Lindsay's particular concern, which was to get the troops out of Canada. Lindsay showed his political sense by urging the regulars and militia to avoid friction caused by national rivalry.
33. Wolseley, *Story of a Soldier's Life*, II, 224.

than those of the contemporary commander in chief in England: [34] until 1847, the G.O.C. in New South Wales successfully claimed the title of "Excellency"; and the commandants also had been accused of lack of respect for colonial ministers. The treasurer of Victoria, William C. Haines, in consequence had thought it would be difficult to avoid conflict as long as the imperial troops remained in the colony.[35] Similarly, now that the British were withdrawing and leaving the colonies, it must have seemed to Cartier that a British general officer commanding the Canadian Militia might be difficult to handle and might perpetuate friction. Furthermore, as the militia was merely planned as a reserve force in training rather than an army embodied for war, it seemed to need an executive and administrative officer rather than a commanding general. The Canadian government therefore simply ignored Lindsay's advice about appointing a G.O.C. The old system, with an adjutant general in executive command, continued without the provision of any other link with the imperial forces or any other form of centralized command.

There was still, of course, the question of the relation of the Canadian Militia to the general officer commanding the regulars who were pulled back to garrison the naval base and imperial fortress at Halifax. Unless a campaign commander were appointed, the general officer commanding the base at Halifax, who retained the title of "General Officer Commanding British troops in the Dominion of Canada," would presumably be the officer to whom, in accordance with the Canadian Militia Act, the Canadian Militia could be assigned in the event of major war.

After the death of General Windham in February, 1870, in Florida, command of the regulars in North America had passed

34. For example, on the grounds that he would command in war, Major General Sir Thomas Pratt claimed "the management and direction of all military matters, the seeing that the laws and rules laid down by the Government are enforced" (Pratt to Barkly, Nov. 5, 1862, Victoria, Department of Defence, *Printed Papers*, I, 1862–1901). The above evaluation of his claim is from T. B. Millar, "The History of the Defence Forces of the Port Phillip District and Colony of Victoria, 1836–1900" (unpublished M.A. thesis, University of Melbourne, 1957), p. 47.

35. Haines to Pratt, Oct. 21, 1862, Victoria, Department of Defence, *Printed Papers*, I, 1862–1901.

to Lieutenant General Hastings Doyle, who had been a successful commander in Nova Scotia during the Civil War when he
had shown much tact in dealing with border problems. At the
time of confederation, Doyle had been made lieutenant governor
of Nova Scotia. He thus combined civil and military duties, a
plurality of office-holding which had been carefully avoided in
the other provinces and in the Dominion government but was
possible in this instance because of the degree of imperial sentiment in the Maritime Colony. But Doyle also retained command
of all British forces in North America, even during Lindsay's
mission to withdraw the troops.

When Lindsay departed, Doyle toured his command in the
provinces of Ontario and Quebec and reported on the amateur
enthusiasm of the militia and on its lack of an adequate "control
system." [36] He found that the adjutant general of the Canadian
Militia, Colonel Robertson-Ross, believed that when the militia
was called out he—Robertson-Ross—would command it under the
superior control of the general officer commanding the regulars
in North America. Doyle therefore repeated Lindsay's proposal
that a general officer commanding the militia ought to be appointed by the Dominion government. He said that the imperial
authorities were deeply impressed with the necessity for such an
appointment, and that he himself thought it indispensable. In
case of war, Robertson-Ross would then remain an adjutant general, "in which capacity no doubt his local knowledge would be
invaluable." [37] While Robertson-Ross, whose fitness for command
was doubted by Doyle, may have been merely repeating the
opinions of his political masters, personal rivalry between the
British officers commanding the Canadian Militia and their colleagues in command of the regulars in Halifax was only to be
expected and was to recur later. It increased the importance
of the silent political confrontation between the government
of the Dominion and the British government over creation of
control and supervision of the Canadian Militia in time of peace.

36. Doyle to Lisgar, Nov. 25, 1870, P.A.C., R.G. 7, G. 21, Vol. 168, No. 295A,
Vol. 1, 1869–1870.
37. Doyle to Lisgar, Nov. 26, 1870, *ibid.*

Macdonald's government was able to get away with doing so little relative to filling the vacuum created by the British withdrawal and to continue to ignore British advice about the military organization simply because the American menace did not materialize. Before the last British units left Canada, the Americans signed the Treaty of Washington removing outstanding causes of friction with Britain. To Canadians, who must have seemed in British eyes to be naïve in the ways of the international world, this was a good omen that the United States had no territorial ambitions. More important still, it removed their chief anxiety—that a British-American clash might involve Canada. Furthermore, as the British had always prophesied, the Fenian pest faded away as the disbanded American troops settled down to a work-a-day civilian existence. Hence, all that Cartier felt obliged to do immediately to replace the regulars was to station two batteries of militia artillery on continuous service at Kingston and Quebec to care for the stores, handle the guns in vacated fortifications, and serve as schools of instruction. A and B Batteries were the first units of the future Canadian regular army. To command them, Lieutenant G. A. French (who later served in Australia) and Captain T. B. Strange were brought from Britain and given local rank as lieutenant colonels.

Macdonald also persuaded the British government to allow him to use for a very different purpose the loan that had been guaranteed for the construction of fortifications in Montreal and further west. He applied it to the building of the railway link with British Columbia. Henceforward, he was to say that this link was an important contribution to imperial defense, a claim that has sometimes aroused cynical comment. It can, however, be said without fear of contradiction that it was a valuable contribution to the making of Canada and therefore to the eventual military strength of the Dominion.

But Macdonald and Cartier did nothing more in that administration to build Canada's defenses. The construction of the railway absorbed the energy of the Conservative government and also, ironically, through scandals which were connected with it, led to its defeat in 1873. As has been shown, Cartier was more concerned to assert Canadian civilian control over the militia than to lay the foundations for a Canadian military power. On his behalf it can be argued that the Canadian government had many other pressing problems and that improvement of relations with the United States had taken away much of the urgency for defense. It is nevertheless true that Macdonald and the Conservative government had not revealed much comprehension of the fact that independence in the modern world demanded some form of well-organized military strength. A future colonial secretary, the Earl of Carnarvon, realized what was part of the trouble. He told Dufferin, "Cartier, I imagine, was too much occupied with general politics to attend very much to his Department. During his illness and since his death it has been altogether neglected." [38]

The Foundations of a Canadian Military Organization

Since George Brown and others had fought the Militia Act of 1855 and later acts, the new government of Alexander Mackenzie and the Liberals seemed even less likely to take defense seriously. Canadian Liberals were less prone than Conservatives to use oratorical flourishes about the glories of the British connection to bolster their own position and win votes; they had campaigned against waste and corruption, and Mackenzie had repeatedly told the House of Commons that he was determined to reduce the militia estimates. Expenditure on defense always seemed to the Canadian legislator to be the first place to cut costs of government. Thus, a couple of years later, Lachlin Mc-Callum, a Liberal-Conservative member of Parliament opposed to Mackenzie, was to call the small military staff, "locusts eating up the public money." [39]

On the other hand, Mackenzie had been a major in the militia and had served during the Fenian raids; he was always interested in militia affairs. His most recent biographer says that at the time of the withdrawal of the British garrisons he felt there was no

38. Carnarvon to Dufferin, March 26, 1874, P.R.O., Carnarvon Papers, 30/6/26, p. 65.
39. Canada, House of Commons, *Debates, 1876*, p. 1099.

reason why a powerful country like Canada should be defended by the British taxpayer. He was aware that some form of imperial co-operation for defense was necessary for the security of all; but imperial authority should not necessarily mean subservience to imperial dictation. A strong self-sufficient Canada would be an asset, not a weakness, in the imperial chain.[40]

These sentiments must have led Mackenzie to listen more attentively to the advice of the new governor general, the Earl of Dufferin, who as chairman of the recent British Commission on Military Education had had some experience with military problems. The Canadian Liberals resented Dufferin's aristocratic background, suspected his outlook on national questions, and resisted his attempts to play a greater part than they thought he should in the actual government of Canada; [41] but he was a man of great charm and persuasive powers and was not lacking in political insight. Despite clashes with the Cabinet, he established good personal relations with the prime minister, whose apparent sincerity impressed him. As the governor general was the only recognized channel from the War Office to the Canadian government, Dufferin was in a strong position to exercise considerable influence in military matters. The extent of his success in this most difficult field should be set beside the prevalence of friction between the governor and his ministry over many other issues.

At the time of the withdrawal of the British garrisons, the War Office in its wisdom had discontinued the appointment of a military secretary to the governor general on the grounds that one was no longer needed.[42] Dufferin got around that difficulty by obtaining the services of a regular officer as his private secretary. He selected Lieutenant Colonel Henry Charles Fletcher of the Scots Fusilier Guards, a personal friend, whose wife, Harriet,

40. William Buckingham and George W. Ross, *The Honourable Alexander Mackenzie: His Life and Times* (Toronto: Rose, 1892), p. 379; Dale C. Thomson, *Alexander Mackenzie: Clear Grit* (Toronto: Macmillan, 1960), pp. 115–116, quoting Canada, House of Commons, *Debates, 1870;* report of Ottawa *Times,* May 2, 1870, Library of Parliament, p. 1287 ff.

41. David M. L. Farr, *The Colonial Office and Canada, 1867-1887* (Toronto: University of Toronto Press, 1955), pp. 55-56.

42. W.O. to C.O., April 27, 1871, P.R.O., C.O. 42/685; W.O. to C.O., July 24, 1871, *ibid.,* C.O. 42/703.

a daughter of Lord Romney, would be a companion for Lady Dufferin in the midst of the bourgeois society of North America. Colonel Fletcher had joined Dufferin on the Commission on Military Education and was a signatory of the second report dated July 14, 1870. Fletcher had visited the Union Army during the war when he had pitched his tent close to McClellan's and had been invited to stay as long as he wished. He knew the potential military strength of the United States. He now worked with Dufferin to bring Canadians to realize the need to put their military house in order.[43]

Fletcher lectured to militia groups and wrote articles and memoranda which were circulated to members of the government and the opposition. Answering those who argued that friendly relations with the United States made defense expenditure wasteful, he said that history showed that peace was only a temporary state of affairs. The small size of the United States Army and its deployment along the Indian frontier and sea coasts did not mean that it represented no threat, but rather that it should be regarded as the nucleus for a larger force in the event of war. Canada must have a force not only capable of defending the country against external foes and of acting as a last resource for the maintenance of law inside the country, but also, "far in the background, to be a symbol of the state which pertains to all nations aspiring to rank as such among their compeers." [44] Dufferin reported later to the commander in chief that Fletcher had "contributed materially to the revival of a military spirit among the [Canadian] authorities." [45]

When Mackenzie took office, however, decline had already set in, and information soon began to reach England that the militia and fortifications of Canada were in a bad state.[46] The Duke of Cambridge had already suggested that the solution was to try to

---

43. Dufferin to Carnarvon, April 2, 1875, in C. W. de Kiewiet and F. H. Underhill, eds., *The Dufferin-Carnarvon Correspondence, 1874–1878* (Toronto: Champlain Society, 1955), p. 141; General Sir Fenwick Williams to Cambridge, April 25, 1862, R.A.W.; May 23, 1862, *ibid.*
44. Col. Henry C. Fletcher, "Memorandum on the Militia System of Canada" (n.p., 1873), in P.A.C., M.G. 26, A 1(a), Vol. 100.
45. Dufferin to Cambridge, May 29, 1874, R.A.W., Cambridge Papers.
46. Carnarvon to Dufferin, April 8, 1874, P.A.C., Dufferin Papers, A 408.

get the G.O.C. of Halifax accepted as inspecting officer in Canada.[47] The Earl of Carnarvon, who took over the Colonial Office soon after Dufferin went to Canada, wanted to go much further. He had always been against the withdrawal of the garrisons, and he suggested to Dufferin that they should be got back somehow—for instance, on the pretext of a parade or demonstration. Knowing full well that the Treasury and the War Office were not likely to pay the cost, he asked Dufferin whether the Canadian government might offer to put up part of the money.[48] The governor general was too wise to make a direct approach on such a topic, but he had hopes of achieving something, for since his arrival he had found that Cartier, after passing the Militia Act, had neglected the militia except to use it for contracts for patronage purposes, and Cambridge thought the Liberals "more liberally disposed" than their predecessors. Dufferin's idea was to revise the proposal for a general officer commanding the Canadian Militia. Robertson-Ross, the adjutant general, had applied for more active service soon after Cartier's death in 1873. At that time Dufferin, not long in the country, could only say that he seemed "zealous, energetic . . . high-minded, and honourable." [49] He soon began to think differently. He came to find that Robertson-Ross had been "a most inefficient officer and owed his position to a penchant Cartier entertained for his handsome wife." Reporting later on Robertson-Ross's application for a K.C.M.G., Dufferin stated that during the Fenian raid the Canadian had "wanted to hang all the American prisoners and was only stopped by a peremptory telegram from Lord Lisgar. He left the country upon Cartier's death, very soon after my arrival, having got into a quarrel with a committee of the House of Commons." [50] Dufferin said he thought that if the adjutant general's appointment were upgraded, he might be able to get a

47. Cambridge to Dufferin, June 27, 1873, *ibid.*, A 413.
48. Carnarvon to Dufferin, Oct. 31, 1874, *ibid.*, A 408.
49. Dufferin 183, July 30, 1873, P.R.O., C.O. 42/718.
50. Dufferin to Carnarvon, Nov. 19, 1875, P.R.O., Carnarvon Papers, 30/6/28, pp. 174–175. No confirmation of Dufferin's allegations has been found. They may have been distortions based on hearsay. However, when Cartier had tried to have Robertson-Ross promoted to major-general, he had been opposed by both Macdonald and the War Office (Kimberley to Dufferin, Jan. 15, 1873, P.R.O., Northern Ireland, D 1071. H/H2/4).

better man to command the Canadian Militia. He also promised Mackenzie that if the appointments were converted to a general officer commanding instead of an adjutant general, this "move to bring Canada into line with the rest of the Empire" would mean that none but first-class men would be sent out to fill so important an appointment.[51] This was, however, a promise he was not in future to be in a position to fulfil.

The commander in chief had sent Dufferin a list of colonels who were likely successors to Robertson-Ross,[52] but the governor general thought none of them suitable. Some officers had applied merely because they were already resident in Canada or had married Canadian women and wanted to live in the Dominion. Dufferin was anxious that the new G.O.C. not be "a hoity-toity Gentleman" with a supercilious contempt for colonials or for the somewhat homely type of society which of necessity prevailed in a new country. He thought that the Horse Guards was too inclined to recommend a "deserving officer" who "has claims." What was needed was "the very best man," not only a good soldier but a person of reserve, of tact, of temper, willing to work in due subordination to the minister of militia, and yet capable of inspiring such confidence in the government that he could get his own way in matters relating to his profession. The Duke then recommended Wolseley—but only in an effort to get him out of England. Wolseley had other views, so the choice fell on a second-string officer, Major General Sir Edward Selby Smyth,[53] and the commander in chief approved the appointment.

The arrangements had been made informally and unofficially, and Dufferin had to ask Carnarvon to warn the Duke that the Canadian government would expect the nomination to be made through the proper channel, that is, through the governor general. He said it was understood that the imperial government would pay Smyth as a major general, and the Dominion would

51. Dufferin to Mackenzie, Feb. 18, 1874, P.A.C., Dufferin Papers, A 409; Dufferin to Cambridge, March 27, 1874, R.A.W., Cambridge Papers; Canada, House of Commons, *Debates, 1875*, p. 29.

52. Cambridge to Dufferin, Jan. 22, 1874, R.A.W., Cambridge Papers.

53. Carnarvon to Dufferin, April 21, 1874, P.R.O., Northern Ireland, D 1071, H/H2/5.

then add enough to make his salary equivalent to that of a full general, plus the usual allowances.[54] But all that Smyth was in fact to get from the War Office was the "attached pay," which meant his "half-pay." Dufferin thought that in view of the advantage to the British connection and of the fact that the selection had been left to the commander in chief and the colonial secretary, Smyth should have had more. He passed on Fletcher's suggestion that the G.O.C. of militia ought also to command the garrison at Halifax.[55]

As soon as Smyth was appointed, Dufferin took the next step toward re-establishment of the British military position in Canada. He put the G.O.C. up to writing a letter which, by showing the need for schools of instruction for the militia and the total absence of "the military element which even the presence of one British battalion in the dominion would so readily and so practically diffuse among the population," could be used as an argument for the return of a regiment.[56] Mackenzie appeared to be convinced, perhaps because he hoped that Britain would pay the cost. However, on a visit to London he found that the Conservative government there, although strong, would not be able to reverse the policy of withdrawal because the commercial interests, the landed classes, and the general public were bitterly antagonistic to Canada. He therefore concluded that to ask for an imperial garrison would be to risk humiliation.[57] The plan was dropped.

Nevertheless, the appointment of Selby Smyth was seen by the War Office as a chance to restore its influence in Canadian military affairs. First, Dufferin had to ward off an attempt by Captain O'Grady Haly, A.D.C. to the general officer commanding British troops in North America, to have Smyth report to the War Office through Halifax. Dufferin thought that Smyth should

---

54. Dufferin to Carnarvon, March 26, 1874, P.A.C., Dufferin Papers, A 406.
55. Dufferin to Carnarvon, June 9, 1874, P.R.O., Northern Ireland, D 1071, H/H1/4; Dufferin to Carnarvon, July 23, 1874, P.R.O., Carnarvon Papers 30/6/27; Dufferin to Carnarvon, Aug. 23, 1874, *ibid.* Smyth got £800 from Canada and £450 attached pay (Dufferin to Carnarvon, April 21, 1874, *ibid.*, 30/6/26, and July 30, 1874, *ibid.*, 30/6/27).
56. Selby Smyth to Dufferin, Nov. 24, 1874, P.A.C., Dufferin Papers, A 413.
57. Mackenzie to Dufferin, June 25, 1875, *ibid.*, A 411.

report direct to the Horse Guards.[58] Next Smyth was sent advisory memoranda by the two officers with best knowledge of the country, Lindsay and MacDougall. Although these went through the Colonial Office, MacDougall also wrote Smyth a long private letter in which he implied that the War Office was intending to correspond with him officially and directly on the subject of reorganization of the Canadian Militia. Dufferin hastened to tell Carnarvon that this would not do. It would put his ministers' backs up; they would feel that their servant was being subjected to extraneous pressures. He pointed out that this was particularly serious because the subject of military expenditure was distasteful to them, to the Canadian Parliament, and to the Canadian people.[59]

Selby Smyth had had distinguished colonial service in India, South Africa, and Mauritius. He thoroughly understood the nature of his relationship with the Canadian government, and he won the confidence of the ministers. His long, erudite, but rather verbose reports on the Canadian Militia pulled no punches regarding its deficiencies in organization, training, and equipment. But at the time of his appointment a severe economic blight had struck the country, and he found military appropriations severely cut, from about $1.5 million to as little as $500,000, the lowest point reached at any time after confederation. Rifles and clothing were in poor condition, and there was insufficient money to train all the men permitted under the law. Smyth therefore proposed to reduce each of the rural militia battalions to a single headquarters company in order to use the budget to train the more effective militia in the towns. His recommendation was rejected because it would have political repercussions, but he did succeed in reducing the unnecessarily large number on district staffs, even though such a move was unpopular. At the same time he pointed out the need for a larger staff at militia headquarters where he had to personally sign every requisition, "from a gun to a snow shovel." He also pressed, but unsuccessfully, for perma-

58. Dufferin to Cambridge, Dec. 11, 1874, R.A.W.; also undated memorandum [1874?], R.A.W., Cambridge Papers.
59. Dufferin to Carnarvon, April 23, 1875, in de Kiewiet and Underhill, eds., *Dufferin-Carnarvon Correspondence*, pp. 147–148.

nent companies of Canadian regulars to staff training schools for the militia. The earlier schools had collapsed upon the withdrawal of the British garrison whose units had staffed them.[60]

The most important development during Smyth's tour of duty was the opening of a military college in Kingston. Preparation for this had been undertaken before he was appointed. Fletcher had proposed in his "Memorandum on the Militia System," published in 1873, that officers should be trained in Canada. Colonel Walker Powell, acting adjutant general, recommended a Canadian military college in the militia report of January, 1874. Mackenzie accepted the proposal soon afterward. In the belief that what was needed was an institution suitable for the colonial society in which it must flourish, the college was to be modeled on West Point, rather than on Sandhurst and Woolwich. It was to train "scientific" officers for the engineers and artillery as well as "ordinary" officers for the infantry and cavalry. It would produce Canadian officers for the staff and so obviate the need to import British regulars, but its graduates would be prepared for civil as well as military employment because Canada had as yet no need for large numbers of officers. Though Smyth's first reaction had been that it was overambitious for a country with no regular army, he supported the college energetically.[61]

Like all the other officers whom the Duke of Cambridge recommended for service in Canada, Selby Smyth had been invited to write unofficially to his patron to report on his work. At first, however, he let his official reports speak for themselves and kept in touch only occasionally with General Sir Richard Airey, the adjutant general of the British Army. Not until he had suffered frustration for two years did Smyth avail himself of the Duke's invitation, and even then he used letters to Cambridge only to let off steam.[62] He was also wise enough not to raise issues in public with his political superiors. Although he made some ene-

60. J. F. Cummins, "General Sir Edward Selby Smyth, K.C.M.G.," *Canadian Defence Quarterly*, V (July, 1928), 403–411.
61. Dufferin to Cambridge, April 30, 1874, P.A.C., Dufferin Papers, A 408; Smyth to Cambridge, June 27, 1876, R.A.W., Cambridge Papers; Fletcher, *Memorandum on the Militia*, pp. 8–12; "Militia Report for 1873," Canada, *Sessional Papers*, VII, 1874, No. 5, pp. xiii–xiv.
62. Selby Smyth to Cambridge, Feb. 1, 1876, R.A.W., Cambridge Papers.

mies,[63] Smyth nevertheless obtained the respect and admiration of the great majority of Canadian officers and men, whose great fighting potential he, like many of his successors, fully appreciated. The first Canadian G.O.C. was a pleasant companion and a born raconteur, and he made a secure place for himself in Canadian society. When he resigned to further his own career in 1879, it was with the plaudits and good wishes of the Canadian Parliament and the Cabinet alike.[64] He was to be the only one of the eight British generals who commanded the Canadian Militia as G.O.C. to serve out his term and to leave without being dismissed. Selby Smyth showed that it was possible for a British officer to work satisfactorily under a Canadian government.

The problem of devising an effective military organization for the new Dominion, however, had been made difficult by the fact that in Britain as well as in Canada financial and constitutional considerations had outweighed those of strategy. Fear of an American attack led to the correct decision that Canadian strategic policy must be defensive. But the difficulty lay, as always, in the assessment of the degree and reality of the danger. How much money and effort should be diverted from other real needs to defense?

This question led to another. Where were such decisions to be made—in London or in Ottawa? To have hope of success, a defensive Canadian strategy must be part of an imperial strategy that would assume an offensive posture. But imperial policy, even if not actually aggressive or dangerously provocative, seemed to some Canadians to have aims that were not clearly concerned with Canada's interests. It was therefore extremely important that Canada retain the right to make even minor decisions about the nature and amount of the Dominion's military effort. Nothing less than absolute control was possible if autonomy was to be preserved. On the other hand, British strategists feared that if

63. One such enemy was Colonel George T. Denison, whom Smyth alienated by failing to give official encouragement or even to order copies of the prize-winning book on cavalry that was to make this Canadian Militia officer a widely recognized authority on the subject. George T. Denison, *Soldiering in Canada: Recollections and Experiences* (Toronto: Macmillan, 1900), pp. 196–199, 240. Denison believed Smyth was reluctant to sponsor an amateur soldier.
64. Canada, House of Commons, *Debates, 1879,* II, 1631.

Canadian politicians were involved, Canada's defense preparations by their inefficiency and inadequacy would endanger the
security of the whole Empire, including Canada.

A major obstacle to the establishment of a sound military relationship for these purposes arose from the nature of the British
military command itself. As yet, Canada had no experienced
senior officers and no effective command structure. For the sake
of efficiency it was desirable that British officers should be appointed to command and train the Canadian Militia. This
arrangement, however, was difficult to operate harmoniously because of a technical problem. Although the authority of Parliament over the British Army had long been established and had
recently been confirmed by the Cardwell reorganizations, the
continuance of the office of commander in chief and its retention
by a member of the royal family, the Duke of Cambridge, concealed to some extent the fact that military command was no
longer part of the royal prerogative. In fact, not only was the
financial and administrative control of the army exercised by the
political chiefs in the War Office, but the military command itself
in peacetime Britain was more of an administrative than an
operational affair. On the other hand, when forces were sent out
of Britain for service overseas, even to colonial garrisons, the
officer appointed to command them was given much greater
authority than a local commander at home because of the problems created by distance. He was, in effect, an operational or
executive commander rather than merely an administrator.

British soldiers, however, were apparently unable to realize
that the command of forces raised by a self-governing dominion
was quite different in nature from the command of British forces
sent overseas or of auxiliary imperial troops raised in non-self-
governing territories. Dominion forces in time of peace were,
from the point of view of the dominion, internal or domestic
forces which must be kept under full political control. Their military command structure must be administrative rather than
operational, and their commander must defer to the authority of
the government that raised them.

The raising of the Canadian Militia thus brought formidable political, social, and financial questions concerning service overseas that were different from normal British military experience. Not merely was there the customary difference of opinion about the extent to which political control could go without harming military efficiency; there was an added complication that the "political interference" came from a government that was different from that which the soldiers actually served. Since many of the British officers sent to Canada in the early years went only because they had personal reasons for taking on an unattractive job that promised no fighting (except with political superiors), they were often not of the highest quality. It is not surprising, then, that the Horse Guards, the British soldiers sent to Canada, and even some Canadian soldiers were unable to understand the nature of the new military relationship within the Empire. They could not comprehend any form of relationship between Britain and Canada except one based on unrestricted military command.

In these circumstances it is remarkable that Fletcher, Dufferin, Mackenzie, and Selby Smyth did so much to fill the void left by the departing British regulars. Dufferin succeeded more than any other governor general of this era in alerting his prime minister that the Dominion had inescapable responsibilities in regard to defense. Mackenzie, although the leader of a party that was rabidly anti-military and suspicious of British imperialism, did more than might have been expected of him. By appointing a British G.O.C. to command the militia he reversed Cartier's policy; he set up a military college to train officers; and at the time of his defeat at the polls, he was privately considering other military instructional units. These were important achievements that must be set against the better-known story of drastic reductions in the militia estimates during the middle of his term of office. Financial stringency, it is true, seriously undermined the efficiency at the company level of the Canadian forces that had turned out so promptly against the Fenians and the Métis. Liberal efforts to oust political rivals intrenched in the militia also created harmful precedents for the future exercise of patronage. But these things, for which Mackenzie and the Liberals cannot be held solely responsible, should serve to make more significant their achievements in regard to the G.O.C. and the military college.

Cartier's Militia Act and the ensuing contributions of Mackenzie had thus outlined the foundations for a sound Canadian military system to suit the political realities of the country's new status. The first Dominion at the outset had established a principle that was to be basic in the Commonwealth of the future—that the constituent nations must have full and unquestioned control of their military affairs and of their own forces. Without that degree of autonomy the British dominions could not have matured and the Commonwealth's full military potential could not have been developed. But since dominion control of foreign policy was still a long way off, since foreign and defense policies are inextricably mingled, since neither Canadian nor British military and political leaders yet knew how to operate the new form of military partnership, and since Canada was not yet prepared to defend herself or to contribute sufficiently to the common defense, military autonomy long rested uncomfortably on the shoulders of the young Dominion.

4

A Naval Mirage—Imperial Defense, 1870–1897

A Naval Imperial Strategy

The withdrawal of the British garrisons from the self-governing colonies marked low water in the decline of Britain's interest in imperial matters and coincided with the turn of the tide. Outraged by what they regarded as a deliberate attempt by the government to goad New Zealand into secession by leaving the colony exposed to the Maoris, the "Cannon Street Colonists," members of the New Colonial Society in London, began agitation in 1869 which soon stirred up new interest in the Empire and affected government policy. When Disraeli made imperial consolidation the theme of his Crystal Palace speech in 1872, the Empire became a rallying cry for the Conservatives, and imperialism entered the realm of practical politics in Britain.[1]

This new British imperial appetite in the last quarter of the nineteenth century coincided with increasing international rivalry on the continent of Europe and with keener European competition for colonies. In the 1870's and 1880's, British fear of Russian intrusion into India reached a new peak as a result of Russian activity in Central Asia. Although Anglo-German imperial rivalry did not become the dominant theme of international politics until the first decade of the twentieth century, the pace of colonial expansion quickened after Germany came on the African scene. The demand for tropical products and the discovery of medicines that could check tropical diseases led to

1. John E. Tyler, *The Struggle for Imperial Unity, 1868–1895* (London: Longmans, 1938), pp. 1–5.

intense competition for the opening up of Central Africa, hitherto known to Europeans only at the mouths of its rivers. Competition developed for the acquisition of Pacific islands; rivalry for concessions to trade (dating back to the 1840's) with the ancient empire in China became sharper.

These conditions led British governments, for the first time since 1815, to look upon all colonies as important strategic assets and as contributors to world-wide military policies.[2] But the problems of an expanding British Empire and its defense were inextricably related to a greater need for Britain to live by trade in an increasingly competitive world and to anticipate the moves of rivals. The need was the more urgent because the margin which an earlier start in the Industrial Revolution had formerly given to Britain was rapidly being lost as other European nations became industrialized. Technical changes also added complications in a vital sphere. Steam power, armored ships, and rifled guns which since earlier in the century had threatened the traditional foundations of British sea power—namely, superiority in the numbers of wooden men-of-war and in the art of fighting them—were creating new problems for naval strategists and tacticians. The doubts thus raised about Britain's naval hegemony seemed the more serious because a revived interest in an empire scattered over the seven seas inevitably involved a reconsideration of the role of sea power.

The importance of sea power as a bond of empire had been fully recognized in the eighteenth century and had been consistently applied in the realm of strategy. In the early part of the nineteenth century, during the period of so-called colonial garrisons, the safeguarding of sea communications had continued to be an essential element in the planning of colonial defenses; but this policy had been taken for granted and had not developed into a theory. However, once British garrisons were withdrawn, sea power became something more than an essential element in the preservation of the Empire. There was now a tendency to

2. Fieldhouse, "British Imperialism in the Late Eighteenth Century," pp. 44–45.

assume it to be the only way in which power could be applied to that end; military force on land was often relegated to a secondary and minor place.

Moreover, it soon became clear that insofar as the self-governing colonies were concerned, military power was likely to be at a low ebb for some time. For when the colonies got over the shock of the removal of British troops, they discovered that they preferred to remain without them. When a Conservative government succeeded the Liberals in 1874, the colonial secretary, Lord Carnarvon, explored the possibility of having the garrisons called back, only to find that the colonies which had deplored their departure would not consider their return if they had to pay. The War Office on grounds of economy was as opposed to the idea as were the colonists.[3] Except for a few garrisons in naval bases, British regulars had left the self-governing colonies forever.

The continued existence of the British Empire, therefore, had now to depend more than ever on the navy. Inevitably this raised important questions. Who would pay for those remaining bastions of Empire defense—the warships that were becoming yearly more expensive? Who would control them? Should the colonies take up any part of the burden, and, if so, under what kind of an arrangement? These were fundamental issues in the discussions about imperial strategy between the Franco-Prussian War and World War I. Beside such problems, developments in other directions which were actually to prove of greater significance for the future of the British Commonwealth were passed over lightly.

The Royal Navy was, of course, paid for by the taxpayers of the United Kingdom and directed by their government. Unlike command in the British Army, command in the Royal Navy, at home and abroad, in peace and in war, was by the nature of the service executive as well as administrative. When British naval forces were sent overseas it was not necessary, as it was with land forces, to put them under a different form of command by appointing an executive commander. Naval forces everywhere

3. Donald M. Schurman, "Imperial Defence, 1868–1887" (unpublished Ph.D. dissertation, Cambridge University, 1955), pp. 66–67.

served under the direct operational control of the Admiralty. There was therefore less confusion about the command control of naval forces to serve the needs of the colonies.

At the same time, it was harder to contemplate associated naval forces under the control of colonial governments. The colonies had been slow to arm themselves on the sea. In 1839 the Maritime Provinces had appealed to Britain for ships to protect fisheries, and two small vessels went out at British expense. In 1856 when the Canadian legislature budgeted funds for a fisheries protective service, the Opposition leader, George Brown, attempted to amend the resolution to read that the naval protection of the province was a duty devolving upon the imperial government and that the province did not need a naval establishment. He was unsuccessful, but many Canadians believed him right on the grounds that the need for a navy grew out of the treaty-making power in which Canada had no voice.[4] In the same year, news that a Russian frigate was off Cape Horn had led the colonial governments in Sydney and Melbourne to acquire and operate a few naval vessels, but only for a brief period.[5] Thus, the colonies had moved hesitantly into the business of providing their own naval defense.

Nine years later, in line with the Commons' resolution of 1862 on self-government begetting self-defense, and to accommodate the aspirations of the colony of Victoria, the British Parliament passed the Colonial Naval Defence Act of 1865 to encourage the formation of colonial naval establishments for local defense purposes. These would be tied in with the Royal Navy. By this act, colonial governments were authorized to acquire warships for local protective services only; crews and personnel would be either provided by the Royal Navy or raised by the colony, but without expense to the government of the United Kingdom in

4. Ruth F. Grant, *The Canadian Atlantic Fishery* (Toronto: Ryerson, 1934), p. 121; see also Province of Canada, *Journals of the Legislative Assembly of Canada, 1856*, XIV, 716–717; L. P. Brodeur referred to British monopoly of the treaty-making power in this connection at the Colonial Conference of 1907 (G.B., P.P., 1907, *Minutes of Proceedings of the Colonial Conference, 1907*, LV, 139 [Cd. 3523]).

5. Arthur W. José, *The Royal Australian Navy, 1914–1918: The Official History of Australia in the War of 1914–1918* (Sydney: Angus & Robertson, 1928), IX, xv.

either case.[6] In the following two years, to counter Fenian raids, the Province of Canada operated small gunboats on the St. Lawrence River and the Great Lakes to supplement three small British warships. The Canadian vessels were manned by nucleus crews from the Royal Navy supplemented by Canadian volunteers.[7] The question of control did not become an issue with the imperial government, possibly because the danger was real. About the same time, in connection with the Maori War in New Zealand, the Australian colony of Victoria commissioned a sloop. However, apart from these small beginnings, the Colonial Naval Defence Act remained virtually a dead letter. In 1868, for instance, a proposal was originated by a New Zealand colonist, W. Fitzherbert. He contended that a squadron of the Royal Navy should be permanently stationed in the South Pacific because the colonies there depended entirely on their oceanic trade, and that the cost of the squadron should be shared between them and England. The proposal came to nothing.[8] Sir Frederic Rogers, the colonial secretary, commented that Fitzherbert's proposal would relieve the imperial exchequer but would give the colonies a voice in the movement of ships that would dangerously divide the command of the fleet. A more important objection was that the degree of danger from enemy ships in the Pacific did not warrant such dispersion. The naval defense of Australia therefore remained solely a British obligation.

Thus far, steps toward colonial assumption of a share of their own naval defense had been concerned only with narrowly limited interests, especially harbor defense and border protection. This was an extension of the concept of "colonial defense," the policy of garrisoning particular localities. The small warships added were virtually floating batteries to cover territorial waters.

6. 28 Vict., c. 14; B. A. Knox, "Colonial Influence on Imperial Policy 1858–1866: Victoria and the Colonial Naval Defence Act, 1865," *Historical Studies, Australia and New Zealand*, XI (Nov., 1963), 61–79.

7. Gilbert N. Tucker, *The Naval Service of Canada: Its Official History* (2 vols.; Ottawa: King's Printer, 1952), I, 42–43; "Return . . . II, December, 1867," Monck to Cardwell, June 8, 1866, in Canada, *Sessional Papers, I, 1867–1868*, Vol. 7, No. 37; *ibid., II, 1869*, Vol. 6, No. 75, p. 142.

8. José, *Royal Australian Navy*, p. xvi; Henry L. Hall, *Australia and England: A Study in Imperial Relations* (London: Longmans, 1934), p. 227; Harrop, *England and the Maori Wars*, pp. 314–317; P.R.O., C.O. 209/209.

As this extension of defenses out to sea came at the time when the land fortifications themselves were passing from British garrisons to colonial militia or other forces, it was in keeping with that policy that the new harbor defense ships should be vessels provided by the colonies.

In 1867, however, something entirely new appeared. Captain J. C. R. Colomb, a retired officer of the Royal Marines, in *The Protection of Our Commerce and the Distribution of Our War Forces Considered,* called for an Empire-wide naval strategy.[9] In this paper, and in others in the following years, Colomb challenged both the strategy of "colonial garrisons" on the one hand and the concept of "fortress England" on the other. He emphasized the need for naval strength to protect the widespread commercial sea lanes upon which the British Empire depended for its very existence. As these sea lanes were common to all, all should contribute to their protection. Colonial naval forces were of value only as "the second line of colonial defence." The central naval forces of the Empire for protecting the sea lanes should be "under the control of one directing head." [10]

In the Australian colonies, which were the chief target of Colomb's advice, he was called by the Melbourne *Leader* a "fussy busy-body." The *Queenslander* and the Sydney *Morning Herald* echoed the sentiments. The Australian colonies, the *Herald* said, must first protect themselves. "New South Wales . . . cannot . . . be asked to pour her defenders into Ceylon or the West Indies, nor would she expect to be similarly assisted. The only movable troops are those of the Imperial army. They ought to be shifted from one threatened or assailed place to another, as the occasion demands." Furthermore, it was Britain's duty to maintain "the imperial roads," i.e., the sea lanes along which British reinforcements would go. Colomb's reply was that

9. Howard D'Egville, *Imperial Defence and Closer Union: A Short Record of the Life-Work of the Late Sir John Colomb* . . . (London: King, 1913), p. xiv; John C. R. Colomb, *The Protection of Our Commerce and Distribution of Our War Forces Considered* (London: Harrison, 1867).

10. John C. R. Colomb, *The Defence of Great and Greater Britain* (London: Edward Stanford, 1880), pp. 10–12, 35, 38, 45, 84–87, 90, 93, 101–108, 120, 128, 132–133.

this argument meant "England does not expect every man [i.e., the colonies] to do his duty, but every man expects England to do hers." "If this be a correct view," he said, "it is as well the whole Empire should know England has not prepared to do so." "The problem of Imperial security cannot be solved by disintegrating that which is common to all; it is a burden resting proportionately on every fragment of the Empire, and distinctions are not those of responsibility but simply of practical ability." [11] Thus, well before Admiral Mahan gave it prominence, Colomb and his brother, Vice Admiral Philip Colomb, preached the doctrine of a centrally controlled naval command that was to be identified later with the "Blue Water school" of strategy and defense and that came to dominate British naval, and even military, thinking. This doctrine gave powerful support to a new movement to centralize the Empire.

Centralized Defense Planning

Concern about the effect of steam on the navy's capacity to perform the duty of guarding the sea lanes led to the next development in defense planning. In 1873 Colomb called attention to the need for protection of ports scattered at convenient distances around the world where coal should be stockpiled for the use of the Royal Navy. The Admiralty showed no great interest, but Colonel W. F. D. Jervois, who had reported on Canadian defenses in 1864 and had advised New Zealand in 1871, produced a paper in 1875 which mentioned this problem.[12] He was sent to Australia to examine the defenses there. As a member of the Jervois-Scratchley Commission he now proposed that major offensive action at sea should be left to the Royal Navy, that local defense could be provided by shore batteries, and that the richer colonies might provide a few swift ironclad gunboats for the protection of coastal commerce and a few torpedo boats or launches to assist the coastal batteries. All floating defenses, however,

11. *Ibid.*, pp. 93 f., 93 n., 107–109.
12. Schurman, "Imperial Defence," pp. 56, 90.

even those manned by colonial naval reserves authorized by the Naval Defence Act of 1865, should come under the command of the Royal Naval Squadron in Australian waters.[13]

The only result of Jervois's report was the fortification of harbors by the Australian colonies, including the fortification of the principal naval coaling station at Newcastle. But even this was done "without any undue haste." [14] However, in 1877 when Russia attacked Turkey, the old British fear of a Russian seizure of the gateway to the Mediterranean was revived, and by early 1878 the Queen and some ministers were ready to go to war. Victoria even considered abdicating if the country did not show its mettle. The fleet steamed toward the Bosphorus, and Disraeli brought Indian troops to Malta; but the prime minister's own resolution not to let things go too far and Russian exhaustion eventually brought about the negotiation of a settlement at Berlin. It had been a near thing, and the crisis had caused some heart-searching about the state of Britain's defense of her Empire. Hence, the colonial secretary, the Earl of Carnarvon, persuaded the secretary of state for war, Gathorne Gathorne-Hardy, to set up an interdepartmental committee to look into the matter. The committee was under the chairmanship of a former first sea lord, Admiral Sir Alexander Milne, and had General Sir John Lintorn A. Simmons, inspector general of fortifications, as a member. Thus was the Admiralty for the first time brought directly into colonial defense planning.[15]

The Milne Committee was instructed to concentrate on "the more important ports" as an emergency expedient. It discussed the proportions which colonial and imperial treasuries should contribute to defense and came to the conclusion that there might be considerable variation in the proportion from one case to another, even as much as from 1 to 9 to 9 to 1 according to each port's interest in imperial trade. It said that the proportion in

13. Lt. Col. Sir George Sydenham Clarke, ed., *The Defence of the Empire: A Selection from the Letters and Speeches of Henry Howard Molyneux, Fourth Earl of Carnarvon* (London: John Murray, 1897), p. 158; José, *Royal Australian Navy*, p. xvi.

14. Maj. Gen. Sir William F. D. Jervois, *The Defence of Great Britain and Her Dependencies* (Adelaide: Government Printer, 1880), p. 23.

15. Schurman, "Imperial Defence," pp. 96–103, 130.

each case could not be decided by a departmental committee.[16] On May 2, 1879, the immediate crisis having passed, and after the committee had done much to hasten the construction of those harbor defenses in the colonies which it declared necessary and immediate, it was dissolved.[17] Its deliberations had shown most clearly that there was need for a permanent policy and also for a permanent body to advise the government on the apportionment of defense costs which the committee had felt itself inadequately constituted to undertake.[18]

Instead of a high-level political committee, however, which would have had to be in close touch with both the Cabinet and all the colonial governments, the British government decided on another device. In July, 1879, it set up the Royal Commission for the Defence of British Possessions and Commerce Abroad. Carnarvon, now out of the Colonial Office but still fired with determination to come to grips with the colonial defense problem, was its chairman. This resort to a royal commission may have been adopted to give some degree of independence of approach to a ticklish situation in which the British Cabinet could obviously no longer give direct orders to colonial governments.

In its terms of reference, the Carnarvon Commission was instructed to see whether an organized system of defense was needed "in addition to such general protection as can be afforded by our naval forces," and whether such defense should consist of permanent works manned by garrisons of imperial or of local troops, of both combined, or of local naval organizations. It was also to consider whether and in what proportions the cost of such measures of defense should be divided between the imperial government and the colonies to which they related, or whether they should be wholly defrayed by the imperial government or by the colonies.[19] The title given to this commission in the War

16. Memorandum by Stafford Northcote, May or June, 1878, National Maritime Museum, Greenwich, Milne Papers.
17. Milne to Carnarvon, Aug. 11, 1879, *ibid.*
18. Memorandum by Stafford Northcote, May or June, 1878, *ibid.*
19. Schurman, "Imperial Defence," p. 140; Earl of Carnarvon, *Royal Commission to Enquire into the Defence of British Possessions and Commerce Abroad* (3 vols.; London: War Office, 1880–83). Hereinafter cited as Carnarvon Commission Report.

Office List of Committees shows, however, what people thought its chief purpose was. It was listed as "Royal Commission—Defence of Colonial Ports and Coaling Stations." [20]

Carnarvon's intention was to recommend nothing "beyond what was clearly necessary." Privately, he thought that Jervois, although a good scientific officer, was inclined to great extravagance in his proposals for fortifications. He hoped that the Australian governments would, "for their own sake, provide the necessary defences and we shall get the benefit of them" for the protection of naval bases; and he believed that a scheme of "more or less adequate co-operation" with local forces could be worked out. But he realized that in the crown colonies, and also in colonies further advanced but not yet able to foot the bill, the imperial government might have to provide the fortifications needed by the colonial defense forces.[21] The commission's Third Report, produced in 1882, declared that no fixed proportion could be established for the assessment of the mother country and her colonies for defense. For the present, the Royal Navy must remain a charge against imperial funds, the report said. These funds must also provide a portion of the charge of fortifying and garrisoning the bases essential to the navy. Colonies ought, however, to undertake the defense of their commercial ports and to contribute to the protection of naval stations. As colonial prosperity grew, their share of the cost of these defenses also would grow.[22]

A change of government soon after the commission began its investigations had jeopardized its very existence. Gladstone and his Liberal colleagues had allowed it to continue its work, but only because it would have been impolitic to dissolve it summarily. The commission's usefulness had clearly diminished since it could no longer count on the support of the British govern-

20. G.B., W.O., "List of Committees," No. 235A, W.O. Library.
21. Carnarvon to Milne, Dec. 16, 1879, National Maritime Museum, Greenwich, Milne Papers.
22. Carnarvon Commission Report, III, 30. The important third volume was not used by scholars until 1947 (Graham, *Empire of the North Atlantic*, p. 279 n.) In addition to the copies in the Public Record Office there is a printed copy of the Carnarvon Commission Report in the War Office Library and a draft as well as a printed copy in the National Maritime Museum.

ment. Although some of its findings were included in the Report of the Colonial Conference of 1887, the Carnarvon Commission Report itself has never been published.[23]

But even had it not suffered this political blight, it is doubtful whether a royal commission of this kind could have solved the knotty problems of the apportionment of defense costs which had been put to it. It had not included either representatives of the colonies, whom Carnarvon had considered and rejected, or any of the pioneer thinkers in the imperial defense field, as the *Morning Post* had suggested.[24] Moreover, it was not equipped to carry out negotiations with the colonial governments which would have been necessary in order to work out joint defense arrangements. Those negotiations were becoming more similar to the diplomatic contacts between independent states than to the earlier relations between a metropolitan state and its subordinate colonies.

Nevertheless, despite these difficulties, the Carnarvon Commission's work was a landmark in the history of the defense of the Empire. Not merely did it systematically accumulate invaluable information about specific local colonial defense problems (which had been done previously, by the War Office, though only on a small scale), and not only did it place special emphasis on the coaling stations that the navy now required to perform its functions, but also—and what was new and significant—it looked at the question of imperial defense as a whole, overriding both the departmentalization that plagued the British government and also the differences of interest between the mother country and the various colonies. It was the first and most important step toward a permanent organ of the British government for the supervision of colonial defense measures.[25]

In 1883 the Carnarvon Commission handed in its report, and its responsibilities in regard to colonial defenses were returned

23. Schurman, "Imperial Defence," pp. 150–153.
24. *Ibid.*, p. 143.
25. *Ibid.*, *passim*; see also Meredith J. Rooney, "Aspects of Imperial Defence: The Relevance of the 1879 Royal Commission on the Defence of British Possessions and Commerce Abroad" (unpublished B.Ph. thesis, Oxford University, 1963).

for a time to the War Office and the inspector general of fortifications.[26] On August 9, the report, modified in accordance with suggestions by the inspector general, was approved by the Defence Committee of the Cabinet, a body representing the various departments concerned. Money was voted by Parliament for some of the projects, but some colonies objected to some of the proposals and "promises not in line with the report" were therefore made to them.[27] As a result, articles by W. T. Stead in the *Pall Mall Gazette* in the autumn of 1884, which were written on the assumption that the Carnarvon Report had been suppressed, discussed the navy's role in imperial defense. These helped to mold public opinion and to warn the government of the need for action to reverse a serious decline in British fortunes. For after the Berlin settlement in 1878 had patched up the Balkan problem for a time, annihilations at Isandlhana (January 22, 1879) and on the retreat from Kabul (September 3, 1879) and defeats at Laing's Nek and Majuba Hill (January and February, 1881) had sapped British confidence and undermined her prestige abroad. It is true that Wolseley's victory at Tel-El-Kebir (September 13, 1882) taught a new respect for British military prowess that was to last until 1899;[28] but the defeat of a British-led Egyptian Army (November 5, 1883) and Gordon's fate in Khartoum in January, 1885, formed the backdrop for a Russian incursion into Afghanistan (March, 1885) that once again brought England close to war with this old adversary. Inquiries from the colonies poured in to ask advice about defense measures in view of panic-inspired rumors that Russian raiders were loose on the high seas. These required joint decisions of the Colonial Office, the Admiralty, and the War Office, and interdepartmental communication was too slow to meet the emergency. Therefore, on the initiative of

26. Schurman, "Imperial Defence," p. 216.
27. "Report of the Committee on Colonial Garrisons," G.B., W.O., Confidential Papers, A 66/1886. Lord Carnarvon was apparently not at first aware that his report had been approved and acted upon. He claimed later that he began to agitate for the release of the report in 1883 when he believed that nothing was being done about it (Carnarvon, *Defence of the Empire*, pp. xiii, xiv).
28. W. C. B. Tunstall, "Imperial Defence, 1870–1897," *CHBE*, III, 242, 248; Robert C. K. Ensor, *England, 1870–1914* (Oxford: Clarendon Press, 1936), pp. 60–61, 63, 69, 79.

H. Robert Meade, the assistant undersecretary of state for the colonies, the Colonial Defence Committee was established.[29]

This new body had prestige because it was a subcommittee of a Cabinet committee, namely the Colonial Committee, about which little is known. The War Office, the Admiralty, and the Colonial Office were represented on the subcommittee, and it was thus in some ways a revival of the Milne Committee on a more permanent footing and with a closer connection to the Cabinet and the War Office. It apparently regarded itself as a continuation of the Carnarvon Commission because it took over and continued that body's manuscript minute book with almost no break. Although it was still only consultative and advisory, the Colonial Defence Committee was in a stronger position than either the Milne Committee, which was temporary, or the Carnarvon Commission, which had been largely ignored because the Liberals feared it might usurp the functions of the executive. Furthermore, the Colonial Defence Committee obtained a clear-thinking and energetic permanent secretary, Captain George Sydenham Clarke, R.E.

From 1885, then, there was continuity in the discussion of imperial defense questions, and there now existed a means of countering the departmentalism of the service administrations. Even so, the new committee failed to overcome the dangerous tendency to engage in independent planning and action. Nor did it solve the even more difficult problem of securing colonial cooperation.[30] Until 1895 it produced no statement of the principles governing imperial defense, and its activity was restricted to the collection of information about the defense of ports and other localities and to the provision of advice upon request. Nevertheless, the Colonial Defence Committee was less parochial in its outlook than the service departments; it looked at questions from both a military and naval point of view; and it gave continuing attention to the part that British colonial territories should play

29. Report of the Colonial Conference of 1897, "History of the Colonial Defence Committee," P.A.C., Governor General's Papers, G. 21, No. 168, 1897.
30. Norman H. Gibbs, *The Origins of Imperial Defence* (Oxford: Clarendon Press, 1955), p. 10.

in the defense of the Empire. It was the ancestor of the future Committee of Imperial Defence, of which it was eventually to become a subcommittee.

The Naval Defense of Australasia

The earlier Russian war scares in 1877–1878 had created alarm in all the colonies where since the laying of the cables in the 1860's and the 1870's foreign news no longer seemed like ancient history. In Australian newspapers there were rumors of Russian plans to attack British colonies in the Pacific. Jervois in 1877 advised the government of Victoria that there was no danger of a major attack, except in the improbable circumstances that Britain should cease to control the seas; but he said that depredation by enemy cruisers was possible,[31] and he advised Sir Henry Parkes, premier of New South Wales, to buy an ironclad.[32] Parkes, after having secured the approval of the legislature for the purchase, withdrew the measure temporarily until he could be certain of Admiralty approval. But the collapse of his government soon afterward put an end to the project.[33] In March, 1878, however, the secretary of state for the colonies circulated a secret warning that the dangerous situation in Europe might lead to raids on the colonies by small enemy squadrons. When the Canadian government, concerned about ports on the Gulf of St. Lawrence and the Bay of Fundy, asked for the protection of fast cruisers, it was told that colonies must provide their own naval vessels for local defense. Next year, however, the danger having subsided, the Canadian Privy Council ruled against large expenditures for defenses at Esquimalt.[34] The New Zealanders had not been as greatly disturbed, but their government had asked for guns and had agreed to install the larger ones recommended by the War Office. Colonel Scratchley, Jervois's associate, when called

31. Victoria, Department of Defence, *Printed Papers*, I, 1862–1901, No. 46.
32. Jervois to Parkes, May–July, 1877, Mitchell Library, Sydney, Parkes Correspondence, XIX, 420–440.
33. Sir Hercules Robinson to Carnarvon, Telegram, July 23, 1877, New South Wales, *P.P.*, 1877–1878, III, 295.
34. Report of the Privy Council of Canada, May 16, 1879, P.A.C., Macdonald Papers, M.G. 26, A 1 (a), Vol. 100.

upon to report on defense, recommended harbor defenses against cruisers and a permanent militia to include a naval brigade.[35]

How serious the Russian danger had been it is difficult to say. Sir Edward Thornton, British minister in Washington, warned the Foreign Office on May 7, 1878, that Russia was attempting to acquire privateers in the United States to attack North Atlantic shipping; and intelligence reports in 1884, on the eve of a new crisis, purported to confirm that there had actually been plans for Russian attacks on Australian ports in 1877–1878, but these latter reports were only based on hearsay.[36] However, what is important is that the effect of the crisis on the Australian colonies was lasting.

Jervois's concept of Australian defense had been based on a division of responsibility between the Royal Navy and the colonies in which it was contemplated that the latter would not only provide defenses for their own ports but would also contribute vessels to aid in the protection of their own coastal trade. Protection of a coastal trade that was common to several colonies obviously implied an agreed division of responsibility between individual colonies or some other kind of joint effort. Therefore, in 1881, while the Carnarvon Commission was still sitting, a conference of the Australian colonies was held at Sydney to discuss this problem. This Inter-Colonial Conference recommended the building of land defenses at Australian expense, but proposed that an approach be made to the Admiralty for an increase in the Royal Navy's Australian Squadron "at the exclusive charge of the Imperial government." South Australia, where Jervois was now governor, was the only colony to suggest that the colonies, and not Britain, should pay for the proposed additional ships. Soon

35. Colonial Secretary to Agent General, New Zealand, May 17, 1878, New Zealand Archives, Letter Book IV; New Zealand, *Appendix to the Journals of the House of Representatives*, 1880, A-4.

36. Leonid Ivan Strakhovsky, "Russia's Privateering Projects of 1878," *Journal of Modern History*, VII (March, 1935), 22–40; B. R. Crick and Miriam Alman, eds., *A Guide to Manuscripts Relating to America in Great Britain and Ireland* (Oxford: Oxford University Press, 1961), p. 395; Confidential Memorandum (M.S.), Victoria, Department of Defence, *Printed Papers*, I, 1862–1901, No. 27; Millar, "History of the Defence Forces," pp. 225–226. For a full account of an earlier scare, see Duncan MacCallum, "The Alleged Russian Plans for the Invasion of Australia, 1864," Royal Australian Historical Society, *Journal and Proceedings* (Sydney, 1958), XLIV, 301–321.

afterward, Victoria, one of the wealthier colonies, ordered three small warships from England for local harbor defense. If New South Wales did not do the same thing, it was probably only because the presence of the Royal Navy's squadron and base at Sydney gave that colony a feeling of greater security.[37]

To regulate these incipient colonial navies, the First Lord of the Admiralty, Admiral Sir Astley Cooper Key, laid down on February 27, 1884, that colonial-owned naval vessels, commissioned in accordance with the Colonial Naval Defence Act of 1865, must fly the blue ensign with the colonial badge on the fly. In time of war such ships would come under the senior Royal Navy officer on the station. Their status as vessels of war had been communicated to foreign powers.[38] But when Victoria's new warships, *Victoria, Childers,* and *Albert,* sailed from England in 1884, the agent general of that colony quite improperly ordered their commander, against his better judgment, to hoist, not the blue ensign, but the white. The Admiralty promptly ruled that these Victorian ships were not entitled under international law to be classed as naval vessels outside the territorial waters of Australia, especially as they had not been commissioned in accordance with the Colonial Naval Defence Act of 1865. Orders were therefore sent to Gibraltar that the ensigns must be hauled down. Even when the colony formally complied with the terms of the act, Cooper Key continued to raise difficulties about the status of the vessels, alleging that he feared lest the Admiralty might incur some improper expenses. He also pointed out that the vessels could not be given up-to-date information on signals and regulations and that questions of precedence and relative rank might arise if they met Royal Navy vessels on their journey to Australia.[39]

For these reasons, and because he said he feared that colonial navies would be unable to keep abreast of modern developments,

---

37. Tunstall, "Imperial Defence, 1870–1897," pp. 235–236; Carnarvon, *Defence of the Empire,* p. 158; G.B., *P.P.,* 1887, *Proceedings of the Colonial Conferences,* 1887, II. *Papers Laid Before the Conference,* LVI, 817 (C. 5901–1).
38. A. Cooper Key, "Status of Colonial Ships of War," Feb. 27, 1884, in New Zealand Archives, Colonial Naval Defence Papers, 1885–1886, No. 1.
39. *The Naval Forces of the Colony of Victoria and the General Question of the Status of Colonial Ships of War* (1884), Admiralty Library, P. 627.

Cooper Key proposed the organization of a special Australasian Squadron which would be provided by the colonies and used for the defense of ports, but under Admiralty control.[40] He therefore instructed Rear Admiral George Tryon to take command of the Australasian Squadron of the Royal Navy and to negotiate with the colonies about an increase of naval strength in Australian waters. Tryon was also to work out an agreement with the colonies about the relation of their new harbor defense ships to the Royal Navy, by which the colonial ships would be put under his command but would be "especially appropriated to the defence of ports."[41]

In Canada, Britain had ceased to make any contribution to the Fisheries Protection Service, and provision had been made in the Militia Act since 1863 for authority to raise a marine force on lines similar to the militia. But marine companies that had existed in Canada West before confederation, and at Halifax for a little longer, had ceased to exist; and when the Fenian threat declined the few small gunboats that had patrolled the St. Lawrence and the Great Lakes had been decommissioned.[42] However, elsewhere the question of colonial navies had now become urgent. The New Zealand government had asked for the latest type of ironclad cruiser to be stationed in New Zealand waters; in return for control of the ship's activities, the government had offered to pay 3.5 per cent interest on the cruiser's original cost, 100 per cent of its expenses in New Zealand, and two-thirds of the total cost of crew and maintenance.[43] The Australian colonies had begun to take advantage of the provisions of the Colonial Naval Defence Act to establish and pay for their own small fleets. In addition to Victoria, which now had seven small war vessels, South Australia and Queensland had taken steps to establish navies and to man them from naval reserves,

40. A. Cooper Key, "Naval Defence of Our Colonies," Oct. 28, 1884, Admiralty Library, P. 735, and in New Zealand Archives, Colonial Naval Defence Papers, No. 2, and also Derby to Governor, June 19, 1885, inclosure, G. 24, Governor, Confidential In-letters.

41. G. Tryon, "With Reference to Colonial Vessels of War," Nov. 28, 1884, Admiralty Library, P. 735.

42. G.B., *P.P.*, 1907, LV, 139 (Cd. 3523).

43. New Zealand, *Appendix to the Journals of the House of Representatives*, 1885, A-6.

and New South Wales had the question under consideration.[44]
The Australian navies all had the benefit of the experience of
retired Royal Navy officers and men who manned them, and in
general they followed British naval practices and tradition; but
these seamen were not recognized by the Royal Navy and were
not included in its plans or training. However, some of the colonial vessels, notably *Protector* bought by South Australia, were
much more modern than the Royal Navy vessels then on the
Australian Station.[45] The Admiralty saw that there was obvious
advantage to be derived if this growing force was at its disposal.
Even though the danger against which this force was directed
might not yet be great, the precedent of its use by the Admiralty
could be useful for the future.

Tryon was quick to realize that Cooper Key and the Australians
were really far apart in their ideas. Even before leaving England
he had said that the Australians might be unwilling to surrender
control of their new ships. He had thought they might be brought
to accept a ten-year agreement by which they would pay for
extra ships for the Royal Navy's Australasian Squadron which the
Admiralty would build and man on their behalf. He believed
they would agree to the extra ships serving under the commander
in chief of the Royal Navy's Australian Station, provided the
ships were not allowed to leave the station except with Australian
consent. He suggested that all the Australian war vessels might
fly the white ensign, but he also thought that the colonies might
possess ships for other purposes.[46]

When the discussions opened in Australia in March, 1885, the
Australians took the stand that Tryon had anticipated. Their
harbor defense vessels, they said, were intimately tied to their

44. Evan Macgregor to the Undersecretary for the Colonies, May 4, 1885,
Admiralty Library, P. 735.
45. *Official Year Book of the Commonwealth of Australia, 1901–8* (Melbourne: McCarron, Bird, 1909), pp. 1084–1085; G. L. Macandie, *The Genesis
of the Royal Australian Navy* (Sydney: Government Printer, 1949), pp. 23, 45–
51. *Protector* had a speed of fourteen knots, like the much larger imperial flagship, *Nelson*, but was fully instead of partially armored and had better guns.
46. Tryon, "With Reference to Colonial Vessels of War." This memorandum
was addressed from 5, Eaton Place, S.W., Nov. 28, 1884. Tryon left for Australia
in December.

coastal fortifications which were under colonial control.[47] Hence, in May, Tryon was authorized to make proposals on the lines he had indicated earlier. The atmosphere for an agreement was now more favorable because of growing international tension. In fact, Victoria had by this time offered its three new warships (which happened to have arrived at Malta on the way to Australia) for service in the Red Sea campaign; and Queensland, although it had horrified Tryon by suggesting desecrating the white ensign by putting a "distinguishing badge" on it, had proposed that the colonies collectively should pay for colonial ships.[48] Cooper Key therefore suggested that officers and men for extra ships should be provided by the Admiralty in return for a fixed annual contribution by the colonies, and that these ships should have the status of Royal Navy vessels but should be assigned to Australian defense duties under the orders of the commander in chief of the station.[49] The colonial secretary told the governor of New Zealand that the vessels supplied by the colonies would be "appropriated especially for the defence of the ports to which they belong." [50]

The British Conservatives returned to office in June, 1885. In September the exact function of Australian defense vessels was defined officially in line with Tryon's ideas. The Admiralty now said that although the defense of harbors was a purely local problem to be undertaken by each colonial government, the protection of ships trading in Australian waters was of benefit to all the Australian colonies and its cost should therefore be shared among them. In peacetime the vessels assigned to this task "should be employed in the usual routine duties of the station in common with the rest of the Imperial squadron," but in time of war they should be employed for the protection of the Australasian floating trade. There should never be divided responsibility. The commander in chief of the station should always be

47. G.B., *P.P.*, 1887, LVI, 818 (C. 5901–1).
48. Memorandum of Sir W. Griffiths, April 27, 1885, New Zealand Archives, Colonial Naval Defence Papers, No. 7.
49. Evan Macgregor to the Undersecretary of State for the Colonies, May 4, 1885, Admiralty, P. 735.
50. Derby to Governor, New Zealand, June 19, 1885, New Zealand Archives, 92/4, Governor, Confidential In-letters.

in sole command. The Admiralty was, however, prepared to promise that the Royal Navy Squadron now in Australian waters would not be reduced when the additional vessels for the protection of trade in Australian waters arrived from Britain. The extra ships would be five cruisers and two torpedo boats, which after ten years would be put at the disposal of the colonial governments.[51] What was now being proposed was not Admiralty control of harbor defense ships, but rather Australasian contribution to vessels available for general naval purposes but restricted to Australasian seas.

Tryon submitted these terms to the Australian governments on December 24, 1885. The following April he met the premiers of Queensland, New South Wales, and Victoria on board the flagship *H.M.S. Nelson* in Sydney Harbor, and he received communications from other colonies not personally represented. All except Victoria were now willing, in principle, to pay for the additional vessels. Victoria insisted that the vessels should be constructed at British expense.[52] Further negotiations followed, but the problem was still unresolved when the first Colonial Conference met in London in August, 1887, to coincide with Queen Victoria's Golden Jubilee. Additions to the naval squadron in Australasian waters therefore became one of the chief problems on the agenda.

Naval Problems at the Colonial Conference of 1887

The conference met in April and May of 1887. Representatives of the crown colonies were present along with those of the self-governing dependencies only on the first day. The aim of the conference was somewhat vague. There was a general belief that the security of the Empire would be enhanced if each part assumed its full responsibility. "Science had made the colonies more vulnerable," and the Admiralty, unwilling to accept greater financial responsibility for peripheral defenses, pressed for a settle-

---

51. R. D. Awdrey, "Local Defence and Protection of Floating Trade in Waters of the Australian Colonies," Sept. 9, 1885, Admiralty Library, P. 735.
52. G.B., *P.P.*, 1887, LVI, 818–819 (C. 5901–1).

ment of the arrangements for the naval defense of Australia. But it did not present a very convincing case for a centrally directed naval strategy. Sir John Downer of South Australia pointed out that the request that the colonies should contribute to the costs of fleets for the protection of the floating trade was a new departure and would have to be made in a form acceptable to the various legislatures. His colony, reversing its previous stand, now supported Victoria's view that the colonies should pay only for the maintenance, and not for the construction, of the additional vessels to be added to the Royal Navy's Australian Squadron. The result was that the conference haggled about the payment of the interest on construction costs. The Australians were accused of ignoring the fact that Britain was already paying the full cost of the existing Australian Squadron.

On the other hand, close questioning revealed that the Admiralty was intending to charge against the colonies not only the pensions of men employed on the extra ships, but also the full pay of reservists who were to be stationed in Britain; these reservists were to be occupied there but held ready to send to Australia in an emergency in order to bring the ships up to full war establishment. The Admiralty also wanted to claim credit for the fact that it would pay for the cost of training extra boys recruited into the navy to replace sailors sent to Australia. Ultimately, after hard bargaining, it was agreed that the colonies would pay only the interest on the cost of construction and a fixed charge for maintenance, but not the capital costs. After a ten-year period the ships would revert to Britain.

Apart from these financial disputes the chief problem for settlement in 1887 was the question of naval command. For good strategic reasons the Admiralty insisted on undivided control. For good political reasons the colonies wanted a guarantee that the ships would not be taken away without their permission. The First Lord of the Admiralty, Lord George Hamilton, twisted and turned in every direction in his efforts to avoid giving a rigid guarantee to the Australians. When he brought the final draft of the agreement for approval it simply stated that the extra ships were to be under the commander in chief but assigned to duty in Australian waters. However, the Australian delegates insisted on the addition of a clause stating categorically that the ships might be "employed beyond those limits only with the consent of the Colonial Governments." [53] Soon after the conference, all the Australian colonies including Queensland after a delay, ratified the agreement by which five fast cruisers and two torpedo gunboats were to be added as auxiliaries (there never was, strictly speaking, an auxiliary squadron) to the imperial ships on the Australian Station under the control of the commander in chief. There was to be no reduction of the strength of the Royal Navy ships in Australian waters.[54]

Tryon's original suggestion that the colonies should continue to possess and control naval vessels for local purposes still stood; he had also emphasized the need to train Australian seamen. As a result he is justly regarded as the father of the Royal Australian Navy. The agreement that command of the extra ships by the Royal Navy should be subject to certain restrictions, which he had originated, was also an important concession to colonial sentiment.

But what seemed at the time to be the most important outcome of the conference was the precedent for a colonial contribution to imperial defense. Sir Henry Holland, the secretary of state for the colonies, wrote: "We do not regard this question in the light of a mere bargain between the mother country and the colonies, but as the starting point of a new policy—the first step towards a federation for defence which will not only add strength to the Empire, but tend to find its members in a closer union." [55]

On the other hand, throughout the conference discussions, the Canadian delegates, under instructions from Sir John A. Macdonald, had taken the attitude that this naval question did not concern them, for though Canada was by far the largest colonial

53. *Ibid.*, p. 508.
54. Imperial Defence Act, 1888 (51 & 52 Vict., c. 32), inclosed in Queensland, *Naval Defence of Australasian Colonies*, 1891, A.W.M. Library, Queensland, Miscellaneous. New Zealand's ratification is in New Zealand, *Statutes*, No. 39, Dec. 23, 1887. By it New Zealand undertook to pay £20,000 a year for ten years. This led to economy measures in land defenses.
55. H. T. Holland, "Proposed Increased Australasian Squadron: Remarks on Discussion at the Colonial Office, 5 April, 1887," April 23, 1887, Admiralty Library, P. 735.

owner of shipping, naval defense was the responsibility of Great Britain alone. For Canada, naval defense was not the paramount issue, as it was for Australia. Following lines on which Macdonald had testified before the Carnarvon Commission, the Canadians claimed their best contribution to imperial defense was the development of their internal resources and especially the building of a railway to link the Atlantic and Pacific.[56]

The Naval Imperialists

A reasoned and convincing defense of the Admiralty case for a centralized Empire naval strategy had been noticeably lacking in the discussions in London in 1887, and there had been no attempt to engage in a general discussion of the imperial defense problem. But in the ensuing years, as public interest in the navy grew, the strategic questions involved were elaborated by the Colomb brothers and by other writers such as Clarke, who had been secretary of the Colonial Defence Committee since 1885. In an article entitled "The Navy and the Colonies" in the *United Service Magazine* in November, 1890, Clarke declared that the colonies derived an incalculable benefit from the protection given by the Royal Navy, that this benefit was beyond the capacity of their own local navies, and that its effectiveness depended on the unity of naval action.[57] A year later, Sir John Colomb, moving a resolution on colonial sea commerce and British naval responsibilities in the House of Commons, declared that colonial commerce was increasing so rapidly that it would soon equal, if not surpass, that of the United Kingdom, but that while the British taxpayer provided £14,215,100, the total naval expenditures of the "outlying empire" amounted to a mere £381,546, mainly for the provision of harbors and similar facilities and services.[58]

Clarke and Colomb provided the strategic arguments which Admiralty spokesmen had failed to produce at the conference.

56. Tunstall, "Imperial Defence," pp. 238–240.
57. Reprinted in Lt. Col. Sir George S. Clarke and James R. Thursfield, *The Navy and the Nation, or Naval Warfare and Imperial Defence* (London: John Murray, 1897), pp. 41–50.
58. G.B., *Hansard* (March 2, 1891), CCCL, 1951.

Their first postulate of imperial defense was a navy able to maintain imperial communications; but though the navy was the defensive force of the Empire, it must be strategically offensive, seeking the enemy's battle fleet to destroy it. The idea of sending two army corps to serve with a foreign continental army was called a "vain dream." The army should be used for "conjunct expeditions." During earlier wars Britain and India had provided most of the troops, but the colonies could now contribute as many as 90,000 men. The Empire should be divided into strategic areas corresponding to the naval stations of the fleet, and colonial troops should be ready to serve outside their own territory in the area to which they belonged.[59] Naval imperialists in Britain now wanted the extension of the "vitally important principle" that had been established in the agreement of 1887, which was described as "the first practical recognition" of "an obligation on the part of the Colonies depending on commerce to contribute to the maintenance of H.M. Navy." [60] And they believed that the colonies as a whole had evinced an earnest desire to assume a share of the imperial burden.[61] The Colonial Defence Committee on May 19, 1896, setting out the principles of colonial defense based on the maintenance of supremacy at sea coupled with local defense, stated that since the completion of fixed defenses it attributed less importance to small colonial navies. It said that it was "generally difficult to obtain from floating harbour defences an effect commensurate with the outlay entailed upon them." This memorandum was widely circulated by Joseph Chamberlain in June, 1896.[62] Clarke pressed for a new conference to explain to the colonies why each member must contribute to the naval strength of the whole.

In Australia, however, although the naval arrangements made

59. George S. Clarke, "Imperial Defence," read at the Royal Colonial Institute, Feb. 11, 1896; printed in Clarke and Thursfield, *Navy and the Nation*, pp. 32–34.
60. George S. Clarke, *Imperial Defence* (London: Imperial Press, 1897), pp. 187–188.
61. *Ibid.*, p. 193.
62. Colonial Defence Committee, Confidential Memorandum 57M, May 19, 1896, P.R.O., Cab. 8/1/2. The Colonial Defence Committee will hereinafter be abbreviated as C.D.C.

in 1887 had gone smoothly into effect, they had actually not aroused that enthusiastic response which Clarke's thesis required. Soon after the new extra ships arrived on station in 1891 they were absorbed into the Australian Squadron. Fears were widely expressed that if a crisis should come, the Royal Navy Squadron might depart and take the auxiliary warships with it.[63] In 1893 the Legislative Assembly of New South Wales complained, wrongly as it happened, of an alleged breach of the naval agreement when one of the auxiliary vessels was used in Samoa without specific approval by the Australian governments.[64] The existence of feelings of that kind led the Duke of Devonshire in a speech in the Guildhall in London to refer sarcastically to the uselessness of navies "hugging the shore" for local defense. In this speech, on December 3, 1896, he told the British Empire League that he had been instructed by the Colonial Defence Committee, of which he was chairman, to inform colonial citizens about the principles upon which the committee's plans were based. According to newspaper reports, these principles were the "maintenance of Great Britain's supremacy at sea upon the basis of a system of Imperial defence against attack from sea at all places likely to be attacked." "The Committee," added Devonshire, "would advocate the creation [in the colonies] of fixed adequate defences and troops sufficient to cope with any possible enemy." He also asserted that "it was the duty of the colonies to provide for adequate defence." [65] Devonshire's speech, which was based on the Colonial Defence Committee's memorandum of May 19, 1896, was taken to mean that he thought restricted use of the auxiliary squadron to Australasian waters, agreed upon in 1887, was a violation of sound strategy. That restriction had been introduced, however, because only on such terms could the Australian electors be brought to pay for additions to the Royal Navy. The guaranteed presence of the auxiliary vessels had given Australians a sense of security. But it had evidently done so at

---

63. José, *Royal Australian Navy,* p. xix.
64. Tyler, *Struggle for Imperial Unity,* pp. 157–158.
65. Toronto *Globe,* Dec. 4, 1896.

the expense of what the Colonial Defence Committee considered strategically necessary—the ability of the Admiralty to concentrate all available resources against the enemy's main battle fleet.

Imperial Federation

Inspired by Devonshire's address, the Lord Mayor of London, who was present, suggested that a fine present for Queen Victoria on the occasion of the sixtieth anniversary of her accession to the throne would be a scheme of absolute and perfect Empire unity. The need for closer political ties within the Empire, if imperial defense was to be made really effective, had long been argued, and the naval imperialists had been among the earliest and most outspoken propagandists for a reversal of the decentralizing processes begun by Gladstone's Liberals. In 1880 Colomb himself put the matter bluntly: "Imperial representation lies at the root of the problem of imperial defence." [66] Professor Burt has shown that between 1874 and the first Colonial Conference, similar ideas were also advanced by C. W. Eddy; Sir Julius Vogel, a New Zealander; F. P. de Labillière, an Australian; S. W. Kelsey; the Marquis of Lorne; and W. E. Forster, the first president of the Imperial Federation League.[67] Although some thought, rather naïvely, that until political arrangements could be achieved, the "Colonies might for the present delegate such control to the English Parliament in the confidential trust that Parliament will see to it that Colonial interests do not suffer," [68] most imperial federationists believed with Captain Colomb that "some sort of Federation for defence is necessary to enable naval and military authority to develop in peace a settled plan for the defence of our Empire in war." [69]

66. Colomb, *Defence of Great and Greater Britain*, p. 10.
67. Alfred LeRoy Burt, *Imperial Architects: Being an Account of the Proposals in the Direction of a Closer Imperial Union* (Oxford: Blackwell, 1913), pp. 126–133.
68. George Baden Powell at the Royal Colonial Institute, quoted in *The Colonies and India*, June 16, 1882, National Maritime Museum, Greenwich, Milne Papers.
69. John C. R. Colomb, "Imperial Federation—Naval and Military," *The Journal of the Royal United Service Institution*, XXX (1886), 857. Hereinafter *The Journal of the Royal United Service Institution* will be abbreviated as *R.U.S.I. Journal*.

The Colonial Conference of 1887 had been called as a result—at least in part—of the urgings of the creators of the Imperial Federation League set up in Britain in 1884. The league had branches in the colonies, though strangely enough not at first in Toronto which was soon to be regarded as the home of Canadian imperial sentiment. Not all the members of the league were convinced federationists, and there were wide differences of opinion about the form that federation should take. It is probable that although most of the colonial members of the Colonial Conference of 1887 were imbued with the desire for some sort of closer association or closer union with Britain, few, if any, were federationists in the fullest political sense of the term.

The colonial secretary, when summoning the 1887 conference, had specifically ruled out federation from the agenda; and the British prime minister, the Marquess of Salisbury, in his address to the conference, when stressing defense as the most important item on the agenda, had spoken of what he called a *Kriegsverein,* an undefined form of association for defense purposes. In fact, the lukewarm attitude of the British government toward all positive suggestions for any form of closer association beyond the specific defense contributions which they were seeking is said by an authority on the imperial defense movement to have given a setback to the imperial sentiments of many colonials at the conference.[70] Delegates who came to London thinking themselves imperialists learned something about their own underlying colonial nationalism. Nevertheless, the conference was generally regarded as a great and successful step toward tightening the bonds of empire. Lack of progress in drafting any kind of constitutional relationship was explained away as a result of the pragmatic British approach and their dislike of paper constitutions.

But in the following years the Imperial Federation League was split between those who sought a customs union and those who wanted federation chiefly for defense; it found itself unable to agree upon a draft proposal for federation. Lord Brassey, one of the earliest advocates of an imperial naval policy, when writing in 1892 on "Imperial Federation for Naval Defence," said that

70. Tyler, *Struggle for Imperial Unity,* pp. 116, 120–121.

it did not seem feasible to admit the agents general of the colonies to the Cabinet, that the admission of colonial life peers to the House of Lords would obviously be inadequate, that colonial representation in the House of Commons was fraught with difficulties, and that the Commons would not be likely to surrender control of foreign policy to an Imperial Privy Council. He had therefore come to believe that only an advisory Council for Imperial Defence was possible.[71] The contemporary activity of Irish nationalist M.P.'s must have dampened enthusiasm in Britain for colonial representation at Westminster. No one wanted a colonial bloc that might seize the political balance of power in the United Kingdom. The result of the divisions within the league, and of doubt about the practicability or advisability of imperial federation, was that in 1893 a group of its members, claiming that its work of public education was done and that it had completed its original purpose, quietly arranged the league's dissolution without informing the branches in the dominions that the question was being considered. Nevertheless, many imperialists continued to believe and profess that the erection of imperial institutions was only a matter of time; and those imperial federationists who favored the creation of imperial institutions for defense created the Imperial Federation (Defence) League to work for cash contributions for the army and navy.[72] The Imperial Federation League, despite the brevity of its existence, had in fact done much to stimulate public interest in the need for improvements in the defense of the Empire; it had also planted the idea that there was a close connection between an effective system of imperial defense and the political reorganization of the Empire.

Sir George Sydenham Clarke, the secretary of the Colonial Defence Committee, thought it essential for the effective preparation of an imperial defense policy that there should be a standing committee to which the colonies would have access. He believed that the Colonial Defence Committee could serve the pur-

<hr />

71. Thomas Lord Brassey, "Imperial Federation for Naval Defence," *Nineteenth Century*, XXXI (Jan., 1892), 95–96.
72. Tyler, *Struggle for Imperial Unity*, pp. 199–211.

pose if colonial agents general were made ex officio members and if the colonies were given the right to appoint representatives.[73] Clarke thought there also ought to be area defense councils meeting annually in various parts of each strategic region, keeping in touch with local defense committees and in direct communication with the standing committee in London with which the colonial agents general would be associated. The area councils would keep proper records and collect intelligence information. They would take note of "military progress or backsliding." Conferences of the whole Empire would be held in London every five years to deal with "larger questions of national [i.e., imperial] defence." [74]

Clarke had argued in 1894 that no "organic change" was being proposed.[75] But in 1896 he admitted that his principles did "practically imply the federation of the Empire for the purposes of defence. If political federation by groups of colonies existed the task would be simplified. There is no reason, however, why organization for Imperial defence should be delayed." [76] In answer to the criticism that his proposed councils would be useless because they would have no executive power, Clarke argued curiously that the only thing needed was mutual understanding. Good will and an earnest desire to co-operate abounded. "Light and leading alone are needed to enable the immense resources of the Empire to be rendered available for purposes of war and . . . the impulse must come from the mother country." [77]

Naval Questions at the Colonial Conference of 1897

Despite the fact that the Imperial Federation League had collapsed and that the secretary of the Colonial Defence Committee was obviously hedging about admitting his belief that

73. George S. Clarke, "Imperial Defence," in Francis P. de Labillière, *Federal Britain: Or Unity and Federation of the Empire . . . with Chapter on Imperial Defence by Major Sir George S. Clarke, R.E., K.C.M.G.,* (London: S. Low Marston & Co., 1894), p. 147.
74. Clarke and Thursfield, *Navy and the Nation,* pp. 38–39.
75. Clarke, "Imperial Defence" (1894), p. 147.
76. Clarke and Thursfield, *Navy and the Nation,* p. 38.
77. *Ibid.,* p. 39.

some kind of political federation of the Empire was necessary, Joseph Chamberlain, who had become colonial secretary in 1895, was less reticent about having commercial union adopted as a step toward his ultimate objective—the political re-centralization of the Empire.[78] The occasion of the Queen's Diamond Jubilee in 1897 therefore seemed to him a favorable opportunity to further imperial unity by calling another colonial conference to discuss various problems, including defense.

To the assembled ministers, Chamberlain declared that every war in the Queen's long reign had at bottom a colonial interest. He also maintained that had it not been for the Royal Navy, Canada would have had to make concessions to her neighbors, the United States, Japan, and Russia, and so would have become to a great extent a dependent country. He therefore speculated imaginatively about various proposals for military and naval co-operation that would make imperial defense more effective and would help to reduce the great financial burden that Britain carried almost singlehanded. Referring to the Australian Naval Agreement, he mentioned that an offer of a naval contribution from Cape Colony was to be presented later; and he said pointedly, "Canada has made no offer." He then asked the representative of the Admiralty, Captain Beaumont, a naval member of the Colonial Defence Committee, to explain in what ways the Admiralty wanted to modify the naval arrangements with the Australian colonies. Beaumont pleaded that he had not been instructed to give the Admiralty's point of view, but he expressed his own personal opinion that it was objectionable that the agreements should restrict to Australasian waters both in peace and in war the ships provided by the colonies in Australasia. But when asked to explain clearly the strategic grounds upon which such limitations were objectionable, he blundered instead into an assertion that the Australian ships in peacetime ought to be used for visits to the Pacific islands for imperial purposes. Some of the Australian premiers and Richard Seddon of New Zealand hastened to protest that they already saw all too little of the ships and that this hampered their attempts to gain popular support

78. Graham, "Imperial Finance, Trade, and Communications," p. 445.

for the policy of contributions. Chamberlain, realizing that Beaumont was not helping his case, dismissed him, saying that he must appeal to the Admiralty for an authoritative statement about the restrictions limiting the use of the fleet in time of war.

At this point, Sir Wilfrid Laurier, who had been silent while the Australians were explaining their reasons for insistence upon restrictions, intervened to say that they had not answered the general question which had been presented to them, namely, whether they would contribute to the "general fund for the protection of the Empire at large." Chamberlain hurriedly interjected that Britain was prepared to defend the colonies, but that he thought the naval authorities should not be hampered by "political restrictions" in time of war. When Laurier insisted the Australians had in fact shown themselves willing only to make contributions "for a particular purpose," the secretary of state referred to the writings of the American naval officer-historian Captain A. T. Mahan. Laurier then said that he himself thought the Australian attitude not "unwise," but he insisted co-operation was all that was politically possible for them. Challenged about Canada's own position on naval defense, he said the question had not been discussed in Canada. Hitherto it had been an academic question. Now that it was put as a practical one, "no doubt Canada will consider it and give an answer."

The Australians promptly retorted that Canada should make a contribution because then their own people in Australia would be the more willing to approve a naval contribution. Laurier's reply was that Canada was in a different position from the Australian colonies: it was "an inaccessible country." By this time it was clear that the Australians were unlikely to change their minds about refusing a contribution for "general purposes"; Captain Beaumont, who had apparently stayed on after his dismissal or had returned, intervened with, "I should like to say, sir, that so far as I know there has been no desire to alter the agreement." Beaumont then finally withdrew.[79] There is no doubt that Cham-

---

79. G.B., C.O., *Proceedings of a Conference Between the Secretary of State for the Colonies and the Premiers of the Self-Governing Colonies . . .* 1897 (London: H.M.S.O., 1897) (C. 8596), pp. 5, 54–64, P.A.C., G. 21, No. 168.

berlain had stage-managed the conference extremely badly, and that he had raised the strategic question prematurely.

When the naval defense question came up again later during the conference, C. C. Kingston, representing South Australia, tabled a proposal made by Captain W. R. Creswell, the colony's naval commandant, which proposed the creation of a naval reserve of seamen in the Australian colonies instead of a contribution toward ships. Chamberlain, however, interjected at this point that the First Lord of the Admiralty, G. J. Goschen, was very anxious to discuss naval defense with the premiers. He went on, "and of course he will be able to give us much more definitely than we could get the other day, the views of the Government on the whole subject." [80]

However, when Goschen, accompanied by Admiral Sir Frederick William Richards, appeared before the conference, the former began by saying the Admiralty had been impressed by reports of the conference's discussions of the many difficulties which beset any other forms of colonial contribution, and that their lordships were therefore content to let the earlier agreement with the Australians stand. He said that though the contribution, £126,000, was not large enough to assist to any important extent, he valued the tie. Cape Colony was making a proposal that showed "the development of that system." He would be glad to open negotiations with Canada. But he went on to say the Admiralty would prefer to have a free hand to conduct the defense of Australia on the same strategic principles as those followed in the defense of British ports, principles which excluded any undertaking to attach ships to particular ports.

In reply, Sir George Turner of Victoria declared that a rumor, which appeared to have foundation, had spread the idea that the Admiralty actually wanted a free hand in wartime to send the Australian ships tens of thousands of miles from Australia; and Seddon of New Zealand added that it was not a mere rumor— the Duke of Devonshire had advanced this argument in his Guildhall speech, and other admirals on the station had preached the same doctrine. Goschen replied that the Duke's intention

80. *Ibid.*, p. 124.

had been only to ask for freedom to move the vessels within Australian waters, and that his speech had been merely a plea for an aggressive naval policy.

After Goschen had rejected the Creswell plan for an Australian naval reserve, Chamberlain turned once more to Laurier and suggested that he should have a private interview with the First Lord on the naval question. The Canadian premier, however, to the professed astonishment of Goschen, said the naval question did not have the same importance for Canada as for some of the other colonies, and that Canadians, although they lived beside a powerful nation, had no thought of war. "We look upon our conflicts with them . . . as family troubles which mean nothing very serious." Sir Gordon Sprigg of the Cape Colony, on the other hand, demonstrated his colony's sentiments by an offer of a contribution to the Royal Navy without conditions.[81] "Family troubles" in South Africa might, of course, necessitate help from the mother country.

So although imperial sentiment in all the colonies, even in Canada, was strong, it had not produced a greater willingness to make positive contributions to the more centralized system of imperial naval defense which had received official approval in Britain. Sir John Colomb, in an article in 1897, said Australians had been roused to patriotic fury by the Kaiser's telegram to President Kruger and had made an itinerant German band play "Rule Britannia" all day long, but they had not offered to increase their contribution to the Royal Navy.[82] In practice, an imperial navy, supported by colonial financial contributions but under British direction and control, had little appeal for most colonials at a time when colonial nationalism was developing. Australian political leaders, who had taken a cautious step in the direction of defense co-operation, were afraid lest further centralized control might appear to leave their cities too much exposed to bombardment. They therefore wanted to have some voice in defense priorities.[83] This right had not been conceded by Chamberlain's

81. *Ibid.*, pp. 140–147.
82. John C. R. Colomb, "British Defence: Its Popular and Real Aspects," *The New Century Review*, I, No. 4 (April, 1897), 313–320.
83. Hall, *Australia and England*, pp. 244–246.

proposals. Despite Cape Colony's gesture in offering an unconditional contribution, the Australians in 1897 merely renewed
their former contribution on the same terms of restriction—
namely, that it was to be devoted not to the general naval
strength of the Empire but to the protection of Australasian
interests in Australasian waters. This arrangement would, of
course, help to relieve the burden for Britain if it allowed British
effort to be diverted elsewhere. But the agreement did not permit
reduction of British effort in Australasian waters.

"Imperial Defense"

By the 1890's, then, the teachings of the Colomb brothers and
their like, powerfully reinforced by Mahan, had found wide acceptance. For many people, the defense of the scattered British
Empire was primarily a naval problem, for which, as "the seas
are one," a single over-all strategic defense policy was necessary.
"Imperial defense" had therefore come to mean something more
specific than merely the defense of the Empire. It was a slogan
with a double meaning: it emphasized the importance of the
naval component in over-all defense planning, but also was based
on the expectation that colonies were expected to play their part.
Since the great rivals of the Royal Navy were still only found in
strength in European waters, it made good sense to concentrate
fleets to control the North Atlantic, as in earlier centuries. Outlying parts of the Empire, although expected to protect both
themselves and the vital naval bases on which world-wide sea
power depended, were now better off and could be expected to
contribute to the central naval strength of the Empire at the
vital point. It was argued that by so doing they would help to
insure that the enemy could launch only minor raids against
them. If they were temporarily incapacitated or overrun, British
retention of control of the seas would mean they could eventually
be relieved or recovered. This line of thought had led to the Australian policy of naval contributions. The Australasian colonies
could only be reached by sea and were therefore especially concerned with naval defense. In their case, the implied moral obli-

gation to contribute to the general naval defense of the Empire appeared to coincide with their own immediate interest.

Even in the case of these Australasian colonies, however, the naval doctrine had not been accepted in its fullest form. No naval policy, whatever its basis in strategic theory, could give absolute protection. Though it could be pointed out that this rule applied also to British ports, Australians were aware that the remoteness of their position, and the fact that major raids might therefore be the more serious, made a difference. Hence, they had insisted upon adulterating the pure doctrine of the naval imperialists by demanding restrictions upon the movement of the ships which they contributed to the Royal Navy in Australasian waters.

So the presence of Russian warships in the Pacific, which had made Australians willing to contribute to the navy, had also worked to limit the degree of their acceptance of the policy of a single, centralized control of the fleet. Electorates, unaware of or unimpressed by the logic of the strategists, were insistent upon retaining some control of the ships they had bought for their own defense. Moreover, Canada, which could not be defended by sea and which would be less easily recovered even though British control of the seas was complete, was less impressed by the arguments of the naval strategists. Canadians were aware that the Empire was a sea-trading organization for which the sea-lanes were vital arteries, and they knew that a good part of their livelihood depended on free passage. But like all the colonials, they also knew that the other independent nations that supplied British consumers, and that were just as dependent upon free passage for their goods, could obviously not be asked to contribute to maintain the freedom of the seas. It was clear to them, too, that Britain was more dependent upon imports than the Canadians were upon exports. Even without colonial contributions, Britain would have to keep up a fleet in order to retain her position and prestige and to preserve her many formal and informal imperial interests in which they had almost no share. While the colonies realized the many benefits they derived from a connection with Britain that they could not afford to lose, they believed they were not compelled by their own immediate or long-term interests to contribute to Empire defense in time of peace. The fact that navies took a long time to build did not move them. Nor did the moral argument that all should share the burden have much effect. For although they were repeatedly told they were sheltering practically free under the British umbrella, they could reply that they were committed by British policies in the making of which they had had no voice, and that Britain had world-wide interests which they did not share. It was now too late to reverse the development of colonial autonomy. Without some form of policy-sharing, defense-sharing was unacceptable. Imperial federation had made little headway and the political arguments of colonial nationalists therefore offset the strategic arguments of the naval imperialists.

In both Britain and the colonies the nub of the problem was financial. It was the increasing unwillingness of the British taxpayer to pay for the growing cost of the navy that by 1897 had added very powerful force to the strategic argument for a sounder defense organization. When Chamberlain admitted that all he wanted was a token contribution, he weakened his case by revealing his hand. A token contribution that was insignificant would not relieve the British taxpayer to any appreciable extent, but it would provide a precedent that might lead to a future surrender of colonial autonomy in the vital defense sphere. After such a revelation, Chamberlain was fortunate to come out of the conference with the colonial contributions at their old level. In fact, he had to accept a compromise that satisfied neither the Treasury which wanted more money, nor the Admiralty which wanted no restrictions, nor the colonial nationalists who wanted to control their own defense policy and to insure the preservation of their hard-won autonomy. In view of the rising tide of colonial nationalism, the slogan "imperial defense" had proved to be a naval mirage.

More serious still, the "imperial defense" theory had had the unfortunate effect of reducing the already overly small interest and participation of the colonies in naval affairs. After the making of the Naval Agreement of 1887, the navies of the Australian colonies—the continued existence of which Tryon had approved

—went into a decline. The blame must be attributed to the colonies as well as to the Admiralty. On the one hand, the Australians believed they were making adequate appropriation to their naval defense through the auxiliary vessels which were to be used especially for defense of Australasian interests. On the other, although the official policy was that colonies were still expected to provide for their own local needs (especially harbor defense) by the maintenance of small local navies, the Royal Navy gave colonial navies little encouragement or help once it had obtained the extra ships. Nor had the Royal Navy any real interest in the colonial naval reserve schemes which from time to time were advocated by writers on imperial defense. Thus, although the theory was that the colonies should be encouraged not only to make naval contributions to the general defense of the Empire by sea but also to their own local defense by "an active naval force," in practice very little of the kind materialized. The concept that imperial defense was primarily a question of sea power had helped to kill infant colonial navies without breathing life into the political institutions necessary to support the concept of centralized control of imperial defense. Had the Admiralty presented its case more effectively at the conferences, it is possible that the colonial delegates might have been more willing to accept the idea of centralized naval defense. But the Admiralty did not do so partly because it did not understand its own case and partly because Admiralty spokesmen were incapable of producing a clear statement on naval needs. In these circumstances, the colonial leaders, who were quite clear about their political aims, could not be won over.

5

The Bombardment Bogie, the Sudan, and Canada

Mackenzie and the Russian Crisis of 1878

When the chief danger to the Empire changed from the American menace of the 1860's to a wider naval danger in the late 1870's, Canadian defense problems were inevitably affected. The confrontation of Britain and Russia over the integrity of Turkey in 1877–1878, which had led to attempts to put the ideas of the naval imperialists into practice throughout the Empire, had caught Mackenzie's logical but leisurely program for the creation of a Canadian military establishment before it had laid the foundations for an effective, trained force. In place of the declining American threat in mid-continent, there had now appeared the specter of Russian naval bombardment or raids on the Canadian Atlantic and Pacific coasts. The Canadian government had already been warned by General Selby Smyth, the G.O.C., that Canada's ocean ports were practically defenseless.[1] Albert N. Richards, the lieutenant governor of British Columbia, on receiving news of the European crisis, also drew the Dominion government's attention to the vulnerability of British Columbia if the Russians should come; he asked to borrow guns from naval stores to defend the Esquimalt naval base. Dufferin immediately reported this to the secretary of state for the colonies; but a week before the warning reached him, Hicks Beach had, in fact, already sent out a secret circular to all the colonies urging them

1. "Militia Report for 1879," Canada, *Sessional Papers*, XIII, 1880, Vol. 5, No. 8, p. xiv.

to take precautions against possible Russian raiders.[2] In Canada there were rumors that a Russian steamer crammed with men and guns had arrived in Maine to arm privateers against British shipping in the Atlantic and to prepare to bombard Canadian ports. Details were vague. The ship was a German vessel, *Cimbria*, hired to transport Russian sailors from the Baltic to man privateers purchased in the United States.[3] The news was electrifying because, outside of Halifax, Canadian ports had only a few guns of ancient model. Its effect was out of all proportion to the actual danger.

Mackenzie's first reaction had been to ask the Admiralty for the protection of fast cruisers stationed in the St. Lawrence. This was on May 4, 1878. At the same time his Cabinet talked about the problems of installing up-to-date guns on both coasts. None were available in Canada.[4] They would have to be brought from Britain. A week later, Mackenzie, worrying lest the United States might take advantage of British preoccupation in the Levant, asked the governor general to cable a request that if hostilities became imminent, prompt information should be sent to Canada from the Colonial Office. "No imperial aid," he said, "will avail us on the inland waters and we can do without it if we are only kept well informed."[5]

It was a typical Canadian reaction to the old American danger: sheer Canadian courage would defend the homeland against invasion. But as the border was unfortified and the militia unorganized, these were little more than brave words. Canada's

2. During the Crimean War a naval hospital had been established at Esquimalt; in 1865 a Stores Establishment and in 1872 an Ordnance Repair Shop were authorized (Major F. V. Longstaff, *Esquimalt Naval Base: A History of Its Work and its Defences* [Victoria: Victoria Book Store, 1941], pp. 20–22; Dufferin 56, March 11, 1878, P.R.O., C.O. 42/753; Hicks Beach, Secret, March 20, 1878, P.A.C., R.G. 9, II A 6, Vol. 1, p. 21; Hicks Beach to Governor General, May 11, 1878, inclosing Colonial Miscellany 35B, April, 1878, P.A.C., G. 21, No. 165, Vol. 3 (b), 1868–1869).

3. "Militia Report for 1879," pp. xliv–xlv; Memorandum by A. Campbell, minister of militia and defense, April 21, 1880, P.A.C., R.G. 7, G. 21, Vol. 76, No. 165, Vol. 4 (c); Strakhovsky, "Russia's Privateering Projects of 1878," p. 26.

4. Report of the Committee of the Privy Council, approved by Dufferin, May 4, 1878, P.A.C., R.G. 7, G. 21, Vol. 75, No. 165, Vol. 3 (b); Summary Report, June-July, 1878, P.A.C., Macdonald Papers, M.G. 21, A 1 (a), Vol. 100.

5. Mackenzie to Dufferin, May 11, 1878, P.A.C., Dufferin Papers, A 411.

security in the interior of the continent actually lay in the fact that the Americans lacked both military preparations and hostile intentions. The United States made no move.

However, at the time of the crisis the danger on the coasts seemed urgent. The Colonial Defence Committee feared lest the loan of naval guns for Esquimalt might expose them to loss; but it agreed to a temporary loan until permanent fortifications and guns were installed.[6] The Canadian Cabinet then decided to spend $150,000 on setting up coastal batteries, and Mackenzie asked Dufferin to inform the Colonial Office what was being done. He said he was determined that Canada should stand on her own feet. "We will not ask the Imperial Government for anything as we think Canada should have, and does have, pride enough to be above shirking her duty in providing for the defence of her own coasts. We are part of the Empire and will bear our share of its burdens as well as we share in its glories."[7] This was consistent with the attitude he had always taken in less threatening times.

But the Canadian prime minister had not yet realized how much coastal defense could cost. He was soon given warning. The Milne Committee, set up in England to recommend emergency and temporary protective measures for the colonies, suggested that Canada should spend £50,000 at once on the defense of Sydney and Saint John. This was about $250,000, that is to say $100,000 more than the Cabinet had considered necessary for the protection of all ports on both coasts. The Canadian ministers were appalled. They said it would be far cheaper to let the Russians destroy everything.[8] They called in their own expert adviser, General Smyth, who, being pressed to economize, suggested that the expense might be reduced by using old smoothbores "rifled" in Canada. Since coming to Canada, Smyth had investigated expedients of that kind in order to find a way for the colonies, with their small resources and lack of ordnance factories, to produce heavy weapons for themselves. He was to

6. Colonial Miscellany 35, April, 1878, inclosed in Hicks Beach to Governor General, May 11, 1878, P.A.C., G. 21, No. 165, Vol. 3 (b), 1868–1869.
7. Mackenzie to Dufferin, June 11, 1878, P.A.C., Dufferin Papers, A 411.
8. Dufferin to Hicks Beach, n.d. [1878?], *ibid.*, Microfilm 1140, p. 215.

claim later that his successful rifling of smooth-bores in Canada had attracted favorable attention in the British press and also in India and Australia. But the Milne Committee did not approve his proposals.[9]

It had no sympathy with the G.O.C.'s difficulties with a government that was determined to keep defense costs to a minimum. Re-bored smooth-bores, it said, would not be able to pierce the thinnest armor at the closest range.[10] Then came a second blow. The Admiralty, rather belatedly toward the end of July, 1878, gave its answer to Canada's request for fast cruisers on the Atlantic. Existing arrangements to protect Atlantic shipping were thought quite adequate for the present; but if war should come they would be stepped up. In view of the very large mercantile marine possessed by Canada, the Admiralty said it presumed the Dominion would take steps to protect its own ports and shipping.[11] Mackenzie's proud boast that Canada would do its bit in imperial defense was proving very expensive to live up to.

By this time the crisis had in fact passed. The Congress of Berlin in June–July, 1878, had worked out a settlement of the immediate issues with Russia. It was expressed in the Treaty of Berlin, 1878. There was now less urgency to undertake the defense measures that had been proposed for the colonies. The hotly debated question about the type of gun to be installed in Canadian ports was left unsettled for a time. The colonial secretary complimented Mackenzie through the governor general on "the creditable spirit shown by my [his] Ministers when the Empire was threatened"; Dufferin agreed, saying, "They [the ministers] really deserve some commendation for what they did." In fact, Canada had only spent $10,000 as a result of the emergency; but the governor general knew that money was tight and he appreciated what Smyth had been able to achieve despite his government's reluctance to spend money on defense. He was also aware that the British government could be equally difficult

9. "Militia Report of 1879," Canada, *Sessional Papers*, XIII, 1880, Vol. 5, No. 8, p. xlvi.
10. Report of the Canadian Privy Council, Jan. 23, 1879, P.A.C., Macdonald Papers, M.G. 26, A 1 (a), Vol. 100.
11. Summary Report, Canadian Privy Council, June–July, 1878, *ibid.*

about appropriating money for defense purposes. On the same day that he spoke sympathetically of Smyth's difficulties about money, he had to tell Mackenzie that Hicks Beach was finding it hard to get the British Cabinet's approval for a grant of $375,000 to match Canada's $750,000 for a new dock proposed for the naval base at Esquimalt.[12]

Three weeks later, at the end of September, the Canadian Cabinet, which had just rejected a proposal that the naval commander in the Pacific should take precedence over the lieutenant governor of British Columbia, agreed to purchase the large-caliber guns for the Eastern ports. But Mackenzie coupled with this decision an order that work should be discontinued on the earthworks built by the Canadian inspector of artillery, Lieutenant Colonel de la Chevios T. Irwin, R.A., to protect the guns at Esquimalt.[13] Faith in big guns to defend ports, but reluctance to provide adequate protection against the landing parties that might put guns out of action, was typical of colonial reaction to the raider problem. Nevertheless, it must be noted that Mackenzie's government had agreed to buy the larger guns after the tension had eased. This was therefore not an emergency measure performed out of panic. It was an extension of his program of military development. The military experts knew that once the guns were installed they would have additional arguments to use in favor of defense works.

The international crisis had raised other proposals of a very different kind which also bore on the question of the provision of some kind of regular force in Canada. As soon as it seemed possible that Russia and Britain might go to war, individual militia officers began to apply for commissions in the British Army. The number of applications was not great, and the War Office was not very encouraging, but when he forwarded the applica-

12. Dufferin to Mackenzie, Sept. 2, 1878, P.A.C., Dufferin Papers, A 409; Dufferin to Hicks Beach, Sept. 4, 1878, *ibid.*, A 407.
13. Mackenzie to Dufferin, Aug. 8, 1878, *ibid.*, A 411; Dufferin to Hicks Beach, Sept. 28, 1878, *ibid.*, A 407. Lt. Col. Irwin had erected at Esquimalt a battery of one eight-inch, nine-ton gun, two sixty-four pounder, sixty-four cwt. guns, and three seven-inch, six and one-half-ton guns (Memorandum, "Defence of Canada," April 21, 1880, P.A.C., R.G. 7, G. 21, No. 165, Vol. 4 [c]).

tions, Dufferin had proposed raising troops in Canada for imperial service.[14]

Dufferin had been influenced by evidence of patriotic enthusiasm in Canada and by approval from Britain. Early in 1877 a Canadian Militia officer, Colonel Thomas Scoble, had proposed the raising of four battalions in Canada for imperial service. In 1878 Colonel Fletcher, addressing the Royal United Service Institution, suggested a mixed British and colonial force if war came.[15] General Patrick MacDougall, now G.O.C. in Halifax, forwarded the idea to the War Office and Wolseley gave it public support.[16] MacDougall stressed "the moral and political effect . . . as inaugurating a *Bund* for the defence of the Empire to which England and her Dominions should contribute *pro rata* against these Pan-Slavistic and Teutonic ambitions by which the Country is supposed to be threatened." However, the secretary of state for the colonies, Hicks Beach, who raised the question unofficially with Dufferin, indicated that the plan's success would depend upon it appearing to be a spontaneous Canadian offer backed by both political parties; he also warned the governor general against premature recruiting.[17] Sir Robert Herbert, the permanent undersecretary of state for the colonies, probably because he remembered that MacDougall had fallen foul of Cartier, then reminded his minister that the general officer commanding in North America did not have the confidence of one of the Canadian political parties. The matter was referred, through Dufferin, to the Canadian ministers;[18] but it had not come to anything when the crisis eased in June, 1878. Its immediate effect, however, was to encourage the Colonial Office

14. Dufferin 47, March 4, 1878, and Dufferin 128, May 13, 1878, P.R.O., C.O. 42/753.
15. Littleton to Hubert, April 26, 1877, *ibid.*, C.O. 42/749; Col. Henry Charles Fletcher, "A Volunteer Force, British and Colonial, in the Event of War," *R.U.S.I. Journal*, XXI (1877), 642.
16. MacDougall to W.O., April 24, 1878, P.R.O., C.O. 42/755; Garnet I. Wolseley, "England as a Military Power in 1854 and 1878," *Nineteenth Century*, III (1878), 454.
17. W.O. to C.O., May 6, 1878, P.R.O., C.O. 42/775; Hicks Beach to Dufferin, May 10, 1878, P.A.C., Dufferin Papers, A 409.
18. W.O. to C.O., May 6, 1878, P.R.O., C.O. 42/755.

and the governor general to urge the building of a permanent force in Canada.

While the international crisis was at its height, troubles of a different kind had brought home the need for a more effective military force at the Canadian government's command. Quebec strikers rioted in June 1878, and the only troops available to deal with them were the handful of men at the artillery school in the Citadel. The militia, called out for such an emergency, might be unreliable. The situation was so grave that Colonel Strange, commandant at the school, had to order his men to fire. Mackenzie approved the shooting saying, "If he erred, it was in not sooner firing on the mob"; but even though he must have been aware that without them it might be necessary to take the risky step of calling out the militia, he went on to state that on no account should the aid of the imperial troops in Halifax be sought to deal with an internal problem of this kind.[19]

Dufferin at once seized the opportunity provided by this incident to push his case that Canada should have a more effective military force. He drew attention to the need for a force to maintain order in the chief centers of population,[20] and when shortly afterward he raised the matter a second time, he coupled it with Canada's "military obligations" to the Empire. In reply, the prime minister agreed that he would recommend whatever Canada could afford "to advance a sense of unity in the Empire." [21] To drive the point home, the governor general sent his prime minister a copy of Thomas Brassey's talk to the Royal Colonial Institute in London on June 7, 1878, in which the future First Lord had advocated the creation of naval reserves in the colonies.[22]

Three very different plans to give Canada a more effective defense force were studied by Mackenzie. The first was the reestablishment of militia schools; these could be staffed by Canadians with the help of British officers. The second was a

19. Mackenzie to Dufferin, June 11, 1878, P.A.C., Dufferin Papers, A 411.
20. Dufferin to Mackenzie, June 18, 1878, *ibid.*, A 409.
21. Mackenzie to Dufferin, Aug. 5, 1878, *ibid.*, A 411.
22. Dufferin to Mackenzie, Aug. 7, 1878, *ibid.*, A 409. "Brassey's pamphlet," as Dufferin called it, was *A Colonial Naval Volunteer Force . . .* (London: Longmans, Green, 1878).

system of calling out militia units for two or three months' service. The third was a plan advanced by General Selby Smyth, but actually suggested to him originally by Dufferin. Dufferin had proposed that the Canadian Militia should be integrated with the British Army by the establishment of a permanent Canadian regiment, of which one battalion would serve with a linked battalion in Britain. As an afterthought, Dufferin added that British and Canadian battalions might be exchanged. The third scheme was not spelled out in detail, but it was obviously a much more expensive undertaking than either of the other two. It is surprising, therefore, that Mackenzie allowed this third plan for a Canadian regular force to be sent to London for examination. But when he sent it, he insisted that submission to the British government did not mean the Canadian government could be assumed to be committed to it in any way; and he added that so basic a question as the integration of the Canadian Militia and the British Army could not be considered until after the forthcoming election. Significantly, he made only one definite statement on the whole subject. That was to reject flatly any sort of proposal for bringing a British regiment to Canada. He did so on the grounds that there were no barracks available. When the regulars had been withdrawn and military property and land reserves had been handed over to Canada, it had been stipulated that if ever the British came back, barracks would be provided at Canadian expense.[23] Mackenzie obviously had no intention of recommending that Canada should pay anything toward the return of a British garrison. However, he was prepared to explore means by which Canada could develop land forces and so, indirectly, increase the military strength of the Empire as a whole.

One other powerful argument was now found by Dufferin and the Colonial Office to support the case for a more effective military force in Canada. The Marquis of Lorne, son-in-law of the Queen, had been designated as Dufferin's successor. It was alleged that unless adequate state befitting the Princess Louise

23. Mackenzie to Dufferin, Aug. 5, 1878, P.A.C., Dufferin Papers, A 411; Dufferin to Mackenzie, Aug. 6, 1878, *ibid.*, A 409; Dufferin to Hicks Beach, Aug. 8, 14, 1878, *ibid.*, A 407.

were provided, Queen Victoria might not allow her to come to Canada. The British Cabinet was said to want assurances on this point. Dufferin supported the request, saying that he had himself been embarrassed by the ill-discipline of militia escorts and that, after an incident when one of the guard commanders had been drunk on duty, he had stopped asking for them. The princess must obviously be treated with more decorum. He therefore suggested embodying the governor general's Foot Guards, a smart new militia unit uniformed like the Coldstream. Another means of providing a proper ceremonial guard would be to bring "A" Battery from Kingston to Ottawa. Mackenzie protested that while he was anxious to insure proper ceremony for the Queen's daughter, the electorate might object to her coming to Canada if it meant extra expense. He therefore refused to move the battery from Kingston. He also said that the Foot Guards could not be embodied because they were all clerks and messengers employed in the government service.[24]

The crisis of 1878, coupled with other contemporary problems, had thus brought to a head the military problems created by the establishment of responsible government in Canada and by the subsequent withdrawal of the garrisons. It had quickened the pace for the development of Canadian defense capability as an indirect contribution to the defense of the Empire as a whole, and it had led to individual Canadian offers of service in the imperial forces and to proposals that an imperial force should be raised in Canada. Before the crisis Dufferin had told the Duke of Cambridge that the prime minister had "shown by the establishment of the military college that he is anxious to go as far as he dare in placing the military condition of Canada upon a satisfactory basis."[25] He and Hicks Beach had therefore been encouraged when the crisis came to use the Russian bogie, contemporary internal disorders, the need for a royal state for Princess Louise, and the signs of martial ardor shown by militia officers' applications for active service, to press Mackenzie to set

24. Dufferin to Mackenzie, Aug. 14, 1878, *ibid.*, A 409; Dufferin to Hicks Beach, Aug. 14, 1878, *ibid.*, A 407; Mackenzie to Dufferin, Sept. 4, 1878, *ibid.*, A 411; Dufferin to Mackenzie, Aug. 31, Sept. 9, 1878, *ibid.*, A 409.
25. Dufferin to Cambridge, Oct. 15, 1877, R.A.W., Cambridge Papers.

up a permanent Canadian military force closely linked with the British Army. Mackenzie had ignored suggestions that he should develop a naval reserve and had temporized on the question of forces linked with the British Army; but he had proceeded to strengthen Canada's own defenses, even though the panic had subsided, and he had temporarily adjusted his defense planning to face the possibility of an overseas threat instead of an American invasion. Whether he would have gone faster than his successor in any of these directions had he not been beaten at the polls, it is impossible to say. Some of his plans were to mature five years later under John A. Macdonald.

The reaction to proposals for closer imperial defense ties, however, did not differ radically from one Canadian political party to another. Sir Francis Hincks, formerly a Conservative minister of finance, put the matter quite clearly in a private expression of his own views which, he said, were shared by Dufferin. Hincks argued that Canada was no expense to England. The Halifax garrison, he said, was maintained for imperial, not Canadian, purposes. Canada had no desire to interfere in foreign politics and would take her chance on war, preparing only to defend herself. Canada would not contribute to imperial military, naval, or diplomatic expenditures. If on that account Britain chose to cast Canada off, she would be forced, against her own desires, into the American union. Englishmen could not wish for such an aggrandizement of the United States as well as the loss of the fisheries and "the finest harbour in the world" at Halifax. Cyprus and Asiatic Turkey would be small compensation for such a loss.[26] Certain members of the Conservative Opposition thus did not differ in any large measure from the main lines of Mackenzie's defense policy.

Macdonald, the Imperial Naval Bases, and an Imperial Reserve

Nevertheless, Macdonald's return to power in October, 1878, seemed a good omen for the imperial defense cause. There was a

26. Hincks to Dr. J. S. Drennan, July 31, 1878, P.R.O., Northern Ireland, DOD 729/39.

tendency to associate Canadian parties with those of the same name in Britain, and the Conservatives thus appeared to have a greater concern than the Liberals for Britain and the Empire. Macdonald himself was better known in England than Mackenzie and had made more important contacts on his visits. Socially he was on good terms with the governor general. He had been friendly with Colonel Fletcher, Dufferin's military secretary, who had successfully advanced the case for a Canadian military establishment, and he had danced the cotillion with Fletcher's wife, Lady Harriet, at Rideau Hall parties. During the recent crisis he had told the British chancellor of the exchequer that he thought it an opportunity to set up "a regular force—closely connected with the imperial army, and worked up to the same standard of training and discipline. Without this Canada will never add to the strength of the Empire and must remain a source of anxiety and weakness." [27]

Immediately after the election, Macdonald pleased Dufferin immensely when "of his own accord [he] intimated his conviction of the necessity for the establishment of a permanent force." He thought it necessary because of "communistic troubles" in the United States. It is true that at the same time he rejected the construction of coast defenses, a naval reserve force, and the acquisition of cruisers—because times were bad and because he said he wanted to concentrate on the constitution of a land force.[28] Still, Macdonald seemed ready to take up Mackenzie's military program, which had been interrupted by the crisis, and to concentrate on laying the foundations for Canadian military strength, but with greater emphasis on defenses designed to resist raiders from across the border rather than along the coasts. Dufferin sent him a copy of the Brassey article about the colonial naval reserve with which he had earlier tried to influence Mackenzie,[29] but it did not alter Macdonald's apparent intention to place more emphasis on defenses in the interior. However, as the

27. Macdonald to Sir Stafford Northcote, May 1, 1878, in Sir Joseph Pope, ed., *Correspondence of Sir John Macdonald* (Oxford: Milford, n.d.), pp. 239-242.
28. Dufferin to Hicks Beach, Oct. 12, 1878, P.A.C., Dufferin Papers, A 407.
29. Dufferin to Hicks Beach, Oct. 12, 1878, *ibid.*

British government had sent Lieutenant Colonel J. W. Lovell, R.E., commanding royal engineer at Halifax, to report on the defenses at Esquimalt, the Canadian Cabinet agreed to send Lieutenant Colonel T. B. Strange, R.A., from the artillery school at Kingston to help draw up defense plans. But work on the defenses at Esquimalt was not then renewed.[30]

Concern about defense, generated in both Britain and the colonies as a result of the scare of 1878, had thus opened a new chapter in Canadian defense policy. When the panic in Canada died away as international tension eased, the Colonial Office was not prepared to let the matter rest or to await developments from Macdonald's professed determination to concentrate on land forces. With the Carnarvon Commission in England investigating the whole question of the defense of overseas possessions, imperial defense was kept very much a live issue. The commission had no authority in Canada, but because of its example the older influences exercised by the War Office and the Admiralty worked more vigorously through the Colonial Office and the governor general. These various agencies were now aided by the presence in Canada of a senior officer as G.O.C.; he in his turn was stimulated by frequent advice from the commander in chief, the Duke of Cambridge, who had ignored lesser lights like the former adjutant general, Colonel Robertson-Ross. Despite the fact that the Duke had no official responsibility in relation to Canadian defense, he continued to the end of his career to show great interest in it—especially in the organization and discipline of the militia. It was from these various sources, rather than from the British Cabinet, that initiative came in the early 1880's for the improvement of Canada's defenses.

British authorities had now realized that the defense ties of the Empire could not, and should not, be severed as neatly and completely as Cardwell had apparently believed necessary. In the face of growing international complications, there were several areas in which colonies could relieve the burden of respon-

30. Report of the Canadian Privy Council, May 16, 1879, P.A.C., Macdonald Papers, M.G. 26, A 1 (a), Vol. 100; Hicks Beach to Lorne, July 3, 1879, P.A.C., R.G. 7, G. 21, No. 165, Vol. 3 (b), 1868–1869.

sibility which the mother country had rather lightly assumed for the defense of the Empire as a whole. It is true that Canada steadfastly refused to accept the role in which, as time went on, the Australasian colonies were cast—namely, as financial contributors to naval defense.

Neither Canada nor the Admiralty showed much interest in the building of the colonial naval reserve which many imperialists advocated; but Carnarvon had pointed out that colonies could be expected to help defend naval bases. In Britain, however, Halifax was thought too important to be left to Canadian care, and only the Admiralty was at this time concerned about the base at Esquimalt. Furthermore, it was difficult to persuade the Dominion government to assume sole responsibility for the base in British Columbia. The Carnarvon Commission itself had, in fact, expressed two conflicting views about Esquimalt. The majority believed it too remote to be supplied or supported in time of war because two coaling stations would be needed to bridge the 7,400-mile gap between it and the Falkland Islands, the nearest British possession on the way from Britain. No islands or bases could be acquired on that route. The majority of the commission showed that not only did Esquimalt's proximity to the United States make it indefensible against an American attack, but also that another enemy could take advantage of American neutrality to launch an attack on a scale that could only be resisted by very strong defenses. As the base could not be supplied after war broke out, and as it would obviously be impossible to maintain it on a war footing during peace, the majority on the commission thought the fleet's base ought to be transferred to another station in the Pacific. It was realized that future civil development in British Columbia might make fortifications expedient; but for the present, powerful fortifications should not be built at Esquimalt, nor should it be garrisoned.

However, Britain had used influence freely to bring about confederation in 1867 and to secure the admission of British Columbia in 1871. A British order-in-council required Canada "to secure the continual maintenance of the naval station at Esquimalt," and the Admiralty had encouraged the Dominion to build a large graving dock there. There were forceful political reasons for the construction of defenses sufficiently strong to defend Esquimalt against any enemy except the United States. The commissioners therefore stated that if the Canadian government could be persuaded to provide the defenses and the garrison, Britain should provide the armament and give professional advice.[31]

Admiral Sir Alexander Milne and Sir Henry Barkly dissented. They believed that Esquimalt would not be in serious danger if attacked by a small squadron from any country other than the United States. If the squadron were withdrawn, such an attack would become likely. They argued that as Canada was required by the order-in-council to secure the maintenance of the base, all that remained to be decided was whether the defense would be undertaken by the home government "as at present" or by the Dominion. They admitted that the Pacific Squadron in the event of war might withdraw to the China seas, and that this, because of prevailing winds, would entail an 8,000-mile journey, one so long that it would have to be made almost entirely under sail. Nevertheless, they argued that a proposal to remove the Pacific Squadron from the base was *ultra vires* for the commission and was an infringement of the functions of the executive departments of state. The squadron should therefore remain and the base should not be abandoned.[32]

However, Sir John A. Macdonald, when he appeared before the commission, had been careful to deny that the Canadian grain trade needed protection by the fortification of Esquimalt. He had suggested that defenses were needed only for the protection of the imperial naval base. It seemed unlikely, therefore, that Canada would build the proposed works for the western base. Hence, the one area in which effective development seemed possible under Macdonald was in building up land forces—not for coastal defense, for which purpose the militia could hardly be concentrated quickly enough to repel local raids, but for their ancient role of defense of the land border against the United

---

31. Carnarvon Commission Report, III, 23–25.
32. *Ibid.*, III, 32–33.

States. Since Canadians were firmly convinced that the need for defense against the Americans would only arise from British imperial policies, the building of land forces appeared to them to be as much a contribution to imperial defense as to the defense of Canada itself. It may be argued that Canada's contribution to the defense of the Empire should be measured by this standard rather than by the neglected naval contribution. A second problem was the means by which trained Canadian manpower could be put to the service of the Empire as a whole. The Carnarvon Commission had mentioned such a contribution to imperial defense, but it was as yet a remote contingency, one that occupied the minds of some of the more imperially minded Canadians and was—as Macdonald repeatedly asserted—likely to become important only when Canadians became convinced that the Empire had need of Canadian aid. Oddly enough, however, the first attempt after the 1878 scare to obtain a Canadian contribution to imperial defense came in this outer area of possible development.

Pressure for a Canadian contribution to the British Army had mounted steadily. For instance, the new governor general, the Marquis of Lorne, submitted to the Canadian Cabinet a proposal to embody a reserve in Canada of fifty-six companies of seventy-five rank and rifle each, organized in seven battalions which "when called out for training" would be paid by the imperial government. Lorne asked General Sir Patrick MacDougall, who was going to a War Office conference on army organization, to bring up there the question of a Canadian imperial reserve.[33] The proposal continued to receive support in certain quarters in Canada. One of the products of the patriotic fervor of 1878 had been the Militia Institute formed in Toronto, with a library and social club for militia officers.[34] On Saturday, October 25, 1879, Scoble gave a paper there on "The Utilization of Colonial Forces in Im-

33. Memorandum by F. de Winton, secretary to the governor general, to the Privy Council, Oct. 21, 1879, and Lorne to Macdonald, Nov. 16, 1879, P.A.C., M.G. 26, A 1 (a), Vol. 80, pp. 274, 282, 294.
34. Lt. Col. J. Hyde Bennett, "In Retrospect," the Canadian Officers Club and Institute, *Selected Papers,* No. 41 (Toronto: Military Publishing Company, 1946), p. 17. This militia institute must be distinguished from its better-known successor, the Canadian Military Institute founded in 1890, now the Royal Canadian Military Institute.

perial Defence" and proposed a regional grouping of forces throughout the Empire to supply garrisons to British fortresses.[35] One feature of Scoble's scheme was interesting and significant. He proposed that the imperial reserve in Canada should be maintained at imperial expense. His explanation for taking such liberties with the revenues of Great Britain is curious evidence of the unreality of much imperialist thinking in the colonies. He said, "The *British Taxpayer* is the 'bugaboo' that has always stood between the motherland and the colonies; but it is the growing belief that this unreasoning person has ceased to exist. . . ."[36] Despite this facile proposal for shifting the expense, Scoble's plan was not universally popular in Canada. Many officers were afraid that a permanent force would supplant the militia in public esteem. Nevertheless, in his report for 1879, General Selby Smyth had included a plan very similar to Scoble's and had added the idea of sending the battalions of the reserve for three years' training in England.[37]

As the scheme for an imperial reserve in the colonies had wide connotations, the War Office was not able to give it immediate support. The colonial secretary therefore sent it to the Carnarvon Commission with a copy of Scoble's pamphlet.[38] Lorne also sent for the commission's use a memorandum containing Selby Smyth's and MacDougall's favorable opinions; but he added his personal opinion that a regular force was not at present a practical proposition and that only a part-time reserve force should be considered.[39]

Sir John A. Macdonald was in London in 1880. Being friendly with Lord Carnarvon, with whom he had worked to get the British North America Act through Parliament, he agreed to appear as a witness before the Commission on Imperial Defence to state his views. As the lines on which he was to be questioned

35. Thomas C. Scoble, C.E., was later editor of the Winnipeg *Nor'Wester*. There is a copy of his paper in the library of the Royal Canadian Military Institute, Toronto.
36. Lt. Col. Thomas C. Scoble, *The Utilization of Colonial Forces in Imperial Defence* (Toronto: Canadian Military Institute, 1879), p. 8.
37. "Militia Report for 1879," pp. xxxi–xxxiv.
38. Hicks Beach to Lorne, April 12, 1880, P.A.C., R.G. 7, G. 21, Vol. 76, No. 165, Vol. 4 (c).
39. Lorne to Kimberley, May 17, 1880, *ibid.*

were apparently agreed upon in advance, his answers must have been carefully thought out; and as the commission was meeting in secret, he was not speaking for public consumption, though it is possible he thought the testimony would eventually be published. He said he believed that war between England and the United States was becoming less likely every year, and if it did come it could only be through "causes entirely unconnected with Canada." Professional soldiers had convinced him that the Americans could invade Canada at any point they chose. But he defended his pet project, the Canadian Pacific Railway, which he had represented as a contribution to imperial defense, by saying that even if it were cut by an American invading force, it would continue to serve for the export of grain from the prairies to the west. Significantly, he told the commission that he preferred not to contemplate the possibility of an American war at all. As for general imperial defense, he thought that no "system" could be laid down to divide responsibility between England and the colonies. A war with a European power—for instance, Russia—would not be likely to involve anything in which Canada was interested, but it would expose the Canadian coasts, though only to temporary raids. He was convinced that "it would be extremely unwise in time of peace, when there is no immediate danger of war, to attempt negotiations for a contingent of military or naval force to be furnished by the Dominion in aid of such a war," because the Canadian people and the Opposition in Parliament would oppose it. He had no doubt, however, that in the event of war the affection of the people of Canada for the mother country would, "on the spur of the moment . . . and [with] patriotic enthusiasm," raise 10,000 men. The Canadian government had no objection to the recruiting in Canada of an imperial reserve, although it warned against the ancient nuisance of widespread desertion to the United States. Macdonald did not say it, but he obviously assumed—as was proposed in all the Canadian plans for an imperial reserve—that the imperial government would pay the cost.[40]

40. Alice R. Stewart, "Sir John A. Macdonald, and the Imperial Defence Commission of 1879," *Canadian Historical Review*, XXXV (June, 1954), 134.

It was, of course, the question of cost that caused this scheme for an imperial reserve in Canada to be rejected by the War Office. All the Canadian proposals amounted to was a return to the old garrison system, with Britain paying the cost, but with troops raised in Canada and permanently located there. In November all the suggested schemes for an imperial reserve were finally rejected in Britain on the grounds that although they presaged developments of great importance for the future organization of the military forces of the Empire, they were at present impractical. It was held that before they were examined there should be a discussion of the wider implications of such schemes. Kimberley, however, showed in a minute the real reason for rejection: "The radical unsoundness of the whole scheme is that the Canadians don't propose to pay anything towards the expense." [41]

MacDougall, who had produced the original, detailed plan, was not quite yet defeated. He appealed to the Duke of Cambridge, saying that a telegram from the adjutant general at the Horse Guards foreshadowed the withdrawal of one of his regiments, which would have the unfortunate political effect of further weakening the British connection. He noted that when British troops garrisoned Montreal, only English fashions prevailed; but now that they were gone, he had been "painfully struck in noticing how 'Yankee' it had become." He thought the home government had been unwise to turn down his proposal for an imperial reserve.[42] Kimberley replied that if the state of things was as MacDougall had described, a regiment or two in Canada would make no difference. And he had always thought, he said, that Halifax was garrisoned for imperial purposes on account of its importance as a naval station.[43] A Liberal colonial secretary had given the knockout blow to this early attempt to produce an imperial military reserve in Canada. But it is unlikely that the British Conservatives would have been any more willing at this time to finance land forces in the colonies.

---

41. W.O. to C.O., Dec. 10, 1880, P.R.O., C.O. 42/765.
42. MacDougall to Cambridge, Dec. 21, 1880, R.A.W., Cambridge Papers.
43. Kimberley to Cambridge, Jan. 7, 1881, *ibid*.

The Duke of Cambridge and the Canadian Militia

The Queen's cousin, Field Marshal H.R.H. George, Duke of Cambridge, commander in chief of the British Army, had an anomalous role in imperial defense. His office had been subordinated in 1870 to the secretary of state for war, who directed policy and controlled the military budget. But as head of the army the Duke was still responsible for its military efficiency. Cambridge's hold on military promotions gave him a strong claim to the allegiance of regular officers. No promotion above the rank of captain was made without reference to him. As he had a very retentive memory, he knew the officers of the army far better than anyone else. He did not control all appointments, but his knowledge of the qualities and availability of candidates also gave him great influence in this sphere. His eminence and integrity undoubtedly kept the British Army free from political jobbery which another royal commander in chief, the Duke of York, had eliminated earlier in the century.[44] Cambridge's dislike for the reforms desired by soldiers like Wolseley, who had had a greater experience of war, and his insistence upon promotion by seniority, because it was least likely to "upset" the army, have given him the reputation of being what today would be called a "Colonel Blimp." However, even if he did not know modern war, the Duke knew his army, and he had a sincere belief that it must be protected as the chief pillar of the monarchy and the Empire.[45]

The Duke was an indefatigable correspondent and kept in touch with British regular officers everywhere, giving advice and inquiring about their problems. He also corresponded with colonial governors about military problems. His usual practice was to ask men going out to colonial appointments "to keep in touch,"

44. Richard Glover, *Peninsular Preparation: The Reform of the British Army, 1795–1809* (Cambridge: Cambridge University Press, 1963), pp. 148–152.
45. Giles St. Aubyn, *The Royal George, 1819–1904: The Life of H.R.H. Prince George, Duke of Cambridge* (London: Constable, 1963), pp. 185–189 and *passim*, Lord Redesdale, *Memories* (London: Hutchinson, 1915), II, 700. In 1856, Cambridge was gazetted the "General Commanding in Chief" but was usually called the "Commander-in-Chief," an appointment he did not receive officially until 1887 (St. Aubyn, *The Royal George*, p. 108).

and many of them, for one reason or another, did so. His correspondents, civil and military, often sought his aid, and he frequently urged them to undertake specific policies. However, his influence upon policy must not be exaggerated. Usually all that he could do was to bring problems to the attention of the appropriate secretary of state. Back at the time of the withdrawal of the garrisons, the Duke's correspondence with Canada had dropped off sharply, but he had continued to be worried about its military weakness and to concern himself with the Canadian Militia. He was free with advice, though sometimes he apparently urged his correspondents to be careful lest it became known that he had interfered.[46] The Duke regarded the command of the Canadian Militia as the key to Canada's part in imperial defense.

The militia was indeed the only Canadian contribution to the defense of Canada as well as of the Empire. General Sir Patrick MacDougall's appointment in 1878 as general officer commanding British North America with headquarters at Halifax had created one technical difficulty in regard to the relation of the militia to the over-all defense problem. It was always assumed that if war came, the Canadian Militia would be put under the command of the Halifax commander. If it had not been for this possibility, the small Halifax garrison would not have merited an officer of MacDougall's rank. But MacDougall as a lieutenant general was junior to Selby Smyth. Smyth informed Dufferin that he presumed he would not be expected to serve under an officer who was his junior. The governor general passed the memorandum on to the Duke of Cambridge for information and comment.[47] Smyth, however, was also dissatisfied for other quite different reasons. Because of his lack of success in impressing his views about militia problems on the Canadian government, he had sought employment elsewhere, preferably in South Africa. Macdonald wanted him to stay on in Canada, and Smyth eventually agreed to do so, but only in order to further Cambridge's efforts to insure the appointment of another regular officer as his

46. That the Duke briefed Lorne orally before he left England to become governor general is clearly revealed in Lorne to Cambridge, Feb. 8, 1880, R.A.W., Cambridge Papers.
47. Dufferin to Cambridge, April 17, 1878, *ibid.*

successor and so to promote the development of the militia's efficiency.[48] In the nineteenth century, before the abolition of purchase, British officers could not be detailed for duties against their inclination; and after purchase was abolished, this situation tended to persist when the appointments were in the service of another government. The governor general was anxious to get an officer "more known to the world." But this was difficult: men who were highly distinguished in the service looked for posts which were "more distinctly military." [49]

To strengthen the British influence over the Canadian Militia, Cambridge had already suggested that Selby Smyth should report "from time to time" to MacDougall in Halifax.[50] It was probably the Duke who now recommended that the two commands held by these men should be combined under MacDougall as G.O.C. in Canada, with a subordinate officer stationed at Halifax. "There would be no interference on our part with their control of their local forces and no increased cost to the Dominion government." [51] Dufferin was consulted and pointed out that the G.O.C. of the regular troops in North America stationed in Halifax took over the administration of Canada when the governor general was absent. If he were put in command of the militia, which was subordinate to the minister of militia, he might find himself both over and under the minister.[52] This purely technical difficulty might have been easily overcome by making some different arrangement for the administratorship, but there was a greater political obstacle in that the amalgamation would be unpopular in Canada. In fact, the Canadian ministry turned it down because the militia men feared they might become secondary to the British and Canadian regular soldiers under the G.O.C.'s command.[53] The voluntary militia was jealous of its primacy in the Canadian military organization and succeeded in killing attempts to incorporate it more fully into a British-commanded force. Lorne hinted, however, that the plan to integrate

48. Selby Smyth to Cambridge, Jan. 27, March 4, July 10, 1879, *ibid.*
49. Stanley to Cambridge, Feb. 23, 1880, *ibid.*
50. Cambridge to Beach, Dec. 30, 1878, *ibid.*
51. W.O. to C.O., Jan. 7, 1880, P.R.O., C.O. 42/765.
52. Lorne, Confidential, March 29, 1880, *ibid.*, C.O. 42/760.
53. Lorne to Cambridge, Feb. 8, 1880, R.A.W., Cambridge Papers.

the Halifax garrison and the Canadian Militia should be revived when the new incumbent as G.O.C. of the militia had completed his tour of duty.[54]

Meanwhile, the selection of a suitable successor to Selby Smyth was of paramount importance. Following the rejection of the Duke's plan to put the Canadian Militia under MacDougall, the Canadian Cabinet did what Selby Smyth had long feared. It proposed the appointment of a militia officer as G.O.C., James William Domville, who was on the Royal Artillery retired list as a major general, although the extent of his professional service was his education at the Royal Military Academy at Woolwich. Domville, a Conservative M.P. for King's County, New Brunswick, was a colorful and influential officer in the militia.[55] The War Office hastily replied that a regular officer, Major General R. G. A. Luard, was better qualified and was recommended by the Duke of Cambridge. The Cabinet, having consulted the former prime minister, Alexander Mackenzie, about the way in which Smyth was appointed, and having learned that the Duke had recommended Smyth after receiving a request from the Canadian Cabinet, accepted Luard's nomination.[56] Luard had actually been considered for the appointment back in 1874, along with Middleton who was to succeed him five years later. Before Smyth had emerged as a candidate at that earlier time, Luard had been rated by the Duke of Cambridge below Colonel Fletcher (who presumably refused) and also below Middleton. The Duke of Cambridge thought the experience which Luard had had as a deputy inspector of volunteers would serve him well in Canada; he was sure that Luard was active and intelligent, but he was doubtful of his temper. Macdonald was to find out later that someone had wanted to get Luard out of England.[57] The new G.O.C. was to prove an unfortunate choice, who hindered rather than helped the task of increasing the militia's value for the defense of Canada and the Empire.

54. Lorne, Confidential, March 29, 1880, P.R.O., C.O. 42/760.
55. Lorne, Telegram, March 16, 1880, *ibid.*
56. Lorne, Telegram, March 25, 1880, *ibid.*; Lorne, Telegram, April 3, 1880, and Lorne 101, April 10, 1880, *ibid.*, C.O. 42/761.
57. Macdonald to Knutsford, Aug. 18, 1890, in Pope, ed., *Correspondence of Sir John Macdonald*, p. 474.

Lorne and an Imperial Depot

The governor general held a very important but delicate position in the imperial system. In theory he was a constitutional head of state and must accept the policy of his ministers. But as he was also the only channel of communication with the Colonial Office, he was in a position to exert considerable influence. Being in some ways a servant of the Colonial Office, he had to serve two masters, but he had to do it without giving his ministers room to complain that he had other loyalties.

The Marquis of Lorne was quite as active as Dufferin in his efforts to persuade his government to do something about defense. But whereas Dufferin had stressed the development of Canadian forces, Lorne emphasized the need for closer military ties with Britain. To some extent their contrasting positions reflected opinions supposedly held by Mackenzie and Macdonald, the respective prime ministers with whom each governor general had to work.

Dufferin had been ambitious to play a part in the real government of Canada, and only his political sense and experience had saved him from going to extremes which would have caused an irrevocable breach with his Liberal ministers. Lorne, appointed governor general when only thirty-three years old, and with much less experience of politics or administration, derived great advantage from Canadian pleasure at the appointment of the Queen's son-in-law to Ottawa. Macdonald's frequent professions of imperial sentiment also supposedly made his task easier. But Lorne was less sensitive than Dufferin to the political atmosphere in Canada. Disappointed by British rejection of the plan for an imperial reserve, he was equally frustrated by the Canadian government's apathy.

Lorne was greatly influenced by General MacDougall, who commanded the regulars at Halifax, especially when he began to find that Luard, the commander of the militia, was an irritant rather than a stimulant. It may be for this reason that although he had previously favored a part-time reserve, toward the end of

1881 Lorne changed face and revived the plan for a regular force. In a letter to Sir Adolphe Caron, minister of militia and defense, Lorne stated that the value which Canada placed upon her present political connection with Britain must be determined by her capacity for self-defense. From time to time, he said, isolated projects had been sent by individuals to Britain, but there had been nothing comprehensive. He therefore suggested establishment of a committee to discuss imperial defense co-operation on the principle that Britain might be willing to provide the money if Canada offered the men. The development of torpedo training for coastal defense could be examined, and the committee might suggest what part of the cost the imperial government should defray. With regard to the stationing of a regular regiment on Canadian soil, the committee could explore what the imperial government might be willing to contribute if a depot were made available by Canada and the officers of the regiment were Canadians. Lorne apparently hoped that Canadian initiative might help to loosen the purse strings. "What is wanted in England is knowledge of what Canada would propose." [58] But at this time it was probably merely wishful thinking on his part to believe that a greater relevation of Canadian interest in defense would change British determination not to pay more for Canadian defense forces.

A month later, however, he had something more definite to suggest. Britain had become involved in the trouble in Egypt, and MacDougall had told Lorne that he again feared that one of the British regiments in Halifax would be withdrawn because of needs elsewhere. The general had proposed that it should be replaced by a regiment of the Canadian Militia. If the Canadian government approved, he would propose to the War Office that a militia regiment embodied for the purpose should be paid by Britain. In a later memorandum MacDougall added that it was cheaper for Britain to maintain troops in Halifax than in Britain or in any other colony. As Halifax was only eleven days' sailing from Britain, the garrison there could be withdrawn for imme-

58. Lorne to Caron, Dec. 20, 1881, P.A.C., Macdonald Papers, M.G. 26, A 1 (a), Vol. 100.

diate service in any emergency, provided that arrangements existed for promptly replacing it by the embodiment of Canadian militia. He believed that people of Canada valued the presence of the imperial garrison as a symbol of their connection with the Empire, and he said that he had found the Duke of Cambridge was willing to keep the garrison up to strength. He claimed he had now also learned that Childers, the secretary of state for war, was willing to establish and pay for a depot in Canada for the "Royal Canadian Regiment," i.e., the Prince of Wales's Leinster Regiment (Royal Canadians), provided the Canadian government would provide the barracks. One battalion would be maintained permanently in Canada to recruit for the others stationed elsewhere for imperial purposes. There would be no difficulty as long as Canadian recruits would accept imperial rates of pay.[59] The Leinsters had originally been raised in Canada as the 100th Regiment in 1858, but they had been entirely removed from the country within a few years and the regiment had quickly lost all connection with the land of its birth. A Royal Canadians' depot in Canada could serve the purpose of reinforcing Halifax and would have the additional advantage of providing permanent forces inside Canada.

The War Office wanted to know whether a sufficient number of recruits could be found for the Royal Canadians in Canada.[60] In pressing for the retention of imperial troops in Halifax—since otherwise it would cease to exist as a military base—Lorne had already told the Duke of Cambridge that recruiting would be difficult. It was hard enough to get recruits for the Canadian batteries at thirty-five cents a day with comfortable barracks. It would be easier to raise French-Canadians, but they also would want a greater financial inducement.[61] Kimberley at the Colonial Office was concerned about who would bear the cost of garrisoning Halifax by embodying of the militia.[62] In his opin-

59. Lorne to Macdonald, Jan. 31, 1882, P.A.C., M.G. 26, A 1 (a), Vol. 82; memorandum by MacDougall, Feb. 27, 1882, *ibid.*, Vol. 100; MacDougall to Lorne, Feb. 28, 1882, *ibid.*, W.O. to C.O., May 15, July 10, 1882, P.R.O., C.O. 42/773.
60. W.O. to C.O., June 15, 1882, P.R.O., C.O. 42/773.
61. Lorne to Cambridge, March 23, 1882, R.A.W., Cambridge Papers.
62. W.O. to C.O., June 15, 1882, P.R.O., C.O. 42/773.

ion the Canadians should only be called out in the event of a European war "directly affecting the safety of Canada." The War Office, however, now agreed that the cost should be borne by the mother country.[63]

The proposal of an imperial depot was referred by Caron to Colonel Walker Powell, a Canadian with long experience on the militia staff and many connections, who had held the post of adjutant general since 1874 and could be expected therefore to give an opinion which would combine professional knowledge with a Canadian point of view. In a long reply Powell put the Canadian case clearly and forcefully. Speaking first of the cordial relations between Britain and Canada, he went on to say that any form of parliamentary representation between them seemed impossible as they had such divergent interests. If so, there could be no closer union than that which now existed. Canada could have no voice in the direction of affairs in Great Britain and had even less interest in the affairs of distant colonies. Neither could Canada have a share in the direction of British foreign policy; therefore, it must "Have a career [policy?] marked out for it and depend upon assistance being forthcoming during time of peril." The Dominion, however, was liable to be attacked during any war between Britain and a foreign power, "and the lives and property of Canadians might be placed in jeopardy, not as a consequence of their own acts, but because a blow struck on this continent would add to the desolating influence of that war. In such case, even should assistance be given by Great Britain, it would not prevent the sacrifices which invasion by a hostile army would demand." It was obvious that more provision must be made for the defense of Canada, but that increase must depend upon the ability of the population to contribute in excess of expenditure on development of the economy. It was difficult for a young country to develop its resources. At the same time, there was no point in saying that the potential enemy (i.e., the United States) was "strong." "The fact remains," Powell said, "that Canadians have been planted here for a purpose, and that they must continue to have faith in their ability

63. W.O. to C.O., July 10, 29, 1882, with Minutes, *ibid.*

to assist in the defence of their homes and country." Halifax
should remain a British base, but the idea of setting up a Canadian depot for the Royal Canadians had less obvious advantage
for Canada:

The sentiment maintained as the basis and reason for the proposal
points more to Imperial than Canadian interests. . . . The depot of
the Royal Canadian Regiment, if stationed here, must continue to
be under [British] army control and pay, and could therefore not
fulfil all the conditions of a corps [regiment] for local use. . . . The
proposal must be looked upon as a measure for Imperial purposes
only.

Powell went on to say that a scheme for dovetailing Canadian
and imperial service might not work. Young Canadians might not
wish to serve abroad on any rate of pay, let alone that of the
imperial army, when opportunities for work at home were plentiful. The Royal Military College at Kingston, now in successful
operation, provided a suitable basis on which to build a superior
military education at a minimum expense to the country. It was
a training establishment for the permanent forces and a model
for other schools for non-commissioned officers. Powell therefore
agreed that the imperial government should make use of Canada
as a cheap and healthy station for troops, but he was against the
proposal for recruiting in Canada in time of peace.[64] In a printed
revision of the memorandum, sent to Macdonald in May, 1882,
Powell added that it was better to retain the militia force than
to trust to two or three imperial regiments stationed at one end
of the country. "Such a policy would draw too much attention
to the United States, and to our want of organization." [65]

Supported by this powerful brief from the senior Canadian
permanent soldier, Macdonald was ready by August, 1882, with
his answer to the proposal to take Halifax over temporarily from
the regulars. He said that the Egyptian trouble was too remote
to justify calling out the militia under the act. There was at
present no war, and it was impossible to say that there was any

64. Walker Powell to Caron, March 22, 1882, P.A.C., Macdonald Papers,
M.G. 26, A 1 (a), Vol. 100.
65. Powell to Macdonald, sent May 11, 1882, *ibid.*

present or immediate danger of it. Certainly there was no threat to Canada. If England were engaged in any serious war, Canadians could be trusted to do their share. If the Halifax garrison were removed at Canada's request, there was no guarantee that it would be returned. But if war actually broke out, a request from England for the provision of troops for the defense of Canada would surely "bring down the house" and secure a warm response.[66]

Lorne was disappointed. At a time when the reserves had been called out in England, Canada would not do what seemed to him "an obvious duty," and he regretted that when such "serious work" was at hand the Canadian government should want to be prompted by the imperial authorities. A Canadian initiative would have had the best effect. Nevertheless, he told Macdonald that he would do his best to get an imperial proposal in the form which, he said, the prime minister had suggested. Macdonald hastened to set him right.[67] He told the governor general that the imperial government should take no initiative to ask Canada to do anything prematurely. To call out troops, Parliament would have to be summoned. Ever since the Fenian raids in 1866 he personally had believed in the need for a permanent force, but he was not sure that all his colleagues in the Cabinet agreed with him.

Some time earlier, however, Macdonald had stated his belief that Britain would be allowed to settle with Arabi Pasha without getting involved in a European war. Lorne now found he was right. It was clear that Britain would not now want reinforcements for Halifax.[68] The whole plan for re-introducing a British regiment, or for taking over the Halifax base, therefore collapsed.

Caron and Luard

At the height of the Russian scare, Dufferin had said, "Nothing could be more satisfactory than the spirit evinced both by the

66. Macdonald to Lorne, Aug. 4, 1882, *ibid.*, Vol. 82.
67. Lorne to Macdonald, Aug. 5, 1882, P.A.C., *ibid.*
68. Macdonald to Lorne, Aug. 8, 1882, Lorne to Macdonald, Aug. 10, 1882, *ibid.*

military engaged in manoeuvres [in Montreal on the Queen's birthday] and [by] the enormous crowds of spectators assembled to witness them." [69] But this emotional fervor was temporary. By 1880 Lorne thought a "good Fenian scare" was needed to promote a military program; [70] three years later Luard said the government would not budge unless a "scare" frightened them.[71] Once again, as the Duke of Cambridge had complained back in 1874, there was "want of interest . . . in these peaceful times." [72] If blame is to be assigned for failure to appropriate enough money for defense, Macdonald's government cannot be held solely responsible. The electors and the men they sent to Parliament felt that Canada could not afford unnecessary luxuries.

Where Macdonald was at fault was that when funds were short he did not take adequate care to insure their best use in providing good foundations for Canada's future security. For that objective, his selection of Adolphe Caron as minister of militia and defense on November 8, 1880, was unfortunate. Caron was a lawyer and politician with little special knowledge of, or interest in, the department he was called upon to administer. Under the parliamentary cabinet system this is not unusual and is not necessarily a disadvantage. One of Macdonald's reasons for having Caron in his Cabinet must have been that he would help to rally French-Canadian support. Macdonald needed him much as he had needed Cartier earlier. But Caron did not have Cartier's stature. It was rumored Caron carried out "shady political jobs" that the prime minister wanted to keep clear of; [73] and certainly Caron was widely known to be a political wire-puller. A future G.O.C. said he had used, solely to assist party interests, the funds that Parliament had voted for the militia.[74] Through imprudence and obstinacy he regularly got into scrapes from which his own persuasive eloquence—and his leader—as regularly rescued him.[75]

69. Dufferin to Cambridge, May 29, 1878, R.A.W., Cambridge Papers.
70. Lorne to Cambridge, Dec. 8, 1880, *ibid.*
71. Luard to Cambridge, April 21, 1883, *ibid.*
72. Cambridge to Dufferin, Jan. 22, 1874, *ibid.*
73. Middleton to Cambridge, March 1, 1889, *ibid.*
74. Herbert to Cambridge, April 11, 1892, *ibid.*
75. Donald G. Creighton, *John A. Macdonald*, II: *The Old Chieftain* (2 vols.; Toronto: Macmillan, 1952, 1955), p. 523.

His long tenure of the office of minister of militia and defense therefore cast a blight on the growth of Canada's military strength. Cartier had taken the office to insure that Canadian autonomy was established in this important sphere and to secure Canadian control of an important political asset. Caron was more narrowly concerned with keeping the Conservative party in power. Macdonald's appointment of Caron to militia suggests that the prime minister had little concern for the welfare of that department and regarded it chiefly as a valuable source of political patronage.

Major General Richard Amherst Luard, who had come to Canada as G.O.C. a few months before Caron took the portfolio, was an almost equally unfortunate choice. As he had applied for the post earlier, in 1874, while he was assistant military secretary in Nova Scotia, he probably had private reasons for wanting to take up an appointment in Canada which had obvious disadvantages. The Duke of Cambridge was well aware of Luard's bad temper, but he had nominated him at short notice in 1880 in order to keep the post open for a British regular. Although there were very good reasons for having a regular officer as G.O.C. and for forestalling the appointment of a less experienced militia officer who might be a party hack, Luard was personally quite unsuitable. After one brief look at the militia he hastened to inform his royal patron that he was unfavorably impressed.[76] This was not merely a new-broom reaction. He continued to be extremely critical of the rural companies, though he came to admit that there was something to be said for the urban militia. But his words are not entirely clear, and he seems to have been reluctant to admit that officers of the urban regiment had any merit:

The men are excellent material, good—willing—sober—intelligent, but the officers are ignorant and so careless of orders and any system of command that if called out in their present state for service disaster would, in my opinion, be the sure result. When I say this I mean the *Rural* portions of the force—which are the Majority—the City Corps are good.

76. Luard to Cambridge, Sept. 12, 1880, R.A.W., Cambridge Papers.

In the same letter he found the cavalry "rough," the artillery "very creditable," the infantry "fine in physique," but he added without restricting the comment to rural companies, "the weak point is the officers and N.C.O.'s." Within twelve months of his arrival in Canada, his public criticisms of the militia in camp "had led to the papers opening up [on him] . . . in full chorus," and he thought he might have to give up his appointment. Apparently he was already writing to his patron with a view to a new job, for he said, "I hope Y.R.H. will give me credit for trying to improve the Force I was sent out by Y.R.H. to command." [77]

No one questioned Luard's sincerity and professional knowledge, nor his desire to strengthen the militia, but despite his previous experience with English volunteers, he failed entirely to understand the difference between the Canadian volunteer militiamen and regular soldiers. He had no sympathy whatever for the fact that the militia made sacrifices to train for the service of their country. He was scornful of their lack of competence in drill and also of their uniform and equipment. He was quite insensible of the need to handle them tactfully. He never understood that he must do so because, unlike regular soldiers, they could resign. He browbeat officers in front of the men, a poor practice in any army but particularly so in a militia where leadership depended more upon prestige than upon discipline. Worse still, he was ill-tempered and often found fault on inspections merely out of bad humor. He may have modeled himself on his patron, the Duke of Cambridge, who was a notorious martinet. But the circumstances were somewhat different. Luard did not have the prestige of a member of the royal family. The result was that he was attacked by the Liberals in the Canadian House of Commons in 1882. They found that Luard's conduct gave them a chance to get at Caron. [78]

Luard's relations with the minister were, however, already bad

77. Luard to Cambridge, July 8, 1881, *ibid.*
78. Canada, House of Commons, *Debates, 1882*, pp. 1293–1302; Denison, *Soldiering in Canada*, pp. 246–248; Morton, "The General Officer Commanding in Canada," pp. 30–33. It is not true that the explanation of Luard's ill-temper is that he was old (see Creighton, *The Old Chieftain*, pp. 339, 349). At fifty-two on appointment, he was younger than his successor and both of his predecessors.

enough. He complained that Caron interfered with discipline and wanted control of promotions. In answer to this, Caron strove to have the Militia Act amended to permit the appointment of a retired officer as G.O.C. He would thus have eliminated consultation with the Duke of Cambridge. As this could have been taken as a slight upon the Duke, Lorne was horrified. His secretary wrote a formal memorandum to the Privy Council of Canada to point out the serious effect of the proposed omission of the requirement that the G.O.C should be an officer on the active list. The only names of men who were being mentioned as successors to Luard, if he should retire, were Strange and Laurie, retired regular officers living in Canada, and Domville, the former Woolwich cadet, all of whom were now out of touch with current military developments. Lorne showed that under the present system the Canadian government, if it were not satisfied, could refuse to accept the commander in chief's nomination. Their new proposal, however, would open the door to a political appointee becoming G.O.C.[79] When the matter was put to the Duke of Cambridge, he said the two secretaries of state (colonies and war) agreed with him that the choice of an officer to be placed at the disposal of the Canadian government "must rest with us here," which was obviously true only insofar as an active officer would require permission to take up the appointment. Ignoring the limitations of his position, he added that he could not accept the suggestion of the Canadian government that a retired officer should be eligible.[80]

Since Lorne was afraid the feud between Caron and Luard would affect the popularity of imperial officers in Canada, he recommended that the G.O.C. be withdrawn. The Duke of Cambridge said he could not withdraw Luard before his term expired; but he then went on incautiously to ask for the right to appoint a successor if Luard retired on his own initiative.[81] Nevertheless, the Canadian Cabinet accepted the governor general's

79. De Winton to Privy Council, March 7, 1882, P.A.C., M.G. 26, A 1 (a), Vol. 83, p. 299; W.O. to C.O., June 26, 1882, P.R.O., C.O. 42/773.
80. Cambridge to Lorne, July 3, 1882, R.A.W., Cambridge Papers.
81. Lorne to Macdonald, June 9, July 18, 1882, P.A.C., M.G. 26, A 1 (a), Vol. 82, pp. 111, 142.

advice against a Canadian G.O.C. Macdonald informed him that the section of the Militia Bill relating to the general officer commanding would remain unaltered.[82] Then, through the intervention of the speaker of the House of Commons and of Colonel Gzowski, a distinguished civilian engineer who was president of the Rifle Association and the senior Militia Staff engineer, Caron was induced to apologize to Luard. The apology was accepted.[83]

Meanwhile, efforts to strengthen Canada's defenses had been making slow but significant progress. In 1882 the Canadian government, fearing that in the event of war ammunition might not be available from Britain, set up a government-owned cartridge factory in Quebec. A few years later this arsenal, the first in a self-governing colony, began to turn out artillery rounds.

One of Luard's first reactions to the condition of the Canadian Militia had been to state that he would press for the establishment of militia schools.[84] This was, of course, not a new proposal. It had been made repeatedly since the withdrawal of the garrisons when the departure of the regulars took away the instructors upon which the schools had relied. In 1883, however, a new Militia Act at last empowered the creation of a small Canadian Permanent Force of 750 men to staff schools of instruction. A cavalry school was set up at Quebec, and infantry schools at Fredericton, St. Jean, and Toronto. Legal authority was also given for a quartermaster general (he was not to be appointed until 1893). The delay in carrying out the necessary step of setting up a permanent force to provide for the other arms the quality of instruction that had already had a useful effect on the artillery can be attributed primarily to the government's unwillingness to assume the expense. But it was also due to the conflict between the Canadian supporters of the militia and those officers who wanted a regular force or who would have accepted one at England's expense, and who would have welcomed the return of the garrisons. Delay must also have been caused by the friction between the minister and the G.O.C. In fact, it is possible that

82. Macdonald to Lorne, March 10, 1883, R.A.W., Cambridge Papers.
83. Lorne to Cambridge, April 20, Aug. 6, 1883, *ibid.*
84. Luard to Cambridge, Sept. 12, 1880, *ibid.*

the militia schools were more the work of the adjutant general, Colonel Walker Powell, than of the G.O.C. himself.

Luard promptly complained to the governor general about the officers who had been appointed to staff the new schools. He said that one of them had been convicted for drunkenness. Macdonald investigated and informed Lorne that of twenty-three officers appointed, five were graduates of the Royal Military College at Kingston, four were ex-regulars, five had been trained by General Strange and Colonel Irwin in the artillery schools, and Colonel Otter had been especially pointed out to be a first-class officer by Luard himself. The "drunken officer" was a French-Canadian who had been convivial as a cadet at a New Year's party. Macdonald admitted frankly that this officer, a grandson of Sir Etienne Taché, had been appointed for political reasons; and it would appear that there were seven other such "political" appointments. Macdonald knew, however, what Luard refused to accept—that the very existence of the schools, and even of the militia, depended on keeping political support. Nevertheless, to make sure of efficiency, he gave strict instructions that all commandants of artillery batteries should go to Aldershot for training and that all combatant officers should go there before getting promotion.[85]

Within a very few months Luard was in trouble again. He publicly rebuked Lieutenant Colonel Arthur Williams, a militia officer and a member of Parliament, for arguing with a superior officer, Colonel Gzowski, at lunch in the officers' mess, after an inspection in which Luard had been as caustic as ever. This time, Luard made remarks which were taken as being derogatory to the House of Commons. Williams "made a grievance" of the matter, and the press of both parties took up the hue and cry against Luard. The G.O.C. talked of resigning and tried to get another appointment. Failing in that, he wanted to stay on as G.O.C. until the following July when he would be eligible for promotion to Lieutenant General, "which would be quite a nat-

85. Lorne to Macdonald, June 21, 1883, Macdonald to Lorne, July 10, 1883, P.A.C., M.G. 26, A 1 (a), Vol. 82; Lorne to Cambridge, Aug. 6, 1883, R.A.W., Cambridge Papers.

ural time to retire." [86] A few newspapers took his part, saying that Caron, by wanting a private soldier with a vote to be addressed with "the Pinaforic 'if you please,'" had made the Canadian Militia look ridiculous.[87] The G.O.C., having succeeded in securing the withdrawal of Colonel Williams' charges against him, went to England on leave, promising to resign.[88] He was given an appointment at Aldershot. But after he left Canada the question of his status was brought before the Canadian House of Commons. Conservatives as well as Liberals at once arose to accuse him of conduct that would have been impossible in England. He had his defenders, especially among military-minded Canadians, but no one could deny that he lacked tact and that he had not understood the nature of his command.[89] He had done much to endanger the military ties between Britain and Canada.

On the other hand, under Caron the militia continued to be in a sorry state. The militia estimates, cut to the bone by the Liberals, had risen in the first five years of Conservative rule, but they did not reach the early Liberal figures until 1883 saw the creation of the Canadian Permanent Force. Militia companies were far below strength and were starved for money and equipment. Company musters were padded by the inclusion of old men and striplings. Some colonels repeatedly failed to turn out their companies for drill and inspection, even when it was authorized, which was not every year. The number of men reported as having been drilled in 1883, a peak year, was 21,863 out of an establishment of about 37,000; the establishment figures presented in the annual report gave a false impression of the size of the militia.[90]

The root of the matter was that Canadians had no real fear of attack. Had it not been for the enthusiasm of a small minority, there would have been no militia at all; and the discouragements

86. Lorne to Cambridge, Oct. 7, 8, 17, 1883, R.A.W., Cambridge Papers; Luard to Cambridge, Dec. 5, 1883, *ibid.*
87. Montreal *Witness*, Feb. 12, 18, 1884; Toronto *Globe*, Feb. 18, 1884.
88. Lansdowne to Cambridge, Feb. 4, 1884, R.A.W., Cambridge Papers.
89. Canada, House of Commons, *Debates, 1884*, pp. 738–753; Lansdowne to Cambridge, March 31, 1884, R.A.W., Cambridge Papers.
90. Stanley, *Canada's Soldiers*, pp. 247, 264.

were so enormous as to insure that those who did train were zealots. Canadian prime ministers used the force as a vehicle for patronage, a cheap means of rewarding those faithful followers of the party who happened to have a military interest. Smyth, Luard, and later G.O.C.'s all deprecated this Canadian practice as being subversive of discipline and efficiency; but to ride rough-shod over enthusiasm in an attempt to stamp out abuses and enforce a greater efficiency, as Luard did, was to drive out the men whose interest made possible Canada's only organized military force. It was a blow struck at the political foundations of the militia's existence.

The outcry against Luard had brought new demands in press and Parliament for a Canadian G.O.C. However, long before Luard left Canada, the Marquis of Lansdowne, who had succeeded Lorne, had had his eye on a possible successor. This was Colonel Fred Middleton, an unsuccessful applicant in 1874, who had a French-Canadian wife and who therefore wanted to go to Canada despite the well-known unsatisfactory nature of the appointment and the low pay of £800. As he had been commandant at Sandhurst for many years, Middleton seemed a satisfactory candidate.[91] Landsdowne warned the Duke of Cambridge against proposing a name before he was asked to do so. At the same time he hoped to prevent the Canadian Privy Council from announcing its own selection.[92]

While off-the-record talks were proceeding, however, somebody leaked the news to the press that Middleton was to be appointed. The Canadian Cabinet had in fact not yet given its approval.[93] Three weeks later, Caron reported to Macdonald that the only candidates to be considered in Cabinet were Middleton and Major General Laurie, but his own choice was the former because although Laurie had been on the Active List until 1882,

91. Lansdowne to Macdonald, Jan. 22, 1884, P.A.C., M.G. 26, A 1 (a), Vol. 84. Middleton had even been willing to accept the inferior appointment of adjutant general (Dufferin to Mackenzie, Feb. 18, 1874, P.R.O., Northern Ireland, D 1071, H/43/1).
92. Lansdowne to Cambridge, March 31, 1884, R.A.W., Cambridge Papers.
93. London *Times*, April 5, 1884, P.A.C., Macdonald Papers, M.G. 26, A 1 (a), Vol. 84.

he had actually been "farming and manufacturing" in Canada for twenty-two years and was out of touch. Caron said that the Royal Military College and the militia schools needed proper supervision, which the former commandant of Sandhurst could provide. Moreover, a G.O.C. should stay for five years only, but Laurie's political influence would mean that he would become a permanent appointment. Furthermore, he might, after his appointment, be "struck off the list of Imperial Officers." [94] Laurie, a former deputy adjutant general in Nova Scotia, had connections with a minister of a provincial administration. He was also strongly supported by Sir Charles Tupper, who was about to go to London as high commissioner.[95] Selby Smyth, an impartial witness, had thought Laurie "an indifferent officer, very self-asserting, and plausible . . . superficial and not of sterling military spirit or worth." [96] Macdonald and Lansdowne therefore waited until Tupper had "left Ottawa for good" before the Cabinet decided to choose Middleton.[97]

Lansdowne fought hard to prevent this decision from being issued as an order-in-council. From the beginning of the negotiations he had taken the stand that the Duke should be asked to suggest names for informal discussion, but that the Canadian Cabinet should make no official recommendation lest it lead to lobbying. In other words, although he admitted that the choice rested with the Canadian government, he wanted it to appear as if it were made by the Duke of Cambridge.[98] On the grounds that "any discussion as to the fitness of a particular officer ought to be unofficial," he succeeded in having the Privy Council order so worded that it showed that Middleton had been selected unofficially in correspondence between the governor general and the Duke.[99] It was a Pyrrhic victory and quite empty, and it was

94. Caron to Macdonald, April 25, 1884, *ibid.,* Vol. 200.
95. Lansdowne to Cambridge, May 11, 1884, R.A.W., Cambridge Papers.
96. Smyth to Cambridge, Dec. 6, 1877, *ibid.*
97. Lansdowne to Cambridge, May 11, 1884, *ibid.;* Lansdowne 112, May 26, 1884, P.R.O., C.O. 42/777.
98. Lansdowne to Macdonald, Jan. 22, 1884, P.A.C., M.G. 26, A 1 (a), Vol. 84.
99. Dufferin to Cambridge, May 19, 1884, R.A.W., Cambridge Papers; Lansdowne 112, May 26, 1884, P.R.O., C.O. 42/777.

to prove disadvantageous in the end. But Lansdowne, like all other British officials, always strove to preserve the symbols of British control. By contrast, Macdonald and Caron appear in this exchange as both realistic and responsible. Despite their use of the militia as a means of patronage, they had been wise enough to keep the top appointments out of politics.

The Canadian Defence Commission, 1884–1885

The important decision expressed in the Militia Act of 1883, to create a small Canadian Permanent Force, pregnant as it undoubtedly was for the future, had little immediate effect on the problems of Canadian and imperial defense. Meanwhile, Canada had agreed (in 1880) to furnish the Carnarvon Commission with information about its resources and defenses as a basis for military planning; and by 1882, with the exception of Quebec, the provinces had done so.[100] This was little more than an increase in the scale of reports made to the War Office for several years past. It could not answer the problems of local defense. As the Carnarvon Commission was not expected to do more than make general recommendations, implementation would depend very much on local initiative. Lorne, perhaps inspired indirectly by Carnarvon, therefore proposed the establishment of a committee to look at the problems of the defense of Canada. Nothing happened until 1882 when Edward Blake, a leading member of the Opposition, asked the government in the Commons to produce the exchanges that had taken place with Britain since 1878 on the subject of defense. Blake did not follow up this initiative, and his move may have been merely a parliamentary tactical device to embarrass the government. But by it he forced Caron to reply that as the pertinent correspondence going back to before confederation was most voluminous, it would take some time to submit the papers. For security reasons, some papers could not be put before the House; but Caron said that it had been decided

100. Lorne, Secret, Jan. 20, 1880, *ibid.*, C.O. 42/760, Index 12947, registered, 1629, "Destroyed by Statute"; Lorne, Secret, Nov. 13, Dec. 29, 1880, Jan. 21, 1881, March 13, 1882, *ibid.*, C.O. 42/763, 766, 771.

to establish a Canadian committee (or commission) on defense.[101] It seemed as if at last a proper examination of Canadian defense policy would be made.

The chairman of the new committee was to be the governor general's secretary, Viscount Melgund, a future governor general as the Earl of Minto. The other members were General Middleton, the G.O.C.; Colonel Panet, the deputy minister of militia and defense; and Lieutenant Colin Campbell, a retired naval officer who had been a civil servant in Canada for twelve years. Campbell was to act as secretary. The brunt of the work fell on Melgund and Campbell. The committee was instructed to examine the militia documents and advise the minister on those which could be presented to Parliament and those which should be reported only to the government. The committee was specifically enjoined to concern itself only with "the flanks," that is, the Atlantic and Pacific coasts, and with the question of the division of responsibility between the imperial and Canadian governments. The defense of the American border and the state of the militia were thus deliberately omitted from its terms of reference, either in deference to American susceptibilities if news of its activities leaked out, or because Caron and Macdonald had become convinced that no good could come of investigating an insoluble problem. The committee was also instructed that it was not to concern itself with the discussion of "particular places." Despite this exclusion it was, in fact, the Canadian counterpart of the Carnarvon Commission. But it was not to deal with details of defenses and it was to go about its business by collecting and collating pertinent documents and not by taking the evidence of witnesses. It was, indeed, a very limited investigation.[102]

Melgund's correspondence with Campbell, instructing him about the work of collection and copying, shows that he wished to use the committee to force the government to put its military house in order, but that he had no preconceived idea of the way

101. Canada, House of Commons, *Debates, 1882*, Feb. 15, 1882, p. 38. The words committee and commission are both used indiscriminately for this and for the 1898 commission.

102. Colonial Defence Commission, 1884–1885, P.A.C., Minto Papers, Pt. III, Pamphlets Letter Book, Vol. 1 (Microfilm A-130).

in which this should be done. After reviewing the exchanges between Canada and Britain when the Milne Committee made its recommendations, he concluded that "speaking generally . . . Canada would be expected to defend her coasts against any roving expedition; but that in the case of an attack *in force* on any important point, or a landing in force on her coast, she might count upon the assistance of the Old Country." Therefore, coaling stations for Her Majesty's ships should be protected.[103]

Campbell hoped to push the government to examine the topic which had been denied to the committee—the defense of particular places. His own solution for the defense of the coasts was a marine militia force.[104] He worked busily, obtaining the pertinent documents from the department and copying those which could not be retained. He collected other relevant material such as defense reports and blue books from the Australian colonies. The committee's report to the minister, prepared by early 1886, consisted principally of a calendar of the documents about "Fortifications, armaments and ammunition, and other modes of defence, and the organization of the Militia of Canada, for the protection of this portion of the Empire against Foreign attack." It had not concerned itself with the use of the militia as a support for civil authority except insofar as the recent North-West expedition would appear as a special report of the department. The committee had selected papers concerning pay, clothing and equipment, and training of the militia only "partially, as regards general questions of efficiency for defensive purposes," a limitation imposed partly by its terms of reference (but even more by the magnitude of the task) and partly by the sensitive nature of the subject. Its report was printed for limited distribution only,[105] and it was not presented to Parliament, which apparently had forgotten the committee's existence amid the more exciting questions arising out of the campaign in the North-West. A shelf of

103. Melgund to Colin Campbell, Jan. 17, 1885, Campbell to Melgund, Feb. 26, 1885, P.A.C., R.G. 9, II B 2 (71), Vol. 32.

104. Correspondence between Colin Campbell and Lord Melgund, Colonial Defence Commission, 1884–1885, P.A.C., Minto Papers, Pt. III, Pamphlets Letter Book, Vol. 1 (Microfilm A-130).

105. Canada, Committee on the Defences of Canada, *The Defences of Canada,* Jan. 1, 1886 (Ottawa: Maclean, Roger, 1886).

documents in the Public Archives remains a sterile monument to the committee's work.

Canada and the Sudan

While Melgund and Campbell were busily collecting defense papers and having many of them laboriously copied, some Canadians were sweating, and a few even dying, on an imperial expedition in Egypt. General Gordon's plight in Khartoum had forced Gladstone to send General Sir Garnet Wolseley to rescue him. Wolseley, remembering the boatmen who had helped him to reach Manitoba in 1870, asked for Canadian *voyageurs* to help him up the Nile. *Voyageurs* were now an extinct breed, but the governor general's office, with the Canadian government's approval, recruited backwoodsmen and Caughnawaga Indians, and Caron promised to find French-Canadians and a chaplain. The Canadians worked on the Nile in civilian clothes under contract with the British government.[106] They did no fighting. But they were organized as a paramilitary unit under officers who were members of the militia. They were commanded by Lieutenant Colonel Fred Denison, who was appointed by the governor general, Lord Lansdowne, at Wolseley's request.[107] This was, however, a British expedition, and the Canadians, properly speaking, were not a military component of it. All that Canada had done was authorize recruiting for noncombatant service.

The recruiting of the *voyageurs* caused some old soldiers in Canada to smell powder. Laurie, recently disappointed in his quest for the command of the militia, applied for the *voyageur* command.[108] When Lansdowne told him that the post was filled, he applied to the British government for the command of any

106. Lansdowne to Macdonald, Sept. 2, 1884, P.A.C., M.G. 26, A 1 (a), Vol. 84.

107. Charles P. Stacey, ed., *Records of the Nile Voyageurs, 1884-85* (Toronto: Champlain Society, 1959), *passim;* Charles P. Stacey and E. Pye, "Canadian Voyageurs in the Sudan, 1884-5," *Canadian Army Journal,* V (Oct., Nov., Dec., 1951), No. 7, 61-73; No. 8, 58-68; No. 9, 16-26; Lansdowne to Macdonald, Sept. 4, 1884, P.A.C., M.G. 26, A 1 (a), Vol. 84.

108. Lansdowne to Macdonald, Sept. 2, 1884, P.A.C., M.G. 26, A 1 (a), Vol. 84.

Canadian force to serve in "Turkey." (He meant Egypt but either his geography was weak or he was out-of-date.) The War Office replied that no such force was being planned.[109] When the situation in the East deteriorated, Laurie was back on the scent and could not be diverted until the North-West expedition in Canada was in the offing. A little after Laurie's application, Colonel Arthur Williams of Port Hope, Luard's old antagonist, telegraphed directly to the high commissioner in London to offer the 46th East Durham "regiment" of militia for service with the British. He claimed that he had the approval of the militia authorities. The War Office asked officially whether Laurie and Williams had the backing of the Canadian government. By this time the flow of similar applications had reached such proportions that the governor general suggested that they should all be channelled through the Militia Department.[110]

This proposal might have had implications of commitment. Macdonald therefore advised Lansdowne that the militia could not be called out under the Militia Act for service in the Egyptian expedition; the proper way for the imperial government to recruit in Canada would be under the British Mutiny Act, or rather under whatever imperial statute had taken its place. Lansdowne duly advised the Colonial Office on the lines Macdonald had suggested. Macdonald thought, quite erroneously it would seem, that the governor general could act by virtue of his imperial commission as commander in chief, as had been done when the Royal Canadians were recruited just after the Crimean War. He had forgotten that the governor general was not commander in chief by imperial commission and that Cartier had insured that his functions in that regard were held by a Canadian statute. Macdonald had thus maintained the stand that he had taken five years earlier when he appeared before the Carnar-

109. W.O. to C.O., Dec. 24, 1884, P.R.O., C.O. 42/779, Index 12946, indorsed, "Destroyed by Statute."
110. G.B., P.P., 1884–1885, *Correspondence Regarding Offers by the Colonies of Troops for Service in the Sudan; and Letters of Lord Wolseley on the Service of the Canadian Voyageurs in the Nile Expedition*, LII, 569–669 (C. 4324, C. 4437, C. 4494). The whole question of Canadian offers of service in Sudan is discussed in Charles P. Stacey, "Canada and the Nile Expedition," *Canadian Historical Review*, XXXIII (Dec., 1952), 319–340.

von Commission. Britain's small imperial wars were not Canada's concern.[111]

Far away in Sydney, rumors of these happenings had a strange result. Sir Edward Strickland, who had retired as commissary general and had gone to live in Australia only five years before, read an inaccurate report by Reuter's in the Sydney *Morning Herald* which said that six hundred Canadians were going to Britain to take over garrison duties while British troops went to rescue Gordon. The next day, when the paper recorded Gordon's death, it printed a letter from Strickland calling attention to "a grand opportunity . . . offered to Australia of proving, by performing a graceful, a loyal and a generous act, that she yields not to Canada . . . in loyalty and affection towards the mother country." [112] Gordon's fate had aroused strong feelings throughout the Empire. William Bede Dalley, acting premier of New South Wales, seized upon Strickland's idea, and without stopping to think the matter over telegraphed to the imperial government an offer of a contingent for service in Egypt. So, New South Welshmen went to the Red Sea in the first colonial expeditionary force to fight in an imperial war.

Dalley, a little later, having refused a knighthood, was made the first colonial member of the British Privy Council.[113] He had earned this unique honor, for he had created a precedent of tremendous importance for the British Empire. Victoria, South Australia, and Queensland made similar offers which were politely declined on the grounds "that more troops would not be required until Autumn." New Zealand apologized for not having followed suit but said that if the need continued and war with Russia followed, the colony would promise one thousand well-trained men to serve in the Sudan or elsewhere.[114]

111. Charles P. Stacey, "John A. Macdonald on Raising Troops in Canada for Imperial Service, 1885," *Canadian Historical Review*, XXXVIII (March, 1957), 37–40.

112. Sydney *Morning Herald*, Feb. 11, 12, 1885; B. R. Penny, "The Age of Empire: An Australian Episode," *Historical Studies: Australia and New Zealand*, XI (1963–1965), 33–42.

113. Stanley Brogden, *The Sudan Contingent* (Melbourne: Hawthorne, 1943), pp. 9–10.

114. Robert Stout to Agent General, New Zealand, May 22, 1885, New Zealand, *Appendix to Journals of the House of Representatives*, 1885, A-7.

Frequently in the years that followed, imperialists referred to the Sudan expedition as the beginning of a new age in which the self-governing colonies contributed to imperial defense. As a consequence of the Australian offers, the War Office rejected Canadian proposals to permit the recruiting in Canada of troops who would be paid out of the imperial treasury. It said that the forces already under orders for Egypt were enough for present needs. If operations were prolonged until "next Autumn," the secretary of state for war would be glad to reconsider the Dominion's proposals.[115]

Macdonald's suggestion had only been that the imperial government should recruit in Canada. When Sir Charles Tupper, the Canadian high commissioner in London, intervened to urge the sending of the Canadian Permanent Force, Macdonald rebuked him severely on the grounds that the Sudan was not Canada's business. However, Queen Victoria and public opinion in England made no distinction between offers by a colonial government to finance contingents, offers to permit recruiting, and offers by individuals in the colonies. Even the title of the parliamentary paper on the subject spoke of "offers by the colonies." This attitude caused Macdonald some immediate embarrassment which had to be explained away in a vigorous exchange of letters.[116] But an impression had been made on the public mind, and especially on those imperialists who wished to believe that all the colonies had offered troops, and it was never erased.

The precedent that had been established was not merely for colonial aid in imperial wars, but also that colonial aid should be at the expense of the colony. It was ironical that this important development should have come through a journalist's error; and in the case of the Sudan, there was room to doubt whether any colonial aid was justified. Certainly Canada, as Macdonald had made quite clear, had no interest in Egypt. The Australian colonies, dependent upon the Suez route, were more concerned, but that route was not seriously threatened. The War Office had

115. W.O. to C.O., Feb. 16, 1885, in G.B., *P.P.*, 1884–1885, LII, No. 21 (C. 4324).
116. Stacey, "Canada and the Nile Expedition," pp. 331, 333–340.

little need of the colonial contingent, and when it got to the Red Sea the fighting was practically over. Nevertheless, the precedent was to have far-reaching consequences.

Esquimalt

Meanwhile, the 1885 crisis with Russia had reawakened concern about the Esquimalt naval base. Lovell's and Strange's reports had been supplemented by one by Colonel Crossman, R.E., who had been sent around the Pacific in 1881 to talk to colonial naval and military authorities at Esquimalt, Hong Kong, Singapore, Penang, Labuan, and Fiji. Copies of his report reached Ottawa in 1882 along with Lovell's,[117] but no action had yet been taken by the time the British set up the Colonial Defence Committee in 1885. Hence, its second memorandum on May 2 called attention to the exposed state of Esquimalt, where the incompleted earthworks (which were inadequately protected on their flanks) [118] were already in disrepair. The committee recalled that at the Carnarvon Commission's hearings the Admiralty had attached importance to the base because it was the only one in the North Pacific; and Admiral Sir Astley Cooper Key confirmed that the Admiralty still considered Esquimalt to be essential. But the committee had apparently forgotten that the Admiralty had said Esquimalt would not be convenient in the event of a war. It argued that since naval forces based on Esquimalt would help to protect the coasts of British Columbia, its defense ought to be undertaken by Canada. The committee proposed the use of marine mining equipment for the defense of the Pacific Coast harbors.[119] The G.O.C. in Canada, General Middleton, called upon to advise the Canadian government, proposed that a hundred regular marine artillerymen should be stationed at Es-

117. W.O. to C.O., June 15, 1881, P.A.C., R.G. 7, G. 21, No. 165, Vol. 4 (c), 1880–1887; C.O. to Governor General, July 27, 1882, *ibid.*
118. Maj. Gen. J. W. Laurie, "The Protection of Our Naval Base in the North Pacific," *R.U.S.I. Journal*, XXVII (1883), 357–381.
119. C.D.C., Minutes, Confidential Memorandum, No. 2 M, May 4, 1885, P.R.O., Cab. 11/27.

quimalt, but at the expense of the imperial government.[120] The question of who should pay thus remained unsettled.

Commissions in the British Army for Colonials

The crisis of 1884–1885, which had led to Admiralty interest in controlling the incipient colonial navies that had been projected after the earlier crisis and had also forced Britain to set up the Colonial Defence Committee to cope with problems that were becoming too much for the Colonial Office and other departments to handle separately, had had other important consequences. It strengthened colonial connection with the British Army in an indirect way. The War Office did not want colonial contingents, but it had found itself very short of officers. The 1885 difficulties therefore opened the gates for young colonials to serve in the army. In the early part of the century, although the Royal Navy had offered cadetships on colonial governor generals' nominations, the system of the purchase of commissions had effectively blocked any extension of this practice to the army. The only way for young colonials to get military commissions was through the normal English channels—personal influence and purchase—and a boy often had to be sent to a "crammer" in England. Few colonials found their way by these routes into the army, and it was often alleged that their colonial origin set them at a disadvantage. Joseph Howe, the Maritimes leader, had once said that he would rather see his sons "thrown overboard" than have them strive to rise in the British Army.[121]

The first breach in the walls of privilege that barred colonials from the army had been made when Selby Smyth in 1879, working through the Marquis of Lorne, persuaded the War Office to offer four commissions annually to graduates of the new Canadian Military College.[122] In 1885 the Red Sea crisis caused a

120. Note on Privy Council Order 1050 F, "Defences of British Columbia," Nov. 25, 1885, P.A.C., R.G. 7, G. 21. No. 165, Vol. 4 (b), 1880–1887.
121. Joseph A. Chisholm, ed., *The Speeches and Public Letters of Joseph Howe* (Halifax: The Chronicle Publishing Co., 1909), II, 289.
122. W.O. to C.O., Oct. 28, 1878, P.R.O., C.O. 335/13, Index 12946, indorsed, "Destroyed by Statute"; Lorne to Cambridge, June 6, 1879, R.A.W., Cambridge Papers.

substantial, though temporary, increase in this number. Then in 1886 a War Office committee proposed that two commissions each, one infantry and one cavalry, should be offered to Cape Colony, South Australia, New South Wales, Victoria, Queensland, and New Zealand. In March the War Office announced its approval.[123] Canada was omitted because of the commissions already offered to the Royal Military College, but Lansdowne pointed out that in relation to Canada's size and resources, the four for R.M.C. were not enough for Canada and that the Canadian Militia was excluded altogether. Hence, six more commissions were offered to Canada.[124] Through these small openings colonials began to climb to high rank. These were, however, individual contributions to the defense of the Empire.

Thus far the colonies' own military forces were primitive and inefficient, and no way had been found to link them effectively with the British imperial defense effort. Between 1778 and 1885 a fear of Russian bombardment, followed by Britain's entanglement in Egypt and the Sudan, had forced the Canadian government to look more carefully at its defenses. Yet, apart from some reforms in the militia that were of greater promise than immediate value, and apart from a very limited governmental inquiry into the history and background of defense policy and its relation to imperial defense problems, nothing was done in these years to strengthen Canadian defenses. At the same time, Canada's military relations with Britain were seriously endangered because the individuals concerned on both sides were unsuitable for the delicate and important work in which they were employed. The single positive achievement, the opening of the way for colonials to get regular commissions in the regular army, did nothing to improve the imperial connection in a direct way. But it may have had important though intangible results by showing that colonials were good officer material.

123. G.B., W.O., "Committee. Commissions in the Regular Army Offered to Officers in the Colonial Forces," Confidential Papers, A 43/1886.
124. Lansdowne 420, Nov. 1, 1887, P.R.O., C.O. 42/791; W.O. to C.O., Dec. 13, 1887, *ibid.*, C.O. 42/792.

6

Rebellion in the Canadian West
and the Canadian Militia,
1885–1895

The North-West Rebellion

Disaffection in the West among Métis and Indians served to divert the attention of those military-minded Canadians who might have otherwise continued to agitate for Canada to emulate New South Wales and send a contingent to the Red Sea. At three days' notice, Major General Frederick Middleton, newly appointed to command the Canadian Militia, was ordered to go west to look over the situation. When he recommended the use of force, the Canadian government authorized him to command the first purely Canadian military operation. Within reach of the rebels, there were only Northwest Mounted Police and the Winnipeg militia consisting of one battalion of infantry, one troop of cavalry, and one battery of artillery. The Canadian Pacific Railway tracks from the East were not yet completed: there were four gaps in the line through the rough bush country north of Lake Superior. Canada had no military transport, supply, or medical services. However, the minister, Adolphe Caron, ordered Middleton to mobilize militia units in the East and move them to the Prairies with men of the new Canadian Permanent Force to preserve order and suppress the leader of the rebellion, Louis Riel. He told Middleton: "Travel night and day. I want to show what the Canadian Militia can do." Despite great difficulties and shortages, made worse by temperatures as low as twenty degrees below zero, the movement of troops to the Prairies was successful. It was a remarkable achievement. The first detachment reached

Winnipeg after less than a week of traveling. Less than two months later the last unit moved all the way by rail, eighty-six miles of track having been laid hurriedly to link Winnipeg with the East.

Middleton's rapidity of movement forestalled a more serious general rising of the Western Indians. Indeed, with the Canadian Pacific Railway completed to the Prairies, Riel had no hope whatever of permanent success. But Middleton suffered early temporary setbacks and moved more slowly in the field than he had done when concentrating his force in the West. He had over five thousand troops, mostly militia, but including 363 officers and men of the Canadian Permanent Force. He also had 550 Northwest Mounted Police. The militia were untrained, barely more than raw recruits; one observer described the police as "whisky detectives" instead of soldiers. The regulars suffered an unduly high proportion of the casualties and probably made a contribution to the success of the operations out of all proportion to their numbers. Middleton's difficulties with such green troops were formidable; an early reverse might have had serious consequences. Furthermore, he made tactical errors in addition to acting with what would have been regarded as excessive caution if he had had experienced troops. Nevertheless, by July 2 the rising was crushed.

Middleton's success probably saved Macdonald's government from defeat. Pro-government papers lauded Middleton to the skies. He was given $20,000 and a knighthood and confirmed as a major general. In addition, the British government also gave him a distinguished service pension of £100 a year and he was thanked by both houses of Parliament at Westminster. Nevertheless, the campaign had shown up the weaknesses of the Canadian military establishment. The militia had, it is true, done much better than might have been expected when its experience and training are taken into account. But if the outbreak had proved more serious, it is probable that Canada would have had to call on Britain for help. In view of the recent developments over the Red Sea crisis this would have been a great humiliation.

However, Middleton's quick victory served to gloss over the

weaknesses in training and supply that had been revealed, and
to postpone remedial action rather than to expedite it.[1] Further
development of the Canadian Militia to build upon the improvements introduced by the Act of 1883 was therefore checked.
Moreover, Middleton found that Canadians as a whole were
thrilled by the success of "their boys," and in consequence they
began to feel that they had no more need for British or, as they
were and are sometimes wrongly called, "imperial" officers. At
the same time, the Canadian Opposition attacked him fiercely
and spread critical rumors about his conduct of the campaign.
His enemies said that partly because he felt an exaggerated need
to nurse his raw militia troops, he had lacked drive, and that it
was two militia colonels who, without his orders, had launched
the victorious assault at Batoche. The documents do not sub-
stantiate this charge. But one of the officers concerned was
Arthur Williams, M.P., who had moved the vote of thanks for
Selby Smyth, who had been insulted by Luard, and who had
volunteered a regiment for service in Egypt. Williams died in the
West on active service. It was alleged that his illness was made
worse by Middleton's tyrannical treatment. Middleton retorted
that Williams had been unable to withstand the strain of war.
These exchanges show that despite his supposed detachment, a
British officer was not necessarily more insulated from Canadian
political strife than was a Canadian. So both Middleton's success
and the ensuing controversies helped to strengthen popular demand for a Canadian to be G.O.C.[2] They did little to further the
improvement of the Canadian Militia in the near future.

Caron, for his part, had shown what he could do when the
need was urgent. His private papers in the Public Archives of
Canada are more concerned with general politics than with the
administration of the department. However, there is one volume
of papers which covers his conduct of the expedition to the

1. Charles P. Stacey, "The North-West Campaign, 1885," in *Introduction to
the Study of Military History for Canadian Students* (Ottawa: Queen's Printer,
1955), pp. 75–85; Stacey, *The Military Problems of Canada: A Survey of Defence
Policies and Strategic Conditions Past and Present* (Toronto: Ryerson, [1940]),
p. 64; Stanley, *Canada's Soldiers*, p. 258.
2. Canada, House of Commons, *Debates*, 1885, IV, 3074; Middleton to Cambridge, Jan. 18, 1886, R.A.W., Cambridge Papers.

North-West. Collected in response to an order for a return to the House of Commons in 1886, the papers show that in this matter he acted with great firmness and expedition.[3]

Less choleric and consciously more cautious than Luard, Middleton managed to avoid real trouble for the next two or three years. He enjoyed his prestige as a victor and basked in the favor of a government that was well-disposed toward him. At times he found government support uncomfortable, especially when Caron began to ask favors for his friends. But without alienating the minister, he managed to avoid being besmirched with political mire. This is remarkable because he actually held the lowest opinion of Caron, and indeed of almost all French-Canadians. He thought them poor soldiers. This opinion contrasts markedly with that of Strange who had commanded them in the Alberta Field Force which was in the Western column and who, as he had served in Quebec, presumably knew them better. The G.O.C. thought the passions which Riel had aroused could only lead to the destruction of the Dominion. "I am convinced," he wrote, that "this country can never be a success as long as the French language is kept equal [*sic*] with the English. I hold these ideas though I married a French-Canadian who, by the way, fully agrees with me." [4] He told the commander in chief that his wife, "a most decided English woman now and not so careful as I am," might speak her mind bluntly.[5] But she does not appear to have given offense. His views suggest that although discreet, he was politically naïve and had little understanding of Canada. He was unsuitable as the military leader of a country composed of two distinct linguistic groups. A regular soldier from Britain who could not rise above such antipathies lost much of the advantage that might be expected from one who came from outside the country.

British Officers in Colonial Service

But it was not on account of these deficiencies that the British government now tried to remove Middleton when he was at the

3. P.A.C., M.G. 27, I D 3, Vol. 199.
4. Middleton to Cambridge, Jan. 18, 1886, R.A.W., Cambridge Papers.
5. Middleton to Cambridge, Aug. 30, 1885, *ibid.*

height of his glory. It was a bureaucratic decision not directed at him personally. The abolition of the system of the purchase of commissions, which had obvious value in its long-run effect on efficiency and professionalism, had disturbed the whole pay structure and organization of the army. To recompense officers who had thus lost a vested interest, army pensions had been introduced. This brought certain complications as far as service with colonial forces was concerned. In the long run a most important effect of abolition would be that British officers could be ordered, rather than invited or entreated, to take colonial postings. But there were more immediate difficulties arising from the effect on pay and pensions. The British government was anxious to restrict its financial obligations. In February, 1886, a British interdepartmental committee had met the agents general of all the self-governing colonies except New Zealand and had secured their agreement to the principle that the imperial government should not bear the full cost of the pensions earned when officers were serving colonial governments.[6]

The reorganization included age-limit retirements, and Middleton was affected. Macdonald protested on his behalf. He called the decision "absurd." Middleton, he said, was engaged in the training and disciplining of an important branch of the military forces of the Empire and was educating himself for future command and responsibility. If this regulation persisted, it would be harder than ever to attract British officers to colonial service. Macdonald said that an Australian colony had also protested and that the secretary of state for war, W. H. Smith, had promised that the regulation would be amended. He then went on to show that the case of Colonel Strange was even worse. When Strange was a "herdsman and Bacchus" he had drawn his half-pay. When he accepted a call to serve in the North-West which he "could not with honour refuse," his half-pay had been stopped and he had been called upon to refund a half-year's portion already received.[7] Thus, in its efforts to strengthen control over colonial military forces through service officers, the British government made the employment of British officers more difficult.

6. P.A.C., R.G. 7, G. 21, Vol. 75, No. 4 (a).
7. Macdonald to Lansdowne, Aug. 3, 1886, P.A.C., M.G. 26, A 1 (a), Vol. 86.

Another problem was the question of command in mixed forces. In 1880 at the time of the Carnarvon Commission, the War Office had pressed for a general rule that mixed forces would always be commanded by British officers. The Colonial Office had had to remind it that this might lead to the junior officer in command of a small British detachment giving orders to a very senior colonial general. When the War Office would not yield the point, the question had been left unsettled, but with a Colonial Office suggestion that in case of difficulty the "telegraph should be resorted to." [8]

During negotiations leading to the Colonial Conference it was announced that arrangements had been made to improve the conditions of employment of British officers in the colonies. Officers on the active list would not be paid from British funds when in colonial service, but if the secretary of state for war approved, they could count that service toward their promotion and retirement as though it were service with the British Army. Retired pay earned in colonial service would be charged against British funds. Officers who retired while in colonial service would immediately draw their pensions for service prior to their colonial appointment, and on retirement from colonial service they would receive retirement pay for the period of colonial service prior to their retirement from the army. Officers on the retired list who accepted a colonial appointment would retain their pension "unless the Secretary of State deems fit." No service under a colonial government subsequent to retirement would earn pension chargeable against imperial funds. The Treasury could not resist adding the observation that this arrangement "involved a further and very important concession to the colonies at the cost of the British taxpayer." [9] The colonies were no doubt expected to show their gratitude by reciprocal military concessions at the conference.

The employment of British officers to improve the "auxiliary forces" of the Empire and the question of employing colonial

8. W.O. to C.O., Oct. 25, 1880; C.O. to W.O., Nov. 4, 1880, Jan. 22, 1881; all printed in Carnarvon Commission Report, III, Appendix, No. 8.
9. Welby to Financial Secretary of the War Office, Nov. 19, 1886, in G.B., P.P., 1887, LVI, 892–893 (C. 5901–1).

forces outside the colony to which they belonged were among the most important topics on the agenda of the first Colonial Conference, which had been largely inspired by "the patriotic action of the colonies in offering contingents of troops to take part in the Egyptian campaign." It had indeed been called more for the purpose of promoting military co-operation than for the naval co-operation which was its more important result.[10] Salisbury, in his opening speech, told the delegates, "the extension of the Empire may from time to time require portions of it to incur danger on account of interests which are not their own." [11] In view of this frank profession of empire-building, it is hardly surprising that despite the great surge of imperial feeling which the Golden Jubilee and Colonial Conference produced, there were no colonial commitments to provide troops for future wars. In fact, the conference did little more than exchange information about the nature of colonial military development. It arranged in principle for a common inspecting officer for the land forces of the Australian colonies and it listened to a War Office proposal concerning precedence and commissions. The War Office proposed that colonial forces should take precedence after British forces and should arrange themselves according to the seniority of the colony. It further suggested that colonial officers should be granted a Queen's commission, but that that commission should only be honorary in regard to the regular army unless the officer concerned was called out to serve with the regular army. These proposals were to be taken home for consideration by colonial governments.[12]

The conference had not settled the vexing questions of command in war. But however reluctant the War Office might be—at this time often with good reason—to consider colonial auxiliaries as the equals of British regulars, that problem would eventually solve itself because the calling out of colonial forces,

10. Sir Samuel Griffiths to Sir Henry Holland, March 28, 1887; Holland to Governors of Colonies, July 23, 1887; Stanhope, secretary of state for war, to Governors of Colonies under Responsible Government, Nov. 25, 1886; all in Maurice Ollivier, *The Colonial and Imperial Conferences from 1887 to 1937* (Ottawa: Queen's Printer, 1954) I, 5, 8–13, 37.
11. *Ibid.*, I, 16.
12. G.B., *P.P.*, 1887, LVI, 528–529 (C. 5901–1).

and the terms on which they would serve, could only be in conformity with the consent of the colonial government. Unresolved also were the conditions for the employment of British officers in the colonies, about which the War Office had made its concessions in the preliminary correspondence. After the conference was over, the War Office, adhering strictly to the letter of the principles of the new regulations, confirmed that Middleton was to be retired. It then offered to nominate a competent officer to replace him.[13] Middleton was despondent. He had accepted the appointment on the understanding that it would last for five years and that he would have his British half-pay on top of his salary of £800 from the Canadian government. Stoppage of the half-pay meant that his anticipated income had already been cut by a total of £1,300.[14]

Macdonald's request that Middleton should stay on as G.O.C. after retirement from the army drew from the War Office a statement of the reasoning behind its action. It said that there was no legal objection to the employment of a retired officer. But it went on,

> there is evidently a disposition on the part of the colonies to put their forces on a sound footing and at no distant date many of them would be able, and as instanced in the Soudan Campaign, eager, to assist the mother country by placing contingents of troops at her disposal should she be engaged in any considerable war. They must also be largely relied upon to act in concert with Imperial troops in defending coaling stations. It is therefore very essential that the military systems, organization, and armament of the Imperial government and the colonies should as far as possible be uniform.

The G.O.C. of colonial forces should be informed about all the latest improvements in the British Army. A retired officer would be "out of touch" and might permit a lack of uniformity that could be dangerous. Moreover, if a small force of British troops went to aid in a colonial campaign, such as that which had recently taken place in Canada, the officer in chief command,

13. W.O. to C.O., Sept. 15, 1887, P.R.O., C.O. 335/17, Index 15385, indorsed, "Destroyed by Statute."
14. Middleton to Cambridge, Oct. 15, 1887, R.A.W., Cambridge Papers.

being retired from the British Army, would be incapable of giving any command to the British troops.[15]

An officer who had gone to Canada to serve for five years not yet completed, and who had fought a successful campaign there, could hardly be adequately covered by that explanation. Furthermore, a colonial government that was responsible for its military forces had a right to keep for a reasonable time a G.O.C. in whom it had confidence. The command in Canada was not an ordinary army appointment. But the War Office was quite oblivious of the Canadian position and also of the strength of Canadian resolution. Lansdowne had to remind the War Office that the G.O.C., although recommended by the commander in chief, was appointed by the Canadian government, was paid out of Canadian funds, and held his appointment subject to the will of the Canadian Parliament. It was not therefore within the province of the War Office to terminate his employment or to appoint his successor. There might be disadvantages in the appointment of an officer on the retired list, but these would not necessarily apply to prolongation of command by one still in service. The Canadian Militia Act did not provide that the G.O.C. must be on the active list, only that an officer from the active list should be appointed.[16] When the War Office continued to demur, Lansdowne telegraphed curtly, "We wish to retain Middleton." In the Colonial Office this wire was minuted, "Compelled to acquiesce." [17] The Duke of Cambridge then helped Middleton to get part of his retired pay, £420 a year.[18]

In a parallel case in Australia in 1888, however, the War Office was more successful. South Australia wished to reappoint Major General M. F. Downes as its commandant. Downes had held the appointment from 1877 to 1882 and had been placed on the retired list of the British Army on October 22, 1884. He had since served as secretary of the Department of Defence of Victoria. The undersecretary of state for war, referring to the Middleton

15. W.O. to C.O., Oct. 19, 1887, P.R.O., C.O. 42/792.
16. Lansdowne 387, Oct. 10, 1887, *ibid.*, C.O. 42/791.
17. Lansdowne, Telegram, Dec. 21, 1887, *ibid.*
18. Middleton to Cambridge, Jan. 30, 1888, R.A.W., Cambridge Papers.

case, repeated the same arguments and said that the appointment of an officer from the retired list could not be approved. South Australia protested that General Downes had been the original source of inspiration for a South Australian offer of troops for the Zulu War (which had not been accepted), that he had been continuously employed and had kept up to date, and that the forces in South Australia were already drilled on English methods and armed like British soldiers. The war secretary retorted that retired officers who accepted civil employment at home had deductions made from their pensions. For service in the colonies they got their pensions in full, but he added that this was on the understanding that colonies employed only officers on the active list for military duties. Downes was given the appointment as commandant in South Australia, but unlike Middleton he did not get his British superannuation while holding the appointment.[19]

The War Office was genuinely anxious to improve the efficiency of colonial troops and to make future co-operation with British forces more effective. Not unnaturally, it was not able to think of these aims in terms of co-operation between forces or troops of equal status. In the arrangement for payment of pensions to officers in civil employment in the colonies, it had agreed to financial aid which was in fact a form of subsidy and had abandoned one means which could be used to cut down its own pensions bill. If this arrangement were also to include colonial military appointments, another means of economizing would be lost. Furthermore, retired officers would be more independent than those on the active list. The War Office was thus motivated partly by desire to extend its control (and perhaps also by the desire to find employment for British officers on the active list) as well as by financial considerations. It therefore appears to have gone back on the general principles of the understanding proposed to the Colonial Conference. The War Office regarded colonial forces as "auxiliaries." It wanted these auxiliaries to be provided at the expense of the colonial governments for military co-operation in the general interest, but at the same time it

19. "Copy of Correspondence Between the Secretary of State for War and the Colonial Office with Regard to the Employment of Major-General Downes," in G.B., *P.P.*, 1890, (129) XLIII, 175–191.

wanted them to be as much as possible under its own control. What it ignored, as usual, was the fact that the colonial governments by their control of the purse regulated the nature and degree of the co-operation that they were willing to give, and that they were always anxious lest their autonomy be infringed. Herein lay an insuperable barrier to the War Office's pretensions.

Caron's Report on Canadian Defense, 1888

Shortly before Caron set up the Canadian Commission on Defence in 1884, Cooper Key's memorandum, "The Naval Defence of our colonies," which was to initiate the movement that led to the Australian naval contributions, was sent to Canada. By it, Canada was in effect invited, along with the other self-governing colonies, to make cash contributions to the Royal Navy.[20] In August, 1885, when it seemed that the Australians were going to accept the proposals forthwith, Tryon, at the instance of Lord Augustus Loftus, the governor of New South Wales, sent copies of his revised proposals to the governor general of Canada. In his accompanying letter he said there was a danger that independent colonial navies might compromise the Empire. He suggested that colonies should be taken into "our confidence as to maritime strategy," and he added that colonial navies needed identical discipline, instructions, and practice. But he admitted that the Canadian situation was different from that of Australia, partly because of the rivalry between the southern hemisphere colonies, but also because the United States might object to the growth of a Canadian section of the Royal Navy. More politically minded than most naval officers and more inclined to take into account contemporary affairs, Tryon had heard rumors of a proposed union of all English-speaking peoples,[21] presumably the idea of Goldwin Smith. Although Tryon was rather wide of the mark in thinking that a wider union of that kind might settle the problem of the defense of Canada, he was shooting in the right direction

20. A copy of the memorandum, dated Oct. 28, 1884, is in the governor general's papers, P.A.C., R.G. 7, G. 21, Vol. 75, No. 165, Vol. 4 (b).
21. Tryon to Lansdowne, Aug. 27, 1885, *ibid.*

when he inferred that American proximity must govern Canadian defense policy and must influence the possibility of contributions to the navy. A larger North American auxiliary squadron subsidized by Canada on the lines of that about to be set up in Australia would obviously have been regarded with grave suspicion in the United States.

Lansdowne presumably forwarded Tryon's missive to his ministers. If so, nothing developed from it. Early in 1887 when the Colonial Conference was in the offing, he took up the question again. He found that the Canadian government had very decided views on the subject. It replied that the Canadian people would not tolerate large expenditure for military and naval purposes and that Canada had already made substantial contributions to the strength of the Empire by organizing its militia and by building the Inter-Colonial and Canadian Pacific railways. These—but especially the latter—would be available as imperial military lines of communication. With a small population Canada could not be expected to do more. Lansdowne's own personal opinion was that it could, but it is noteworthy that he thought the Canadian effort should be made in the sphere of local defense.[22]

The Sudan crisis and the North-West expedition had diverted attention from the unsettled problem of the defense of Canada and from the work of the defense commission set up in 1884. Melgund, the commission's chairman, had been busy as chief of staff in the North-West and had then left for England to enter politics. However, the new Colonial Defence Committee set up in London as a result of Sudan pressed the colonies to establish local defense committees.[23] In Canada, Caron kept putting the matter off. He had not yet reported to Parliament on the findings of the defense commission. Therefore, Colin Campbell, its secretary, who had been left on his own, took it upon himself to produce a synopsis of the salient points in the defense correspondence and send it to the governor general.[24]

22. Lansdowne to Holland, March 11, 1887, *ibid.*
23. Stanhope to Lansdowne, Nov. 18, 1886, *ibid.*
24. The synopsis is in the governor general's papers, dated Jan. 15, 1887; see also in the same file, Campbell to Capt. Wheatfield, March 27, April 7, 1888, *ibid.*, Vol. 76, No. 165, Vol. 5.

After the Colonial Conference in 1887, when Canadian refusal to contribute to the navy had been made clear to everybody, Lansdowne returned to the question of Canadian defense. He once again urged the government to establish a Canadian defense committee with a professional officer as its secretary and with subordinate local defense committees in various places. Soon afterward he was shown a draft of a report which Caron proposed to submit to the Cabinet. All that Caron was proposing, he found, was another defense commission of inquiry similar to the Melgund Commission. Lansdowne then succeeded in persuading Caron to set up instead a standing defense committee "substantially in accordance with the recommendations of the secret circular" from the Colonial Defence Committee. He even hoped that a regular officer might be appointed as secretary of this new committee, though he realized that this would probably only be possible if the appointee were a graduate of the Royal Military College at Kingston and if he were paid only a small salary. He also noted that there was much apathy in the country at large about defense, almost an admission that Caron was doing about as much as could be expected.[25]

Caron's long-delayed report was finally presented to the Cabinet on January 23, 1888. He referred to a memorandum from the governor general on November 19, 1886. This had called attention to Colonial Office dispatches upon defense in 1880, 1881, 1883, and 1885, to which the Canadian government had as yet made no reply; it also had asked for the government's opinion on the creation of a colonial naval force along Australian lines. Caron also referred to a Colonial Defence Committee circular for the preparation of local defense plans, to a War Office inquiry into possible Canadian contributions to surveys for the defense of Esquimalt, and to a dispatch from the naval commander in charge of the North America station proposing the formation of torpedo companies. He then said that in the Anglo-Canadian agreement on defense which had preceded confederation there had been no definite contract, only an understanding that Can-

25. Lansdowne to Caron, Dec. 20, 1887, *ibid.;* Lansdowne, Confidential, Jan. 30, 1888, P.R.O., C.O. 42/795.

ada would spend from $300,000 to $1,000,000 annually on the militia. He said that in the twenty years since confederation $27,026,224.55 had been spent. After a long account of development of the military system in Canada, he offered his considered opinion that Canada need not at present make more provision for naval defense than the small fisheries protection service now existing. In an emergency this service could be expanded through embodiment of the hardy seafaring population of the Dominion. The Canadian Pacific was a national highway that was "emphatically a contribution to the defences of the Empire" as well as of Canada. As regards the "external defences" of the Dominion, he admitted that little had been done; but he pleaded that the financial resources of the country would not warrant any considerable outlay. No action had yet been taken concerning the formation of torpedo companies, but this subject could be investigated by a new defense committee which he proposed to establish within his department. The committee would consist of the G.O.C., the adjutant general, the commandant of the Royal Military College, and the inspector of artillery; there also would be local committees in each district. The general officer commanding in Halifax had not been included because "Canada is too large and Halifax is at one end." [26] Lansdowne agreed, "[c]onsidering the circumstances of this country," that it would be undesirable to have the general from Halifax as president of the committee.[27]

Caron had rejected General Middleton's suggestion that he should get a regular officer from England to be committee secretary. Instead, he agreed to accept Lieutenant John Irvine Lang, R.E., a graduate of the Canadian Royal Military College and a "very clever young officer," who was attached to the garrison at Halifax but was at that time in British Columbia assisting in surveying and designing defense works at Esquimalt.[28] The gov-

26. Caron, "Report on the Defences of Canada," Jan. 23, 1888, P.A.C., Privy Council 384, Orders-in-Council, Minute; also in P.A.C., R.G. 7, G. 21, Vol. 76, No. 165, Vol. 5.
27. Lansdowne, Confidential, Jan. 30, 1888, P.R.O., C.O. 42/795.
28. Middleton to Cambridge, Jan. 30, 1888, R.A.W., Cambridge Papers, Lieutenant Lang (later called Lang-Hyde) had a distinguished career in the Gold Coast and Nigeria as a military engineer.

ernor general made arrangements with the commander in Halifax to have Lang's part-time services made available without extra cost to British funds.[29] The immediate result was the resignation of Campbell, who refused to serve under Lang. Leaving for Boston, Campbell complained to the governor general that he had been removed "for no cause shown except *trop de zèle*." He said that his aim on the commission had been to show that the British government had repeatedly pressed the question of defense, and especially of the navy, upon the Canadian government. Caron had "so slight appreciation" of Her Majesty's government's wishes concerning defense that "the Home Government may never know how faithfully I have tried to manifest their just demands upon my native country." [30] Campbell was typical of many of those who served the Canadian government in defense matters. Their divided loyalty helps to explain why Canadian politicians were reluctant to make commitments and to intrust important aspects of Canadian policy to the care of men whose allegiance lay elsewhere.

The War Office had urged the Colonial Office to arrange for the Canadian Militia to support the Halifax garrison. A second result of the announcement of the Canadian defense committee was that Lieutenant General Sir John Ross, the general officer commanding in Halifax, said that his plans for the defense of the base could not now rely on the militia because it might be required elsewhere by the Dominion Committee of Defence, of which he was not a member.[31] However, at the governor general's invitation, Ross visited Esquimalt and the Canadian militia schools, and joint exercises were arranged with the militia in support of Halifax. Militia officers were also brought for training in the Halifax citadel.

Ross, however, was signing his letters "Commanding troops in Canada" and even "Commanding troops in the Dominion of Canada." [32] Until 1908, Hart's *Army List* placed the British lieu-

29. Lansdowne to Holland, Feb. 24, 1888; Knutsford to Lansdowne, April 24, 1888, P.A.C., R.G. 7, G. 21, Vol. 76, No. 165, Vol. 5.
30. Campbell to Capt. Wheatfield, March 27, April 17, 1888, *ibid.*
31. Knutsford to Lansdowne, March 15, 1888, *ibid.*
32. Ross to Cambridge, June 26, Oct. 16, 1888; Middleton to Cambridge, March 1, 1889, R.A.W., Cambridge Papers.

tenant general commanding in Halifax under a list of staff for "Canada, comprising all the Provinces adjacent thereto." This might possibly apply in the event of an attack on Canada, but it was not the actual situation in peacetime. Naturally enough, Caron was careful not to do anything that might seem to further the idea that the militia was under the supervision or control of a servant of the British government. It was for this reason that he had hesitated to have the general officer commanding British troops in Halifax as chairman, or even as an ordinary member, of the defense committee. When the new governor general, Lord Stanley of Preston, invited Ross to meet Caron, the talks were cordial and Stanley reported, "We are all friends." But the results had been unsatisfactory for the purpose of the closer association he had in mind.[33] "They will not spend money here and everything is tinged with politics," he explained.

These various difficulties partly explain the lack of progress with the defense committee. But there was another contributing factor as well. Middleton's opinion was that "defence here should be at both ends and perhaps Quebec as it would be impossible for this country to attempt defence against the United States, nor do I think it necessary as I very much think that the two English-speaking nations will never fight one another again." [34] Furthermore, he had been given only an oral order to convene the new Committee of Defence and no terms of reference for it. When the committee met early in 1889, all that it could do was draft a letter asking for instructions.[35] It never met again.

The explanation for this dormancy as given later to the Canadian Cabinet was that one of the members of the committee, the commandant at the Royal Military College, was changed, and that soon afterward the G.O.C. retired. It was therefore deemed advisable to wait until the new G.O.C. could report on his new command, which was not until December 15, 1890. What actually happened was that the commandant at the Royal Military College was removed and his place given "unceremoniously" to

33. Stanley to Cambridge, Dec. 2, 1888, *ibid.*
34. Middleton to Cambridge, Jan. 30, 1888, *ibid.*
35. Middleton to Cambridge, March 1, 1889, *ibid.*

Major General D. R. Cameron, a son-in-law of Sir Charles Tupper.[36] Also Middleton got into hot water over some furs he had seized as booty during the North-West expedition. Charles Bremner, the trapper from whom the furs were seized, was later declared by a Saskatchewan court to have been held by the rebels "under duress." Middleton's excuse that he had never received the furs, and that in any case it had been customary to collect spoils of war in India and China, did not go down very well in Canada. The Liberal Opposition renewed their attacks upon him, and this time he was not as staunchly defended by the government. Caron said the G.O.C. had made an error of judgment; and Macdonald thought the general had behaved foolishly.[37] The scandal inevitably revived the old question of the command of the Canadian Militia. Although Middleton had in fact been the Canadian Cabinet's own nominee, Lansdowne, it will be remembered, had insisted on concealing this fact as much as possible. So when Middleton was in trouble, the practice of British nomination of the G.O.C. was again attacked, and there was renewed pressure for the appointment of a Canadian. Meanwhile, the new Committee of Defence was stillborn.

Macdonald and the State of the Militia

By 1891 the Canadian military establishment was in bad shape. Back in 1878 Macdonald had told Dufferin that he would concentrate on the land forces. Now, after twelve years of his administration, the militia had wasted away for want of supplies. As General Herbert, the next G.O.C., was to tell the Duke of Cambridge after the "Old Chief" died in 1891:

Whilst upholding in the strongest manner politically the idea of the integrity of Canada, as a portion of the British Empire, he would do nothing practically for the defence either of the Dominion or of the Empire. He looked upon money, voted for militia purposes, only as a means of gaining political party ends, but he was honest enough

36. *Ibid.*
37. Canada, House of Commons, *Debates, 1890*, II, 4732–4761; Macdonald to Lorne, Aug. 18, 1890, in Pope, ed., *Correspondence of Sir John Macdonald*, p. 473.

to keep that use of it within strict limits, and consequently cut down the militia estimates to the lowest possible figure.[38]

But this form of honesty only served to increase the difficulty of keeping the militia equipped and trained.

The small Canadian Permanent Force was capable neither of serving as an example to the citizen soldiers nor of training them. Some 54 per cent of the force had served less than two years, 35 per cent less than one year, and only 17 per cent were available as non-commissioned officers and instructors. Low pay and poor conditions of service led to large wastage by men buying themselves out or deserting to the United States. From June, 1890, to June, 1891, when the establishment was 966, the average total effective strength had been 887. During this period, 201 men completed their engagement, but only 122 re-enlisted, while 152 deserted, 128 were convicted by court-martial, 103 bought their discharge, forty-one were discharged as unsuitable or unfit, and eight died.[39] The officers were either political appointees or former British officers who had stayed on when the garrisons left, often because they had married Canadian women. They had no hope of promotion or pension, and they now frequently had large families to maintain with no professional prospects.[40]

The militia itself was in even worse shape. Uniforms, equipment, and weapons dated back to the American Civil War period and were in bad condition. The little money available had been spent on pay and armories or given to particular units for political reasons. Standards of drill and training were generally poor. As the infantry and cavalry schools were organized too long a time after the garrisons departed, they had not gained the prestige and *esprit* of the older artillery batteries and had less influence for good upon the militia. Establishment for the battalions was low, 252 all told, and there were too many non-commissioned officers and bandsmen, so that often there were only fourteen files on parade.[41] "Dinners and convivial meetings . . . supposed

38. July 6, 1891, R.A.W., Cambridge Papers.
39. Canada, *Sessional Papers*, XXV, A, 1892, "Militia Report for 1891," Vol. 12, No. 19, pp. 1–2, 12–13.
40. Herbert to Cambridge, April 19, 1891, R.A.W., Cambridge Papers.
41. Herbert to Cambridge, July 6, 1891, *ibid.*

to keep up the spirit of the force" were frequent, and the city companies tended to become social and political clubs.[42] Regular officers like Herbert were not always able to appreciate the need for a strong social basis for volunteer units. The Act of 1868 and subsequent acts were sound enough, but many of their provisions had fallen into disuse, so that the 40,000 men who were popularly supposed to be in training were a figment of the imagination or of propaganda.[43] When a lecturer at the Royal Colonial Institute mentioned this fact, the chairman, Sir Charles Dilke, "abused Canada" by describing the Canadian Militia as a "mere paper force," thus arousing Lieutenant Colonel George T. Denison, who was present, to fury. This Canadian Militia officer hotly attacked those like Goldwin Smith who had alleged that Canada would not attempt to defend herself against the United States, and he asserted that the spirit of Canadians was unchanged from the days of 1812.[44] Canadian newspapers reported these exchanges, and clippings were brought to the desk of the man who had ultimate responsibility, Sir John A. Macdonald.[45]

Colonel Owen, the speaker who had stirred up the dispute about the militia, had pointed to other deficiencies in Canada's defense policy:

The Dominion of Canada [he said] gives no contribution towards the defence of her commerce, nor has she done much towards the defence of her coast, either on the side of the Atlantic or Pacific, leaving these principally to the protection of our navy. On the Pacific coast the magnificent harbours of British Columbia still wait the necessary works and guns for want of agreement between the Dominion and the mother country.[46]

Despite his professions of belief in the Empire and in the British connection, Macdonald had done little or nothing to increase Canada's part in imperial defense. His willingness to permit re-

42. Herbert to Cambridge, April 19, Oct. 21, 1891, *ibid.*
43. Herbert to Cambridge, Dec. 27, 1891, *ibid.*
44. Col. J. F. Owen, R.A., "The Military Defence Forces of the Colonies," *Proceedings of the Royal Colonial Institute,* XXI (1890), 320–325. His brother, Fred Denison, had heatedly rejected a similar description of the Canadian Militia at the same institute in 1885 (Stacey, *Records of the Nile Voyageurs,* p. 144).
45. St. John *Sun,* and Toronto *Empire,* July 11, 1890, in P.A.C., Macdonald Papers, M.G. 26, A 1 (a), Vol. 332.
46. Owen, "Military Defence Forces . . . ," p. 291.

cruiting for the British Army in Canada has frequently been regarded as a proposed Canadian contribution. But he was not ready to assume any of the costs. He never accepted the principle that Canada had any obligation to protect Canadian mercantile interests at sea or to defend imperial naval bases. He was as careful of Canadian autonomy in military matters as were Laurier and Mackenzie King. He was consistent and sound in his assertion that the militia could only be called out for the defense of Canada, perhaps a wise attitude in view of the fact that the authority for calling it out had been left deliberately vague. If Canada were invaded, there would be no room for differences of opinion. But no provision had been made for lesser, or for more remote, emergencies.

Macdonald had no faith in any form of imperial federalism as a political solution for the structure of the Empire. Never at any time did he make more than a vague profession of belief that Canada's strength was a contribution to the strength of the Empire as a whole; and this could always be interpreted within his concept of the relationship with Britain as that of two autonomous "kingdoms." His failure to build up the military strength of the Canadian kingdom can be accounted for in the first place by the fact that he concentrated on expanding and consolidating the Dominion by other means, and in the second place by the fact that there was no real military threat to the successful achievement of that end. Even his use of the militia for patronage purposes can be explained, if not excused, on these grounds. His chief problem was the presence of two peoples in one nation. For all but about fourteen months of his nineteen years as prime minister of the Dominion, he kept a French-Canadian as his minister of militia and defense, and possibly as a counterpoise to the British officer who, until experienced Canadians were available, must head the force. It seems that this was the old game of checks and balances at which Macdonald was adept.

Even with all its deficiencies, the militia could be thought strong enough to cope with any of the tasks it was likely to face. Only for a short time, around 1878, did Macdonald fear a renewal of Fenian or other border raids. He was less unwilling than Mackenzie to fall back on the use of British troops from Halifax to deal with civil unrest, e.g., that caused by strikers at Lingan in Cape Breton Island in March, 1883. But he said then that the regulars should be replaced by militia as soon as possible.[47] By and large there was not likely to be any disturbance the militia could not handle. The idea of external danger to Canada from the south, as long as Britain was not seriously challenged, was incredible; if Britain got into war with the United States, the danger was irresistible. On the coasts, defense against any attack was merely peripheral and not vital. During Macdonald's period of office, British involvement in Egypt and the Red Sea area was principally, if not solely, due to an inflammable mixture of imperialism and Gladstonian bungling. It did not directly concern Canada. The most serious ruffling of British relations with the United States in this period came as a result of Canadian tariff policies and controversy over fishing rights in which Canada was concerned. The fisheries dispute began about 1885, and in 1887 the Fisheries Commission worked out a modus vivendi with Canada calling the tune. This temporary settlement was renewed from year to year until 1909.[48] When Canadian-induced disputes with the United States could be settled with such relative ease, there was little incentive to build up Canadian defenses merely in order to strengthen Britain's diplomatic hand for general imperial purposes.

Macdonald's refusal to make contribution to the navy was of a different order from his failure to strengthen the foundations of the militia. Not so dependent on sea communications as the Australian colonies, Canada could have made cash contributions to a North American Squadron only at the cost of making the United States apprehensive. Navies and the men to man them could not be built up as rapidly as armies. Yet the concept of a marine militia or reserve had never caught on. The story of the worthless hulk, *Charybdis*, stripped of its ordnance stores when

47. P.A.C., M.G. 26, A 1(c), Vol. 83, pp. 324 ff.; W. A. Stewart MacNutt, *Days of Lorne: From the Private Papers of the Marquis of Lorne 1878–1883 in the Possession of the Duke of Argyll at Inverary Castle, Scotland* (Frederickton, N.B.: Brunswick Press, 1955), pp. 198–199.
48. Harry C. Allen, *Great Britain and the United States: A History of Anglo-American Relations, 1783–1952* (London: Odhams, 1954), pp. 527–531.

given to Canada for the training of reserves in 1880,[49] showed how little regard the Admiralty had for colonial naval reserves as potential reinforcements for the fleet. Caron made an alternative proposal. If the necessity arose for the naval defense of Canada, all that need be done would be the rapid enlargement of the fisheries protection force of two steamers and six schooners "by the embodiment of the hardy sea-faring population of the Dominion." [50] His was a landsman's myth. Still, it is noteworthy that it came after the fisheries dispute with the United States had been temporarily resolved.

Hence, there appeared to be less need to build up a colonial navy in Canada than there was in Australia. And without a colonial navy, the step to colonial naval contributions at one jump was much too big to take. It is obvious that the propaganda of the naval imperialists carried little weight in the vast Canadian land mass.

Herbert and the Canadian Militia

To British and colonial imperial defense enthusiasts, the solution for the difficult problem of securing colonial co-operation in the defense of the Empire was to develop some form of political federation which would allow colonies a voice in foreign policy.[51] Practical politicians were almost all of an opposite opinion because they could see the enormous obstacles in bringing federation about in face of colonial insistence upon the retention of autonomy. But already by the 1890's the ground was being prepared for a quite different solution of the problem—though the exact nature of that solution was not yet clearly understood. When the appointment of a new G.O.C. was being discussed in 1890, Sir John Macdonald wrote to the governor general: "No one is more impressed than I with the importance, nay the necessity of the Canadian Government being completely *en rapport* with the Imperial military authorities on all matters connected

49. W.O. to C.O., Oct. 4, 1880, P.R.O., C.O. 42/765.
50. Canada, Orders-in-Council, Jan. 23, 1888, P.A.C., Privy Council 384.
51. E.g., Thomas Bland Strange, *Gunner Jingo's Jubilee* (London: Remington, 1893), pp. 540–544; H. Armytage, "Federation and Defence," *Young Australia*, IV, No. 7 (July, 1890), 141.

with the national defence." [52] Autonomous dominion governments could, if they wished, maintain co-operation in defense matters without political or military integration or previous commitment. Standardization of equipment, of course, was realized to be essential for successful co-operation between British and colonial forces. It had been recommended by the Carnarvon Commission "to avoid serious embarrassment in war"; but the commission had also noted that it was an expensive undertaking.[53] It is not surprising, therefore, in view of the Canadian government's reluctance to spend money on the militia, that Macdonald did not try very hard to put this principle into practice. Macdonald and his colleagues and successors made a valuable contribution by refusing to be stampeded by popular clamor into appointing as G.O.C. a Canadian who would have lacked experience and prestige, and who might also have political connections. Such an appointment would have made uniformity between British and colonial forces much more difficult to achieve.

In 1890 Macdonald also resisted the very heavy British pressure to accept a British nomination forthwith. Almost before Middleton had resigned, the Duke of Cambridge telegraphed the name of Colonel Ivor Caradoc Herbert of the Grenadier Guards as his successor. Macdonald told the governor general firmly that the Dominion government would make the appointment, but that as in the past his Royal Highness's advice would be received with deference. There were in fact four applicants for the post, all British. The other three were a Colonel Cavaye, "who spoke to someone when passing through," Colonel Hewett, the former commandant at the Royal Military College, Kingston, and Colonel Cameron, who was then commandant of the college.[54] The

52. Aug. 20, 1890, in Pope, ed., *Correspondence of Sir John Macdonald*, p. 475.
53. G.B., W.O., [Earl of Carnarvon], *Royal Commission to Enquire into the Defence of British Possessions Abroad* (London: War Office, 1880–1883), I, 9, 47–50, II, 31, 184.
54. Cambridge to Stanley, July 18, 1890, P.A.C., M.G. 26, A 1 (a), Vol. 90, p. 141; Stanley to Cambridge, Aug. 5, 1890, R.A.W., Cambridge Papers. "Cavaye" was probably Colonel Cavaye, secretary to the Duke of Connaught, the commander in chief of the army in Bombay. A fifth officer had been mentioned, Colonel Robinson, son of a former chief justice of Upper Canada, and one of the Duke of Cambridge's military secretaries; but it was not expected that he would be interested.

former governor general, Lord Lorne, also stepped in to bring his powerful influence to bear upon Macdonald. He urged the appointment of a regular officer, "despite Middleton's *faux pas*," and also that the authorities in Britain, by which he undoubtedly meant the old Duke, should have a voice in the appointment.[55] The governor general was even more outspoken. He told Macdonald that the militia law was excellent, the personnel on the whole were good, but that arms and discipline were inferior. "No one . . . wished to see Canada a great military country, no one would wish to see the estimates largely increased," he said, but a smaller and more efficient force would be preferable to what now existed. "It is openly said that the disposal of the money voted for the Militia is not always that for which it is voted, nor is it influenced only by consideration of the well-being of the force or of its equipment." Men were firing arms that were unsafe. "If we do not keep our eyes open and our hands fairly ready we may have a bitter awakening someday." He said that he would produce a formal memorandum on these points if it was desired; he had not done so hitherto because he had been trying to get Caron to take the initiative himself.[56] However, much of this heavy pressure seems to have been unnecessary. Macdonald was already determined to appoint a regular officer and was merely waiting to discuss the matter in Cabinet.[57] The Duke's nominee, Herbert, was to be the new G.O.C. So despite the shortcomings of earlier British appointees and the political difficulties that had ensued, and despite British pressure which increased suspicion that control was intended, this important link between the Canadian Militia and the British Army was preserved and with it some hope of fostering efficiency and conformity to British practice.

The continuing weakness of Canadian land forces at a time when reform was in the air in Australia and New Zealand was a challenge to both the War Office and the Canadian government. To remedy the situation Herbert seemed an excellent

55. Lorne to Macdonald, July 27, 1890, P.A.C., M.G. 26, A 1 (a), Vol. 90.
56. Stanley to Macdonald, July 21, 1890, *ibid.*, A 109.
57. Pope, ed., *Correspondence of Sir John Macdonald*, pp. 473–475.

choice. Herbert had had a distinguished career in operations in Egypt and as an attaché at St. Petersburg. His qualities are illustrated by the fact that on retirement from the army he went on to an equally distinguished career in politics and received a peerage as Lord Treowen. He was able and energetic and got to know the militia far better than did his predecessors. He rapidly became respected in it, except by a small minority. But his first great advantage was incidental. A change in the Canadian government opened the way for progress. Macdonald died in 1891 and was buried in Kingston with a show of pomp provided by the Canadian Permanent Force and Canadian Militia, both of which he had largely neglected. After he was gone there was a housecleaning and a struggle for power. In consequence of scandals uncovered in the Department of Public Works, Caron was eventually transferred to become postmaster general in 1892, despite his efforts to stay in the militia department. Herbert then found that the fluidity of the political situation and the weakness of the government helped him to regain control of things which his predecessor had allowed to slide into the hands of the minister. Caron's successor, Mackenzie Bowell, was one of the militia officers who had been dismissed by MacDougall twenty-three years before. As a consequence, he might have harbored a grievance against British regulars, but Herbert found him amiable, honest, and willing to learn. There seemed good hope for reform at last.[58]

Herbert was also helped by growing complications abroad. Early in 1891 he noted uneasily a change at the court where he had recently served. The Tsar of Russia signally honored the president of the French Republic; and Herbert feared that an alliance might isolate Britain.[59] Of even greater assistance to him in his purpose was a growing Canadian suspicion about American intentions. The American attitude on the Canadian tariff and several petty border incidents that arose from it, bitter negotiations over the Bering Sea dispute, and the noisy agitation of anti-British minorities in the United States made Canadians

58. Herbert to Cambridge, Oct. 30, Dec. 24, 1892, R.A.W., Cambridge Papers.
59. Herbert to Cambridge, April 19, 1891, *ibid.*

somewhat more willing to look to their defense forces, even though they regarded most of these problems as of British rather than Canadian concern. By July, 1892, Anglo-American relations had deteriorated so much that there was talk of rescinding the Rush-Bagot Agreement. The Admiralty vetoed the move, but only because it thought it would react against British interests to take so drastic an action when the Americans had better facilities for construction on the Great Lakes.[60] Herbert did not think that the Americans would "ever deliberately initiate an aggressive military policy against Canada." He said that they understood a *"Finanz-krieg"* better than a "real war"; but he was glad to take advantage of the contemporary state of feeling to further his purpose—the strengthening of Canadian land forces. Already in 1891 he had improved the militia camps by placing them directly under headquarters control.[61] Aided by the growing Canadian suspicion of the United States, he then set to work to overhaul the Canadian Permanent Force. In 1892 the cavalry, artillery (formerly with no organization above the battery or its equivalent), and the infantry were set up as regiments. In 1893 the practice of sending officers and men to England for courses was resumed on a regular basis. In 1894 the new Royal Regiment of Canadian Infantry was brought together in camp at Lévis.[62] A British regular officer, Major Percy Lake, was appointed quartermaster general in 1893 with the local rank of lieutenant colonel.[63]

To give Canada a more effective military force, the militia itself had to be reformed and reorganized. From the beginning, Herbert had been aware that reform would mean the reduction of a large number of higher ranks and of the political patronage they represented.[64] He had therefore held back his first annual report until Caron was out of the way lest the minister make use of it to try to save his own place by forcing Herbert's resignation. The new minister, Bowell, accepted the report after

60. Admiralty to C.O., June 25, 1892, P.R.O., C.O. 42/812.
61. Herbert to Cambridge, Oct. 21, 1891, April 11, 1892, R.A.W., Cambridge Papers.
62. Stanley, *Canada's Soldiers*, pp. 265–269.
63. W.O. to C.O., May 23, 1893, P.R.O., C.O. 42/819.
64. Herbert to Cambridge, July 6, 1891, R.A.W., Cambridge Papers.

Herbert had toned down criticism of the staff.[65] Bowell thereby virtually committed himself to reform. A tour of inspection in Herbert's company opened his eyes to "the terrible state of military impotence into which this country has fallen. Empty stores, barracks and fortifications going to ruin and money spent for no other purpose than to provide for political supporters." [66] However, as a result of another Cabinet shuffle, Bowell was replaced by James C. Patterson, a younger man with little experience or influence, who horrified Herbert by his indolence. The soldier was shocked that the minister stayed in bed until 11 A.M. or 12 noon. Even so, as Patterson was impressionable, Herbert hoped to be able to continue with the reform program that he had marked out. And he made one great step forward. He succeeded in getting Patterson to agree to a settlement of the negotiations over Esquimalt.[67] In a very optimistic frame of mind, Herbert went to England to get the British government to accept the proposed settlement.

Esquimalt and Halifax

To reach an agreement on Esquimalt with Patterson "in less weeks than the previous years of discussion" was a personal triumph for Herbert. The question had been on the table for fifteen years and under discussion for eight.[68] The story of the protracted negotiations illuminates British and Canadian views on imperial problems. The Admiralty had insisted against contrary opinion that Esquimalt was an essential naval base and must be defended, but it had continued to assert that the defense of naval bases was not its business. New coal mines at Nanaimo caused Canada to become concerned about defenses.[69] But protection of coal that might be used by enemy navies could also be regarded as an imperial matter. However, British policy aimed at persuading Canada to accept a larger share of the costs. There-

65. Herbert to Cambridge, April 11, 1892, *ibid.*
66. Herbert to Cambridge, Oct. 30, 1892, *ibid.*
67. Herbert to Cambridge, Dec. 24, 1892, June 21, 1894, *ibid.*
68. Aberdeen, Confidential, Feb. 12, 1895, P.R.O., C.O. 42/829.
69. Smith to Chapleau, March 28, 1885, P.A.C., R.G. 7, G. 21, Vol. 76, No. 65, Vol. 4 (c).

fore, as has been said earlier, the Colonial Defence Committee proposed in 1885 that Britain should assist Canada to build the defenses which, following the Carnarvon thesis, would be available if Britain had need of them.[70] In 1886 a War Office committee offered a compromise. If Canada would construct and man the defenses, the committee suggested, the British government should then provide armament and appoint a commander.[71]

In 1887 "C" Battery, a permanent unit of the Canadian Artillery authorized in 1883, arrived in Victoria from Kingston. As it was not possible for Canada to find enough regular artillerymen to man the guns on a permanent basis, the Admiralty agreed in 1888 to lend Canada seventy-five Royal Marines, including fifteen submarine mine experts, at an annual charge of £6,978. Britain would supply the arms and ammunition in the first instance, would build mine stores, and would supervise the works; Canada would build defense works, maintain a garrison, provide barracks for the garrison, and keep the guns and defenses in repair.[72] Caron's reason for placing "C" Battery in Victoria had been to stimulate the growth of the Canadian militia system in British Columbia. He obtained a promise that the British marines would instruct the militiamen in the use of mines and torpedoes, and he admitted that this arrangement signified an apparent Canadian interest in the defense of the base. The Royal Marines selected for Esquimalt were sent to Chatham for training; when they completed their course, however, they were not sent to Canada because barrack accommodations had not yet been provided for them there. Caron had balked at providing the housing at Canada's expense. Local wage rates made it imposssible to use the militia to man the guns, but the minister was said to be still trying to find Canadian Permanent Force artillerymen.[73] As Canada had

70. C.D.C., Memorandum No. 2 M, May 4, 1885, P.R.O., Cab. 11/27.
71. G.B., W.O., "Report of Committee on Colonial Garrisons," Confidential Papers, A 66/1866, Para. 35.
72. Longstaff, *Esquimalt Naval Base,* p. 46; C.O. to Admiralty, Sept. 8, 1888, P.R.O., W.O. 32/500/57, Gen. 1482; Admiralty to C.O., April 4, 20, 1889, *ibid.;* C.O. to Governor General, May 2, 1889, *ibid.*
73. Précis of Privy Council Report 1902 G in reply to C.O. dispatch, May 2, 1889, P.A.C., R.G. 7, G. 21, No. 165, Vol. 4 (b), 1880–1887; Privy Council Report 1960 G to C.O., June 24, 1889, *ibid.;* Stanley, Confidential, Aug. 13, 14, 15, 1889, P.R.O., C.O. 42/800; C.O. to W.O., Sept. 23, 1889, P.R.O., W.O. 32/500/57, Gen. 1483; C.O. to Stanley, Nov. 7, 1889, *ibid.;* Stanley to C.O., Dec. 31, 1891, P.A.C., R.G. 7, G. 21, No. 165, Vol. 6 (b), 1890–1896.

not yet formally agreed to hire the marines, the base remained virtually defenseless.

The Admiralty argued that by the proposed arrangement for Esquimalt, more was being done for Canada (which already had an imperial base on its East coast) than for any other colony. Hong Kong, Singapore, Mauritius, and Ceylon paid for all their works of defense, barracks, etc., and also made "military contributions." Caron retorted that the base was being defended for imperial purposes. As a result of the haggle over paying for the garrison, no progress was made with the defense works that Canada had agreed to provide. In January, 1892, Lord Stanley, the governor general of Canada, advised the colonial secretary that nothing more could be expected from Caron who was not likely to stay long in office. He would have been transferred already had it not been for the delays that had followed the death of Macdonald.[74]

Then in the same year the Admiralty suddenly announced that its offer of marine artillerymen as instructors did not mean it would assume responsibility for the defense of the base. A Colonial Office minute pointed out that their lordships were in fact asking Canada to pay for certain gunners who were to be kept in England and employed there and were only to be sent to reinforce the base in an emergency: [75] this was the same policy that had been followed by the Admiralty during the negotiation of the Australian naval contribution.

The Esquimalt discussions had been in this state of impasse for some time before Herbert reported that he would attempt to work out a compromise. Sydenham Clarke, secretary of the Colonial Defence Committee, feared lest through lack of knowledge of the background Herbert might agree to unacceptable changes.[76] What Herbert had in view was an increase in the British government's contribution to the defenses in return for a definite limitation upon its ultimate obligations. Canada would provide sites

---

74. Knutsford to Stanley, Nov. 7, 1889, P.A.C., R.G. 7, G. 21, No. 165, Vol. 5, 1888–1889; Nov. 31, 1891, *ibid.*, Vol. 6 (a); Stanley to Knutsford, Jan. 22, 1891, *ibid.*, Vol. 6 (b), 1890–1896; W.O. to C.O., Dec. 18, 1890, P.R.O., W.O. 32/500/57, Gen. 1482.
75. Admiralty, April 18, 1892, P.R.O., C.O. 42/812.
76. G. S. Clarke, Minute on Canadian Commons' Debates, May, 1892, P.R.O., C.O. 42/811.

and £10,000 toward barrack buildings. Those already built would be taken over at a valuation in part payment. Canada would contribute half of the estimated cost of £60,000 for the defense works and half of the annual cost of maintenance, which was expected to run to £1,000 a year. Canada would pay £7,000 a year for seventy-five marines to be lent by the Admiralty and would arrange in addition to have one hundred Canadian Permanent Force artillerymen ready for immediate transport to Esquimalt in an emergency. The local militia would be reorganized to provide an additional four hundred men when needed. But the base would be under British control. Herbert also congratulated himself that the works would be built by Britain, which would serve to eliminate the graft so common in Canadian public life.[77]

Herbert's success in getting constructive proposals from Patterson and the Canadian Cabinet after all the obstruction that had been evident on both sides was a tribute to his diplomatic skill. But he found the settlement of apparently easier problems on the opposite coast a more difficult matter. Esquimalt was useless in an American war and of doubtful value in any other conflict; to secure Canadian support for it was therefore an empty triumph. On the other hand, the British base at Halifax was probably already more powerful than was necessary in the event of either an American or a European war as long as Britain remained mistress of the seas. In 1889 a local garrison defense committee, which had been appointed in response to a Colonial Defence Committee directive, had stated its opinion that the only danger of an attack on Halifax would be as a consequence of war with the United States, and then, in view of the weakness of the United States Navy, their only fear would be of a land attack. Ignoring the great difficulty involved in such an attack, the local committee pointed out that defense of the Canadian frontier required close co-operation with the Canadian Militia.[78]

77. Memorandum, "Defence of Canada," Jan., 1899, P.A.C., Minto Papers, M.G. 27, II B1, Vol. 9, Pt. II, p. 6; Herbert to Cambridge, Dec. 24, 1892, R.A.W., Cambridge Papers.

78. C.D.C., "Report of Local Committee, Halifax," April 8, 1889, No. 31R, P.R.O., Cab. 11/27.

Hence, when Herbert sought to have militiamen trained in submarine mining by the experts in the Halifax garrison, the War Office delayed answering for two years because it wanted in exchange some more positive agreement, preferably in the form of legislation, that Canada would supply the militia as reinforcements if Halifax were attacked.[79] In 1894, when the Halifax defense scheme was sent for revision to the Colonial Defence Committee, nothing had been done, and the need for arranging for reinforcements from the militia had to be mentioned again.[80]

The root of the trouble in developing a defense plan was that the real function of Halifax in relation to Canada's interests was as a naval base from which a British fleet could threaten American shipping and the American coast. Such a potential result from maintaining the force there presented Canada with grave misgivings. Canadians had good reason to want to avoid irritating their great neighbor; they found it difficult, therefore, to accept the idea that they must support measures that, if the worst happened, would only provide opportunity for a British naval offensive against the United States while their own land frontier was threatened. In view of this dilemma, Canadian lethargy in providing military support for the base is understandable, if not necessarily justifiable. Apparently no one in Britain or Canada thought of the Halifax base as a necessary link in the communication from North America to Britain rather than in the reverse direction. Any suggestion that its value might be connected with Canadian participation in European wars would have alienated large sections of the Canadian population. Halifax's actual use in the future was therefore not anticipated in these discussions.

The Fall of Herbert

Neither the Halifax nor the Esquimalt agreements were yet complete. There were to be further squabbles about details, and

79. Stanley, Telegram, June 25, 1891, P.R.O., C.O. 42/806; W.O. to C.O., June 30, 1891, *ibid.*; Stanley, Confidential, Dec. 19, 1891, *ibid.*; W.O. to C.O., Feb. 10, 1892, *ibid.*, C.O. 42/813; Stanley, Confidential, April 29, 1892, *ibid.*, C.O. 42/811; W.O. to C.O., Feb. 6, Nov. 18, 1892, *ibid.*, C.O. 42/813.
80. C.D.C., Minutes, "Halifax Defence Scheme, Jan., 1894," July 4, 1894, P.R.O., Cab. 11/27.

neither agreement was to be long lasting. But when Herbert returned from England with a British acceptance in principle of the Canadian government's proposals for Esquimalt, he seemed to have gone a long way toward finding a solution for one of the most vexing problems of co-operative imperial defense. He was therefore taken aback when he found himself slighted in every possible way by Patterson. He learned that because an election was in the offing, the reductions in district militia staffs that he had arranged had been cancelled during his absence. As a result, he jumped to the conclusion that the Cabinet had also changed its mind about the Esquimalt agreement. However, mistakenly feeling secure in a belief that he could not be summarily dismissed by the Canadian government without the previous sanction of the commander in chief, he ignored vexations which he believed were deliberately introduced in order to get him to resign.[81] Through Lord Aberdeen, the new governor general, Herbert obtained a confrontation with Patterson. By this means, mutual misunderstandings were removed. Herbert then reported to the Duke of Cambridge that Patterson liked him personally, but that the young Cabinet member was a very difficult man with whom to work. Herbert also put his finger on probably the most important difficulty in the way of militia reform at that moment: a new trade depression had made reduction of expenditures once again inevitable.[82] The reconciliation of the G.O.C. and the minister meant that progress toward the Esquimalt agreement went ahead again, though there were still some disputes, notably over Canada's refusal to pay the transportation costs of the families of the marines.[83]

Although Herbert had been reconciled with Patterson, he had, in fact, begun to run into the same kind of trouble that his predecessors—and also commandants in other colonies—had experienced, namely, opposition from the militia units which he had wanted to reduce. His efforts to reduce the proportion of

81. Herbert to Cambridge, Nov. 28, 1893, Feb. 8, 1894, R.A.W., Cambridge Papers.
82. Aberdeen to Cambridge, Feb. 13, 1894; Herbert to Cambridge, June 21, 1894, *ibid.*
83. Aberdeen, 33, Feb. 4, 1895, P.R.O., C.O. 42/829.

officers and non-commissioned officers and to enforce proper qualification for promotion had brought upon him the wrath of political colonels in the House of Commons. When he spoke in French in Quebec about the *esprit* shown by the Canadians who had gone overseas to defend the pope as "Pontifical Zouaves," he pleased his French-Canadian audience but annoyed Orangemen. His dismissal of the inefficient and absentee militia colonel of a Belleville unit led to accusations that he was persecuting a sick man who had gone to the United States for the sake of his health. Finally, he suspended the adjutant general, Colonel Walker Powell, for signing—without the initials of the minister and while Herbert was ill—an important order which cancelled summer training in order to pay for new rifles. This action was followed by his departure to England "on leave." In the ensuing debate in the House, the disciplinary powers of the G.O.C. were discussed at length, and some members even argued that he had no right to suspend an officer from duty. Herbert's reason for suspending Powell was never given to the House. His letter to the minister was marked "Confidential" and could not be communicated because Powell had not given his side of the story. Whatever Powell's fault may have been—and it may be that he had been too long in his appointment—the fact that he had served as senior or second senior officer in the Canadian Militia for thirty-two years made Herbert's arbitrary action against him seem tactless and perhaps even arrogant.[84]

A year was to pass before the public learned of another incident which had been carefully hushed up at the time it occurred. Herbert, having read in the newspapers that Britain needed reinforcements for the garrison at Hong Kong, proposed to Patterson that Canada should supply them from the Canadian Permanent Force. The minister, without consulting his colleagues or sounding out the Colonial Office, rushed off a telegram making an offer. The War Office, which apparently had no desire to have four companies of Canadians thrust upon it, promptly rejected the proposal. This rejection came to the great relief of Sir John Thompson, the Canadian prime minister, who when he had

84. Canada, House of Commons, *Debates, 1894,* II, 5496–5497, 6155–6190.

heard of Patterson's offer had felt obliged to give it official confirmation. However, Sir Robert Meade, permanent undersecretary for colonies, wanted to grasp an opportunity to "gush" over what could be represented as yet another magnificent gesture by a colony to come to the aid of the mother country. But the Liberals were in office in England, and their secretary of state for war was Campbell-Bannerman, who, typically, had regarded the proposal from the first as an unwarranted intrusion by Herbert, a soldier, into political matters. He therefore opposed publicity, and Lord Rosebery, the colonial secretary, agreed with him.[85]

After a period of leave in England, Herbert resigned without returning to Canada. The circumstances of his going are clouded in mystery. A new militia minister, A. R. Dickey, who had succeeded when Patterson was sent to Manitoba as lieutenant governor, told the Commons that Herbert had not resigned, but that he did not expect him to return as G.O.C.[86] There is a possible explanation of Herbert's decision not to return to fight his case. In England he found that his patron, the Duke of Cambridge, on whom he had previously depended for protection, was himself on the point of being forced out of the command to which he had clung for so long. It was one of the last acts of the Liberals in Britain before losing office themselves. Aberdeen's dispatch asking for nomination of a new G.O.C. for the Canadian Militia arrived in England only a few days before the Duke's resignation took effect.[87] Herbert had also lost the confidence of the Conservative government in Canada; and his greater enemies, the Canadian Liberals, were soon to take over. Furthermore, he had little faith in Lord Aberdeen, the new governor general, whose liberal ideas were poles apart from his own.

Herbert's efforts to strengthen the Canadian Militia had been aimed primarily at strengthening the Empire, and perhaps inevitably they had come to seem to imply infringements upon Canadian autonomy. His letters to the Duke show that in the negotiations about Esquimalt he looked forward to the establish-

85. Guy R. MacLean, "The Canadian Offer of Troops for Hong Kong," *Canadian Historical Review*, XXXVIII (1958), 275–283.
86. Canada, House of Commons, *Debates*, 1895, I, 2137.
87. Aberdeen, Telegram, June 16, 1895, P.R.O., C.O. 42/830.

ment of a British base on Vancouver Island and the complete withdrawal of Canadian artillerymen.[88] Much as the Canadian government wanted to transfer to Britain the bill for building defenses, it could not favor complete loss of control. Esquimalt, unlike Halifax, had been partly constructed and was partly maintained by Canada. In the East, Herbert wanted to put the Nova Scotia Militia permanently under the orders of the general commanding British troops in Halifax. To create a precedent for this action, he deliberately seized upon the occasion of the funeral of the prime minister, Sir John Thompson, to hand over the militia for three days and to attach Canadian staff officers from Ottawa to the Halifax staff.[89] It was an interesting and successful experiment in imperial co-operation, prophetic of future co-operation in war; but Herbert was out of touch with political reality if he thought it could be applied permanently in time of peace. How far Herbert's imperialism had made him *persona non grata* in Canada is not clear. His fall suggests that a British regular officer had to be more than a good soldier, and even more than a successful diplomat, if he would succeed as G.O.C. of the Canadian Militia. Patterson wrote in testimony to Herbert's soldierly qualities: "In a democratic country such as Canada it is hard to dissociate the Militia Force from the Active Politics of the hour. Herbert is a soldier and not a politician." [90] A British G.O.C. of the Canadian Militia, if he did his job energetically, could hardly avoid appearing to act in imperial interests. Therefore, he inevitably raised problems of civil control of military power, and when these were added to an appearance of imperial interference in colonial affairs the result was a head-on conflict which the soldier was bound to lose. Although the imperial G.O.C.'s, whose aid could not yet be dispensed with, did much to stimulate the military spirit and disseminate military knowledge, and although they strengthened the imperial zest of those Canadians who were already imperially minded, the incidents in which they became involved stirred a contrary feeling in many

88. Admiralty to C.O., Dec. 13, 1892, *ibid.*, C.O. 42/812.
89. Herbert to Cambridge, Jan. 16, 1895, R.A.W., Cambridge Papers.
90. Patterson to Aberdeen, Jan. 24, 1895, *ibid.*

nationalist breasts. As for the development of Canada's land forces, Herbert had managed to reorganize the tiny Canadian Permanent Force, but he had failed with the militia, which was still a long way from being an army ready-trained and organized to take the field. The naval bases at Esquimalt and Halifax were not yet defended as he had hoped they would be. Nevertheless, he had made a great contribution to Canadian military development. He could not do more because Canadians were not yet spurred by a sense of urgency. European dangers were too remote.

Herbert's failure was, however, due to something more than the existence of strong ideas in the War Office about the need for control of the army that was being built up in Canada in a completely new setting. The British government was preoccupied with larger questions of defense of the Empire and failed to look at the particular problems of Canadian defense. Britain failed to do so partly because it had not yet set up a proper command system for the army at home. It had also failed to arrange for effective military and naval co-operation, especially in the joint presentation of defense policy and requirements to the British Cabinet. In view of these shortcomings of a government which had long experience of war and international politics, it is not surprising that the less experienced government in Ottawa also failed to examine all the implications of Canada's defenseless position and did not organize a military system capable of coping with them. Perhaps the greatest obstacle to Canada's military progress was a lack of clarity about the nature of the danger. The dangers that threatened the Empire and the comparatively minor insurgency that disturbed Canada internally might, after all, yet be secondary to a closer menace—an American invasion. Until the reality of any one of these dangers was established, Canadian defense planning was always difficult. Military co-operation with Britain in time of peace led inevitably to squabbles and frustration.

7

"The Necessity for an Army as well as a Navy . . ."

Naval imperialists in the last quarter of the nineteenth century frequently minimized the role of land forces in imperial defense; and historians, impressed by the significance of sea power, have been inclined to follow suit. However, during that period the British soldier was continually marching or fighting in colonial wars. The North-West Frontier of India saw fighting almost all the time; British troops also were in Afghanistan (1878–1880) and Burma (1885) to secure the possession of India. In South Africa the army fought the Gaika and Galeka War (1877), the Zulu War (1879–1880), the First Boer War (1880–1881), and the Matabele War (1893). Further north, British troops were busy in Egypt and the Sudan (1882–1885 and 1898–1899), in Gambia (1891–1892), in Ashanti (1873–1874 and 1895–1896), in Sierra Leone (1899), and in Somaliland (1900–1901). In all these little wars the navy played the important but nevertheless passive role of maintaining communications. Yet in 1896 a soldier, Captain Walter Haweis James of the Royal Engineers, found it necessary to speak at the Royal United Service Institution on "The Necessity for an Army as well as a Navy for the Maintenance of the Empire." The Colomb brothers and several admirals were there. They rose in quick succession to defend vigorously what one of them nevertheless admitted was an epidemic of "naval fever." The navy, Sir John Colomb said, was "your only line of defence in a sea empire, for the protection of the oceans and seas in the world. There is no other, there can be no other." [1]

1. Capt. Walter Haweis James, "The Necessity for an Army as well as a Navy for the Maintenance of the Empire," *R.U.S.I. Journal*, XL (1896), 707. Captain James was the author of *A Handbook of Tactics* (London: Gale and Polden,

Despite this powerful naval broadside, Captain James was not overwhelmed. He was fortunate to have in the chair an influential backer, the new commander in chief of the British army, Lord Wolseley, who spoke approvingly of his thesis. Wolseley and James were concerned not so much with the small colonial wars, like that which the army was currently fighting in Ashantiland, but with the possibility of a major European conflagration. They feared that Britain might have to fight continental powers whose armies were swollen by conscription. James calculated that with a population of thirty-eight million, the total of the available troops at home, including reserves, was 531,000. Of these, only the regulars were available for an expeditionary force. When allowance was made for about 15 per cent being unfit or not fully trained, he thought that Britain would be able to field 150,000 men, a mere handful by contrast with the armies of the European powers.[2] James thus saw a little farther than the naval imperialists. If the Royal Navy failed to deter an enemy, he might have to be fought on land. But for that purpose the army simply did not exist. Here was the Achilles' heel of reliance upon a maritime strategy. Sea power was important. But if the army were neglected, sea power by itself might not be enough. James therefore made certain proposals for increasing the size and effectiveness of the British Army. In view of the fact that the danger which he postulated was to become a reality in 1914, his views and suggestions must be given some credence by historians who have the advantage of looking at them with hindsight.

James also criticized the colonies for not doing what they could and should to furnish land forces for the defense of the Empire. He said that with a population of ten million, the colonies had only 91,000 troops, very few of whom were regulars. Canada, with a population of five million, had 32,000 in its militia and only a thousand regulars. It can be seen that on a strict numerical proportion with Britain, the colonies could have provided 140,000 troops, of whom about 40,000 would have been

1883, etc.); he later wrote *Modern Strategy* (Edinburgh: Blackwood, 1903, 1904) and *The Campaign of 1815, Chiefly in Flanders* (Edinburgh: Blackwood, 1903).
2. James, *Handbook of Tactics*, p. 700.

permanent force soldiers. In each case, half would have been Canadians. It should be noted that according to *The Army Book for the Empire*, a semi-official publication from which James seems to have got his statistics, Canada had 200,000 men who had served with the colors and who, by the Canadian Militia Law, were liable for service in defense of Canada.[3] Nevertheless, James's evidence, based on troops actually in training or on immediate recall, shows that there was wide difference between the numbers of soldiers immediately available in the colonies as compared with those in Britain.

In fact, the disparity was actually considerably greater than he stated. His figure of 91,000 colonial soldiers, taken from a compilation published in 1893, includes 48,315 for Canada, Victoria, and New South Wales, the three biggest colonies.[4] The remainder could not possibly bring the number up to 91,000. Three years earlier a more precise table had given the strength of colonial land forces as 78,000. One of the tables appended actually gives 79,967, or almost 80,000. This figure, however, is also not a safe one with which to work. For among other discrepancies there is the fact that it includes a total of 38,238 for the Canadian Militia in a year in which only about 8,000 actually performed the quite inadequate training in camp.[5] Variations in the figures given by these advocates of greater military preparation can be explained by the difficulty they experienced in obtaining and interpreting data. Yet, however inaccurate and unreliable the figures may be, the fact is that the imperialists obviously understated their own case. Another method of comparison was provided by Sir Charles Dilke when his paper on the strength of colonial forces was given at the Colonial Institute. He declared that whereas Britain spent £38 million on defense, and India spent £20 million, the colonies altogether spent only £2 million. Dilke's figures included the cost of the navy which was still regarded as largely a British

3. Lt. Gen. W. H. Goodenough and Lt. Col. J. C. Dalton, *The Army Book for the British Empire: A Record of the Development and Present Composition of the Military Forces and Their Duties in Peace and War* (London: H.M.S.O., 1893), p. 482.
4. *Ibid.*, pp. 481–485.
5. Owen, "Military Defence Forces . . . ," pp. 278, 303; Canada, *Sessional Papers*, XXV, A, 1892, Vol. 12, No. 19, pp. 3, 15.

responsibility and was by far the greatest element in the defense budget. But they emphasize the difference in the size of the burdens borne by the mother country and her colonies.[6] According to a Canadian statement, the amount of taxation devoted to military purposes in Britain in 1894 was 23.6 per cent as compared to 14 per cent in the United States, 37.3 per cent in Germany and 27.5 per cent in France. For the British colonies the percentages were Cape Colony, 8.3 per cent; Natal, 26.6 per cent; the Australian colonies altogether, 4.5 per cent; and New Zealand, 2.6 per cent. In 1895 Canada spent 5.8 per cent of her budget on defense.[7] Thus, apart from Natal which had local native problems, it was freely admitted that all colonies spent much less on defense than did European countries. The explanation usually given was that they had other needs—for instance, public works —and less responsibility. Moreover, they were in less immediate danger. By this reckoning, Canada's defense contribution was one of the largest. Canada at this time was the only federally organized member of the Empire, and provincial spending was presumably not taken into account in recording the amount of the budget of which defense was a part. The percentage of all government spending was thus less favorable to Canada than these figures suggest.

Britain and Colonial Land Forces

Such small forces as existed in the colonies in the 1890's were not at the disposal of the imperial government. Cartier's careful consolidation of Canadian control of the Canada Militia had anticipated the position taken by all colonies on this subject. There were arrangements for putting colonial forces under the command of a British general in the event of war, but colonial forces were provided primarily for the defense of the colony. Plans for assignment to a British commander were based on the assumption that colonial troops would be attached as auxiliaries to a British relieving force. Apart from a few militia colonels

6. Owen, "Military Defence Forces . . . ," p. 316.
7. Canada, *Sessional Papers, XXXIII,* 1899, Department of Militia and Defence, "Report for 1898," Appendix H, Vol. 13, No. 19, p. 57.

"anxious for excitement or notoriety," who (probably without asking what the men in the ranks thought) spasmodically volunteered their units for service with British expeditionary forces,[8] few people considered that the colonial forces should be established for service outside their own borders unless, perhaps, it was in their immediate vicinity. Colonial governments had no responsibilities in the many small colonial wars fought by Britain in remote lands. In larger conflagrations the extent to which a colony would participate was a matter for its own decision. Colonial forces were part of a system of imperial defense only if and when their political masters and colonial electorates chose to make them available.

The Right Honorable Hugh Childers, who had been a civil servant in Victoria, and who had also headed both the War Office and the Admiralty, had hailed in 1890 "the tendency of the last few years to concentrate the control over our military and naval forces." As he said this when he was chairman of the session of the Royal Colonial Institute in London at which Colonel Owen spoke on "The Military Defence Forces of the Colonies,"[9] Childers might be assumed to have been referring to centralized control over colonial forces as well as of those at home. In fact, however, he was wrong in both instances. The Colonial Defence Committee established in 1885 exercised no control; and the Admiralty and the War Office operated quite independently of each other and were to continue to do so for many years. A Joint Naval and Military Committee of serving officers was used from time to time on an *ad hoc* basis to attempt to solve problems which called for co-operation between the two services. In 1895, however, the Cabinet had to set up a defense committee to make another attempt to pull them together, though without appreciable success.[10] Childers' satisfaction at the moves toward concentrated control was merely typical of the wishful thinking of imperial defense enthusiasts. Concentrated control of the land

8. Macdonald to Tupper, March 12, 1885, in *Canadian Historical Review,* XXXIII (Dec., 1952), 336.
9. Owen, "Military Defence Forces . . . ," p. 325.
10. Zara Shakow, "The Defence Committee: A Forerunner of the Committee of Imperial Defence," *Canadian Historical Review,* XXXVI (1955), 36–44.

forces of the British Empire was a very remote objective, and one that was indeed quite out of reach in time of peace.

For many reasons, imperial organization for the use of colonial land forces in the service of the Empire was even more difficult to accomplish than organization of an imperial navy. Not only was there no simple but powerful strategic theory like the doctrine of sea power (supremacy at sea is the key to colonial defense, and unity of command is imperative since the seas are one), but the various land forces were scattered and rarely came into contact. The land forces had much less need than the navy for complicated equipment, and their chief function of local defense did not require as much preliminary planning. Furthermore, the War Office was even less adequately organized than the Admiralty for planning strategy and military development.

In 1890 the Hartington Royal Commission offered a proposal to establish a new department, free from executive functions, which would control the army and plan its employment in war. The relationship of the proposed department to the commander in chief of the army, the Duke of Cambridge, was deliberately obscure because the authors of the plan feared to offend him. At the same time, Campbell-Bannerman, a Liberal member, wrote a minority report against the proposed reform: he thought it might be a step toward the establishment of a Prussian-type general staff which would endanger civilian control of the army. When the enforced resignation of the Duke of Cambridge in 1895 opened the way for a change of the kind proposed by the commissioners, his successor, Wolseley, who objected to civilian interference, resisted efforts to elevate a board or council that would reduce his status.[11] There was also the Department of Military Intelligence, set up in 1873, but it did not have the authority a general staff would have carried, and was responsible only for the collection of information. In 1886 a mobilization section was added, but there was no provision for the special task of preparing the army in peace for its role in war. In fact, until after the South African War of 1899–1902, there was no

11. Ensor, *England 1870–1914*, pp. 291–292; St. Aubyn, *The Royal George*, pp. 282–287.

adequate staff at the War Office to plan Britain's own military strategy and make preparations for war, let alone to guide or direct colonies on the part they should play in a future war.

The channel of communication from the War Office to the colonies was through the Colonial Office, whose efforts to improve colonial defenses were powerfully aided after 1885 by the Colonial Defence Committee. However, in the early 1890's the committee was still only in the stage of collecting information and calling for local defense plans. These it returned through the Colonial Office with comments collected from the War Office and the Admiralty. This piecemeal procedure inevitably meant that the defense problems of the colonies were still looked at separately, even though, it is true, they were now examined through imperial spectacles and, as time passed, with the benefit of a widening experience. The committee did no over-all strategic planning and little over-all strategic thinking, except insofar as it accepted the prevailing doctrine of the overriding importance of sea power. The local defense plans which it examined were naturally defensive rather than offensive, and though there were references to the idea that offense was the best form of defense, such concepts affected defense planning only in limited ways. Apart from occasional reference in speeches to the future "expansion of the Empire," the general approach of British statesmen, and even more of colonial statesmen, was defensive. Hence, although sea power would make possible the defense of the center and outlying parts of the Empire and would also permit the launching of counterattacks, the use of colonial forces for such purposes was at first rarely considered except as a vague future possibility or as a vague proposal to seize potential enemy bases nearby.

There were many reasons for these limitations in planning. First, colonial forces were not considered competent to undertake offensive operations. Second, colonial resistance might have developed against any premature discussion of such proposals. Third, and probably most important of all, the international situation had not yet crystallized sufficiently to identify the Empire's chief potential enemy; the scale of future expeditionary forces that might be required had thus not yet been realized.

Ever since the withdrawal of the garrisons, Britain had used her influence through those means that remained to her to persuade the colonies to build up forces to fill the gap left in their defenses. The Colonial Office, the governors in the colonies, the Colonial Defence Committee, the Admiralty and the War Office, the commander in chief, G.O.C.'s, commandants, and other regular officers in colonial service—all worked steadily toward this end. Colonial conferences and pressure upon visiting statesmen moved in the same direction. Even the subtle flattery of charming society hostesses was called into play in Britain. But it was the colonial governments themselves that had the final word in defense planning, and they were already very much harassed by the financial problems and by the local demands incidental to the development of new countries. Furthermore, they were extremely sensitive about their freedom of action. British influence must be exerted tactfully lest it have the reverse effect to that intended. Ultimately, the development of colonial land forces depended upon convincing colonial electorates of the need to spend more money on defense.

Colonial Attitudes

The factors influencing defense policy in the various self-governing colonies differed greatly. In Canada, as has been seen, the dominating concern was the uncomfortable nearness of a potential enemy. But as time went on the United States seemed less and less likely to resort to aggressions unless aroused by British policies unconnected with Canada. Traditional and inherited Canadian determination not to be swallowed up by the United States stimulated a certain interest in preparation to resist an invading force that would probably be overwhelming if it came; but it was difficult in peacetime to cast Canadians in the role of a "forlorn hope" merely to strengthen British diplomacy vis-á-vis the United States. Coastal defense was relatively less important than land defense for Canada; and military reinforcement from the interior, being likely to arrive too late to prevent raids or invasion, seemed hardly worth preparing. Provision of land forces to furnish military power to complete the pattern of Canadian autonomy was a concept that had little appeal. A few military enthusiasts were inspired to press for a more vigorous defense policy, usually with the idea of strengthening the British Empire as a whole or of preparing to resist the United States. But many of these men were possibly motivated by the desire for military rank, for soldiering as a pastime, or for the good fellowship of the militia unit. Political patronage in the militia, which flourished so vigorously and to which regular soldiers objected so much, was not the chief reason for the existence of the militia, but it helped to make its existence possible, even if it also tended to make the militia less efficient.

In Australia and New Zealand, on the other hand, distance from potential foes was the dominant factor in the planning of defense and meant that these countries relied upon sea power. Despite frequent professional reassurances about the impossibility of a major invasion, fear of bombardment or raids persisted and led to debates about the nature and size of the forces that should be used to deter or oppose them. Progress from guns for defense of bases, to fortifications, and then to garrisons went much faster in Australia than at Esquimalt where a similar problem existed. In Canada these steps quickly brought fortification to protect ports as well as naval bases, partly to deny their use to the enemy, but probably even more to give immediate comfort to local inhabitants. Australia, with no internal security problems other than industrial unrest, and with no danger of a large-scale invasion, moved more slowly to build infantry forces, although these forces were often the most popular among those elements of the population interested in military service. The Australian colonies therefore still had a considerable proportion of unpaid volunteers in the early 1890's. In New Zealand the veterans of the Maori wars felt less need for professional military guidance and help, especially as the domestic danger receded. But there as everywhere else, when the guidance and example of professionals was lacking, the efficiency of unpaid volunteers declined more rapidly than that of any other kind of troops. When the fortifications had been completed, the need to man and support them led to proposals for a partially paid system and to a request for a senior British officer to improve efficiency.

In South Africa warlike native tribes and the militant Boer republics which employed a form of citizen military service had compelled the British colonies at the Cape and Natal to develop citizen forces but at the same time to rely heavily upon British regulars. The importance of the Cape as a naval station on the route to India and the discovery of diamonds and gold in South Africa served to strengthen British interest in maintenance of the military position in the colonies and in retention of the naval base.

These circumstances, varying from colony to colony, did not, however, have as much effect in bringing differences in the development of land forces as they had had on naval policy. In fact, the various self-governing colonies showed remarkably similar trends in their military development, for the attitude toward defense of colonials everywhere had certain elements in common. All self-governing colonies, even those in Australia which in the early 1870's had wanted to keep British garrisons and pay for them, had quickly become reconciled to their departure. The colonial attitude on this question was clearly expressed by a British officer, Major General Thomas Bland Strange, who had commanded one of the Canadian artillery batteries. After his retirement and his subsequent recall for service in the West, Strange went on a world tour and visited Australia. While there he told the premier of New South Wales, Sir Henry Parkes, that he agreed with what Sir Henry had said fourteen years earlier: namely, that it was better to do without British regulars. Strange wrote:

1st: Had the defence of the Colonies been left to the Imperial Government, the task would have been ignored and the great colonial cities would today lie as much at the mercy of an invader as Liverpool or Newcastle-upon-Tyne. 2nd: If even a corporal's guard of imperial troops were in the colony it would be an excuse for political economies [by colonial governments] today. Why pay for colonial defence? The Imperial Government are bound to support that corporal's guard to the last man. 3rd: The *amour propre* of the colonial soldier would suffer if he saw his soil even nominally protected by an

Imperial detachment. In short the presence of Imperial troops would kill local effort and would itself be inadequate. . . . But you have said all this in better words than me.[12]

Although naval strategists would have objected to one possible implication of Strange's argument—namely, that the particular defense of mercantile seaports should be given priority in defense—no one could dispute his thesis that withdrawal of the garrisons had forced consideration of self-reliance upon the colonials, and that the results could in the long run only be beneficial.

The principle asserted by Strange—that colonies must train their own manpower for defense, which had also been held as a minority opinion by Admirals Tryon and Creswell in regard to colonial naval defense—was to become the generally accepted rule on land. Colonial attempts to get British garrisons back for particular purposes (for instance, to bring marines to Esquimalt) were exceptions that do not deny this rule. The immediate question was whether colonies would make adequate provision for their own defense and whether they would make it in a form that would also contribute in the most satisfactory possible way for the general security of the Empire as a whole.

The result had been the development of the colonial "militias" and "partially-paid forces," which were not a direct borrowing from British experience but which were something quite different. The British Militia was a purely infantry force, a second line of defense to the regular army, but used principally as a source of recruits for the regular army. It had never been a successful organization. The colonial militia was more akin to the British yeomanry and volunteer movement, but it was actually modeled on practice in New York, Massachusetts, and Connecticut.[13]

In ultimate aim if not in immediate achievement, it was an army complete in itself and able to act independently until relieved. So fifty years before Lord Haldane created the British

12. Strange to Parkes, Aug. 23, 1887, Mitchell Library, Sydney, A 68, "Public Men of Australia," pp. 140–141.

13. Canada, Province, Adjutant-General's Office, Col. Baron George de Rottenburg, *Report on the State of the Militia of the Province of Canada, 8 Jan. 1857, Appendix No. 3 to the Fifteenth Volume of the Journals of the Legislative Assembly of the Province of Canada* (Toronto: Queen's Printer, 1857), para. 1.

Territorial Army in 1907 to include all arms in a citizen, part-time force, Canadian citizen-soldiers were mastering the technical mysteries of artillery training. An anonymous Canadian writer claimed that it took the second South African War to demonstrate to the War Office that clerks and farmers could become first-class mounted artillerymen in their spare time.[14] One reason for the delay may have been British inheritance of the ancient tradition that heavy weapons must not be put into the hands of the masses. The British Honourable Artillery Company, which claims sixteenth-century origin, does not disprove the idea that the colonies learned earlier than Britain that a modern democratic state can rely heavily on part-time citizen-soldiers.

Another point of similarity between colonies was in the degree of their response to the need for land forces. By the early 1890's, when some colonials were beginning to realize that international problems were increasing the need for colonial armies, Canada, with about half of the colonies' white population of ten million, had rather less than half of the total of colonial land forces. However, other colonies had been slower than Canada to abandon reliance upon unpaid part-time volunteers; in 1890 Australia still had many more of them than of "partially-paid" troops, and the issue in New Zealand was still fluid. It is the Australasian unpaid volunteers that account for the larger numbers in the southern colonies. But forces of that kind, although cheaper, were notoriously even less efficient than militias. Permanent forces, which amounted to one thousand in Canada and to 2,158 scattered through the other colonies, were about equally insignificant everywhere.[15] In general, then, it can be said that the degree of response to defense planning had been roughly the same in all the colonies.

Similarity of development was undoubtedly furthered by di-

14. The Bombardier (pseud.), "The Father of the Canadian Artillery," *Canadian Defence Quarterly*, II, No. 1 (Oct., 1924), 8.

15. The nomenclature used to describe the various kinds of troops varies somewhat from one colony to another. Furthermore, figures for all the different colonial land forces are not available in published documents for any one year. The figures given by Owen in his "Military Defence Forces . . . ," Appendices I–IV, do not tally from one of his tables to the next; but, along with figures in *The Army Book,* they give a general picture which is probably reasonably accurate.

rect borrowing from each other. The colonies began to get to know what was being done elsewhere, especially after the contacts made at the Colonial Conference of 1887. Information was sought from the experience of West Indian militia forces, and the Canadian Militia Act was a model upon which many built. Requests for information about defense organization and policy began to pass from one colony to another. In the late 1880's steps were being taken in several colonies, notably in New Zealand and Queensland, to put the Canadian system into effect. This process aided the ultimate adoption everywhere of a system which provided for universal obligation to service in defense of the colony but for the actual training of only a limited number of partially paid volunteers in time of peace.

British Influences

Similarity between the colonies was also fostered by British officers who served in one colony after another, and by private tourists like General Strange, whose influence has been mentioned above. These also carried with them British military experience, which thus became a part of colonial tradition. The number of army officers on the active list serving in the colonies in 1886 (mainly as instructors) was forty-four, of whom ten were in Canada.[16] Among these were the Australian commandants and the Canadian G.O.C.; because of their positions, their influence was even greater than that of the instructors. In addition, there were other means for the transference of British military institutions and practices. Many retired regular soldiers settled in the colonies and were prominent in the citizen forces. In Toronto the Canadian Military Institute founded in 1890 made much use of military visitors as speakers who passed on their knowledge and experience in formal lectures which were then published to spread their message to far parts of the country.

Colonial governments were well aware that military efficiency depended on professional knowledge, skill, and organization, and that the natural place for them to turn for these attributes was Britain. It was only to be expected that the Canadian *Regulations*

16. Melbourne *Age*, Nov. 27, 1886.

and Orders for the Active Militia should be drawn directly from the British Queen's Regulations. A few changes in the earlier paragraphs made them suitable for the militia; but perhaps the most noticeable and significant difference from the Queen's Regulations was the parallel French translation in Canada.[17] From the beginning of the century the Canadian Militia used such British training manuals as were available. In the middle of the nineteenth century, military manuals were chiefly concerned with peacetime drill and were not as detailed, even in that limited sphere, as they were to become later. Nor were they obligatory. A colonel had considerable latitude in the way he drilled his regiment. There were many manuals produced by individual officers which were not official publications produced by a military staff. Wolseley's *The Soldier's Pocket Book,* a manual of military organization and tactics published in 1869, which was the best-known predecessor of the *Field Service Regulations* of the twentieth century, broke new ground. As it was actually long unpopular in Britain with certain conservative-minded senior officers who did not like Wolseley,[18] it is possible that it was followed at least as much and as early by the Canadian Militia as by the British Army. Published first in 1880, Otter's *Guide* on the organization and interior economy of a militia regiment became the standard text on that subject in Canada. It was written by a Canadian who believed there was nothing in the administrative organization of a battalion of the British Army that could not be adopted and faithfully imitated in the Canadian Militia except for imperial rates of pay and imperial scales of punishment. The guide shows at once the degree of adherence to British models; but it also suggests that if Canadians began to produce their own manuals, divergence might develop in the future unless it were checked.[19]

17. *Regulations and Orders for the Canadian Militia, 1870* (Ottawa: Queen's Printer, 1870).
18. Wolseley, *Story of a Soldier's Life,* II, 226.
19. Lt. Col. William D. Otter, *The Guide: A Manual for the Canadian Militia, Infantry, etc.* (Toronto: Willing and Williamson, 1880); Otter, "The Administrative System of a British Regiment (Infantry) and the Adaptation of the Principles of That System to the Active Militia of Canada," Canadian Military Institute, *Selected Papers from the Transactions . . . 1892–3,* II, No. 5,

The widespread adoption of British types and styles of uniforms and of British military practices and traditions is evidence of the great influence of Britain upon colonial forces. While these adopted characteristics did not necessarily mean the transference of British military experience and technical knowledge, they are more important than many civilians realize, since such things are important elements in the building of military spirit, tradition, and morale. More important still was the adoption of the British regimental system with its pride in colors and battle honors. From the eighteenth century the British Army had held fast to its uniform in hot and cold climes and had only grudgingly made concessions to climate—more so, indeed, to the cold of Canada than to the heat of India. Colonial units adopted British fashions, especially the green of the rifle regiments. But the scarlet of the infantry, chosen by the Toronto Grenadiers, and the tartans of the Scots regiments were also popular. Arms and equipment were obtained from British stores because it was cheaper and more convenient. There seems at first to have been no express permission for adoption of details of British-style uniforms; but in Canada the governor general ordered that volunteer cavalry and artillery should wear blue, and rifle regiments green, and that the "coats be of the tunic shape, such as is now prescribed for Her Majesty's Forces." [20] There is evidence of colonial punctiliousness in correct British procedures, although there were occasional lapses. Pressure for the adoption of British regimental customs, uniforms, and other traits usually came from the officers and other ranks of the militia. At times there was official resistance to the popular pressure—e.g., for the adoption of Scottish traditions in the artillery. One British Columbia group that wanted the kilt was told facetiously by the G.O.C. to join the artillery, and then, when the Russians came, to seek permission to man the guns without wearing their trousers.[21] Even-

32–46; J. F. Cummins, "General Sir William Otter," *Canadian Defence Quarterly,* III (1925), 25.

20. Province of Canada, *Public General Orders,* Aug. 16, 1855.

21. Herbert to Cambridge, Oct. 30, 1892, R.A.W., Cambridge Papers. The early arrangement for the use of British arms and accoutrements is given in the "Militia Report for 1870" (Canada, *Sessional Papers,* IV, 1871, Vol. 4, No. 7, p. 147).

tually, the tartan was worn by thousands of Canadians whose ancestors had never seen any heather.

But the official British attitude on the adoption of styles in uniform peeped out when French-Canadian units wanted to adopt the gray of the old Ancien Regime militia and of the Zouave uniforms in which men from Quebec had gone to defend the pope in Rome in 1870. Dufferin told the minister of militia that the recommendation of the commander in chief was that the militia regiments of Canada should be assimilated as far as possible in uniform and general appearance with British regiments, who in case of war "will have the honour of standing by them in the field of battle." [22] This may also have been intended to deceive the enemy by making him think the militia were British regulars. Some French-Canadians thought the refusal of the authorities to permit the recruitment of Zouave and Chasseur units of the militia accounted for slowness in recruiting among them.[23] On the other hand, adoption of uniformity with the British regiments and the development of regimental alliances, which was known before the official introduction of the practice by Dundonald in 1904, helped to foster the military spirit in Canada and to facilitate twentieth-century military co-operation.[24]

The Influence of Jervois

The British officer who had had the greatest influence upon the development of defense policies in the colonies in this period was Lieutenant General Sir W. F. D. Jervois who served in turn in the Cape, the United Kingdom, Canada (on brief visits only), the Straits Settlements, Australia, and New Zealand. After he had taken a second look at the problem of the defense of Canada, Jervois had accepted the principle of greater reliance upon

22. Dufferin to Vail, Dec. 19, 1874, P.A.C., A 413, Microfilm 1146; W.O. to C.O., Feb. 22, 1875, P.R.O., C.O. 42/738; MacNutt, *Days of Lorne*, pp. 240–241.
23. L.G. D'Odet D'Orsonnens, *Considérations sur L'Organisation Militaire de la Confédération Canadienne* (Montreal: Duvernay et Dansereau, 1874), p. 49.
24. Richard A. Preston, "The Transfer of British Military Institutions to Canada in the Nineteenth Century," in William B. Hamilton, ed., *The Transfer of Institutions* (Durham, N.C.: Duke University Press, 1964), pp. 81–107.

the militia. However, he did not give the same advice in Australia and New Zealand where the threat came from the sea. In New Zealand, as in Canada, the guns mounted as a result of the scare of 1878 had soon been declared not only useless but in a defenseless state if fortifications and an adequately trained force were not also provided. The colonial secretary, Hicks Beach, therefore recommended that the government of the colony consult Colonel Scratchley, R.E., a Jervois man, who was being sent out to the colony "with view of securing, as soon as possible, the proper protection of the armaments in question." [25] Soon afterward, the Colonial Office circulated information about the alleged growth of the Russian fleet in the Pacific,[26] and Jervois proposed an Australasian conference. The New Zealand ministers, saying that their views had not yet sufficiently matured to justify their being represented, declined the invitation. However, Scratchley had persuaded them to make a preliminary allocation of £9,000 to begin fortification of their four principal ports in order to render them capable of repelling attacks by one or two hostile cruisers.[27] Fortifications were always more popular with taxpayers because they gave visible evidence of measures taken for defense. They also seemed to offer economies in manpower.

In 1882 Jervois became governor of New Zealand where he was now able to exercise more directly those powers of persuasion which had recently been very effective in South Australia. He worked on nerves by pointing out that as Australia increased her defenses, New Zealand became more vulnerable. Against some who argued that there was no danger, he asked, "Why, then, has New Zealand volunteers?" He persuaded his government to spend the huge sum of £400,000 for forts, not merely to protect naval bases, but also to prevent an enemy from seizing a port to use as a base against other parts of Australasia.[28] Since

25. Hicks Beach to Governor, Jan. 10, 1880, New Zealand Archives, G. 2/2, Governor, Confidential In-Letters.
26. F.O. Circular, March 6, 1880, *ibid.*
27. Robinson to Hicks Beach, Jan. 31, March 9, 1880, New Zealand Archives, G. 26/1, Governor, Confidential; Kimberley to Governor, June 28, Nov. 6, 1880, G. 2/2, Governor, Confidential In-Letters.
28. W. F. D. Jervois, *The Defence of New Zealand* (Wellington, 1884), *passim.*

a later Colonial Defence Committee report was to admit that from 1877 to 1887 Russia had only two cruisers in the Pacific,[29] Jervois's advice can now be seen to have been questionable. New Zealand's static defenses, like those in Australia, seem to merit the description which Sir George Clarke, the secretary of the Colonial Defence Committee, applied to forts in Bermuda: "monuments of misapplied ingenuity." [30]

Jervois's professional experience, it will be remembered, went back to the era of the fortifications craze in Britain in the 1850's and 1860's. He had placed more emphasis on militia forces for the defense of Canada West only after his first report had been subjected to Gladstone's criticisms and when the provincial government seemed willing to accept responsibility for control of Lake Ontario.[31] He had been closely connected with the Carnarvon Commission's efforts to fortify coaling stations. And he, more than anyone else, had been responsible for expanding that program in Australia into an elaborate system of fortifying major ports. But he was rapidly outdated. His great powers of persuasion might have been better devoted to securing the improvement of a system for training and mobilizing New Zealand land forces which were as severely criticized by inspecting officers as were those of Canada.

At the same time, his most determined colonial opponents were probably equally wrongheaded. Scratchley's original proposal of extensive fortification had been as bitterly opposed by the supporters of the volunteer movement in New Zealand as by those who wanted to see a permanent force. The colony, it was said, had more experience of wars than most colonies and also had more retired officers settled in it. There was therefore no need to follow the advice of Scratchley and the practice of Australia by borrowing money from England in order to fortify ports; there was no need for academic tests for officers as Scratchley

29. C.D.C., Miscellany 405, Naval Intelligence Department, "Memorandum on the Defence of Esquimalt," Dec. 11, 1896, P.R.O., Cab. 1/2.
30. Quoted by James R. Thursfield, "The Higher Policy of Defence," *National Review*, XL (1902–1903), 830.
31. Jervois, [*Second*] *Report on the Defence of Canada* (1865), p. 9.

had advocated; knowledge of languages, mathematics, and the
civil service test, it was contended, had not been of much use to
those British officers who had recently been defeated by the
Boers.[32] This was a pronouncement of volunteer doctrine in its
most extreme form.

However, once the fortifications were built, Jervois's disciples
among the regular soldiers advocated the building up of land
forces. In 1887 Major General Henry Schaw, who had just retired as deputy inspector general of fortifications, advised the
colony that its military requirements were now quite different
from what they had been; the struggle with the Maori being
over, an external danger had taken its place, but fortification and
the projected "colonial addition to the fleet in these waters" had
made invasion improbable. Schaw said that raiders were still
possible. Therefore, there was need for more trained troops.[33]
One New Zealand commentator agreed that New Zealand ought
to have a permanent militia, but he objected to its being commanded by British officers who, even if they had the highest
attainments, might fail where "officers with special qualifications" (i.e., New Zealanders) would succeed.[34] Some New Zealanders were apparently not entirely happy about following
British professional military guidance and were determined to
keep the New Zealand forces as free from British control as
possible.

The New Zealand government, anxious above all to cut
expenses, was nonplussed by all these conflicting views and opinions. It rejected the Colonial Defence Committee's recommenda-

32. J. Stormont Small, *Suggestions Relating to the Defence of New Zealand,
and the Re-organization of the Volunteers* (Auckland: John Henry Field, n.d.),
p. 4; see also Julian J. D. Grix (pseud.) [Cpl. D. Batley, N.Z.A.V.], *The Defence of New Zealand* (Wellington: Naval and Military Institute, 1891).
33. Schaw, "Defences of the Colony," Nov. 8, 1887, New Zealand, *Appendix
to the Journals of the House of Representatives*, Session II, 1887, A-7. As the
report was tendered three days after it was requested it must have been prepared in advance, perhaps at the instance of Jervois. Schaw had been in New
Zealand since March.
34. Maillard Noake, *To the Taxpayers of New Zealand: How We May Save
£50,000 a Year by Reorganization of Our Forces* (Wanganui: "Herald" Co.,
1887).

tion that a local professional defense committee should be established to advise it. Clarke saw this rejection as a move to preserve Jervois's influence.[35] But at the same time New Zealand did little to put into effect either the recommendations of General Schaw, or those of General Bevan Edwards a little later, for the establishment of a "partially-paid force." The reason for this lack of action was that the New Zealand Parliament was unwilling to provide the necessary funds.[36] On Jervois's advice the colony had already spent nearly £500,000 upon material which, according to the secretary of the Colonial Defence Committee, was "absolutely valueless without a proper organization to handle and maintain it. If this were fully realized in the colony it is impossible to believe that there would be any general reluctance to undertake the small changes necessary to render the forces of New Zealand available for the purposes of war." [37] But the New Zealand ministers, not surprisingly, were reluctant to add more to the enormous sums that had already been put into forts and to the money that was now being paid for naval subsidies. This was partly because forts and ships could be seen and therefore gave more confidence to taxpayers who had not appreciated the fact that forts had to be manned by trained men. Their reluctance also stemmed from their suspicion of new proposals which seemed to contradict what they had been told by other experts only a little earlier. As the forts were more elaborate than necessary, and as they rapidly became obsolete, hindsight suggests that some of the money might have been spent to better effect on land forces to help preserve the military spirit and military experience of the colony. But as in the United States at this time, money for land forces was harder to get from the taxpayer, and colonial legislators had little appreciation of the need to keep up a military establishment as a necessary part of colonial autonomy.

35. Jervois to Colonial Secretary, March 8, 1888, Minute by G. Clarke, P.R.O., C.O. 209/248.
36. C.O. to Governor, Aug. 4, 1889, with Minutes, New Zealand Archives, G. 2/7, Governor, Confidential In-Letters.
37. Onslow, Confidential, Oct. 14, 1890, Minute by G. Clarke, P.R.O., C.O. 209/250.

British Material and Technical Aid and Political-Military Disputes

Encouragement of self-reliance and the fostering of colonial defense measures did not mean there was now no requirement for British aid and guidance. The colonies still lacked military matériel and military experts. On the eve of the Colonial Conference of 1887, Britain had listed the military aid given to the colonies. Between 1881 and 1886 military materials had been supplied from obsolescent stores at reduced prices as follows: New South Wales, £66,486; Victoria, £66,104; South Australia, £32,486; and Canada, £32,486. Canada had also received four muzzle-loading cannon at one-third of their value. Despite the loan or gift of one or two small naval vessels during this period, the Melbourne *Age* thought that the Ordnance Department had been more liberal than the Admiralty; but it admitted that if the total of military aid to the colonies had been greater, there would have been a British parliamentary demand for retrenchment. It noted also that the list had been padded by the inclusion of supplies to imperial bases and to non-self-governing colonies; but the newspaper was grateful for that which was received.[38]

British material aid was, however, small in amount when compared with that which some colonies were themselves spending on their defenses. The chief effect of aid was to encourage colonies, always hard-pressed to find money for arms, to persist in their policy of relying on obsolescent equipment. The reduced prices were, indeed, less an act of generosity than they seemed. They actually served to relieve the British taxpayer of part of the cost of re-equipment with more modern weapons. But the British government objected when, in their turn, colonial governments disposed of arms which they no longer required: such arms were inclined to find their way into the possession of native tribes with whom the British soldier was at war.

Material aid also was probably much less important than the professional guidance which Britain, as long as there was little

38. Melbourne *Age*, Nov. 27, 1886, p. 13.

cost to the British taxpayer, was willing to supply. British officers sent to aid colonies found everywhere the same great need for their services and skill; but they all reported that they had to struggle against political interference, deficient and unserviceable equipment, poor standards of drill, and legislatures that were unwilling to appropriate money. On the other hand, colonial politicians were often suspicious of the objectives of British officers. Naturally enough, these officers thought of their task as the building of auxiliary arms for the British forces in terms of general imperial purposes; they were not concerned with developing forces peculiarly devoted to the defense and interests of the colony. Not infrequently these differences of approach led to disputes between soldiers and politicians that were so widespread as to suggest they were an inevitable outcome of attempts to give British military guidance to colonies where responsible government had brought control of defense matters entirely into local hands. Long before the well-known Hutton and Dundonald incidents in Canada, clashes in all the colonies had shown that the notorious tactlessness of some British officers was an irritant, even if not the chief cause of friction. Sir Thomas Pratt's opinion in 1862, before withdrawal of the garrisons, has already been quoted.[39] In 1881 Major W. W. Spalding of the Field Battery of New South Wales Permanent Artillery offered the services of his battery to the British government for duty in South Africa without prior reference to the colonial government. Colonel Richardson, commandant of the forces, improperly passed the offer on directly to the governor on what the Premier called the "assumption that he stands in some peculiar relation to your Excellency which relieves him from Ministerial control." Sir Henry Parkes told the governor that any future violation by the commandant of the principle of ministerial control would be treated in the same manner as would any similar violation by any other servant of the government.[40]

When officers were brought out to reorganize the military

39. See p. 68, n. 34, above.
40. Henry Parkes, Minute for Governor, "Ministerial Control of Forces Maintained by the New South Wales Government," March 16, 1881, in Victoria, Department of Defence, *Printed Papers*, I, 1862–1901, No. 9 B.

forces in Victoria in 1884, the commandant, Colonel T. R. Disney, R.A., claimed that since the governor by his commission was commander in chief of the forces and therefore his superior officer, in accordance with military usage he was the only individual to whom he, as commandant, should report. The governor supported Disney and had to be told that Section 40 of the Discipline Act stated that "governor" meant "governor in council." [41] Disney also claimed a special position by virtue of his Queen's Commission in the regular army. When the minister, T. F. Sargood, sought copies of his orders, Disney told the minister that he could get his own clerk to copy them out and paste them in a book. The minister, unable to obtain information from Disney, asked a subordinate officer for it, upon which the colonel promptly objected to being bypassed. Disney's professed purpose was to eliminate political interference in the forces; the minister's was to assert the supremacy of the civil power. [42] Sargood outmaneuvered Disney by appointing a retired general, Major General M. F. Downes, in a civilian capacity as secretary of the Department of Defence of the Colony and by persuading the governor to accept his interpretation of the law; [43] also the British colonial secretary recommended that the Department of Defence be placed clearly under the control of the minister of defense, except for matters of discipline. [44] But such a division of functions was not easy to maintain.

Lieutenant Colonel Francis John Fox, R.A., who had been appointed to command the New Zealand Militia, presented a report with proposals for the militia's reform. The report, however, was ignored by the government of New Zealand, at which the governor, the Earl of Glasgow, a retired naval officer, rashly stepped in by virtue of his commission as commander in chief

41. *Ibid.*
42. Correspondence, Minister of Defence and Military Commandant, in Victoria, *Votes and Proceedings of the Legislative Assembly, Session 1885* (Melbourne: John Ferres, 1886), II, 907–926; "Memo. in Reference to the Correspondence Between the Minister and the Military Commandant [1885]," in Victoria, Department of Defence, *Printed Papers,* I, 1862–1901, No. 26.
43. Millar, "History of the Defence Forces of the Port Phillip District and Colony of Victoria."
44. "Ministerial Control of Colonial Forces [n.d.]," in Victoria, Department of Defence, *Printed Papers,* I, 1862–1901, No. 9 A.

and supported his professional colleague. The origin of the trouble was that Fox had mentioned inefficient militia officers by name, had advised the reduction of inefficient companies, and when his advice was not followed had accused the minister of playing politics. Prime Minister Seddon, who was minister of defense, refused to allow Fox freedom from political control. He replied to Glasgow that the government could not spend large sums of money "at the suggestion of every military officer who may, from time to time, occupy the position of Commander of the Forces in New Zealand without, at any rate, submitting the proposals to Parliament"; he also said that Fox had asked for large powers which really belonged to the minister and Parliament. Fox was denied the title of commandant, which actually had as yet no sanction in the law, and the governor was told firmly that "in respect to command of the Colonial Forces, of course the Governor is Commander-in-Chief thereof, but . . . the Minister for Defence had the control of and is responsible for" them. Seddon said that Fox appeared to be trying to force upon the colony an "imperial defence policy" which would be "an infringement of the rights of the people of the colony."

Robert Meade, undersecretary in the Colonial Office, took the side of the prime minister against Glasgow and Fox. He thought that disbandment of some of the militia corps would seriously discourage the volunteer spirit in the colony; he also felt that Fox would probably have got his way on this matter if he had not tried to hold a pistol to the minister's head. Meade said Fox was too young for the job, and he thought the War Office ought to be given a hint to select more experienced and tactful men. "Where so much remains to be done in developing the country, it is a great thing to get them to spend anything on defence, and it is very undesirable to set up the Horse Guards as a model for a small colony." The Earl of Ripon added: "Colonel Fox is, I do not doubt, a good soldier, but he does not understand his position as Commandant in a Self-Governing Colony." Fox was before his time. What he wanted is now accepted—that the G.O.C. should be more the adviser and less the servant of the minister of defence. The New Zealand Defence Act of 1895 largely adopted his proposals.[45] British attempts to foster colonial military co-operation thus only slowly overcame local political resistance.

Colonial Armies and Their Employment

Lack of standardization, of co-ordination, and of plans for mutual help among the separate forces of the several colonies in Australia was one of the most obvious weaknesses in the whole colonial defense system. At the Colonial Conference of 1887 some of the Australian colonies had therefore asked for inspection by a British general. Hence, in 1889 Major General J. Bevan Edwards, the commander-designate of the British forces in Hong Kong, was invited by the Australian colonies and New Zealand to report on their land forces.[46] The avowed aim of his inspection was the improvement of the Australian colonies' land forces and the co-ordination of their efforts for the defense of Australia. However, as in Canada, though for different reasons, there were doubts in certain quarters in Australia about the reality of the need for land forces for defense. In Canada these doubts arose from the inescapable fact that the United States had a preponderance of power. In Australia they came from the inevitability of relying upon the navy. In both cases the result was the same: apathy, objection to taxation for military purposes, and disputes about the nature of the military effort that was actually needed.[47] Nevertheless, the military preparations that began in the 1890's in Australia—like those in Canada—although also hesitant, and perhaps even reluctant, and although also of little immediate

45. New Zealand Archives, G. 26/4, G. 2/8, G. 17/1063, *passim;* P.R.O., C.O. 209/254; Randal Matthew Burdon, *King Dick: A Biography of Richard John Seddon,* (Christchurch, N.Z.: Whitcombe and Tombs, 1955), pp. 213–218; David Fieldhouse, "British Colonial Policy and New Zealand, 1891–1902," MS Collection of Documents, Canterbury University College, 1956, pp. 238–266; New Zealand, *Appendix to the Journals of the House of Representatives,* 1893, H-196.

46. Victoria, *P.P.,* "Correspondence Relating to the Inspection of Colonial Forces by an Imperial General Officer, 1887–1889," 57/1889.

47. Victoria, *P.P.,* and South Australia, *P.P.,* "Report of Major-General Bevan Edwards on the Military Forces of Victoria with a Memo. Containing Proposals for the Re-organization of the Australian Forces," 139/1889, and 118/1889, 118A/1889.

value for the purpose of the defense of the Empire as a whole, were steps toward the building of a tradition, an organization, and an experience that was to be the basis of future dominion military strength.

The primary purpose for which General Edwards advised that the Australian forces be reorganized was the defense of the continent. But the Colonial Defence Committee saw the matter in a different light. When Bevan Edwards said that 30,000 or 40,000 men were needed for the defense of Australia, the committee disagreed. It believed that the relative danger in the South Pacific did not warrant such large armies. "No British territory is so little liable to aggression as Australia. . . . Territorial aggression on a large scale [would be] impossible." Yet the committee strongly supported the proposal for large land forces. Trained Australian troops, it said, would be useful to serve the purposes of the Empire elsewhere. "The possibility of being able to take a vigorous offensive action at the outset of a war against points which might subsequently prove menacing would be a strategic advantage of the first importance." [48]

Not all British soldiers believed that such planning for overseas expeditions was sound. Major General Strange, who knew the colonies and was closer to the Australian political scene than was the Colonial Defence Committee, while admitting the force of the theory of the "offensive defence," said that it was not a logical strategy for England, much less for the colonies. The colonies would not entertain it. They had, it was true, sent troops to the Sudan, but there had been a violent reaction at home against that action. Chinese Gordon had been called by the Sydney *Bulletin* a "sainted nigger butcher"; and Dalley, who sent the troops because of Gordon's plight, had been labeled in Australia "an ass in a lion's skin." [49] Colonials had a different idea of soldiering from that of the British regular. Every man in a colony was needed for the development of a vast territory. The proper line of development, therefore, said Strange, was militia

48. South Australia, *P.P.*, "Remarks by the Colonial Defence Committee on Major-General Edwards's Report," May 16, 1890, 145/1889.
49. Strange, *Gunner Jingo's Jubilee*, p. 533.

artillery for defense, and dispersion rather than concentration.[50] Strange's formula for defense—a dispersed militia artillery—stemmed from his experience in command of the Canadian Artillery. It was true that artillery required more training than either cavalry or infantry and therefore would receive first priority when money was short. But in the long run the advice was misleading, for the true path for Australia must be toward balanced forces that could be flexible in employment. Nonetheless, Strange was probably correct in his assumption that the colonies were not yet ready to spend money in peacetime on forces that were intended to be used primarily for overseas expeditions.

Colonial sensitivity on this point was shown by bitter attacks on Major General Edward T. H. Hutton, the commandant in New South Wales, for his alleged attempts to "imperialize" his troops in order to fit them for service in India or elsewhere. His defense was that he was simply trying to combine efficiency with economy.[51] Yet Major General Sir A. B. Tulloch, the commandant in Victoria, who worked closely with Hutton, admitted that the ultimate aim was to send forces overseas. While it was recognized that colonial troops would not be ready for imperial service at the beginning of a war and would perhaps be inadequate at the outset even for home defense, he believed that if the colonies were not crushed at once, they would be able to produce many battalions of infantry and mounted troops within four months. Tulloch argued that the effect of the Sudan contingent, for which the number of recruits had been "incredible," had been unfortunate because a considerable section of the Australian community had thought that the Arabs were fighting for liberty. Nevertheless, he believed that a war in India or Russia would be different and that the independent spirit of the colonists would serve to bring out the "old fighting strain." [52] No doubt these same comments could have been applied in greater or lesser degree elsewhere. When the need was established, the will to fight

50. Strange to Parkes, Oct. 29, 1889, Mitchell Library, Sydney, A 907, Parkes Correspondence, Vol. 37, pp. 116–117.
51. *Journal of the Imperial Federation League,* VIII (Nov., 1893).
52. Maj. Gen. Alexander Bruce Tulloch, *Australia's Share in the Empire and Its Defence* (Melbourne: Victoria United Services Institution, 1894), pp. 20–21.

would be there; but each self-governing colony would have to be convinced of the validity of the cause before it would support an overseas expeditionary force.

Despite these differences of opinion, progress toward the integration of Australian land forces was rapid. On October 26, 1894, an Inter-Colonial Military Conference was held at Sydney to produce a scheme for the defense of Australia. Its suggestions were considered by the Colonial Defence Committee in London and amended at a second Inter-Colonial Military Conference in Australia at which Hutton presided in 1896. The final report stated that the defense of Australia rested on the navy, and that as it was supreme in those waters no sizable raid could be mounted until it had been "worsted." In view of the impossibility of providing complete protection for every port and place of landing, Australia must devote its resources in the first place to the security of essential naval bases. For this purpose, a federal military force that could be concentrated anywhere should be created, and there should be a Federal Council for Defence and a general officer commanding. The Australian colonies should adopt a rifle with the same caliber as that used by the British forces. An ammunition factory should also be established. Simplification of drill for colonial troops, which was requested by South Australia, was thought unnecessary; and the question of uniforms for the federal force was left in abeyance.[53] But it was soon found impossible to create the effective central directing authority necessary to act on behalf of the various colonies without taking a more radical step. The Commonwealth of Australia was established in 1901, largely to meet this problem.

Integration of the Australian land forces was one of the big steps taken in the nineteenth century toward the creation of dominion armies. It was comparable in importance to the creation of the Canadian Militia in mid-century, which had similarly preceded a confederation of colonies, and also to the use of

53. G.B., Admiralty, "Australian Federal Defence, 12 Feb. 1896," Confidential Papers, P. 627; Maj. Gen. Sir E. T. H. Hutton, "A Co-operative System for the Defence of the Empire," *Selected Papers of the Canadian Military Institute*, VIII (1896–1897), 102–103; Col. J. M. Gordon, "The Federal Defence of Australia," *R.U.S.I. Journal*, XLII (1898), 136.

volunteers from the New Zealand Militia to deal with the Maori problem. Australian military development, incidentally, was a step toward the provision of colonial forces for the defense of the Empire. Many imperial defense enthusiasts indeed saw the military integration of the Australian colonies and the political federation which followed hard upon it as stages on the road to the federation of what General Strange called "The Disunited States of the British Empire." Imperial federation, which had been dying, was therefore given a new lease of life. The arrangements for the co-ordination of Australian military effort were, however, an expression of Australian national development rather than of imperial solidarity. Railway-building in Australia had now made mutual support for defense possible and had helped to increase the strength of a national sentiment. Noticeably, New Zealand, separated by the Tasman Sea, once again stayed out of an inter-Australian defense organization. Even though the Japanese menace was not yet taken very seriously, emphasis on the need for the defense of the continent of Australia, rather than on the need for expeditionary forces, had made military integration acceptable to colonial electorates. Australian developments for self-defense appear to compare favorably with the slow progress being made in military reform in Canada up to the middle of the 1890's, but it must be remembered that the Australian military federation was as yet only a plan which brought Australia up to a level of military development that Canada had reached a generation earlier. Much still remained to be done in both countries.

Major Sir George Sydenham Clarke, in his essay on "Imperial Defence" published in 1897, summed up proposals for organizing colonial forces for imperial purposes. As he was secretary of the Colonial Defence Committee, his ideas carry the hallmark of the British government at a time when Chamberlain had taken up the torch for the military organization of the Empire. Clarke placed most emphasis and devoted most space to naval questions, but he also said: "Organization for Imperial defence demands that all doubts be removed, that the functions of colonial troops should be clearly defined, and that the full measure of their possible activity should be exactly known." Hailing the naval agreement of 1887 as the first practical recognition of colonial obligations, he said that propositions for the use of colonial land forces had been prepared for discussion at that conference but had not been brought forward for discussion. He thought the time was now ripe. These propositions were that colonial forces should have a standard obligation to serve for defense of their own colony, and, with the assent of the colonial government and in the event of that government providing the means, to aid Her Majesty in any wars in which she might be engaged. Arrangements should be made for conditions of discipline and command over colonial troops. The British Regular Army would serve anywhere in the world; colonial forces could be used for garrisons and reinforcements.[54] Few at that time would have believed that when the great emergency did come, Australians and Canadians would scorn to be used only as "garrisons and reinforcements."

Meanwhile, it is clear that the problem of colonial military development and of colonial attitudes to the organization of land forces for imperial defense was largely similar everywhere, even though circumstances differed enormously. The Australians and New Zealanders developed citizen forces that had much in common with the Canadian Militia and had no close counterpart in Britain. All colonial troops depended heavily on British technical and professional aid. All found that that technical aid tended to lead to political disputes with the mother country. None were yet prepared to spend as much on defense as British advisers thought necessary. Nor would any of them do so until the reality of the danger was made clearer.

54. Clarke, *Imperial Defence* (1897), pp. 191–193, and *passim*.

8

Hutton and a Canadian National Army

A New Look for Canadian Defense Policy

General Herbert's misfortunes appeared to suggest that Canada, the most important daughter nation in the Empire, might have difficulty in responding to the demand for military and naval reform and reorganization which had begun to be heard elsewhere. However, four unrelated events in 1895 and 1896 had quickened the pace of military development there also. The first of these was the Duke of Cambridge's resignation as commander in chief. Though its effect was not immediate, this cleared the way for military reform in Britain and removed what had come to be a most questionable influence on military affairs in the colonies. The second was Joseph Chamberlain's appointment as colonial secretary which brought new vigor to the Colonial Office and initiated an attempt to reunify the Empire. The third was the Venezuela crisis which, though soon over, gave Canada a galvanic shock not unlike that of 1878, but in a more sensitive area—on the American border. The fourth was Dr. Frederick W. Borden's appointment as minister of militia. A surgeon who had long been interested in the militia, Borden was determined to make it more effective. These four events were followed by the exposure of the new Liberal prime minister, Wilfrid Laurier, to the infectious fever of imperialism at the Diamond Jubilee and the Colonial Conference in London in 1897. His reactions there indicated that a new deal might now be coming in Canadian defense policy.

President Cleveland's provocative Special Message to Congress on December 17, 1895, had seemed very likely to escalate the

Venezuela border dispute into war between Britain and the United States. Attention turned at once to the condition of Canadian defenses. It is now known that Chamberlain, who had become colonial secretary in June and who was the real power in the Conservative government in England, was determined to see that Anglo-American relations did not deteriorate too far.[1] But the British armed services departments and the government and people of Canada, not being in the British government's confidence, were compelled to assume that the worst might happen. Their fears were confirmed by noisy groups in the United States who, as a later intelligence report stated, were determined to seize this opportunity to "wipe Europe off the Continent."[2] The Canadian government was aroused from its lethargy about defense. With unusual vigor, and without waiting for parliamentary approval, it sent the quartermaster general, Colonel Percy Lake, to buy modern Lee-Enfield magazine rifles in England and to ask what support the Royal Navy could give to the militia.[3] To thinking soldiers, however, it seemed obvious that a strictly defensive policy would result in the loss of Canada as soon as the United States had time to raise and train an army to take it.[4] The commander in chief, General Lord Wolseley, believed with Wellington that "Whichever [country] holds the inland seas will hold Upper Canada"; hence, when the War Office received the request from Colonel Lake it was anxious to find out how much the Admiralty would do on the Great Lakes. The secretary of state for war convened a meeting of the Joint Naval and Military Committee which had been established to discuss particular problems and enterprises involving co-operation between the services but which had hitherto had little result. This joint committee came to the conclusion that even with naval assistance on the Great Lakes, only Lake Ontario, and perhaps Erie, could be held; it also stated that British military

1. Ensor, *England 1870–1914*, p. 230.
2. Capt. C. B. Levita to Col. Latham, Nov. 1, 1898, P.R.O., W.O. 106/40, B 1/7. "Operations in a War with the United States," 1901.
3. Percy Lake, "Naval Action in the Defence of Canada on the Great Lakes," *ibid.*, B 1/5.
4. Sir John Ardagh, D.M.I., to the Joint Naval and Military Committee, March 30, 1896, *ibid.*

assistance would be needed to secure Montreal. The committee concluded that the St. Lawrence canals must be controlled. But the most important result of its deliberations was the reassertion of the doctrine that the security of Canada could only be insured in the long run by an invasion of the United States.[5]

The War Office at once dispatched Major Hubert Foster, R.E., to reconnoiter "likely landing places" on the coasts of Maine and Massachusetts and to draw up plans for an offensive.[6] In April of the previous year, Foster had made the first major report on the strategy of Canadian defense since Jervois. He had suggested that in the event of war the Americans would attack between the Richelieu River and Lake Ontario and on the Niagara frontier.[7] Although the Admiralty was apparently willing to pursue the idea of offensive action, it pointed out that if the navy was to help on the Great Lakes as well, the right bank of the St. Lawrence must be in British control.[8] At the height of the crisis, the Conservative government, which was still in power in Canada, had taken steps to meet the emergency without waiting to assemble Parliament; and the Liberals had made no serious objection. The Department of Militia planned that in the event of war, Ogdensburg would be seized and also, if possible, Plattsburgh, while at the same time the militia would hold fast on the Niagara frontier; but the immediate support of two or three British Army corps (that is to say, about 100,000 men) would be required.[9] But not until February 2, 1898, did the commander in chief in Britain approve plans for offensive operations, including coastal landings, and then with the proviso that New York City, and not Boston, should be the main objective of the attack. A month later, however, the First Sea Lord refused to comment further on the War Office's plans. He said that the situation was

---

5. "Report of the Joint Naval and Military Committee," April 23, 1896, *ibid.*
6. W.O., to Admiralty (n.d., 1896?), *ibid.*; Col. E. A. Altham, "Comments on Capt. Haldane's Memo.," March 13, 1902, *ibid.*, B 1/1; Maj. W. R. R. Robertson, "Memo on the Defence of Canada," March 15, 1901, *ibid.*, B 1/7.
7. Robertson "Memo on Defence of Canada," March 15, 1901, *ibid.* Foster's first report has not been located.
8. Evan MacGregor to C.O., June 4, 1896, *ibid.*, B 1/5.
9. "Comments by Colonel Lake on Captain Haldane's Memo. 1902," *ibid.*, B 1/1.

changing too rapidly.[10] The reason for the Admiralty's change of heart was the steady growth of American naval power.

British hesitation was not due to realization of the futility of trying to defeat the United States by seizing a small part of its territory. That strategy had been unsuccessful in the eighteenth century when the United States was very much smaller and weaker; saner counsels in Britain were to admit within a very few years that it was even less possible now; but in 1896–1897, instead of being realistic, British soldiers preferred to blame the weak state of the Canadian Militia for the impossibility of vigorous action against the United States. "The chief points of weakness in Canada are inherent and insuperable," wrote Sir John Ardagh, the director of military intelligence at the War Office. He added that the Canadian Militia was deplorably inefficient in training and entirely unprovided with auxiliary necessities for the field. He did not note that Britain herself had only skeleton arrangements in many supporting services and that Canadian requirements in this respect were less urgent than Britain's since it was always assumed that Canadians would fight at home. He went on to say that Canadians were not disposed to bear the burden of their own defense but preferred to rely on the home government; as a result, he thought Canadian defense a "futile strain." Ardagh regretted that Britain had not succeeded in arousing the Dominion to a consciousness of the glaring imperfections of its military forces. Without reform it would be premature to plan operations in detail. There was much patriotism in Canada, but Canadians were living in a fool's paradise. He concluded: "It would be imprudent and impolite to take Canadian ministers into our confidence . . . more than can be helped, in a matter of this kind which should be treated as far as possible with secrecy, particularly as regards the part British troops would play across the Atlantic." [11]

This last sentence shows a fatal flaw in British military thought. Sir John probably feared that any British force sent to Canada

10. Robertson, "Memo on Defence of Canada," March 15, 1901, *ibid.*, B 1/7.
11. Sir John Ardagh, "Naval Action in Defence of Canada, Strategic Attack on the American Coast," Dec. 14, 1897, *ibid.*, B 1/5.

would meet defeat. He apparently believed that ministers responsible to the Canadian people could allow themselves to be committed to raise and deploy forces that would co-operate with British troops (which might never arrive) without having knowledge of, or a voice in, the nature of the action to be taken. Such action, however, would be incompatible with responsible government. Central control of the Empire's forces might become necessary in a great emergency; but Canada could hardly be expected to regard as such an emergency, and as the reason for jeopardizing her hard-won autonomy, a crisis in which the United States had been provoked, whether legitimately or not, by British policies that were not Canada's concern.

When Ardagh expressed these views, the crisis had long been over. On February 2, 1897, the Treaty of Washington had referred the Venezuela boundary problem to arbitration. But the tension had stirred Canadians temporarily from their customary apathy on defense matters, and although this was quickly forgotten by the press and the public, the soldiers were determined to make what they could of it in order to revitalize the Canadian Militia.

Little progress could be made at once. Major General William Julius Gascoigne had been appointed to succeed Herbert as G.O.C. This was after the resignation of the Duke of Cambridge in England, but before Wolseley had established his claim to be sole military adviser to the secretary of state for war. Gascoigne was lethargic and had little influence at home. He tried to get Canadian officers admitted to the "Royal Staff College" [*sic*] at Camberley, but without success; and to defend Canada during the crisis he had borrowed obsolete guns from Halifax. He steered clear of controversy, and he did not show the same energy as his predecessor in visiting militia units. It seems likely, therefore, that it was not the G.O.C. but someone else, possibly Colonel Lake, the quartermaster general, who persuaded the Canadian government to buy for the militia the best rifles available. It is true that Gascoigne had been firm in vetoing an application by Colonel James Domville, the irrepressible commanding officer of the 8th (New Brunswick) Hussars, to take a company to the

Sudan to build and operate a steamboat, a railway, and a telegraph service for the British Army; but that veto had probably served only to antagonize some militiamen, including some government supporters, without pleasing the rest.[12]

Furthermore, the G.O.C., despite his caution, had fallen even more quickly and deeply into the political mire than had his predecessors. He had been used by the new minister, Borden, to get rid of some of the Conservatives who held more than nine-tenths of the militia commands. On the other hand, he had annoyed Liberal Orangemen by permitting troops to parade for the funeral of Archbishop Taschereau. His part in the dismissal of General Cameron, son-in-law of the leader of the Opposition, from the Royal Military College at Kingston also brought him into great disfavor with the powerful Tupper family, to which the commandant was related by marriage.[13] The root of the trouble was that the G.O.C.'s salary was too low to attract a more distinguished officer. This was now fully realized in Canada, and a bill to increase the remuneration offered had been introduced in the Commons as part of Borden's plans to put new life into the militia. But, even though Gascoigne knew that the government intended to push the increase through immediately, he supinely resigned. The Canadian Cabinet, obviously convinced that he was not the man they wanted, recommended that his resignation be accepted.[14]

The Diamond Jubilee

The victory of Wilfrid Laurier at the polls in 1896, hard on the heels of the Venezuela crisis, had posed a challenge to imperialists in Britain and in Canada. As a French-Canadian, Laurier was unlikely to be swayed by racial sentiment for the

12. Aberdeen 10, Jan. 8, 1896, P.R.O., C.O. 42/838; W.O. to C.O., March 20, 1896, *ibid.*, C.O. 42/845; Aberdeen 64, 66, Feb. 22, 24, 1896, *ibid.*, C.O. 42/838; Aberdeen, Telegram, April 3, 1896, *ibid.*; W.O. to C.O., May 28, 1896, *ibid.*, C.O. 42/839.

13. Canada, House of Commons, *Debates, 1896*, First Session, II, 5345, 6637, 6737–6742, 6766; *ibid., 1897*, II, 4802; [*Canadian*] *Military Gazette* (Ottawa), Jan. 5, 1898, p. 11.

14. Aberdeen 109, 119, April 23, 29, 1898, P.R.O., C.O. 42/857.

preservation of ties with the mother country; indeed, in his earlier life he had looked forward to an independent Canada. Furthermore, like most French-Canadian politicians, not even excluding the ministers of militia, Cartier and Caron, Laurier had shown no great interest in defense, except in the patronage associated with it. "The fact is," he told the Colonial Conference in 1897, "I take very little interest in military affairs even in my own province. . . ." [15]

Yet when he went to England, the image that Laurier projected outside the conference hall was not that which might have been expected. Although he never missed an opportunity to tell his British audiences that he was proud of being a Canadian, and especially of his French ancestry, he indulged in the fashionable imperialistic rhetoric of the day. By 1897 imperial federation had been considerably discredited by its advocates' failure to agree upon a plan, but emotional imperialism was at least as strong as ever; furthermore, it was widely believed that a federal solution, although apparently only possible in a remote future, must be the only eventual alternative to imperial disintegration. Laurier may have desired to meet his Ontario supporters half way, and he was a sincere admirer of the values and standards of English public life. He was also moved by the pageantry of the Diamond Jubilee parades and by the great naval and military displays. But when he said that he looked forward to the time when a French-Canadian would take up a seat at Westminster, his political opponents on both the imperialist and the nationalist extremes thought that his head had been turned by his reception in England.

However, O. D. Skelton has shown that Laurier's knighthood was thrust upon him by Chamberlain against his own inclination; and we know that Laurier was aware, at least in later life, and perhaps also at the time, that vigorous social pressure was being put upon the colonial visitors. "We were dined and wined by royalty and aristocracy and plutocracy and always the talk was

15. C.O., Miscellany 111; *Report of a Conference between the Right Hon. Joseph Chamberlain and the Premiers of the Self-Governing Colonies of the Empire . . . , June and July, 1897*, Confidential, Sept., 1897, p. 74.

of Empire, Empire, Empire." It was hard, he complained, to stand up against the flattery of a gracious duchess. What had probably happened there was that Laurier, who was as responsive to audiences as are all great orators, had reacted to the growing imperial sentiment in Britain by speaking of the expectation of eventual federation.[16] What he probably saw in 1897, however, was a future free association of the nations of the Empire in a form that would appeal to Canada, something quite different from Chamberlain's hopes. It was more like Macdonald's concept of "two kingdoms" but on a multilateral basis. It was also less clearly thought out.

With regard to the immediate problem of imperial defense, Laurier largely followed what Macdonald had told the Carnarvon Commission. Macdonald had said that if England were in real need of aid, Canada could raise 10,000 men. According to Laurier's political opponent, Sir Charles Tupper, Laurier was more oratorical than Macdonald on this theme, perhaps because his pronouncements were made in public meetings. Tupper told Lord Minto that Laurier had said, "England had proved at all times that she can fight her own battles, but if a day were to come when England was in danger, let the bugle sound, let the fire be lit on the hills, and in all parts of the Colonies, though we may not be able to do much, whatever we can do will be done by the Colonies to help her." [17] These words do not appear in the published version of Laurier's address to the Royal Colonial Institute on June 18, 1897,[18] in which Tupper alleged they were uttered; and Tupper repeated them for political advantage to allege that Laurier had gone back on his word. But even though these exact words may not have been used, those who heard Laurier's public addresses in England appear to have been impressed by signs of an imperial vision.

16. Oscar D. Skelton, *Life and Letters of Sir Wilfrid Laurier* (2 vols.; Oxford: Oxford University Press, 1922), II, 65–72, 82; Skelton, *The Day of Sir Wilfrid Laurier: A Chronicle of Our Own Times* (Toronto: Glasgow, Brook, 1920), pp. 180–181; John W. Dafoe, *Laurier: A Study in Canadian Politics* (Toronto: Allen, 1922), pp. 56–57.
17. Tupper to Minto, Sept. 23, 1902, P.A.C., Minto Papers, Box MM, No. 33.
18. Sir Wilfrid Laurier, [address], June 18, 1897, *Proceedings of the Royal Colonial Institute*, XXVIII, 356–358.

In the conference, Laurier was less expansive. Chamberlain wanted precise commitments and made suggestions that had far-reaching implications. At the opening of the sessions he spoke of possible "interchangeability between the whole forces of the Empire . . . chiefly for the purpose of drill and instruction. . . ." He added, "Yet if it were their wish to share in the dangers and glories of the British army and take their part in expeditions in which the British army may be engaged, I see no reason why these colonial troops should not, from time to time, fight side by side with their British colleagues. That . . . is not a recommendation which has any pressure behind it; it is merely a suggestion." [19] Although Laurier steadfastly opposed naval contributions and centralization of control, he was apparently not immediately repelled by this patent effort to get Canadian soldiers to fight in Britain's little imperialist wars. When the proposal for troop exchanges was raised by Captain Nathan, the secretary of the Colonial Defence Committee, in the ordinary conference sessions, Laurier said he thought that it would be acceptable to Canada under an act of Parliament but that he could give no assurance on his own. Nathan then revealed that following a proposal made by General Herbert for an exchange of artillery units between Britain and Canada,[20] an experimental exchange had already been tried between the Halifax garrison and the Fredericton militia. Encouraged by this evidence of the Canadian government's co-operative attitude, and by the fact that Laurier had not been put out by the revelation of the experiment which he had either not known about previously, or had forgotten, Chamberlain offered to send an official proposal for a permanent exchange system. But Nathan intervened to suggest that it would be more convenient if the proposal came from Canada. To this Laurier replied rather noncommittally, "Oh, very well." The conference believed that the problems of discipline and pay would present little legal difficulty; and all present were agreed that there should be an attempt to take the basic

19. Ollivier, *The Colonial and Imperial Conferences . . .* , I, 134–135.
20. Memorandum of Maj. Gen. I. J. C. Herbert, Ottawa, May 10, 1894; "Report of Colonial Conference, 1897," Appendix VIII, Enclosure 1, P.A.C., G. 21, No. 168, 1897.

step of arranging for uniformity of military law. Furthermore, the British government announced an offer to sell discarded Martini-Henry rifles to the colonies on favorable terms. (Canada, which had recently bought modern Lee-Enfields, was excluded from this offer.) Finally, Laurier agreed with the other delegates that it was desirable to standardize on .303-inch small arms ammunition.

Captain Nathan then introduced the question of local defense schemes. He said that Victoria, New South Wales, and Natal had submitted their schemes annually to the Colonial Defence Committee for revision, that Tasmania and New Zealand had no scheme, or only an old one, and that the only Canadian plan was one prepared by the British military authorities in Halifax.[21] There was discussion about the Canadian Military College, which Laurier claimed had been a success until a few years before, since when its commandant, General Cameron, "had let it run down a little." Nathan, obviously well-informed, said, "We cannot understand here how it is that the appointments in the Permanent Force are not necessarily given to cadets of Kingston college, . . . it seems to us that the Dominion government ought to encourage the college in the same way as the Imperial government does." Laurier agreed that this seemed reasonable but claimed that he was not informed on the subject. But he must have been aware that permanent and militia commissions in Canada had been used as political patronage by the Conservatives and that his own party was now trying to evict its opponents.

Lastly, Laurier himself brought up another proposal to coordinate the Empire's military effort. Some Toronto citizens had suggested that the British Regular Army should recruit in Canada. Laurier said that in the present economic slump, despite the differential in wages, men might volunteer. But once again he admitted that he did not know much about the matter. It was at this point that he told the conference that he took little interest

21. It was at this point that Nathan proposed, for security reasons, that discussion of military matters be confidential, and Chamberlain stated that they would not be published. The dominion governments later refused to permit publication for fear of political repercussions. The full text was not released until 1960.

in military affairs. He could not give an opinion whether imperial recruiting could function along with the proposed scheme for the exchange of units.[22] Laurier obviously lacked interest in, and knowledge of, military matters; but his willingness to go along with all these various plans for co-operation between the Empire's forces is shown by the fact that many of these arrangements were promoted in Canada in the next few years. The Venezuela scare, the Diamond Jubilee vision of Empire solidarity, the increasing isolation of Britain and therefore of the colonies, the Franco-Russian entente, and the Kaiser's telegram to Kruger, all helped to make Laurier's government carry on with the defense measures begun by the Conservatives in their last days of office. The result was that in Canada in the 1890's, as in Britain in the 1870's, military reform was the work of the Liberals rather than of their more imperially minded predecessors.

The first effort to put into effect one of the conference's proposals for improved military co-operation—the exchange of military units—was, however, not an unqualified success. In the summer of 1898 an exchange of artillerymen between Quebec and Halifax was arranged on the principle that each country would pay for the cost of its own detachment. The Dominion government agreed to the exchange, subject to the condition that it should be given no publicity. The British general commanding in Halifax reported that the exchange worked well: the behavior of the troops left nothing to be desired; and the men of the Royal Canadian Artillery in Halifax, receiving double the British soldier's pay, showed no tendency to save the difference but instead were delighted to treat their less fortunate British comrades. However, General O'Grady Haly later told the Elgin Commission that the British artillerymen in Quebec were dissatisfied at not getting the Canadian rate of pay. It was found inexpedient to repeat the experiment because Canada had too few troops ready-trained to take over duty in the Halifax garrison, and the Minister of Militia was not convinced that the British artillerymen would carry out adequately the instruction normally given by the Canadian artillerymen. General Hutton,

22. C.O., Miscellany 111, *Report of [Colonial] Conference, 1897*, p. 74.

who arrived in Canada when the exchange was in operation, thought that Canadian Militia officers were not sufficiently qualified to go on exchange and were not helped by it. He preferred to send militia troops for training in Halifax and Esquimalt. Hence, the wider scheme which Chamberlain now wanted —exchanges with Britain by which "the Mother Country should have the option of employing Colonial field units (other than garrison artillery) on Field Service Abroad" and of keeping them until the end of campaigns in which they participated—fell through.[23]

The Leach Commission

While under the influence of the emotions aroused by the Diamond Jubilee, Laurier seems to have been persuaded, perhaps in private discussion, to breathe life into the long dormant scheme for a committee to report on Canadian defense. The actual initiative came from the British general commanding in Halifax, Montgomery-Moore, who, some time after the prime minister got back to Canada from the imperial conference, addressed a letter to him to recommend peacetime measures for the defense of Canada. Gascoigne forwarded a copy of this letter to the minister of militia, Dr. Borden, who submitted it on February 24, 1898, to the Cabinet, which then asked for the advice of the imperial authorities on the subject. This stronger Canadian interest in defense may have been the result of the government's recent decision to take a firm stand against American encroachment in the Yukon territory where gold had been discovered. On April 13, Chamberlain, gratified that the idea of a defense inquiry had thus been initiated in Canada, suggested an investigation by three British Army officers and one naval officer, who

23. W. F. Seymour to Hutton, Oct. 23, 27, Dec. 24, 1898, P.A.C., M.G. 21, G. 3, Hutton Papers, Vol. 5, pp. 646–647, 649, 686–687; "Interchange of Military Units Between the Colonies and the Mother Country," P.R.O., Cab. 11/124; "Scheme for Interchange of British and Canadian Army Units," P.R.O., W.O. 32/814/058/2528/1900; G.B., *P.P.*, 1904, *Report of His Majesty's Commissioners Appointed to Inquire into the Military Preparations and Other Matters Connected with the War in South Africa; Minutes of Evidence, . . . ; Appendices . . . ,* XL, para. 8558 (Cd. 1790).

were to be paid by the imperial authorities but given traveling and subsistence expenses by Canada.[24] Gascoigne was to have presided over this commission, but he had now resigned. The officer designated to succeed him as G.O.C., Major General Edward T. H. Hutton, thought that a defense commission independent of the G.O.C. would have more influence and would also strengthen his hand in reforming the militia. The presidency therefore went to Major General E. P. Leach, V.C., C.B., R.E., who had recently served as senior engineer officer at Halifax and who, while there, had prepared two valuable reports on the defense of Montreal, the potential objective of earlier American plans and attacks.[25] The prospects of effective action were strengthened on May 15, 1898, when Chamberlain summarily replaced Aberdeen by a governor general more to his taste, the Earl of Minto.[26] Formerly Viscount Melgund, Minto was the soldier who had been the leading member of the earlier Canadian Defence Commission and Middleton's chief of staff in the North-West expeditionary force in 1895.

To avoid arousing "the susceptibilities of the Yankees," and at the same time to avoid giving the Canadian public the impression that there was any suggestion of imperial interference with the militia, Hutton recommended that the committee be called "The Commission upon the Inter-Oceanic Communications of Canada for Imperial Purposes and their Defence," a reference to the recent development of trade with China.[27] But the name "Commission [or sometimes Committee] of Defence" was actually used. The Canadian government insisted on adding the minister of militia and the minister of fisheries to the commission, additions which the Admiralty, and perhaps the War Office also,

24. Montgomery-Moore to Laurier, Nov. 3, 1897, Militia Docket 16461, P.A.C., Militia Department, R.G. 9, II B 2 (71), Vol. 32; Chamberlain to Aberdeen, April 13, 1898, P.A.C., R.G. 7, G. 21, Vol. 77, No. 165, Vol. 6 (c). For a discussion of the significance of the Yukon crisis in imperial defense developments, see Penlington, *Canada and Imperialism* . . . , pp. 81–131.

25. Hutton to Minto, March 30, 1899, P.A.C., Minto Papers, M.G. 27, II B 1, Vol. 15, p. 15; W.O. to C.O., June 16, 1898, P.A.C., R.G. 9, II A 6, Vol. 5, p. 2066.

26. Skelton, *Life and Letters of Sir Wilfrid Laurier*, II, 85.

27. Hutton to Sir John Ardagh, director of military intelligence, June 12, 1898, P.A.C., Hutton Papers, M.G. 21, G. 3, Vol. 4, p. 364.

thought would bring no extra strength to the inquiry and which they therefore accepted with ill-concealed reluctance.[28] The commission was instructed to consider the possibility of a closer connection between the colonial and British forces, to examine local defenses, to submit to the minister a detailed scheme of defense for Canada, to report on the organization of the militia and plans for mobilization, and to suggest additional things that could be done to complete a scheme for defense.[29] It assembled in August, 1898, traveled across Canada, and interviewed forty prominent militia officers. Its report was ready in draft by December. Hutton kept in touch with the commission at every stage, and all its recommendations were, as he admitted privately, "made in direct collusion" with him.[30]

The Leach Report was premised on the need to defend Canada against an American attack which would come in the event of an Anglo-American war. It assumed that the United States, now experienced in war, could within a week launch 3,000 regulars and 2,000 militia in raids on Canada. After two months it would have 10,000 regulars and 40,000 militia available. The first few weeks would not be serious, but the Canadian Militia was declared inadequately organized to meet later attacks by all arms. Until improvements were made it would have to act on the defensive. Under the Militia Act of 1868 the command of the militia in the event of war devolved upon a general officer commanding in Canada, who would thus be vested with the supreme command of all Her Majesty's troops, imperial as well as local. For the purpose of the defense scheme which the commission now proposed, the executive command of Canadian troops would of necessity devolve in the first instance upon the general officer commanding the militia. When a field force was organized and formed after preliminary mobilization, the question of its command "must rest with the military authorities." This statement implied that the appointment of a commander of a force that

28. Admiralty to C.O., July 27, 1898, C.O. 42/859.
29. "Instructions to the Committee on Military Matters in Canada," 1898, MS Copy, P.A.C., R.G. 7, G. 21, Vol. 77, No. 165, Vol. 7.
30. Hutton to Minto, March 30, 1899, P.A.C., Minto Papers, M.G. 27, II B 1, Vol. 15, p. 15.

would be primarily Canadian would be made by the War Office
—in other words, by the British government. The report went on
to say that the extent to which Canadian officers could be appointed to the staff of army corps and divisions with higher
formations would depend upon the amount of training they had
received in time of peace. But at present, as there were no
adequately trained Canadian officers, British officers would have
to be appointed. It was not certain that any could be spared, or
that they could arrive in time. If they came to supersede the Canadians who had been appointed temporarily, it would lead to
jealousies. The second part of the report consisted of recommendations for the reorganization of the Canadian Militia to
remedy this sad state of affairs.[31]

Hutton told Nathan, secretary of the Colonial Defence Committee, that the defense scheme was only an "academic exercise"
until the militia was reorganized and trained. He lamented that
as both parts of the report must be strictly confidential, they
could not be used to arouse public opinion on the question; but
he added that the War Office, the Colonial Office, and "above
all your Committee, can impress the importance of the recommendation with all the weight that attaches itself to your
eloquent pen." [32] John Buchan, in his book on Minto, is responsible for the statements, which others have repeated after him,
that the report of the Commission of Defence was pigeonholed,
that Minto could only get access to it after repeated demands,
and that Hutton never saw it at all.[33] What actually happened
was that Charles L. Panet, who had been appointed secretary to
the commission in January, worked to prepare the necessary
copies which were not ready until March 30.[34] Meanwhile, also
in January, Hutton told General W. F. Seymour, the general
officer commanding the British garrison in Halifax, that as the
reports were secret they would never see the light of day but

31. Defence Committee, Canada, Reports No. 1 and No. 2, 1898, P.A.C.,
Tunney's Pasture, G.H.Q., C.E.F. Section.
32. Hutton to Nathan, Jan. 9, 1899, P.A.C., Hutton Papers, M.G. 21, G. 3,
Vol. 7, pp. 1043–1071.
33. John Buchan, *Lord Minto* (London: Nelson, 1924), p. 127.
34. Deputy Minister's Report Book, No. 16861 (11924), Jan. 12, 1899, No.
12014, March 30, 1899, P.A.C., Militia Papers.

would be "consigned consequently to the traditional pigeon-hole and docketed P.A. [put away]." He revealed that he had therefore put the principal recommendations of the commissioners into his annual militia report.[35] Hutton also told Seymour that he had asked Borden whether he could comment upon the commission's recommendations before they were considered by the Cabinet.[36] He also must have written to tell Chamberlain the same thing, for before the report had been sent to England, Chamberlain replied with the extraordinary suggestion that he would ask the governor general "in a public despatch" to request his ministers to publish Leach's report.[37] The colonial secretary apparently wisely reconsidered this proposal to appeal to public opinion, for no such improper dispatch was sent. Meanwhile, Hutton got Dr. Borden, the minister, to promise that as G.O.C. he would receive the report *"officially"* before Minto sent it to England. He told Minto that he would feel slighted if this did not happen.[38] As he already knew full well the contents of the report, he obviously wanted it sent to him officially so that he could attempt to force the government to act. Buchan's idea that Hutton did not "see" the report arises from the fact that Borden apparently did not fulfil this promise to send it officially to the G.O.C. and did not let him comment on it publicly.

Minto found that when the report was ready the Cabinet did not have time to give it full consideration. This was because several ministers were then in Washington negotiating with the American government, evidence enough that the emergency had passed. Minto therefore forwarded it to England with his own views. These were to the effect that the Canadian public would be dissatisfied if provision was not made for the defense of Winnipeg; that any proposal to give the general officer commanding in Halifax any degree of control over the Canadian Militia in time of peace would be resented; but that that officer ought to be kept informed about the state of the training of the

35. Hutton to Seymour, Jan. 15, 1899, P.A.C., Hutton Papers, M.G. 21, G. 3, Vol. 5, pp. 694–696.
36. Hutton to Borden, Feb. 20, 1899, *ibid.*, Vol. 8, p. 1294.
37. Chamberlain to Hutton, March 14, 1899, *ibid.*, Vol. 7, p. 974.
38. Hutton to Minto, March 30, 1899, P.A.C., Minto Papers, M.G. 27, II B 1, Vol. 15, p. 15.

forces that might come under his command in the event of war. He also thought that many of the commission's recommendations might be rejected by his government on the grounds of expense; and he pointed out that in time of peace a voluntary militia could not be as efficient as regulars.[39]

Hutton and Borden

The report of the Leach Commission was shelved, but this was not due solely to the Canadian government's desire to suppress it. It occurred because of two related events: the onset of the worst clash yet between a G.O.C. in Canada and a minister of defense, and the outbreak of the South African War in 1899. "Curly" Hutton's fight with Borden was caused by the same kind of difficulty as had led to all previous collisions, and like the earlier affairs it stemmed chiefly from the fact that the G.O.C. could not adequately serve two masters. The Hutton "incident," as it has come to be called, is better known than earlier disputes because Hutton was a more distinguished and a more energetic officer than his predecessors. One of the ablest members of the "Wolseley Gang," as the followers of the commander in chief were known, he also had other important contacts. He was an A.D.C. to the Queen, a former schoolmate and friend of the governor general, Lord Minto, and a former Australian commandant whose success in dealing with similar difficulties in New South Wales had given him great, perhaps overweening, confidence. On the other hand, the minister, Dr. Borden, was much more concerned with the state of the militia than any of his predecessors had been, and he was proud of the fact that he had already introduced important reforms to increase the number of men who trained and to impose strict limits on the length of service of militia commanding officers. Most important of all, the question of Canadian participation in the South African War made the pretensions of the G.O.C. of greater moment since they seemed to bear directly on Canadian government policy in this

39. Minto to Chamberlain, April 5, 1899, P.A.C., R.G. 7, G. 21, Vol. 77, No. 165, Vol. 7.

important sphere. Lastly, the quarrel, when it was resolved by the G.O.C's resignation, was not allowed to be decently buried. Laurier and Chamberlain, protagonists on opposite sides, both wanted to follow the usual course and let Hutton "go on leave"; but Minto, in order to pillory Laurier's government, insisted on the publication of the reasons for the resignation. However, the blame was not, as Minto appears to have believed, all on the side of Laurier and Borden.[40]

Before he went to Canada, Hutton had set out the principles upon which he intended to work. In a paper on *A Co-operative system for the Defence of the Empire,* which he had read to the Royal Colonial Institute in 1898, he had described the concept of voluntary defense co-operation that had been worked out for the separate Australian colonies during his service in New South Wales and had suggested their extension to the Empire as a whole. He declared, somewhat prematurely, that nothing "fresh" had been necessary in Australia (i.e., no political federation); but he added that the British Empire was different. He went on,

It may be taken for granted that the only plan of co-operative defence which would be acceptable to Great Britain and to her colonies would be based on a representative system . . . some system of defensive-offensive alliance, or Federal Agreement which shall include the creation of a central controlling council having, in peace, the limited administrative powers necessary for the organization and maintenance of the federal force agreed upon, and in war, its control and distribution.

Apart from this proposal for an imperial federal council, a co-operative system for the defense of the Empire would follow

40. Norman Penlington, "General Hutton and the Problem of Military Imperialism in Canada, 1898–1900," *Canadian Historical Review,* XXIV (1943), 156–171. See also Warren Perry, "Military Reforms of General Sir Edward Hutton in New South Wales, 1893–96," *The Australian Quarterly,* XXVIII, No. 4 (Dec., 1956), and "Military Reforms of General Sir Edward Hutton in the Commonwealth of Australia, 1902–04," *Victoria Historical Magazine,* XXIX, No. 1 (Feb., 1959).

Mr. Penlington notes that Hutton frequently boasted that he had overthrown the government in New South Wales (p. 158). The general exaggerated his own importance because defeat of the Dibbs government in the elections of 1894 during Hutton's period of command was largely the result of a financial crisis. However, what Hutton had done in New South Wales which had bearing on his work in Canada was to have the status of the military secretary reduced, thereby making him subordinate to the commandant instead of, as heretofore, to a minister (Perry, pp. 5–6).

the lines of the federal defense scheme proposed for Australia (which at first had no federal political council), and would include a general scheme of defense, co-operative defense agreements, and an allotment of federal troops on the basis of population.[41]

Hutton's aim in Canada was to reorganize and reform the militia and to give it the necessary services so that it would be an independent force, complete in all arms—a Canadian "national army" as he styled it. He deliberately adopted the phrase "national army" as his "best line" to use in speeches to arouse the martial spirit in Canada because he thought that the national idea would appeal to Canadians and would bring them to insist upon reform.[42] Secondly, he sought to reduce the control exercised by the department over the militia. He persuaded Borden to accept a new administrative structure, by virtue of which the G.O.C. became solely responsible to the minister for everything except finance, a new allocation of responsibility which was published in a chart in the militia report.[43] Hutton expected that this would get rid of improper political interference.

Hutton soon found that Dr. Borden's new regulations about the length of tenure of militia commands, which had been introduced before the G.O.C. arrived in Canada, were harder to enforce against the few Liberals who held commands than against the many Conservatives. Colonel James Domville, M.P., onetime candidate for the G.O.C.'s position, had recently turned from Conservative to "Liberal-Conservative" and was supporting the Laurier government. He was alleged to be now a hopelessly negligent and inefficient commander. It took Hutton a year to remove him as commanding officer of the 8th (New Brunswick) Hussars. Next the minister struck two names from a list of officers already warned to attend a Militia Staff Course. When Hutton informed the officers concerned that they had been removed on account of their political activity on behalf of the Conservatives,

41. Hutton, "A Co-operative System for the Defence of the Empire," in *Selected Papers of the Canadian Military Institute*, VIII (1896–1897), 104.
42. Hutton to Minto, Nov. 20, 1898, P.A.C., Minto Papers, M.G. 27, II B 1, Vol. 15, pp. 8, 46; Hutton to Nathan, Jan. 9, 1899, P.A.C., Hutton Papers, M.G. 21, G. 3, Vol. 7, p. 1045.
43. Canada, *Sessional Papers, XXXIII, 1899*, "Militia Report for 1898," No. 13, Paper No. 19, Appendix G.

he, on his part, came dangerously close to dabbling in politics. When he sought to insure the elimination of political patronage from the purchase of horses, he again virtually allied himself with the Opposition.

Hutton's determination to build a force to serve the Empire entangled him in disputes with some of those in Canada who sympathized with him in this aim. He antagonized certain militia colonels, and especially the volatile Sam Hughes, M.P., by opposing their wish to raise Canadian forces for service with the British Army in Africa. He took this stand because Chamberlain and Minto preferred to have the Canadian government commit itself to the raising of a force rather than merely to permit the recruiting of individuals. Ultimately it was this issue that destroyed Hutton because he attempted to appeal over the heads of the ministers to Canadian imperialists. It was then discovered that he had given secret orders to the members of the militia staff that they were to keep certain matters from the minister and that they were to report to the G.O.C. whenever the minister approached them. Hutton's "national army" thus seemed likely to slip from Canadian control. The crisis came with the publication in the press of an official letter about a plan to send a contingent to South Africa which was being discussed in Cabinet. Hutton may not, as his enemies believed, have inspired the leak in order to force the hand of the government; but his stirring speeches had aroused a martial spirit which worked toward the same end.[44]

Hutton's Fall

Laurier was furious that an officer subordinate to the Canadian government should appear to determine Canadian policy. Quite apart from the fact that his interference in this matter hurt the French-Canadian support on which the Liberals relied, no government which claimed to be autonomous could tolerate so independent a servant. Hutton's determination to appeal over the heads of the government to the people is shown repeatedly

44. Buchan, *Lord Minto,* p. 142.

in his private letters, and he was alleged to have told Cabinet ministers of this intention. If, as the future minister of militia, Colonel Sam Hughes, alleged, Hutton told Laurier that Canadians "would not go to South Africa, were not wanted, and would be a menace," [45] he was also guilty of irresponsible mendacity to serve Chamberlain's political objectives: for a little later Hutton wanted to take Canadians to South Africa as a self-contained unit under his own command.[46]

Like other G.O.C.'s before him who also had fine military qualities, Hutton had many supporters in Canada. But there was suspicion on both sides. This was shown early in his tour of duty when he was inspecting militia on a firing range and was called upon to fire the first shot. An irreverent Canadian soldier gave him a blank cartridge.[47] Hutton turned down the Herbert plan for an exchange of units between Britain and Canada on the grounds that the Canadian Permanent Force was an instructional cadre and the militia were not trained well enough to replace British regulars, an opinion which was probably true but not necessarily relevant. Nevertheless, despite his ill-concealed contempt for the quality of the forces under his command, Hutton's soldierly qualities succeeded in winning him the respect of many of the militia officers and men, and especially those in Ontario who were aroused by the flood of anti-Boer propaganda to demand that Canada intervene. However, the British reverses at Stormberg, Magersfontein, and Tugela River—the "Black Week" of 1899—undermined Canadian confidence in the efficiency of British generals and this reflected back on the Canadian G.O.C. A horse-purchase dispute was used as a pretext for dismissing him. Two days before he was forced to hand in his resignation, Hutton struck back. He demanded a royal commission "to report on the administration of the Department of Militia and Defence"; and before he left the country, at a farewell dinner in Toronto

45. Penlington, "General Hutton and the Problem of Military Imperialism in Canada," pp. 164–165.
46. Hutton to Minto, Sept. 3, 1899; Minto to Hutton, Oct. 12, 1899; Hutton to Minto, Oct. 16, 1899, P.A.C., Minto Papers, M.G. 27, II B 1, Vol. 15, pp. 107, 116, 119–120.
47. Hutton to Nathan, Jan. 9, 1899, P.A.C., Hutton Papers, M.G. 21, C. 3, p. 1044.

given him by those who had supported him,[48] he denounced the government he had served.

Hutton went off to an operational appointment in South Africa regretting that he had not been able to do in Canada what he had done in Australia—that is, to prepare the gound for participation in a militia system of co-operative defense that would be applicable to the whole Empire.[49] A year later he was still planning to "have a go" at the reorganization of the militia system in Britain to make co-operation with Canada and Australia possible.[50] His appointment in 1902 to command the army in the new Commonwealth of Australia gave him a chance to work on this plan. But his own words at that time show that he had had no change of heart about the nature and purpose of the militia armies of the British Empire. In a draft of preliminary chapters for a narrative of Minto's career he wrote, "We on the spot alone realized the magnitude of the stake for which we played: none could share the risks we had to face together . . ."; and he added, "Difficulty of realization lay—as usual—with the political leaders. They were slow to grasp that the problem of the defence of the Empire, or of any part of it, could only be solved by all portions undertaking a similar system of organization, training, arms and equipment. . . ."[51] Events of the future were to prove him wrong and to show that the politicians could accept standardization and preparation for co-operation, provided they were convinced of the need for these things. What they feared was something else that Hutton earnestly wanted, namely central control. They feared that this might mean central direction of policy for British interests. Had Laurier seen a letter that Hutton wrote to Minto early in 1902, his natural suspicions of such an arrangement and of Hutton would have been quite properly increased. Hutton said that French-Canadians must fear "the day

48. Penlington, "General Hutton and the Problem of Military Imperialism in Canada," p. 170. Hutton's dismissal came as a result of charges that he and Colonel Kitson of the Royal Military College for political reasons had purchased horses from Opposition supporters.

49. Hutton to Minto, Feb. 27, 1900, P.A.C., Minto Papers, M.G. 27, II B 1, Vol. 16, p. 40.

50. Hutton to Minto, Jan. 16, 1901, *ibid.*, Vol. 17, p. 27.

51. Hutton, "Narrative of Minto's Career," (1923), *ibid.*, Vol. 19, p. 19.

will dawn when an Australian Army will land in Vancouver, a British Army at Quebec, and a South African Army at St. John, New Brunswick, who together will force the French-Canadian of the future to forever hold his voice should his efforts to force the tri-colour upon Canada make such efforts necessary." [52]

Sir Edward Hutton had much military lore to teach the amateur soldiers of the colonies, but he did not understand the political situation in the Empire. He regarded the Canadian command not as a Canadian national military organization but as a district of the British military command system. Sir Frederick Borden, on the other hand, wanted to apply in Canada a structure similar to British military organization under the War Office. [53]

G.O.C. Militia versus General Commanding Troops, Halifax

Hutton's attempt to strengthen his command of the militia also brought him into conflict of a different kind with the general officer commanding British North America in Halifax. The current incumbent of the office, General W. F. Seymour, claimed that the G.O.C. in Halifax was commissioned by Britain to command all troops in Canada, including the militia. The claim was exaggerated, but it was true that the Leach Defence Commission assumed that, as the law stood, the militia should be put under the Halifax commander in the event of war. Colonel Percy Lake commented that the Dominion government had not always been ready to acknowledge the effect of the "law," and he thought that care should be taken lest by implication it was suggested there was any doubt on the subject. [54] General Seymour, alarmed by Hutton's activity, and perhaps by the Leach Commission's own proposal that at the outbreak of a war the G.O.C. of the Canadian Militia must inevitably have a preliminary command, complained that he was not receiving reports about defense

52. Hutton to Minto, Jan. 10, 1902, *ibid.*, Vol. 17, p. 58.
53. Minto to Chamberlain, June 6, 1900, P.R.O., W.O. 32/815/058/2422/251207/1900.
54. Lake, Minute, May 4, 1900, "Relative Position of G.O.C. Canada and G.O.C. Canadian Militia," *ibid.*, W.O. 32/815/058/2372/116077/1900.

problems and forces which, he claimed, might come to him in due time; he also asked pointedly whether it was his duty to submit a report on the G.O.C. along with all other officers in Canada. Someone in the War Office, apparently suspicious of Hutton's arrogance, was at first inclined to sympathize with Seymour. "Difficulty occurs," reads a minute, "particularly if the officer in what may be called the junior position [the command of the militia] should happen to be constitutionally deficient in every atom of tact—and constitutionally incapable of even acquiring and exercising even the elements of it." [55] But when General Seymour began to communicate with the Canadian ministers directly, bypassing the governor general whom he had accused of supporting Hutton's pretensions, Wolseley, the commander in chief, and Lansdowne, the secretary of state, both forcibly expressed their disapproval. [56]

The wrangle went on for a long time, and files on the subject piled up in the War Office. After Hutton had left, Seymour attempted to reassert his position as adviser to the Canadian government and commented adversely on its renewed flirtation with the idea of appointing a Canadian as G.O.C. of the militia. Ultimately the dispute led to Seymour's own resignation, protesting as he went that he had not actually sought to command the militia, only to challenge Hutton's claim to be the adviser of the Canadian government which was in conflict with his own instructions. [57] Seymour had, in fact, become almost mentally unbalanced on the subject; and his complaints cannot be taken too seriously. But the incident served to demonstrate once more the unsatisfactory nature of the structure of military command in Canada. Dundonald was to claim a little later that the Halifax commander, although now only a colonel with the temporary rank of major general, was still signing himself "Commanding Troops, Canada," when the G.O.C. himself was a full major general and would presumably be in supreme command of both

55. "Position of the G.O.C. [Canadian] Troops, 1899," *ibid.*, W.O. 32/815/ 058/2309/143907/1899.

56. "Position of the G.O.C. [Canadian] Troops, 1900," *ibid.*, W.O. 32/815/ 058/2380/133036/1900.

57. "Lord Seymour and His Position in Canada," *ibid.*, W.O. 32/815/058/ 2525/258673/1900, 32/815/2372/116078/1900, and 32/815/058/133036/1900.

imperial and Canadian troops in event of war with the United States until a more senior general arrived to take over. The War Office therefore proposed that the officer commanding troops in Halifax should be called "Officer Commanding, Regular Forces, Canada," and that the G.O.C. of the militia should be styled "Officer Commanding Canadian Troops, Canada," which did not entirely remove the ambiguity.[58] The anomalous conflict of command was only satisfactorily eliminated by the complete withdrawal of the Halifax garrison.

Weakness in Imperial Defense and Canadian Defense Policy

The South African War, which had created some of the problems that put an end to Hutton's efforts to bring Canada into the imperial military fold, was in the long run to start a chain of events leading to rather different and more effective solution of the Empire's defense problems. Even before the South African War broke out there was plenty of evidence that the Empire's defense difficulties were insoluble without a radical shift in policy and opinion. *The Army Book for the British Empire*, which carried semi-official authority, claimed there were already signs of the growth of "wider views and a deeper insight"; and it stated:

The increase of knowledge of these conditions in the Colonies is marked, and the earnest efforts which are being made in some of them to bear their part in guaranteeing national security are among the most satisfactory signs of the times. The solution cannot be dictated and is possible only by arriving at an understanding of the real needs of the Empire as a whole, and of the mutual interdependence of its scattered positions.

But it admitted, "The great problem [of imperial defense] has not yet been completely solved." [59] A few months before the Colonial Conference of 1897, Clarke wrote, "The older ideas of Colonial Empire have given place to a nobler conception—that

58. Lt. Col. E. A. Altham, A.G.M.G., June 16, 1902, "Relative Position of G.O.C. Canadian Militia and O.C. Troops, Canada," *ibid.*, W.O. 32/815/058/2653/144394/02; W.O. to C.O., July 5, 1902, P.R.O., C.O. 42/858.
59. Goodenough and Dalton, *The Army Book*, p. 12.

of union on terms of equality. Already there are signs that the influence of the Colonies is beginning to react on the Mother Country . . . the idea of a United Empire . . . has everywhere gained ground." [60]

These optimistic forecasts, and this vision of an imminent state of equality, were premature. After the 1897 Conference, Hutton wrote that despite the recommendations of the conference ten years earlier, "The military defence of the Empire on any comprehensive scale has practically remained *in statu quo.*" He said the Colonial Defence Committee was still not authorized to prepare "any broad scheme for the military defence of the Empire, nor to formulate any joint system or organized defence in which all Her Majesty's dominions shall take a share." The Colonial Defence Committee had given valuable advice, and much money had been spent on piecemeal defense, but there was no over-all plan. To account for this situation, Hutton blamed the excessive emphasis that had been placed on "supremacy at sea" as "the basis of Imperial defence." He said the result of the emphasis put on this doctrine was that the colonies had "ceased to disquiet themselves" or to tax themselves to provide naval forces.[61]

On the Canadian side the story was much the same. The militia suffered not merely from the effects of political interference and long neglect, but also from lack of staff, transport, supply services, and medical services.[62] The Esquimalt arrangement was unsatisfactory. The base had been placed under the control of the general commanding British North America who was thousands of miles away at Halifax; but his responsibility was in effect shared with the government of Canada, who paid for the garrison and provided reinforcements, and with the Admiralty who provided the marines and used the base.[63] By 1897 the militia in Nova Scotia had been issued with Lee-Enfields,[64] but in order to guarantee their attendance for training in the garrison it was

60. Clarke, *Imperial Defence* (1897), p. ix.
61. Hutton, "Co-operative System for the Defence of the Empire," pp. 98–102.
62. C.D.C., Secret Memorandum 59M, "Defence of the Dominion," March 27, 1896, P.R.O., Cab. 11/27, C.D.C. Minutes, 1885–1908.
63. Aberdeen 33, Feb. 4, 1895, P.R.O., C.O. 42/829.
64. P.A.C., R.G. 9, II B 2 (71), Vol. 33.

necessary to pay the men, and the Colonial Defence Committee thought that Britain should not assume this charge.[65] These evils and difficulties all stemmed from past or present divided control and responsibility. Their elimination was unlikely until Canada became fully aware of her responsibilities, and until Britain realized that imperial control, even in a disguised form, was unacceptable to the dominions.

65. C.D.C., Minute 17/3/98, P.R.O., Cab. 11/27.

9

The Boer War, the Reinvigoration of
Imperialism,—or of Colonial Nationalism?

The Call to Arms

Events in South Africa diverted everyone's attention before there had been enough time to carry out the recommendations of the Canadian Defence Commission and so to fulfil the agreements upon military standardization and co-ordination of military effort made at the Colonial Conference in 1897. During 1899, Britain's relations with the two Boer republics, badly strained by the ill-treatment of British citizens in the Transvaal, deteriorated rapidly as the high commissioner, Sir Alfred Milner, and the president of the Transvaal, Paul Kruger, became convinced that a solution could only be reached through war. Public opinion in Britain was greatly inflamed, and the imperial sentiment which flared up there was reflected far and wide throughout the self-governing colonies. The nature and extent of colonial aid in war became a hotly debated issue, and, as in 1885, offers of service began to pour in from English-speaking individuals and militia units. French-Canadians, however, remained aloof and skeptical: foreign and imperial entanglements had little appeal for them. In Britain on June 8, 1899, the commander in chief, realizing the implications of these things, told the secretary of state for war, Lord Lansdowne, "It would create an excellent feeling if each of the Australian colonies, Tasmania, and New Zealand, furnished contingents of mounted troops and that Canada should furnish two battalions of foot." [1]

The commandant in New South Wales, Major General George

1. G.B., *P.P.*, 1904, XL, 262 (Cd. 1789).

A. French, and the G.O.C. in Canada, Major General E. T. H. Hutton, both general officers on loan from the British Army, began to discuss publicly the possible composition of colonial aid. Queensland and other Australian colonies sent offers of troops to Britain.[2] However, General Sir Redvers Buller, who had been appointed to command the force being assembled for South Africa, hoped to recruit irregulars from among the men expelled by the Boer Republics, and he was "rather reluctant to accept . . . overseas" (i.e., non-South African) colonials, who would be given the British rates of pay, lest he might then not be able to carry out his plan to recruit the South Africans at a higher colonial rate. He proposed that small units of colonial infantry should be attached to British regiments. After the war, he claimed that in the belief that all colonials could ride he had intended to use them as mounted infantry.[3] However, Lansdowne could not recall that Buller had intended to mount the colonials.

The colonial secretary, Chamberlain, seizing the opportunity to publicize the loyalty of the colonies, sent similarly worded letters to all colonial governors, setting out the terms on which offers of service would be accepted. Making no distinction between those colonies which already had officially made offers and those in which, thus far, offers had only been made by individuals, he asked that colonial troops should be organized in infantry units of not more than 125 men each, with only one officer of the rank of major in charge of each colonial contingent. They should be equipped and transported to South Africa at either their own, or their colony's, expense. On arrival they would be taken on to imperial pay at the port of disembarkation. They would be sent home at British expense on completion of service and would be entitled to British casualty allowances. Ignoring the fact that some colonial ministries had not yet made their

2. Buchan, *Lord Minto*, p. 137; G.B., *P.P.*, 1904, XL, Vol. I, paras. 8019, 8021, 8025 (Cd. 1790). Hutton's plans were published, possibly without his instigation in *The [Canadian] Military Gazette* (Ottawa) of Oct. 3, 1899. General French had been inspector of artillery, Canada, from 1870 to 1873, and commissioner of the Northwest Mounted Police from 1873 to 1876.

3. G.B., *P.P.*, 1904, XLI, paras. 15277, 15279, 21138, 21139, 21140, 21141 (Cd. 1791).

minds up about sending aid, Chamberlain concluded his telegram to every governor in the same words: "Inform accordingly all who have offered to raise volunteers." [4] This was not merely, as a contemporary noted, an official British request for colonial contingents; [5] it was a deliberate attempt to put pressure on the slower colonial governments by appealing over their heads to the growing number of militant imperialists who had pressed for colonial participation in the coming war.

The War Office's telegrams were badly worded and misleading. Because they seemed to imply that cavalry was not wanted in a war in which, as everyone knew, mounted men would be invaluable, [6] they had the effect of confusing the very people to whom Chamberlain intended to appeal. Someone in the War Office probably believed that colonial cavalry would be inadequately trained by British standards and also had no proper appreciation of the role that mounted infantry would play.

After the war, Lansdowne was to allege that colonial attachment to regiments "was very much approved at the time by the colonies and it was a reasonable one"; [7] but in saying this he completely ignored the fact that the Canadian government, having bowed to the clamor of Canadian imperialists, had agreed that it would send not small units but a battalion one thousand men strong—twice as many as had been requested—on condition that the unit be kept together as much as possible under its Canadian lieutenant colonel. [8] Thus, Laurier, yielding to the imperialists' demands three days after the war began, had insisted on a qualification which appealed to national sentiment in Canada. Lest this be thought contrary to the ideas of the colonial imperialists, let it be remembered that when the contingents from the separate Australian contingents reached South Africa,

4. Canada, Department of Militia and Defence, *Supplementary Report: Organization, Equipment, Despatch, and Service of the Canadian Contingents During the War in South Africa, 1899–1900* (Ottawa: King's Printer, 1901), Pt. II, p. 1.

5. William Sanford Evans, *The Canadian Contingents and Canadian Imperialism: A Story and a Study* (Toronto: Publishers' Syndicate, 1901), p. 57.

6. G.B., *P.P.*, 1904, XL, para. 124 (Cd. 1789).

7. *Ibid.*, XLI, para. 21138 (Cd. 1791).

8. Canada, Department of Militia and Defence, *Supplementary Report . . . the War in South Africa*, Pt. II, p. 4.

anticipating the creation of the Commonwealth of Australia which did not then exist, they formed an Australian regiment.[9] Although this may have been organized mainly for the convenience of the British staff at Cape Town,[10] it found favor with the colonial troops because nationalism was already a vigorous growth even among those imperially minded colonials who had volunteered for service in South Africa. This paradox was difficult for people at that time to understand.

Laurier at first resisted the call to send Canadians to South Africa, partly because he knew that Quebec was indifferent to imperial sentiment, but also because he thought that Britain's need was not great enough to warrant Canadian aid. One of his ablest supporters, Henri Bourassa, was adamantly opposed to any Canadian participation in an imperial war and broke with his chief on this issue. Another French-Canadian member of the government, Israel Tarte, who remained in office a little longer, thought that aid should not be sent without Canada "voting in the Imperial councils." [11] In New Zealand, the prime minister, Richard Seddon, took up with zest the project to send troops, but only because he thought it a step toward a voice "in the council of the nation at home." [12] There was thus a general belief throughout the colonies that colonial aid to Britain should be conditional. British losses in "Black Week" and the cry that the Empire was in danger overcame some of the hesitation brought by these desires for conditions; but as the war went on, colonial interest declined and governments left the equipping and even the recruiting of later contingents to the British government or to private individuals, doing less out of colonial funds than they had done at the beginning of the war. They also

9. Arthur W. José. "The Empire that Found Itself," R.U.S.I. Library Pamphlets, 1901, 10/21/8, p. 39.

10. Warren Perry, "The Military Life of Major General Sir John Charles Hoad," *The Victorian Historical Magazine*, XXIX (Aug. 1959), 169.

11. "Tupper's Memo. to H.E. on the South African War, 23 Sept., 1902, Referring to a Speech Made by Tarte at St. Vincent de Paul, 28 Oct., 1900," P.A.C., Minto Papers, M.G. 27, II B 1, Box MM, No. 33.

12. A. J. Harrop, *New Zealand after Five Wars* (London: Jarrolds, n.d.), p. 82. For a general account of the New Zealand contribution, see *The New Zealanders in South Africa, 1899–1902* (Wellington: New Zealand Department of Internal Affairs, War History Branch, 1949).

became less willing to alter their British pay rates to bring them up to colonial standards. Furthermore, from all the other colonies only about 30,000 men all told went to South Africa; this compared to 50,000 men from the South African colonies themselves. And it was a small part of a grand total of 450,000 men.[13] Canada's contribution was about 8,300. However, this number included 5,000 troops raised by Britain or Lord Strathcona without cost to the Dominion, as well as the battalion which garrisoned Halifax to release the Prince of Wales's Leinsters (Royal Canadians) for war service.[14] When the Commonwealth of Australia was created, its government held back from further war effort on the pretext that its legal position was not clear.[15] All these things serve to show that the colonies made only qualified, limited, hesitant, and declining contributions.

The reason for this relative lack of support was that the South African War was not the Empire emergency about which imperialists had warned. The Empire was not threatened at the center, nor was it even seriously faced with irremediable damage in any of its parts. A small people, of European race, armed with modern weapons, and with an early local superiority in numbers had proved more able to resist the British Army than the primitive tribes that the Empire had faced in recent years. If that situation could not be handled easily, it was not because the Boers presented any real threat to the integrity of the Empire. Although it is possible that the war might have been won by the Boers in the early weeks if they had moved rapidly into Cape Colony and had won more effective German support, that possibility could not have been absolutely prevented by any degree of colonial commitment or colonial aid. Colonial support, however small, was needed only because, as the Canadian G.O.C., Major General O'Grady Haly, reported, "The chief object . . . was to demonstrate to the world that England could not be at-

---

13. G.B., *P.P.*, 1904, XL, p. 76, paras. 141–142, (Cd. 1789).
14. Charles P. Stacey, "The Development of the Canadian Army," in *Introduction to Military History* (Ottawa: Queen's Printer, 1955), p. 20. The Elgin Commission reported that 7,368 Canadians went to South Africa, including 1,238 raised for the South African Constabulary (G.B., *P.P.*, 1904, XL, para. 76 n. [Cd. 1789]). The difference is explained by the Halifax garrison.
15. *Ibid.*, XL, paras. 8252–8253 (Cd. 1790).

tacked without the assailants having the colonies to reckon with at the same time, and that in the colonies there are, without there being what might be called the nucleus of a standing army, citizen soldierly forces which are to the Empire a formidable strength." [16] To fulfil that purpose the colonies' support was sufficient.

It was also adequate for the object that Chamberlain, Minto, Hutton, and the like had in mind; but it is doubtful whether any of Britain's potential enemies were impressed. Indeed, the demonstration of support may have been necessary not so much to show European nations that Britain in isolation was still not alone, as to offset the moral disadvantage suffered by the British Conservative government when it was accused of bullying a small colonial people. But the charge that the South African War was unprovoked imperialist aggression served to discourage full colonial support for Britain's cause.

The Colonial Achievement in South Africa

Nevertheless, European observers ought to have been impressed by the celerity of the colonial responses. The first New Zealand contingent sailed in fourteen days, even though the men had to be collected from all over the country and even though much of their equipment had to be specially made.[17] The first Canadian contingent, composed of men from militia units across Canada from Prince Edward Island to British Columbia, embarked sixteen days after the orders were issued. All were volunteers. The Permanent Force made a large contribution, but many of the volunteers were little more than raw recruits who had joined in order to seek excitement in South Africa. The contingent was formed into a Second (Special Service) Battalion of the Royal Canadian Regiment under the command of Lieutenant Colonel W. D. Otter of the Canadian Permanent Force. It arrived at Cape Town on November 29, 1899, and after a period

16. O'Grady Haly, March 27, 1901, in Canada, Department of Militia and Defence, *Supplementary Report . . . the War in South Africa*, Pt. II, p. 192.
17. Ranfurly to Chamberlain, Oct. 23, 1899, New Zealand Archives, Governor, Confidential, G. 26/4.

of training and picket duty on the line of communication it went into action at Paardeberg in February, 1900, five months after it had first been called into being. However, as enlistment was only for twelve months, and as many of the men had no wish to extend it, the Second Royal Canadian Regiment was withdrawn from operational service in September to return to Canada.

A second Canadian contingent had been offered only one week after the first, but it was not accepted by the War Office until after "Black Week." This contingent was organized into two regiments of Canadian Mounted Rifles and their batteries of field artillery. With Strathcona's Horse, raised at the private expense of the founder, and with the twelve squadrons of skilled horsemen raised in Canada for three years' service with the South African Constabulary, these later arrivals saw much campaigning in the later stages of the war when the main Boer armies had been defeated and the difficult task of clearing the country of irregular commandos had to be carried out.[18]

What should also have been noted in Europe was that the performance of the colonials in South Africa compared not unfavorably with that of their British comrades, even though the latter included more regulars and fewer recruits. By the time the overseas colonials got into action, the British had learned through severe losses that they were fighting a kind of war for which they had not been adequately prepared either by organization or training. New lessons had to be assimilated. In some ways, therefore, the colonials started on a level similar to the British regulars. The colonials learned to respect the professional training and experience of the British and benefited greatly from it; but numerous witnesses who appeared before the Elgin Commission of Enquiry into the conduct of the war testified to the fighting qualities of the men from the colonies. Field Marshal Lord Wolseley, who did not fight in South Africa, went so far as to state that he believed they would have stood up against European regulars. "The colonial contingents would have fought anybody, but I should not extend that same expression of opinion

18. Stanley, *Canada's Soldiers,* pp. 280–285.

to the very large bodies of men we sent out from here." [19] He meant, presumably, men recruited in Britain for the duration of the war, and not the British regulars. However, Wolseley had never fought in Europe and cannot be regarded as a conclusive witness. The commissioners themselves described colonials as "half soldiers by their upbringing," a rather exaggerated concept; but they emphasized their need for training and discipline.[20] Thus, the fighting quality of colonial troops seems to have impressed, and perhaps surprised, many British regular officers.

The only significant qualification made by the Elgin Commission on these eulogies was in regard to the efficiency of colonial officers. It declared that colonial units were greatly improved "by attaching to them officers from the Regular Army." Many witnesses went still further and said that colonials fought better when under British Regular Army commanding officers and adjutants,[21] though some admitted that colonial officers who had had training in England were nearly as good as British regulars.[22] Graduates of the Royal Military College, Kingston, were classed by one witness along with regular officers; but another said that although they were well trained, they lacked experience in handling men.[23] Some witnesses said that all colonial officers were excellent; another complained of their intemperance.[24] These generalizations cannot all be taken at their face value, and indeed some were mutually contradictory. But they pointed to the fact that the colonies lacked a supply of experienced officers.

In view of Hutton's experience in Australia and Canada and his command of a mixed force from both countries in South Africa, his opinion might be expected to carry weight. But when

19. G.B., *P.P.*, 1904, XL, para. 146 (Cd. 1789); paras. 9128, 9133, 9134 (Lord Wolseley, 10346) (Cd. 1790); XLI, paras. 13253 (Lord Roberts), 20011 (Maj. Gen. Baden Powell) (Cd. 1791).
20. *Ibid.*, XL, para. 149 (Cd. 1789).
21. *Ibid.*, XL, 80, para. 147 (Cd. 1789); para. 10234 (Lord Roberts) (Cd. 1790); XLI, paras. 12767, 12768 (Maj. Gen. Baden Powell) (Cd. 1791).
22. *Ibid.*, XL, 452 (Major, the Marquis of Tullibardine), paras. 8444, 8446, 12744 (Cd. 1790).
23. *Ibid.*, XL, paras. 258, 259 (Cd. 1790); XLI, paras. 12769, 12812 (Cd. 1791).
24. *Ibid.*, XL, 454, paras. 12741, 19543, 19564 (Cd. 1790).

he wrote to Minto that Canadian officers "do not seem to possess a military instinct to the same degree as the others [the Australians]" and blamed this on the intrusion of politics into the Canadian Militia, his statement was possibly a reflection of his anger over his dismissal by the Canadian government and the fact that he was angling for a command in Australia.[25] Six months later he told the governor general of Canada that both Canadian and Australian troops were much improved after his tours of duty in those countries and that the Canadians showed up better because they were better organized.[26]

The following is perhaps one of the most useful pieces of evidence about the adaptability and efficiency of colonial officers and also about British attitudes on the subject. Although at the outset the secretary of state had said that, apart from sixteen men who were to be under instruction, it was unthinkable that Canadians should be added to the imperial staff, many were in fact selected for staff employment in the field.[27] Colonial officers obviously suffered initially from lack of training and experience, but the record suggests that they learned much faster than some British G.O.C.'s in past years would have believed possible.

Little information is available to permit more detailed comparison of the training of the British and colonial forces, but evidence of the practice of breaking up artillery units and using them indiscriminately may be an indication that they were regarded as interchangeable. On the other hand, it can also be taken as proof of a desire to intermingle inexperienced colonial gunners with regulars. For example, "E" Battery of the Royal Canadian Field Artillery was scattered along the line from

25. Hutton to Minto, Aug. 18, 1900, P.A.C., Minto Papers, M.G. 27, II B 1, Vol. 16.

26. Hutton to Minto, Feb. 8, 1901, *ibid.*, Vol. 17, p. 29. As Hutton had served in Canada more recently, this appears almost as if he were claiming all the credit for himself. However, he was not referring to himself, as has been alleged, when he spoke of "the dashing leader" under whom they had been "privileged to learn" (see Stanley, *Canada's Soldiers*, p. 286). That reference was to Colonel E. A. H. Alderson, who was to become commander of the Canadian Expeditionary Force in 1914 (Hutton to Lessard, Oct. 14, 1900, in Canada, Department of Militia and Defence, *Supplementary Report . . . the War in South Africa*, Pt. II, p. 94).

27. Canada, Department of Militia and Defence, *Supplementary Report . . . the War in South Africa*, Pt. II, pp. 4, 7, 30–31.

Kimberley to Vryburg; its commanding officer acted for six weeks as officer commanding the Western District at Vryburg. There he commanded a battery with a right section consisting of two guns of the Royal Field Artillery, with a center of two guns of the Royal Canadian Field Artillery, and with a left section of two guns of the Royal Australian Artillery. Major G. Hunter Ogilvie, the Canadian officer who had this "almost unique" experience of a mixed command, found that the English gunners were a "well-balanced and a well-seasoned lot" and that their horses were larger, while the Canadians and Australians were physically bigger and more athletic men and their horses were faster and lighter in the bone.[28] Unfortunately he made no further comment on training and efficiency. His silence when there was integration to this extent may suggest that the colonial gunners were adequately trained on British lines and to British standards. Mounted troops were also mixed. Certain irregular mounted units, like the Bush Veldt Carbineers, were made up by transferring men to them from various colonial units that elected to stay in South Africa when their comrades returned home. But the standards and practices of the carbineers were not those of regular cavalry; and so this example of integration also provides little comparative evidence about the nature and quality of colonial training.

Equipment and Supplies

In view of the fact that standardization of equipment, weapons, and ammunition had been urged over and over again since the point was first raised by the Carnarvon Commission, and that there had recently been a resolution on the subject at the Colonial Conference of 1897, surprisingly little appeared in official reports to indicate the extent to which this problem affected the integration of colonial troops into British armies. Equipment problems in war had not yet become as important as they are in more technically advanced days. Colonial troops almost all arrived in South Africa fully equipped either by their own govern-

28. *Ibid.*, p. 150.

ment or by private subscription, and little difficulty seems to have arisen from the differences that must have existed. Perhaps the most serious problem was that the Australian "digger" hats resembled those of the Boers and occasionally attracted fire from their own side.

Australia had been deficient in ammunition when the war began, and Major General G. A. French blamed the War Office for not placing orders with contractors until they were received from the colonies. He added that the War Office treated the colonials as if they were strangers instead of part of the defense force of the Empire.[29] New Zealand had been loath to wrap capital up by stockpiling ammunition; and the commandant of her forces, Lieutenant Colonel Pole Penton, argued that the imperial government ought to have maintained an adequate reserve.[30] Shortage of war matériel in the colonies was an obvious weakness; and reliance on Britain for supplies when Britain was herself mobilizing for war meant that colonial orders had less chance of being filled.

Canada manufactured much of her own matériel except for field guns and (though strangely these were not mentioned as exceptions) the Lee-Enfield rifles that had been bought in quantity in the panic of 1896. At the outbreak of the South African War, however, only arms and Oliver "equipment" were in store, and orders for clothing and other equipment had to be hastily filled.[31] Lieutenant Colonel W. D. Otter, who commanded the First Contingent, thought the Canadians were as well equipped as any troops in South Africa, that their Lee-Enfields had stood up well to the test of use in action, but that their Canadian-designed Oliver "equipment" was unsatisfactory because it galled and

29. G.B., *P.P.*, 1904, XL, paras. 8104, 8111 (Cd. 1790).
30. *Ibid.*, XL, para. 8658 (Cd. 1790).
31. *Ibid.*, XL, para. 8380 (Cd. 1790); Canada, Department of Militia and Defence, *Supplementary Report . . . the War in South Africa*, Pt. I, p. 13. This "equipment," i.e., the infantrymen's carrying harness, had been designed by Surgeon Major Oliver, a veteran of the Red River expedition. Although favored by Wolseley and Redvers Buller, it was never adopted for the British Army. Luard tried unsuccessfully to persuade the Canadian government to adopt it for the militia. General Hutton finally succeeded in obtaining it in 1898 (Morton, "The Canadian Militia, 1867–1900," pp. 273–274, 316).

pinched.[32] He preferred Canadian boots; but not everyone agreed with him.[33] Canadian prairie wagons were described by a gunner as "far and away the best transport in the army" and were the envy of the British soldier. South African wagons were also said to be superior to the "heavy cattle-killing concerns in use in the British corps." [34] Canadian canvas duck uniform was cool, but the trousers caused chafing; the Canadian greatcoats lacked pockets and had a loose belt that was easily lost. The heavy Western Canadian stock saddle compared unfavorably with the lighter equipment of the Boer commandos.[35] Clearly there was room for standardization and for improvement of equipment on the basis of experience; but the lessons to be learned were not all on one side.

Colonial units, being an integral part of the British Army in South Africa, received British rations. A contract for meat was put out to the South African Cold Storage Company, which in 1901 bought large quantities of meat in the Argentine and caused Australian producers to complain that they were not getting a "due share" of the orders. Public opinion in Australia became greatly agitated, and repeated references were made in the press to the support that Australia had given in the war. On the other hand, there was some feeling that colonial support had not been given on the condition of sharing orders for supplies for the army. This point of view was expressed in the Sydney *Daily Telegraph* on January 29, 1902. The Australians were appeased a month later when the Imperial Supply and Cold Storage Company, another contractor to the army, cabled a promise to order from "the various British colonies." [36] Although it had not assumed unmanageable proportions in this war, here was a prob-

32. Canada, Department of Militia and Defence, *Supplementary Report . . . the War in South Africa*, Pt. II, p. 12.

33. G.B., *P.P.*, 1904, XL, paras. 8501 (Cd. 1790); XLI, para. 12596 (Cd. 1791).

34. Lt. E. W. B. Morrison, *With the Guns in South Africa* (Hamilton: Spectator, 1901), pp. 171–172.

35. Stanley, *Canada's Soldiers*, p. 287; Col. Otter's Report, Jan. 26, 1901, in Canada, Department of Militia and Defence, *Supplementary Report . . . the War in South Africa*, Pt. II, pp. 12–13.

36. Feb. 23, 1902, C.A.O., Prime Minister's Department, C.P. 103, S. 12, B. 3.

lem that would become more serious in the future. Control of war production entailed not merely obtaining the best and cheapest supplies for the army but also maintaining domestic production and home morale. When several separate self-governing colonies were fully engaged, this problem would become more complicated.

Legal Problems of Military Co-operation

The legal implications of sending colonial troops to serve overseas raised problems about the authority for their dispatch and also about jurisdiction over them in the field. With regard to the first point there was a recent precedent of interest. In 1899, as a result of the Fashoda crisis, the War Office had considered plans for taking over St. Pierre and Miquelon, the French islands in the St. Lawrence, in the event of war with France. Troops from the garrison at Halifax would be used in the first instance, but it was proposed to reinforce them shortly by Canadian Militia. The governor general, Lord Minto, thought that Section 79 of the Militia Act gave no authority for Canadian troops to be used outside the Dominion except perhaps for pursuit into the United States. He drew a careful distinction between what he called a "sentimental offer" of troops for service in the event of a European war, and the question of whether the Queen had the right to call out the militia for service on other expeditions outside the Dominion. Laurier consulted the Cabinet on this question on March 25, 1899, and the ministers of justice and of militia, D. Mills and F. W. Borden, agreed that under the Militia Act the Queen could order troops to any part of the world in time of war. Laurier told Minto that in the case of the French islands, he personally advised against the use of French-Canadians, "but in saying this he in no way qualified the right of the Imperial government" to call out the militia for service outside Canada. He thought that the original framers of the act had had no idea of service overseas, but only in the possibility of a war with the United States. However, he declared that the law was quite clear.

Minto then read to Laurier Macdonald's letter of February 9, 1885, written at the time of the Sudan crisis, in which he had said that Canadian troops for overseas service should be recruited by Britain into the Regular Army; but the prime minister adhered to his opinion.

This puzzling Cabinet decision was thought in the War Office to have been a result of the fact that no single militia regiment was sufficiently efficient for employment overseas as an operational unit. To take offers of volunteers from a militia company for reinforcement of British regiments would be a very different thing.[37] But this does not explain why Laurier should have proposed to interpret the Militia Act in such a way that if Britain had been prepared to pay the whole cost the Canadian Militia could be drafted for overseas service in any war. It is possible the Canadian ministers had an eye to the future of these strategically placed islands, and were therefore not unwilling to have them garrisoned by Canadians, and that this governed their opinion.

The South African War was, however, something very different from the occupation of St. Pierre and Miquelon and more akin to the "sentimental offer" of troops to which Minto had referred. Two questions affected this issue. First, part of the cost was borne by Canada and therefore would require the assent of the Canadian Parliament. And second, any large use of Canadians in an overseas campaign not clearly a Canadian concern, whether the men were supplied from the militia or by direct enlistment, would inevitably become a political matter subject to parliamentary comment. There could therefore be no question of the British government calling for Canadians for the South African War in the name of the Queen. When he yielded to political pressure and agreed to send the First Contingent, Laurier took the curious attitude that as the expense was not large and would not be a precedent, it would be no departure

37. "Question of the Use of Canadian Troops for Reinforcement of Or Occupation of Miquelon and St. Pierre," P.R.O., W.O. 32/275/266, Canada 100/91823/1899.

from constitutional practice for the government to act without calling Parliament into session.[38] Presumably he sent the contingent on the assumption that as the Queen could call out the militia and even send it overseas, the Canadian Cabinet, acting in her name, could do the same thing.

In South Africa the colonials became subject to the British Army Act and were subject to the provisions of Queen's Regulations. As their numbers were relatively few, as all were volunteers, and as many of them had served in colonial militias and were accustomed to military law, few difficulties occurred. But one famous incident illustrated the anomalous legal position of the colonials and revealed a degree of detachment on the part of a colonial government that was unlikely to persist. Some Australian officers were court-martialed for the murder of prisoners of war. "Breaker" Morant and the others involved had gone to South Africa with Australian units and had been transferred to the Bush Veldt Carbineers, one of the mounted units organized to round up the irregular Boer forces. A recent investigator has shown that evidence was given that the carbineers had instructions to take severe action to deal with Boers caught wearing khaki and that they had been discouraged from taking prisoners. The Australians were convicted of the murder of some prisoners but were acquitted of responsibility for the murder of a German missionary which had occurred when they were in his vicinity.

It was reported that the Australian prime minister, Sir Edmund Barton, believed that Australia could not expect to be informed about the trial of Australian soldiers in South Africa except as a courtesy. When the prisoners, facing the death sentence, attempted to communicate with Australia, every obstacle was put in their way by the army authorities. Telegrams appealing to the Commonwealth and state governments were suppressed. In the last hours before the execution, Kitchener and other senior officers, who alone could have ordered a stay of execution to give time for Australian opinion to be heard, are said to have deliberately made themselves unavailable in the depths of the

38. Stanley, *Canada's Soldiers*, p. 280; Canada, Department of Militia and Defence, *Supplementary Report: . . . the War in South Africa*, Pt. 1, p. 2.

Veldt. Afterward, when Australia did ask questions, Kitchener allegedly gave a false reply.[39] It was the belief of F. M. Cutlack, the distinguished author of one of the volumes of Australia's official history of World War I who has looked into the matter recently, that Morant and an associate were executed to placate the German government which was incensed over the murder of the German missionary, a charge on which the court had actually found the Australians "not guilty." The Australian government, diverted by Kitchener's deception, did not pursue the matter; and public opinion was soon distracted by other events, such as the problems of the new federation, the end of the war, and the death of Queen Victoria. But from time to time in the years that followed, the treatment of Breaker Morant was brought up in the Australian press. Cutlack believes that Morant's fate, and the British Army's handling of his case, explains why the Australian government and people took such a strong stand against the death penalty for Australian troops in World War I, and were therefore in favor of a legal code for Australian troops that differed from the British code.[40]

At the time of the South African War, colonial troops fighting with the British Army had no such special status. Major Lenehan, an Australian who commanded one of the Bush Veldt units, was cashiered for concealing thirteen murders similar to those with which Morant was charged. Lenehan was reprimanded by Kitchener, was relieved of his command, and was sent under escort to Cape Town for repatriation. When he reached Australia, General Hutton dismissed him from the militia. Lenehan did not complain about his treatment, but the Australian government initiated inquiries. It was assured by Kitchener that the escort provided for Lenehan was for his protection because the Boers were incensed by the murder of prisoners. Lenehan later

39. Frederic M. Cutlack, *Breaker Morant: A Horseman Who Made History* (Sydney: Ure Smith, 1962), p. 103.

40. *Ibid.*, p. 22 and *passim;* Lt. Trent G. R. Witton, *Scapegoats of Empire* (Melbourne: D. W. Patterson, 1907); Adelaide *Advertiser*, March 28, 31, April 3, 7, 1902; Commonwealth of Australia, *P.P.*, II, 137; I. F. Thomas to Hon. E. Barton, May 9, 1902, C.A.O., Prime Minister's Department, C.P. 103, S. 12, B. 5. Some Canadian soldiers in France were executed during World War I without word being given to the Canadian government.

submitted to the imperial authorities claims for back pay and gratuities as well as for compensation for loss of personal belongings; but these were rejected. However, the Commonwealth authorities reinstated him in their military forces.[41] Obviously, it did not occur to colonial troops to complain about being subjected to British military discipline until such time as they found themselves victimized. The Bush Veldt Carbineers were British units organized from colonial volunteers and therefore not liable for special status. Yet it was inevitable that colonial governments must eventually take an interest in the protection of their citizens against judicial abuse or arbitrary treatment.

The Effects of Going to War

In the crucibles of war nations mature rapidly. Participation in the South African War had effects on all the colonies, and especially on Canada, out of all proportion to the size of the effort made or to the degree in which they were involved. Although the racial disputes that had erupted over the sending of troops to an "imperial war" had distracted some popular attention in Canada, there was widespread pride in the achievements of Canadian soldiers on a distant field of battle. Four Victoria Crosses were won by Canadians, and the newspapers published stories of Canadian dash and bravery. Though this war was not a severe testing by comparison with the next great upheaval in which the nations of the British Commonwealth came of age, it nevertheless served to give Canadians, and other colonials as well, a new outlook on the world. To some contemporaries the crisis about participation had seemed to pose the question whether Canada would move toward a new place in an integrated Empire or fall back on the road to colonial subjection. In fact, neither of these was the real destination. Instead, the war opened a path toward nationhood, but at the same time racial animosities were aroused which sowed fertile seeds of national disintegration in Canada.

41. Case of Major Lenehan, C.O., Bush Veldt Carbineers, C.A.O., Prime Minister's Department, C.P. 103, S. 12, B. 6.

For the present, however, although the imperialists had not yet had all their say, the trend was set toward national status. So, as the twentieth century dawned, Canada had found that it could not easily stand aside from distant world problems. Even when a dispute was not of its immediate concern, the emotional involvement of some Canadians could drag the country into it. Canada had given the first signs that it could not be left out of any reckoning to which it had made a contribution. Furthermore, Canadians had begun to realize that their own defense problems must be regarded in wider terms than merely those of their own safety against a possible, or an unlikely, American attack. It was therefore important that Canadian soldiers had gained on the South African veldt an experience of modern war and of military organization and routine that was bound to affect the defense policies and military development of their country and the Empire as well. But the significance of these things was not immediately apparent.

For the problems of the defense of the Empire, the South African War provided no complete answer. It was true that the theory of sea power, which had been elevated into an articulate doctrine by the Colombs and translated into a world-wide creed by Mahan, appeared to have been substantiated. Britain's navy had kept the local war isolated, had maintained communications and supplies until victory was achieved, and had prevented other powers from dabbling in troubled waters. All this was convincing evidence, not merely of the significance of sea power upon the course of history, but even more of the fact that it could deter war by preventing the expansion of the conflagration.

Yet sea power by itself had not been enough. Navies have the self-evident limitation that they cannot project themselves inland and win victories. Sea power can seldom dominate nations; it can only keep open the routes over which land forces and supplies travel to the theater of operations, and deny those routes to the enemy. Hence, whereas the South African War appeared to confirm Mahan, this war that followed so soon after Captain James spoke to the Royal United Service Institution effectively proved the thesis of that address. The "necessity for an army as well as a navy" was now made obvious by the tragic early humiliation that British arms had suffered and by the length and severity of the struggle.

Furthermore, if Britain found so much difficulty in suppressing two small republics, how would her forces fare in the event of a major European war? Some consolation might be sought from the fact that this was a different kind of war, that the open veldt was very different from a thickly populated European theater of war, and that the Boers were not an ordinary people but one that was (as the Elgin Commission described colonials generally) "half military by upbringing." Making every allowance for the fact that these conditions might never be repeated, it was still clear that the British Army had been caught ill-prepared and that it might be found wanting again. The prestige of British soldiers in the field had been high in the last two decades of the nineteenth century. But this was when they had frequently fought savage tribes who were armed only with spears. However, the ordinary British soldier's prestige had not suffered as much in South Africa as that of his leaders. Hence, quite apart from the fact that Britain had a disadvantage in numbers of trained men, which was yet another problem, there was clearly also doubt about the army's adaptability, about its ability to face European troops with modern weapons, and even more about its basic organization for planning operations and supplying and maintaining forces in the field. A thorough investigation was inevitable. The Elgin Commission of Enquiry into the conduct of the war was a necessary step; and plans to reform the military establishment in Britain were under consideration even before the commission had reported.

Yet, even before the war ended, reform had suffered its first great rebuff in the most vital field of all, interservice co-operation. After the disasters in South Africa it had been proposed that the defense committee of the Cabinet, which looked at defense problems as a whole rather than as separate naval and military concerns, should meet regularly and have a secretary. But the First Lord of the Admiralty, Lord Goschen, opposed the plan.[42]

42. P.R.O., Cab. 1, Box 3, No. 53, Nov., 1900.

The Admiralty had no immediate concern with the prosecution of the war which was still in progress, and it could see little advantage to be gained by exposing itself to the limitations upon its freedom of action which a permanent defense committee might impose.

In addition to interservice co-operation, a second valuable development could be the perpetuation of the imperial co-operation that the war had produced. The conflict had created a new spirit in the colonies. Something might now be done to bring them closer to the mother country. So wrote Chamberlain to Minto in March, 1900; at the same time he asked whether the colonies would like to be consulted in connection with the terms of the peace settlement. As he went on to say that annexation and eventual self-government had already been planned, it would seem that "consultation" meant to him in fact little more than "information," as indeed it was to mean to British officials and governments for many more years. Chamberlain also asked whether the time had not now come for an imperial council to advise the secretary of state for the colonies, much as the Indian Council advised the secretary of state for India. Questions of defense, in particular the number and character of forces to be permanently maintained by each colony, would be considered by this council. Chamberlain's reference to India was typical— and unfortunate. The Canadian government could not relish undertaking so far-reaching a commitment to a body which might claim to dictate the size of Canadian forces in return for little more than Canada's right to be told as much as Britain wished to tell. Still less could Canadians appreciate being asked to accept a development modeled on Britain's rule of her great Eastern dependancy. Inevitably, Minto's reply was "disappointing" to Chamberlain.[43] But this idea of an Empire council was to crop up again.

The colonial response to the call for aid in 1899 and the realization that in a greater emergency the colonies might help to redress the balance against Britain in a European war, had,

43. Minto to Chamberlain, March 2, 1900, P.A.C., Minto Papers, M.G. 27, II B 1, Vol. 14, pp. 55, 60.

however, reinvigorated those who called for imperial centralization. The Imperial Federation (Defence) League, heir of the defunct Imperial Federation League, had become convinced by 1900 that political federation must be an inevitable consequence of imperial defense contributions. The colonies, said one of the league's Australian members in 1902, were not doing enough; militia forces and fortifications were now only for local defense, and the Canadian Pacific Railway was a commercial enterprise. If proposals for contributions for imperial defense caused the colonies to secede, "the connection which now exists is hardly worth having." [44] The Elgin Commission had also concluded that the most significant lesson of the war was that there was "throughout the Empire, in the United Kingdom, its colonies and dependencies . . . a reserve of military strength which, for many reasons, we cannot and do not wish to convert into a standing army, but to which we may be glad to turn in our hour of need as we did in 1899." The commission said there had been no preparation or plan for utilizing those resources when the war broke out, and it felt that not enough was yet being done to put matters on a better footing in the event of another emergency. It balked at the thought of attempting to make the British Empire a great military power in the continental sense; but it had faith in the strength and unanimity of loyalty of the Empire "if properly used within the limitations which circumstances impose." [45]

When that report was written, an attempt following the South African War to capitalize on imperial sentiment at the Colonial Conference of 1902 had in fact already proved a partial failure. However, as the full text of the conference discussions was not published, the degree of success and failure was not known to the general public and perhaps not to the members of the Elgin Commission, despite their eminence. The significance of those discussions must be considered later.

The South African War had found Britain isolated with most

44. H. B. Bignold, *The Burden of Empire, by an Australian* ([Melbourne?]: Imperial Federation Defence League, 1902), in State Library of Victoria, Melbourne.
45. G.B., *P.P.*, 1904, XL, para. 155 (Cd. 1789).

European nations hostile to her, and the British Army had shown obvious signs of weakness. Colonial military aid was thereby made to appear the more important: troops from the self-governing colonies, including Canada, could become a valuable addition to British strength in time of need. It had been demonstrated that despite lack of experience, colonials quickly became first-class fighting men. Long tutelage under British officers had familiarized them with British military organization and methods and with British military law so that they could be relatively easily integrated into a British force. The Canadian government had assumed that it had the right to send organized bodies of volunteers to serve in a British expeditionary force, and this right had not been challenged. The Morant and Lenehan affairs might, however, have suggested to those few people who heard of them that the legal position of colonial troops in British service was not clear; but when all colonials were volunteers no serious problem was encountered. The need for the standardization of equipment throughout the military forces of the Empire, which had long been realized, had been demonstrated in practice; but the differences that existed had not proved serious. Lastly, large numbers of colonials, including Canadians, had been inspired by a great wave of imperialist sentiment to volunteer to come to Britain's aid. When the war ended the voices calling for imperial defense planning were loud.

Amid the imperialist clamor there were, however, signs suggesting a great need for further essential military reforms in the colonies as well as in Britain. What is more, the full development and application of colonial strength in war required national, rather than imperial, development. The greatest weakness in the colonial contingents had been the officers sent with them, especially their lack of staff training. War experience, though relatively brief, had temporarily eased the situation. But many of those colonial officers who received the best of all military schooling, active service, returned to civilian life after leaving South Africa. The need for officer training in the colonies was apparent. Secondly, the small colonial contingents that fought in this war had been on British pay; many of the initial costs had also been paid by Britain. If future colonial aid were to be impressive in amount, colonial governments would have to assume a greater share of the burden than they had shown themselves willing to do in South Africa. Although popular enthusiasm in the colonies had been maintained and even increased as the war had progressed, governmental interest had declined partly because the war was not clearly of colonial concern. The poverty of British leadership in the early months of the war had also discouraged colonial governments from making any irrevocable commitment of colonial forces to British command in time of war to serve the ends of British policy. Furthermore, the publicity given to colonial military prowess had generated a national enthusiasm that bade fair to rival, and even to outgrow, the temporary wartime imperial patriotic fever. The lessons of the South African War for Canada were that military reform was urgently needed, that British military co-operation could serve to provide it, but that Canadian control of Canadian military forces was as imperative as before, if not more so.

10

The Defeat of Imperial Defense Centralization

The Colonial Conference of 1902

The postwar move to give a more enduring form to the patriotic imperial spirit shown in the colonies in 1899 had three parts. The first was a plan to provide a pool of colonial troops for imperial purposes so that unlike the situation on the eve of the conflict just ended, British "offensive or defensive schemes abroad" could be based on knowledge of what aid the colonies could give.[1] The second was the amendment and expansion of the Australasian naval agreements. The third, which would have given cohesion to the whole imperial system of defense, was a proposal to set up an imperial supervisory body. The coronation ceremonies planned for King Edward VII provided Chamberlain with an opportunity to gather the statesmen of the Empire together once more for a great colonial conference in London in which he hoped that these proposals would be carried forward as a step toward the reunifying of the Empire.

The colonial secretary arranged the agenda on defense questions much more skilfully than in 1897 and insured a better statement of the principles of naval strategy. To attempt to obtain an imperial military reserve of the kind that the War Office preferred, he also planned to make good use of an enthusiasm which the prime minister of New Zealand, "King Dick" Seddon, had developed for such a force. But it was typical of his lack of finesse that when he knew that opposition was strong, he men-

1. Colonel P. H. N. Lake, former quartermaster general in Canada, referred to "offensive schemes" in his evidence before the Elgin Commission. G.B., *P.P.*, 1904, LX, para. 1120 (Cd. 1790).

tioned at the very outset—but did not pursue—the third of the above proposals which should have either been left to grow from other developments or else been made the theme of the whole conference. In his opening speech Chamberlain apparently could not resist the temptation to recall what Laurier had said in 1897: "If you want our aid, call us to your councils." He then said that he looked forward to that "council of Empire" [2] which Laurier, through Minto, had recently rejected during the war and which in his more recent public speeches Laurier had ruled completely out of court.

Laurier's flirtation in 1897 with the vague prospect of an eventual imperial federation had attracted far more attention than it deserved; it also had attracted much more attention than had his many forthright statements about colonial nationalism made at the same time. He and his supporters had no desire for involvement in international complications, and his reference to consultation on foreign policy can only have been intended as an explanation of why Canada had not accepted anticipatory commitment; it cannot have been a request for a place at the imperial council table in the immediate future. Federation was not palatable to most colonials, though some would have tolerated a limited development in that direction. But all of them suspected that Britain was unlikely to yield any real share in policy-making, and so their comments on the subject often took the form of provocative statements or rhetorical questions. Chamberlain, by pretending to call Laurier's bluff, appeared to have scored a point at the beginning of the conference. If there had been any real substance in British willingness to share the control of defense and foreign policies with the colonies, his move might have had some force. But point-scoring for its own sake had no value.

In 1902, much more than in 1897, Laurier had made his position perfectly clear in public speeches and private letters before he left Canada for London. The war in South Africa had made him wary of a more vigorous imperial defense policy. His government did not believe that "in the varying conditions

---

2. Julian Amery, *Life of Joseph Chamberlain* (London: Macmillan, 1951), IV, 421; C.O., Miscellaneous No. 144, "Confidential, Conference Between the Secretary of State for the Colonies and the Premiers of Self-governing Colonies: Minutes . . . ," Oct., 1902, pp. 2-4.

of the Colonies . . . there can be any scheme of defence applicable to all." His "mind was firmly made up" that he would not "go into military expenditure any more than we have done in the past." When an opponent, Francis W. Caulfield of Victoria, expressing the hope that he had been misquoted on these things in a report in the *Colonist*, pointed to the "strategic axiom that a piecemeal defence is an ineffective defence even for its own purpose," and argued that there was a "moral obligation of every part of the Empire to contribute to the Imperial Navy which is the common safeguard of all," Laurier replied curtly, "the report which you have read . . . is quite correct." [3] Laurier knew that some imperialist groups in Canada were well aware of the difficulties in the way of achieving their ends. The Toronto branch of the Navy League believed that a comprehensive scheme of imperial defense would involve a common defense fund, a general imperial tax, and an imperial representative body to fix the tax and control its expenditure. But it also thought that these arrangements might ultimately prove impracticable and was resigned to the fact that there was certainly at present no consensus in Canada to warrant the expectation of early consummation. Therefore, it only advocated schemes for the training of seamen and for subsidizing merchant ships. [4] The Toronto *Globe* reported to Laurier that it had received no remonstrances against his proposed course of action, and he was assured that the strength of the "imperial faddists" had been much exaggerated. As a result of the war, they had begun to think they had it all their own way recently and had begun to think themselves "invincible Good Britishers," but he was told that even the Tories were growing weary of men like George Parkin, "the only man of force in the combination. The rest are children." [5] Laurier was warned that the Conservatives hoped that, in order to conciliate Quebec, he would reject a British offer of imperial preference in exchange

3. Francis W. Caulfield to Laurier, March 12, 1902, Douglas Library, Queens University, Laurier MSS, Microfilm, F. No. 1, Ser. A, Reel 56, p. 63610; Laurier to J. S. Willison, April 14, 1902, *ibid.*, p. 64256.
4. "Memorandum . . . for the Consideration of the Government of Canada," April 11, 1902, *ibid.*, Reel 57, p. 64474.
5. John Lewis to Laurier, April 16, 1902, *ibid.*, p. 64339. Parkin was the headmaster of Upper Canada College, Toronto. In the absence of Colonel George T. Denison, he was the leading member of the Imperial Federation League.

for Canadian commitments on defense. His political opponents would then, it was alleged, use such a rejection to split Canada on racial lines.[6] But their hope was indeed a two-edged sword, for any offer that Britain might make would almost certainly include a proposal for free admission of her manufactures into the colonies, and that would mean the end of protection for Canadian industries—a step that would be unpopular in many of the quarters upon which the Conservatives depended. More important still was an opinion held in some quarters that Laurier's stand would not have the effect of weakening the Empire. The Vancouver *Province* compared him with Macdonald as a statesman who had strengthened imperial ties.[7] Thus, Laurier's policy was not a personal idiosyncrasy or a racial quirk. He had much support in Canada, even outside his own party, for his proposed stand against any movement "to bring the colonies into the vortex of expenditure which Great Britain's situation and warfare make incumbent upon her." [8]

If Chamberlain's reference to Laurier's "call-us-to-your-councils" speech was a move to isolate Canada, it failed miserably. Indeed, it probably had an opposite effect by showing the different colonial prime ministers what they had in common with each other. The reference to a "council of Empire," without any convincing indication of the benefit it could bring to the colonies, simply served to put before the delegates the idea that the limited defense proposals of the War Office and Admiralty might have unforeseeable complications and might lead to automatic commitment in the event of Britain going into an unpopular war. Chamberlain thought the council would be advisory in the first instance; but, in his own words, he felt that after that "preliminary step, it is clear that the object would not be completely secured until there had been conferred upon such a Council executive functions and perhaps also legislative powers; and it is for you to say, gentlemen, whether you think the time has come when any progress whatever can be made in this direction." [9]

6. Willison to Laurier, June 10, [1902], *ibid.*, Reel 58, p. 65765.
7. Vancouver *Province*, March 18, 1902.
8. Laurier to Willison, April 14, 1902, Douglas Library, Queens University, Laurier MSS, Microfilm, F. No. 1, Ser. A, Reel 56, p. 64256.
9. C.O., Miscellaneous No. 114, Confidential, *Colonial Conference, 1902 . . . Minutes of Proceedings . . .* ([London: Colonial Office, 1902]), pp. 2–4.

Throughout the sessions the gentlemen gave him their answer by pointedly ignoring his proposal for a council of Empire, even though there were at times references to the need for some closer political or administrative contacts.

Chamberlain's biographer commented that had the dominions been prepared to make "large-scale contributions to Imperial Defence," their claims to a voice in the control of its expenditure would have been "only too readily granted." [10] What he meant by "only too readily" is not clear; but the phrase suggests that Mr. Amery thought the concession would have been either unwise or inconsequential. However, it cannot be believed that in return for what would have inevitably been relatively small contributions, the British Parliament and Cabinet would have yielded to the colonies an effective voice in foreign policy, for this would have had the effect of a veto. Nor can it be believed that the Admiralty and War Office would have accepted any appreciable degree of colonial "interference." So colonial refusal to contemplate progress toward a centralized defensive system for the Empire was due to more than merely the colonial niggardliness that Mr. Amery inferred. It was caused by the difficulties obviously inherent in co-operative control of defense without complete centralization in every other related sphere, where such a development was utterly impracticable. Defense centralization would have removed control of a large block of expenditures from the colonial legislatures. It would have done so without any real concession of a voice in the policy for which the contributions had been made. Colonial legislatures were no more willing than the British Parliament to accept any reduction of their status, powers, and military omnipotence.

An Imperial Reserve

In the first proposal for improving the defense of the Empire —the establishment of imperial reserves in the colonies—the effect of colonial nationalism was more apparent. The war had highlighted the potential value of the reserves of manpower in the self-governing colonies. Could these reserves be tapped on a

10. Amery, *Life of Joseph Chamberlain*, IV, 425.

permanent peacetime basis? When this question was raised in the House of Lords on July 19, 1900, Lord Lansdowne, the secretary of state for war, said that the initiative should come from the colonies.[11] Colonel Hubert J. Foster, R.E., quartermaster general to the Canadian Militia, who had had a lot to do with the enrolment of the Canadian contingents, was doubtful about the possibilities. He told Major Altham, one of the D.A.A.G.'s at the War Office, that it was the emergency that had induced men to enlist. "Good men will not bind themselves to join the army whenever called on and take part in some foreign war for which they may feel no strong call. The wave of enthusiasm rises for a definite crisis and soon falls when it is past. I am sure that it is already down in Toronto, the very focus of its original intensity." [12] Foster did not attempt to disentangle nationalist from imperialist sentiment in the motives that made men enlist for South Africa; but he was aware that commitment to a "foreign" war in which Canadians had no interest would discourage men from enlisting in peacetime.

This point of view was not clear to other British officers in colonial service, nor even to all colonial statesmen. During the war, when Britain had asked New Zealand for permission to recruit in that dominion in order to tap the resources revealed by the dispatch of the contingents, the reply received was that the colonial government's political interests would be hurt by recruitment at imperial rates which were lower than those received by the contingents already in South Africa. Yet the New Zealand government admitted that many New Zealanders might be willing to join up even at the lower rate of pay.[13] Arising out of this exchange, out of the fact that New Zealand had found it difficult to equip her contingents adequately, and probably even more out of Seddon's desire to obtain a voice in imperial policy, the New Zealand prime minister sent to the governor on May 11, 1900, a "tentative proposal rather than a policy" for the estab-

11. C.D.C., Memorandum 271M, P.R.O., Cab. 8/3/1.
12. Extract from Foster to Altham, Nov. 7, 1900, in C.I.D. File, "Canadian Troops for Imperial Service in War," P.R.O., Cab. 11/121.
13. Ranfurly to Colonial Secretary, Confidential, Feb. 26, 1900, New Zealand Archives, G. 26/5.

lishment in peacetime of an Imperial and colonial reserve force of all arms which would be equipped by the imperial government, with the colonies paying half of the interest on the capital required, and for which the imperial government would pay three-quarters of the cost when the reserve was "on service or in camp." He believed that in New Zealand 8,000 to 10,000 men could be raised for such a force.[14]

Possibly by coincidence, three days earlier Major General G. A. French, commandant of the New South Wales Forces, had put up to his premier a suggestion for a "war reserve in the colonies." French argued that the enthusiasm for the current war showed that Canada would be able to produce a reserve of 75,000 sailors and fishermen for the fleet, and that Australia would provide a few sailors and also "horsemen." Ten thousand reserves at £10 per annum would cost only £100,000 as against £1,000,000 for the same number of British regulars.[15] French gave his scheme to the newspapers in both England and Australia, and he claimed that it was received with favor in the press of both countries and also by leading colonials. However, his attention was called to King's Regulations forbidding officers to communicate with the press, and the whole arrangement was halted. He was to complain to the Elgin Commission: "I do not think that helped the defence of the Empire in any way."[16]

Seddon's proposal had somewhat more success. It was incorporated in an amendment to the New Zealand Defence Act, 1900, to permit the government to transfer volunteers from other New Zealand forces into an imperial reserve earmarked for service outside New Zealand at the same rate of pay as that then received by the Fifth New Zealand Contingent in South Africa. The reserve would be paid either "at the cost in all things of the Imperial government" or by an arrangement for cost-sharing between the New Zealand government, the imperial government,

14. Seddon to Governor, May 11, 1900; Governor to C.O., May 28, 1900, New Zealand Archives, NA 26/5, Governor, Confidential.
15. Maj. Gen. G. A. French, "Defence Scheme (Australian Mounted Men)," May 8, 1900, C.A.O., Prime Minister's Department, Canberra, C.P. 103, S. 12, B. 3.
16. G.B., *P.P.*, 1904, XL, para. 8132 (Cd. 1790).

and the governments of any other colonies involved in operations in which the reserve was engaged.[17] Six months later the secretary of the Colonial Defence Committee took up the idea, saying that it had been proved that the colonies could produce men for expeditionary forces. Thus, Canada might furnish 20,000, South Africa 3,000, Australia 14,000, and New Zealand 3,000, making a total of 40,000 to supplement 120,000 men available from the United Kingdom. He recommended that plans should be made to use such a force in "all conceivable wars," such as one with the United States, with France, with Russia, with France and Russia together, with France and Spain, with France, Spain, and Portugal, with Germany, or with China, etc. But he opposed a proposal by Lord Brassey that the imperial government should subsidize such reserves maintained in the colonies for service in imperial wars. This, said Nathan, would be unfair to the British taxpayer who was already supporting the navy, the imperial fortresses, and the coaling stations. On the other hand, he thought it not desirable to press the colonies for a formal commitment of a specific number of troops for particular purposes. It would be better for the colonies to offer aid than for Britain to demand it under the terms of an agreement. But it was essential for planning to know the numbers of colonial troops that would be available should their governments decide to provide them. The general principle, he said, might be the subject of a colonial conference, but he declared that a "general Council of Empire"—that is, a permanent or executive body to deal with standardization and similar problems—was undesirable since these things could be adequately covered by the Colonial Defence Committee which had military members. However, he added that the president of the committee would like it to be strengthened by the addition of members who could speak with authority for Canada, Australia, New Zealand, and South Africa.[18]

Nathan did not make clear how planning could be accom-

---

17. *Statutes of New Zealand, 1900,* No. 69, para. 12.
18. M. Nathan, "Colonial Co-operation in Imperial Defence," Aug. 16, 1900, C.A.O., Prime Minister's Department, C.P. 103, S. 12, B. 3.

plished if there was no certainty of commitment, nor how colonial governments could be brought to take part in preliminary arrangements which might have the effect of committing them morally (or by implication) without giving them a voice in the making of foreign policy. Furthermore, his proposal differed from Seddon's on a crucial point: who would bear the cost of the reserve? A contemporary War Office proposal that British reservists who had emigrated to the colonies should be retained on reserve lists, as was done only in India, showed the depth of the chasm between British and colonial thinking on this question of cost. In making this suggestion to Australia, the War Office said it wanted the colonies to assume the cost of paying emigrant reservists. This would have meant that the reservists would receive as much as a colonial militiaman although their obligation would be to serve in Britain's wars rather than in the defense of Australia.[19] Any such arrangement would obviously alienate large sections of the Australian electorate.

When the New Zealand Defence Act of 1900 with its plan for an imperial reserve was considered by the Colonial Defence Committee, the proposal that a colonial reserve serve at the expense of the imperial government was rejected. The committee noted that if the reserve were paid by New Zealand, there would be no need for inspection. The reserve should be drawn from inland districts, not from those who already contributed to the defense of ports. Chamberlain, sending the committee's "weighty" arguments to New Zealand, commented that the New Zealand government might in its own interests wish to free its hands of this "hard and fast rule" about payment. He said that in order to give time for the New Zealanders to reconsider the question, Her Majesty would not be advised to veto this bill which the committee had described as "the first organized effort of the people of a great self-governing colony to create a force which shall be available for service wherever the Empire may require it."[20]

On the eve of the conference, the secretary of state for war,

19. C.O. to Governor General, Aug., 1901, *ibid.*
20. C.D.C., Memorandum 271M, P.R.O., Cab. 8/3/1; Chamberlain to Ranfurly, Sept. 6, 1901, New Zealand Archives, G. 2/12, Governor, Confidential In-Letters.

St. John Brodrick, asked the Colonial Defence Committee's opinion about imperial reserves. He was advised that in order to get assurances about the size of the colonial forces that would be available, the colonies should be told "in confidence" the general nature of the duties which their contingents would be expected to undertake.[21] How far could such information be spread when foreign policy secrets were not even shared by all members of the British Cabinet? Was it possible to make plans to meet every conceivable war situation? How could machinery be set up to cope with continually changing situations? Would the colonies accept anything less than a full sharing of the direction of foreign policy? Would they, indeed, entertain any form of commitment at all?

Once more the discussions about imperial defense had come full circle. Responsible government meant that colonial governments were chary of surrendering control of the destiny of their peoples. Britain wanted a blanket assurance of aid because only thus could the full resources of the Empire be harnessed for imperial defense and, it was said, simultaneously for the defense of colonial interests. The colonies must therefore take on trust Britain's assessment of danger and Britain's conduct of foreign policy, particularly so since they had no means of performing these tasks for themselves. The Colonial Defence Committee's suggestion that this information gap be bridged by the circulation of confidential memoranda was not pursued at the conference apart from Chamberlain's casual, or incautious, reference to a "Council of Empire." But an imperial reserve had already been rejected by the Colonial Defence Committee, and the colonies were obviously suspicious of such a plan.

So before the conference discussions began, the dissimilar views of Seddon and the Colonial Defence Committee on the payment of, and implications arising out of, an imperial reserve had already reached an impasse. Nevertheless, at an early session of the conference, the secretary of state for war mentioned New Zealand's resolution that an imperial reserve in every colony be financed by mutual agreement. He claimed that the idea

21. *Colonial Conference, 1902,* III, 203–205.

arose not merely from the experience of the recent war but from twenty years of imperial development. Listing the 570,000 man peacetime forces of the home government to show that the mother country was doing her part in imperial defense, he said that the "permanent force" (he actually meant the militias) in Australia amounted to 27,000, in Canada to 38,000, in New Zealand to 17,000, and in South Africa to 100,000. He said that although these colonial forces were a moral force for the support of the Empire, they were not one on which the Empire could rely to the exclusion of its own regular troops. He declared that the colonials had defects which destroyed their potential value. The Canadians were good fighting material but untrained; Canada had no trained staff and no system for training staff officers; and the Dominion had, by a little idiosyncrasy, recently adopted a new rifle (he meant the Ross, adopted because Canada could not get a license to manufacture Lee-Enfields) which, though it took the same caliber ammunition as the British rifle, was of a different pattern. The Australian forces varied greatly in quality. Brodrick suggested that one-fourth of these colonial forces should be specially trained as an imperial reserve whose services would be "absolutely pledged," but only in the event that the government to which they belonged should offer assistance to the imperial forces in case of emergency—a rather peculiar contradiction in terms which at once eliminated the absolute nature of the pledge. He did not want to discuss details in the conference, but he estimated the total cost, divided among the colonies, to be £180,000 per annum, and he pointed out that Britain had added £9 million to the peacetime estimates for the army since 1900.[22] His plan obviously envisaged the colonies financing the scheme, though he did not make this especially clear.

Although this was a conference of prime ministers, Laurier, knowing his own knowledge was limited on the subject of defense, arranged to take his minister of militia and defense, Sir Frederick Borden, to the defense sessions with power to speak but not to vote. Borden replied to Brodrick by saying that the larger colonies had recently "shown their sympathy" for the

22. *Colonial Conference, 1902*, pp. 81–85.

British position in a most practical manner. He protested against the minister's criticisms of the Canadian Militia which, he said, were based on one or two extracts from the last report of the general officer commanding, Major General O'Grady Haly, and he claimed that the militia had been much improved in the past five or six years. He declared that the new Ross rifle was "as good as, and in some respects better than, the service rifle in this country." (Brodrick at this point interjected an incredulous "Is that so?") Borden then went on to say that he could not subscribe to a proposal for a reserve force because it would have a derogatory effect on the militia staff. Instead, he offered further improvement of the militia. In regard to defense costs generally, Borden protested that Canada had more than kept her word in carrying out the tacit understanding of 1867 that she would spend $1,000,000 annually on the militia. She was now spending $2,000,000 without counting the costs of the South African War and of the wartime garrison at Halifax.

Sir Edmund Barton, prime minister of Australia, also expressed doubts about the raising of an imperial reserve force. However, he stressed the need for standardization and said that it might be necessary to sacrifice something for efficiency, a barbed shaft aimed at Canada's Ross rifle. He then proposed two resolutions urging standardization to imperial patterns and the erection of arms factories in the colonies. Seddon, expressing his disappointment at the Canadian attitude, tried to infer that Australia would support his reserve scheme because British generals in Australia, Major General French and Major General Hutton, had commented favorably on it. Barton therefore told him flatly that in the discussion on the Defence Bill "scarcely a voice had supported the inclusion of provision for service outside of Australia." Even so, Seddon insisted that Australia's exposed position made a striking force necessary. Brodrick, however, put the real issue clearly by saying that if the colonial governments were to have the power of deciding whether the reserve would be used, the colonies must pay for it. If, however, the reservists were to be at the call of the imperial government, then it was a fair subject of discussion whether the imperial government should not meet some portion of the charge. But he made no offer to bear the whole cost.[23]

Brodrick then negotiated separately with the prime ministers of New Zealand, Cape Colony, and Natal, and succeeded in getting their agreement in principle to a scheme by which the War Office would pay £6 a year per man for a colonial reserve to serve on call in South Africa, China, and Canada. The War Office wished to add Europe and the North-West Frontier of India (where great wars were at that time thought less likely), but Seddon was only willing for the obligation of automatic service to be extended to the Pacific islands. He also objected to a South African proposal that the colonial reservists should be attached to British regiments. At this point the conference went into private session and no records were kept. According to Chamberlain's biographer, however, the colonial secretary proposed there that the colonies should be intrusted with the defense of certain areas and with the control of all troops, imperial and colonial, in those areas; but he thereby pleased neither the War Office nor the colonial prime ministers.[24] Therefore, when the subject was brought back to open session, "owing to the conditions which now exist," Seddon withdrew his resolution. The project of an imperial reserve was dropped from the agenda.[25]

Seddon, however, was persistent. He raised the matter again with the Colonial Office after the conference ended. Eighteen months passed before he got a reply, which was to the effect that the War Office now thought that any plan for automatic commitment to particular areas would present grave difficulties as there was no central authority in which the colonies were represented. To make a separate agreement with one colony might impede the establishment of such an authority for all. Therefore, the War Office now preferred that New Zealand should develop its own force for service anywhere by specific consent of the colonial government, but to be maintained solely at the charge

23. *Ibid.*, pp. 85–101.
24. Amery, *Life of Joseph Chamberlain*, IV, 427.
25. Brodrick to Chamberlain, Aug. 11, 1902, in *ibid.*, IV, 427–428.

of the government of New Zealand.[26] Seddon's failure to make a bilateral arrangement shows clearly that not even a colonial prime minister as determined to co-operate as he was could overcome the chief obstacle. This was that the British government's real objective was relief from the financial burden, or the acquisition of at least a token colonial commitment to assume a part of costs that might in due time be increased; although the colonial secretary had been induced to hold out the vague prospect of some share in foreign policy and of control of defense forces, it was clear that there were powerful forces in the Admiralty, War Office, and Foreign Office that would resist any such move.

When Chamberlain found his proposals blocked generally on the imperial reserve, and also, as will be seen, by Canada on proposals for naval contributions, he lectured the colonial prime ministers on their duty to "educate" their electorates, a tactic which must surely have irritated them. He went on to declare that if the colonies were independent, defense would cost them vast sums. "Public opinion in these colonies must be very backward," he said. The colonies should recognize that they were relieved of these outlays by the imperial government, and they should therefore offer to share the burden in as generous a spirit as possible.[27] This quite impertinent attempt to tell the prime ministers what they should say to their electorates shows Chamberlain at his worst.

A discussion on a New Zealand resolution to set up a system for cadet entry into the imperial forces from the colonies revealed that the gulf between the British and colonial governments was matched by an even greater one between the societies of the mother country and the dominions. When complaints were made of the practice whereby British officers were required to live up to a standard beyond a point they could support on their pay and allowances, Chamberlain retorted quite tartly that he would not discuss conditions in the British Army in the con-

26. Seddon to Secretary of State for War, Sept. 6, 1902, inclosed in Lyttelton to Ranfurly, April 8, 1904, New Zealand Archives, G. 2/15, Governor, Confidential.

27. *Colonial Conference, 1902,* pp. 38, 99; Amery, *Life of Joseph Chamberlain,* IV, 428.

ference, a reply that suggested what British reaction would be to any future colonial voice in defense and foreign policy. Brodrick, however, intervened to explain that since there were three or four applications for every commission, Parliament was not disposed to increase remuneration in order to open the officer rank to other classes of society without private means. He admitted that some colonial officers were not "comfortable in regiments," but he ascribed this to individual personality problems and he complained that whenever a colonial was upset, public opinion in the colonies was incensed. He went on to say that standards of entry were under consideration, perhaps a tacit admission that they were low and that social fitness was the major criterion of selection.[28]

The problems that would arise from greater integration of colonial with British forces were forcibly illustrated by a minor incident that occurred during the conference itself. The Australian Coronation Corps, which had gone to London for the coronation of King Edward VII, was confined to barracks by Major General Trotter, the officer in command of the troops taking part in a review of colonial troops by the Prince of Wales on July 1, 1902. This occurred despite the protests of their own commanding officer, Lieutenant Colonel St. Clair Cameron, that the order should have gone through him and that the Australians were not subject to the discipline of the British Army Act. It took the combined efforts of the Australian prime minister, Sir Edmund Barton, of the Australian minister for defense, Sir John Forrest, of the commander in chief, Field Marshal Lord Roberts, and of the secretary of state for war, St. John Brodrick, to reverse the order which was admitted to have been due to a misunderstanding "not on Colonel Cameron's part."[29] Military discipline often appears to onlookers or subordinates to be arbitrary. Colonial troops might claim the right of appeal to their own government, an authority to which the military command under which they served was not responsible. This would upset

28. *Colonial Conference, 1902*, pp. 168–169.
29. C.A.O., Prime Minister's Department, C.P. 103, S. 12, B. 5; Adelaide *Advertiser*, July 3, 7, 1902. Cameron was a "difficult, quarrrelsome" man (information from Major Warren Perry).

the normal chain of command and normal military procedure and would introduce a new complex civil-military relationship. Here was a problem of imperial defense co-operation that would need special handling. As Captain R. Muirhead Collins, Australian secretary of the Department of Defence, told Hutton in another connection, Australian ministers would never agree to any proposal to give control or implied control over Australian troops to any but the Commonwealth authorities.[30]

The Naval Agreements

Meanwhile, the limited centralized control of colonial fleets arranged by the contributions system had also been threatened. The Australasian Auxiliary Squadron Agreements, concluded in 1887, had been set up to last for ten years from the time of the arrival of the vessels on station, which was in 1891. They were therefore due to expire in 1901. In 1897 Chamberlain's attempt to secure an increased contribution had failed, partly through the ineptness of his presentation of the Admiralty's case. Since that time, however, opposition to the agreements in Australia had become much more articulate, having been focused by discussions about the effect of federation on the remnants of the old local colonial navies which the agreements of 1887 had supplanted but not entirely destroyed. The man behind the movement for the revival of the local colonial navies by the creation of an effective federal force was Captain W. R. Creswell. As naval commandant of South Australia, he had been responsible for the presentation of a scheme for an Australian naval reserve in place of naval contributions at the 1897 Colonial Conference and had received scant attention. On August 5, 1899, a conference of the naval officers of the Australian colonies, including Creswell, had assembled at Melbourne to consider the naval defense of Australia. The conference members agreed that the effect of reliance on the Royal Navy and on the naval agreements had been to shrivel up the local navies which were now almost

30. Collins to G.O.C., Aug. 6, 1902, C.A.O., M.G. 84, Ser. 2, 10 B, B. 56, File 2688/02.

completely defunct. They complained that the auxiliary squadron had not carried out one of the functions stipulated for it in 1887—the training of Australians in seamanship—because the vessels of the squadron were designed for operational duties and were not training ships; vessels in reserve had been laid up in Sydney and no attempt had been made to utilize them for the benefit of the reserve naval force. "There has, consequently, been no advance in Australia's ability to undertake any honourable share in her sea defence," the conference members concluded. "Twenty or fifty years hence Australia's ability for sea defence—self-defence— . . . will be as today, as it was ten years ago." Therefore, on the grounds that the defense of Australia depended chiefly on sea power and that it was proper that Australians should be encouraged to participate in it, the conference members recommended a reserve scheme. Different from 1897, the reserve scheme was, for the present, proposed as an addition to the subsidization of the auxiliary squadron and not as an alternative to it.[31] Here in a nutshell was the colonial case against the imperial sea power thesis and indeed against the whole concept of imperial defense. Centralization was a corrosive influence that could destroy the power and will of self-governing colonies to contribute to their own defense and so to the defense of the Empire.

Publication of the report of this conference stirred the wrath of the London *Times* which, in two articles on September 28 and October 6, 1899, pontificated on the orthodox doctrine of sea power and thundered that if the Admiral commanding the Australian Station had presided at the conference he would have prevented the propagation of such fallacies as had been propounded. A separate colonial fleet, manned mainly by amateurs, would be expensive to maintain in time of peace and absolutely ineffective in war, the *Times* said.[32]

To counter the *Times* articles Creswell, or one of the other

31. Commonwealth of Australia, Senate, *Report of the Conference of Naval Officers Assembled at Melbourne, Victoria, to Consider the Question of the Naval Defence of Australia*, No. 27, printed Sept. 11, 1901, reprinted in Macandie, *Genesis of the Royal Australian Navy*, pp. 69–74.
32. *Ibid.*, p. 74.

advocates of local navies, elaborated their case. The rebuttal declared that there was no reason to believe that an Australian navy would be semi-independent: the homogeneity of the Australian force with the "National [Royal]" navy would depend on the administrative ability of the Admiralty, which must show itself to be the Admiralty of the Empire, not merely of the United Kingdom. It said that as sea supremacy could not be absolute, the needs of Australia were not necessarily identical with the rest of the Empire. The auxiliary squadron had been set up in recognition of these needs but was now always regarded as merely a direct contribution to the fleet strength of the Empire. Politically there was no reason to believe that Australia would stand aside from any cause that might be the Empire's. But why should Australia be defenseless if a future "Little Englander" government in the United Kingdom neglected the fleet?[33] Captain Creswell then elaborated on a scheme for the progressive development of an Australian naval force in a report which he entitled, "The Best Method of Employing Australian Seamen in the Defence of Commerce and Ports." In this he argued that Australia needed a special type of ship for local defense rather than the Royal Navy ships which were designed to fight all over the world. He also denied that Australians were poor seamen, a charge that had been advanced in order to pour ridicule on the idea of a local navy.[34]

The Australian prime minister, Edmund Barton, asked the governor general to seek the opinion of the commander in chief of the Royal Navy's Australasian Squadron, Rear Admiral Sir Lewis Beaumont. It was Beaumont who at the Colonial Conference of 1897 had presented the ineffective statement of the Admiralty point of view. As might be expected, he was strongly opposed to Creswell's ideas. He rejected the notion that the federal government should create or maintain naval reserves. He said instead that Australia should "cause to be maintained on the

33. Australia, Department of Defence, "Notes for Reply to *Times* Articles," *Printed Papers, Naval, 1885–1908*, Vol. I, No. 28.
34. W. R. Creswell, "The Best Method of Employing Australian Seamen in the Defence of Commerce and Ports, 28 Sept., 1901", in Macandie, *Genesis of the Royal Australian Navy*, Appendix 1, pp. 300–308.

Australian Station" a fleet of at least six cruisers in commission, which should be under the command of the admiral of the station, with crews subject to the Naval Discipline Act and on the same terms of engagement as in the Royal Navy.[35] Hopetoun, the governor general, in a personal letter to Barton, added his own argument. "You can't 'locate' sea power. Trafalgar would have had the same effect if fought in the West Indies. . . . Our purely local efforts should be confined to the protection of our harbours. . . ."[36]

Sir John Forrest, the minister of state for defense, advised the prime minister against the formation of an Australian navy. Forrest was influenced in part by the strategic argument, "There is only one sea to be supreme over, and we want our fleet to be mistress over that sea," but even more by the fact that an Australian navy would be very costly. His recommendation favored an extension of the Naval Agreement.[37] But he added that if all other federations and colonies of the Empire could be brought to agree to the principle of "one fleet for the Empire's Naval Defence," . . . "it would be necessary for the British Dominions beyond the Seas to be adequately represented at the Admiralty." Thus, it was clear in these pre-conference exchanges that Australia was prepared to support the resolutions that Seddon had circulated in March. These resolutions were in favor of increasing and improving the Australasian Squadron with "the extra cost of maintenance to be defrayed in the same proportion as provided under the existing agreement and on a population basis."[38]

When the Naval Agreements came up for discussion at the Colonial Conference of 1902, the First Lord of the Admiralty, Lord Selborne, anticipating the doctrines later preached by Ad-

---

35. Commonwealth of Australia, Senate, *P.P., Naval Defence of the Commonwealth of Australia*, 22/1901. In a passing phrase, Beaumont said, "The future may see the creation of an Australian Navy," but the rest of his memorandum shows that he thought it a very remote future.

36. Hopetoun to Barton, Aug. 2, 1901, Australian National Library, Barton Papers.

37. John Forrest, "Memorandum on Naval Defence," March 15, 1902, in Australia, Department of Defence, *Printed Papers, Naval, 1885–1908*, Vol. I.

38. Premier's Office, Wellington, New Zealand, March 10, 1902, C.A.O., Prime Minister's Department, C.P. 717, S. 1, Vol. 32.

miral Sir John Fisher, presented a powerful brief for a centralized naval strategy and control. He argued that the word
"defence" had no place in naval thinking, that the task of the fleet
was to seek out the ships of the enemy and destroy them. "It
follows from this that there can be no localization of naval forces
in the strict sense of the word . . . [and] in time of war there
must be only one authority with full power and responsibility
to the Empire to move the Ships, to concentrate them where
they can deal the most effective blow against the forces of the
enemy. . . ." But he agreed that the Australasian agreement
had faults. It was simply a financial agreement that gave the
Australasians no personal interest in the Navy. Therefore, he suggested that efforts should be made to recruit colonial officers
and men into the navy. One or two cruisers should be manned
exclusively by them. He suggested there should be an Australasian branch of the Royal Naval Reserve in New Zealand and
Australia, and he added that the ships should be available for
service anywhere in Far Eastern waters rather than only in
waters near the shores of those countries.[39]

Speaking for New Zealand, Seddon disdained the idea of a
local navy but thought a naval reserve an absolute necessity. He
was also willing to give the Admiralty a freer hand in the movement of the ships of the auxiliary squadron, but he pointed out
that colonies had burdensome development costs that the mother
country did not have. He said that some form of representation
for the colonies was desirable, but that participation in war
should be voluntary and not as a result of an agreement.[40] His
arguments were quickly reinforced by Laurier who said, "As
I understand it, he [Seddon] rather spoke in the same direction
as I do now, that it would be difficult for the colonies to assume
any more burdens than they carry at the present time." Sir Edmund Barton added, "Australia stands in precisely the same
position [on this question] that Canada and New Zealand do."
He said the reason Australia was not planning "a Navy of our
own," for which there was much support, was that he would

39. *Colonial Conference, 1902*, pp. 19–21.
40. *Ibid.*, pp. 21–26.

find very great difficulty in finding the money for the purpose.[41]

However, after separate negotiations with each of the prime ministers, the First Lord was able to tell the conference that the Cape Colony and Natal had offered £50,000 and £35,000 respectively, without conditions; Newfoundland had offered £3,000 a year to maintain a naval reserve; Australia and New Zealand had offered £200,000 and £40,000 a year, respectively, which was half the cost of the maintenance of an improved naval squadron to operate in "the Eastern Seas" and to establish a branch of the Royal Naval Reserve. The Dominion of Canada alone had not been able to make any suggestion for a naval contribution; but Laurier had told Fisher that Canada was contemplating the establishment of a local navy.[42]

Apart from Canada's continued refusal to recognize any obligation to support an imperial navy, this result seemed a triumph for Chamberlain and, even more, for Selborne. Despite the obvious trend toward local navies and the general belief that colonial development made larger defense expenditures completely out of the question, Australia and New Zealand had stepped up their contributions and had taken away the restriction which bound the ships that they provided to narrow limits in Australasian waters. They had also agreed to accept the elimination of the earlier distinction between the Royal Navy's Australian Squadron and the auxiliary squadron, which had in fact never been much more than theoretical. The Admiralty made concessions in the direction of training part-time sailors, manning some of the ships with colonials, and offering colonial cadetships.

The Verdict on Imperial Defense Centralization

At the Colonial Conference of 1902, Chamberlain, who is said to have been misled by Toronto imperialists into the false step

41. *Ibid.*, pp. 27–30.
42. *Ibid.*, pp. 173, 175–176, and Appendix VIII, pp. 263–265. Tucker believed that the reference was to a naval reserve rather than to a Canadian navy and concluded that the evidence invalidates any idea that the formation of a Canadian navy entered the field of practical politics in 1902 (Gilbert Norman Tucker, *The Naval Service of Canada: Its Official History* [Ottawa: King's Printer, 1952], I, 109).

of introducing the idea of centralization of imperial defense, had found a willing "colonial chore-boy" in the person of "King Dick" Seddon whose flamboyant expansionist policy in the islands of the South Pacific, coupled with New Zealand's strategic loneliness, had led him to seek a voice in Britain's foreign and imperial policies. Seddon, although an advocate of New Zealand's interests, was a less mature colonial nationalist than either Laurier or Barton. When on one occasion Laurier began to ask him a question beginning, "In your country . . . ," Seddon interrupted him by saying firmly, "In our *colony*. . . ." [43] But not even Seddon was willing to accept either unlimited commitment to war as a result of British policies, or the absorption of colonials into British regiments, which the Cape Colony and Natal, smaller, more dependent on Britain, and even less mature than New Zealand, accepted unhesitatingly.

Creswell's proposals, which Barton had rejected before the conference began, had offered full co-operation with Britain on the sea, but had looked forward to the full development of an Australian navy. Barton had accepted the contrary naval contributions policy, but only because it was a less expensive way of getting the naval protection that Australia needed. This, the one major achievement of 1902 toward a sharing of the burden of imperial defense, covered half the cost of the whole Australian Squadron and freed it from its earlier restriction to Australian waters. But the Admiralty's attempt to interest Australians in joining the navy did not do much to exploit the fact that Australians had a real incentive to defend themselves by sea. Moreover, colonial offers of naval contributions were almost invariably accompanied by simultaneous intimations of a desire for some form of representation in London. This condition was echoed in one form or another by British spokesmen, but apart from Chamberlain's vague but disturbing suggestion of a Council of Empire no specific proposal to achieve this end was made. It is noticeable, in fact, that argument about defense co-operation tended to go in a circle. Colonial aid in defense must, it was said, lead to representation in the councils of the Empire. When

43. *Colonial Conference, 1902,* p. 56.

aid was not immediately forthcoming, the opposite argument
was produced: representation must come first in order to make
colonial aid possible. It was obvious from the debate that defense arrangements which included colonial commitments would
also have to include political innovations. These would be of a
nature that would not only threaten the power of the colonial
parliaments but would also, if the commitments were to be made
acceptable to colonial electorates, have to arrange the surrender
of some of the power of the British Cabinet and Parliament and
some of the exclusive control of the service departments over the
services. Those who pressed imperial defense schemes upon the
colonies with promises or hints of surrenders of this nature were
either deliberately deceiving the colonials or were themselves
guilty of gross self-deception. Thus, the southern seagirt colonies,
whose dependence on the navy had made them go part way to
meet British proposals for centralized control of imperial war
defense forces, were nevertheless not completely sold on all imperial defense schemes.

On the other hand, Laurier, who had become the archenemy
of the imperialists during the recent war, had steered a difficult
course between Quebec nationalism on the one hand and Ontario imperialism on the other; he had found a middle way which
satisfied most moderate and rational Canadian opinion and was
to prove satisfying to colonial opinion everywhere in the future.

The stand of the Canadian ministers on the defense problem
was explained in a memorandum presented when the conference
ended. The proposals for defense centralization were rejected,
"not so much from the expense involved," but because the ministers thought they "would entail an important departure from
the principles of Colonial self-government." After explaining that
the measure of local independence granted from time to time
by the imperial authorities was valued because it had led both
to material progress in Canada and to the strengthening of ties
with Britain, the memorandum went on to agree that as Canada
advanced in wealth it should make "more liberal outlay for those
necessary preparations of self-defence which every country has
to assume and bear." It was reasonable that the taxpayers in

Britain should seek to be relieved of some of the defense burden; and Canada, in the development of its own militia system, would be found ready to respond to that desire by taking over some of the services in the Dominion hitherto borne by the imperial government. It was agreed that Canada's expenditures on the militia were evidence of good intentions. Perfection had not yet been attained. "If defects exist, there is every desire on the part of the Canadian government to remove them, and for this purpose the advice and assistance of experienced imperial officers will be welcomed and all reasonable efforts made to secure an efficient system." At present, expenditures were limited to the military side, but a system for training naval reserves also was contemplated.[44]

Like Sir John A. Macdonald, every colonial minister believed that if Britain was in real need, the colonies would come to her aid. But to make preliminary commitments to do so without there being evidence of danger and without leaving the specific decision of participation in war to the colonial peoples seemed to many to be a diminution of the sort of responsible government that they had won and cherished. It was not enough to argue that the colonies must surrender their autonomy for the general good, or because in the future they themselves might be in danger. Nor would colonial electorates agree to financial burdens just because the British elector was finding them too heavy. Not merely did this argument raise the old bogie of "no taxation without representation"; it was also not within the range of practical politics. Admirals and generals naturally pressed for more weapons and more men under their control. That was their purpose in life. But Chamberlain, Brodrick, and Selborne were practicing politicians. Reducing the defense burden was one way for them to win elections. Yet they must have been aware that this same principle also applied in the colonies. In the slogans of imperial defense they had found a good rallying cry that could serve them well; but it is not surprising that they did

44. *Ibid.*, pp. 261–262, Appendix VII, "Memorandum by the Canadian Ministers Concerning Defence, 11 August 1902"; also in Canada, *Sessional Papers*, XXXVII, 1903, No. 12, Paper 29a, Appendix VI, pp. 82–83.

not succeed in selling it to the colonies. The imperial enthusiasm generated by the South African War was insufficient to overcome the growing nationalism of the great colonies; neither could it persuade them to accept a military recentralization of the Empire.

11

British Military Reforms and Canadian Defense Problems

The decade after the South African War saw Britain torn by internal upheavals that were not far short of revolutionary. In 1906 a long Conservative hold on power was broken, and the Liberals began the first steps beyond Tory paternalism and Liberal laissez faire toward the democratic welfare state. They were plagued by labor disruption; and in the background a deeply divided Ireland, teetering on the brink of civil war, exercised a malevolent influence on affairs at Westminster. Meanwhile, by the end of the nineteenth century, the rise of American and Japanese sea power in the Pacific had made it clear that it was no longer possible for Britain to control the world's oceans by dominating European waters. About the same time a new specter appeared. Until the last few years of the old century Germany had not been counted among Britain's potential foes, and as late as 1902–1903 the two countries were still co-operating in diplomatic ventures. However, in 1904, casting off Salisbury's "splendid isolationism" and Chamberlain's Germanophile leanings, the Conservatives reached an understanding with the ancient enemy, France. Three years later, following this Conservative initiative, the Liberal government completed the diplomatic revolution by coming to terms with France's new ally—and Britain's most feared rival of half a century—Russia. Henceforward, Germany became Britain's number one enemy. But the alienation of the devious and bombastic Kaiser Wilhelm II had not been caused by Britain's move toward the Franco-Russian *Entente* (which must therefore not be regarded as the sole cause of the German menace). German hostility was amply demonstrated. The *Entente* had the great advantage that Britain would not have to face the Kaiser's megalomania alone; but it also meant that henceforward Britain would be more rapidly drawn into any major war that broke out on the Continent.

These epoch-making developments greatly disturbed British strategic thought, and consequently they changed her plan of organization for the defense of the Empire. Until the South African War, military policy had followed a memorandum written in 1888 by the secretary of state for war, Edward Stanhope. While rejecting an earlier restriction of the army's function to home defense and the reinforcement of the colonies, Stanhope nevertheless envisaged expeditionary forces only for service outside Europe. He had ruled that the sending of an army corps to Europe was improbable. The French *Entente* in 1904 radically altered that situation and made it possible that a British Army might once more have to fight on the Continent. The old rival strategic concepts—security behind the naval shield or reliance on the army and land fortifications—were challenged, not merely by the German naval program which threatened to upset the balance of sea power, but even more by a growing possibility of British involvement on land. Disagreement eventually developed between the advocates of three different strategies: "conjoint" expeditions against Germany in the Baltic and elsewhere, British maritime landings on nearer German and Belgian coasts, or full participation with the French on the Western Front, each of which represented a revolution from pre-1899 planning. In the decade from the *Entente* to the outbreak of war, Britain's chief military problem was to determine the exact nature of the new commitment and to create the armies to honor it.[1] Domestic problems, and particularly economic and financial stringency, made a solution difficult to achieve.

British military reform, spurred by the lessons of the South African War and by continuing Russian hostility, had preceded the appearance of a serious German menace. The war had shown shortcomings in officer training and a shortage of trained man-

1. John E. Tyler, *The British Army and the Continent, 1904–14* (London: Arnold, 1938), pp. 9–24.

power; but an even more immediate and obvious need was more effective military direction at the top. Several witnesses suggested that the Cabinet's defense committee had given no consistent leadership,[2] and Sir John Ardagh, the director of military intelligence at the War Office, told the Elgin Commission in November, 1902, that Britain needed an army general staff. About the time of Ardagh's testimony, Lord Selborne reversed the Admiralty's previous stand against improved machinery for consideration of military problems jointly with the War Office. He and the secretary of state for war sent a memorandum to the prime minister which recommended the replacement of the Cabinet committee by one that would authoritatively and expertly consider all problems that had naval, military, and political implications. Balfour, who had recently replaced Salisbury as prime minister, was impressed. In December, 1902, he radically reorganized the Cabinet's Defence Committee by adding service members and by commencing to attend it regularly himself. From November, 1903, he took the chair.[3]

Lord Esher, a confidant of the new King Edward VII, a member of the Elgin Commission, and a penetrating critic of army administration who preferred the anonymity of backstairs influence to the hurly-burly of political or administrative life, had been influential in determining Balfour's action. It was he who also persuaded the prime minister to appoint a committee of three, with Esher himself as chairman, to investigate the structure of the War Office. The other members were Admiral Sir John Fisher, recently returned from the top seagoing appointment in the navy, the Mediterranean Command, and Sir George Sydenham Clarke, formerly secretary of the Colonial Defence Committee. All three were men of great energy, insight, and patriotism.

The War Office (Reconstitution) Committee placed a wide interpretation on its terms of reference. It started with the prem-

2. Maurice V. Brett, ed., *Journals and Letters of Reginald Brett, Viscount Esher* (4 vols.; London: Nicholson & Watson, 1934–1938), I, 360–361, 376–377, 378–379.
3. Maurice P. A. Hankey, *Diplomacy by Conference: Studies in Public Affairs 1920–1946* (London: Ernest Benn, 1946), pp. 84–85.

ise that the newly reorganized Defence Committee was a sound
move for the improvement of the higher direction of war planning
and ought to be made permanent and more effective in order to
co-ordinate the work of all departments of state concerned with
the conduct and preparation of war: that it should, in fact,
"fulfil the functions of a General Staff." As Britain was a naval
and colonial power, the Defence Committee should have a much
wider interest than the Great General Staff in Berlin which was
concerned only with the army. Because ultimate authority in
Britain rested with Parliament and the prime minister, the Defence Committee should also differ from the German example
(which was responsible only to the Emperor as commander in
chief) by having the prime minister as its president. "No body of
experts, however highly trained and qualified would carry sufficient weight without him; and he should have absolute discre-
tion in the selection and the variation of the committee's
members." But because prime ministers have heavy responsibility
in many other fields (and future prime ministers might not be
sufficiently interested in defense), a "permanent nucleus" in the
shape of a secretarial staff should constitute a "department" under the prime minister. The duties of the "nucleus" would be to
consider all questions of imperial defense from the point of view
of the navy, the military forces, India, and the colonies; to obtain
and collate information for the several departments concerned;
"anticipating their needs as far as possible," to prepare documents required by the prime minister and the Defence Committee; and to furnish such advice as the Cabinet might request
in regard to defense questions involving more than one department of state.[4] The secretariat of experts would thus have room
to undertake the study of any defense problems that it thought
necessary, but it would not interfere with the business of the
departments or usurp the executive authority of the Cabinet.
This ingenious formula made the reorganized Defence Committee generally acceptable to the service departments, the ministers, and the House of Commons, despite the suspicion that all

4. G.B., *P.P.*, 1904, *Report of the War Office (Reconstitution) Committee,*
VIII, Pt. I, paras. 1–10 (Cd. 1932).

of these were accustomed to show toward any new body that seemed likely to infringe their powers.

In 1904, after some hesitation, Balfour took the necessary step. By Treasury minutes he set up a secretariat for the Defence Committee and so put it on a permanent basis. The new committee thus had certain important advantages over previous bodies of a similar nature. It amalgamated the composition of the old Cabinet Defence Committee and the professional Joint Naval and Military Committee, which now lapsed. Being a prime minister's committee it was free from some of the stringent secrecy which restricted the activities of Cabinet committees. Its secretariat, a novelty in the Cabinet system, gave it continuity and permanence and also permitted experts to enjoy initiative in the study of defense problems. Furthermore, the annual vote for its maintenance made possible for the first time a regular Commons debate on defense as a whole instead of on its separate military and naval aspects.[5]

Shortly after Balfour had shown his personal interest in the committee by taking over the chairmanship, he announced that henceforward, he, as the prime minister, would be its only permanent member and that he would invite to each meeting whomsoever he thought might be concerned. He said the advantage of this plan was the very great elasticity that it would give to the committee.[6] It would mean, however, a potential increase in the prime minister's power, and although it would bring more thorough treatment of defense problems and a means of overcoming departmental rivalries, the prime minister's aggrandizement might have excited some suspicion and jealousy. Balfour therefore explained the move away by suggesting that the new format had been designed to make possible the inclusion of colonial representation. It happened that the Canadian minister of militia had

5. Gibbs, *Origins of Imperial Defence*, pp. 18–21; John Ehrman, *Cabinet Government and War, 1890–1940* (Cambridge: Cambridge University Press, 1958), p. 29; Hankey, *Diplomacy by Conference*, pp. 84–85; Franklyn Johnson, *Defence by Committee: the British Committee of Imperial Defence, 1885–1959* (London: Oxford University Press, 1960), pp. 53–58, 69–71; Major-Gen. Sir George G. Aston, *Memories of a Marine: An Amphibiography* (London: John Murray, 1919), pp. 244–245.

6. G.B., House of Commons, *Debates*, March 4, 1905, 4th Ser., Vol. 146, Col. 157.

come to England to discuss his new Militia Bill. Balfour had suggested that the arrangement which he had proposed would enable the committee to be expanded on occasion "so as to include the representatives of our great Colonies and India." It thus constituted the first attempt to form a constitutional machine dealing with imperial concerns, and one in which representatives of the Empire beyond the seas might take their part.[7] Borden's visit had provided a convenient opportunity for initiating the new movement. The committee agreed that Borden should sit as a member. This proposal made the prime minister's new plan for the Defence Committee more acceptable than it might otherwise have been. Borden's visit had been Balfour's opportunity. This valuable new committee, which had been made possible in part by the accidental coincidence of a colonial problem, greatly strengthened Britain's machinery for defense planning.

Balfour and Colonial Representation on the Defence Committee

Balfour stated in the House of Commons his claim that the advisory character of the Defence Committee might help to overcome the former reluctance of the self-governing colonies to commit themselves to imperial defense planning.

I think [he said] that one of the great merits of the Defence Committee is that it has no executive authority at all. It has no power to give an order to the humblest soldier in His Majesty's Army, or the most powerless sloop under the control of the Admiralty. I think that is especially valuable from a point of view not yet touched upon— namely, the relations between the Defence Committee and those self-governing Colonies of the Empire over which no office in this country has any control at all. I hope that when any problem of defence which touches them nearly comes up, and even when they take a closer interest in the problems of Imperial defence as a whole, we may have the advantage of their assistance in our councils. But I am certain that the self-governing Colonies will never allow any representative of theirs to come to the Defence Committee if the

7. G.B., House of Commons, *Debates*, Aug. 2, 1904, 4th Ser., Vol. 139, Col. 618; Kenneth Young, *Arthur Balfour: The Happy Life of the Politician, Prime Minister, Statesman, and Philosopher* (London: Bell, 1963), p. 224.

Defence Committee with that addition had the smallest authority to impose obligations, financial, political, military, or naval on the colonies which they represent. But we are so constituted that the only thing the Defence Committee may give, either to a Department at home or to the Cabinet or to the Colonial Governments, is advice.[8]

In saying this, Balfour did not anticipate the rule he was shortly to lay down that no one except the prime minister had a right, either personal or ex officio, to sit on the Defence Committee. Colonies seeking the committee's advice could obviously be invited to attend particular meetings when their problems were discussed. But how could they use it to offer regular counsel if each attendance was only by invitation of the prime minister of Great Britain? Balfour had apparently ignored the significance of the fact that the prime minister's absolute control over the Defence Committee was acceptable in England only because he was ultimately responsible to the electorate; but a British prime minister was not responsible to colonial electorates. A right of occasional attendance at Defence Committee sessions would not satisfy those in the dominions who sought a voice in the direction of imperial foreign and defense policies; and it would suggest a degree of commitment that would worry other colonials. However, from its third meeting the new Defence Committee took for itself the title "Committee of Imperial Defence." [9] This was an accurate description insofar as the committee was to "take a closer interest in the problem of Empire Defence as a whole" (to quote Balfour's explanation to the House of Commons on August 2, 1904).[10] But the new committee was not "imperial" in the sense of including colonial representation.

Balfour's announcement about colonial representation had been inspired by Borden's attendance, and he admitted to the King that he had deliberately invited Borden in order to set a precedent of "great imperial significance"; but he said, "Unfortunately it appears that this particular gentleman is of rather

---

8. G.B., House of Commons, *Debates*, Aug. 2, 1904, 4th Ser., Vol. 139, Cols. 618–619.

9. Gibbs, *Origins of Imperial Defence*, p. 18.

10. G.B., House of Commons, *Debates*, Aug. 2, 1904, 4th Ser., Vol. 139, Col. 618.

inferior quality—but we shall be careful what we say before him!" [11] Borden's visit was thus to be a precedent for a great experiment in imperial co-operation and trust; but he was himself not to be trusted. Sir Frederick could have been excused if, had he known Balfour's attitude, he had himself expressed some doubts about the British prime minister's personal qualities. He had some grounds for doubts since questions about British withdrawal from Canadian naval bases and about the sending of Canadian regiments to India were raised without warning at the committee meeting which he attended. When he got back to Canada, he had to ask that the discussion on these subjects be expunged from the minutes. His attendance was always afterward used to mark the first step toward making the Defence Committee "imperial." His disclaimer shows that it should rather be taken as evidence that the committee was not "imperial" at this time and that there were serious obstacles to it ever becoming imperial. Not the least of these reasons were British lack of confidence in colonial ministers and British unwillingness to consult them fully.

That the committee was not imperial in composition was re-emphasized two years later. In 1905, at the request of the Australian government, the Committee of Imperial Defence prepared a defense plan for the Commonwealth which, as sent out in 1906, omitted certain points that Australian naval officers persuaded their prime minister were necessary in Australia's interest. Deakin complained (in a private letter to Richard Jebb) that the C.I.D.'s plan was only notable for the condemnation of any and every plan to allow Australia a floating defense of any kind on any terms. He also noted that Australia had not been consulted by Britain about the New Hebrides convention with France, even though these islands were only British because of earlier emphatic protests. He added, "What can we do with such people?" [12] Deakin tried at the Colonial Conference of 1907 to

11. Young, *Arthur James Balfour*, pp. 224–225.
12. Deakin to Jebb, July 23, 1906, Australian National Library, Jebb Papers. New Zealand disassociated herself from the complaint about non-consultation (E. J. Tapp, "Australian and New Zealand Defence Relations, 1900–1950," *Australian Outlook*, V [Sept., 1951], 165–175).

obtain colonial representation on the Committee of Imperial Defence. That it was necessary for him to attempt to obtain this privilege shows that hitherto the committee had been British, not imperial.

At the Colonial Conference of 1907, Haldane explained the operation of the committee on which there was no fixed membership: "I always attend it, but I am not a standing member of it." [13] Campbell-Bannerman, the prime minister, had stated that so far only two important questions affecting self-governing colonies had been discussed, thus implying that there was no need to summon dominion representatives regularly. He said that whenever colonial questions were discussed a representative of the Colonial Office attended and that a colonial representative could be summoned as a member when any question was submitted by a colony. He had not said that the representatives of a self-governing colony were present whenever their interests were involved. The committee had discussed Halifax defenses in 1903 and 1905 without calling for Canadian representation. As will be seen later, the discussion of Canadian defense was on one occasion deliberately hidden from Canada. Deakin's resolution read: "That it is desirable that the Colonies should be represented on the Imperial Council of Defence. That the Colonies be authorized to refer to the Council for advice any local questions in regard to which expert assistance is deemed advisable." [14] Elgin got this watered down to read that "whenever so desired, a representative of the Colony which may wish for advice should be summoned to attend as a member of the Committee during the discussions of the questions raised." [15] The dominions thus did not receive a general right to attend all sessions. Richard Jebb, who made a contemporary study of the Colonial Conference of 1907 and knew many of its members, wrote that at the request of New Zealand, Australia, and the South African colonies, Haldane's address on military defense was published at once. He also said that Canada dissented from the Australian Resolution, but that

13. G.B., *P.P.*, 1907, LV, 189 (Cd. 3523).
14. *Ibid.*, LV, 715 (Cd. 3524).
15. *Ibid.*, LV, 65 (Cd. 3523).

the objection was not officially recorded.[16] Certainly Laurier had thought a resolution was not needed; and Frederick Borden said that it was already "settled" that colonies would be summoned when questions concerning them were discussed and that the resolution was therefore unnecessary.[17] After his experience in 1903, representation on the Committee of Imperial Defence was a subject on which he was no doubt sensitive. The situation in 1907 was that Canada did not want the commitment to British policies that membership of or attendance at the committee sessions would incur; at the same time, Britain was prepared to concede neither full membership nor dominion attendance when dominion interests, either general or local, were involved, except in those cases when a dominion sent in a request for advice.

Frederick Borden and the Command of the Canadian Militia

Sir Frederick Borden's summons to England to attend the Committee of Imperial Defence meeting had been a result of reports that he was planning to consolidate the government's control over the militia by opening the command to Canadian officers and so to diminish British influence. While British organization for defense was being improved, Canada, impelled also by the lessons of the South African War, had similarly undertaken a reorganization of her defenses. The war had given some Canadian officers valuable military experience, and some people felt that the time was not far distant when a Canadian would be qualified to be the general officer commanding. The command proposal was just one part of the whole scheme of reform. It would however, break an important military link with Britain, and it could be argued that Canadian officers promoted through the militia and even through the Permanent Force would normally not have enough training and experience for the task. Hence, when Chamberlain heard of Borden's intention in April, 1903, he took the unusual step of suggesting that before the bill

16. Richard Jebb, *The Imperial Conference: A History and Study* (London: Longmans, Green, 1911), II, 151.
17. G.B., *P.P.*, LV, 188–189 (Cd. 3523).

was introduced in the Commons Borden should come to England to discuss it. As Borden could not leave while the Canadian Parliament was in session, this effectively delayed the measure for a year.[18] But Chamberlain's intervention backfired. It led to the bill becoming more radical than originally intended. By the time it was discussed in the House, Britain had introduced sweeping changes in her own army organization that gave Borden ideas and precedent for extending civilian control in Canada. And the Dundonald "incident" had hardened his resolution.

Meanwhile, when Borden reached England to discuss his proposed bill, Chamberlain had left the Colonial Office and the Esher Committee was in session. There was some disagreement afterward about what occurred at the Committee of Imperial Defence meeting on December 11, 1903. But it was certainly agreed by all parties that the Militia Act should be amended to permit a Canadian officer to command. It was also suggested that because of the shortage of trained Canadian staff officers, three British regulars should be assigned to Canada to work under the G.O.C., but under the over-all control of the Canadian government. Their duties would be to prepare for war during peace and to undertake "general direction" (which could only mean command) when war began. To train Canadians for staff work, two places at the Staff College at Camberley should be made available, and trained Canadian staff officers should be accepted for service on the imperial staff. The committee also discussed with Borden the vexing problem of the relative ranks and precedence of British regular officers and Canadian Militia officers; and it suggested that inspection of the militia by a British officer would help to guarantee efficiency and preserve the link with the British Army. On all these things Borden was given a good hearing and probably got much of what he sought. It may have been as a result of his satisfaction that he was incautious enough to discuss matters on which he had not been instructed, namely the taking over of the Halifax and Esquimalt garrisons and the rais-

18. Borden to Minto, April 13, 1903, P.A.C., Minto Papers, M.G. 27, II B 1; Chamberlain to Minto, April 20, 1903, in Canada, House of Commons, *Debates, 1904,* July 11, 1904, IV, 6365.

ing in Canada of two battalions of infantry, one of which would serve in India.[19]

In Borden's report on the results of the meeting, he declared that he had said he had no present intention to appoint a Canadian as G.O.C., but he had said that His Majesty's British government had exacted no conditions in return for agreeing to open the command of the militia to Canadians, to rank Canadian Militia officers with British regular officers in the normal way by seniority in rank, and to offer six regular commissions in the British Army to the Canadian Militia. The colonial secretary, Lyttelton, said that Borden's version was the correct one and that the War Office report, which differed from it, had not been made until eleven days after the meeting when its rapporteur had "composed the minutes on the theory that what he thought ought to have been arranged was arranged." Nevertheless, although Governor General Lord Minto said that he agreed with Borden "theoretically," Minto opposed the proposed change in the law governing the command. He said he believed that "most thoughtful Canadians" would also object to it, partly because it would destroy the hopes of Canadian officers "who have served with us," and partly because the Canadian forces would deteriorate. He thought that a change when imperial relations were in a delicate state might be very injurious.[20] If Minto was trying to suggest that Canadians who had served with the British Army would be prejudiced by loss of opportunity to return to command the militia, he needed to look back at the record. No Canadians in the Regular Army had been willing to accept the command. But he was, of course, simply looking for arguments to strengthen his case. As Sir John Anderson, principal clerk in the Colonial Office, minuted his dispatch on the subject, "Lord Minto will not understand that a quasi-independent command-in-chief is incompatible with complete ministerial responsibility." [21] British soldiers and imperialists refused to recognize that civil control of military power, now more firmly intrenched in

19. "Committee of Imperial Defence," Dec. 11, 1903, P.A.C., R.G. 7, G. 21, No. 270, Vol. 1, Pt. 1.
20. Minto, Telegram, Jan. 5, 1904, P.R.O., C.O. 42/896.
21. Minto, Confidential, Jan. 15, 1904, *ibid.*

the United Kingdom by the abolition of the office of commander in chief, was proper also in a self-governing colony.

Neither Borden nor the Committee of Imperial Defence had authority to commit their respective countries to these agreements. The War Office's version of the meeting was forwarded to Canada to ask for the attitude of the Canadian government. This report included statements that the meeting had agreed that it would be "advantageous to have a Canadian regular infantry regiment with two battalions, one serving in Canada and the other in India," and that it would also be advantageous to have occasional inspections of the Canadian defense forces by British regular officers of high rank. But it did not include reference to an understanding that the crown would have the right to appoint a senior officer in time of war. When Borden had returned to Canada he had found that some people objected to his having taken a seat on the committee.[22] It was for this reason that in February, 1904, he had asked Minto to arrange that the references to Halifax and Esquimalt be expunged from the minutes of the committee. The Canadian Cabinet then approved the minutes, excluding the reference to the bases. The transfer of a Canadian regiment for service in India was not mentioned at all.[23] The minutes of the Committee of Imperial Defence, which stated that Borden had said the Dominion government was anxious to take over the bases, were indorsed to the effect that Borden wished it to be understood that he had not assented.[24]

Minto, however, was determined to retain some form of imperial supervision of the Canadian forces. He proposed a scheme for more practical co-operation between the British forces and the forces of the Dominion government: he suggested that the new Canadian Chief of the General Staff should report to an inspector general of Canadian forces, who, as an imperial officer, would be in direct communication with the governor general. He explained to the Colonial Office, "it is necessary to bear in mind that the inclination of my government will be to obtain

22. Minto, Telegram, Dec. 22, 1903, *ibid.*, C.O. 42/895.
23. Minto, Memorandum of Conversation with Borden, Feb. 29, 1904, P.A.C., M.G. 27, II B 1, p. 92.
24. Minto, Confidential, March 4, 1904, P.R.O., C.O. 42/896.

as much military control as possible for themselves with a minimum of Imperial influence." [25] His proposal was based on a
false hope. The Canadian government was not committed to appoint a British regular officer as an inspector general of its land
forces, and in fact did not do so at first. An inspector general,
like the Chief of the General Staff, must serve only the responsible
government of the country. Borden said there would not at first
be much for an inspector general to do and that therefore the
office could be held by a Canadian. He appeased Minto by saying that when the reorganized militia was in working order, the
post should be held by a British officer. The pay would be $6,000,
the same as that of the former appointment of G.O.C., but it
would be understood that in the case of emergency the Chief
of the General Staff would assume command of the militia.[26]
Minto's scheme to perpetuate the vestiges of British military control thus came to nothing.

By his Militia Bill, introduced on March 17, 1904, Borden intended to open the command of the militia to Canadians, to rank
British officers with officers of the Canadian Militia according to
the date of appointment, to cancel the arrangement whereby
the general officer commanding the Halifax garrison would command in the event of war, to replace King's Regulations with
regulations drafted in Canada, to increase the Canadian Permanent Force from 1,000 to 2,000 of all ranks, to increase the pay
of regulars and militia, and to lengthen the annual drill camps
from sixteen to thirty days.[27] However, Minto noticed that in the
first reading, the provision for the crown to appoint a British
regular officer to command in the event of war had been omitted.
He brought this to Borden's attention and received a promise
that it would be inserted. But the Commons would only accept
the provision when it was assured that, in effect, the appointment would be made by the Canadian Cabinet.[28] The act
provided that His Majesty might appoint a British regular officer

25. Minto, Confidential, April 11, 1904, *ibid.*
26. Minto, Secret, July 9, 1904, *ibid.*, C.O. 42/897.
27. Canada, House of Commons, *Debates*, 1904, I, 205–208, March 17, 1904.
28. Minto to Lyttelton, March 21, 1904, P.A.C., R.G. 7, G. 21, No. 270, Vol. 1,
Pt. 1; M.G. 27, II B 1, Vol. 9, Pt. 2, pp. 59–64.

to command the Canadian Militia when it was called out on active service; but only the governor in council, i.e., the Canadian Cabinet, could authorize the calling out.[29] The implication was that the Cabinet would also approve the selection of a commander and it could be argued that appointment by "His Majesty" would be by advice of his Canadian Cabinet, and not his British Cabinet. As this point was not cleared up, both sides could accept the formula. This was a radical departure from the intention of the Committee of Imperial Defence. Borden then told Minto that, following the lines of the Esher Report, he had decided to establish a Militia Council to administer the militia. The council would have the minister as chairman and four military and two civilian members, and the command structure of the militia would be entirely Canadian in composition.[30]

The War Office commented that consent to a Canadian G.O.C. had been given on the understanding that appointment to the command in war would be made "by the Crown" (which it thought would mean by the British government); it also complained that the bill did not give British regular officers authority over Canadian Militia officers, which, it alleged, was part of the bargain over regular ranks. It argued that "fully trained officers should always take command." Lyttelton disagreed that the Canadians had not kept their part of the bargain. He said it was intended to implement the bill by regulations and that the full agreement was therefore not included in it, that the War Office could not insist on Canada accepting British staff officers because Canada would only take them on an exchange basis, and that although Canada might accept a British officer as "first military member" of the council, it would not hand over all the best-paid jobs in the new staff organization to the imperial government.[31] Major General Parsons, the British commander in Halifax, proposed that the militia should be under an independent authority responsible only to the governor general, by which he probably also implied that both the Halifax garrison and the

29. *Statutes of Canada, 1904,* 4 Edw. VII, c. 23, paras. 70–72.
30. Borden to Minto, March 29, 1904, P.A.C., Minto Papers, M.G. 27, II B 1, pp. 63–66.
31. W.O. to C.O., May 16, 1904, P.R.O., C.O. 42/890, Minuted.

militia should remain under British supervision. However, the War Office, no doubt because it knew that the British garrison at Halifax would soon be withdrawn, and because it did not wish to keep a senior officer there, dissented.[32] The Canadian government was careful to assert that if the militia were put under a British regular officer in time of war it should be one who was senior to its general officer commanding.[33] The act, with amendments, became law in November, 1904, and was put into effect immediately.

In its protection of Canadian control over command of the militia in war, the new act had gone much further than Borden had apparently originally intended, and further than the Committee of Imperial Defence had recommended. It also went further to establish Cabinet and ministerial control over the militia in peacetime than was the case with the British model which Borden had supposedly copied. The Army Council in Britain had inherited those ancient royal prerogative powers exercised in recent years by the secretary of state for war. The Militia Council did not get the same degree of independence. It was permitted only to advise the minister of militia and defense, who was in supreme control subject only to the supervisory direction of the Cabinet. This new Canadian system of militia control was a legacy of the old distrust of imperial officers and of British control. However, by bringing the minister and senior officers together, the Militia Council greatly reduced friction or hid it from public knowledge. The new system proved to be a more efficient method of administering the militia than the former method of control by the G.O.C. and deputy minister under a minister.[34] It also prepared the way for more harmonious co-operation between British and Canadian military authorities.

Meanwhile, Borden had brought the Canadian Militia closer to Hutton's idea of a "national militia army." On October 29, 1903, an order-in-council had transferred the Engineer Services

32. W.O. to C.O., June 3, 1904, *ibid.*, C.O. 42/899.
33. Minto to Lyttelton, March 21, 1904, P.A.C., R.G. 7, G. 21, No. 270, Vol. 1, Pt. 1.
34. Capt. L. R. Cameron, "Constitution of the Army and Militia Councils and the Creation of the Imperial and Canadian General Staffs," Canadian Army Historical Section, March, 1958, pp. 4–5.

Branch and the Militia Stores Branch from civil to military control and placed them under the G.O.C.[35] In the following years the organization of the Royal Canadian Engineers, the Canadian Army Service Corps, the Canadian Ordnance Corps, and the Militia Signal Corps made it virtually complete in all arms. A Corps of Guides had provided officers for intelligence, and the minister had also approved certain proposals that would aid cooperation with British forces. Establishments were to be based on British war establishments, and the whole Canadian force was to have service dress and equipment of British pattern.[36] Some Canadian newspapers had pressed for a distinctly Canadian uniform, but the G.O.C., the Earl of Dundonald, believing that the majority of militia officers were "very British in sentiment," prepared dress regulations on British models in order to "carry on the old traditions."[37] Moreover, even before the Committee of Imperial Defence recommended that Canadian officers should go to the Staff College at Camberley, the practice had commenced. Up to 1903, colonials who attended Camberley had got there by entering the British Army; and they had not always been very successful. Field Marshal Sir William Robertson noted in his biography that in the 1890's, when staff college standards were very low, only two officers were dismissed from the course, one who refused to grow a mustache in accordance with Queen's Regulations, and the other who was a "young man from the Overseas Dominions who, both by ordinary education and natural ability, ought not to have been sent to the college, for he could never hope to be equal to a position of responsibility."[38] After the South African War the first officer to go to the Staff College from colonial forces was Major D. I. V. Eaton from Canada, who attended from 1903–1904. In 1905 it was found that Canadian officers could not keep up with other officers on the

35. Stacey, *Military Problems of Canada*, Appendix B, "Military Reforms After 1898."
36. Memorandum on Relations of G.O.C. and Minister of Militia, June, 1903, Douglas Library, Queens University, Dundonald MSS, Microfilm.
37. Dundonald to Col. Altham, March 6, 1903, P.A.C., Tunney's Pasture, Cummins Papers.
38. Sir William Robert Robertson, *From Private to Field Marshal* (London: Constable, 1921), p. 174.

course, mainly because they had not had preliminary coaching by specialists in their profession known popularly as "army crammers." A special short course at the Royal Military College of Kingston was therefore designed to avert that difficulty as far as possible.[39]

The Earl of Dundonald as G.O.C.

Borden's explanation for the need to revise the Militia Act was that the old one (only slightly revised in 1883) had served since confederation, that the militia had grown since then, and that many circumstances had changed. He noted that the system of command by a British general officer had never worked well. When he first planned amendment he may have been merely trying to appease the more nationalistic members of his own party, and he was probably not yet motivated by his own experiences with the contemporary occupant of the command. But before the act went through the Canadian House of Commons in the fall of 1904, the G.O.C.'s behavior had led to summary dismissal and had amply justified the minister's case.

Dundonald was a descendant of Admiral Thomas Cochrane, Earl of Dundonald, who had a spectacular naval career in the early nineteenth century. The twelfth earl had joined the Life Guards, had served in the Nile expedition in 1884–1885, and had then enjoyed peacetime soldiering with his regiment until he became its colonel in 1895. When the South African War broke out he had given up his colonelcy, obtained a staff appointment in South Africa, and eventually commanded cavalry brigades which included irregulars and volunteers. With these he had gained a popular reputation for dash. He became a voluble advocate of the military virtues of the part-time soldier. Dundonald had won many admirers among the officers and men of the Canadian contingents. He therefore seemed in 1902 to be a suitable choice as G.O.C. of the Canadian Militia. In his first annual report he said that he had decided to leave out ceremonial pa-

39. "Annual Report of the Militia Council," Canada, *Sessional Papers, XIV,* 1906, No. 35, p. 24.

rades in order to concentrate on instruction to fit the soldier to take the field.[40] This sounded like admirable doctrine for a part-time force.

Before he accepted the appointment, Dundonald had been pointedly told the Canadian government's views on his subordination to the minister of militia.[41] But from the first he resented ministerial control. Although energetic and affable, he was tactless and vain. He reveled in the adulation of his military followers. His record in South Africa and his fondness for lecturing on the glories of the British connection soon made him the hero of the Canadian Opposition who exploited him against Laurier, a persistent critic of the military enthusiasm aroused by the war. Dundonald appeared to have no understanding of the delicacy of his constitutional position. Thus, he appeared on what was virtually a Conservative platform in a Vancouver meeting about the Alaska boundary dispute with the United States, heedless of the fact that this question was likely to become an election issue. On another occasion he approved the use of Macdonald's slogan, "A British subject I was born—a British subject I shall die," on a recruiting pamphlet for a new company of Glengarry Highlanders.[42] His first direct major clash with Borden came over the publication of his annual report. The second part of the report contained a proposed defense scheme which raised questions of policy and involved questions of expenditure. Borden thought these were outside the province of a departmental annual report and told Dundonald that they should not be published. He suggested that Part II be compared with the report of the Leach Commission which, he said, had been approved by the War Office and adopted by the Canadian government.[43]

In reply, the G.O.C. prepared a long memorandum on the nature of his relations with the minister in which he complained that he had never made his report confidential. He said it was

40. Department of Militia, "Annual Report," in Canada, *Sessional Papers,* XXXVII, 1903, No. 13, Paper No. 35, p. 36.

41. Minto, Telegram, Feb. 26, 1902, P.R.O., C.O. 42/888.

42. Douglas D. M. B. H. Cochrane, the Earl of Dundonald, *My Army Life* (London: Arnold, 1926), pp. 244, 256.

43. Jan. 31, Feb. 21, 1903, Douglas Library, Queens University, Dundonald MSS, Microfilm.

not true that it should be compared with the 1898 report since almost none of that earlier report had yet been implemented. He then went on to say that Laurier had told him that the defense of Canada "was not worth bothering with or spending money on. . . . Canada has nothing to fear from any non-American power," and in any case was "guaranteed by the Monroe Doctrine." He said the prime minister had told him that it was useless to prepare defenses against the United States because resistance would be futile, and in fact there was no danger of an attack. The militia was only a means of "keeping the Jingoes quiet." Laurier had said that the people of Canada agreed with him on these things. Dundonald thought this attitude explained the actions of the Cabinet and of Borden which, he said, did not coincide with the views expressed by the prime minister at the Colonial Conference in 1902.[44]

Dundonald sent a copy of his report to Colonel Altham at the War Office and said that the minister would be heckled in Parliament until he had put its recommendations into effect. He said the new Intelligence Department and Corps of Guides were organized only on paper and would not be effective until money was appropriated. The Intelligence Department was "merely a farce." Canada was not organized for defense, and the defense scheme was ineffective because munitions were not available. The War Office forwarded Dundonald's report to the Colonial Office where Chamberlain minuted it that Canadian defenses were "thoroughly unsatisfactory" and noted that Dundonald was "gloomy." [45] The Colonial Office then inquired about the implementation of the Leach Commission's report. Minto forwarded the Canadian government's reply, which was to the effect that the defense plan in the first part of the report had not yet been considered because of pressure of work, but that much of the second part concerning the reorganization of the militia had been put into effect, and the rest was either soon to be adopted or still

44. "Memorandum on the Relations of the G.O.C. and the Minister of Militia," n.d., *ibid.* An appendix lists fourteen recommendations of the Leach Commission that had not been carried through. It is not clear to whom this memorandum was addressed.
45. W.O. to C.O., March 6, 1903, P.R.O., C.O. 42/895.

under consideration. There had been improvements at Headquarters, and an assistant quartermaster general, district staff
adjutants, and an intelligence staff had been appointed. An Ordnance Department was to be set up. The Medical Corps had
been organized in 1899. There was an inspector of musketry, a
musketry school, and a supply of one thousand rifles per month.
There was also a new Army Service Corps. The defenses at Kingston, Montreal, Quebec, Saint John, and the lower St. Lawrence
had been strengthened. Minto, however, in a private letter,
practically said that the Cabinet's minute was "misleading, not to
say false"; and Dundonald's private communications to the War
Office were to the same effect.[46]

Five days after sending this Cabinet minute, Minto reported
that Borden had told him that about a year earlier a committee
consisting of himself, Sir Richard Cartwright, and Sutherland
had been appointed to consider the Leach proposals, but that
nothing had come of it. Minto doubted whether it had ever met.
Borden admitted he was not expert enough to express an opinion on the points raised by Leach. Minto thought the Cabinet's
memorandum "extremely plausible and in some points entirely
misleading in respect to the view it presents of the improvements
undertaken by the Department of Militia." A Colonial Office
minute to Sir John Anderson said that "plausible" was not the
right word. Read in conjunction with Dundonald's report, it
seemed "ludicrous." [47]

Anderson blamed Canadian political life. He said that as the
United States was now building a regular army there was no
longer any excuse for Canada not to defend herself. The Leach
plan had been made when the United States regular army was
smaller. If Borden was puzzled by its proposal that Canada
should prepare to resist a potentially overwhelming attack with
forces that were inevitably inadequate, the growth of the United
States Army must have added to his concern, and not lessened it.
Anderson, at least, saw that no effective solution could be found
by insisting upon British direction of the militia. He said that

46. Minto, Secret, April 20, 1903, *ibid.*, C.O. 42/892 and Minutes.
47. Minto, Secret, April 25, 1904, *ibid.*

Canadians were quite right to refuse to permit the G.O.C. to be independent of the minister, and that if the G.O.C. attempted to educate public opinion without the concurrence of the minister he was guilty of insubordination. The old G.O.C. system in Canada had only led to squabbles, whereas in the Cape and Natal, in which local governments had chosen their own commandants, the results had been far more satisfactory. There was no legitimate means of informing the Canadian public about the inefficiency of the Canadian government. Anderson believed that as Britain was responsible for the defense of Canada, she had a right to know that the Canadians were doing their best, and he suggested that if Britain obtained the right to inspect the Canadian Militia, she would have the right to remonstrate about its condition.[48] His argument would have been more convincing if he could have shown that Britain could effectively defend Canada against the United States, or if he could have persuaded Canadians to believe that strengthening their defenses would aid Britain's diplomacy and act as a deterrent.

Plans for War with the United States

Dundonald's insubordinate attitude was made ominous by its bearing on this problem—security against the United States. It was serious for Canada that military planning in England did not yet reflect the amelioration of Anglo-American relations that had become a basic principle of British foreign policy and had been reciprocated in the United States since Secretary of State John Hay took office in 1898. The War Office had continued to revise its studies of Canadian defense in an American war. In 1901, after reviewing the Leach Commission's report for the War Office, Major W. R. Robertson, the head of the foreign section of the Intelligence Department at the War Office and the future wartime Chief of the Imperial General Staff, had said that if Britain were engaged in a European war, the United States might be tempted to take advantage of its superiority over Canada in numbers and resources. For a popular war the Americans could raise

48. W.O. to C.O., May 4, 1903, *ibid.*, C.O. 42/895, Minute.

2.5 million levies. Robertson thought that a "land war on the American continent would be, perhaps, the most unprofitable and most hazardous military enterprise that we could possibly be driven to engage in." But he argued that this fact, coupled with the great increase in British responsibilities, made it more essential than ever that Canadian forces be put on an efficient footing for defense. As regular troops could not be sent from Britain early enough to be of use, offensive action must depend on the navy.

A deputy assistant adjutant general in the Directorate of Military Intelligence, Colonel H. A. Lawrence, agreed. But he thought that the occupation of New York City or Boston, though humbling to American pride, would scarcely convince the Southern or Western states that the nation was beaten. America's vital part was her trade. He therefore believed that although it would be impossible to starve the United States into submission, the loss of foreign trade would be a blow "felt from one end of the country to the other." Offensive action should come later. Troops should first cover Montreal and then operate up Lake Champlain against Springfield, Hartford, and New Haven. Robertson had given no indication of the way he thought such a war could be won; but another War Office study which collected these opinions together said that the weakness of a republic lay in its political constitution. A democracy was proverbially unstable, and without popular support no democratic government could continue for very long a war which entailed sacrifices from every member of the community.[49] Colonel Hubert J. Foster, R.E., who had served at Halifax, then with the Canadian Militia, and was now attaché in Washington, believed that a vigorous Canadian defense would disappoint the invader and would "possibly tire him out." With Canadian patriotism, which he compared with that of the South in the Civil War, and with the assistance that the mother country was pledged to give, there

---

49. Capt. A. Haldane, staff captain, "Military Policy in a War with the United States," March 12, 1902, P.R.O., W.O. 106/40, B 1/1, brought up to date, Jan. 15, 1903.

was no reason why Canada should not resist an invasion successfully.[50]

These studies of the problems of an American war were proper exercises for British staff officers; and, in view of the tough nut they tried to crack, the futility and even fatuity of their proposals were excusable. Some military observers who knew the United States well were not as convinced that the Americans would tire or would treat the war lightly. Captain Arthur Hamilton Lee, R.A., who had also served at Halifax and at the Royal Military College in Kingston, thought that war with the United States meant the inevitable loss of Canada: once the Americans were aroused they would not stop short of victory. Colonel Kitson, who went from commandant at the Royal Military College at Kingston to be military attaché in Washington, agreed.[51] But even these officers thought it Canada's duty to strengthen herself against a preliminary American invasion.

The realization that Canada was defenseless permeated all staff papers, but true to form the soldiers were not prepared to admit defeat in advance. Colonel Charles E. Callwell, in a thirty-eight-page memorandum on the defense of Canada prepared by December 2, 1903, for the director of military intelligence at the War Office, declared that in a fight to a finish "we should lose Canada." The Canadians were totally incapable of defending themselves for more than a few weeks, he asserted, and a military force sent from the United Kingdom would be overcome by sheer weight of numbers after some months. He argued therefore that it was essential to use Britain's advantage of being able to send warships up the canals to the Great Lakes; but the ships should go at once. And he said that it would be necessary to avoid arousing in the American people the idea that their national honor was at stake. His assessment of the preponderance of American strength was fully confirmed by a reconnaissance of

50. Col. H. J. Foster, "A Study of the Strategical Considerations Affecting the Invasion of Canada by the United States," 1904, *ibid.*, B 1/8.
51. E. A. Altham, "Comments on Haldane's Memo.," March 13, 1902, *ibid.*, B 1/1. Captain Lee enjoyed a long public career and was created Baron Lee of Fareham.

the United States carried out in 1904 by a Canadian in the British Army, Lieutenant Colonel G. M. Kirkpatrick, R.E. Throughout all studies, dependence on the navy for the defense of Canada against the United States was made quite clear. The navy would be used partly for rushing reinforcements to Nova Scotia and the St. Lawrence, partly for controlling Lake Ontario, and partly for attacking American shipping and the American coast. The quartermaster general at the War Office, Colonel J. M. Grierson, after reading the reports of Callwell and Kirkpatrick, therefore decided to raise the question of the defense of Canada before the Committee of Imperial Defence.[52]

The Canadian government's reaction to the Alaska boundary question reveals the complexity of its attitude to defense against the United States. This crisis differed from others of earlier years in that it was more clearly an issue between the two North American countries and was not an outgrowth of British international problems. Some American historians, though not all, have believed that Roosevelt was prepared to go to the length of using force if he had not got his way. Canada was thus put in jeopardy, but this time not as a result of British policy, nor because the United States wished to take advantage of British preoccupation elsewhere. It was endangered solely because the American president wanted territory that Canadians believed belong to them. However, Laurier is said to have been reconciled to the loss of the Canadian case. His government did not, as Canadian governments had done so often before, hastily arm and appeal for British aid. It appears never to have thought in terms of physical resistance. In his book on British-American relations, H. C. Allen has shown that "for the future neither Canadian nor any other subordinate interests would in the last resort be allowed by the British government to stand in the way of Anglo-American accord." [53] Laurier did not regard the adverse decision as a consequence of Canada's military weakness. He chose instead to accept the inevitable result and to exploit polit-

52. C. E. Callwell, "The Defence of Canada in a War with the United States," Dec. 2, 1903, *ibid.*, B 1/3. An anonymous realist in the War Office indorsed this memorandum, "Then why should [we] start at all?"
53. Allen, *Great Britain and the United States*, p. 600.

ically the general Canadian belief that Britain had betrayed Canadian interests. He asserted that Canada must control her own foreign policy in areas vital to her interests. But that day was still a long way off.

The significant point of his response for the immediate future was that it made clear Canada's attitude toward military preparations. If the Canadian government was unwilling to look to its defenses in a dispute with the United States about what it regarded as its legitimate rights, it was even less likely to agree to arm at the response of a British G.O.C. in order to strengthen the British position generally. Although never prepared to provide adequately for defense against the United States, Canada up to this time had relied on Britain to defend her interests. Now that Britain could not do so, or would not do so, she blamed Britain rather than her own vulnerability. Canadians continued to watch closely any British surrender that might affect her—for instance, any slackening of the Rush-Bagot Agreement on the Great Lakes; [54] yet they nevertheless tacitly accepted, as did Britain, their dependence upon American good will, of which, ultimately, they would be the greatest beneficiaries. Canadians were thus in a confused state of mind about the problem of defense against the United States. They were inclined to ignore the relation of diplomatic strength to military preparedness; they were anxious that Britain should not reduce her guard and should continue to give them diplomatic and military support; but they were equally anxious that nothing should be done to provoke the United States and so make diplomatic contact more difficult.

One of the weaknesses of British military planning at this time was that the professional soldiers who undertook it were not given political terms of reference; therefore they speculated improperly without regard for American intentions. Had they been given a proper premise on which to write, much of this planning for impossible situations would not have occurred. All these staff papers were secret documents in the files of the War Office, but

54. Col. John Adye, General Staff to D.M.O., "Armed Vessels on the Great Lakes," Nov., 1907, P.R.O., W. O. 106/40, B 1/15.

they undoubtedly influenced the thinking of British regular officers including the Canadian G.O.C. The problem of defense against the United States was therefore sufficient to make the Canadian government regard with suspicion and fear Dundonald's independence and his fondness for the public platform. It probably learned quite early that he had indorsed a memorandum on the subject of defense against the United States which the chief Opposition military critic, Colonel Sam Hughes, had sent to the secretary of state for war. The G.O.C. himself described Hughes as "honest and able, a good officer," but "eccentric and extravagant in his views and language." He said Hughes was "for many years the chief supporter of the imperial connection from a military point of view," and one of those chiefly responsible for forcing the hand of the government to send Canadians to South Africa. Hughes's memorandum had deplored the fact that previous plans for war with the United States were merely defensive. He proposed the seizure of the area from Sackets Harbor to Portland, leaving most of Maine on the flank. The War Office declared Hughes's scheme quite impossible because a hostile Maine would be on an exposed left flank; and it reproved Hughes for giving the proposal to a journalist, L. J. Amery, when, as a militia railway intelligence officer, it was his duty to forward it only to his commanding officer.[55] But Dundonald was equally at fault in passing Hughes's proposal to the War Office and the commander in chief, thus bypassing the government which he served.

When explaining to the commander in chief why he had supported Hughes's plan, the G.O.C. had said that his aim was "imperial military control" of Canada.[56] This was not a passing fancy. Dundonald's autobiography reveals that he believed that he had powers similar to those of his patron, the commander in chief himself. Even when Field Marshal Lord Roberts was unceremoniously bustled out of that office and it was abolished in

55. Dundonald to Field Marshal the Right Hon. Earl Roberts, April 27, 1903, Douglas Library, Queens University, Dundonald MSS, Microfilm; Hughes to Secretary of State for War, March 30, 1903, *ibid.;* "Colonel Hughes's Paper on Canada's Defence, 1904," P.R.O., W.O. 32/275/266, Canada 205.
56. Dundonald to Roberts, April 27, 1903, Douglas Library, Queens University, Dundonald MSS, Microfilm.

1904, Dundonald did not see it as a lesson for his own situation. He thought that a colonial command was different from one in England in that it could only be subordinate. His pretensions became especially embarrassing to Laurier, and perhaps dangerous to Canada, when they were coupled with a belief in an anti-American defense policy which the government was unwilling to follow.

As in previous cases, the G.O.C.'s conflict with the minister came to a head over patronage. Borden seems to have grown more circumspect with time in his handling of militia patronage; but the minister of agriculture, Sydney Fisher, in whose riding the G.O.C. wished to raise a new company, and who happened to act for a time as minister of militia, was less cautious. Dundonald's complaint of political interference in the commissioning of officers for the unit had some substance in that, although men of both parties were appointed, one of Fisher's particular political enemies was repeatedly rejected. But Dundonald was overly persistent in trying to get his way, and then he put himself quite in the wrong by airing this grievance in a public speech. His dismissal was inevitable, but after it he stayed on in Canada in order to embarrass the government. Laurier had to request that he be recalled. Even after his return home he continued to make mischief by what seem like ill-founded accusations.[57] Dundonald's behavior may not have been the cause of Borden's determination to abolish the G.O.C. system; but it confirmed his belief that no other course was possible. It revealed once more that when a self-governing colony had views on foreign and defense policy that differed from those of the mother country, a British officer's loyalty to Britain could make him an undesirable colonial servant.

The dismissal of Dundonald was caused by his own personal qualities, especially his lack of tact. But it also arose out of the peculiar nature of the G.O.C. appointment. A military command was extremely difficult in all the self-governing colonies. All co-

57. Grey to Laurier, July 11, 1905, Douglas Library, Queens University, Laurier MSS, Microfilm, F. No. 1, Ser. B, Reel 184, p. 203128; Grey, Telegram, July 15, 1905, P.R.O., C.O. 42/901.

lonial governments were jealous of any interference by an imperial officer. Large sections of the colonial public and press saw nothing in an appointment from Britain but "feathers and gold lace." And there was a widespread belief that discipline was of minor importance. The result was repeated discouragement. Necessary reorganization was often opposed on political grounds.[58] Success in the face of such problems required qualities beyond those possessed by most British officers.

Halifax and Esquimalt and the Defense of Canada

General Grierson's decision in November, 1904, to refer the Canadian defense problem to the Committee of Imperial Defence came some time after the main lines of future policy had been laid down earlier by Admiralty decisions about the two British naval bases in Canada. Admiral Sir John Fisher, concerned about the possibility of war with Germany, had discounted dangers elsewhere and planned the concentration of the Royal Navy nearer home in line with the strategic doctrine that its first objective was the destruction of the enemy's main fleet. He had already decided that British naval strength in the Pacific and Caribbean must be reduced. This contraction of power affected the future of Halifax and Esquimalt and inevitably had repercussions on Canadian defense problems and on imperial military relations. For although Halifax was considered primarily an imperial naval base, and although Esquimalt was also usually assumed to be maintained primarily for imperial purposes, both places gave a sense of security to those Canadians who lived on the coasts. Indeed, it was on this account that Canada had been induced to share the cost of Esquimalt's construction and maintenance.

The future of Esquimalt had, in fact, already been in doubt before Fisher decided to redistribute the fleet. The Admiralty's contract to supply marines at Canada's expense was due to expire in April, 1900. Long before that time their lordships had made

58. Governor of New Zealand, to C.O., Sept. 24, 1906, New Zealand Archives, G. 26/6, Governor, Confidential. This letter recommended Maj. Gen. J. M. Babington, retiring commandant, for the C.M.G.

it clear that it would not be renewed. The Royal Marines had been found to cost about half as much again as the £7,000 that Canada had agreed to pay, and the Admiralty had never been happy about departing from their rule that the defense of naval bases was not the Admiralty's business and should not come out of naval funds. Hence, in 1898, there was a conference about the future of Esquimalt, especially about the unsatisfactory sharing of responsibility between Canada, the War Office, and the Admiralty. It was agreed that although defense of the naval base was a Canadian responsibility, since the Dominion would for some time be unable to garrison it, the War Office would take over operational responsibility for ten years. Canada accepted this arrangement and admitted liability to provide sites for defenses.[59]

The War Office then questioned whether the garrison was adequate and how the civilians in the neighborhood could be fed in the case of an attack. In consequence, Colonel E. A. Altham, an assistant quartermaster general at the War Office, proceeded to make the first thorough study since the 1880's of Esquimalt's strategic significance. His conclusions came as a shock. They cast grave doubts on the value of the base. He recalled that the Carnarvon Commission had itself been ambiguous on the subject and that the Admiralty's belief that the base was not tenable against an American attack had been held consistently. Although the Colonial Conference of 1897 had not discussed strategy, it had ruled that the protection of the Pacific Squadron at Esquimalt was a Canadian government responsibility and had encouraged Canada to expect local naval aid if it should be needed. He concluded that Esquimalt's only value was as a naval base. If it were not needed for that purpose, its defense was a waste of men and money. He suggested, however, that as Britain had pressed Canada for twenty years to develop the base, her influence with Canada would be harmed if the base were now abandoned. He therefore recommended that Esquimalt should be strengthened.[60] Altham's report made it clear that the British

59. Minto, Secret, Feb. 8, 1901, P.R.O., C.O. 42/881.
60. Altham, "Memorandum on Esquimalt," April 29, 1902, P.R.O., W.O. 32/275/266, Canada, 189.

government, and particularly the Admiralty, had taken advantage of Canadian concern about local defense to obtain financial support for a marginal imperial naval base. On the other hand, Canada had spent money freely on Esquimalt despite the fact that it gave no direct protection to the commercial shipping in Victoria Harbor. It had done so in the belief that the fleet would defend the Pacific coast. Withdrawal of the fleet in accordance with imperial requirements would now nullify the local defensive value of the base.

Nevertheless, when Borden arrived in England to discuss his Militia Bill at the end of 1903, he was told that Britain proposed to withdraw entirely from both Halifax and Esquimalt. He apparently was asked whether he thought Canada would take over the bases. Although the question had not yet been considered by the Canadian Cabinet, he said Canada was anxious to take over the stations.[61] But since both nationalists and imperialists would be likely to object, there were obvious difficulties. The former would oppose spending money on defenses which could be called imperial, and the latter would resist moves that might diminish the ties with Britain. This latter position was, indeed, put forcibly by the governor general, the Earl of Minto, to the Colonial Office. He resisted the proposal on the grounds that the question could not be treated solely on military grounds. The effect of such a transfer on the colony's feeling for the mother country should be considered. The Colonial Office was less sure that the garrisons were really bonds of Empire.[62]

In view of all these difficulties the question was shelved and a year passed after the withdrawal was proposed. Then in December, 1904, it was reported that Borden had openly stated that Canada was prepared to relieve England of the task of protecting the Dominion in peacetime. Minto had gone. The new governor general, Earl Grey, a less militant imperialist, said he would inquire whether the minister had Cabinet approval for his statement.[63] A month later, however, he complained that the War

61. Minto, Confidential, March 4, 1904, P.R.O., C.O. 42/896.
62. Minto, Secret, June 18, 1904, *ibid.*
63. Grey, Telegram, Dec. 30, 1904, *ibid.*, C.O. 42/897.

Office and Admiralty were being permitted to interfere with, and nearly wreck, a national policy by announcing the withdrawal of the garrisons without giving him time to squeeze "a decision out of Laurier to supply Canadian replacements." [64] He found that the chief cause of the Canadian government's slowness was the problem of getting enough regular troops to man the garrisons. The Militia Act had to be amended to double the Permanent Force. Canada had to ask for a postponement of takeover, had to arrange to receive transfers from the British Army, and had to hire British Engineer Companies on a temporary basis.[65]

Although Canada undertook to accept the bases, debate continued about their value. As usual, the War Office and Admiralty were at odds. In military eyes, an overland attack on Halifax from the American border had always been unlikely, and the War Office had "always assumed that His Majesty's Navy undertook the responsibility of protecting British possessions from such organized sea attack." Existing defensive arrangements were therefore based on the assumption that the Admiralty would intercept an attacking naval force.[66] But it was against Admiralty policy to accept responsibility for defending bases. The Committee of Imperial Defence was therefore requested to investigate the strategy for both places. It came to the conclusion that Halifax, because it would be remote from possible spheres of operations, had little strategic importance except in a war with the United States. In a European war it would be liable to raids, but only by one or two cruisers. The situation would be very different in a war with the United States, and defense against battleship attack should be the standard. Esquimalt, on the other hand, was declared useless in a war with the United States because it could not be defended. The decline of the Russian fleet since the war with Japan made its retention as a fortified base now unnecessary. The Pacific Squadron should be based on Hong

64. Grey to Ommaney, Jan. 23, 1905, P.A.C., M.G. 27, II B 2, Vol. 6, No. 10.
65. Grey, Telegram, Jan. 20, 1905, P.R.O., C.O. 42/900; W.O. to C.O., Jan. 28, 1905, *ibid.*, C.O. 42/904; W.O. to C.O., Aug. 17, 1905, *ibid.* Grey 286, Sept. 2, 1905, *ibid.*, Index 17727, indorsed "Destroyed by Statute."
66. Director of Military Intelligence to Director of Naval Intelligence, Dec. 22, 1902, P.R.O., W.O. 106/40, B 1/2.

Kong.[67] Halifax had thus been held only because of its value in a war with the United States, while Esquimalt would have had to be abandoned at the outset of such a war. Now that an American war was less likely, both places were to be abandoned. But abandonment had been decided upon before these strategic appraisals were made, and the Committee of Imperial Defence investigation served chiefly to cast doubt on earlier policy, especially on the construction of Esquimalt.

The strategic papers on the bases were considered by the committee on April 5 and 12, 1905, and were discussed in relation to the defense of Canada. Mr. Balfour asserted that Canada had a right to support by all the forces of the Empire. He said it was accepted General Staff opinion that the defense of Canada against the United States required the control of the St. Lawrence river and of Lake Ontario; but since the navy believed that even if ships could be passed to the Great Lakes they would soon be outnumbered, every care should be taken to avoid giving the United States an excuse to revoke the Rush-Bagot Agreement. General Grierson suggested the stationing of submarines at Halifax to cover the St. Lawrence estuary; but Admiral Sir John Fisher pointed out that this would be regarded by the Americans as a provocation. Alfred Lyttelton, the colonial secretary, then stated that Canada had already asked for an explanation of the withdrawal of the Pacific Squadron from Esquimalt and would certainly ask questions about a reduction of the North American Squadron. He therefore wanted to be able to reassure the Canadian government that promises of aid given by Cardwell in 1865 and Chamberlain in 1896 would be kept. He thought that it was necessary to explain that the recent changes in the distribution of the fleet were designed to increase the efficiency of the naval defense of the Empire as a whole, including, of course, that of Canada. At the second meeting a week later, however, he reported that as Canada was not acquainted with the existing defense scheme, there was no need to communicate to her any changes that were contemplated. The committee thus simply

67. C.D.C. Memorandums 346M and 347M, "Strategic Conditions of Halifax and Esquimalt," May 4, 1905, P.R.O., Cab. 11/27.

decided to reaffirm the general principles of protection for colonies and to proceed on its own to study the effect of the redisposition of the fleet on local defense schemes.[68]

Three months later, because the War Office and the Admiralty were still unable to agree where the responsibility for the defense of Canada really lay, the Committee of Imperial Defence discussed the Admiralty's answers to certain questions that had been put to it. The Admiralty refused to accept responsibility for the control of Lake Ontario at the outset of a war with the United States. General Grierson therefore suggested that Canada should finance and maintain torpedo craft at Halifax for this purpose and that these should be considered her contribution to imperial naval defense. This was opposed by Austen Chamberlain, the chancellor of the exchequer, because it was an encouragement to Canada to return to the old idea of local defense only. With Balfour's support, Chamberlain said that he looked forward to a time when the dominions would possess their own navies ready to co-operate with the Royal Navy in time of war. He knew this was against the Admiralty's concept of "one absolute control," but he believed that colonies would never contribute large sums for ships so long as they exercised no control over the expenditure of funds or the distribution of ships. Sir John Fisher, although nettled by this direct onslaught against his sacred principles, showed no willingness to yield and extend the fleet's protection in Canadian waters. To a further question about control of the lower St. Lawrence, he declared simply that the Admiralty had no intention of repudiating its responsibilities, but that this must be "interpreted reasonably." The navy could stop fleets, but not individual vessels. And he said the Admiralty had no advice to give Canada to show how to secure command of Lake Ontario in time of peace without violating the provisions of the Rush-Bagot Agreement.[69]

In considering the relation of these problems to the Canadian attitude on imperial defense and her acceptance of British lead-

68. "The Defence of Canada," C.I.D., 69th and 70th Meetings, April 5, 12, 1905, P.R.O., W.O. 106/40, B 1/4.
69. "Defence of Canada," C.I.D., 75th Meeting, July 13, 1905, *ibid.*

ership, it is of interest to note that in 1902 the Admiralty had ruled that the loss of Esquimalt would not be of strategic significance,[70] and in 1903 it had stated that in the event of a war with the United States at a time when relations with a European power were uncertain, it proposed to abandon the sea command in the Atlantic to the American fleet.[71] The defense of Canada had always been dependent on British sea power, and the difficulties implicit in asserting that power against a great land power had now been made infinitely greater by the growth of the United States Navy to a position second only to that of the Royal Navy. In these circumstances the Admiralty now virtually refused to consider war against the United States a practicable proposition. The War Office, on the other hand, was inclined to take the attitude that however unlikely it might be, the danger must be studied. But study invariably brought up the fact that the prosecution of such a war depended primarily on the Royal Navy; and this navy already virtually declared its unwillingness to act in defense of Canada. In view of this impasse, the War Office was left to draw the conclusions that the brunt of a war with the United States would fall on Canada, even though the war might be entirely unconnected with her as it would have been in 1895; that Britain was pledged to defend Canada with all her resources (as well she might if a war were not Canada's concern); that Canadian defenses were in poor condition; and that Britain had "the right to demand from Canada that she take adequate steps for her own defence and that these be communicated to the Imperial government." [72]

It is perhaps noteworthy that about the same time, when considering the strategic value of Halifax and the need to maintain its defenses, the British General Staff had refused comment on its potential value as a naval base except to say that it "would seem to be of importance," but had dwelt on its value as a port for the reinforcement of Canada. As the Naval Intelligence

70. Admiralty to W.O., April 19, 1902, *ibid.*, W.O. 32/275/266, Canada 189.
71. Admiralty Mo567, June 29, 1903, quoted in W.O. Intelligence Department, "Strategical Conditions in the Caribbean and West Atlantic, 1903," Sept. 17, 1903, *ibid.*, W.O. 106/40, B 1/17.
72. "Conditions of a War between the British Empire and the United States," 1908, *ibid.*, W.O. 106/40, B 1/20.

Division at the Admiralty had said that reinforcements could not be sent for six months, it seemed clear that the United States might attempt to seize the port at the beginning of a war.[73] The significance of these views is that no one in Britain was apparently yet thinking of Halifax's value as a port of embarkation for goods and supplies *from* Canada in the event of a European war. The Admiralty, which still wanted a centrally controlled navy, had washed its hands of the means by which, if the dominion supported that navy, it would protect its own coasts and would furnish supplies and men for a war outside North America. Presumably the Admiralty expected Canada to make adequate provision for the defense of Halifax. While the Admiralty thought that the control of bases could be completely decentralized, it held that control of ships must remain absolutely centralized. Furthermore, these strategic plans, which were not all communicated to the government responsible to the Canadian people, were based on the assumption that the general security of the Empire took precedence over the security of any of its outlying parts. Canada was expendable. This kind of assumption, which involved complex assessments of the degree of danger, made it difficult for a dominion government to accept British direction of imperial defense and foreign policy.

73. "Remarks on the Halifax Defence Scheme, 1908," May 14, 1908, *ibid.*, W.O. 106/40, B 1/19.

12

Military Co-operation and Naval Decentralization

Britain's diminishing concern with defense against the United States, which was bound to affect Canadian military policy in one way or another, came in combination with some signs of a growing understanding of the colonial point of view. An anonymous and undated typewritten memorandum in the files of the Committee of Imperial Defence, which discussed "Possible methods of employing troops from self-governing colonies in a Great War," suggested that troops from all parts of the Empire could be concentrated in any sphere of operations including North America; but it contemplated no action in Europe. The writer added that there seemed no hope of achieving such concentration through a centralized defense system. The best that could now be done was to prepare the legal arrangements that would be necessary for the employment of colonial troops. The fact that this document was not printed and circulated like most others suggests that it was not yet fully accepted as a firm policy. But it indicates the dawn of a new approach to the problem of imperial defense.[1]

The impossibility of forcing the colonies into an imperial defense straitjacket of British design was beginning to be widely realized. By 1904 Chamberlain admitted that he had been wrong in his aims at the conferences.[2] A year later he wrote:

I know by experience how sensitive the colonials are to anything which appears to be criticism, or even a suggestion, as to their local

1. "Colonial Troops for Imperial Service in War," P.R.O., Cab. 11/121. A reference to Chamberlain suggests the date of this document to be 1903.
2. Chamberlain to Minto, Aug. 17, 1904, P.A.C., Minto Papers, M.G. 27, Vol. 14, p. 135.

action. . . . My own experience and my conversations with the representatives of the colonies have rather altered my views as to the best way of securing acceptance of proper responsibility for Imperial Defence by the colonies. I see that there will always be difficulty in getting the Colonies to contribute to our expenditure. It arouses the question of taxation without representation and encourages a local agitation against what is called a "tribute." If I were in my old office I should try to find out whether it would not be possible to arrange a plan whereby each Colony should have its own Army and Fleet, in which of course it might be hoped that it would take a patriotic interest and towards which it might contribute much larger sums than it would to an English army or an English Fleet. Of course such an arrangement must be accompanied by some agreement as to what is to happen in the event of war, and must secure the certainty that the colonial Fleet and Army would work as an integral part of the main Imperial force. It would be necessary that they should drill and exercise together under certain conditions. This is a little vague but you will, I think, understand the general idea.[3]

An agreement on an automatic commitment to war, however, was still a difficulty. What Chamberlain had apparently not yet realized was that Britain was not in a position to insist upon that condition as a prerequisite for colonial autonomy in defense measures. Sir Frederick Pollock, the distinguished British jurist, told Laurier that Chamberlain had been wrong to introduce proposals of contributions for defense at the Colonial Conference of 1902. Pollock suggested "some central Imperial regulation and organization of purely voluntary and spasmodic assistance." This kind of ambiguous phrase that might have meant much or little clouded all discussions of imperial defense relationships. Laurier would not accept it. He said that voluntary assistance as in South Africa was possible, but not direct and systematic contribution; and he enlarged on the fact that Canada was free from alarms of war. It would be time enough to discuss the subject when the conditions of danger arose.[4]

The appointment of Earl Grey to succeed Minto as governor general of Canada in November, 1904, helped to further under-

3. Chamberlain to Grey, May 20, 1905, P.A.C., Grey Papers, M.G. 27, II B 2, Vol. 6.
4. W. A. S. Hewins, *The Apologies of an Imperialist: Forty Years of Empire Policy* (London: Constable, 1929), II, 121.

standing of Canada's point of view. Both governors were anxious
to strengthen imperial ties, and both were charming and on good
terms with Laurier; but Minto, a soldier with Conservative ties,
thought in terms of military centralization, while Grey, a Liberal
politician, had a more subtle understanding of colonial autonomy. As Laurier said, he gave "his whole heart, his whole soul,
and his whole life" to Canada;[5] and when he returned to England in 1907 Lord Esher found him still "bubbling with
enthusiasm" about the country and his projects.[6]

When Sir John Colomb and the Imperial Federation (Defence) League, called attention to dominion slackness in defense
and urged the British prime minister to introduce a representative
system for the Empire to stimulate it,[7] Grey told him privately
that Laurier hoped to make Canada "the natural route between
Australasia and the United Kingdom" and that this, if successful,
would be another contribution to imperial defense. Laurier's
idea, a revival of Macdonald's claim that the Canadian Pacific
Railway was a contribution to imperial defense, had only marginal value in face of growing dangers to Britain at sea; but
Grey went on to counsel Colomb to "avoid irritating references
to what the United Kingdom has done in the past for Canada
and instead [to] give Canada credit for the possession of a manly
respect and generous Imperial spirit."[8] This was sage advice.
Frequent British criticism that the dominions were not bearing
their fair share of the cost of imperial defense could have little
effect unless Britain was prepared to retaliate by withdrawing
her ancient offer of protection of the colonies in the event of war.
This she was not likely to do, and for reasons that were not
entirely sentimental. The fact was that the imperial connection
was not a one-sided benefit. The connection with Canada had
a certain prestige value for Britain and also potential military
value under certain circumstances. These values could not be

5. *Dictionary of National Biography, 1912–1921* (London: Oxford, 1927),
p. 278.
6. Esher to M. V. Brett, May 21, 1907, Brett, ed., *Journals and Letters of
. . . Esher*, II, 237.
7. Colomb, Memorandum, Dec. 10, 1904, Douglas Library, Queens University,
Microfilm, Laurier Papers, F. No. 1, Ser. B, Reel 184, pp. 202860–202865.
8. Grey to Colomb, Feb. 16, 1905, P.A.C., M.G. 27, II B 2, Vol. 12, No. 12A.

measured. They could not be used as yardsticks to decide imperial defense contributions. Canada was in a good position to put her own price tag on what she would pay for the British connection.

In the past her evaluation had differed from Britain's because it was affected by a different judgment of the effect of American proximity and of the best way to meet it. Now that there was less room for disagreement on that score, and now that Canada was hesitantly accepting complete responsibility for her own peacetime defenses, it was beginning to be realized that Britain, and not Canada, might need help in the event of war. But British military organization and thinking was not yet readjusted to digest this different approach to the question of imperial defense.

Alfred Lyttelton's famous imperial council minute in 1905 suggests that the Colonial Office itself did not yet understand the way in which opinion in the colonies was developing, especially in Canada. The silent rejection of Chamberlain's proposed imperial council in 1902 had apparently not made much impression. What Lyttelton proposed was something very little different. Chamberlain had apparently thought of an all-embracing council. Lyttelton suggested that as the Committee of Imperial Defence was now dealing with defense problems, a commission might be established on a permanent basis in London to deal with other matters between meetings of the colonial conferences, which he thought could now be more appropriately named imperial councils. He was encouraged by the fact that Seddon was reported to be in favor of an "imperial council"; and he received sympathetic replies from Australia and South Africa.[9]

Grey tried to sell the idea to Laurier by asserting that Lyttelton had approached the problem as one who regarded Canada not as a colony but as a sister nation, which would be satisfactory to all self-respecting Canadians.[10] When Laurier was slow to reply, Lyttelton appealed to him again by saying that he had

9. London *Times*, Oct. 17, 1905.
10. Grey to Laurier, Nov. 3, 1905, Douglas Library, Queens University, Laurier MSS, Microfilm, F. No. 1. Ser. B, Reel 184, pp. 203302–203305.

made the proposal "without pressing it" because he thought it more appropriate for an Empire that was, as Laurier had said, "an aggregate of free nations under one crown." He believed that the Empire could not have the unity of a single state under a single legislature and executive authority, but that it had, and ought to have, a greater unity than that of wholly independent states settling their relations by ordinary methods. The question to be solved was how free nations under one crown, and therefore in permanent alliance, could most effectively act in harmony.[11]

Lyttelton's proposition rested on the assumption that the Committee of Imperial Defence was already a representative defense commission; but this was, as has been shown, only partially correct. His proposal was in line with Deakin's request for colonial representation on the committee, but Deakin's request disproved Lyttelton's basic assumption. Sir Charles Lucas, an assistant undersecretary in the Colonial Office at the time, has said that Lyttelton's dispatch is essential reading for anyone who would trace the growth of imperial unity.[12] It also illustrates the growing strength of colonial nationalisms. Lyttelton, a nephew of Gladstone, was a lawyer and a Liberal-Unionist. As colonial secretary he accepted responsibility for the controversial scheme of importing Chinese labor into South Africa. He was greater as a cricketer than as a statesman, and he was not far-sighted enough, or sufficiently liberal in his political philosophy, to make a drastic innovation in imperial constitutional relations. Lyttelton stated the problem correctly, but he did not find a solution. Like Sir Charles Lucas and most of their contemporaries, his mistake was that he thought the only possible solution for the problem of the defense of the Empire was "imperial unity."

Laurier's opinion was that the use of a new title, "imperial council," would be deemed to indicate a significant step from the current informality of the colonial conferences and would

11. Lyttelton to Grey, Oct. 23, 1905, *ibid.*, p. 203308.
12. In a letter to Edith Lyttelton, *Alfred Lyttelton: An Account of His Life* (London: Longmans, 1917), pp. 312–313.

therefore introduce further constitutional change rather than mark the end of a stage already reached. He also thought that an "imperial commission" would conceivably interfere with the working of responsible government. He preferred to leave things as they were.

Laurier's rejection of the imperial council was due to something more fundamental than a desire to avoid commitment and expense, and it was more than a result of his racial background and dependence upon French-Canadian votes, important though these things were. Sandford Fleming, who was not an extreme Canadian nationalist, told Australian Prime Minister Alfred Deakin that, although less pretentious measures to draw the units of the Empire closer had never met with opposition, there was little support in Canada for the idea of an imperial council.[13] Some Canadians like G. R. Parkin, a close associate of Milner and the "kindergarten" imperialists, wanted a federal union and would have accepted a council as a step toward it; but the thinking of even Canadian imperial federationists was tinged with nationalism. One federalist, describing himself as "one who has with the millions suffered the stigma of colonialism for over seventy years," urged Laurier to insist on securing

from the British Crown complete federal autonomy so that the stain of Colonialism shall be for ever removed from Canada and that Canada be raised to a standard of equality co-equal and co-relative in voice as regards the making and unmaking of wars within the purview of the Empire. Then and then only will Canada be prepared to furnish her due proportion in harmony with other portions of the Empire in self- and united defence, and any contributions at the present moment would only entangle and endanger the growing nationhood of Canada.[14]

An imperial council did not satisfy this demand at all. It did not go far enough or fast enough. When the question was discussed at the Colonial Conference of 1907 (which had adopted the name "Imperial Conference"), Laurier succeeded in obtaining

13. Fleming to Deakin, April 4, 1907, Douglas Library, Queens University, Laurier MSS, Microfilm, F. No. 1, Ser. A, Reel 111, p. 123517.
14. G. O. S. Conway, Stanfield, Ont., to Laurier, March 27, 1909, *ibid.*, Ser. A 139, p. 154071.

a virtual admission that an imperial council might really be an imperial parliament, that is to say a restricted form of legislative union. Deakin of Australia, Ward of New Zealand, Jameson of Natal, and the Colonial Secretary Elgin, all agreed that they could accept no departure which would diminish the authority of existing governments.[15] The proposal of an imperial council had thus been a vague and ill-thought out proposal of imperial federation. Canadians had more experience of federation than anyone else at the conference, and they knew that however carefully spheres of interest were marked out, there would be difficult problems of overlapping jurisdiction. They knew better than anyone else, too, that a federal arrangement would be exceedingly difficult to set up. A true federation, giving foreign and defense policy to an imperial parliament, would have required the surrender of certain powers by the British Cabinet and Parliament. It would have attempted to produce a single foreign policy for self-governing states separated by thousands of miles of ocean, with very different interests in many fields, and with different racial backgrounds. Laurier had good reason for refusing to plunge into these uncharted waters.

To create a council and commission as a halfway house on the road to federation, however, had the obvious disadvantage that it might remain a step toward an impossible but ultimate closer federation. This would leave the colonies in the position where they would receive some information, give advice, make commitments to help, but have little influence on the course of events, and certainly not a veto, even when these events affected colonial interests more than Britain's. Deakin himself recorded privately that all the colonial prime ministers except Ward were determined not to give up any authority to their high commissioners; neither would they permit the commissioners to take part in any conference which hinted of being of a truly representative character. Deakin also said that the proposed commission or secretariat should be no more than a "Clearing House for the Empire." [16] Thus, none of the colonies was prepared to

15. G.B., *P.P.*, *Minutes of Proceedings, Colonial Conference, 1907*, LV, 95, 98, 102, 105 (Cd. 3523).
16. Deakin to Jebb, Sept. 10, 1907, A.N.L., Jebb Papers.

accept representative machinery for common imperial defense planning.

However, the assumption of greater control and responsibility, and the passing of the belief that Canada's first duty was to plan resistance to an American attack, eased military relations with Britain. Although some Canadians saw the switch in Britain's attitude to an American war as a new reason for not spending their money on fleets and defenses,[17] the government actually showed a greater, not a lesser, interest in defense. Canada sought the appointment of Lieutenant Colonel Percy H. N. Lake, in whom it had confidence, as its Chief of the General Staff. When the War Office demurred on the grounds that he was not due for promotion, Grey urged that the difficulties be surmounted as his appointment was required by imperial, as well as local, interests. He said that Lake possessed "exceptional tact, as well as great ability, [and] he is able to induce Canadians to accept his advice, and his wife has Canadian relations." Lake was appointed for six months, but the Army Council was willing to promote him to brigadier general when Canada agreed to keep him for four years.[18] In January, 1905, arrangements were made for Canadian officers to attend the Camberley Staff College (as in the past), and in June the Canadian Cabinet approved the inspection of the militia by a British officer. On the same day it agreed that Canadian officers who graduated from the Staff College could serve in the War Office, but it asked that their places in the Canadian Militia be taken by British staff officers.[19] Before agreeing to second officers to Canada, the War Office, anxious for military efficiency but possibly still thinking in terms of influence, sought an assurance that the Chief of the General Staff would be a British officer. Lake's appointment answered this condition. In the interests of the officers who might go to Canada,

17. L. G. Power to Laurier, Feb. 5, 1905, Halifax Club, Douglas Library, Queens University, Laurier MSS, Microfilm, F. No. 1, Ser. A, Reel 83, pp. 94512–94518.

18. W.O. to C.O., Feb. 18, 1905, P.R.O., C.O. 42/904; Minto to Borden, Dec. 18, 1904, P.A.C., M.G. 27, II B, Vol. 8, p. 147; Grey to Lyttelton, Jan. 6, 1905, *ibid.*, R.G. 7, G. 21, Vol. 152, No. 270 A, Vol. 1 (a); F. W. Borden, "Appreciation of the Services of General Lake," Nov. 5, 1910, *ibid.*, No. 270 B, Vol. 2 (a).

19. Lyttelton to Grey, April 17, 1905, *ibid.*, Vol. 259, No. 416; Grey 209, June 21, 1905, P.R.O., C.O. 42/901.

the War Office asked for details of the terms of service offered them in order to insure that they would not lose financially. It then arranged to supply three staff officers, eight artillery officers, six engineers, two infantry officers, eight Army Service Corps and departmental officers, and, if required, veterinary corps officers.[20] A scheme which Dundonald had planned for the alliance of British and Canadian regiments went ahead, and the War Office permitted Canadian Militia regiments to adapt the badges of British regiments.[21]

The resolution of another question that had vexed relations for some time helped to make co-operation easier. Since 1879, Canadian Militia Regulations had laid down that British regular officers serving with the Canadian Militia would take precedence from the date of their militia rank. To offset the effect of this rule, a promotion in local rank was usually given British officers serving in Canada, and by courtesy they were also given precedence informally within each rank. Under Hutton, "to establish clearly the position of imperial officers," the regulations concerned had been revoked and all British officers were given precedence over militia officers of the same rank. When he left, the old regulations were restored. There was an immediate outcry from the War Office on behalf of British officers who, if they received no step up, lost seniority by being seconded to serve in Canada. However, Chamberlain agreed that British regular officers serving in Canada must have Canadian Militia commissions; and the Canadian government's contention, that provision in Queen's Regulations for the precedence of British regular officers serving with Canadian Militia troops applied only on active service, was supported by the British law officers of the crown. When Borden went to England in December, 1903, he secured a promise that British regular and Canadian Militia officers should have equal authority and seniority. The root of the problem lay in the fact that in Canada the small Permanent

---

20. W.O. to C.O., Dec. 31, 1904, Nov. 2, 1905, P.A.C., R.G. 7, G. 21, No. 270 B, Vol. 1 (a).
21. Grey 25, Jan. 20, 1905, P.R.O., C.O. 42/900; Dundonald, *My Army Life*, pp. 216–221; Grey to Ommaney, Jan. 23, 1905, P.A.C., M.G. 27, II B 2, Vol. 6, No. 10.

Force was not a separate army but was considered part of the militia. In April, 1905, the Army Council stated that Halifax could not be handed over to officers of the Dominion until the relative position of British officers and the Permanent Force officers of the Canadian Militia had been clarified. This opened the way for its further proposal that there should be equal authority and precedence between British regular officers and the Canadian Permanent Force, and that the non-Permanent Force Canadian officers should have the same status as the British Militia. Borden announced that the Canadian Militia was delighted with this arrangement.[22] It had the incidental and indirect effect of making clear the distinction between the Permanent Force and the Canadian Militia.

Another step toward improved British-colonial military co-operation was initiated by Australia in March, 1905. The Australian government suggested that to give wide experience and promote a feeling of common interest there should be a system of officer interchange between the United Kingdom, Canada, India, and Australia. As the Australian proposal was that each government should pay its own officers and their expenses, it differed from earlier arrangements for the loan and seconding of personnel. During negotiations the original Australian suggestion for three-year exchanges was altered to one year. A little later it was raised to two years. On July 29, 1905, the Imperial Defence Committee approved officer exchanges because they were free from the difficulties involved in the larger schemes, still being proposed from time to time, of exchanging units. In August, Borden strongly indorsed the principle of officer exchanges but thought that for the present it should be limited to three officers from each country. By January, 1906, all the governments concerned had agreed in principle. The scheme was quickly put into operation and was soon working well, although through a misunderstanding one Canadian officer in Australia was at first paid by both governments. Eventually it was ar-

22. "Relative Ranks of Imperial and Canadian Officers," P.R.O., W.O. 32/815/058/24221/251207/1900; P.A.C., R.G. 7, G. 21, No. 25, Vol. 1, *passim;* W.O. to C.O., March 9, Oct. 8, 1901, P.R.O., C.O. 42/886.

ranged that an officer would be paid by the host country and the money recovered.

In the *Official History of Australia in the War of 1914–18,* C. E. W. Bean says the exchange system was set up "in accordance with the suggestion of the Imperial Conference." [23] This is a common error. By the time the Imperial Conference sat in 1907, the system was in operation and the conference simply indorsed it. Australia could only spare one officer to each of the other countries, but Deakin said they would like to extend the practice. At the same time he put forward an interesting colonial point of view on these exchanges: "We wish, if possible, that our men should be put to do the work; they may fail, or they may do it imperfectly and that will have to be provided against, but we believe that without the actual pressure of active responsibility upon them you will not test their capacity and they will not learn the limits of their own knowledge." [24] It has been seen that earlier another Canadian condition for exchanges of officers was that British officers should always be supplied to take the place of Canadians who could ill be spared for duty in Britain. Colonial forces thus gained experience in two different ways, by being employed in Britain, and by borrowing experienced officers.

The presence of Canadian intelligence diaries for the years 1905 to 1907 in the Australian Archives suggests that yet another kind of intercolonial military contact existed at this early date.[25] Colonel W. T. Bridges, the Australian chief of intelligence, received the diaries from the Canadian Chief of the General Staff —possibly directly. Bridges had a connection with Canada, having begun his military career at the Royal Military College in Kingston before his parents moved to Australia. He visited England and the War Office in 1906, and it may have been at this time that he made arrangements to secure the diaries. The in-

23. Charles E. W. Bean, *The Story of Anzac* (Sydney: Angus & Robertson, 1921), I, 9.

24. "System of Interchange of Imperial and Colonial Military Officers," P.A.C., R.G. 7, G. 21, No. 270, Vol. 1, Pt. 2 (a); C.A.O., M.P. 84, Ser. 1–15, B. 55, *passim;* "Proceedings of the Colonial Conference of 1907," C.A.O., Prime Minister's Department, C.P. 717, Vol. 34; Bridges to Deakin, Jan. 24, 1907, *ibid.,* C.P. 103, S. 12, B. 6.

25. "Canadian Intelligence Diaries, July 1905–November 1907," *ibid.* M.P. 153, S. 10–1, B. 56d 3.

formation they contained, which was arranged in sections headed Canada, the United States, Foreign, and General, had no particular concern for Australia. The Australian Archives also include Canadian Militia Orders for 1905–1906 and the minutes of the Militia Council of Canada for June 13, 1905.[26] These diaries, orders, and minutes may have been sent as a sample of the conduct of military affairs in Canada; but they are typical of the kind of exchange which was to become a feature of the Commonwealth military system a few years later.

Brigadier General George Aston of the General Staff in South Africa, who had set up a staff officers' committee in Durban to further the defense co-operation of the four South African colonies and to prepare the way for creation of a South African Defence Force if union was successfully achieved, states in his biography that he exchanged military information with Canada, Australia, and New Zealand. Although in another article he said that he instituted monthly letters in South Africa after the Imperial (Defence) Conference of 1909, the reference in his biography clearly implies that liaison had been established before that conference met.[27] Contact between the military forces of the self-governing dominions thus had begun to grow up spontaneously before the Imperial Conference of 1909 established the rules.

These measures to improve the efficiency of Canadian forces and to further military co-operation within the Empire were not designed on Canada's part (as one might assume from some interpretations of Canadian history) to improve defense against the United States now that Britain was prepared to do less than before to defend Canada. The 1883 Militia Act had provided for service "within or without the Dominion by reason of war, invasion, or insurrection or danger thereof." This had been interpreted to mean that troops would be raised and trained only for the defense of Canada and for possible counterattacks into the United States. The defense of Canada had not hitherto been

26. *Ibid.*, M.P. 153/10, S. 10–1, B. 56d.
27. Aston, *Memories of a Marine*, p. 269; Aston, "The Committee of Imperial Defence: Its Evolution and Prospects," *R.U.S.I. Journal*, LXXI (Aug., 1926), 460.

expected to require expeditions overseas. Borden told the Colonial Conference that Canada could now prepare "for any supreme struggle which might take place." The militia could now be called out for service "in Canada and also beyond Canada for the defence thereof at any time which appeared so advisable . . . by reason of emergency." A new clause had been introduced that Parliament must approve every time.[28] Although the inclusion of this clause providing for recourse to Parliament for authority to mobilize could be regarded as protection against involvement in an "imperial" war, it was at the same time part of a silent revolution which permitted Canada to take part in a great war on its own volition.

That revolution resulted not so much from British direction and example as from growing national sentiment that was already affecting the military development of the larger dominions. Australia had been as quick as Canada to institute a system of untrammeled control over her own armed forces by setting up a Council of Defence, a Naval Board, and a Military Board in the Defence Acts of 1903 and 1904. Hutton, when appointed to command the Australian forces in 1902, claimed that he had not pressed for the appointment of experienced imperial officers to his staff because he knew that "Australians could be reckoned on." But Australia lacked trained officers, and Hutton opposed the establishment of a Militia Council on the grounds that Australians, unaided by imperial officers, would be unable to enforce discipline in face of local political pressures and personal influence. Hutton also believed that a British inspecting officer without power to command would not meet present needs.[29] There was some truth in Hutton's arguments; but a colony naturally resents imperialist opinions of this kind and believes that the only way to deal with such a problem is to grasp the nettle firmly.

28. G.B., *P.P.*, 1907, LV, 102 (Cd. 3523); *Statutes of Canada, 1883*, Vict. 48, para. 61, and *1904*, 4 Edw. VII, c. 23, paras. 70–71.
29. Maj. Gen. Edward T. Hutton, *Military Forces of the Commonwealth of Australia. Second Annual Report with Appendices*, in Australia, Commonwealth, Parliament, *Records of Proceedings and the Printed Papers*, II (1904), 277 (25).

By 1906 the inspector general of the Military Forces of the Commonwealth, Major General H. Finn, remarked in his report that Australia had "practically decided against the engagement of Imperial Officers to fill the higher and more important positions of command and administration in the Australian Forces." [30] Assumption of responsibility for, and of control of, their own military forces by the dominions, and the consequent reduction of civil-military conflict and of imperial-colonial friction, made possible colonial military developments which had been difficult under a centralized system of imperial defense.

A General Staff for the Empire

On the military side, by far the most important development in this period both for Britain and for future Empire military quarters and the other in commands and districts. The staff on continental lines. Hitherto, the staff system in the army had varied from one command to another and had had no organic unity. A staff officer simply meant an officer with an appointment at the headquarters of the army or of a part of it. There was no planning body and no common system of planning. In 1906 Haldane set up a new General Staff with two parts, one at headquarters and the other in commands and districts. The staff throughout the army would engage in the study of military problems and would disseminate a common doctrine for solving them. It would be an instructional body as well as a war planning staff. Its function was to advise commanding officers, not to command. It therefore did not remove the ultimate responsibility of a commanding officer, but it enabled him to draw upon the combined thinking of the best brains in the army. To avoid the danger that the staff officers would become a clique, Haldane warned against their losing touch with the rest of the army. They did not belong to a separate "staff corps," and they were required to return periodically to regimental duty. As the new General

30. *Military Forces of the Commonwealth, Maj. Gen. H. Finn, Inspector General, Report* (Sept. 1, 1906), in *ibid.,* II (1906), 117 (77).

Staff was to be a part of the machinery designed for national defense planning, the Chief of the General Staff was to be represented on the Committee of Imperial Defence.[31]

When recommending the introduction of the general staff system, the War Office (Reconstitution) Committee had stated that it was aware that its proposals violated "traditions engrained in our Army system." [32] But the principle of selection by merit to which it referred had to be adopted despite possible objection on the part of the officer corps. For merit was the essence of the general staff system. Since tradition and reputation die hard, one of the problems of the General Staff would be to convince observers at home and abroad that the system of selection had changed and that merit was now a significant factor in officer promotion and appointment in the army.

As with the Committee of Imperial Defence, the principle that the General Staff was an advisory and not a command organization naturally suggested the idea that it might be extended to the self-governing colonies as well as throughout the commands of the British army. But the new British General Staff was slower than the Defence Committee to add the word "imperial" to its title. It did not do so for three years. The reason was, perhaps, a fear that an imperial military organization, formed by separating the command organization from the administrative side, might naturally be regarded with more suspicion by colonials. Hence, the General Staff proceeded at first only to urge the value of the general staff system to the whole Empire. It did so in a paper prepared for the Colonial Conference of 1907.

The chief of the General Staff, General Sir Neville G. Lyttelton, an elder brother of Alfred Lyttelton, the colonial secretary, realized that it was necessary to avoid arousing the susceptibilities of the colonials. He therefore emphasized that the General Staff knew that "it is impossible (at any rate at present) to learn in advance the exact number of troops which might be placed in the field [by dominions] side by side with the home army." But he

31. Anon., "The Development of the General Staff," *Army Review*, I (1911), 18–22, quoting Army Order 233, Oct., 1906.
32. June 28, 1905, P.R.O., Cab. 1/5/743.

indicated the advantages that would accrue to the safety of the whole Empire from good military co-operation. The more that the forces of the Empire could be brought together for training, education, and the development of "community of thought," the better would they be able to cope with the peculiar military problems of what he called a "federation of widely scattered nations." He hoped, therefore, that the new General Staff would embrace officers from all parts of the Empire and would form a "bond of union in regard to military thought throughout its length and breadth. . . ." [33] A second General Staff paper indicated the need for standardization and co-ordination, and urged uniformity in war establishments. In British war establishments the tactical unit of infantry was the battalion, but in Canada it was the regiment. The mounted unit varied considerably throughout the Empire both in name and in strength. Some colonies had not brigaded their artillery batteries, and others had no arrangements for forming ammunition columns. The paper suggested that United Kingdom War Establishments should be adopted because the British General Staff had better facilities for investigating the problems involved and because the colonial forces should be organized to meet the most important requirement—namely, a general war.[34]

In presenting these papers to the conference Haldane emphasized that there was no intention to present a rigid pattern, which was impossible in the varying circumstances of the colonies, but that there should be a common end in view and a common conception. This could only be provided by the most skilled advisers, and he said his main purpose in addressing the conference was to suggest that the new General Staff receive as far as possible an imperial character. The General Staff officer, "trained in a great common school, recruited, it may be, from the most varying parts of the Empire, but educated in military science according to common principles, . . . would be at the disposition of

33. "The Strategical Conditions of the Empire from the Military Point of View," in G.B., *P.P.*, 1907, *Papers Laid Before the Colonial Conference*, LV, 718–721 (Cd. 3524).

34. "The Possibility of Assimilating War Organization Throughout the Empire," in *ibid.*, pp. 722–727.

the local government or of the local Commander-in-Chief . . . for giving advice. . . ." Exchange of staff officers would help to solve particular local problems. An exchange of staff officers could make "the work of the General Staff in the largest sense the work of a military mind which surveyed the defence of the Empire as a whole . . . [and would] bring about that uniformity of pattern in organization and in weapons, and in other details regarding military matters, which is to some extent essential if there is to be effective co-operation in a great war." He reminded the assembled ministers that a general staff was a purely advisory organization in which command was not a function.

Sir Frederick Borden wished to know whether it was intended that the General Staff at the War Office, which would be responsible to the British government, the Army Council, and the secretary of state for war, was to be linked with the general staffs in the self-governing colonies of the Empire and would claim authority throughout the Empire. Haldane said that it was a training school to produce experts in military planning and operations and would not have "independent authority." On the understanding that officers of the general staffs in different dominions would be responsible only to the dominion government and not to the secretary of state for war, Borden was prepared to indorse the proposal; and Deakin (Australia) and Ward (New Zealand) agreed that the British General Staff (not yet called "Imperial") as outlined would not infringe their control of their own local general staffs. General Botha, who perhaps missed some of the point of the discussion, said that if the Empire was to expand still more, the development of military organization was one of the important factors for expansion. At a later session Laurier and Borden again asked for assurances that selection of general staff officers would be subject to the approval of the dominion concerned. Borden also asked whether general staff officers in dominion armies would be eligible for appointment to the Imperial General Staff, and if so whether their selection would be subject to the approval of the dominion government. Haldane replied, "We should take nobody whom you did not recommend out of your General Staff. None of us would, of course, bind ourselves one way or the other . . . , but we should take over here in the ordinary course naturally anybody you recommended as being well qualified from your General Staff, and at your request we should send you somebody whom you liked." With these assurances, a resolution recommending the establishment of a general staff for the Empire was carried unanimously.[35]

The self-styled "Imperial" Conference of 1907 thus approved the principle of co-operation and rejected commitment. This revolutionary departure was to be the basis of the military structure of the future Commonwealth. The details had not yet been worked out; there was to be wide difference of interpretation of the principles that had been adopted; and there were to be difficulties in obtaining universal acceptance of the principle within the British Army, let alone in the Royal Navy which had not yet admitted the possibility of accepting such principles. But henceforward Empire co-operation, rather than imperial organization, was to be the aim. The fact that this was to be achieved through an organization that was to call itself an "Imperial" General Staff, but that lived up to that description only in part, was to be responsible for blurring the extent to which the aims of the military centralizers had yielded to the demands of the colonial autonomists.

It is not exactly certain who was responsible for this fundamental change. Perhaps no single individual conceived the idea. Haldane personally drafted the Army Order of September, 1906, outlining the General Staff and suggesting its suitability for extension to the dominions. He is therefore usually given the credit for inaugurating the idea of military co-operation between the armies of the Empire. Without any knowledge of military organization when he came to the War Office, he had a powerful intellect, great experience in administration, and a quick grasp of the principles of the new regime introduced by the Esher Committee. General Lyttelton signed the paper which presented the concept to the dominion prime ministers. He had come fresh to the post of Chief of the General Staff at the War Office without

35. G.B., *P.P.*, 1907, LV, 94–128 (Cd. 3523).

knowing anything of the changes that were being introduced
and had no part in their initiation, but he accepted them so
thoroughly that when Kitchener in India applied them only up
to the divisional level Lyttelton was severe in his criticism of that
powerful and independent character.[36]

Charteris says that Major General Douglas Haig, director of
military training at the War Office from August, 1906, recommended to Haldane that the General Staff be extended and
developed into the Imperial General Staff for the Forces of all the
Empire, and that Haldane gave him full support.[37] However,
Haldane in his *Autobiography* appears to suggest that Haig arrived in London after the idea was conceived.[38] Haig's inability
at a later date to comprehend the desire of the dominion forces
under his command to serve during the war as "national units"
shows that he really had no understanding of the importance of
dominion national sentiment. His contribution was probably that
of suggesting the means by which a common military doctrine
could be disseminated. Haldane is more likely to have been the
inaugurator of the idea of co-operation without commitment.[39]

An Australian Navy?

Naval development had hitherto seemed to be moving in the
opposite direction—toward centralization rather than voluntary
co-operation. The Australasian Naval Agreement of 1903, drawn
up as a result of the decisions made at the Colonial Conference in
the previous year, had provided that the Admiralty would maintain an Australasian Squadron to cover the Eastern seas and that
half of the cost would be provided by the two self-governing
colonies, Australia and New Zealand. The abolition of the old
auxiliary squadron, in which those colonies had had a proprie-
tary interest, and the reintroduction of colonial naval contribu-

36. Sir Neville Gerald Lyttelton, *Eighty Years: Soldiering, Politics, Games*
(London: Hodder & Stoughton, 1927), pp. 274–275.
37. John Charteris, *Field-Marshal Earl Haig* (London: Cassell, 1929) p. 43.
38. *Richard Burton Haldane: An Autobiography* (London: Hodder & Stoughton, 1929), p. 199.
39. Dudley Sommer, *Haldane of Cloan: His Life and Times, 1856–1928*
(London: Allen and Unwin, 1960), p. 226.

tions to a single fleet which they had firmly rejected in 1887 soon proved to be unpopular in Australia. Furthermore, the strategic controversy still simmered. Even before the agreement was put into effect a distinctive Australian point of view was put forward by Senator Sir A. P. Matheson at the Royal Colonial Institute. Matheson said the Admiralty and the imperialists claimed that only a centralized naval force had any value, and that, as Britain found the burden intolerable, the colonial subsidy should be increased. He argued that Australia, on the other hand—as Sir George Clarke was said to have admitted—could not rely on Britain for her sole protection. Since it was apparently inadvisable to restrict British ships to local waters, Australia felt the need for an Australian fleet. This would reduce the burden on the British taxpayer and would also fulfil Australia's duty to the Empire to defend herself. Matheson said the choice lay between a subsidized British squadron under Admiralty control but confined to Australian waters, and an Australian squadron manned by Australians and under Australian control. Australians deprecated Admiralty control, partly because of neglect in the past and partly because they thought the Admiralty was out of date. The question of subsidizing a British "fleet of offence" could be considered later when the British government had formulated a scheme for imperial control of imperial politics.[40]

Meanwhile, however, what was left of the former state navies had continued to decay. Oral promises were said to have been made by Lord Selborne to Chamberlain that the officers of the old colonial navies would not be forgotten; but Vice Admiral Sir Arthur Fanshawe, R.N., commander in chief of the Australian Station (1902–1905), had not heard of them. His understanding was that the Admiralty would be unable to assume the cost of the pensions of any who transferred. He was willing to take on only the former naval commandants—as recruiting agents at salaries of £300 a year.[41] Three drill ships and one other ship in the squadron were to be manned by Australasian personnel re-

40. Senator Sir A. P. Matheson, "Australia and Naval Defence," *Proceedings of the Royal Colonial Institute*, XXXIV (March 10, 1903), 194–246.
41. Australia, Defence Department, *Scheme for a Permanent Force and Naval Reserve of Australia and New Zealand*, 1903, Naval Archives, Victoria Barracks.

cruited for five years at Royal Navy rates of pay plus a colonial bonus. To set up the recruiting organization, Fanshawe sought the aid of Captain Creswell, the director of the Australian Naval Forces.[42]

Creswell was not satisfied with these plans. In October, 1905, he was asked by the minister of defense what the Commonwealth of Australia itself should have in the way of a navy. His reply was three cruiser-destroyers (large oceangoing destroyers), sixteen torpedoboat destroyers, and five torpedoboats. He said these were not for action against hostile fleets or squadrons, which were the responsibility of the imperial fleet, but purely for use as a defensive second line to give security to naval bases, populous centers, principal ports, and commerce. A month later Creswell rejected the use of submarines on the grounds that they were still in the experimental stage, were slow, and were normally considered as supplementary to surface craft.[43] In his annual report, Creswell pointed out that Australia must plan on the assumption that in war the Pacific fleet was likely to be far away from Australian waters on vital service. There would therefore be danger from single cruisers against which a local defense fleet was necessary as an addition to, and not a replacement for, the Royal Navy.[44]

Creswell's proposal of an Australian fleet had wide support. A speech published by the Imperial Federation League of Victoria argued that it would be a more effective contribution to imperial defense than subsidies and more "in keeping with our [British] national history and traditions. . . . We have now reached our majority, we are claiming the full rights of nationhood, and we should not shirk the full responsibilities inevitably connected with its attainments." The continuance of subsidy would interfere with the growth of national pride.[45] So, as in

42. Fanshawe to Chapman, March 5, 1904, C.A.O., M.P. 178, Ser. 1–1, c. 2.
43. Australia, *P.P.*, 1905, [Capt. W. R. Creswell], *Defence of Australia*, II, 311 (66/1905).
44. Australia, *P.P.*, 1906, *Report of the Director of the Naval Forces on the Naval Defence of the Commonwealth of Australia for the Year 1905* (Melbourne, Jan. 1, 1906), II, 45.
45. Capt. the Hon. C. Carty Salmon, M.P., *An Australian Navy: A Necessary Part of Imperial Defence* (Melbourne: Imperial Federation League, 1905).

Canada, Australian imperial federationists wanted national forces under dominion control. They were motivated by concepts of colonial nationalism that British imperial federationists found hard to comprehend.

The commander in chief of the Australian Station concurred that Australia was not doing enough for naval defense, but his proposal was simply that the Australian contribution, about 42 per cent of the cost of the squadron, should be increased; and he made this assertion several times in public speeches. Alfred Deakin asked the Colonial Office whether the admiral's dissatisfaction with the amount of the colonial contribution was shared by the Admiralty. He said there was concern in Australia because the grant was not applied to any specific Australian purpose and because the squadron was not especially Australian. Imperial sentiment languished due to the fact that the ships were rarely seen in Australian ports. He therefore suggested that Australia should provide coaling stations instead of the subsidy and should co-operate in maintaining a service of fast mail steamers employing naval reserve men. He ventured the opinion that those parts of the Empire which made no naval contribution might change their policy to a scheme such as he proposed. The Admiralty hastily replied that it was not dissatisfied with the agreement and that the Committee of Imperial Defence had been asked to discuss the whole plan of defense for Australia.[46]

Deakin began to keep a file of the problems arising out of the agreements. It included Creswell's criticism of the Admiralty's proposal to send the first-class protected cruiser *Powerful* to replace the first-class armored cruiser *H.M.S. Euryalus*. The Admiralty's explanation of this offer was lame. It said that sometimes a supposedly inferior vessel proved itself superior as a fighting machine; but in order to live up to the exact wording of the agreement it would substitute *H.M.S. Monmouth*. When a report of this exchange of letters reached the *Age*, there was public indignation in Australia. The governor general protested against the leak in security, and Deakin had to make excuses.

46. G.B., *P.P.*, 1907, LV, 769–773 (Cd. 3524); also in Australia, *P.P.*, II, 83, 98/1906).

Deakin also complained that *Cambrian* was detached to go to South America, far outside the agreed zone, and that inefficient ships were sent to the Australian Squadron.[47] Prime Minister Seddon of New Zealand similarly protested that "to strengthen the fleet" the Admiralty sent out vessels that were actually weaker than those in service before.[48] There were many other complaints. An offer of obsolete ships to form an Australian navy was for Creswell the strongest prima facie evidence that imperial policy was opposed to any Australian naval development.[49]

Admiral Fanshawe stated in 1905 that the plan to recruit colonials into the fleet (which sometimes appeared to be the only aspect of the naval agreement, apart from the subsidies, in which the Admiralty was interested) was proving successful; [50] but a year later Deakin found that instead of the expected 700 men, only five officers and 299 men had been recruited into the Australian branch of the Royal Naval Reserve in three years.[51] Furthermore, the restriction of Australian personnel to specific ships in the squadron hampered their movement and limited their training.[52] The naval agreement was also unpopular in New Zealand, though less so than in Australia, perhaps because Seddon took every opportunity to strengthen public interest in it.[53]

The Admiralty's replies to all these charges and complaints were singularly devious. It said that the agreement was being "loosely observed," that it was against sound strategy to divide the sea into zones; but, recognizing the value of the agreement, it was prepared to carry out its obligations loyally.[54] Thus, instead of taking steps to insure that the Australians saw their ships regularly and got their money's worth, the Admiralty fell back on a dogmatic statement of those naval principles which a decade

47. C.A.O., Prime Minister's Department, C.P. 290, S. 15, B. 1, *passim*.
48. Seddon to Governor, Dec. 27, 1905, New Zealand Archives, G. 26/6, Governor, Confidential In-Letters.
49. Creswell to Deakin, 1905, C.A.O., M.P. 178, Ser. 1–1 C2, 05/11047.
50. Fanshawe to Secretary, Admiralty, May 19, 1905, New Zealand Archives, R.N.A.S. 12, p. 14.
51. July 13, 1906, C.A.O., C.P. 290, S. 15, B. 1.
52. Australia, Defence Department, "Historical Outline of the Australian Naval Forces, Dept. of Defence," Naval Archives, Victoria Barracks, 500/1/1.
53. Governor to C.O., Sept. 7, 1906, New Zealand Archives, G. 26/6, Governor, Confidential.
54. C.A.O., Prime Minister's Department, C.P., 290, S. 15.

earlier its representative had been unable to express at the Colonial Conference. To use wartime strategic principles to justify the detachment of a single ship in peacetime was an absurdity. The Admiralty made little effort to remove Australian anxiety that when war came the fleet would steam over the horizon and leave Australian cities and Australian shipping to their fate. Although complete safety could not be guaranteed (for that would be impossible), the Admiralty could have harped less on the one-fleet theory and taken a little trouble to assure the colonies that when war broke out the navy would deal with enemy raiders and with local protection as well as with the enemy's main fleet. This was what actually happened in 1914.

Early in 1906 Creswell was instructed by the minister of defense to go to England to inquire into the latest naval developments. The governor general was asked to request that he be given information about naval matters and an opportunity to view naval maneuvers. The minister also asked that he be shown confidentially the recommendations of the Committee of Imperial Defence in reply to Australia's request for a scheme of local defense.[55] On his return, Creswell reported that when he visited Sir George Clarke, the secretary of the C.I.D., he left with the impression that Clarke was not averse to his proposals. However, unlike his military colleagues, Creswell was not asked to appear before the committee. At the Admiralty, Sir John Fisher told him that the Royal Navy was capable of taking care of the whole British Empire, but that he could quite understand the Australian desire to take part in the defense of Australia. The lords of the Admiralty left on a tour of inspection the day after he called on them and offered him no help. Hence, with the aid of the agent general for Victoria, Creswell had to act on his own initiative to obtain information from Osborne, Dartmouth, and Keyham for use in connection with the establishment of a school of naval science at the University of Melbourne. He applied to the Colonial Office for permission to extend his stay in order to attend

<hr/>

55. Australia, *P.P.*, 1906, *Instruction of the Minister of Defence to Captain W. R. Creswell Relative to His Visit to England to Inquire into the Latest Naval Developments*, II, 65 (81/1906).

naval maneuvers; but their letter in reply left him no option but to act on his original instructions and return home early in July.[56] The reason for this shabby treatment of Creswell was that although British naval opinion was bitterly divided about Fisher's strategic and technical ideas, it was united in opposing Creswell's colonial navy policy.

The report of the Committee of Imperial Defence on Australian defense arrived in Australia about the same time as Creswell. It reiterated the naval thesis about concentration against the enemy's main fleet and asserted that the enemy would similarly concentrate. Therefore, the use of enemy armored cruisers in Australian waters was as unlikely as the use of battleships. Nothing more than a raid by three or four vessels and five hundred men need be feared, and local military forces should be organized to oppose them. Dealing specifically with Creswell's proposals for a local fleet, it said that destroyers had no value for the protection of ports and were not worth the cost. There was therefore no strategic justification for the creation of a local force of destroyers. If in the future a need arose, the Admiralty would provide them as part of its general responsibility for the strategic distribution of the naval forces of the Empire. It was no doubt advantageous to have ships manned by Australians, but the employment of a naval force as "a purely defensive line" was a misapplication of maritime power and opposed to every sound principle of naval strategy. The old colonial defense vessels were obsolete, but the Committee of Imperial Defence had hitherto hesitated to recommend their suppression because they were an inspiration to local naval interest. The new naval arrangement would eventually produce ships "specially manned and officered by Australians . . . in the Royal Navy." [57]

The committee was afraid that a return to local navies would produce less over-all naval strength, would lead to inefficiency,

56. *Ibid., Report of the Director of the Naval Forces [Capt. W. R. Creswell, C.M.G., on a Visit to England in 1906,* II, 67 (82/1906)]. Certain critical references to the C.I.D. and to Admiral Fisher in the typescript copy of Creswell's report in the Naval Archives at Victoria Barracks were not printed in the parliamentary paper.

57. *Ibid., Report of the Committee of Imperial Defence Upon a General Scheme of Defence for Australia,* II, 165 (62/1906).

and would weaken British central control. It was apparently unable to agree that Australian interest in a fleet of its own would produce bigger and better results than would a system of money contributions to the Royal Navy. The future of the Australian navy, and of colonial naval subsidies, had therefore to be dealt with at the forthcoming Colonial Conference in 1907. There Australia submitted a resolution: "That the provisions of the Naval Defence Act, 1902, be reconsidered." New Zealand's resolution was typically different: "That the question of an increased contribution by the Australasian Colonies to the Australian–New Zealand Squadron should be considered together with other matters respecting Colonial Defence." [58]

But the first lord, Tweedmouth, who was completely under the thumbs of his professional advisers, had nothing useful or constructive to add. The Admiralty clearly thought discussion of technical naval questions with the colonial prime ministers was pointless. Tweedmouth tried to get Deakin, who had presented the resolution, to open the discussion. When pressed to give the Admiralty's point of view first, he said that he offered not a sketch of a new organization, like Haldane, but a completed picture. The Navy had never failed. He therefore asked for confidence: "You should put your trust in us now." All the Admiralty wanted was complete control in war and peace. Their lordships would welcome colonial assistance but did not come "as beggars" to the conference. If colonial assistance were not given, it would still defend the colonies to the best of its ability. Contributions were acceptable in kind—for instance, dockyards and facilities—as well as in cash. The navy would even be willing to accept the co-operation of small colonial craft such as it would find inconvenient to send out from Britain. It is noticeable that the vessel Tweedmouth suggested as suitable for the colonies was the submarine, the one least likely to become the nucleus of a colonial fleet.

Deakin replied that Australia was opposed to monetary contributions, but he felt insufficiently expert to decide upon the best alternative. Sir Joseph Ward, however, was satisfied with the

58. G.B., *P.P.*, 1907, LV, 738 (Cd. 3524).

contributions system for New Zealand. As the agreement was a tripartite arrangement, all parties should agree to an alternative. The Admiralty therefore simply sat tight. Ward complained to the conference after private discussions, "Lord Tweedmouth has not, to me personally, or at the Conference, given any indication as to what the Admiralty favours." Deakin also sought suggestions. As the Admiralty had none to offer, the delegates returned home with the contributions system still in operation. But its days were clearly numbered.[59] Centralized imperial defense in time of peace was becoming as unworkable on the sea as on land. In that sphere in which Australia and New Zealand had once taken the first steps toward imperial defense centralization by their cash contributions to the Royal Navy's Australian Squadron, Australia was now moving toward the looser Canadian pattern.

The "Imperial" Conference of 1907 Points the Way

To Haldane the 1902 conference was a failure in military matters "because of the desire of the old War Office to centralize authority." [60] He must have been disappointed that the 1907 conference did not tidy up details which had to be dealt with more fully two years later. Yet, even though the conference had, in fact, done little more than indorse the arrangements for military cooperation that had recently come into existence—often as a result of colonial initiative—it had marked a stage in the development of the future Commonwealth military system. Although there was still room for difference of interpretation on what had been decided, Haldane had found a formula which could cover the War Office's desire to continue to exercise supervision, and perhaps suzerainty, over colonial forces, as well as the Canadian desire to retain complete control of its own forces. Haldane had also succeeded in pushing through the Committee of Imperial Defence the resolution on colonial representation, although by the time of its passage the resolution had been weakened to remove real representation. In this modified form Laurier had al-

59. *Ibid.*, pp. 128–151, 469–483.
60. Haldane, *Autobiography*, p. 199.

lowed it to go ahead without insisting that his opposition become a veto. He objected to the formality of a resolution which might have the effect of binding the dominions to all kinds of future action.

On the naval side, the British had failed to make constructive suggestions. But Laurier had been driven to resort to his weakest arguments. He had defended Canada's refusal to make cash contributions to the navy by pleading that Canada was a struggling community, an argument that in days of growth and prosperity no longer had its earlier force. Jebb said that Laurier could have made a good case against Admiralty insistence on complete control, but that he did not do so because it would have committed him to creating a fleet unit instead of doing nothing at all.[61] He said that Laurier seemed against commitment in advance, "even though the assent of the Colonial Parliament were a condition precedent of such action"; and he declared that this was due to French-Canadian nationalism and isolationism.[62] Canada, however, had as yet no apparent need for naval defense except against the United States, in which case it would have been very indirect and of doubtful effectiveness. Appropriations for a colonial navy were therefore difficult to obtain. Laurier was not aware of any urgent danger. When Australia, which was more exposed at sea, had not yet produced a naval policy other than the objectionable system of contributions, it was not for Canada to give a lead. Although the nearest danger to Canada—that from the United States—was receding, Canada had by 1907 not merely begun to reorganize on land but had accepted, though not without suspicion, British proposals for guidance as between equal partners. The Dominion had at last taken a responsibility for all of her own defense preparations and for all defense establishments on her soil. These were not munificent measures, but they were significant ones. The year 1902 had seen the rejection of military centralization; 1907 pointed to the principle of military co-operation. It was the navy, and not Laurier, that was out of step. Imperial centralization for

61. Jebb, *The Imperial Conference*, II, 171–174.
62. *Ibid.*, II, 148–149.

defense had been abandoned as completely as imperial preference. In defense matters the road toward voluntary Commonwealth co-operation had been clearly indicated.

A Common Military Education

In the two years immediately following the Colonial Conference of 1907, when good progress was made toward defense co-
operation within the Empire, especially on land, two ideas that
were complementary, but also in conflict, influenced those who
were responsible for the Empire's security. The 1907 conference
had been told by the General Staff at the War Office that "the
very essence of a military system in a great federation [*sic*] of
territories is the power of combination for a common end, and
when those communities are separated from each other by the
sea, such combination is wholly dependent on the possession of
maritime command." [63] The memorandum went on to point out
that "naval supremacy is powerless, unaided, to bring a great
war to a successful conclusion," and that the Empire, with vast
land frontiers and continental responsibilities, must have military
as well as naval forces for local defense and also for mutual support in time of emergency.[64] The first of these statements included
a false premise about the nature of the Empire. The British Empire now lacked those political bonds that would have facilitated
effective combination in a centralized military and naval command in time of peace; and there was little precedent for any
other form of close peacetime co-operation between autonomous
political entities. Furthermore, as the possibility of a war on land
grew, the second view came to possess greater force. And armies
happened to have less need for centralized command during
peace. Combination for a common end on a basis of co-operation
rather than of centralization was facilitated.

Nevertheless, the 1907 conference's agreement to co-operate

63. "The Strategical Conditions of the Empire from the Military Point of View"
(paper prepared by the General Staff), in G.B., *P.P.*, 1907 (*Papers Laid Before
the Colonial Conference, 1907*), LX, Appendix IV, 718 (Cd. 3524).
    64. *Ibid.*, pp. 718–719; *Imperial Conference: Correspondence Relating to the
Proposed Formation of an Imperial General Staff* (London: H.M.S.O., 1909),
Pt. I, pp. 8–9 (Cd. 4475).

militarily, so that the dominions' strength might be deployed in the event of a great war, matured very slowly. Lord Esher, the leading civilian authority on military affairs, tried to hurry things. The dominions had great need for expert staff officers to train staff instructors for their forces, but the innovation of a modern General Staff organization had created an increased demand for staff officers in Britain. Esher thought that the enlarging of the Staff College at Camberley could solve both problems and that the dominions might help to pay for the cost of extending buildings "with a view to the special training of dominions' officers." Believing it inappropriate for the mother country to make such a proposal, he approached Botha in the hope that the Boer general's military interest would induce him to raise the matter. When Botha rebuffed him, he turned to Laurier. But the Canadian prime minister's interest was much less than Botha's. He apparently did not even bother to reply.[65]

Esher's proposal was premature. It was too much like a step toward dominion subsidies for British-controlled imperial institutions to be accepted easily. It was also too precipitate. The dominions' use of the Staff College at Camberley would at first be small and might not be permanent. Large initial capital grants could hardly be expected of them. But by indicating the importance of a common system of staff training and education, Esher had pointed in the right direction.

Soon after the 1907 conference, the need for an adequate arrangement for producing colonial staff officers was re-emphasized. No qualified colonial officer had been nominated to Camberley in 1908.[66] The small trickle which had begun so recently had apparently dried up. A partial explanation of this situation was that suitable officers were in short supply in the dominions, and there were many competing demands for their services. For instance, Canada's assumption of responsibilities at Halifax and Esquimalt meant that there would be fewer officers available for training. Colonial officers also were inadequately

---

65. Brett, ed., *Journals and Letters of Esher*, II, 234–236.
66. W.O. to Governor General, Feb. 22, 1908, P.A.C., R.G. 7, G. 21, No. 270, Vol. 1, Pt. 4 (a).

prepared for the entrance examination. Canada had had a pre-staff college training course at the Royal Military College at Kingston in Hutton's time, but it had lapsed and had to be revived. Australia had set up such a course at the University of Sydney in 1906 with Colonel Hubert J. Foster, p.s.c., R.E., formerly quartermaster general in Canada, as director of military science. There were many colonial officers who had had experience in the South African War, and there should therefore have been little difficulty in finding a few colonial students each year for Camberley. But until the ideas and intentions of the War Office were known, the dominions naturally moved slowly and cautiously.

Furthermore, although co-operation was to be the keynote, the War Office obviously still had to take the initiative. However, the War Office regarded dominion aid as a secondary problem, the solution of which must follow effective military reform in Britain. It had therefore turned first to the reorganization of the training of the British Army.

For many years the army's "bible" had been Wolseley's *Soldier's Pocket Book,* a private commercial publication. In 1902 a volume entitled *Combined Training* had been produced as an experiment. Then in 1906 Wolseley's volume was supplemented by the official *Field Service Pocket Book.* When Douglas Haig took up his appointment as director of staff duties at the War Office in November, 1906, he was instructed to work out a central doctrine for the army. Following lines originally proposed by Colonel G. F. R. Henderson, author of *Stonewall Jackson and the American Civil War,* and which had also been given the imprimatur of the Esher Committee, Haig brought out a more complete training manual for all arms. By 1909 his *Field Service Regulations, Part I, Operations* was ready. It was quickly approved and adopted. Although he did not continue to receive as much support in high quarters when preparing *Part II, Organization and Administration,* that second volume eventually followed. Haig thus gave the army a tactical doctrine and an organization that fully utilized the lessons of the South African War, and his manuals were to serve usefully through World War I despite many unforeseen aspects of that greater conflict.[67]

Haig also worked out the details of the secondary plan for military co-operation between the mother country and the dominions. General Sir William Nicholson, who had replaced Lyttelton as Chief of the General Staff in 1908, embodied these in a draft which was circulated to the dominions on January 15, 1909.[68] Nicholson's memorandum enlarged upon the agreement of 1907. The ideal which he set before the dominions was that all their military forces should be made capable of acting together as parts of a whole. He argued that this could be achieved only if they were organized and trained by a single General Staff, which must be an entity, which recognized only one head, the C.G.S. in London, and of which there were local branches in the dominions forming parts of the whole and springing from the central body.

Nicholson was well aware that a structure of this kind could create difficulties. He suggested therefore that on all purely military questions the local sections must be "guided" by a Chief of the Imperial General Staff; but he knew that such "guidance" might seem incompatible with control by dominion governments.

The solution of this difficulty, [he wrote] would appear to be that, while the chiefs of the local sections of the General Staff [must] keep in close communication with the Chief of the Imperial General Staff, they cannot receive orders from him. He will keep them informed as to what are considered the correct general principles; and they will advise their governments as to the best method of applying these principles to local conditions, and as to the risk of departing from them. When their advice is not accepted, it will be their duty to carry out whatever their respective governments may order.[69]

This was a simple but subtle formula which it was hoped would permit the creation of a single military staff for the Empire.

To set up this Imperial General Staff and to co-ordinate the

67. Col. John K. Dunlop, *The Development of the British Army, 1899–1914* (London: Methuen, 1938), pp. 291–293.
68. Haldane, *Autobiography*, p. 200.
69. G.B., *P.P.*, 1909, LI, 635–636 (Cd. 4475).

activities of its parts, Nicholson proposed occasional general conferences and the careful selection and training of General Staff
officers. Education in a common doctrine was suggested as a
substitute for centralized command. He recognized, however,
that dominion governments would not be willing to continue to
rely only on staff officers sent out from Britain. He therefore
proposed a system of officer exchanges for training purposes. He
also believed that eventually the dominions would want to set
up their own institutions to train staff officers. He thought that if
they did, their colleges should work even more closely with Camberley than such an institution as Quetta in India was already
doing in all things except entrance examinations. Nicholson
recommended that dominion staff colleges should have entrance
qualifications similar to Camberley's and an identical curriculum.
Furthermore, the head of a dominion staff college should have
served on the central body of the Imperial General Staff at the
War Office, and a proportion of its instructors, perhaps one-third
as at Quetta, should be Camberley graduates.[70]

Nicholson elaborated his proposal in an appendix to the submission to the Imperial (Defence) Conference of 1909 which was
entitled, "The Education and Training of Officers Preparatory to their admission to Staff College." Governments should
look into the feasibility of setting up their own "national educational establishments calculated to meet their own military
requirements . . . [and] not . . . limited to their permanent
forces only." [71] In this paper he probably had in mind the example
of the cadet college in Kingston. At that level, the possibility of
diversive nationalistic indoctrination and of the development of
different military techniques was not a serious problem; but
Nicholson's proposal that there should also be dominion staff
colleges, if adopted prematurely, might have led to divergence
in training and organization unless the Imperial General Staff
controlled them. However, Nicholson expected the Imperial
General Staff would be a tightly knit entity—a single body under

70. *Ibid.*, p. 637.
71. *Ibid.*, p. 641, Appendix, paras. 3, 4.

a single command—throughout the Empire, and that it would closely control the training of all the Empire's armies.

The British Army Council wanted even greater integration. It wished to revive the proposal for peacetime exchange of military units. But Nicholson was opposed to this because he was aware of the difficulties. He said that the obstacles in the way of such exchanges were "almost insuperable" because colonial troops were mainly part-time soldiers, because the dominions were not anxious to have British troops, and because the colonial forces would want to keep their higher pay.[72] The plan was, in fact, too costly. Co-operation in peacetime must be along less ambitious lines.

Simultaneous with the issuing of his memorandum, Nicholson called a conference of General Staff officers from the dominions and India to meet at Camberley, ostensibly for training on a "staff-ride." [73] These officers were mainly senior members of the British army. Nicholson summoned them to give them a preview of the proposals that were being put to the governments which they served; and this preliminary conference shows something of his approach to the problems. Nicholson saw that a general staff permeating the Empire could maintain uniformity and prepare the way for co-operation in war. But could military matters be sufficiently separated from political problems to permit an imperial general staff to be a single entity? Nicholson apparently took the usual attitude of the soldier that certain questions were purely military and should be left entirely to a professional imperial general staff. His preliminary conference of staff officers was an experiment to show how it would operate.

If Nicholson had any qualms about the difficulties that might hamper the development of a single general staff for the Empire, he must have been pleased by the promptness of the Canadian reply. On February 10, 1909, the Canadian Cabinet approved his proposals in principle. But this was misleading. What it

72. W.G. Nicholson, C.G.S., Minute, May 10, 1909, "Interchange of Military Units Between Self-Governing Colonies and the Mother Country," P.R.O., Cab. 11/124, 1898–1909.
73. Aston, *Memories of a Marine*, p. 269.

actually approved was Nicholson's qualifying condition that control by responsible ministers would be safeguarded. And the Canadian Cabinet went on to add that Sir Frederick Borden wanted to have it definitely laid down that communications from the Chief of the Canadian section of the General Staff, other than those on routine or ephemeral questions, should be submitted to the minister for his concurrence before being dispatched. Thus, although Nicholson had emphasized that a general staff was to be an Empire-wide entity for professional matters, the Canadian government had seized upon the other side of the proposal and had replied by flatly reasserting its determination to control its own forces.

Nevertheless, as Canada could not spare more than four officers a year for staff training, the Canadian government thought that a Canadian staff college would not be worthwhile. Canada would prefer to continue to send officers to Camberley in accordance with existing arrangements and would be prepared to pay an equitable share of the extra cost of buildings and instructors. To meet the need for preliminary (or pre-staff college) military education, the functions of the Royal Military College at Kingston would be extended, making use of the services of British officers from the Imperial General Staff.[74] Thus, Canadian inability or unwillingness to assume the expense of a staff college opened the way for the general use of senior military educational institutions common to all the Empire. Through a common staff college, a common doctrine could be disseminated. Such a college was acceptable to Canada, but chiefly because absolute Canadian control of military forces was to be assured. A common military education need not mean a single command or automatic commitment to war.

Australia's Quest for a Naval Policy, 1907–1909

Meanwhile, the success of the Admiralty's attempt to preserve imperial unity on the seas by forestalling Deakin's request at the

74. Governor General of Canada to Colonial Secretary, Feb. 13, 1909, in G.B., *P.P.*, LI, Appendix No. 4 (Cd. 4475).

1907 conference for a reconsideration of the 1903 Naval Agreement was proving to be a Pyrrhic victory. The old Australian fear of Russian cruisers was now being replaced by an even greater fear of the rising power of Germany. Although he approved of Fisher's naval concentration in European waters to meet this menace, Creswell, the director of Australian Naval Forces, said that Germany's ambitions in the Middle East and the Pacific threatened Australia. He continued to urge Deakin to alter the agreement. Furthermore, it was clear that Britain's traditional two-power standard would be less effective for the defense of Australia if one of the two allied enemy powers were situated in the Pacific; and Creswell believed that Japanese dislike for the White Australia policy might one day move her to attack Australia in alliance with Germany, and perhaps with China.[75] Although the Anglo-Japanese Treaty prevented immediate danger from that source, Australians, and to a lesser extent New Zealanders, were uneasy about Japanese intentions after Tsushima.[76] Creswell therefore argued that Australia's future safety might depend on her own naval strength.

To prepare the way for that eventuality, he thought that Australia should begin at once to build a local fleet which would supplement the Royal Navy, co-operate with it, and protect an Australia that would be "naked of sea defence" if the navy were called away to fight the main body of the enemy in distant waters. The naval concentration in British waters that was already taking place was sound enough; but the fleet's strength in Australian waters had been reduced, ships had been transferred to the China Station, and battleships had been withdrawn from the Far East. The local state navies, which the government that had drawn up the Naval Agreement in 1903 had promised to revive, were still in decay. Their ships were old, their armament was outdated, and some could not even get up steam. Creswell declared that an Australian navy would add to the strength of the

75. Creswell to Deakin, March 6, 1907, in Macandie, *Genesis of the Royal Australian Navy*, pp. 176–182.
76. D. C. Sissons, "Attitudes to Japan and Defence" (unpublished M.A. thesis, University of Melbourne, 1961), pp. 27, 50; Patricia Lissington, "New Zealand and Japan: Relations Until December 1941" (New Zealand War History Section), pp. 1–3.

Empire. It should be "in many respects a branch of the Royal Navy." Officers and men should be interchangeable with the Royal Navy. But the Australian Naval Forces should be "independent of the lines of communication of the Empire's base" and "a complete entity in themselves." However, Creswell had made no reference to the crucial question of command in war except in a memorandum which he had written before the 1907 conference took place. He had then said that Australian surrender of all power of naval action or authority or responsibility on Australian coasts was a matter for decision by the Australian Parliament, a point of view which was unpalatable in the Admiralty.[77]

Deakin was loath to accept the full implications of Creswell's thesis. He was opposed to "little Australians who think nothing of a flotilla unless it is cut off from the Royal Navy, which to me appears a fatal mistake"; and he consciously tried to balance Creswell by leaning a little to the other side.[78] Accordingly, he acknowledged the force of the Admiralty's case for a single strategy and a centralized command which would give unfettered use of forts and port facilities, communications systems and ships throughout the Empire for over-all strategic purposes including the defense of colonial merchant shipping. Yet he also believed that a naval defense policy should appeal to Australians and receive their full support. He therefore proposed to the Admiralty that the subsidy, which was so disliked in Australia that it had caused the Barton government to lose favor in 1903, should be devoted to furnishing one thousand men for the fleet and to the building and manning of submersibles, or destroyers, or similar local defenses, as proposed by the Colonial Conference. At Creswell's suggestion he added that until these local defense vessels were built, two cruisers of the Royal Navy should be retained on the Australian Station and two more should be bor-

77. Creswell, "Notes on the Proposals with Reference to the Naval Agreement Contained in the Admiralty's Letter of 18th February, 1907," in Macandie, *Genesis of the Royal Australian Navy*, pp. 173–175; Memorandum of March 6, 1907, in *ibid.*, pp. 176–182; Memoranda to the Minister of Defence (Hon. T. T. Ewing), Sept. 11, 26, 1907, in *ibid.*, pp. 187–195.
78. Deakin to Jebb, June 4, 1908, A.N.L., Jebb Papers.

rowed and maintained at Australian expense for training purposes.[79]

Creswell had already rejected submarines on the grounds that they were unsuitable for Australia's operational and training needs. Although Deakin admitted he was not competent to decide such a technical question, he had included them in his proposal in the hope of helping to secure Admiralty acceptance.[80] The Admiralty preferred that the dominions should acquire submarines because they were less suitable than large surface vessels for forming the nucleus of local fleets. It therefore replied that Deakin had not mentioned retention of cruisers in Australian waters when he was in London, and it added that if the new proposal required a definite pledge to maintain particular vessels permanently on the station, the agreement could not be amended but must be reviewed as a whole. In a cabled elucidation the colonial secretary said the Admiralty had explained that their control of the Australian flotilla was considered indispensable on account of probable international difficulties as well as for strategic reasons; but such control would not necessarily mean the removal of the flotilla from Australian waters.[81]

In an important speech on defense policy in the House of Representatives several hours before this Admiralty cable was received, Deakin had demanded an Australian navy. He said that the defense of Australia depended on the sea and he admitted the force of the Admiralty's strategic arguments. But Australia's defense problem was a special case to be viewed in the light of a special set of circumstances because "the squadron in these seas may at any time be removed to the China or Indian Seas." He said that at the Colonial Conference in 1907 Campbell-Bannerman had made the extremely pregnant statement that the control of naval defense and foreign affairs must always go together. From this it could be deduced that as Australia had no

79. Admiral Fawkes to Admiralty, Oct. 1907, in Macandie, *Genesis of the Royal Australian Navy*, p. 208.

80. Deakin to Jebb, June 4, 1908, A.N.L., Jebb Papers; Deakin to Dilke, April 27, 1908, B.M., Add. MSS, 43877.

81. G.B., *P.P.*, 1908, *Correspondence Relating to the Naval Defence of Australia and New Zealand*, LXXI, 154, 156, 158 (Cd. 4325).

voice in foreign policy, she was not obliged to take any part in imperial naval defense. It also implied "with equal clearness . . . that when we do take a part in naval defence we shall be entitled to a share in the direction of foreign affairs." After outlining the reasons why both the Admiralty and a section of the Australian people had been dissatisfied with the Naval Agreement, he told of his offer at the conference to build "local floating defenses" at the full expense of Australia. The Admiralty had been willing for Australia to have a local protection fleet that could serve with the imperial squadron but had only accepted its restriction to local waters because it wanted the financial contributions. Deakin suggested that the interests of the Empire would be best served if the Admiralty were to forego the contributions and if Australia were to have its own squadron flying the white ensign with the southern cross, with arrangements for interchange of officers, promotions, and inspections, and with unity of command in the event of war at the option of the Australian government. In reply to the charge that the sea was an unfamiliar element to many Australians, he claimed that "in the finest navy the world possesses," Australians "stood well above the average" in examinations and tests. Australian ships for the protection of the Australian coasts would be engaged in the defense of the Empire just as much as if they fought at the mouth of the Thames. The government of Canada, he concluded, did not conceal the fact that it did not intend to pay a subsidy to the Royal Navy.[82]

Deakin's speech forced the Admiralty's hand. Their lordships, in the course of a long, drawn out exchange of letters, demanded that there should be no misunderstanding about single control in war, complained that out of a thousand sailors only 350 would be left in the Royal Navy after the local vessels were manned, declared that they had "difficulty in comprehending the extent of the scheme as sketched by Mr. Deakin," and continued to pretend that Australia's aim was harbor protection and not an embryo Australian seagoing fleet. Nevertheless, they offered, in the absence of contributions, to help with the creation of the

82. Australia, *Parliamentary Debates*, 1907–1908, XLII, 7509–7526.

Australian navy, provided there was no additional charge upon United Kingdom revenues.[83]

In Australia, debate about naval policy continued, and the instability of Australian governments delayed a decision. Powerful opposition to Deakin's program came from a professional source. The University of Sydney had appointed to its new position of director of military science, Colonel Hubert John Foster, a staff college graduate of the Royal Engineers. The purpose of the appointment was to provide training for citizen force officers to prepare them for staff duties.[84] Foster's lectures were often published in the Sydney *Daily Telegraph* and the Melbourne *Argus*. Sometimes they were published as pamphlets. Foster argued that the defense of the Empire as a whole was important to Australia because she depended on sea trade. The best defense was the Royal Navy and a British striking force. Wars in Europe and on the coasts of the Atlantic were too far distant to be within Australia's scope, but Australia was in a strategic position for other theaters, for instance, the Suez Canal area. Australia should therefore follow the example of India which, he said, furnished troops for imperial purposes "without dictation." He inferred that Australia's military effort should be devoted to this end rather than to a local navy.

In a reply published officially with Foster's, Creswell said that Foster's aim had been "political"—to attack government policy. He argued that the British Admiralty's scheme would lead to the distraction of its efforts in war if it had to worry about distant places like Australia. The Australian plan would have immense advantage to the Empire since it would make unnecessary the diversion of a force to aid Australia. Creswell declared that the Pacific and Australia did not seem to exist for Foster. But with Japan's current rate of naval expansion, she and Ger-

---

83. G.B., *P.P.*, 1908, LXXI, 37–38, 46 (Cd. 4325); Admiralty to C.O., April 16, 1909, P.R.O., C.O. 418/75.

84. Hubert J. Foster, R.E., was deputy assistant general in the Intelligence Branch at the War Office from 1890 to 1895. He then served at Halifax and with the Canadian Militia. From 1903 to 1906 he was military attaché in the United States. In 1907 he was appointed Challis Director of Military Science at the University of Sydney by arrangement with the War Office and the Colonial Office.

many would have an overwhelming preponderance over Britain in capital ships when the Anglo-Japanese Treaty was due to expire in 1911.[85]

In August, 1908, a fleet of American warships sent by President Theodore Roosevelt to show the flag around the world was invited by the Australian government to call in Australian ports. It was the largest display of naval power ever seen in those waters. Naval interest was stimulated in Australia; but an even more important result was that Australian attention was drawn to the contrast between the American fleet's ascendancy and the decline of British sea power in the Pacific. Six months later Creswell told Senator Pearce, minister of defense in the Labour government that had ousted the Deakin government in November, 1908, that not one penny of present Australian expenditure was available to prevent destruction of the trade and business life of the Commonwealth by a raider. Australia was being told, "you want no navy, no floating defence, because the Royal Navy is supreme in all seas and nothing can approach your shores. No invading force could venture afloat whilst the British Navy exists"; yet, on the other hand, "the same authority" called for organization of Australian defense forces into "field armies" ready to give the invader short shrift. The reconciliation of these statements, alleged Creswell, was that it was necessary for Australia to have troops that would be available for overseas service. He thought it unfortunate that this reason could not be put in more straightforward fashion. He believed that future aggression on a great scale was sufficiently probable to require military training for every Australian; but he added that as Australia's frontier was the sea, she must also have the sea force best fitted to aid in her defense against such a serious menace.[86]

The Fisher government had by this time made its decision. Three river class destroyers were to be ordered in Britain to form

85. Col. Hubert Foster, R.E., *The Defence of the Empire in Australia* (Melbourne: Rankine, Dobbie, 1908); Australia, P.P., 1908, *The Defence of Australia by Col. H. Foster, Director of Military Studies, Sydney University, Together with Remarks Thereupon by Capt. W. R. Creswell*, II, 363 (35/08).
86. Creswell, Confidential Memorandum on Naval Defence, Feb. 4, 1909, Naval Archives, Victoria Barracks; Creswell to Pearce, Feb. 22, 1909, in Macandie, *Genesis of the Royal Australian Navy*, pp. 222–229.

the nucleus of an Australian navy, and one of the vessels was to be assembled in Australia. The Admiralty, which in practice now meant the First Sea Lord, Sir John Fisher, had become so concerned about the growing German menace that it was more than glad to be freed from any necessity to keep ships in Australian waters; its opposition to an Australian navy weakened. The idea of a fleet of submarines had been given up.[87] In fact, Fisher was opposed to an Australian fleet that would consist solely of destroyers able only to "chase raiders up rivers." He favored bigger vessels that could be used offensively at sea.[88] Senator Pearce planned that Australia should possess cruisers as well as destroyers.[89] It was reported from London that the First Lord, Reginald McKenna, was pleased with the Australian proposals.[90]

In regard to the knotty question of command, Pearce's personal belief was that in war the command of the Australian squadron should pass to the Admiralty; but he was aware that this question had to be dealt with carefully because of "political sentiment."[91] Andrew Fisher, the prime minister, therefore added to the draft a proposal outlining the method by which the vessels would come under the control of the British senior naval officer. Each commander of an Australian vessel would be furnished with sealed orders to be opened upon declaration to him by the senior naval officer in the area that a state of war or emergency existed.[92] Creswell suggested an addition to the preamble of the proposed agreement to show that naval development in Australia was needed to make its people efficient at sea and to enable Australia to assist the United Kingdom with ships as well as men.[93]

The Australian program thus had a long-term objective of

87. Macandie, *Genesis of the Royal Australian Navy*, pp. 219–220; Capt. R. M. Collins, Australian Government Office, London, to Pearce, Feb. 5, 1909, A.W.M., Pearce Papers, Vol. 7.

88. J. F. G. Foxton, *The Evolution and Development of an Australian Naval Policy* ([Brisbane]: United Service Institute, Queensland, Sept. 3, 1910).

89. Pearce to Collins, May 26, 1909, A.W.M., Pearce Papers, Vol. 7.

90. Collins to Pearce, April 23, 1909, Pearce to Collins, May 12, 1909, *ibid.*

91. [Pearce] to Collins, March 15, 1909, *ibid.*

92. Draft by Pearce to Secretary, Department of External Affairs, March 23, 1909, Naval Archives, Victoria Barracks; Atlee Hunt to Secretary, Governor General, April 10, 1909, C.A.O., Prime Minister's Department, C.P. 290, S. 15, B. 1.

93. Creswell to Andrew Fisher, (n.d.), Naval Archives, Victoria Barracks.

great significance for the development of the British Common-wealth defense system. Moreover, as J. S. Ewart, the Canadian nationalist propagandist, told Laurier, all the dominions except New Zealand, whose situation was exceptional, had now come to accept the policy which Canada had hitherto followed alone—the development of their own forces independent of those of the mother country.[94] In Australia the balance had apparently swung against imperial naval centralization.

94. J. S. Ewart to Laurier, March 27, 1909, Douglas Library, Queens University, Laurier MSS, Microfilm, F. No. 1, Ser. A, Reel 139, No. 15084.

13

The Dreadnought Crisis and Its Effects

The 1909 Scare and Dominion Navies

In Britain, for the sake of economy and in order to avoid provoking further German competition, the Campbell-Bannerman government had not fully carried out the Cawdor-Fisher naval building program that had been announced in 1905–1906. But during the winter of 1908 the Admiralty became convinced that Germany, by pushing forward her announced program and by building secretly, could soon outnumber Britain in capital ships. There was only certainty of German capability to outbuild Britain, of course, and not of her intention or conspiracy to do so; [1] but there was so much evidence of German hostility that even a pacific-minded British government like that of Campbell-Bannerman could not ignore the danger. McKenna at the Admiralty therefore asked for six dreadnoughts. He got Cabinet approval for four, with four more to be built later if the need remained. To get the Commons and the public to accept an inflated naval budget along with the Liberal party's social reform measures, it was necessary to reveal the government's suspicions about German plans and intentions. A surge of fear followed, which produced a vigorous jingoistic reaction, crudely expressed in the slogan, "We want eight and we won't wait." Authority was therefore given for eight dreadnoughts, two more than the Ad-

1. A. J. Marder, *From the Dreadnought to Scapa Flow* (London: Oxford University Press, 1961), I, 177–178, is not convinced that there was a German plot to build. E. L. Woodard, *Great Britain and the German Navy* (Oxford: Clarendon Press, 1935), pp. 203–252, examined the evidence at greater length and, though not able to show positive proof, thinks the existence of the plot likely but that it was foiled by being discovered. Tucker, *Naval Service of Canada*, states that the Admiralty's evidence of German acceleration in construction has never been published (I, 92 n.), and that the British government did not know until later that it was incorrect (I, 95 n.).

miralty had originally requested and more than the government of the day wanted. Although this new program was not strictly adhered to, it was to give Britain a lead that was maintained until war came.[2]

Public opinion was disturbed in the dominions just as much as in Britain. Their reaction is well known and has been described elsewhere.[3] Their slow and deliberate progress toward the creation of autonomous fighting forces was jolted. The naval crisis served to encourage those who supported a concerted imperial defense effort; and the alarm, and its repercussions, were not restricted to those dominions which depended most for their safety on sea power, Australia and New Zealand.

Not unnaturally, the first to react was New Zealand, whose smallness, remoteness, and greater dependence on the Royal Navy had limited her national aspirations and development. New Zealand had never shown much ambition for autonomous naval power, and internal differences of opinion about imperial defense were less extreme there than in the other dominions. Indeed, after the 1902 conference, she had voluntarily increased the contribution to the Royal Navy from £40,000 to £100,000 per annum, and an Admiralty refusal to lend a cruiser for training purposes had not checked the Dominion's preference for centralized naval control.[4] New Zealand's immediate response to the crisis of 1909 was to offer Britain a battleship and to promise that a second would be forthcoming if it should be needed.

A similar offer followed from the Malay States. When the Commonwealth government did not act, private individuals in Australia began to subscribe money and the states of New South Wales and Victoria offered to join together to provide a dreadnought if the federal government failed to do so. In Canada, where the imperialists were in the minority, Sir George Foster, a leading

2. Ensor, *England 1870–1914*, pp. 363–365, 401–402, 412–413, 522–523; Woodward, *Great Britain and the German Navy*, pp. 209–218; Marder, *From Dreadnought to Scapa Flow*, I, 151–185.

3. E.g., in Tucker, *Naval Service of Canada*, pp. 114–120; and more recently in Donald C. Gordon, *The Dominion Partnership in Imperial Defense, 1870–1914* (Baltimore: Johns Hopkins University Press, 1965), pp. 215–241.

4. Crewe to Plunket, Nov. 25, 1908, New Zealand Archives, G. 2/20, Governor, Confidential In-Letters.

member of the Conservative Opposition who before the crisis arose had already put on the Order Paper a resolution calling for immediate financial support for the Royal Navy, was able to arrange for his motion to come up for discussion thirteen days after the British budget-day revelations. The atmosphere was charged with excitement. Sir Wilfrid Laurier said he was willing to adopt Foster's motion if he would amend it to propose that Canada should build a naval service to bear a proper share of the defense of her coasts and trade.

Although extreme nationalist French-Canadian Liberals led by Bourassa were suspicious, although one French-speaking Canadian conservative[5] said that his constituents would agree to no greater expenditure than was necessary to protect fisheries and coastal trade, and although others sought a plebiscite, the consensus in the House was in favor of a greater naval effort. Robert Borden, leader of the Opposition, accepted Laurier's amendments but stated that he wanted a Canadian navy and if the emergency became greater he would favor direct contributions.

The debate in the Canadian House, which brought a unanimous vote for a Canadian naval force, centered upon twin problems that always came up in discussions about dominion support for imperial defense—namely, the control of dominion forces in peacetime, and the degree of the emergency. It showed that although someone in Ottawa circulated a rumor that Ontario, British Columbia, and Manitoba were planning to combine to present a dreadnought to Britain,[6] Canadian feeling, including that of the Conservative Opposition, largely supported building naval forces to remain under Canadian control.[7] But as danger seemed nearer, there appeared to be increasing willingness to yield on this issue. Future organization for the defense of the Empire would thus be likely to be determined by the actions of Britain's enemies, or rather by the construction that the people in the dominions placed upon them.

5. M. Wilfrid Bruno Nantel, member for Terrebonne.
6. Fred Cook, of the London *Times*, to Laurier, April 1, 1909, Douglas Library, Queens University, Laurier MSS, Microfilm, F. No. 1, Ser. A, Reel 139, No. 154232.
7. Canada, House of Commons, *Debates*, 1909, I, 482, 3202; II, 3484–3523.

Meanwhile, the Fisher government in Australia had held firmly to its earlier course. On April 15, 1909, it had presented its plans for an Australian navy. Two weeks later, under considerable pressure from imperialists who contrasted its narrow particularism with New Zealand's imperialism, it proposed an imperial conference to discuss naval defense. The British government had, however, anticipated Fisher by a few hours. Circulating the Canadian resolution as evidence of a change of heart in the Dominion which had hitherto consistently refused to do anything at all for the defense of the Empire by sea, it suggested that the time had come to hold a special imperial conference of defense ministers as provided by a resolution of the Colonial Conference of 1907. The purpose of the conference would be to consider the defense of the Empire as a whole rather than those local problems that had been the concern of the Committee of Imperial Defence. Those who were to prepare the conference were instructed to "think widely" and to embody the principles which should govern naval and military co-operation with the dominions.

Australia and Canada were now both looking toward their own navies; but Britain wanted to take advantage of the New Zealand lead and of the new Canadian attitude. With all the dominions in favor of action, it took only three weeks to arrange the conference; but its opening had to be delayed from early to late July. The reason was that the New Zealand ministers could not leave until their Parliament had met to vote supply: as they were leaders of the contributions school, their presence was important to the Admiralty. Then, one week after the date was settled, as a result of the coalition of all his foes including those who opposed his naval policy, Fisher's government fell. Deakin, who once more became prime minister of Australia as leader of a new Liberal party which included Conservative Free-Traders, promptly offered Britain a battleship.[8] Australia appeared to have changed sides on the naval contributions question, and Canada

8. Governor General of Australia to Secretary of State for the Colonies, June 4, 1909, in G.B., *P.P.*, 1909, *Correspondence and Papers Relating to a Conference with Representatives of the Self-Governing Dominions on the Naval and Military Defence of the Empire*, LIX, 335–392 (Cd. 4948).

appeared to have been isolated for the conference. It seemed as if all the progress made toward dominion co-operation might now be reversed.

When the conference opened the British prime minister, Asquith, made a statement on naval proposals which left the Canadian delegates unclear as to his thinking. He promised them a memorandum which was not immediately forthcoming.[9] In fact, the Admiralty's proposals for naval aid from the dominions had not been circulated until a few hours before the conference met,[10] too late for thorough digestion or for counterproposals. These proposals affirmed that a single navy was preferable for both strategic and economic reasons, but noted that the dominions had grown in wealth, had acquired a national sentiment, and had developed differing aims. Because local defense flotillas of torpedo craft and submarines could not co-operate with the fleet in the wider duties of protecting and preventing attacks from hostile cruisers and squadrons (which in 1907 it had proclaimed unlikely), the Admiralty recommended that a dominion contemplating a navy of its own should provide "a distinct fleet unit." The cost of such a fleet unit would be £3,700,000 and its maintenance would be £600,000 per annum. The vessels already offered to Britain by the dominions should be capital ships of the new type known as "battle cruisers" and should belong to the proposed fleet unit. Hence, no extra cost would fall on the dominion. There should be one common standard of training and discipline, and facilities for refitting and replenishing dominion navies should be shared with the Royal Navy. The memorandum concluded: "It has been recognized by the Colonial Governments that in time of war the local naval forces should come under the general directions of the Admiralty." [11]

In his address to the conference, Reginald McKenna, the First Lord, explained that New Zealand preferred to adhere to the contributions principle, but Canada and Australia wanted to lay

9. Borden to Laurier, July 30, 1909, Douglas Library, Queens University, Laurier MSS, Microfilm, F. No. 1, Ser. A 143, No. 158524.
10. Aston, *Memories of a Marine*, p. 272.
11. Admiralty Memorandum (signed R. McKenna), July 20, 1909, in G.B., P.P., 1909, LIX, 360–363 (Cd. 4948).

the foundations of their own fleets. He then gave more details of revolutionary proposals which revealed that the Admiralty was prepared to abandon its long-held single-navy principle and even apparently to breach its newer strategy of concentration in home waters. McKenna proposed that the squadrons in Far Eastern waters should be remodeled to create a Pacific fleet of three units in East Indies, Australian, and China seas. Each unit would be led by a battle cruiser of the *Indomitable* class, a vessel as heavily armed as the earlier dreadnoughts, but faster and less heavily armored. Each unit would also have three *Bristol* cruisers, six improved river class destroyers, and three C class submarines. It was noted that the Australian and New Zealand offers of battleships had been amended to offers of battle cruisers for service on the Australian and China stations, respectively. Thus, the opposing concepts of small colonial coastal vessels versus contributions for large capital ships, and of colonial control versus Admiralty control, had been settled by a compromise.

Despite the fact that the naval picture had been completely changed from that of 1902 and 1907 by the dominions' offer and by the new British response, the Admiralty repeated its practice of negotiating with each dominion separately, as it had done earlier when the bargaining for money contributions had made it desirable that the dominions should not act together. This procedure suggests that the Admiralty was still not really thinking in terms of full co-operation with the dominions. However, another reason for individual discussions may have been Canada's dislike for negotiations along with other dominions whose problems were very different. Virtually admitting weakness in the Pacific, Admiralty officials told the Canadians that it was hoped that they would provide a fleet unit, including a battle cruiser, for the Pacific Coast. When asked by Brodeur, minister of fisheries, "What about the Atlantic?" McKenna said the English fleet would take care of it.

Brodeur and Borden both informed him that this was quite impossible. They were aware that the Maritime Provinces would be dissatisfied if all Canadian ships were stationed in the Pacific and that the Canadian government could not afford to alienate

Eastern voters. Political difficulties of this kind were not peculiar to Canada. As the Canadian delegation noted, the Asquith government's views on the naval question were just as much governed by domestic political considerations as were those of Canada. What the British government wanted was to be able to tell its supporters, who were hesitant about paying for defense, that more dreadnoughts would have to be built but that the dominions would build three of them and so reduce the cost to the British taxpayer. "This," Brodeur told Laurier, "would be a good electoral platform for them, but hardly with us." Brodeur believed that by telling the First Lord that many Westerners and many recent English immigrants were opposed to defense expenditures, he convinced him that Canadian opposition to the Admiralty's proposals was based on more than just French-Canadian opinion. As a result, when Sir John Fisher launched into an outline of the proposed plan for a Canadian Pacific Fleet with a battle cruiser, the First Lord intervened to say that Canada would not support such a scheme.[12] In Brodeur's view, McKenna "behaved admirably." After his private talk with Brodeur, he had become "willing to abandon the idea of an imperial navy in everything in which Canada was concerned and to advise us how best to carry out the resolution of 29 March." [13]

In its talks with the Canadians the Admiralty agreed that while on strategic grounds a Pacific fleet unit might be desirable in the future, it must be recognized that Canada's double seaboard rendered the provision of such a fleet impossible for the present. It inquired how much Canada was prepared to spend and was asked to provide estimates on the basis of £600,000 and £400,000 per annum excluding the cost of the fisheries protection service but including the cost of the two naval dockyards in Canada which it was proposed that the dominion should take over. The Admiralty advised that the larger sum would provide four *Bristol* type cruisers, one *Boadicea* cruiser, and six river class destroyers to be divided between the Atlantic and the Pacific.

12. L. P. Brodeur to Laurier, Aug. 10, 1909 (in French in the original), Douglas Library, Queens University, Laurier MSS, Microfilm, F. No. 1, Ser. A, Reel 143, p. 158796.
13. Brodeur to Laurier, Aug. 26, 1909 (in French), *ibid.*, No. 159190.

Canada then raised the question of the flag that her navy should fly, and the Admiralty representatives said that they would look into the matter and send their views later. Canada had thus succeeded in obtaining approval in principle for a separate fleet that would not form part of the imperial fleet but would be aided by the Royal Navy to achieve high standards of efficiency. Negotiations for the purchase of vessels and the borrowing of personnel proceeded immediately.

The Australians, in their negotiations with the Admiralty, agreed to provide a fleet unit composed of the type of ships proposed to them, to man these ships as far as possible with Australians, and in peacetime to have them under the exclusive control of the Australian government. "When placed by the Commonwealth Government at the disposal of the Admiralty in war time the vessels should come under the control of the naval Commander-in-Chief." Like that of Canada, the Australian fleet would cost about £600,000 per annum, but the imperial government would provide £250,000 of that amount until such time as Australia took over the whole charge. The Australian fleet unit would form part of the Eastern fleet of the Empire.

Sir Joseph Ward of New Zealand, however, continued to favor an imperial navy. He accepted the fact that Canada and Australia were doing what they thought in their best interests, but he showed that Australia's action affected New Zealand's position. Under the new arrangement, her maritime interests in her own waters would be almost entirely taken care of by the Australian fleet unit. However, New Zealand wanted to retain its connection with the Royal Navy and would therefore contribute a dreadnought "under the control of and stationed wherever the Admiralty considers advisable."

Ward also said that although the proposal for the New Zealand dreadnought to be the flagship of the China fleet was "satisfactory," he nevertheless wanted two cruisers, three destroyers, and two submarines, especially those with New Zealand personnel, to come to New Zealand from time to time. Because of his concern about the effect of Australia's action, but also to secure his own condition for bringing New Zealand manned ships to

New Zealand, when Ward attended his conference with Admiralty officials he presented a written memorandum recalling the meeting of the Committee of Imperial Defence on August 10 when the First Lord had talked about a Far Eastern fleet composed of three parts on the Pacific Station. He showed that when Australia provided an independent unit for this fleet it would supersede the present British Australian Squadron and that that would mean the end of the Australasian Naval Agreement. McKenna replied that the present Naval Agreement would not be renewed, but that in view of the circumstances mentioned in Ward's letter a part of the China fleet would be maintained in New Zealand waters. The battle cruiser, when completed, would visit New Zealand.[14]

Returning to the general session of the conference, the secretary of state for the colonies, Lord Crewe, tried to find a formula which would recognize the full autonomy of dominions over naval forces now conceded to be their own, but which would also establish the principle of organization for mutual aid. According to Brodeur, his Canadian colleagues Frederick Borden and Fielding would have accepted Crewe's proposed resolution which read:

This Conference, while recognizing that the provision made for defence in his Majesty's self-governing dominions beyond the seas is primarily designed for local purposes, and is subject to the conditions imposed by the legislature of each dominion, desires to declare its full acceptance of the principle that the whole of the military and naval forces in the British dominions should be so organized as to render each force capable of performing the most efficient service in any embroglio which might threaten the integrity of the Empire.

Laurier, consulted by wire, was afraid of commitment. He therefore declared the Crewe resolution "impolitic." He preferred to go no further than the Canadian Commons' resolution of March 29. In consequence, Crewe's resolution was withdrawn.[15] If passed it might have had the opposite effect from its author's

14. G.B., *P.P.*, 1909, LIX, 363–368 (Cd. 4948).

15. Brodeur to Laurier, Aug. 13, 16, 19, 1909, Douglas Library, Queens University, Laurier MSS, Microfilm, F. No. 1, Ser. A, Reel 143, pp. 158893, 158899, 159004, 159190.

intentions and might have impeded imperial co-operation by its undue emphasis on local defense, a function which the Admiralty in the past had rejected as unsuitable for true naval forces.

The original advocate of a local fleet, Deakin, appeared to have now been pushed by local political considerations into becoming the leader of those colonials who advocated an imperial navy. But his position was by no means as simple as this statement suggests. A biographer has said that he was both a "sound imperialist" and at the same time "the fervid and outspoken champion of Australia . . . the embodiment of that spirit of colonial nationalism which, though its very existence had hardly begun to be suspected by British statesmen, was already subtly transforming the whole character of imperial relations." Deakin wanted to preserve full dominion autonomy; nevertheless, he thought that just as the Australian states had given up some of their powers to enter upon the larger life of the Commonwealth, so the dominions ought to surrender some of their individual powers in order to take up their share of the responsibilities of Empire. He (and also his biographer) [16] seemingly saw no ambiguity in these positions. They apparently believed that full autonomy was compatible with the surrender of some aspects of power.

Thus, Deakin, while rejecting imperial federation, had no clear alternative in mind except a positive desire for closer imperial unity. His offer of a battle cruiser, and the subsequent agreement that the Australian Squadron would form part of the British Far Eastern fleet, had been a result of his continued desire to gain a voice in the conduct of foreign policy. Although he wished to preserve dominion autonomy, he would have liked to see regular conferences, an imperial council, and an imperial secretariat, through which Australia could exercise an influence on imperial defense and foreign policy. He did not accept the argument that this concession of authority to a central body for these purposes would infringe hard-won dominion autonomy, and that

16. Walter Murdoch, *Alfred Deakin* (London: Constable, 1923), pp. 98–99, 255.

there was no practicable halfway house between the free association of independent states and federation.

On the other hand the Australian Labour party, like the Afrikaaners, the French-Canadians, and indeed many other colonials, had already come to believe that dominion autonomy and central control were irreconcilable. Professor J. La Nauze, a more recent biographer of Deakin, suggests that the story of the Commonwealth of Nations in the ensuing generation seems to demonstrate that the colonials were right and Deakin was wrong.[17] The naval policy of Fisher's Labour government had, in fact, been not very different from that of Deakin's coalition. The Labour party's more unalloyed nationalism had perhaps made possible a more vigorous Australian defense policy. Nevertheless, Deakin's return to power, and his offer of a battle cruiser, had not necessarily reversed the principle of an Australian navy which Fisher had announced. Much depended on the significance that would be given to the term "Imperial Far-Eastern Fleet" and on the arrangements by which the Australian Squadron would pass under its command.

The Admiralty's concessions to Canada and Australia seemed to be a policy revolution of great significance. It yielded colonial control of colonial navies in peacetime. The Admiralty was now apparently prepared to rely on colonial goodwill to put colonial naval forces at Britain's disposal when war came; and it had accepted battle cruisers for the Pacific instead of battleships for the North Sea. The Admiralty had always held that the Pacific dominions had no need for capital ships for their protection because attack could only be on a small scale. Recently it had emphasized the need for strategic concentration of the whole fleet in the North Sea to face the growing German fleet. The 1909 proposals appeared to contradict all these policies. Furthermore, British policy had been largely governed by a desire to secure relief from some of the onerous and growing financial burden of imperial defense, and the Admiralty's proposals seemed to

17. These views are from Professor La Nauze's manuscript of his biography of William Deakin and from talks with the author.

offer none. The *Times,* commenting before the conference began on the offer of battleships, had said that if they were in addition to the Royal Navy, it would mean that the dominions were, in effect, being given the right to decide what size that Royal Navy ought to be; but if they were a substitute for Royal Navy ships, then they would truly represent a "shifting of the burden." [18] However, now that the dominions were to contribute capital ships to new fleets in distant waters where capital ships had hitherto been considered unnecessary, they appeared neither to help redress the balance in the North Sea nor to relieve the British taxpayer.

The origins and purpose of the Admiralty's new proposals are not entirely clear in the available documents, and so they are an interesting subject for speculation. Bordeur was convinced that he had personally won the First Lord over from expecting Canadian participation in an imperial fleet, and there may be some truth in this opinion. But McKenna's concession to Australia is more difficult to understand. It will be remembered, however, that the Admiralty had virtually accepted the principle of a separate Australian fleet before the change of the Commonwealth government led to the dreadnought offer. McKenna, a man of shrewd political insight, may have realized that Deakin's offer did not really represent a fundamental change in Australian opinion and that Australians still looked forward to possessing their own fleet. Sir John Fisher's proclivity for big ships helped to bring the suggestion that if the dominions were to provide fleet units in the Pacific, those units should include the capital ships which the dominions were offering spontaneously.

The explanation of the change of policy may be that Asquith and McKenna did not understand the strategic issues involved and therefore settled on political and financial lines only. What is more surprising is that Admiral Fisher was prepared to regard the new naval arrangement as a personal victory and not as a defeat. He wrote in 1911, "that great fundamental truth [*that the coasts of the enemy are the frontiers of England*] has been swallowed like an oyster by all the Dominions' Prime Ministers

18. London *Times,* May 24, 1909, p. 5.

(KEEP THIS TO YOURSELF AND BURN THIS LETTER!) . . . Don't worry about either the British Empire or the Navy (THEY ARE SYNONYMOUS TERMS!) We are the Lost Ten Tribes of Isarael! WE CAN'T GO UNDER!" [19]

Another statement by Fisher may indicate his real object in accepting this revolution in policy forced upon him by the politicians he usually detested. McKenna and Fisher thought they were engaged in a war of nerves with the German Kaiser and Admiral von Tirpitz, the secretary of state of the Imperial German Navy, in which Britain had undertaken to outbuild Germany in dreadnoughts but in which the margin of safety was not easy to determine. The Anglo-Japanese Alliance and the current belief that war with the United States was improbable meant that there was now no potential enemy naval power in the Far East. Is it not possible that McKenna and Fisher saw the Pacific fleet units as reserves that might pass without being counted in the current naval race?

I am so surprised [Fisher wrote] how utterly both the Cabinet and the Press have failed to see the "inwardness" of the new "Pacific Fleet"! I had a few momentous words in private with Sir Joseph Ward [the Prime Minister of New Zealand]. He saw it! It means *eventually* Canada, Australia, New Zealand, the Cape [that is, South Africa] and India *running a complete Navy!* We manage the job in Europe. They'll manage the job . . . as occasion requires out there![20]

Fisher's acceptance of dominion navies may thus have had a concealed motive that fitted in with his general aim of containing German expansion. He was looking "inwardly" to Europe. A man who was later to refuse to go as naval adviser to Australia because, as he admitted, he would only go as "dictator," [21] was not likely to have been moved by a real understanding of dominion nationalist aspirations or interests. Admiral Fisher may not have anticipated that one of the Australian battle cruisers would soon be assigned to home waters, but he knew that they would relieve

19. Fisher to Edward A. Goulding, June 6, 1911, in Marder, *Fear God and Dread Nought*, II, 374–375.
20. Fisher to Esher, Sept. 13, 1909, in John A. Fisher, *Memories* (London: Hodder & Stoughton, 1919), p. 193.
21. Fisher to Esher, May 27, 1910, in *ibid.*, p. 199.

the Admiralty of concern if the new German battle cruisers got loose in the Pacific. The dominion fleets therefore represented to him an extra margin of safety. Furthermore, the creation of separate dominion navies did not mean that all hope of Admiralty control was lost. Events in the ensuing years show that the Admiralty, like the War Office, hoped that the British service departments could retain a great amount of indirect control even under the new pattern of decentralization.

E. L. Woodward believed that the significance of these new proposals was that as a result of the rise of the German naval menace, "the strategic revolution [had] enforced its own logic" and had strengthened the links that bound the dominions to Britain. "The constituent parts of the British Empire were brought into closer connection in order to meet a common danger." [22] This is only a superficial part of the truth. What was more important was that the German danger had brought a reluctant change of heart in the Admiralty which was to have the incidental effect of helping to establish the future structure of the military relations of the Commonwealth. What must be emphasized is that the strategic situation had indeed enforced its own logic, but that it was the logic of Commonwealth naval cooperation and not what Woodward implies—the idea of "imperial defense." The Canadian gesture of naval support had been followed by an Admiralty concession of dominion control. Although later the Admiralty was to try to turn the clock back once more toward the traditional policy of centralization, it did not succeed. Colomb had once said that Britain's survival was impossible if committed to the guardianship of an imperial navy constituted on the principle of naval disintegration—or, in other words, "naval homerule all round the Empire under the White Ensign." [23] Now that Admiral Fisher, his most practical disciple, had sanctioned that principle, it remained to be seen how much Admiralty control could be retained and whether, if all was gone, Colomb was right.

22. Woodward, *Great Britain and the German Navy*, p. 388.
23. John C. R. Colomb, "Which Way to an Imperial Navy?," *National Review*, XLVII (1906), 684.

The 1909 Defence Conference and the Imperial General Staff

The special Imperial Conference which met in July, 1909, had been summoned chiefly to examine the problems arising from Australian and Canadian naval aspirations; but it was the War Office, and not the Admiralty, that made the better use of the sessions. Whereas the Admiralty circulated its proposals only a few hours before the sessions began, General Nicholson's preparations had been made before the conference was proposed, were more thorough, and took the dominions' views so well into account that the conference's military subcommittee had little more to do than approve his plans and settle some of the technical details.[24] Haldane had planned the presentation effectively. It was recommended to the participating governments that all the expenses of officers on loan should be paid by the employing country, but it was suggested that in the case of exchanges the travel expenses to and from the appointment should be paid by the officer's own government and his pay and employment by the country which employed him. Staff pay was to be at the rate of the country to which the officer belonged, but there should be an attempt to assimilate the pay of the officers on the General Staff in order to overcome the prickly problem of differences between British and colonial rates.[25] Procedure for arranging interchange of General Staff officers was outlined, but it was stated that equality of interchange could not be expected until the military education and higher staff training of dominion officers had been assimilated to those of the British Regular Army.[26] Finally, it was believed that for the senior ranks in particular interchange would have to give way to loan until the general staff system prevailed throughout the Empire.[27]

Coming down to the details of army organization, the War Office recommended that the unit establishments of the Regular Army should be adopted by the dominion, that the first-line

24. Aston, *Memories of a Marine*, p. 272.
25. G.B., *P.P.*, 1909, LIX, 370 (Cd. 4948).
26. *Ibid.*, p. 387.
27. *Ibid.*, p. 379.

transport (ammunition carts and water carts) of units should be on the British pattern, while second-line transport should be of local pattern; that the dominions should adopt the new field service regulations and training manuals now coming into use in Britain; and that the dominions should also adopt, as far as possible, British patterns of arms, equipment, and stores.[28] These arrangements were accepted first by the military subcommittee and then by the representatives from the dominions in general session. The structure of Commonwealth military co-operation had thus been drafted.

But the key to military co-operation was at the top, and the structure of the Imperial General Staff was yet to be settled. Canada had had a general staff since 1904, but it was small and rudimentary. In January, 1909, the Fisher government in Australia had set up a general staff with Colonel W. T. Bridges as its first chief. These general staffs were not modern planning organizations like the Prussian General Staff, although the Prussian model had been adopted in all European armies and in the United States; and both were without organic connection with the new General Staff in London. Since the Australian government was aware of these things prior to the Imperial Defence Conference, it had already sent its inspector general to the War Office to discuss staff organization for the Empire. Colonel J. C. Hoad had attended Nicholson's staff conference in January, 1909, and was much influenced by the imperial defense advocates whom he met during his five-month stay. He drew up and submitted to the War Office, subject to subsequent approval by his own government, a proposal for the creation of an Australian section of the Imperial General Staff which followed the general lines of Nicholson's plan. Appointees to the Australian section of the General Staff were to be specially qualified: they must have graduated from the Staff College and have eight years' service; General Staff appointments were to be provisional, except for the chief and two directors; after appointment to the staff, officers

28. Col. C. F. Hamilton, "Defence, 1812–1912," in Adam Shortt and A. G. Doughty, eds., *Canada and Its Provinces: A History of the Canadian People and Their Institutions* (Toronto: Glasgow, Brook, 1914), VII, 464.

were to go to London for further experience; and a specially qualified Australian officer was to be attached to the Imperial General Staff at the War Office.[29]

When Colonel Bridges came to London to attend the Imperial Conference as military adviser to Colonel J. F. G. Foxton, Hoad returned to Australia. In May, Defence Minister Pearce recommended to the prime minister that Hoad's proposals be accepted. Hoad was ambitious to be the chief of the Australian Staff, and this aim he now achieved.[30] Bridges was to stay in London as the Australian representative on the Imperial General Staff; the chief of the Australian General Staff was to be chief of the Australian section of the General Staff; but the Australians were careful to note that the latter position was to be kept separate and detached from the Military Board in order to avoid linking imperial control and local administration.[31] When the Imperial Conference in July and August approved an Imperial General Staff, the Australian section was immediately inaugurated and was, in effect, amalgamated with the Australian General Staff. So, the Australian chief enjoyed two titles. Although Hoad was not a Staff College graduate, he held the dual position until his death in 1911. The Australian solution was made possible by the fact that the top positions in the Australian forces were already filled by Australians. But it was also in part a consequence of Hoad's ambition and of his susceptibility to British influence, and it satisfied Australian imperial sentiment. Ward in New Zealand also accepted the British proposals for the reorganization of the command of the dominion forces and participation in the Imperial General Staff. The opening of a cadet college in Duntroon to train professional officers suited both Australia and New Zealand.

The Canadian story was quite different. Past willingness on Canada's part to accept British officers to train the militia had had an unfortunate result. Only one of the five appointments

29. G.B., *P.P.*, 1909, LIX, 381, Appendix A (Cd. 4948).

30. White to Bridges, Jan. 15, 1909, R.M.C., Bridges Papers; Foster to Bridges, July 30, 1909, *ibid.*

31. Pearce to Fisher, "Notes on the Australian Section of the Imperial General Staff, 14 May, 1909," A.W.M., Pearce Papers, Bundle No. 4.

designated at the 1907 conference to make up the General Staff in Canada was currently held by a Canadian officer. The deputy minister, L. F. Pineault, showed that, in consequence, Canadian officers were deprived of opportunity to learn the duties to qualify them for General Staff positions. He therefore suggested that good service in the field should be accepted as a qualification for the Canadian General Staff. The minister, Sir Frederick Borden, agreed but added that no unqualified officer would be recommended for the Imperial General Staff. The War Office now offered a command at Aldershot to Major General William Otter, the leading Canadian Permanent Force officer. He declined. He had just been appointed Chief of the General Staff of the Canadian Militia.[32]

After what seemed to be Canada's surprisingly prompt approval of the War Office's proposals for an Imperial General Staff with local sections, the Department of Militia persevered with the task of creating the local Canadian General Staff to train Canadian staff officers, but at the same time it took steps to insure that it suited Canadian aims. In April, Otter drafted a paper outlining the "Organization of the Canadian General Staff" which announced an intention to evolve a Canadian section of the Imperial General Staff out of the Canadian General Staff by a gradual process. Otter laid down no standard of qualifications for appointment to the Canadian General Staff, but he said that only Staff College graduates or, in certain instances, officers who had served creditably on the staff of a force in the field would be appointed to the Canadian section of the Imperial General Staff.

By suggesting the possibility of such exceptions, Otter threatened the standards which the War Office had set down. In September, 1909, after the Imperial Conference, the War Office, having examined Otter's proposals at length, urged Canada to drop them and to set up a local section of the Imperial General Staff at once. At the same time it issued a list of Imperial General Staff officers in Canada, pointedly omitting Otter's name al-

32. Grey to C.O., Telegram, March 18, 1908, P.R.O., C.O. 42/918.

though he was the Canadian Chief of the General Staff and although the Canadian government had proposed in March that he should be one of the four officers (to be increased to six in April) who should form the nucleus of the Imperial General Staff section. Sir Percy Lake, a British officer who was inspector general of the militia and a member of the Militia Council, protested to the War Office against the omission of Otter's name, but it was to no avail. However, when in June, 1910, Otter suggested to the Militia Council that the title "Chief of the Canadian Section of the Imperial General Staff," which was, he said, being used in communications from the War Office, should be promulgated in Canada, he soon withdrew the submission, presumably because he found it unacceptable to his political superiors. Then, in 1911, Otter was made inspector general, an appointment that the British had expected to go to a British regular. Major General Colin Mackenzie, a British officer selected by the Army Council, was appointed by Borden to be Chief of the Canadian General Staff in Otter's place. The War Office promptly told the Imperial Conference that a Canadian section of the Imperial General Staff was now being evolved from the existing Canadian General Staff and that certain officers, including Mackenzie, "may perhaps [be regarded] as constituting the Canadian Section." [33]

Neither Hoad of Australia nor Otter of Canada had the staff qualification required for the Imperial General Staff, but the War Office had accepted Hoad and had rejected Otter. Hoad and Otter had had remarkably similar fighting and administrative careers in the colonial militia; both of them had had the rather sketchy military training of colonial permanent force officers; both of them were pushing "political" generals who were careful to maintain relationships with political leaders in their own country. But Hoad had spent more time in England making professional contacts in high places,[34] and the British military leaders thought that they had won him over to their concepts of imperial

33. Capt. L. R. Cameron, "Constitution of the Army and Militia Councils and the Creation of the Imperial and Canadian General Staffs" (Canadian Army Historical Section, March, 1958); C.O. to Governor General, Aug. 13, 1910, P.A.C., R.G. 7, G. 21, No. 70 B, Vol. 2 (a), 1910–1911.
34. Perry, "Military Reforms of General Sir Edward Hutton . . . ," p. 185.

defense. Otter, on the other hand, was out of favor with the War Office because he had jeopardized the principle that all staff officers should have Staff College training. He had taken a military course in England as a young officer, but in the higher ranks after the South African War he had served mainly in Canada. When offered a senior appointment in Britain he had declined. Most serious of all he had sought to further Canadian local control rather than imperial centralization. Frederick Borden's acceptance of a British general selected by the War Office as Chief of the Canadian General Staff shows that despite the pressure upon him to reappoint a Canadian to that position, he was anxious to get the best-qualified officer to head the Canadian Militia. The fact that the War Office, after having refused to recognize a Canadian C.G.S. as a member of the Imperial General Staff, unilaterally announced the emergence of a Canadian section of the Imperial General Staff as soon as a British officer became C.G.S. in Canada, seems to suggest that it was concerned with something more than merely the qualification of staff officers and the maintenance of efficiency. Canadians had, therefore, cause to fear that the use of the title "imperial" for the British General Staff indicated an intention to set up an organization through which an undesirable influence could be exercised. Hence, the title was never adopted in Canada, even by the more imperially minded government which followed Laurier's.

The Australian General Staff, on the other hand, continued to be styled a section of the Imperial General Staff until 1963, when, without consulting or previously informing the Australians, the British themselves dropped the word "imperial" from the title of the Chief of the British General Staff. Yet the relations of the Australian General Staff with the Imperial General Staff in London during the intervening years differed in no noticeable respect from those between London and the Canadian General Staff. The word "imperial" had—or came to have—no real significance except to assuage the imperialism in Australian sentiment. Sir Frederick Borden's attitude was more realistic and more in line with the way in which the British Commonwealth was actually developing.

Dominion Representation at the War Office

The formal creation of a Dominion Section of the Imperial General Staff in Whitehall proved even more difficult than the creation of sections in the dominions. Occasional colonial visiting officers, like Bridges in 1905 and Hoad in 1909, had been given offices and facilities in the War Office to help them in their particular tasks. From 1909, to complete their staff training, officers from the dominions who had completed the Staff College course at Camberley were attached to various sections of the War Office. Thus, in 1909 Captain C. B. B. White of the Royal Australian Artillery was attached to M.O. 1 (Strategical and Colonial Section), and Captain H. Kemmis Batty of the Royal Canadian Regiment was attached to M.O. 3 (Asiatic Section) which included the United States in its scope.[35] These officers got an insight into British staff methods on the operational side, but they also obtained information about the forces in other dominions, collected official papers for their colleagues at home, made personal contacts which they could follow up in official and unofficial correspondence, kept the War Office informed about colonial developments, and even endeavored to correct what they considered erroneous reporting of their country's point of view in the British press.[36] They were, in fact, acting as liaison officers as well as trainees.

Nicholson's memorandum of December 7, 1908, proposing an Imperial General Staff, had suggested more formal dominion representation in the War Office to serve as a channel of communication and for the study of the methods of education, staff duties, and the latest ideas in organization, strategy, and tactics. As a result, Bridges had gone with Foxton to London in 1909 not only to attend the Imperial Defence Conference but also with the assignment of staying on as Australia's representative on the Imperial General Staff.

35. G.B., W.O., *List and Administrative Directory* (London: H.M.S.O., 1909), p. 41.
36. Brudenell White to Bridges, Jan. 15, 22, 29, Feb. 19, 26, March 4, 25, April 2, 1909, R.M.C., Bridges Papers.

When Bridges had arrived in London he found that no other dominion had yet appointed a representative. He also discovered that although everybody in the War Office assisted him in the heartiest and most cordial manner and opened their files to him, the details of the work of the dominion representatives, their status in the War Office, and similar matters had not yet been considered. An Australian request that a General Staff officer be sent to Australia in exchange for Bridges was rejected by the War Office on the grounds that the work he had come to do was on behalf of Australia. The Australian government thereupon agreed to allow the War Office to assign Bridges to whatever duties it thought fit. This would have reduced him to an inferior status equivalent to that of the colonial Camberley graduates already employed in Whitehall. Bridges declined to accept the change.

Instead he proceeded to prepare for the guidance of the Chief of the Imperial General Staff a paper on the functions and duties of a dominion military representative in Whitehall. Such a representative, he thought, should be a colonel or a major, should have had experience on the central administrative staff in Australia, and should be kept fully informed of developments there by receiving orders, the agenda and decisions of the Military Board, intelligence diaries, etc. He said that he himself had received all these from the Australian General Staff with the exception of the intelligence diaries. But he told Pearce, the Australian minister of defense, that when the War Office had asked him to request Australian suggestions for the amendment of training manuals, the department in Australia had not answered his letter on the subject. He protested that as this was the first time the dominions had been consulted, it would have been wise, as well as polite, to reply. He urged the continuation of the system of representation and emphasized that the officer appointed to replace him should be the Australian representative on the Colonial Defence Committee.[37] His suggestion actually involved official representation of dominion forces on the Im-

37. Bridges to Pearce, 20/6/10, Commonwealth Archives Office, Defence, 1897/2/11.

perial General Staff, something rather different from the attachment of junior officers for training.

Early in 1910 the colonial officers already attached to the War Office were "ensconced" in a separate bureau under the director of staff duties.[38] The Directorate of Staff Duties was concerned with the study and planning of the organization of the army for war and with the co-ordination of staff work. This move, however, was not officially communicated to the dominions until August 31, 1910, when a memorandum based on Bridges' paper set out arrangements for loans, attachments, and exchanges. The duties of the bureau would be to study contemporary methods of military education, training, and staff duties, as well as the latest ideas on organization, strategy, and tactics under the eyes of the Chief of the Imperial General Staff; to give the C.I.G.S. information of local defense arrangements and other local matters in their respective countries; to study the part to be played by local forces in imperial defense; and to correspond on such questions with their local chiefs. On purely technical and routine matters, the dominion representatives would correspond with the authorities in their own countries who were to decide to whom letters should be addressed; and letters from representatives to the dominions "conveying the views of the C.I.G.S. should be initialled by the Directors of Departments concerned or by the C.I.G.S."[39] However, despite the urging of the British, no other dominion followed Australia's lead by sending one of their senior officers. Furthermore, when Bridges was recalled in November to set up the military college to produce officers in Australia, the War Office was notified that it was not the intention of the Australian government to replace him at present.[40] The Australian view of dominion representation in the War Office had been rejected and the Australians had turned back to emphasize national development.

38. Paley to Bridges, from Department of Militia and Defence, Canada, Feb. 6, 1910, R.M.C., Bridges Papers.

39. "Memorandum on the Subject of Loans, Attachments, and Exchanges of Officers of the Regular Army and Officers of the Overseas Dominions, 31 Aug., 1910," P.A.C., R.G. 21, No. 270, Vol. 1, Pt. 5 (a).

40. W.O. to C.O., Nov. 25, 1910, C.A.O., M.P. 84, Bundle 38 A; C.O. to W.O., Dec. 2, 1910, *ibid.*

Loans, Exchanges, Examinations, and Communications

Faster progress toward military co-operation was made in ways that did not require the creation of new institutions. Thus, exchange of personnel developed rapidly. Between 1906 and 1912 about seventy British officers served on loan in Canada for average tours of about three years each.[41] By 1914, thirty-seven were in Canada and an equal number of Canadians were in Britain.[42] This exchange, though not large, was to have an important influence, and the flow of Canadian soldiers to Britain increased substantially as more Canadians reached standards fitting them for service with the British Army. Arrangements for exchange were first made through the governor general's office. The customary practice was for the British General Staff to advise on all attachments but for the branches concerned to make the detailed arrangements.[43] The dominions preferred exchanges to one-sided attachments because the former suggested equality of status, avoided implications of imperial control, and also provided better experience for the colonial officers concerned. Experienced British officers, especially Royal Engineers, were not always available for exchange with less experienced dominion personnel. It was therefore frequently necessary, especially in the early years, for the dominions to borrow British officers for staff appointments and to send their own officers for training rather than for employment.[44] Greater difficulty was found in setting up "indirect exchanges" for unequal periods than with the management of "direct exchanges" for equal periods. But, as the prime minister of New Zealand told his legislators, exchanges of some kind were necessary to promote an imperial spirit as well as to keep dominion forces up-to-date.[45]

41. P.A.C., R.G. 7, G. 21, Vol. 151, No. 270, Vol. 1, Pt. 5 (b), 1905–1933.
42. Lt. Col. Harry D. G. Crerar, "The Development of Closer Relations Between the Military Forces of the Empire," *R.U.S.I. Journal*, LXXI (1926), 446.
43. W.O., List of Committees, Dobell Conference, "Attachment of Colonial Officers to Units (1911)," W.O. Library.
44. Deputy Minister to Governor General's Secretary, Oct. 27, 1909, P.A.C., R.G. 7, G. 21, Vol. 151, No. 270, Vol. 1, Pt. 2 (b), 1909–1910; W.O. to C.O., Nov. 11, 1910, *ibid.*
45. New Zealand, House of Representatives, *Appendix to the Journals of the House of Representatives*, Vol. 1, A 1, p. 4, April 14, 1914.

Another important step toward effective co-operation was the adoption of British examinations by the dominions. This practice had preceded the creation of the Imperial General Staff, having been begun by Lord Dundonald in Canada in 1903. After his time, Canada adopted subsequent revisions of the British syllabus. Question papers were sent out and scripts were sent back for correction. In a few papers which were believed outside the scope of the knowledge of Canadian officers—for instance, in Organization and Administration, Military Law, and Army Medical Organization in Peace and War—the Canadian Board of Examiners at first set alternative questions which were sent to England for correction. As this practice created obvious difficulties for British markers, it was eventually arranged that certain question papers should be sent out confidentially to Canada ahead of time, to permit the substitution of satisfactory alternatives. But from December, 1910, Canada adopted the complete British papers in most of those subjects set in Canada. Australia adopted the British promotion examination in 1909, but with certain exceptions which were, however, soon removed. New Zealand, on the other hand, insisted from the first on adopting exactly the same examinations on the grounds that her military organization was the same as that in Britain. In 1910 the Examination for Tactical Fitness for Command was also offered to and accepted by the dominions.

A paper presented to the Imperial Conference in 1911 pointed out that very satisfactory progress had been made in carrying out the resolutions of the conferences of 1907 and 1909 in which it had been agreed that the education of officers was the bedrock of the formation of the imperial organization. It also reported that the greatest harmony prevailed between the Imperial General Staff at the War Office and its local sections in the Dominion in carrying out this important work.[46] It would have been more accurate, and more revealing, if the paper had noted that the use of British examinations in Canada had preceded the deci-

46. "(C) Examinations for Promotion of Officers of the Permanent Forces of the Dominions," in G.B., *P.P.*, 1911, *Imperial Conference 1911*, *Papers*, LIV, 872 (Cds. 5746–5752); White to Bridges, April 2, 1909, R.M.C., Bridges Papers.

sions of the conferences by several years and that it was carried on by a Canadian General Staff and not by a section of the Imperial General Staff in Canada.

There was a third means of fostering co-operation, namely through direct contact by mail and telegraph. The colonial secretary announced in September, 1910, that routine correspondence, including correspondence relating to military examinations, should go direct from the Imperial General Staff at the War Office to the local sections in the dominions and need not pass through the Colonial Office and the governor general's office.[47] This action anticipated by eighteen months the formation of a Dominions' Section at the War Office to act as a channel of communications.

But British officers in the dominions and dominion officers in London had, of course, always had an official or semi-official contact with their colleagues back home, and the system of liaison letters, which Aston claimed to have initiated in South Africa, had already been put on a wider basis by Haig when he went as chief of the General Staff at G.H.Q., India, in 1909. Haig had written to Hoad in Australia earlier in 1910, and possibly to other chiefs of general staffs in the dominions, to suggest the exchange of regular liaison letters. He gave Hoad information about the formation of the General Staff in India, discussed the institution of the practice of using Australian exchange officers as staff officers with formations, and he reported the progress of Australian officers at the Staff College at Quetta.[48] So, although correspondence dealing with policy continued to go through the old channels, there had grown up a large direct exchange on routine questions, an important semi-official correspondence, and the regular exchange of information between the service departments in the colonies and Britain.

Aided by these various developments, by the time the 1911 conference came to discuss progress toward the establishment

47. Crewe to Grey, Sept. 28, 1910, P.A.C., R.G. 7, G. 21, Vol. 284, No. 541, Vol. 1, 1909–1910.
48. Haig to Chief of the General Staff, Australian Section, June 9, 1910, C.A.O., M.P. 153/10, S. 10–1, B. 56d 3; Hoad to Chief of the General Staff, India, July 6, 1910, *ibid.*

of a defense system for the Empire, the dominions had already done much to put their military systems on a sounder footing. As far as possible they had adopted—for forces that were in the main part-time—the standards and practices of the British Army. Complete assimilation to it was not always possible. Thus, Canada felt that in artillery brigades and transport, because of the existing organization, "or want of it," the War Establishments for the British Territorial Army were an easier standard for the Dominion to achieve "for the defence of Canada" than were the War Establishments of the Regular Army.[49] Nevertheless, as the regular units of the British Expeditionary Force would themselves be backed up in war by British Territorial Army units, the latter's standards were not a serious Canadian shortcoming.

Harmonious solution of many problems of co-ordination was achieved because British soldiers showed great willingness to compromise in the hope of getting the basic principle of co-operation accepted. Major Brudenell White, an Australian officer writing from the War Office, said of the tact the British had used with Hoad: "They are, however, so pitiably afraid of doing anything to retard the progress of the Imperial General Staff that they will expose their souls to any risks!" [50] Insofar as the War Office was aiming at an Imperial General Staff that would be an organic entity, it was to prove only partially successful. But the effect of its conciliatory spirit was that dominion military co-operation was fostered. Furthermore, British soldiers were helped toward a better understanding of the dominions' points of view, though they were not always correct in their assessment of colonial opinion. White reported that the staff officers at the War Office thought they had converted Hoad from "anti-educational, anti-Imperial, and republican sentiments"; but he added that he had told them that the effect on Hoad would wear off as soon as he crossed the fifty-fathom line on his way home. When Hoad got back to Australia he was in fact to inspire newspaper articles criticizing War Office views and the Chief of the Imperial General Staff.[51] There were thus strict limits even to Hoad's sub-

49. Parey to Bridges, Feb. 6, 1910, R.M.C., Bridges Papers.
50. White to Bridges, Feb. 19, 1909, *ibid.*
51. *Ibid.*

servience to British influence. Bridges, a more independent individual, gave a lecture at Camberley on "the crimes the War Office has committed against Australia" and was told after it that he had "rubbed it in"; but he commented, "It is time some one did." [52] Hoad and Bridges were rivals with different views and different political contacts, but both looked at military matters with Australian rather than British eyes. The War Office found Australian soldiers somewhat less hard to get along with than Canadian politicians; but it began to learn rather painfully that dominion soldiers who seemed to be imperialists invariably became colonial nationalists when colonial interests were involved. Technical co-operation was successful only because it recognized colonial aspirations and the colonial sense of identity.

Laurier and a Canadian Navy

All those who attended the 1909 Imperial Defence Conference were agreed upon the desirability of strengthening the Empire's defenses, but their decisions left much room for different interpretations of the principles upon which they had reached an apparent consensus. Furthermore, Empire co-operation had been easier to achieve on land than on the sea. The isolation of colonial armies was virtually complete: the oceans separated them, and, apart from contacts by occasional individuals for whom special arrangements could be made, they rarely came in touch with forces of other parts of the Empire; there had been a fairly long history of loans and exchanges which had given time for the study of problems of status and command; and military personnel, coming rarely into contact with those of foreign powers, were less likely to raise international complications. More important still, in the event of war a dominion obviously had considerable freedom of choice whether or not to commit its military forces, how much aid to give, and which among many courses or fields of action to adopt. It was also likely that there would be adequate time in which to make decisions and to anticipate such problems of co-operation as were expected to arise. All these

52. Bridges to Pearce, April 20, 1910, A.W.M., Pearce Papers, Bundle 6.

conditions made it much easier to plan for the co-operation of land armies in time of peace than to arrange for naval co-operation.

Naval co-operation had to be worked out in very different circumstances. Colonial warships would frequently come into contact with vessels of other parts of the Empire and with those of foreign countries: oceans, far from separating navies, were the highways along which they moved. Communication problems and questions of status and command would not only be of more frequent occurrence but would also be more important. Furthermore, the specialized nature of sea service and the rudimentary state of colonial navies meant that there would be a greater need for professional aid if colonial navies were to be built up quickly. But there had been relatively little experience of aid to local navies on any significant scale. What was even more important was that if war should come, it must involve the fleets with little or no previous warning. And a dominion with a sea frontier or seaborne commerce would be liable to be attacked, whether it wished or not, and would have little scope for deciding the degree of its involvement. The nature of sea warfare would also mean a considerable intermingling of the ships of the different Empire navies. Since all the world's oceans were potential naval battlefields, arrangements for co-operation between allied navies must be worked out in advance and there must be mutual confidence. It was because of these peculiar and difficult circumstances that an imperial naval defense policy seemed necessary and that the Admiralty had clung so tenaciously to the simpler concept of a unified command. On the other hand, proposals for dominion naval support led more forcefully to a demand for a voice in foreign policy.

Britain had made revolutionary concessions to the dominions in 1909 through fear of Germany. Willingness to put them into practice would depend on continued belief in the imminence of danger to the security of the Empire. Only if the dominions also were convinced of the existence of a state of emergency would they be likely to respond or to yield on questions that obstructed co-operation. They had learned enough about the German problem to make them uneasy. At the conference Asquith had sought to allay fear and in so doing had helped to impede progress toward defense preparations. He had said: "I am glad it has not been necessary to suggest that there has been any deterioration in our friendly relations with the other Great Powers of the world; we are on good terms with all, and, so far as we can foresee, there is no imminent cause for quarrel." [53] This statement gave Laurier grounds for believing and asserting that Canada had gone as far as was necessary at the conference; but as Asquith had spoken in confidence, Laurier could not quote him to answer imperialist critics in Canada. Neither Laurier nor his critics had any source of information about the state of foreign affairs other than news reports. Their policies and arguments on defense were inevitably based only on subjective judgment and prejudice. Until a new crisis occurred, the rate of progress toward the implementation of the principles of military and naval cooperation laid down at the conference would thus depend on incidental and unrelated events, such as the rise and fall of governments over domestic matters.

But Laurier's naval policy was based on something more than merely a belief that there was no danger. He refused to identify Britain with the Empire. Although he admitted that when Britain was at war all her dependencies were liable to attack, he did not think that the whole Empire must necessarily go to war. "England, by her position in Europe, was in the past and may be again in the future, engaged in wars which never put her in peril and which do not affect the rest of the Empire." He would not agree to Canada's participation in wars such as the Crimea or the bombardment of Alexandria. "But," he added, "if the day should ever come, which God forbid, that England would be engaged in a life and death struggle, or even in a contest that would tax her energy, she would have to be supported by all the nations of the Empire." [54] Though it did not take care of situations caused by enemy action against an inactive Canada, nor show

53. Brodeur to Laurier, Nov. 9, 1909, Douglas Library, Queens University, Laurier MSS, Microfilm, F. No. 1, Ser. A, Reel 146, No. 161954.
54. Laurier to Rev. Charles W. Gordon (Ralph Connor), March 15, 1910, *ibid.*, Reel 143, p. 188133.

how Canada could hasten adequate preparation for a great emergency, this was a reasonable statement of Canada's position. It was not acceptable to Canadian imperialists because they suspected not only that Laurier meant to do too little to prepare Canadian armed forces but also that he would not necessarily honor his promise to give Britain aid when it was needed. They therefore preferred to have Britain decide when Canada should give aid. In other words, when they were not themselves in power, they trusted Britain more than they trusted the government of Canada.

There were some Canadians of an imperialist frame of mind who believed that the Empire was in a transition stage in which it could not rest. "The final stage will be reached when the Co-ordinate Nations, standing upon the same plane as Great Britain and forming with her the British Empire, shall be represented in a Common Council for Imperial affairs." Answering Laurier in these words, the Reverend Charles Gordon (Ralph Connor, the historical novelist) agreed that that time had not yet come. But he took it for granted that a sincere belief in the integrity of the Empire must mean that despite the apparent contradiction with Canadian autonomy, Canada ought to take part in any British war, "no matter how unjust the war may seem to Canadians." He argued that Canada controlled her own resources and their disposal, but that "at the first beat of the drum" she should "stand alert and pledged to the Empire"—"to her last dollar and her last man." There might be wars in which Canada did not participate because of their insignificance, but there could be none in which she should not participate if necessity arose unless she were prepared to sever the bonds of Empire. As there was as yet no imperial council, the ultimate decision of peace or war must rest with the imperial Parliament.[55]

Gordon was obviously harking back to the South African War; but Laurier told him that his idea of an imperial council was at least half a century ahead of the times. Thus, it appears that even Laurier, like his opponents, could also see no long-term future for the Empire that did not ultimately include some form

55. Gordon to Laurier, April 23, 1910, *ibid.*, Reel 154, p. 170271.

of organic political integration. His counter-argument to Gordon was that in the present state of the development of the Empire, a daughter nation's greatest contribution to the Empire's strength must be to develop her own resources and that she must avoid letting defense preparations impede her efforts in this regard.[56] Obviously, Laurier's case here rested on Asquith's assurance of the absence of a state of emergency. In a great crisis, by Laurier's own reasoning, Canada would be committed to war; but his policy, even in such an emergency, would be to leave the decision to the Canadian government. Gordon, on the other hand, argued somewhat illogically that a Canadian navy "should always be in case of necessity . . . automatically available for the Empire, the control always remaining with the Dominion's Parliament." [57] Imperialists like Gordon were consistent with what he called "the fact of Empire," that is to say, the legal and constitutional condition that the Empire was a political entity, but they did not understand that the dominions were young nations.

Richard Jebb was to write in 1913 that there were then no anti-imperialists left. He thought that the obvious need for defensive strength had left only imperialists of two distinct schools: on the one hand, there were those who believed in the British ascendancy and centralism—that is to say, those who looked at the question from the British point of view; on the other hand, there were those who believed in the Britannic alliance and autonomy—that is to say, those who looked at the problem from the colonial point of view.[58] Jebb ignored colonial nationalism, which was already a powerful force, and his use of the word "imperialist" for his two groups was misleading. The Anglo-Saxon word "Commonwealth" had not yet been adapted for the new version of the Empire. Nevertheless, although there were several distinct shades of opinion which could at that time be properly called "imperialistic," the principal contest had actually come to be waged between those who believed in an alliance of autonomous

56. Laurier to Gordon, April 28, 1910, *ibid.*, p. 170278.
57. Gordon to Laurier, May 5, 1910, *ibid.*, p. 170280.
58. Richard Jebb, *The Britannic Question* (London: Longmans, Green, 1913), pp. 9–17.

nations with pretensions to equality of status and without undesirable entanglements for the member nations, and those who believed in a centralized Empire with the component parts enjoying a voice, if not a veto, in the direction of affairs, but with the mother country exercising a predominant influence at least for the foreseeable future.

Laurier's policy, based on the former concept, would secure for Canada the only international influence that he sought—namely, a commanding voice in Canadian-American relations, upon which he had been determined ever since the Alaskan boundary affair. His Naval Service Act of 1910 was designed to put into practice the principle of the decentralized Empire which he had propounded to Gordon. It proposed a naval force that was completely under Canadian control but which, in emergency, the governor in council could put at the disposal of His Majesty for service with the Royal Navy. If it were so committed, the Canadian Parliament must be called into session within fifteen days.[59]

Laurier's sincerity in intention to fashion a navy for the sake of the Empire may possibly be questioned, but there was no doubt that he intended to begin to build a Canadian navy. Immediately after the Imperial Defence Conference his government, short-circuiting the governor general and Colonial Office channel of communication to save time, had made arrangements to obtain naval aid from Britain. Rear Admiral Kingsmill, director of the Canadian Naval Service, had asked for the loan of naval instructors;[60] Canada had bought the old cruisers *Niobe* and *Rainbow* for use as training ships; and Laurier announced a plan to build a navy of five cruisers and six destroyers. He was immediately attacked in his own province for making concessions to the imperialists.

On the other hand, Sir Robert Borden, leader of the Conservative Opposition, complained in the House of Commons that the proposed Canadian navy was not in accord with the principles

59. 9–10 Edw. VII, c. 43, para. 24.
60. Admiralty to C.O., Sept. 9, 1909, P.A.C., R.G. 7, G. 21, No. 270 D, Vol. 1.

of unity which the Admiralty had preached in 1909, that it improperly made provision for Canadian neutrality which he declared an impossibility, and that it provided inadequately for naval training. Borden therefore called for Canada to offer two dreadnoughts to Britain, and for Canadian participation in a defense council which would give Canada "a voice in the control of war." [61] He declared that the 1909 resolution had not been "entirely satisfactory" to him, but that he had gone along with it because it "seemed eminently desirable" that it should be passed unanimously. He claimed that the resolution had been much criticized and "not altogether . . . along party lines." The most serious criticism of these ideas came from his own party. One of his own Quebec followers, Frederick D. Monk, parted with him on the issue and took a strong stand against any naval aid to Britain for imperial purposes. Borden himself said there was a "cabal" or "cabals" against him. It has been suggested that while in England in the summer of 1909 Sir Robert learned about the seriousness of the international situation.[62] But no supporting evidence is given. How much Borden's decision to break the unanimity achieved in the House in 1909 on the naval question stemmed from the fear of increased German naval building which he cited, or how much it was due to domestic political considerations, remains uncertain.

The Creation of the Royal Australian Navy

Meanwhile, planning for an Australian fleet unit to form part of the Imperial Eastern Fleet was not having an easy passage. Although Australia had been more willing than Canada to cooperate with the Royal Navy, the Australian government had soon discovered that it was necessary to take measures that would protect the identity of its fleet, would insure Australian control,

61. Canada, House of Commons, *Debates*, 1909–1910, I, 1738–1762; Henry Borden, ed., *Robert Laird Borden: His Memoirs* (Toronto: Macmillan, 1938), I, 267–286.
62. Gilbert Tucker, "The Naval Policy of Sir Robert Borden, 1912–1914," *Canadian Historical Review*, XXVIII (1947), 2–3. Tucker seems to be unaware of the great long-term significance of Borden's action in thus breaking the unanimity of the House.

and would, on the other hand, bring certain necessary measures of integration. On the grounds that the fleet unit now planned was larger than the squadron proposed by the Colonial Conference of 1907, the Admiralty sought to reduce the offered amount of personnel interchange and was opposed to Australia's request for full interchangeability and for equal status in all things except pay. It was feared that the officers in a small navy would not have adequate experience of high command to fit them to replace officers of the Royal Navy. This reversal of position was probably also a result of dissatisfaction that the proposed transfer of the Australian Navy to British control on the outbreak of a war still depended on a Commonwealth government promise to act when the time came. Australia insisted that transfer in time of "emergency" would need "prior preparations." [63] Admiralty officials therefore queried the international status of colonial warships and said that another conference was needed to discuss the question.

As the time approached for Australia's new destroyers to sail from England, this matter became urgent. The Admiralty's legal officers declared that the Australian Naval Defence Act could not cover the vessels until they reached Australian waters. Their international status on the high seas, and also the legal basis for administering discipline on the high seas, was therefore in jeopardy. Canada had got around the same problem for *Niobe's* Atlantic crossing by legislating for temporary acceptance of Admiralty commissions and of discipline under British law.[64] Australia could have followed this lead. The Australians were reluctant to do so lest it provide undesirable precedents for the status of their ships and for the future relation of the fleet unit to the Imperial Eastern Fleet. Their law officers believed that the Commonwealth's Naval Act could provide for discipline over Australian officers and ratings outside Australian waters, although perhaps not over those on loan from the Royal Navy.[65]

A closely related issue was the question of the flag that colonial

63. Foxton to Green, Sept. 31, 1909, C.A.O., Prime Minister's Department, C.P. 78, N.D. 105, Bundle 54.
64. Collins to Pearce, Personal, July 29, 1910, A.W.M., Pearce Papers, Vol. 7.
65. Pearce to Collins, Personal, Aug. 29, 1910, *ibid.*

navies should fly. Although adopted only as recently as 1864 as the flag of the Royal Navy in place of the three different colored ensigns formerly in use, the white ensign had come to possess a traditional mystique as the symbol of British sea power. In some circles the idea of imposing an emblem upon the white ensign was regarded as a "desecration." There were, however, precedents for the use of colonial emblems on ensigns. With the passing of the Colonial Naval Defence Act of 1865 the blue ensign had been so modified; and in recent years the Admiralty had not seemed averse to a distinctive form of the white ensign for each colony. At least it had not protested when the proposals to this effect were first made. In 1909, however, it deliberately postponed discussion of the flag question at the conference. Then, in August, 1910, stating that the idea of using the white ensign *without* a distinguishing badge had apparently not occurred to the representatives of the dominions at the 1909 conference, it offered this solution as a means of fostering unity.

The Australian government promptly objected. It instructed its high commissioner in London to press for the Admiralty's recognition of the Australian flag for the new naval unit. He stalled, however, by suggesting a compromise to his own government: that the white ensign be flown at the stern and the Australian flag at the jack staff. But he was told firmly by Senator Pearce by wire: "Government desire Australian flag agreed to. Cannot accept your suggestion." A month later it was decided that pending an agreement on the flag issue, the destroyer *Paramatta* should sail from Britain flying the Australian flag. The positions taken by Australia and the Admiralty in this flag debate were thus exactly the reverse of those taken by the colony of Victoria and the Admiralty back in 1884. Then the colony's ships had flown the white ensign and the Admiralty had ordered that they be struck. The flag question was left unsettled for the present.[66]

At the same time as the Admiralty proposed the use of the

66. Admiralty Memorandum, Aug., 1910, Naval Archives, Victoria Barracks, 185 i, Pt. B; Pearce to High Commissioner, Aug. 29, 1910, *ibid.;* High Commissioner to Pearce, Sept. 7, 1910, *ibid.;* Pearce to High Commissioner, Sept. 9, 1910, *ibid.;* Pethebridge to Cook, Oct. 11, 1910, *ibid.*

white ensign, it set out its considered opinion on the whole question of the status of dominion ships of war. It asserted that the problem presented by the proposed dominion navies was unique; that this problem raised questions about the international recognition of colonial vessels as British warships and of their officers as commissioned officers; that the imperial government should be able to control their actions because they might involve the whole Empire, but that imperial control should be restricted as much as possible; and that the colonial navy's ability to attract good men, the establishment of interchange facilities, and the efficiency of the service depended on satisfactory solution of the status problem. Furthermore, serious questions might arise as a result of the doubts about the capacity of dominion parliaments to legislate effectively to discipline their naval forces outside territorial waters. The solution which the Admiralty now suggested was to establish "What may be called a united Imperial navy . . . subject to whatever limitations may be necessary in order to secure to the Dominion Government as great a power of control as is compatible with one main principle that all the naval forces of the Empire should form a single whole." The Admiralty stated, however, that it did not intend thereby to imply that dominions should cease to own their own ships or to possess the power to refuse their use in peace or war. It simply meant that they should be subject to the same Discipline Act.[67]

The Australian Attorney General's Department had investigated the steps necessary to confer international status as warships of a sovereign state on the vessels of the Australian navy. It declared that, in international law, ships flying the national flag of a sovereign state and commanded by properly commissioned officers were recognized as warships. It argued that the Commonwealth of Australia Constitution Act, and the authority which the governor general exercised under this act in the name of the King, could provide adequate authority. But it declared that the proper flag to be flown by Australian warships was a matter for agreement with the British government, because if any flag other

67. Admiralty, "Memorandum on the Status of Dominions Ships of War," Aug., 1910, C.A.O., M.P. 153, Ser. 11–1, SB 56d 3, 1928/3/4.

than the British naval flag were authorized, the Foreign Office would have to notify all foreign powers (as had in fact been done with the blue ensigns of the colonial navies of the nineteenth century) in order to obtain recognition. It went on to say that as the Australian ships were to be part of the King's navy, there seemed no reason why they should not fly the same flag as British warships.[68] Creswell now agreed that the offer of the white ensign should be accepted. "It is the superior flag of the Empire. . . . Its use by the whole naval power of the Empire is significant of unity . . . the status of Australian ships will be above challenge . . . the Blue ensign is a subordinate flag." [69]

As no Australian minister could go to London before the time of the Imperial Conference arranged for later in that year, the status question was dealt with by a preliminary naval conference between the Admiralty, Canada, and Australia, in which the high commissioner represented Australia. That meeting agreed that to avoid problems arising from the natural desire of the commander in chief of the Far Eastern fleet to command ships of all its constituent units, each fleet unit should normally not leave its own defined station except when arrangements were made by the Commonwealth government and the Admiralty for maneuvers under the Far Eastern fleet commander. Even then the fleet commander would be instructed not to interfere more than was absolutely necessary in a unit's "interior economy." The Commonwealth forces would be placed under British command for general service in time of war only by a formal order of the governor general in council.[70] It was further agreed that similar discipline was advisable for the whole of the Imperial Eastern Fleet. But some difficulty might arise from the difference between the legal position of a sovereign power like Britain and that of a dominion legislature which might not have a fully recognized authority over its own nationals outside its territorial waters. It was therefore proposed that the British Naval Disci-

68. Australia, Attorney General's Department, Minute Paper, 8/2/11, *ibid.*
69. "Creswell, on the Admiralty memorandum on the Status of Dominions Navies, 8.2.11," *ibid.*, B 6d 3.
70. Australian Department of External Affairs to Secretary, Department of Defence, Feb. 15, 1911, Naval Archives, Victoria Barracks, 185 i, Pt. B.

pline Act should be amended to include any dominion ships proclaimed warships by an order of the governor in council. King's Regulations and Admiralty Instructions should be identical for all Empire navies, but it was conceded that a dominion should have the right to make its own regulations. However, the Admiralty could withdraw Royal Navy personnel from service in dominion warships unless all those chapters of the regulations that affected fighting efficiency of a ship had been enacted in identical terms. The Admiralty concluded by earnestly requesting that dominion ships should fly the white ensign, with the dominion flag at the jack staff. But the prickly flag question was left for settlement "by higher authority," [71] that is to say, at the forthcoming Imperial Conference.

Co-operation by dominion navies was discussed when the members of the Imperial Conference of 1911 met with the Committee of Imperial Defence. The First Lord made it clear that the Admiralty's proposal was that dominion fleets should have equal status with the Royal Navy, but that all should constitute an imperial navy, the vessels of which would fly the white ensign at the stern to denote the King's commission and hoist a dominion flag at the jack staff. The Canadian minister of marine and fisheries and minister of the naval service interjected that dominion ships were required by law to fly a blue ensign, and added that the Canadian representative at the naval discussions had been instructed to ask for a white ensign with a Canadian coat of arms or maple leaf in the fly. McKenna retorted that ships with the same commissions should fly the same flag and that a governor general's commission had the same force as one issued by the King.

Laurier then intervened to take strong exception to a statement in an Admiralty paper which proposed that there should be a single imperial navy in time of peace and that a dominion might withdraw its fleet in time of war. He said that the Canadian Naval Act had enacted the reverse of this situation: in time of peace Canada was to have its own fleet which might be placed at His Majesty's disposal in the event of war. He said that the

71. Agreement about the Royal Australian Navy, Feb. 14, 1911, *ibid.*

Admiralty's view reflected the views of a school of thought in the United Kingdom which held that it was the duty of the dominions to take part in all United Kingdom wars. He agreed that this might be the legal situation but said that British institutions were not characterized by logic; and he produced historical evidence, including the Crimean War, to show that Canada might be at peace when the Empire was at war. When McKenna asked about possible attacks on Canadian grain ships, Laurier agreed that a country with which Britain was at war might attack them as British ships. This made the First Lord retort sarcastically that it was apparently the duty of Britain to protect Canadian ships, but not the duty of Canada to do so. Laurier replied firmly that it was still a matter for Canadian decision whether or not Canada would go to war. In that case, said McKenna, a foreign alliance is more favorable to the United Kingdom than the support of the dominions.

The Australian representatives, Fisher and Pearce, tried to calm the atmosphere by suggesting that dominions would have autonomous control, but that anything less than hearty co-operation was inconceivable; and Pearce proposed as a compromise that the question of withdrawal simply be left out. He said that Australia would have liked a seven-pointed star on the ensign but did not feel strongly on the point. Laurier was not mollified. The Admiralty, he said, would prefer a single imperial navy. Asquith then brought the discussion to a close by asking, "Is it not true that Canada would not contribute except to a separate navy?" To this Laurier replied, "That is as far as the Canadian government and the Canadian Parliament would go." [72]

The next day the conference met once more with the Committee of Imperial Defence, and Asquith at once put this discussion on solid ground by conceding that although a single navy was preferable strategically, "political conditions" had to be taken into consideration. He said the United Kingdom would accept dominion naval support upon whatever terms it was offered. Laurier then repeated that although Canada might be

72. C.I.D., Minutes, 112th Meeting, May 29, 1911, P.R.O., Cab. 2/2/2.

technically in a state of war, there was no obligation upon her to participate, except on a decision of the Canadian Parliament. Having stated this as incontrovertible truth (which it undoubtedly was), he declared that Canada was unlikely to fail the mother country. Fisher added that Australia would co-operate cheerfully, but in her own way.[73] Fisher's rider shows that although it had been clear throughout the discussion that Australia was more inclined to co-operate on the seas, there was not, in fact, a great deal of difference between Canada and Australia in their determination to make their own decisions about the extent of participation in war. Laurier had annoyed the British by harping on Canadian autonomy when the degree of danger seemed to them to call only for unity. On the other hand, British unwillingness to rely on Canada's making the right decision when war came, their fear that Canada would be inadequately prepared, and their desire to extract from her advance offers and a blank check did nothing to encourage Canadian naval support.

The agreement reached at the naval conference in February, 1911, was confirmed by the Imperial Conference in June, 1911. It was put into effect in Australia in 1911 and 1912 by amendments to the Naval Defence Act of 1910. The Imperial Conference secured acceptance of the white ensign as the common flag, and in July, 1911, the titles "Royal Australian Navy" and "His Majesty's Australian Ship" were approved by the King. In August the "Royal Canadian Navy" was authorized as the designation of the Canadian fleet.[74] But only in Australia was there progress toward a dominion fleet. New Zealand was content to make contributions in cash and kind to the Royal Navy, and the "Royal Canadian Navy" failed to develop. Debate about whether the proposed new Canadian naval vessels would be built in Canada or England had not been settled when Laurier's government collapsed in September over the question of reciprocity with the United States—an event which Brigadier General Henry Wilson, director of military operations at the War Office, hailed as "the

73. C.I.D., Minutes, 113th Meeting, May 30, 1911, *ibid.*
74. Tucker, *Naval Service of Canada*, I, 156 n. A full account of the naval controversy in Canada is to be found in this book.

most hopeful sign from an imperial point of view that I have seen for a long time." [75]

Laurier's fall was to lead eventually to an impasse in naval development in Canada; but the concept of an Australian navy had already developed far beyond Creswell's early dreams, and it established the pattern for future naval development in the dominions. In 1910 Australia had invited Admiral Sir Reginald Henderson, who had just retired from the command of the coast guard and naval reserves, to make recommendations for the development of the Australian navy. Published in March, 1911, his report contradicted the cherished views of the orthodox in the Admiralty. Henderson said that Australia's naval forces should be large enough to prevent an enemy from landing an invasion force while the British navy was busy asserting its superiority in distant waters. Australia should proceed with the building of the proposed fleet unit, but the ultimate objective should be much bigger—a complete fleet of eight armored cruisers, ten protected cruisers, eighteen destroyers, and twelve submarines. Henderson thus looked forward to a time when Australia would become a minor naval power in its own right. His recommendations about the Naval Board, naval bases, the creation of a naval college, and naval representation on the staff of the high commissioner in London were quickly implemented. [76] Henderson's proposals for a great fleet in the future appealed powerfully to growing Australian national sentiment. The arrival of the fleet unit at Sydney on October 4, 1913, created "a navy within the navy—a logical outcome of a nation within a nation," which, as Senator Pearce pointed out, was the recognized position of each self-governing dominion within the Empire. [77] The Royal Australian Navy consisted of a battle cruiser, *Australia*, three light cruisers, *Melbourne, Encounter* (on loan), and *Sydney*, and three torpedo boat destroyers.

The agreements of 1911 thus marked the completion, on the

75. Maj. Gen. Sir C. F. Callwell, *Wilson* (London: Cassell, 1927), I, 95–96.
76. Adm. Sir Reginald Henderson, *Recommendations* (March 1, 1911), in Australia, Commonwealth, Parliament, *Records of Proceedings and Printed Papers*, II (1911), 87 (7); Henderson to Pearce, Sept. 23, Oct. 12, 1910, Naval Archives, Victoria Barracks, 2102/3/9.
77. Quoted in Macandie, *Genesis of the Royal Australian Navy*, p. 272.

naval side, of provision for dominion autonomy and co-operation in time of peace with voluntary commitment when war broke out. Naval co-operation was assimilated to the arrangements for co-operation on land and was similarly based on the principle of uniformity and a common system of training. But where the naval arrangements differed from those on land was in the effect of the proposed acceptance by Australia and Canada of responsibility for the defense of the waters of the newly defined Australian and Canadian stations. Despite the measures taken to insure that commitment to war was voluntary, acceptance of these naval responsibilities inevitably implied a greater obligation to participate. This aspect of the arrangements was, in fact, little different from the arrangements made by Britain with her allies for allocation of spheres of naval interest, except that the dominion areas were less important and the dominion navies still small or nonexistent. The Imperial Conference of 1911 marked a high-water mark in co-operation for the defense of the Empire in time of peace. The principle on which it was established both on land and sea—the principle of voluntary co-operation in time of peace —had long been Canada's view of the military relations of a dominion with the mother country. Despite the differences between the condition of land and sea forces, the principles that were applied were the same in each case, although international responsibilities caused by greater possibility of contact with foreign powers and their nationals, which fell more heavily on naval forces, called for and received more precise definition in the case of naval co-operation. The end result was a very close conformity between British and dominion navies and the possibility of a single direction and command in time of war.[78]

78. Tucker, *Naval Service of Canada*, II, 154; "The Status of Dominion's Ships of War," C.I.D., No. 83–C, P.R.O., Col. 3/2/2; "Co-operation Between the Naval Forces of the United Kingdom and the Dominion," C.I.D., No. 82–C, *ibid.*; C.I.D., Minutes, 113th Meeting, May 30, 1911, *ibid.*, Cab. 2/2/2.

14

An Empire United but Diverse, 1911–1914

The Dominions and Foreign Policy at the Imperial Conference of 1911

If colonies were to help to resist increasing external dangers by contributing substantially to the general defense of the Empire, their electorates would want a voice in the disposition of their money and in the formation of policies that might lead to war. From 1907 to 1914, when imperial military and naval co-operation was being arranged, the question of sharing the formulation and direction of defense and foreign policy was never out of mind. It has been shown that Deakin's naval policy was designed to secure a voice in foreign policy. Pearce believed that separate navies must be under complete dominion control, except when committed to war, "until some more satisfactory means of determining the foreign policy of the Empire is found." [1] Naval defense, the burning question of the day, was even more closely bound up with the problem of a common foreign policy than was military co-operation. Those who advocated aid to Britain on the seas always ended up by demanding a share in foreign policy-making. The more they were anxious to help, the more forceful became their demands.

Political federation to share control of foreign policy was still considered by most people—even by moderate colonial nationalists—to be an inevitable ultimate goal if the Empire were to survive. But no practicing politician believed federation likely in the foreseeable future, and the British electorate's rejection of imperial preference seemed to have set up a new and insur-

1. Quoted by Macandie, *Genesis of the Royal Australian Navy,* p. 272.

mountable obstacle. Milner had given up public office in 1905 to prepare the ground for imperial federation. But by 1913 the Round Table, which he organized, purported to have disavowed that goal.[2] Imperial federation was realized, even by enthusiastic imperialists, to be too complicated and difficult a step for the immediate future. Hence, what was usually suggested in return for military and naval aid was "a voice in foreign policy," a vague phrase that was usually left undefined.

Because political federation was out of the question, there was a constant search for some means of granting the dominions a say in foreign policy without integrating governments at the legislative or executive level. But foreign policy involved too many political considerations; what had developed was an attempt to integrate defense organization. Defense policy could be considered a matter for professional soldiers rather than politicians. Although dominion participation in defense policy would have been a significant step toward political federation (which was the reason that many federationists wanted it), it could be represented as a lesser step at the technical level without political implications.

It was either believed or pretended that there could be participation by the dominions in defense planning without political involvement—that imperial administrative and consultative defense institutions could have a kind of political half-life. Defense, it was believed, could be lifted above party politics and petty nationalisms. Thus, Esher thought that the Committee of Imperial Defence could include "men of experience in affairs and of independent position": men like Cromer, Minto, Kitchener, Selborne ("if he was not a combative member of the Opposition"), and Earl Grey. "Above all it should include the Defence Ministers of Canada, Australia, and South Africa."[3] His own membership and that of Lord Roberts, and the attendance of Balfour when in opposition, gave some color to this idea. But non-political control of defense organization was at that time, as

2. Carroll Quigley, "The Round Table Groups in Canada, 1908–1938," *Canadian Historical Review*, XLIII (1962), 206, 219.
3. Esher to Lord Knollys, Sept. 10, 1910, Brett, ed., *Journals and Letters of . . . Esher*, III, 22.

always, a dangerous delusion. Ultimate authority must rest with the responsible ministers. Defense policy cannot, in fact, be separated from foreign policy or excluded from political direction. The political implications of the Anglo-French staff talks of this same period are a striking illustration of this principle. Dominion representation on defense matters, even though below the political level, bristled with difficulties. Yet these were ignored by imperial defense enthusiasts.

The creation of the Imperial General Staff had been advocated as a means of achieving institutional development in defense matters within the Empire without arousing political suspicions about federation. It has been seen that the attraction of the proposal to Canada was the reverse of the coin—namely, the suggestion that it involved no surrender of control by the Canadian Cabinet. A second attempt to bring the dominions into defense planning was made through the establishment of the Committee of Imperial Defence. As that body was concerned with defense as a whole, and not just with one service, and as it had a political as well as a professional membership, it seemed the more important. The C.I.D. has, indeed, frequently been interpreted as a big step toward the establishment of a system of imperial defense.

On the contrary, like the Imperial General Staff, the Committee of Imperial Defence was set up in the first place to improve British, rather than collective, defense planning. In this field it helped to make Britain more prepared for war in 1914 than for any previous great war. But its success in that achievement has often been exaggerated and the committee's deficiencies have been glossed over. On the eve of war in 1914 the War Office and Admiralty were still planning very different kinds of operations.[4]

4. John P. Mackintosh, "The Role of the Committee of Imperial Defence before 1914," *English Historical Review*, LXXVII (July, 1962), 490–503, shows that the committee failed to bring about any significant degree of interservice co-operation in planning. This failure is played down in the comprehensive study by Franklyn A. Johnson, *Defence by Committee: The British Committee of Imperial Defence, 1885–1959* (London: Oxford University Press, 1960), where the C.I.D. is described as a "Centre of Strategic Planning" from 1907 to 1911, a chapter heading which is belied by his own dramatic account of the discussions in the C.I.D. at the time of the Agadir crisis (pp. 114–115).

Again like the Imperial General Staff, the Committee of Imperial Defence was not "imperial" in every sense. It dealt with Britain's imperial and colonial interests and with aspects of the defense of the Empire, but it was not imperial in a second and less accurate meaning of the word—"including participation by the dominions." "Imperial" derives from *imperium* and originally meant domination or sway. By a strange inversion it had come to be used to mean the sharing of imperial authority with the dominions. The word "imperial" was, however, used in many different senses. In the *Manual of Military Law,* "Imperial forces" were defined as those raised in a colony by direct order of His Majesty and maintained by a vote of the imperial Parliament. This definition was retained from before the South African War until World War II.[5] However, during World War I, "the Imperials" was the term used by British soldiers when discussing troops raised by the self-governing dominions; Canadians called British troops "the Imperials" (dominion personnel now speak of "the British" or "the Brits"); and to Australians "Imperials" were those Australians who went overseas to fight in the Imperial Expeditionary Force. The use of "imperial" in the titles of British institutions therefore did not necessarily have much significance. When used to mean a sharing of imperial authority with the dominions, it was from the point of view of the many colonials a direct inversion of the original sense of the word.

In the sense of sharing defense responsibilities with the dominions, the Committee of Imperial Defence was far from "imperial." Until the dreadnought crisis drew greater attention to the German problem, there had been no strong sense of urgency to alter the traditional British concern with Empire defense problems centering on the safety of India, the North-West Frontier, etc.— questions of some interest to Australia but of practically none to Canada.

Therefore, until the calling of the Imperial (Defence) Conference of 1909, neither British ministers and defense experts nor dominion ministers and service chiefs had done much to imple-

5. E.g., *Manual of Military Law* (London: War Office, 1914), pp. 194–195.

ment either Balfour's vision of dominion representation on the Committee of Imperial Defence or Deakin's resolution of 1907. At the 1909 conference the general problem of co-operation between the United Kingdom and the dominions had been discussed in full session. Following earlier practice, the Admiralty then proceeded to negotiate details with each dominion separately; but the War Office worked through a conference subcommittee to produce the agreements for uniformity and for the creation of an Imperial General Staff. On the last day of the conference, August 19, the dominion representatives attended a meeting of the Committee of Imperial Defence. The prime minister referred to the Resolution of 1907 and said that although distance made regular attendance at the committee sessions impossible for dominion ministers, he hoped they would be present more frequently than in the past. He pointed out that while there was no desire to interfere with local autonomy, the main problems of imperial defense were common to the whole Empire.[6] The proceedings were formal and the committee simply registered its approval of the arrangements for co-operation made at the conference. There seems to have been no general discussion.

Use of the Committee of Imperial Defence to wind up the conference has been taken to mean that Britain desired to bring the dominions into something more permanent than special—and even than regular—imperial conferences. In June, 1909, Esher had told Balfour that

A note that wants striking hard is that Great Britain is the heritage of these people as well as ours. Not only the abbeys and churches and old domains, but the honour of England and her sea Dominions. Relatively we grow weaker, and they grow stronger, as their populations and wealth increase. If they agree, as they do, in this ideal, is it not time for them to consider what sacrifices they are ready to make? Sea-power is the base on which the Empire rests, and it should not be beyond their wit and ours to discover a practical method by which the burden of Empire can be apportioned. Perhaps you might hint at the permanent representation on the Defence Committee of the Dominions, for Imperial Defence questions.[7]

6. C.I.D., Minutes, 104th Meeting, Aug. 19, 1909, P.R.O. Cab. 2/2/1.
7. Esher [to Balfour], June 9, 1909, in Brett, ed., *Journals and Letters of . . . Esher*, II, 392.

After the conference concluded, Esher suggested to Asquith that the Committee of Imperial Defence should become the *joint* Imperial General Staff.[8] Promise of large-scale dominion support for imperial defense could obviously not be expected without granting them some form of supervision of expenditure. Representation on the Committee of Imperial Defence appeared to be a means of doing this.

Occasional attendance was all that was achieved. But this practice was not new. For many years British service officers in the middle of tours of duty overseas (or after them) had been employed as members of the Colonial Defence Committee. The committee had now become a subcommittee of the Committee of Imperial Defence. On the eve of the Imperial Conference of 1911 it was renamed the Overseas Defence Committee in order to suit the new dignity of the self-governing dominions. When officers of dominion forces visited England, they had attended this committee's meetings for discussion of their problems.[9] But such visits constituted only a small part of the committee's total business, and the Overseas Defence Committee was a technical committee composed of relatively junior service officers. The practice of irregular and occasional attendance at the Overseas Defence Committee therefore met in no way the need for an imperial defense organization including dominion representation. The Committee of Imperial Defence itself remained imperial in name, but only partly so in function, and not at all in constitution, for it was purely British in membership. Too much has been made of Sir Frederick Borden's visit in 1903, which had no long-term significance.

At the Imperial Conference in 1911 there were new efforts to arrange some form of dominion participation in the direction of imperial defense. They sprang from many sources. Australia had protested at not being consulted about the Declaration of London, an international agreement on the laws of naval warfare; imperialists in the British Conservative party complained that

8. Esher to M. V. Brett, Oct. 7, 1909, *ibid.*, II, 412.
9. E.g., Col. W. T. Bridges, Royal Australian Artillery, in C.D.C., Minutes, April 7, 1910, P.R.O., Cab. 8/1/2.

the dominions were building navies, but that there had been no arrangement to bring them under Admiralty control in the event of war; [10] and in New Zealand, Sir Joseph Ward suggested a positive step by announcing that New Zealand "stands for the old flag, a white country, an invincible Imperial Navy, with an adequate share of responsibility, an extension of trade within the Empire, and representation in an Imperial Council." [11] Ward's proposal for representation on an imperial council, however, was flatly rejected by the sister dominions who saw it only as a thinly disguised form of imperial parliament and therefore completely impracticable.[12] Nor would the other dominion leaders indorse representation by high commissioners on the Committee of Imperial Defence. However, it was generally accepted that there must be some discussion of foreign policy at the coming Imperial Conference. Therefore, at the first session Asquith announced that the foreign secretary, Sir Edward Grey, would "speak . . . on the international situation, as far as it affects the Empire as a whole." This would take place in a special session of the Committee of Imperial Defence which would be attended by dominion prime ministers and defense ministers.[13]

The origin of this British invitation to the dominions to meet to discuss foreign policy at the Imperial Conference in 1911 is to be found in the report of a Committee of Imperial Defence subcommittee established to draw up an agenda concerning the naval and military defense of the Empire, and in an ensuing discussion about the dominions' international status during a war in which the United Kingdom might be engaged. The undersecretary of state for foreign affairs, Sir Arthur Nicolson, had stated that if the United Kingdom was at war, the dominions were necessarily at war also: neutrality would mean secession. He said that as the dominions were always asking how they could help, it did not seem to him that they were contemplating neutrality. The First Sea Lord, Sir Arthur Wilson, pointed out in

10. G.B., House of Commons, *Debates*, 1911, XXIV, 990.
11. London *Times*, April 25, 1911, p. 3.
12. John E. Tyler, "The Development of the Imperial Conference, 1887–1914," *CHBE*, III, 433.
13. G.B., *P.P.*, 1911, *Imperial Conference, 1911, Précis of Proceedings*, LIV, 21 (Cd. 5741).

reply that it was undesirable to communicate secret war plans to the dominions if there was any doubt about their attitude. McKenna, the First Lord, then showed that the truth was that the dominions thought they might not necessarily be attacked and that they claimed the right to decide whether they would themselves take part in any attack. As a result of this discussion, the Committee of Imperial Defence had come to the conclusion that it was desirable to have talks on the subject with dominion leaders.[14]

At previous colonial and imperial conferences, foreign policy had been mentioned only in general terms. The Committee of Imperial Defence suggested that in accordance with the precedent of 1909, the members of the forthcoming conference should be invited to attend its sessions because foreign policy could be discussed there in greater secrecy than would be possible in the conference hall itself.[15] Discussion of foreign policy was, however, not normally a function of the committee, and the proposal thus suggested a revolutionary step which, if continued, would have challenged a monopoly of the Cabinet and the Foreign Office, which was certainly not the British government's intention. What it hoped was that the revelation of secrets in the possession of the government would impress the dominion leaders with the gravity of the situation and so would induce them to make larger commitments to imperial defense. The use of the Committee of Imperial Defence as the medium of communication for this purpose would have the advantage of bringing the dominions into a permanent body instead of allowing the exchange to take place in an imperial conference that had no permanent existence.

Regular attendance at sessions of the Committee of Imperial Defence would not, however, have conceded to the dominions an effective voice in foreign policy since that was, after all, outside the committee's province. Furthermore, even within the more limited spheres with which the committee was concerned, dominion influence could be minimized. A contemporary anony-

14. C.I.D., Minutes, 109th Meeting, March 24, 1911, P.R.O., Cab. 2/2/2.
15. P.R.O., Cab. 5/2/3, pp. 94–96.

mous writer, who may have been Lord Esher or someone close
to him, suggested that the reason why the Committee of Imperial
Defence was used for the foreign discussions was that its voting
procedure would insure the preservation of British control. As
votes at an imperial conference were by countries, Britain could
have been outvoted. But at the committee meetings, voting was
by heads. Since the principle on which the committee was established was that the British prime minister could summon whomsoever he pleased to attend, it would always be possible for him
to flood the committee with officials in order to outvote dominion
representatives.[16] In both the conference and the committee, in
accordance with British practice, voting was infrequent and
business was usually carried on by reaching an informal consensus. Even so, an invitation to the dominions to attend the
Committee of Imperial Defence sessions was probably offered
with a careful eye to the future to avoid a possible surrender of
British control of foreign and defense policy if dominion attendance should become formal and regular (and the committee
should become more than merely consultative). However, if the
dominion leaders were as farsighted as the British, they must
have realized that membership on the committee would not give
them the influence which some of them desired.

Grey's statement on foreign policy at the 1911 conference was,
nevertheless, a revolutionary departure. The dominion prime
ministers received fuller information than the House of Commons. Yet they were not told about the military staff talks with
France. These were known only to an inner ring of British Cabinet ministers and not to what Brigadier General Sir Henry
Wilson called "the small fry," among whom he numbered not
only the pacific-minded but powerful Lord Morley, but also
Reginald McKenna, recently appointed First Lord of the Admiralty.[17] Sir Edward Grey told the conference that separate
navies made a single foreign policy more essential than ever.
"We wish to have consultation and I wish to explain as fully as

16. "X" (pseud.), "The Committee of Imperial Defence," *United Empire,*
III (1912), 732. This anonymous article is largely based on a lecture delivered
by Lord Esher at the Royal United Service Institution.
17. Callwell, *Wilson,* I, 106.

I can the present situation of foreign affairs and what our views and prospects are," he said.[18]

The assembled dominion premiers were impressed by the fact that they had been taken into the British government's confidence; but as they had no special knowledge of international affairs, they were not in a position to contribute much to a debate on foreign policy. Therefore, the few comments that were made were based only on their known personal prejudices and on their concept of their own dominion's interest. There was little discussion except about the renewal of the Anglo-Japanese Treaty, which was approved. Laurier's repetition of the fact that Canada was not bound to contribute to a British war aroused the director of military operations, Brigadier General Wilson, to a frenzy. He commented, "Canada is already gone." Wilson was much more favorably impressed by Sir Joseph Ward, who he said had "spoken up like a man." [19] Ward said things that Wilson wanted to hear. The ears of British service officers and imperialists were attuned only to dominion statements that had imperial overtones.

Grey's speech to the premiers on foreign policy was for "information" rather than for "consultation." In 1911 British foreign policy was clothed in great secrecy and was not directly controlled in detail by the British Parliament. This might seem a rational justification for the denial of full participation by the dominions also. But the cases were not directly parallel. The foreign secretary, who directed foreign policy, was ultimately responsible to the British Parliament which could therefore control the Foreign Office, if only in a vague and distant way. But the dominions had no constitutional means of exercising any control at all. Furthermore, Asquith and Harcourt had made it quite clear at the conference that it was unthinkable that there should be any infringement of the right of the United Kingdom to an unfettered control of foreign policy.[20] Participation in a body to discuss but not to decide foreign policy was therefore more likely to obtain dominion commitments than to allow them

18. C.I.D., Minutes, 111th Meeting, May 26, 1911, P.R.O., Cab. 2/2/2.
19. Callwell, *Wilson,* I, 95–96.
20. Ollivier, *Colonial and Imperial Conferences,* II, 59–60.

to exercise influence. The move for joint control of foreign policy, or for some lesser means of co-operation in that field, had come from both British and dominion imperialists. It failed, not merely because the more important governments in the Empire, Britain, Canada, and even Australia, were basically unsympathetic to the idea, but even more because it carried with it built-in difficulties that prevented it from being applied to a congerie of autonomous states.

The question of permanent representation of the dominions on the Committee of Imperial Defence and the question of local dominion defense committees came up when the dominion ministers visited the committee. Laurier said he was perfectly satisfied with things as they were. He did not wish to impose his views on the other dominions, but he thought that high commissioners should not be intrusted with authority on the Committee of Imperial Defence. Andrew Fisher, on the other hand, wanted Australian representation; but he said that it must be by a servant of the government without authority to act on his own, except by direction of his superiors in the Commonwealth. Malan of South Africa went much further. He thought that representation should be by a responsible Cabinet minister. The committee thereupon resolved that "one or more representatives, appointed by the respective governments of the Dominions, should be invited to attend meetings of the Committee of Imperial Defence when questions of naval and military defence affecting the Overseas Dominions are under consideration." It was also agreed that the proposal for a defense committee to be established in each dominion should be accepted in principle, the composition in each dominion being for each dominion to decide.

These resolutions have sometimes been represented as a great step in the development of imperial defense organization, but they actually did little more than renew the resolutions of the Colonial Conference of 1907.[21] The second proposal, about colonial defense committees, was not published in 1911, apparently because some dominions preferred to have it kept quiet.[22]

21. C.I.D., Minutes, 113th Meeting, May 30, 1911, P.R.O., Cab. 2/2/2.
22. *Ibid.*, 118th Meeting, July 11, 1912, P.A.C., M.G. 26, H 1 (a), Vol. 23.

Dominions could be present at Committee of Imperial Defence meetings "as of right" only when matters that directly concerned them were being debated. But this right had narrow limits since it was not made clear how they were to know which subjects were on the agenda. The practice of inviting dominion ministers to attend, which was to increase, was a far cry from dominion representation for full consultation on defense, much less on foreign policy. The extent to which the committee was instrumental in bringing the dominions into the higher councils of the Empire was thus minimal. It has been alleged that the secretariat of the committee was beginning to replace the Colonial Office as the channel of communication between Britain and the dominions on defense matters.[23] The Colonial Office had, indeed, authorized direct communication on routine business between the dominions and the service departments which was growing rapidly in amount. But the Colonial Office remained the normal channel for all important matters. The status of the Committee of Imperial Defence had been enhanced by its use as a means of information on foreign policy during the Imperial Conference, but its normal function in relation to the self-governing dominions had been changed little.[24]

A Need for an Expeditionary Force

On the heels of the Imperial Conference of 1911, a sharp note of urgency was re-injected into the Empire's defense problem when the German demonstration at Agadir brought the likelihood of a Franco-German war closer. But in August, discussions in the Committee of Imperial Defence about the action to be taken to support France in the event of a war with Germany uncovered the fact that the War Office and the Admiralty had completely different plans. Brigadier General Wilson, who had engineered the staff talks with the French as long ago as 1906, and who had not known any details of French plans until very recently,[25] had nevertheless made military arrangements with the

---

23. Johnson, *Defence by Committee,* p. 111.
24. For a contrary view, see *ibid.,* pp. 111, 121.
25. Callwell, *Wilson,* I, 103.

French in expectation that British troops would fight alongside their armies on the Franco-German border. However, the First Lord now complained that he had not been consulted about the provision of naval protection for an expeditionary force and that he could not provide it.[26] The Admiralty had been planning a series of invasions in the Baltic which the War Office declared "hopeless." [27] Furthermore, although the inner ring of Cabinet ministers who had known about the staff talks from the beginning had salved their consciences by pretending that the talks were only technical and did not imply a political commitment, when the staff arrangements were disclosed to the rest of the government in 1912, it was at once clear that Britain's involvement in any Franco-German war was almost a foregone conclusion and that the nature, if not the full extent, of British participation had been predetermined.

The acuteness of the German danger explains why British ministers had been willing to agree to measures of doubtful constitutionality, and might also excuse their anxiety to obtain advance promises of dominion support. But the governments of those autonomous dominions which had insisted that decisions could not be made in advance about commitment to war and about the degree of participation in such a war were now amply justified in the stand they had taken. No free government could buy a pig in a poke without seeming to surrender its liberty of action. To have accepted commitment to British plans when the servants of the British government had not yet agreed upon the broadest outline of possible operations would have been irresponsible political folly.

Nevertheless, the reality of the German menace was working to push aside constitutional and political arguments and to insure voluntary dominion support; and the dominions were anxiously putting their military forces into better shape. When the Imperial General Staff system had been instituted, it had been suggested that inspecting officers of the dominion forces should be British. Dominion governments had avoided the possibility of

26. C.I.D., Minutes, 114th Meeting, Aug. 23, 1911, P.R.O., Cab. 2/2/2.
27. Haldane, *Autobiography*, p. 226.

War Office influence which this might have implied by selecting inspectors general who were relatively junior, or colonials, or British officers whose judgment could be trusted. The British government, however, had also offered something quite different —occasional inspection by very senior officers of the British Army. Canada had declined an inspection by General Sir John French in 1908 on the grounds that the celebrations of the three-hundredth anniversary of Champlain's founding of Quebec to be held in that year would occupy all the available troops; [28] but he was invited to come in 1910. About the same time Lord Kitchener went to Australia and New Zealand on a similar mission. Flattered by the visits of great war heroes of the South African conflict, the dominion authorities apparently forgot their suspicions of British control, and the British government thought the inspections so important that French was called to brief the Cabinet orally before submitting his formal report on the Canadian Militia for investigation by the C.I.D.[29]

French criticized the inadequate organization and lack of military knowledge of the Canadian higher command, stated that the regulations for the proper qualification of officers and N.C.O.'s were not strictly observed, and noted (as MacDougall had protested in 1868) that the rank and file were not compelled to fulfil their engagements. He found the militia not yet really efficient, and he reported favorably only on the artillery and the Royal Military College. But the tone of his report was restrained and he was evidently prepared to give the reorganized system time to develop. His recommendation that the officers commanding the several permanent corps should be entirely under the orders of the inspector general (a British officer) who should not be a member of the Militia Council, savored of an attempt once more to insert a modicum of British supervision. But General Lake, the British officer who then held that post, retorted that as the officers commanding the permanent corps were

28. Grey to C.O., Telegram, Jan. 30, 1908, P.R.O., C.O. 42/918. This great militia rally in Quebec had no training value, but it was a useful publicity stunt for the militia, especially as it was accompanied by a visit of the Royal Navy.

29. Esher to M.V.B., Sept. 14, 1910, in Brett, ed., *Journals and Letters of . . . Esher*, III, 23–24.

commandants of schools of instruction and of organized units, they must be under the orders of officers commanding commands and districts. His own membership on the Militia Council, he said, was a result of special circumstances (he meant his long service and acceptability in Canada) which would not necessarily pertain afterward.[30]

Kitchener in Australia reported enthusiastically upon the Australian system of universal service which had not yet been adopted in Britain; but French judiciously refrained from any comment about that subject in respect of Canada. Both inspecting officers avoided stressing the need to prepare large expeditionary forces. French said that the Canadian Militia was needed for defense against a land attack, "or to furnish contingents to succour other parts of the Empire in the event the Dominion government sees fit, as in South Africa." [31] Kitchener put the purpose of military forces in more general terms and with even less emphasis on expeditionary forces. Recommending an army of 80,000 men for Australia, he said that the need to concentrate the Royal Navy against a major enemy fleet might leave a dominion exposed to invasion. "It therefore becomes the duty of all dominion governments to provide a military force adequate, not only to deal promptly with any attempt at invasion, but also to ensure local security and public confidence until our superiority at sea has been decisively and comprehensively asserted." [32] In 1914 Kitchener was to be one of the first to realize the need for huge armies. If he had already, in 1910, anticipated the possibility of large-scale intervention on the continent, he refrained from drawing the logical conclusion about its effect on Australia's training needs, perhaps because he thought that universal training made any comment on the subject unnecessary.

Three years later, in 1913, General Sir Ian Hamilton reported

30. Gen. Sir John French, *Report on His Inspection of the Canadian Militia*, in Canada, *Sessional Papers*, XLV, 1911, Vol. 21, No. 35 a; Maj. Gen. Sir P. H. N. Lake, *Report on the Best Method of Giving Effect to the Recommendations of General Sir John French, G.C.B., G.C.V.O., Regarding the Canadian Militia*, ibid., No. 35 b.

31. French, *Report on His Inspection of the Canadian Militia*, 1910.

32. Gen. H. H. Kitchener, *Memorandum on the Defence of Australia* (March 1, 1910), in Australia, Commonwealth, Parliament, *Records of Proceedings and Printed Papers*, II (1910), 83 (8).

on military institutions in Canada. In discussing the defensive preparations that Canada should make, Hamilton tacitly depreciated the possibility of an American invasion; yet he talked in his report of a delaying action until the Reserve Militia could be assembled and knocked into shape. However, on the question of expeditionary forces he saw no reason for camouflage. He said that British strategy had always placed offensive overseas action before local defense, and that the call for co-operation overseas was certain to come before many years had passed. He said that Canada should think of the thousands from overseas who would fight on her behalf if she were attacked tomorrow; she should, therefore, prepare herself, according to her means, to do as much for them in return.[33] Colonel Hubert Foster, R.E., the director of military science at Sydney University, was even more blunt. He thought that local citizen forces were unsuitable for the Empire's real need—co-operation in expeditionary forces on land.[34] Despite this official confusion and obscurity about the purpose of land forces in the dominions, the effect of the inspections was to spur efficiency. Upon receiving French's report, Borden promised immediate implementation, and although the Colonial Office was skeptical, there was a rapid advance in military organization in Canada.[35] Eastern Canada was divided into six divisional areas, and it was becoming realized in informed circles, if not openly announced, that one reason for military preparation was the sending of forces overseas.

Robert Borden's Naval Policy

While these reports and comments were being digested, the deteriorating international situation in Europe strengthened the voices of those Canadians who had opposed the creation of dominion navies on the grounds that they would destroy the unity

33. Canada, Department of Militia and Defence, Gen. Sir Ian Hamilton, *Report on the Military Institutions of Canada* (Ottawa: King's Printer, 1913), pp. 12–13, 33.
34. Col. Hubert Foster, *War and the Empire: The Principles of Imperial Defence* (London: Wilkins & Norgate, 1914), p. 215.
35. Hamilton, "Defence, 1812–1912," p. 467; Grey to C.O., Confidential, Jan. 6, 1911, P.R.O., C.O. 42/946.

of command which a sea strategy needed. It was argued that at a time when there was an "almost ruthless concentration" of ships under Admiralty control, British naval officers and officials could obviously not be sincere in their professions in favor of the creation of a Canadian navy. Laurier's defeat was said to have been "solely because [the Canadian people] . . . wanted to remain permanently British." The election was asserted to be evidence that Canada was now ready to listen to the British case. It was argued that the Admiralty should realize that "sinister forces" in Canada had clamored for a Canadian navy in order to get contracts; that "Canada has no need whatever for a navy, while the British Empire—of which Canada is a part—has supreme need for the greatest navy in the world"; but that the Admiralty must tell the Canadian people what was wanted.[36] There was thus considerable pressure to reverse the decision on naval decentralization.

The victor in the election, Robert Borden, had once favored a Canadian unit of a British or imperial navy. But in the debate on Laurier's Naval Bill he had changed face and had recommended direct contributions like those offered by New Zealand and other dominions. His alleged reasons, which he outlined in the House, were based not so much on long-term principles as on the present danger. When he came to power, however, he revealed his intention to repeal the Naval Service Act which had created the Royal Canadian Navy, but he did not immediately announce the gift of battleships which he had suggested during the debate. Instead he led a delegation of his ministers to England for the purpose of "reaching a decision with respect to naval co-operation with Great Britain . . . [which was] not only desirable but necessary." [37] Borden's aim was to secure for Canada a voice in foreign policy.

On their arrival the Canadians were invited to attend a session of the Committee of Imperial Defence. There Asquith and

36. Albert R. Carman, "Canada and the Navy: A Canadian View," *Nineteenth Century and After*, LXXI (May, 1912), 822–823, 827–828.
37. Borden, ed., *Robert Laird Borden*, I, 355; Tucker, *Naval Service of Canada*, pp. 173–177.

Grey described Britain's foreign relations to them but, as Borden noted in his *Memoirs* later, without telling them about the staff conversation with France.[38] The secretary of state for war, Seely, showed the need for a common military doctrine and said that there were now thirty-four British officers serving in Canada and a number of Canadians in England; and Winston Churchill, the new First Lord of the Admiralty, then described and emphasized the naval threat which Germany presented. Asquith concluded by making reference to the Imperial Conference resolutions for dominion representation on the committee and for the establishment of a defense committee in each dominion. This latter proposal had not yet been formally communicated to the dominion governments. Borden replied only briefly, asking for a conference with Admiralty officials.[39]

Borden's objectives were, first, to obtain evidence that could be used to convince the Canadian electorate that the emergency demanded extraordinary measures, and, second, to explore the ground for a means by which Canada's voice could be heard in the making of the Empire's foreign policy. Where he differed from Laurier was in his acceptance of the fact that the danger was imminent and in his belief that Canada's tie with Britain meant inevitable involvement, which therefore made it necessary to insure that Canada's voice was heard in British councils. When he met with Churchill and his advisers, Borden obtained a promise that a statement about Britain's peril and about its naval needs would be given to him in writing.[40] A few days later he was much encouraged by a speech by Asquith in which the prime minister offered to withdraw from the position that he had taken at the Imperial Conference in 1911 when he had declared that the making of foreign policy could not be shared and must be exercised subject only to the British government's responsibility to the imperial Parliament. Asquith now told the British House of Commons: "Side by side with this growing participation

38. Borden, ed., *Robert Laird Borden*, I, 358.
39. C.I.D., Minutes, 118th Meeting, July 11, 1912, P.R.O., Cab. 2/2/3; Borden, ed., *Robert Laird Borden*, I, 358.
40. Borden, ed., *Robert Laird Borden*, I, 238.

in the active burdens of the Empire on the part of our dominions, there rests with us undoubtedly the duty of making such response as we can to their obviously reasonable appeal that they should be entitled to be heard in the determination of the policy and the direction of Imperial affairs." [41] Borden followed up this lead by telling the 1900 Conservative Club in London: "The people of Canada are not the type that will permit themselves to become merely silent partners in such a great Empire. If there is to be Imperial co-operation, the people of Canada propose to have a reasonable and fair voice in that co-operation. I do not doubt but that it is the wish of all the statesmen in the British Isles to accord them that voice." [42]

Nevertheless, although he warned Churchill that everything depended on the cogency of the statement to be put forward about the emergency, the Admiralty's memorandum, when it came, was so inadequate that Borden was convinced Churchill had not given the matter reasonable attention. He told the First Lord that if this was the best case that could be made, it would be idle to expect any results from the government and people of Canada. Churchill then sent him a secret statement which bore the hallmarks of his own pen and which was much more satisfactory. But Borden insisted there must also be a parallel version that could be given to the Canadian public.[43] Churchill's secret memorandum, when read to the Canadian Cabinet, proved most effective. Borden, however, thought the text that was expurgated for publication had not been so well prepared; in particular, it omitted the important statement that capital ships were required.[44]

Churchill's memorandum was secret because it included details of German ship construction gathered from intelligence sources, and also because it gave detailed reasons why an invasion of Germany was not possible. It stated that the effect of a Canadian refusal on the whole international situation would be serious, and it argued that Canadian aid was needed for rea-

41. *Ibid.*, I, 361.
42. *Ibid.*, I, 364.
43. *Ibid.*
44. *Ibid.*, I, 399.

sons of morale as well as for the addition in material strength.[45] Churchill said that Britain could not expedite the naval building program without provoking Germany, but he thought that a voluntary Canadian offer would have the desired effect of countering combined German and Italian construction which was threatening to outdo Britain.[46]

Why Borden thought a British request for capital ships would help his case is not clear. It could obviously have been interpreted by the Opposition as an example of unwarranted British intrusion in Canadian domestic questions. But as a result of Churchill's stand, Borden had to bring in his bill to give £35 million to the Royal Navy without being able to show that Britain had said that amount was necessary. Although Borden opposed and defeated an amendment that would have denied contributions until Canada received a voice in foreign policy, he argued that when Britain no longer undertook to assume sole responsibility for defense, she could no longer undertake to assume sole responsibility for, and sole control of, foreign policy. He said that his statements on this point had been enthusiastically received by British audiences, and that the leaders of both British political parties "had apparently accepted this principle." [47]

Borden refused to tie the emergency gift of battleships to a statement about the future creation of a Canadian navy, which he believed would take fifteen to twenty years to come about. He said that he had been assured that when a Canadian fleet unit was created, the vessels could be recalled by the Canadian government to form part of that unit.[48] If it was possible to take part in the existing naval organization "on self-respecting terms," he questioned the need to build up an expensive naval organization in Canada.[49] He then announced that the British government had assured him that pending the solution of the question of a

---

45. Churchill, Secret Memorandum (in answer to the Canadian government's request concerning the naval situation), Sept. 20, 1912, P.A.C., Perley Papers, R.G. 27, II D. 12. The text is printed in Tucker, *Naval Service of Canada,* Appendix VIII, pp. 394–407.
46. Tucker, "Naval Policy of Sir Robert Borden," p. 6.
47. Borden, *Robert Laird Borden,* I, 404.
48. *Ibid.*
49. *Ibid.*

voice in foreign policy and defense, they would welcome permanent Canadian representation on the Committee of Imperial
Defence. No important step would be taken without consultation
with the Canadian representative, a minister. News of Borden's
statement, with its implications of greater Canadian participation in imperial defense organization, caused a mild sensation
in London.[50]

Borden's assumption that the gift of ships would be followed
by a voice in foreign policy was premature. Although many vague
promises had been made in the British Parliament, there was no
real evidence of any such intention in Britain. As the gift would
have been unconditional, the ships could have been disposed of
at any time without consulting Canada. The invitation to membership on the Committee of Imperial Defence had been issued
because it was believed that the information which dominion
ministers would receive there would educate them in the mysteries of foreign policy. Richard Jebb, who believed the regular
imperial conferences were the closest the Empire could come to
centralization, told Deakin that the Round Tablers, heirs of the
Imperial Federation movement, were saying privately that there
was no intention to give Canada a vote in return for the emergency gift because there was no need to do so. He added that
if Borden hoped to use an offer of a Canadian fleet unit in the
imperial navy to obtain a share in foreign policy-making through
some form of federalism, then "either the permanent [naval]
policy is postponed to the Greek Kalends in Canada, or else
Borden makes way for Laurier." [51]

Nevertheless, Borden continued to insist that Canadian naval
preparations must be accompanied by a share in policy-making.
In a private interview, Borden told Sir Herbert Samuel, an emis-
sary of the Asquith government, that a permanent policy of
monetary contributions for naval purposes was quite out of the
question for Canada. He added that until a means of giving
Canada a voice in the affairs of the Empire were found, her naval
policy except in emergency must be limited to providing naval
bases, graving docks, and small craft for home defense. He be-

50. *Westminster Gazette,* Dec. 9, 1912.
51. Jebb to Deakin, March 21, 1912, A.N.L., Jebb Papers.

lieved an imperial executive that was representative of the whole Empire was unlikely "in our time"; but he hoped that the Committee of Imperial Defence might develop and that through it the dominions might make their voices heard in foreign policy also. His permanent naval policy, he said, "approximated very closely" to Laurier's and would be generally acceptable in Canada, even in Quebec.[52] He spoke in the knowledge that his confidence would be respected. But he thus admitted that he had attacked a Liberal policy with which he was largely in agreement and that in doing so he had shattered the country's fragile unity on the naval issue. Borden differed from Laurier on the desirability of a say in foreign policy. Laurier, like Mackenzie King after him, was anxious to avoid this issue lest it imply commitment. But how could Borden expect a voice in foreign policy through the Committee of Imperial Defence when, as Asquith had informed him, such questions were "not strictly within the purview of this committee"? It had been made quite clear to him that the C.I.D. was purely advisory and that policy was the sole prerogative of the Cabinet. True, he had been assured that any dominion minister sent to London would at all times have full and free access to the prime minister, the foreign secretary, and the colonial secretary for information on all questions of imperial policy.[53] But this offer did not include any promise that dominions could have a formal voice in foreign policy. Access to the prime minister would presumably have permitted Canada's opinions to be heard informally, but the proposal was more akin to diplomatic representation, or to lobbying, than to participation in any organic process of policy-making. It is true also that the offer implied access on a wider and more regular scale than was customary for foreign powers; and Britain and the dominions would presumably have more common problems to discuss. But this proposal of contact at the prime ministerial level pointed to the future Commonwealth rather than to a system of imperial defense. Borden's accession to power, which had

52. Sir H. Samuel, "Canada and Naval Defence," Oct. 12, 1913, P.R.O., Cab. 1/9/478.
53. C.I.D., Minutes, 119th Meeting, Aug. 1, 1912, P.A.C., M.G. 26, H. 1 (a), Vol. 23; Harcourt to Governor General, Dec. 10, 1912, *ibid.*, H. 1(b), Vol. 122, No. 66217–66220.

slowed naval development in Canada, had thus not radically altered the trend of development toward Commonwealth cooperation.

By his determination to use the opportunity of the emergency to secure a voice in foreign policy, Borden set his face against the development of the Canadian naval service which he had told Samuel that he favored. The passage of Laurier's Naval Service Act had been followed by royal approval for the establishment of a Royal Canadian Navy. But in March, 1912, Winston Churchill, reporting to the Commons on naval developments in Australia and New Zealand, added, "The development of the naval policy of Canada is at the moment somewhat uncertain. Until the proposals of the new Dominion Government are formulated, it is not possible to say how far the organisation of the recently constituted Royal Canadian Navy will be modified." He promised Admiralty aid in any scheme to enable Canada to take an effective part in the naval defense of the Empire.[54] However, in single-minded determination to pursue a policy of contributions, Borden proceeded to dismantle the Royal Canadian Navy. Appointments, enlistments, and re-engagements ceased in November, 1912, and men who wanted a free discharge were permitted to leave the service before the expiration of their terms of service.[55] The cruisers *Niobe* and *Rainbow* were paid off and laid up. A Royal Navy Canadian Volunteer Reserve was established, but by the outbreak of the World War I it had attracted only about 250 officers and ratings. So great was the Conservative government's hostility to the idea of a Canadian navy that the title "Royal Canadian Navy," which came into popular usage during the war, does not appear in the annual reports of the Naval Service until 1920 and then only to state that the future of the Royal Canadian Navy was in doubt.[56] Thus, even before

54. "Statement of the First Lord of the Admiralty Explanatory of the Navy Estimates, 1912–1913, 4 March, 1912," in G.B., *P.P.*, 1912–1913, LII, 298 (Cd. 6106).

55. Col. A. Fortescue Duguid, *Official History of the Canadian Forces in the Great War, 1914–1919* (Ottawa: King's Printer, 1938), I, Pt. II, 24.

56. A single exception is the "Report on the Health of the Royal Canadian Navy" in the report of the Department of Naval Service for 1913; see Canada, *Sessional Papers, XLVII, 1913,* Vol. 25, No. 39, p. 21.

the rejection of his dreadnought offer by the Canadian Senate, Borden smothered the Royal Canadian Navy which his political opponents had sired; and both before and afterward he made no effort to set up the local navy which he had professed was his long-term policy.

The fate of Borden's attempt to provide three dreadnoughts for the Royal Navy is well known and need not be repeated in detail here. The Liberals in opposition tied their flag to the creation of a Canadian navy that would be bigger than that proposed in 1910. Borden, seeking to preserve unity within his party, emphasized the emergency. When the Liberals resorted to obstruction, he had to use a closure motion to put an end to a debate that had lasted twenty-three weeks. The Naval Aid Bill was passed in the Commons on May 15, 1911. Two weeks later it was defeated in the Senate. Nevertheless, Borden took no steps to reverse his calculated policy of suppressing a local navy, perhaps because the Admiralty intimated that it would have difficulty lending men and material for the purpose.[57]

Naval Nationalism in New Zealand and Australia

Winston Churchill was pleased that Borden's offer of a money contribution to the Royal Navy had made a "tremendous impression" throughout the Empire. He was therefore exceedingly annoyed when the Royal Navy's commander in chief on the Australian Station, Admiral King-Hall, expressed a desire to see New Zealand join forces with the Australian fleet.[58] Opinion in New Zealand was, in fact, moving in the opposite direction from that in which Borden seemed to be going. One reason was that although the naval contributions had been increased, the Pacific was "almost bare of [British] ships." [59] While Japan had twenty battleships and battle cruisers, nine armored cruisers, and was building seven more dreadnoughts, Britain had only four large

---

57. Tucker, *Naval Service of Canada*, pp. 188–196; Churchill to Borden, Jan. 24, 1913, P.A.C., Borden MSS, O'C. 658.
58. Churchill to Denman, Dec. 13, 1912, A.N.L., Denman Papers.
59. John A. Allen, *A Naval Policy for New Zealand* (Dunedin: Otago Daily Times and Witness, 1912), p. 15.

vessels in the Pacific.[60] Many New Zealanders believed that the subsidy policy was a failure.

Sir James Allen, who became New Zealand's minister of defense in July, 1912, went to England to discuss the question. On the way he called on the Australian prime minister and minister of defense. It was reported that he made it clear that New Zealand wanted the control of Australasian fleets to pass into the hands of the Admiralty in the event of war. However, his purpose in going to England was rather different than that suggested by the report. He intended to obtain an arrangement more satisfactory than the making of contributions so that the national sentiment of New Zealand could be mobilized in support of measures of naval defense. He argued that the plan for contributions was strategically unsound, and he asked the Admiralty to advise Australia and New Zealand on the best ways to concert their naval construction so as to produce fleets which could be integrated with the British vessels in the China seas for training, but which would be handed over to the Admiralty unconditionally when war began. In London, Allen found that he was subjected to what seemed more like influence than advice. This served to confirm his views, which, as he now realized, differed fundamentally from those of the Admiralty.[61]

The battle cruiser *New Zealand,* the Dominion's gift to Britain, was commissioned on November 19, 1912, and soon afterward sailed around the world, calling at New Zealand as had been promised. It was now arranged by Churchill, however, that she would be attached, not to the China Squadron as had been the original intention, but to the First Battle-cruiser Squadron in European waters.[62] It was therefore said by colonials that while Australia and New Zealand had lived up to the Naval Agreements of 1909, the Admiralty had not. It had failed to create the Eastern fleet by sending out the promised armored cruisers and dreadnought. Sir James Allen complained to his prime minister

60. F. M. Cutlack, "Australia and Imperial Defence," *National Review,* LX (Feb. 13, 1912), 995 n.
61. Sir James Allen, *New Zealand and Naval Defence* (Dunedin: [n.p.], 1929), pp. 4–7.
62. Kia Ora, *H.M.S. New Zealand* (n.p., n.d.).

that while the Australian ships were not listed by the Admiralty and could therefore be regarded as additions to British strength, *H.M.S. New Zealand* was so listed and therefore served only to relieve the British taxpayer of the cost of building a ship.[63] The New Zealand and Australian governments both levied charges of bad faith against Britain.[64]

Discontent was increased when the Admiralty, advising New Zealand reluctantly about the kind of ships needed for local protection, said that submarines were unsuitable for New Zealand because they were too difficult to man and maintain. The Admiralty had thus now adopted Creswell's view which it had once bitterly opposed. With a note of sarcasm, Allen told the House of Representatives, "Admiralty opinion *does* vary from time to time . . . we have the right to ask, if in 1909 they were suitable for New Zealand waters, why is it that in 1913 they are considered unsuitable." [65] Massey, the prime minister, said that if no satisfactory agreement were reached with the Admiralty, New Zealand would build a fast cruiser for protection of her own trade; and in 1913 he introduced a Naval Defence Bill which was designed to divert part of the former naval contribution to the training of New Zealand sailors. Many clauses in it were adopted without change from the Australian Naval Act. Massey said that the balance of the contributions would be given to Britain to pay for cruisers to be stationed in New Zealand waters. New ships would be built to form a New Zealand division of the Royal Navy which would be administered by New Zealand in time of peace, but which would by virtue of a clause in the act be handed over automatically to the Admiralty in the event of war.[66]

Thus, New Zealand, irked by the decrease of naval strength in the Pacific which had resulted from the imperial concentration

63. Allen to Massey, June 3, 1913, in Allen, *New Zealand and Naval Defence,* pp. 5–6.
64. London *Times,* Feb. 20, April 13, 28, 1914.
65. New Zealand, *Parliamentary Debates,* Nov. 17 to Dec. 15, 1913, Vol. 167, p. 465.
66. Australia, Naval Defence Act, *Statutes,* 1910, No. 30; New Zealand, Naval Defence Act, *Statutes,* 1913, No. 45. Paragraph 19 in the New Zealand Act arranged for transfer wherever Britain was at war.

against Germany in home waters, had, as a contemporary newspaper said, elected to "plunge into the vortex of armaments" by building its own fleet.[67] The proposal was to create what was called an administrative "division" of the Royal Navy, and not a separate fleet, and to commit that division automatically to Britain's aid on the outbreak of war. But the difference from the Australian pattern was not as great as the name implied. Except for the arrangements for transfer in the event of war, the New Zealand Naval Act was almost identical with that of Australia. The use of the device of a "division" of the Royal Navy was an expression of New Zealand's traditional loyalty but did not in fact mean that there would be much difference from Canadian and Australian policy either in time of peace or in the event of a great crisis.

Although the Admiralty had accepted the principle of an Australian navy, there were points on which it still disagreed fundamentally with the Australians. One was the question of transfer to Admiralty control in the event of war. Australia had suggested that on receipt of a signal from the Admiralty, the Australian Navy Board would order Australian ships to put prearranged war orders into effect; then, until the end of the war or the emergency, the Naval Board would, while keeping the Commonwealth government informed, "act in every way as if they were in the position of a Commander-in-Chief appointed by the Admiralty" and would be the channel of communication between the United Kingdom and the Australian vessels.[68] The Admiralty, on the other hand, continued to press for automatic wartime commitment to Admiralty control for a period of five years. Defence Minister Pearce protested that this would mean that the Commonwealth government would then be merely the United Kingdom's agent to administer its own ships in time of peace but would be deprived of the right to put that fleet at the disposal of the Admiralty when war came.[69] The irrepressible Admiral King-Hall proposed that the Australian vessels should

67. Melbourne *Argus*, Oct. 30, 1913, quoting the London *Daily Telegraph*.
68. [Secretary of Defence] to Secretary, Prime Minister's Department, June 17, 1912, A.W.M., Pearce Papers, Bundle 5.
69. Notes by Pearce, Sept. 24, 1912, *ibid.*, Bundle 3.

be a division of the Eastern fleet and that the commanding officer of either the Australian or the China division should command according to seniority.[70] This attempt at compromise seems not to have found favor.

In November, the Admiralty objected to Australia's proposed "intervention" of the Naval Board in the chain of command in time of war. It stated that except for those Australian ships which were retained for station duties in Australian waters, the Australian fleet should come directly under the Admiralty through the commander in chief. It offered to inform the Australian Navy Board of all important orders and instructions and said that the board's function in time of war would be to act for the Admiralty in all ancillary and administrative matters.[71] When *H.M.A.S. Melbourne* arrived in Sydney, Pearce told its officers that the creation of the Australian fleet to share the burden of defense appealed to Australian patriotism, but that Australians recognized that sectional navies could be "taken in detail by an enemy." The Australian government had therefore come to an agreement with the Admiralty whereby a wireless message would give effect to the system of one control and full co-operation.[72] This agreement marks the final achievement of intimate naval co-operation in peacetime and voluntary commitment to fully centralized control in time of war. This was very different from the views of the advocates of imperial defense. It was an important step in the establishment of the Commonwealth defense system.

A second dispute between Australia and the Admiralty arose as a result of a speech made by Churchill in April, 1914. He was reported in Australia to have said that a battle cruiser was not an essential part of a dominion fleet unit, and that because of the Anglo-Japanese alliance Britain did not need battle cruisers in the Pacific. Pearce termed this a revolution in Admiralty policy and described Churchill's suggestion that Australian ships be sent

---

70. King-Hall to Governor General, Sept. 12, 1912, C.A.O., Prime Minister's Department, C.P. 78, Bundle 54.
71. Admiralty to Governor General, Telegram, Nov. 7, 1911, *ibid.*, Bundle 5.
72. Manuscript report of speech by Pearce, March 20, 1913, A.N.L., Denman Papers.

to home waters as a virtual return to the discarded "contributions" policy. He argued that without capital ships in the Pacific, Britain's diplomatic influence there was nil, and he added that these ships had been promised to Australia in 1909 for training purposes. He admitted privately that the Australian fleet unit was needed in Australia in order to make defense taxation acceptable. He said that the new Admiralty policy should be discussed at the conference table. Australia therefore wanted an imperial conference in Vancouver in 1915 to discuss naval defense.[73]

The controversy showed that a centralized defense organization was difficult, if not impossible, for a group of autonomous states with different strategic interests. Churchill was moved by fear of Germany to discount the long-range danger from Japan. Undoubtedly he was right insofar as the immediate welfare of Britain and the whole Empire was concerned. But Japan was much closer to Australia than to Britain, and the Japanese danger could not be as easily discounted there as it could in Britain. It was inevitable that Australia should insist upon protective measures which, in British eyes, were not of immediate consequence. When, a generation later, the danger feared by Australians loomed over the horizon, and when Britain followed the same strategic policy of concentrating first against a European enemy, it was alliance with the United States and not the defense connection with the British that appeared to Australians to stand between them and a possible Japanese invasion and against actual air attacks. Meanwhile, in 1914–1918, despite the formidable opposition that it had had to overcome in the struggle to be born, the Royal Australian Navy had proved a most valuable strategic asset for the Allied cause.

Dominion Representation in London Fails to Mature

The trend toward colonial naval nationalism had been shown by Borden's public professions and confidential statements about

73. Memorandum by Pearce, April 13, 1914, in Commonwealth of Australia, *P.P.*, 1914, No. 1; Pearce to Denman, May 4, 1914, A.N.L., Denman Papers; E. D. Miller to Denman, June 5, 1914, *ibid.*

a long-term belief in a Canadian navy (which were, however, contradicted by his policy of allowing the Naval Service to wither away), by Australia's jealous call for the use of the Royal Australian Navy in her own interests, and by New Zealand's belated conversion to the principle of a dominion naval division. By way of contrast, new efforts to introduce machinery for central control of military affairs and of imperial defense had some limited success. Bridges's proposal for the attachment of senior dominion officers to integrate dominion armies with the War Office had failed to come to anything. However, junior dominion officers attached to the War Office had served in different sections of the Directorate of Military Intelligence. On April 1, 1912, these officers were brought together in a new Dominions' Section of the Directorate of Staff Duties (S.D. 1), that is to say in the directorate concerned with the organization of the army for war and the co-ordination of staff work. The creation of the Dominions' Section, staffed by dominion officers, was thus designed to co-ordinate the dominion armies for war. A formal section for this work, acceptable to the new government in Canada, seemed an effective way to link dominion military forces with the British Army; and junior officers might serve the War Office's purposes better than seniors who could be more independent of it. The section was to study methods of training and education and strategy and tactics, to supply the C.I.G.S. with information about the dominions, and to correspond with dominion chiefs of staff.[74] On August 26, 1912, the War Office authorized "semi-official" correspondence between the Dominions' Section and dominion authorities to supplement the official correspondence which still passed through the Colonial Office. But in April, 1913, Borden's government disapproved the Australian proposal to open channels of communication that were even more direct. The Canadian government preferred that official communications, other than those on purely routine matters, should continue to pass through the Colonial Office and the governor general's office.[75] Nevertheless, the new Dominions'

74. London *Times*, May 24, 1912.
75. C.O. to Governor General, Aug. 17, 1912, April 10, 1913, P.A.C., R.G. 7, G. 21, No. 270, Vol. 1, Pt. 5 (a).

Section provided a more effective means of handling the increasing volume of military communications between Britain and the dominions.

Another prewar effort to use the Committee of Imperial Defence for the integration of British and dominion effort at a higher level moved more slowly. Borden's statement of intention to have Canada permanently represented on the Committee of Imperial Defence was not followed up until 1914, and despite British pressure to extend the practice, the other dominions continued to shy away from that step because of the difficulty of stationing a minister permanently in London.[76] However, Borden did eventually send a Cabinet minister, George Perley, to act as high commissioner and to discuss defense problems with the British government, especially Canada's participation in the naval defense of the Empire.

Perley's mission has been customarily regarded as the initiation of Canadian representation on the Committee of Imperial Defence, but this is an overstatement. Borden informed the colonial secretary of Perley's presence in London and told him that "if it should be thought desirable by H.M. Government, Mr. Perley should be summoned to attend any meetings of the Imperial Defence Committee which might be held during his visit." [77] The only difference between Perley's attendance and the occasional visits of other dominion ministers in the immediately preceding years was that he went to stay in London for a longer time for the purpose of representing the Canadian government in discussions about defense organizations. Borden's letter to Harcourt shows that he was aware there were no permanent members of the C.I.D. apart from the British prime minister. Furthermore, Perley had no intention of remaining indefinitely as permanent representative on defense matters. Rather, he went to look into the question of the nature of future membership on the Committee for Imperial Defence—whether it should be by a permanent

76. G.B., *Representation of the Self-Governing Dominions on the Committee of Imperial Defence*, Cd. 6560, Cd. 7347; New Zealand, *Parliamentary Debates*, 1914, Vol. 170, p. 437, Oct. 7, 1914; Hunt to Collins, Dec. 17, 1912, A.N.L., Attlee Hunt Papers.
77. Borden to Harcourt, June 6, 1914, P.A.C., M.G. 27, II D 12, Vol. 1.

high commissioner or by a high commissioner with Cabinet rank.[78] It was the outbreak of war with the consequent need for ministerial representation in London to deal with the many problems which ensued that prolonged his stay beyond his expectations. He attended only one meeting of the full C.I.D.—in July, 1914. After the war began, the full committee lapsed and only its subcommittees continued to operate. Most of these dealt with the affairs of the British Isles, and Perley was not a member of any of them.[79] Perley's appointment had not given any greater significance to the word "imperial" in the title of the Committee of Imperial Defence.

Australia carefully watched Borden's attempt to get representation in London. If a Canadian minister were there, Australia might "suffer by comparisons." But the difficulty of distance, and the fact that the C.I.D. was fully realized to be only a technical body, prevented any action. Australia preferred to wait until a new Imperial Conference could attempt to set up some kind of political representation.[80]

Thus, when war came in 1914, the British Empire had not developed the centralized system of imperial defense which had been advocated by many since the first Russian crisis in 1878. Instead, spurred by the darkening international horizon, there had grown up a close degree of integration and co-operation but no form of central organization or of political institutions that might appear to infringe dominion autonomy. No one can say whether imperial defense, had it been attempted, would have been more effective.

78. Perley to Borden, Aug. 8, 15, 1914, *ibid.*
79. Borden to Perley, Cable, Jan. 14, 1915, Perley to Borden, Cable, Jan. 16, 1915, *ibid.*, M.G. 26, H 1(a), Vol. 33; Perley to Borden, Jan. 15, 1915, *ibid.*, R.L.B. 168; Perley to Hankey, Jan. 15, 1915, *ibid.*
80. Collins to Pearce, Oct. 25, 1912, Dec. 3, 1912, A.W.M., Pearce Papers, Bundle 7; Pearce to Collins, Jan. 21, 1913, *ibid.*

15

Commonwealth Defense Co-operation
Matures in War

An Imperial Army?

In conflicts in earlier centuries the manpower of the Empire was dispersed in colonial wars; in 1914–1919 it was concentrated for European or near-European campaigns. Only New Zealand, of all four of the great dominions, had specifically promised in advance to provide an expeditionary force in the event of a general war; [1] but when hostilities became critically imminent, Canada and Australia also offered substantial military aid, and all dominion naval forces were immediately put at the disposal of the Admiralty. Although the quarrel had not been of their making and had developed without their full knowledge, the dominions were automatically at war when Britain made the declaration. South Africa released for duty elsewhere the garrison of British troops that was still in the country despite the fact of union. Within three months of the outbreak of war, the three other dominions had sent expeditionary forces overseas. Britain's naval power insured the safety of the convoys. Totaling 30,000 men from Canada, 20,000 from Australia, and 7,000 from New Zealand, these initial contributions to the British cause were considered in 1914 to be large. Despite the fact that they were recruited largely from civilian life and had so much further to go, the Canadians were in the trenches before Britain's territorial divisions, and the expeditionary forces from Australasia were in

1. Australian arrangements with New Zealand have been said to have constituted an indirect commitment which for political reasons could not be made directly. C. E. W. Bean, *Anzac to Amiens, A Short History of the Australian Fighting Services in the First World War* (Canberra: Australian War Memorial, 1952), p. 25; Bean, *Story of Anzac*, pp. 27–28.

action in Gallipoli before Kitchener's new armies took the field.[2] This achievement compared not unfavorably with Britain's record in sending succor to threatened colonies in centuries past.

The quick response of the dominions showed that in one respect the advocates of imperial defense had been correct: the peoples of the Empire were willing to come to its defense. But Laurier and those who thought like him had always agreed that the colonies would rally to Britain's aid if the danger were real; his opponents' alleged fears that without previous commitment and peacetime centralized control the dominions would be unable to respond adequately in emergency had proved to be unfounded. Although a more vigorous imperial defense program in the prewar years might possibly have brought dominion troops into the field a little earlier, this could hardly be expected when Britain herself was not much better prepared for the scale and kind of war that occurred. Nor is there any reason to be confident that a more fully developed imperial defense organization, particularly one stressing naval centralization as imperial defense enthusiasts urged, would have prevented the war. Even though the Kaiser had noted the rejection of the Canadian Naval Bill with satisfaction, it is unlikely that any dominion action in those years would have altered the tragic drift of events.

These first contributions were, however, to seem a mere trickle by contrast with the flood of men and treasure that the dominions poured out in defense of the Empire as the war dragged on from year to year. From a Canadian population that had been counted at 7,200,000 in the census of 1911, almost 700,000 served with the Canadian Expeditionary Force between 1914 and 1920, most of them with the Canadian Corps on the Western Front. Nearly one-tenth of those who served gave their lives.[3] The voluntary sacrifice of nearly 1 per cent of her total population is stark testimony to Canada's interest in the maintenance of Britain's freedom and of the British connection. The autonomy of do-

2. Col. G. W. L. Nicholson, *Official History of the Canadian Army in the First World War: Canadian Expeditionary Force, 1914–1919* (Ottawa: Queen's Printers, 1962), p. 40; hereinafter cited as *C.E.F.* Charles P. Lucas, *The Empire at War* (London: Oxford University Press, 1923), III, 81.
3. Nicholson, *C.E.F.*, pp. 535, 548; Lucas, *Empire at War*, II, 3, 288.

minions in military matters had thus produced a war effort that could hardly have been bettered by any form of previous imperial defense centralization.

The magnitude of Canada's war effort must not be attributed merely to the fact that Robert Borden, and not Wilfrid Laurier, was prime minister. The Opposition in Canada, as elsewhere, joined with the government in proclaiming loyalty and support for Britain. Crowds in Ottawa, the capital cities of Australia, and Wellington hailed the outbreak of war with the same enthusiasm as those in London, Paris, and Berlin. Only in South Africa, where the Boer War was still a very recent memory, was there any significant dominion resistance to support for Britain in the war; and the revolt of a dissident Boer minority was quickly suppressed by the Boers themselves. This impressive response in the dominions to the call to arms occurred because the German menace, unlike that of the Boers in 1899, appeared to threaten the very heart of the Empire and therefore all its parts. But undoubtedly the fact that the dominions were free to make their own offers spontaneously and voluntarily encouraged a much more wholehearted and persistently determined reaction than if there had been any question of central control or any hint of coercion. That the dominions had not been fully informed about the circumstances leading up to the crisis was ignored or forgotten. What mattered was that there was unanimity in a belief that common Empire interests were endangered. In those circumstances, the military relationship that existed in 1914 was effective.

The manifest unity of the Empire in war, which was acclaimed by the King in a special message,[4] was followed by the rapid introduction of some of the military arrangements that the imperial defense school had long sought. The dominions accepted British over-all strategic direction without question. Strategic planning was the sole responsibility of the British government, which, in the early months of the war, meant by *ad hoc* committees of the British Cabinet. At Britain's behest the dominions

4. Col. A. Fortescue Duguid, *Official History of the Canadian Forces in the Great War, 1914–1919* (Ottawa: King's Printer, 1938), I, 44-45.

undertook local assignments in which they had a special interest, and they consigned their main forces to the theaters of war which the British government designated. Except in the local expeditions, dominion troops were committed to British command and served with larger British formations. Thus, the Canadians training on Salisbury Plain, like the Anzac forces in Egypt, were responsible to British general officers who were in turn responsible to the War Office.[5] On the Western Front, the Canadian and Australian divisions and corps seemed in many respects to be in exactly the same relation to the British commander in chief as were British units.

Some difficulty was experienced in co-ordinating the forces of the dominions with those of Britain because differences still existed in organization or equipment. For instance, the 1st Australian Division did not have the same amount of artillery support at the outset as a British division; and the New Zealand and Australian "division" in Egypt was a peculiar formation with one Australian infantry brigade, one New Zealand infantry brigade, and two mounted brigades (1st A.L.H. Bde. and N.Z.M.R.).[6] Some Canadian equipment was found to be less serviceable than British equipment, especially the Ross rifle which had been adopted a decade earlier because the British Lee-Enfield could not be manufactured in Canada. By 1914 the Ross had become a political sacred cow. When opportunity offered, Canadian soldiers exchanged their Ross rifles for the Lee-Enfields of British casualties in the field. Eventually, the Canadian government agreed to the adoption of the British-type rifle. There was also trouble about other equipment, especially boots. Australian boots were lighter and more comfortable than the British ammunition boot and proved serviceable in the Middle East, only to be found useless in Flanders mud.[7] However, before the war ended, by one means or another, dominion troops had come to be equipped substantially in the same way as British forces, and the appearance of a single imperial army was thereby

5. *Ibid.*, I, 126–127.
6. Lucas, *Empire at War*, III, 79–80; see also Bean, *Story of Anzac*, p. 118.
7. Birdwood to Pearce, Feb. 15, 1917, A.W.M., Pearce Papers, Bundle 5; Birdwood to Pearce, Aug. 20, 1917, *ibid.*

fostered. The prewar program of standardization had indeed been sufficiently effective to permit dominion formations to slip smoothly under British over-all command. The War Office sometimes showed itself unable to make up its mind about what it wanted, as for instance when it vacillated about the question whether the Canadian division should conform to the eight-company battalion of colonial establishments or to the four-company organization of the regular army.[8] Nevertheless, the dominion forces at first readily accepted British direction to bring them into closer conformity.

This dominion willingness to conform tended to make British military leaders assume that the forces from the dominions had been absorbed into the British Army for the duration of the war and could therefore be completely integrated into it. It is untrue that Kitchener threatened the Canadian minister of militia, Sam Hughes, that he would break up the Canadian contingent among British units; and allegations that General Wilson, the British liaison officer at the French G.H.Q., and his friend, General Foch, planned to disperse the 1st Canadian Division when it went to France may have referred only to their proposals for introducing it to operations.[9] But there seems little doubt that the War Office asked Australia to furnish brigades of separate services to be distributed among British formations and that this intention was prevented only by General Bridges' firm reply that Australia was preparing a complete division.[10] The Chief of the Imperial General Staff, General Sir William Robertson, proposed that there should be an imperial army which would be directed in all spheres by the Imperial General Staff.[11] His dream faded, but chiefly because the British Cabinet kept control of British military forces and not because of any reluctance expressed at that time by the dominions. However, Haig believed that the war and

8. Nicholson, *C.E.F.*, p. 38.

9. Duguid, *Official History of Canadian Forces . . .* , I, 126–127. Colonel Nicholson doubts the Kitchener story (*C.E.F.*, p. 35). It was based on a statement made to Colonel Duguid years later.

10. Bean, *Anzac to Amiens*, pp. 26–27.

11. Field Marshal Sir William Robertson, *Soldiers and Statesmen, 1914–1918* (London: Cassell, 1926), I, 174.

its hardships had actually already created an "Imperial Army." [12] Always careful to restrict the loan of British divisions to the French, Haig assumed that he was able to detach dominion divisions freely to other parts of his command.[13] As late as 1918 the Canadian minister for overseas forces, Sir A. E. Kemp, reported that Canadian forces were still afraid that they would be split up in this way and absorbed into British units.[14] At the root of these threats and fears about the dividing up of dominion forces was a British belief that separate organization of the dominion forces should bow to military convenience.

Certain actions or attitudes of some dominion political and military leaders helped to further this illusion of an imperial military structure and an imperial army. General Bridges, who organized the Australian Expeditionary Force, called it "The Australian Imperial Force." [15] Prime Minister Borden talked at first of sending Canadian regiments to enlist as imperial troops in the imperial army with the Canadian government undertaking to provide their equipment, pay, and maintenance.[16]

Major General Sam Hughes, however, had quite different ideas. He refused to call the Canadians an "Imperial" force and chose instead the title "Canadian Expeditionary Force." Yet even he contributed in his own way to the illusion of an imperial army. When he realized that he could not himself command the Canadians in action, he did not insist upon the appointment of a Canadian commander. Instead he sought the best available British officer. When Kitchener recommended a choice from three Canadians serving in the British Army, Hughes refused all of them on the grounds that they were not sufficiently senior and experienced.[17] Once the Canadian government had made its choice of a Canadian Expeditionary Force commander, Kitch-

12. Robert Blake, ed., *Private Papers of Douglas Haig, 1914–1919* (London: Eyre and Spottiswoode, 1952), p. 214.
13. *Ibid.*, pp. 303–304, 305, 319.
14. Kemp to Borden, April 2, 1918, P.A.C., M.G. 26, H 1 (b), Vol. 139.
15. Lucas, *Empire at War*, III, 73. Bridges disliked the word "expeditionary" and preferred "imperial." But "expeditionary" was used for the Australian force in the Pacific and also for the New Zealanders in the Middle East and in France.
16. Borden, ed., *Robert Laird Borden*, I, 452–453.
17. Kitchener to Perley, Aug. 16, 1914, P.A.C., M.G. 27, II D 12, Vol. 1.

ener "designated" its selectee, Major General Sir E. A. H. Alderson, to command the division.[18] The use of the word "designated" suggests that a veil was deliberately drawn over the fact that Canada had made the appointment. The designation of a force commander by the British secretary of state for war served to suggest that the Canadian Expeditionary Force was part of an imperial army.

British officers were indeed often unable to appreciate that, inevitably, dominion forces had a peculiar relationship to the British Army and that dominion governments had special interests that could not be ignored. Thus, the Canadian government was seriously put out during the war by Colonel Edward A. Stanton, the secretary to the governor general. Borden said that Stanton, who had served in "some crown colony or dependency" (he was governor of Khartoum, 1900–1908), believed Canada occupied the "same relative status within the Empire." Regarding himself as "the real ruler of Canada," he was alleged to have sent secret reports on Canadian military matters to the War Office and to have run to the governor general with "silly tales" about military matters in Canada that he did not really understand. English officers serving in the colonies in the past had, of course, frequently been in direct touch informally with the War Office. In Australia, Colonel W. T. Bridges, an Australian officer, had sent "secret" reports based on "tactful" investigations to the British general officer commanding for onward transmission to the War Office. But tactless reports on sensitive politico-military questions could cause a dominion government serious embarrassment. Colonel Stanton was an extreme case, but not without parallel throughout the British forces. The governor general of Canada, the Duke of Connaught, a soldier and a member of the royal family, although very popular in Canada, had no sound understanding of the Dominion's military autonomy and was therefore inclined to commit unconstitutional indiscretions. An earlier secretary, Lieutenant Colonel H. C. Lowther, had gathered impressions about conditions and public opinion in club circles and had presented them in a report for the War Office.

18. Perley to Kitchener, Aug. 29, 1914, *ibid.*; Nicholson, *C.E.F.*, pp. 28–29.

Sir Charles Fitzpatrick, the administrator, after consulting Borden, had refused to sign it. Borden commented, "These professional military men have a remarkable confidence in their own judgment upon matters upon which they may happen to be singularly ill-informed." [19]

It is not surprising therefore that the War Office expected dominion commanders to use the normal military channels of communication through general officers commanding and to approach what it called "colonial authorities" only through its agency. It conceded only reluctantly that General Alderson, when appointed to command the Canadians, could make direct contact with the Canadian authorities. [20] This became the normal pattern for all dominion forces. Thus, General Godley maintained a regular correspondence with Sir James Allen about matters relating to the New Zealand Expeditionary Force, particularly the promotion of senior officers. In British eyes, and to some extent in the eyes of some dominion soldiers, there was a single imperial army which was a homogeneous force under British direction. But in fact the dominion troops served *with* the British Army rather than *in* it and co-operated fully because they shared the same ultimate objective—victory. The degree to which the dominions tolerated British illusions about imperial military centralization was possible only because the war had aroused imperial sentiment. The general will to win, evident on every side, made sectional interests seem petty.

The Appointment and Promotion of Officers

Militia appointments had always been an inexpensive form of political patronage in all the dominions. Possibly it was a result of this practice that the Canadian force arrived in England with an embarrassingly large surplus of officers. [21] But Alderson reported that Canadian officers were "very ignorant and possess

19. Borden to Perley, March 14, 1916, *ibid.*, Vol. 5, p. 142; Borden to Sir George Foster, July 14, 1916, *ibid.*, p. 167; Hutton to Bridges, March 9, 1903, R.M.C., Bridges MSS; Borden, ed., *Robert Laird Borden*, I, 384, 461, 470, II, 603–604.
20. Nicholson, *C.E.F.*, p. 34.
21. *Ibid.*, p. 38.

no power or habit of command. Some of them have got drunk and a few of them have been dismissed for this reason." [22] As Camberley had as yet had only a handful of students from the dominions, lack of experienced officers therefore forced all the expeditionary forces from overseas to rely on British officers for large operational commands and principal staff appointments. Thus, a British officer commanded the Canadian division and, in turn, the Canadian Corps until June, 1917; the important posts of brigadier general, general staff, and of deputy adjutant and quartermaster general of the Canadian Corps were held throughout hostilities by British officers; and the command of the heavy artillery did not go to a Canadian until twenty days before the Armistice.[23] Even at lower levels, few Canadians had sufficient military experience to fit them for appointments like that of G.S.O.I. at divisional headquarters and brigade major. The appointment of British officers to dominion formations was taken as a natural solution to this problem of scarcity of professional experience; but as the war went on the supply of experienced British officers also became inadequate. Canadians worked into such appointments as they gained experience. Sir George Perley, the acting high commissioner, said that senior appointments in Canadian forces on active service ought to be made by the secretary of state for war because "our men are simply part of a great whole." [24] It was generally agreed that the British officers attached to the Canadian forces were of high quality. But this widespread use of British officers had helped to bolster the illusion that there was a single imperial army.

An inevitable result was the common charge that British officers were favored in appointments and promotions. Sam Hughes and Sir Max Aitken, who had an informal brief from the Canadian government to watch over Canadian interests, urged the appointment of Canadians wherever possible. Hughes was most intemperate on the subject. He spoke of the "contemptuousness of

22. Memorandum of points in Gen. Alderson's letter to H.R.H. (returned March 3, 1915), P.A.C., M.G. 26, H 1 (a), Vol. 49.
23. Nicholson, *C.E.F.*, pp. 540–541. The command of the Canadian Royal Artillery and Engineers was held by Canadians from the beginning.
24. Perley to Borden, Jan. 26, 1915, P.A.C., M.G. 27, II D 12, Vol. 3.

some [British] army officers in 1st Division," a criticism that Kitchener indorsed as "extraordinary, even from Hughes." [25] The Canadian minister, while acknowledging that he had no jurisdiction in regard to operational matters, claimed that the Militia Act gave him authority over officer appointments. The matter came to a head when Kitchener requested that J. E. B. Seely, a British politician and former secretary of state for war, should be appointed to command a mixed brigade of Canadian and British cavalry. Prime Minister Robert Borden was as incensed as Hughes because he thought that there were many other men more competent. He declared that the next Canadian mounted command would go to a Canadian.[26] Kitchener did not ease matters by his explanation that his request to appoint Seely had been referred to the Canadian government only through a misunderstanding on the part of his private secretary.[27] He obviously believed that the appointment to the command of a mixed British and Canadian brigade was exclusively his. As it happened, Seely proved to be a successful and popular commander with the Canadians; but Kitchener had been blind to the fact that his appointment would seem objectionable in Canada because British leadership was acceptable only when it was clearly professional and when it met a real need. There was, of course, always difficulty in assessing the fitness and suitability of any individual for command. But in cases where there was doubt, when the War Office tended to lean toward British officers, Canadians naturally favored their own men.

Australian experience was, in the long run, not very different. Nevertheless, General Bridges, who had organized the Australian Expeditionary Force, took the 1st Australian Division to Gallipoli, and its principal General Staff officer was another Australian professional soldier, Major C. B. B. White, the first Australian officer to attend the Staff College course at Camberley. Because Australia had been more willing than Canada to accept British plans for the organization of imperial defense, Bridges

25. Hughes to Kitchener, April 8, 1915, *ibid.*
26. Borden to Perley, Feb. 6, 1915, *ibid.*
27. Perley to Borden, Jan. 26, 1915, *ibid.*

and White were of course well known and highly regarded at the War Office before August, 1914. But neither their experience and qualifications nor their British contacts completely explain why they obtained these operational appointments and were not replaced like the Canadian staff officers who brought the C.E.F. to England. Perhaps the chief reason was that the Australian force was only half as large as the Canadian, and that it served at first in a more remote "colonial" theater where dominion troops formed a greater part of the whole.

But even among the Australians there was a feeling that the British were getting an undue share of the senior appointments. Although some members of the Australian Army Corps objected to the retention in positions of command of "old and inexperienced Australian brigadier generals" after they had brought the troops from Australia,[28] others complained that promotions were kept for British regulars and that Australians were excluded. As a result, the Australian Military Board, on its own initiative, promoted seven Australian colonels serving in the field to brigadier general. The future commander of the Australian Army Corps, Monash, who was one of these, was very much afraid that the British regulars with an eye on their own future careers in the service would succeed in getting the promotions rescinded. Monash wrote to his minister of defense: "Australians here sometimes feel in regard to advancements [that] the idea is that 'no Australian need apply'; the [British] Army clique is very strong here and several appointments for which Australians entertained quite legitimate aspirations have gone to Imperial [i.e., British] officers."[29] The whole incident suggests that when their personal interests were clearly involved, Australians reacted to British appointments much in the same way as Canadians.

The War Office very much disliked dominion promotion of "amateur" generals, and its attitude seemed justified by the experience of the High Command in France which found it very difficult to dismiss dominion generals when it thought them in-

28. Keith Murdoch to Pearce, Sept. 13, 1915, A.W.M., Pearce Papers, Bundle 7.
29. Monash to Pearce, Nov. 18, 1915, *ibid.*

competent in the field.[30] Furthermore, there was some room for doubt about the qualifications of many dominion candidates. Thus, in March, 1916, General Birdwood, the British officer who commanded the Anzac Corps, was of the opinion that no Australian had as yet had enough experience to command a new division then being formed.[31] However, three months later, when the War Office seemed about to make the appointment of the divisional commander without referring it to Australia, Birdwood felt it was his duty to alert the Australian minister of defense.[32] The explanation of Birdwood's seeming change of stance may have been that as he was an officer from the Indian Army and not in with the War Office "clique," he felt no special loyalty to it. But it is also possible that he had by this time learned to appreciate Australia's need to control appointments or that he believed that the Commonwealth would in any case appoint a British officer. Even so, when his own interests were involved, he did not show as much understanding of Australian national pride. Two years later he tried to hang on to the administrative command of the Australian Army Corps along with a British Army command to which he had been promoted.[33] He apparently assumed that since there would be keen competition for the appointment among Australians, it would be better that he should be left in possession of the command. Thus, even a well-intentioned British officer too easily assumed that British appointments to dominion commands were part of the natural order of things.

Active service provided the military experience which the citizen soldiers from the dominions had lacked, and the mass armies of the war inflated demand for staff officers. By the end of the war many colonials held senior appointments. General Godley, the British officer who commanded the N.Z.E.F. throughout the war, noted in his Farewell Order that the fact that British officers on loan to the force had been increasingly re-

30. E.g., General Turner and Brigadier General Ketchen (Blake, ed., *Private Papers of Haig*, p. 140).
31. Pearce to Birdwood, Feb. 4, 1916, A.W.M., Pearce Papers, Bundle 9; Birdwood to Pearce, March 24, 1916, *ibid.*
32. Birdwood to Pearce, June 6, 1916, *ibid.*
33. Hughes to Acting Prime Minister, Cable, June 17, 1918, *ibid.*

placed by New Zealand officers capable of carrying out their duties was "the best possible proof of the disinterested *success* and value of their work." [34] But the Canadian government had come to feel that Canadian officers were not being appointed to staff duties as rapidly as they should be. Haig said the difficulty in training colonials as staff officers was that they did not want to leave their corps.[35] No doubt there was some truth in this statement; fighting men always despise brass hats. But it was also another way of complaining that the Canadians wanted to stay with their own countrymen and not move indiscriminately throughout the army, whereas British officers had no such inhibitions about being employed in colonial units in which they customarily had been employed in the past. Whatever the reason, too few Canadians were given staff training.

In 1917 Sir Robert Borden raised this matter at the Imperial War Cabinet and was told by the C.I.G.S. that it had only recently been brought to his attention.[36] There can be little doubt that part of the reason why staff training was given Canadians so belatedly, and why it was necessary to take up the matter at the highest level, was that many in the War Office thought that staff jobs were the preserves of British regulars who would make a future career in the army. As is made clear in both dominion and British accounts, even when attached British officers were of first-class quality, there still was much chauvinistic hostility directed against them,[37] and this was inflamed by the slowness with which they were replaced by dominion officers. The War Office could always argue that the safety of the dominion troops depended on the military efficiency of the staff and that it alone was the best judge of qualification for staff appointment. Behind such rationalizations there was a false

34. Lt. Col. John Studholme, *New Zealand Expeditionary Force: Record of Personal Services During the War of Officers, Nurses, and First-class Warrant Officers and Other Facts Relating to the N.Z.E.F.* (Wellington: Government Printer, 1928), p. 481.

35. Blake, ed., *Private Papers of Haig*, p. 214.

36. Imperial War Cabinet, Minutes, May 2, 1917, P.A.C., M.G. 27, D 12, Vol. 14.

37. John Laffin, *Digger: The Story of the Australian Soldier* (London: Cassell, 1959), p. 38; Blake, ed., *Private Papers of Haig*, p. 140; William Keith Hancock, *Survey of British Commonwealth Affairs*, I, *Problems of Nationality, 1918–1936* (London: Oxford University Press, 1937), p. 63 n.

premise that there was a single imperial army under British direction and control, and that it followed that British influence over dominion force should be preserved.[38]

Toward a Canadian Army Overseas

The appointment and promotion of officers was one means of securing the integrity and distinctive identity of a dominion's forces. The vigorous interest of Hughes and Aitken in this regard was therefore important, partly to strengthen morale for the general good, but also to insure Canada's control over its own forces for its own purposes as well as for the general interests of the Empire. Despite the fact that a war-inspired imperial spirit had pervaded the Empire and had fostered the concept of a homogeneous imperial army under British command (a concept which the dominion troops themselves shared up to a point), there was paradoxically a firm trend in the opposite direction toward the emergence of dominion forces that were entities in themselves.

There were several powerful reasons for the jealous care with which dominion governments protected their authority. Most important of all was the fact that they inevitably felt responsible for the safety of their troops. An incident arose from this concern when the first New Zealand contingent sailed for the Middle East without convoy. Upon receiving reports that the *Scharnhorst* and *Gneisenau* (seen off the coast of Africa on September 14) were in the vicinity, the dominion government asked that the transports be recalled. The Admiralty insisted there was actually no danger; and the Colonial Office told the New Zealand government bluntly, in terms which angered the ministers, that if the transports did not sail the responsibility was theirs. Resenting this badgering tone, the New Zealand ministers threatened to resign. They were, however, persuaded to accept the Admiralty's judgment; but they were warned immediately afterward by the governor general of Australia, who was worried about the possible effect of serious losses upon Australian public

38. R. B. Bennett, who was Borden's parliamentary secretary, thought Canadian complaints on this score were exaggerated and unjustified (Nicholson, *C.E.F.*, p. 128).

opinion, that the danger was real because the Admiralty itself had stated that the German ships were in New Zealand waters. Amid conflicting advice from the War Office, the Colonial Office, the Admiralty, and the governor general of Australia, the New Zealand ministers again became apprehensive and made renewed appeals for convoy protection. When the Admiralty still refused to provide it, another threat of resignation was needed to induce it to change its mind reluctantly.[39] The official history of the Royal Navy shows that the German cruisers were in fact nowhere in the vicinity.[40] But this story from the "most British" dominion reveals that from the outset of the war dominion governments felt a continuing responsibility for the safety of their overseas forces that could not be lightly brushed aside. Dominion anxiety to retain some degree of control over dominion forces overseas was, therefore, much more than a mere matter of patronage and chauvinism. It was based soundly on the inalienable responsibility of a constitutional government to watch over the safety and well-being of the troops that it dispatched to war, on the need to use these troops for their country's good, and on the necessity for considering local opinion—all factors which the government of the United Kingdom frequently overlooked in regard to dominions, though not at home.

Furthermore, a financial-constitutional principle was also involved. To pay for their war effort, all dominions at first borrowed in the British money market. But Canada soon found it possible to raise ample funds at home.[41] The Canadian government had already decided to bear its full share of the cost of participation in the war by paying, equipping, and maintaining Canadian troops.[42] This meant that it must also be ultimately responsible to the Canadian electors for their employment and their achievements. Other dominions followed this Canadian example insofar as they were able. Although Australia was more

39. W. Downie Stewart, *The Right Honourable Sir Francis Bell* (Wellington: Butterworth, 1937), p. 111; José, *Royal Australian Navy*, p. 153.
40. Julian S. Corbett, *History of the Great War, Naval Operations* (London: Longmans, 1920), I, 144–145, 303.
41. Lucas, *Empire at War*, II, 22.
42. Governor General to C.O., Aug. 2, 1914, in Duguid, *History of the Canadian Forces . . .* , I, 15.

dependent on British loans than Canada, by 1915 the Australian government had also acknowledged its intention to pay for its war effort.[43]

Because accounting separately for the many items of equipment and rations that were supplied through British channels to dominion troops on active service overseas would have been an impossibly complicated business, a rule-of-thumb decision was reached in 1916 that a flat rate per man per day would be charged against the dominion governments.[44] But footing the bill in this way did not remove the ultimate responsibility of the overseas governments. Nor did it mean that dominion governments had surrendered their interest in the administration of matters relating to their troops on active service overseas. When the contingents were originally raised, pay, equipment, and records had naturally been looked after by their respective defense and militia departments. When colonial troops left the dominion, their governments continued to take an active interest in them and, in due course, set up the necessary administrative staffs or departments overseas. Indeed the Canadian minister of militia and defense, Colonel Sam Hughes, crossed to England by a faster ship than the first convoy to supervise personally the arrangements for the establishment of the C.E.F. in England. Although Sir Robert Borden had only allowed him to go on condition that it was understood that he went "on holiday," [45] and although Hughes went in the vain hope of obtaining a military command, his trip helped to establish the principle that the Canadian contingent must have a special relationship to the British War Office and to the British Army.

Hughes established contact with the War Office and, when he left England, appointed Colonel J. W. Carson, a Canadian Militia officer, to be his representative there. Carson acted as liaison between the Canadian Militia Department, the War Office, and the Canadian troops in England. In these tasks he

43. Lucas, *Empire at War*, III, 18; Australia, *P.P.*, *The War: Australian Contingents: Correspondence Concerning the Undertaking by the Commonwealth Government to Bear the Whole Cost*, 1914-15/231, p. 1167.
44. W.O. to C.O., Nov. 4, 1916, P.A.C., M.G. 26, H 1 (a), Vol. 85.
45. Nicholson, *C.E.F.*, p. 34.

was at first aided by Lieutenant Colonel P. E. Thacker, the Canadian member of the Dominions' Section of the Imperial General Staff, or M.O. 8 (Colonial Section) as it was called by this time. Carson's appointment by, and relation to, the Canadian minister of militia and defense meant that liaison and supervision would not become a monopoly of the Dominions' Section as had apparently been vaguely intended by the War Office when the war began. He thus forestalled the possibility of the Canadian Expeditionary Force being brought by that means more closely under War Office control. The section's smallness, and its concern with all the dominions generally, would however probably have made it quite unsuitable for such a task. The Dominions' Section was an early casualty of the war, disappearing from War Office organizational charts early in 1915. M.O. 8 became a censorship department.[46] British control of dominion armies through this section in the War Office thus failed to mature.

Carson sought to command all the Canadian troops in England, reporting to Canada through Perley. He did not achieve this end, but he stayed on in England as Hughes's representative. He was not the only Canadian involved in liaison work and supervision in Britain. When he reported to his minister that the conditions in which the Canadians were encamped on Salisbury Plain were very bad (only the Canadians were in tents and it was alleged that they had been prevented from digging drainage trenches around their tents lest they should interfere with the fox hunting),[47] Borden instructed the acting high commissioner to investigate. Perley replied that he was willing to take up important military matters with the British, but that Hughes had made his own arrangements, Carson's mission had never been explained to him, there was no military man on his staff, and he did not have time to go to Salisbury Plain personally. However, he went on to report on various matters connected with the C.E.F. He said there had been errors in the loading of the transports, and that many of the officers sent with the

46. G.B., W.O., *Allocation of Rooms with Lists of Officials*, Nov. 30, 1914, March 31, 1915.

47. Correspondence arising from Col. Carson's report, Jan., 1915, P.A.C., M.G. 27, II D 12, Vol. 3.

troops were unfit for command and should never have come.[48] Thus, despite the pressure of other war work, the acting high commissioner had a watching brief over the Canadian military forces in the United Kingdom in addition to being the chief official channel of communication with the British government on military as on all other matters. Liaison was thus provided at two levels, but without any formal arrangement for co-ordination. There was considerable overlapping, and the War Office was confused by the situation. All that was really clear was that the Canadian government intended to retain a careful supervision over the C.E.F.

When Lieutenant General Alderson moved with the 1st Canadian Division to France, Brigadier General J. C. MacDougall, a Canadian officer who had been his military secretary, assumed after an interval the command of most of the Canadian troops remaining in England. MacDougall, an officer of the Canadian Permanent Force who at fifty-one was too old for active service, was declared to be "responsible to the Canadian Department of Militia and Defence, Canada, for all appointments to the force, and the training and discipline and all other matters pertaining to and including stores and equipment." As most stores were issued through British Army channels, there was little for MacDougall to do in that regard. Indents were normally submitted in routine fashion by the quartermasters of units.[49] However, this appointment, which overlapped somewhat with Carson's, gave further evidence that the Canadian government was determined to retain direct control over Canadian troops in England as well as to maintain the liaison contacts established by Carson and by Perley.

The Canadian government's concern to watch over the interests of Canadian troops overseas was shown again by the fact that in January, 1915, Borden appointed several unofficial overseas representatives.[50] One of these was Sir Max Aitken, then a Canadian newspaper publisher in London, who was appointed to organize the personnel records of the Canadian forces. The

48. Perley to Borden, Jan. 24, 1915, *ibid.*
49. Duguid, *History of the Canadian Forces* . . . , I, 443.
50. Borden, ed., *Robert Laird Borden*, I, 490.

following September, Aitken was made "General Representative for Canada at the Front"; and in January, 1916, he was authorized to set up a Canadian War Records Section, distinct from the casualty records section, to collate the general historical record of Canada's war effort. Significantly, Aitken at first called himself "the Canadian Eye-Witness." [51] This extraordinary multiplication of the Canadian government's representatives supervising Canadian forces overseas which had been put under British command suggests that the Canadian government, although very anxious and determined to assert its control, was somewhat uncertain of the way in which it should implement its responsibilities.

Military commands do not usually relish attached political representation or interference by their own government, let alone by another. But the Canadian appointments were accepted with as good grace as the War Office could muster. In fact, it began to see that dominion initiative had considerable value. Hughes, who had begun by being a War Office bête noire, was honored in 1916 by appointment as an honorary lieutenant general in the British Army. By that time, however, his irresponsible and inconsistent behavior had made him a political liability in Canada and had insured his dismissal from the Cabinet.

The establishment of the Canadian Corps in September, 1915, with Alderson as its commander, was a recognition of the success of the Canadian division in the field and of Canadian desire to contribute more to the war effort. British corps were rather transitory formations because infantry divisions and other units could be placed under different corps headquarters as the military situation required. The Anzac Corps and Canadian Corps, however, inevitably had greater permanence because of their dominion significance, and this permanence undoubtedly helped to develop their efficiency in the field as well as the *esprit de corps* that came from national sentiment. Although operating under the over-all direction of the British High Command, the dominion corps were henceforward identified as distinctive dominion formations.

51. Nicholson, *C.E.F.*, p. 356.

Behind the Front, administrative necessity was also making for fuller recognition of a distinctive Canadian war organization. The headquarters of Canadian Overseas Military Forces in England, under Sir George Perley, was set up in 1916, allegedly, it has been said, in order to get rid of Hughes.[52] But it is obvious that it was also established to eliminate the confusion that had grown up as a result of the effort to assert Canada's effective control over an overseas military force that had become large. As early as 1915 the Canadian Record and Casualty Department, housed in the Imperial Tobacco Building on the Embankment in London, employed seven hundred persons and was a hive of activity.[53] Retention of administrative control by Canada over Canadian forces including appointments and promotions was thus consolidated, although the operational command and employment of these forces were left to the British High Command. The use of an overseas department headed by a Cabinet minister for this purpose, perhaps unnecessary since it was neither adopted by other dominions nor repeated by Canada in the next war, was a striking reminder that the Dominion's expeditionary force was not merely part of a centralized and homogeneous imperial army but was operating under Canadian supervision.[54]

Lieutenant General A. W. Currie, when Canadian Corps commander, placed great emphasis on the spirit of the corps and on the need to preserve its identity. The British Army, because of a shortage of reinforcements, was compelled at the end of 1917 to reduce the number of battalions in each division from twelve to nine and to increase the number of its armies in the line. The Imperial General Staff proposed in January, 1918, that the Canadian Corps should be similarly reorganized. In order to find a place for the new Fifth Division commanded by Garnet Hughes, son of the former minister of militia and defense, Canadian military headquarters in London, influenced by the Hughes

52. Donald M. A. R. Vince, "The Acting Overseas Sub-Militia Council and the Resignation of Sir Sam Hughes," *Canadian Historical Review*, XXXI (1950), 1–24; *Report of the Ministry: Overseas Military Forces of Canada, 1918* (London: Overseas Military Forces of Canada, n.d.), pp. 1–5.
53. Collins to Pearce, Aug. 18, 1915, Pearce Papers, Vol. 7.
54. Nicholson, *C.E.F.*, pp. 356–357.

clique, favored the reorganization. But this was resisted strenuously by Currie on the grounds that it would destroy the morale and fighting efficiency of the present units in the corps. Currie said that the Canadian Corps was not yet suffering from shortages of reinforcements, that there were not enough experienced Canadian officers to staff the headquarters of an army and of an extra corps, and that there would be difficulty in the future in maintaining the supply of men for a field army. Currie persuaded the Canadian minister for overseas forces to kill the plan.[55]

Currie had refused to support an intrigue to undermine the position of Kemp, the overseas minister, whereby the Canadian organization overseas would have been assimilated to those of Australia and New Zealand. And he refused to take part even though as G.O.C. he would have commanded and administered the Canadian troops in England as well as those in France and would have reported directly to Ottawa. After some preliminary hesitation, however, he favored the establishment of a Canadian section at the British general headquarters in France, the aim of which was to eliminate the need for all questions relating to the appointment, promotion, and posting of Canadian officers to pass through the higher British command with which Canadian forces were serving. This Canadian section at general headquarters began to function in July, 1918.[56] Along with the Canadian Corps in the field and the Overseas Military Council (created in April, 1918) in London, the Canadian section marked high water in Canadian national military development in World War I.[57] The minister and his staff were virtually an Overseas Canadian War Office.

The Australian Imperial Force and Australian Representation in London

Australian war organization overseas was different from the Canadian because the administrative control of the Australian

55. Hugh M. Urquhart, *Arthur Currie* (Toronto: Dent, 1950), pp. 197–203.
56. Nicholson, *C.E.F.*, p. 357; Urquhart, *Arthur Currie*, pp. 214–216.
57. *Report of the Ministry: Overseas Military Forces of Canada*, pp. xi–xii.

Imperial Force (A.I.F.) and of Australian troops in England remained with an operational commander in France, General Birdwood. In July, 1916, the commander in chief, Haig, formally recognized that Birdwood came directly under the Australian Department of Defence in regard to administrative matters.[58] However, Haig's concession of this status accompanied his refusal to permit the creation of an Australian–New Zealand army on the Western Front.[59] The two Anzac Corps, which were authorized in 1916, were rather less permanent formations than the Canadian Corps. Birdwood, following British Army practice, was not as unwilling as the Canadian Corps commander to permit his divisions (which remained under his administrative control) to be used on other parts of the front. After a year's experience of Australian divisions being used piecemeal in this way, however, the Australian government requested formally through the governor general and the Colonial Office that all its divisions should operate in one corps under Birdwood in order to give effect to what it called "the national feeling." [60] This was achieved in November, 1917, when Haig suddenly yielded the point and five Australian divisions were concentrated under Birdwood in the Australian Corps which took the place of his old First Anzac Corps.[61]

The Canadians had always argued that separation undermined their morale; and Birdwood believed that his Australians fought "30% better" side by side with their compatriots.[62] Even the British, when not hard-pressed by reverses to undertake makeshift regrouping, were not unaware of the morale value of dominion national sentiment. Godley's II Anzac Corps, including the New Zealanders, became the XXII British Corps. The New Zealand division, which had formed part of the II Anzac Corps, remained with Godley, who was also the administrative commander of the New Zealand Expeditionary Force. Thus, except for the South Africans, for whom dispersal among British units

58. Birdwood to Pearce, July 4, 1916, A.W.M., Pearce Papers, Bundle 9.
59. Birdwood to Pearce, July 14, 1916, *ibid.*
60. Governor General to C.O., July 31, 1917, *ibid.*
61. Birdwood to Pearce, Nov. 5, 1917, *ibid.*, Bundle 5; see Bean, *The Australian Imperial Force in France,* V, 12–13.
62. Birdwood to Plumer, Sept. 3, 1917, *ibid.*, Bundle 9.

was preferable because heavy losses to a single South African formation might have had serious political consequences at home,[63] the dominions all came to secure, though in different ways, the maximum possible cohesion of their forces at the front despite their commitment to British over-all command. That they were not afraid of the possible consequences was a sign of their national maturity as well as of their devotion to the cause.

The typically different Australian approach to the problem of liaison with the British after the Gallipoli tragedy was an attempt to secure the admission of a senior Australian officer into the councils of the War Office—"right in the middle of the spider's web that was spinning out its thread of death," as Prime Minister Billy Hughes put it. Hughes put the proposal to the C.I.G.S., Field-Marshal Robertson, who was shocked that the officer whom Hughes proposed to send as the Australian representative to the War Office was a militia major; he was even more shocked at the alternative which Hughes offered: that the major should come as a civilian. Hughes countered with, "Then I will make him a general"; and he later alleged that the officer appointed, General Anderson, proved to be acceptable to Robertson chiefly because he had a soldierly figure, stood erect, and had a close-cropped military mustache.[64]

Hughes said that Anderson was a great success. But he had originally been selected because, as a civilian, he would be able to stand up to the soldiers in the War Office better than would another soldier.[65] Anderson was instructed from home that he was subordinate to no one in England but the high commissioner.[66] A year later, however, the Australian government was once again trying to get a senior officer into the War Office.[67] It seems, then, that Anderson may not have been entirely successful, perhaps because he was no longer a civilian. Another complication was that the senior Australian officers in London had become heavily

63. Imperial War Cabinet, Minutes, June 14, 1918, P.A.C., M.G. 26, H 4 (a), Vol. 395.
64. W. M. Hughes, *Policies and Potentates* (Sydney: Angus & Robertson, 1950), p. 156.
65. Hughes to Pearce, May 24, 1916, A.W.M., Pearce Papers, Bundle 3, Folder 3.
66. Hughes to Pearce, June 8, 1916, *ibid.*
67. Birdwood to Pearce, July 30, Aug. 28, Nov. 9, 1917, *ibid.*, Bundle 9.

committed with administrative duties, had come into conflict with each other over overlapping functions, and had intrigued to take over the administration of the A.I.F. from the corps commander in France. A place in the War Office would, it was believed, strengthen the hand of those who were ambitious for this appointment. Birdwood, the A.I.F. commander, naturally opposed their schemes.[68] Not until Monash was appointed director general of repatriation and demobilization in England were these disputes ended. Monash then became, as he had forecast earlier, "the sole representative of the Australian government in relations with the British government relating to the war affairs of Australia that are not purely political." [69]

In June, 1918, at the time when Birdwood was appointed to command the Fifth British Army, it was proposed that there should be an Australian army in the field. Birdwood recommended the plan to Pearce, but nothing more was heard of it.[70] Pearce was, at that time, arranging for Monash to succeed Birdwood in command of the A.I.F. as well as of the corps. However, *The Official History of Australia in the War of 1914–1918* states that had the war continued until 1919, there would have been both Canadian and Australian armies on the Western Front.[71] The history of the dominions' struggle to maintain the identity of their own forces under the operational and administrative command of their own officers, suggests that if there had been dominion armies in the field, they would have been commanded by their own generals and not by British general officers.

Force-Commander Communications with Dominion Governments

It is a cardinal sin in Britain for officers in the regular military forces to communicate with politicians. But in militias the same

68. Birdwood to Pearce, March 12, 1918, *ibid.;* [Pearce] to Mr. Watt, Aug. 29, 1918, *ibid.*
69. Monash to his wife, Aug. 23, 1918, A.W.M., Monash Letters, II, 446.
70. Birdwood to Pearce, Aug. 6, 1918, A.W.M., Pearce Papers, Bundle 9.
71. Ernest Scott, *The Official History of Australia in the War of 1914–1918*, IX, *Australia During the War* (Sydney: Angus & Robertson, 1936), 750–751.

rules cannot apply. In dominion militias, and also in the expeditionary forces sent overseas, many of the officers were themselves politicians. Inevitably they remained in contact with their political friends and with the militia department. General Alderson complained to the governor general of Canada that the Canadian officers who were surplus to establishment in the 1st Canadian Division in England believed they could appeal the disposal of Alderson's decisions over his head to the minister of militia and defense.[72] There was too much politics in the C.E.F., and this was dangerous for discipline and morale. Similarly, as we have seen, Monash wrote to the minister of defense in Australia when he feared the War Office would endeavor to revoke his promotion to brigadier general.[73]

To many British regular officers, direct communication between a dominion force commander and his government constituted a similar breach of the code of officer behavior. However, as has been said, General Alderson, although a British regular officer, realized from the first that he must establish direct contact with the Canadian Militia Department. His Canadians were not mercenaries, recruited like the Germans of the Revolutionary period and paid for by Britain, nor were they like the 60th or Royal Regiment of Foot which had been raised by the British in the American colonies and which was retained on the foreign establishment of the British Army from 1755 to 1824. They were Canadians raised in Canada at Canadian expense. That situation and the need to encourage continued Canadian support made it imperative that he inform the Canadian government directly about all matters relating to the condition and safety of his force. In so doing he demonstrated that the dominion forces had a special relationship to the British Army and to the British command even though they served with it for operational purposes.

When instructing him to keep in touch after his appointment to command the Australian Corps, the Australian defense min-

72. Memorandum of points in Gen. Alderson's letter to H.R.H., returned March 3, 1915, P.A.C., M.G. 26, H 1 (a), Vol. 49.
73. See above, p. 472.

ister, Senator Pearce, told Monash that his predecessors, Bridges and Birdwood, had written him regular "private and personal letters to deal with matters which cannot be the subject of official correspondence." [74] This was perhaps a hint that a force commander was expected to report on matters concerning the force, even if they implied criticism of the employment of their troops by the High Command. Monash agreed to report to Pearce but explained that he had not done so previously when he was a divisional commander because he had not wanted to embarrass Birdwood, the corps commander. Three years of war since he had written about his own promotion had apparently taught him something of the niceties of military behavior regarding communication over a superior's head or behind his back. At this time, Monash was in operational command of the Australian Corps, but Birdwood had not yet yielded the administrative command of the A.I.F. and was in fact hoping to keep it. It is noticeable that Monash assumed that this punctiliousness did not apply to the force commander himself who was in a special relationship to the Australian government, but apparently he had doubts about the propriety of communication by the senior commander in the field. It may be that, as a potential A.I.F. commander, he did not want to encourage a practice of communication by subordinates. Monash therefore obtained the A.I.F.'s commander's consent to his correspondence with Pearce. [75]

Currie always assumed that he was under Haig's orders for operational purposes only and that in all matters of administration he was responsible to the Canadian government directly. When the Overseas Headquarters was set up he apparently did not stop communicating with Ottawa also, though on a considerably reduced scale. [76] Inevitably there were areas when these loyalties overlapped. In his dispute with the Canadian Overseas Headquarters about the War Office's proposal to reorganize the Canadian Corps, Currie obtained the support of Haig, who said

74. Pearce to Monash, June 20, 1918, A.W.M., Pearce Papers, Bundle 7.
75. Monash to Pearce, June 21, Oct. 3, 1918, *ibid.*, Bundle 9. Pearce said that he did not succeed in establishing with Monash the same kind of intimate relationship he had had with Birdwood (information from Warren Perry).
76. Urquhart, *Arthur Currie*, p. 218.

that if any change were made, he would insist that Currie should command the new Canadian Army in the field.[77] But a little earlier, when Haig heard that Currie had reported to Sir Edward Kemp, the overseas minister, that the commander in chief had requested the transfer of some Canadian divisions to British command to help stem the German breakthrough in March, Haig wrote in his diary (without any contradicting comment) that General Horne thought Currie was "suffering from a swollen head." [78] Some weeks later, the Canadian minister of militia, on a visit to the front, raised the matter with Haig and was, in the commander in chief's own words, "shut up" by being told that Currie's protests had kept the Canadians out of serious fighting at a critical time. The charge was not entirely accurate. Currie's Corps headquarters had been left without divisions under its command for less than twenty-four hours before it was made operational again as a result of his protests; but different problems actually had kept out of the line the Canadian divisions that had been detached from the corps for service elsewhere.[79]

What Haig apparently objected to, however, was Currie's appeal to politicians for support. He himself on an earlier famous occasion had had no scruples about intriguing through King George V to get his commander in chief, French, dismissed when he thought him incompetent. But now he found political interference, especially that of Lloyd George, unbearable. To have the interference of dominion politicians added was, for Haig, the last straw. He did not have to conceal his impatience with Canadian politicians, as he must with Lloyd George. He could treat them with the contempt which he thought politicians deserved. Hence, he was neither courteous, nor honest, in his reactions.

Haig was able to take this attitude freely because Canadian politicians could not dismiss him. But he was wrong in believing that they had no right to intervene and also in his failure to explain properly the military reasons for the regrouping of the

77. *Ibid.*, p. 202.
78. Blake, ed., *Private Papers of Haig*, pp. 208, 303–304.
79. *Ibid.*, p. 319; Nicholson, *C.E.F.*, pp. 379–380.

Canadian division. The fact that the regrouping was rescinded so quickly makes one wonder whether it had been as necessary as Haig had held. Haig's feelings about politicians blinded him to the true position of a Canadian force commander and to the nature of the force's relations with the British Army, a subject on which he had never at any time shown himself to be thoroughly instructed.

The Effects of the Independence of Dominion Forces

The independence of the dominion forces, in all except operations, helped them to take up independent positions even in matters that affected operations. Thus, they at times resisted service under senior British officers whom they distrusted or thought incompetent. The R.A.M.C. in Gallipoli was the only service that had a joint British-Australian unit. The Australians demanded the recall of its commanding officer who, they said, lived in comfort on the island of Mudros while his incompetence endangered lives. The Australians were convinced that this man only kept his job because "professional soldiers stick together through thick and thin." [80] In medicine the British were not able to rely on their professional military superiority over the amateur soldiers from the dominions as they could easily do in other fields. In another case that involved purely professional military considerations and concerned operations directly, Currie protested against being placed under Gough, the commander of that Fifth British Army that was to buckle under the German attack in March, 1918. Some British divisional commanders had apparently also expressed the hope that they would not be put under Gough; but Haig had not been influenced;[81] and there is no evidence that any except the Canadians ever got their way. However, during the winter of 1917–1918, the four Australian divisions at the request of the commander of the Australian Corps were transferred to a quiet section of the front in order to

---

80. Keith Murdoch to Andrew Fisher, Sept. 23, 1915, A.W.M., Pearce Papers, Bundle 7.
81. Nicholson, *C.E.F.*, p. 312; Blake, ed., *Private Papers of Haig*, p. 272.

avoid heavy losses and to conserve the corps for operations in 1918.[82]

A degree of independence also permitted the dominion forces to experiment more freely, even in operational matters that came under direct British command. Thus, Currie, the Canadian Corps commander, placed special emphasis on intensive artillery fire before and during an attack across no man's land; in addition to laying down a heavy barrage in front of the advancing infantry, the Canadians paid much attention to the counter-battery role of silencing the enemy guns and preventing them from ranging on the exposed attackers. It was claimed that Canadian counter-battery work equaled, and perhaps excelled, any other on the Western Front.[83] The Canadian Corps also went in for more defensive barbed wiring, which some British officers despised even as late as 1918. Borden, for instance, told the Imperial War Cabinet that a British officer had told Currie that wiring sometimes took second place in the British Army to the building of officers' tennis courts behind the lines. The Canadian Corps put up nearly ten times as much wire as neighboring British corps in the line.[84]

This information was presented to the Imperial War Cabinet by Prime Minister Borden. When the Imperial War Cabinet met to discuss the serious situation caused by the German breakthrough in 1918, Borden sent for Currie and ordered him to tell him the truth, as far as he understood it, about the occurrences of the past few months. Borden then related some of Currie's statements to the Cabinet.

He said that Currie had told him the Germans would not have broken through if the defenses everywhere had been prepared like the Canadian lines—or at all events they would have been stopped at an early stage. He claimed that (although there had been experiments with the concentration of machine gun fire at Gallipoli and in France and although a machine gun corps had

82. Charles E. W. Bean, *The Australian Imperial Force in France . . . 1918* (Sydney: Angus & Robertson, 1937), V, 12–13.
83. Urquhart, *Arthur Currie*, pp. 194–195.
84. Borden, "Memorandum 15 June 1918, Prepared for Speech to Imperial War Cabinet on June 13 and Expanding Some Points Made Then," P.A.C., M.G. 26, H 4 (a), Vol. 395.

been formed), the British still dispersed their machine guns among battalions without adequate co-ordination. The Canadian Corps had now organized its machine guns in companies as tactical units which, he declared, had proved more effective.[85] British machine gunners had indeed had great difficulty in over-coming G.H.Q. opposition to reorganization; and there is some reason to believe that Canadians had pioneered the develop-ments.[86] The British did not adopt this Canadian system until November when the war was almost over.[87] Borden also quoted Currie as saying that the young men on Haig's staff had recom-mended a year earlier that ten corps commanders should be replaced, but that Haig had weakly kept them on during the winter and had only relieved them about the time the German offensive began.

The official histories reveal that the British were well aware an attack was imminent;[88] but Borden said that three days before the Germans attacked, the chief intelligence officer had tipped Currie off not to expect an offensive.[89] Currie had found British intelligence reports to be so misleading in the past, however, that when he read the signature on these, he put them in the waste-paper basket without reading them.

For some time before Currie was called to report to Borden and through him to the Imperial War Cabinet, he had been severely critical of the performance of the British Army, both privately in his diary and also in conversation with General Pershing.[90] Haig had come to hear about Currie's criticisms and resented them. Currie's opinions, which Borden now passed on to the Imperial War Cabinet, were perhaps provoked by the events of

85. Imperial War Cabinet, Minutes, June 13, 1918, *ibid.*
86. C. D. B. S. Baker-Carr, *From Chauffeur to Brigadier* (London: Benn, 1930), tells the British story without reference to Canadian experiments. Canadian claims are expressed in Larry Worthington, *Amid the Guns Below: The Story of the Canadian Corps, 1914–1919* (Toronto: McClelland and Stewart), pp. 11–20, as obtained from Brigadier General Raymond Brutinel, commander of the Canadian Machine Gun Corps.
87. Nicholson, *C.E.F.*, p. 383.
88. Brig. Gen. James E. Edmonds, *History of the Great War . . . : Military Operations, France–Belgium, 1918* (London: Macmillan, 1922), I, 103–113. This was probably a whitewash.
89. Borden, Memorandum, June 15, 1918, P.A.C., M.G. 26, H 4 (a), Vol. 395.
90. Nicholson, *C.E.F.*, p. 380 n.

the previous March and April when Haig had detached divisions from his command and had then made misleading statements about the effect of Currie's protests. This must have severely strained Currie's loyalty to the British High Command. But the significant thing about the criticisms is not so much their origin or their content, the accuracy of which it would be difficult to establish, but rather the fact that they were uttered with impunity and that they could be reported to the British Cabinet. Such a thing would, of course, have been entirely impossible if the Canadians had been fully part of an imperial army.

Haig complained more than once that the colonials looked upon themselves as "junior allies." The secretary of state for war, the Earl of Derby, warned him that they used "the analogy of the Portuguese" for their relationship to the British Army, and he added, "we must look upon them in the light in which they wish to be looked upon rather than the light in which we would wish to do so." Haig said that they regarded themselves as "not part of his army" and "not as citizens of the Empire." [91] He did not understand the position which Borden had explained to Lloyd George, namely that the dominions "fought in the war on the principle of the equal nationhood." [92] This was a concept that was altogether too subtle and complex for his narrow soldier's mind, and indeed for the British concept of Empire at that date.

The Reputation of Dominion Forces in the Field

The expeditionary forces from the various dominions, although fighting with the British Army in World War I and although integrated with it for training and operational purposes, were not part of it administratively. This relative independence fostered the fuller development of distinct national characteristics and marked off the colonials from British soldiers and from each other. Kitchener once astonished Lloyd George by "making jest

91. Derby to Haig, Nov. 2, 1917, in Blake, ed., *Private Papers of Haig*, p. 266; Haig's diary quoted by Nicholson, *C.E.F.*, p. 381.
92. [Borden], Memorandum sent to Lloyd George, April 26, 1917, P.A.C., M.G. 26, H 1 (c), Vol. 163.

and merriment" at the expense of the Territorials as amateur soldiers.[93] After two years of war, dominion forces, which some in the War Office had similarly earlier belittled because they were not composed of professionals, had earned a high reputation for their fighting qualities in battle. Even at the outset of the war, the physique and intelligence of the colonial private soldiers had attracted attention. A Canadian regimental historian claimed that as early as 1915 the British had come to realize that Canadians "were most excellent soldiers," that their artillerymen (especially the "heavies") were the equal of British artillerymen, and that their engineers were superior to British engineers.[94] Lloyd George stated that he believed the dominion forces may have turned the tide in 1915.[95] By the end of the war, when all the Allied armies were largely composed of civilians, Canadian officers (who had originally been criticized even more severely than the men) were acknowledged as being worthy of their fellow countrymen. Some amateurs from the dominions had succeeded in rising faster and further than any British amateur soldier and were pushing at the door to the highest command because they did not have to face as much competition from regulars.

British civilian leaders and critics, doubtful about the ability of their own military leaders, made a point of praising the generals and troops from the dominions. Lloyd George said that the Germans always expected trouble wherever they identified the Canadians; and G.H.Q., when it called them in to try to regain the initiative lost at Passchendaele and also, assisted by British troops, to capture the apparently impregnable Vimy Ridge, had tacitly acknowledged that the Canadians had to be regarded as elite shock troops. By 1918 the British authorities frequently

93. David Lloyd George, *War Memoirs* . . . (6 vols.; Boston: Little, Brown, 1933–1937), I, 341.
94. J. A. Currie, *The Red Watch: With the First Canadian Division in Flanders* (Toronto: McClelland, 1916), p. 183. Currie added that the C.E.F. received relatively little help from the British Army in training, but that, on the contrary, Canadian officers and N.C.O.'s were borrowed to help train Kitchener's new armies, a statement the inaccuracy of which shows the extent of Canadian chauvinism but does not entirely undermine the other opinions quoted in the text.
95. Lloyd George, *War Memoirs* . . . , IV, 3.

borrowed competent Canadian officers to occupy responsible technical places in their forces.[96] In the last months of the war Anzac troops and Currie's Canadians made up almost three-quarters of the British forces who smashed the Germans before Amiens on August 8 and broke the lines that had held so long, thus beginning the advance that brought victory.[97]

The dominions' hard-won military prestige in 1917 and 1918 was a very real thing. It is true that this fighting reputation was earned partly because dominion corps possessed more homogeneity and more permanence than British corps and by the end of the war were also somewhat larger. The Canadian Corps was practically as big as the average British army, which normally included two British army corps. It is also true that this reputation had been won mainly in conditions of warfare on the Western Front that were strange to the British regulars and did not call for much of the same professional expertise that open warfare required, and that it was at a time when Britain had been reduced to the use of whole battalions of low-category men. Yet there is also no doubt that this reputation was based on the natural qualities of the men from overseas and on their growing national pride which had been fostered by independence in administration and even in conducting military operations in the field.

Although the British High Command was irked because it found difficulty in breaking in dominion divisions quickly in emergency because of their national sentiment, in the long run this deficiency was amply offset by the benefit that accrued because these young nations had been able to develop their own individuality. The vital force of dominion national feeling was at least as important as imperial sentiment, though the latter had been cited more often as the source of the tremendous military effort exerted by the dominions.

Political and military leaders in the dominions were fully, perhaps arrogantly, conscious of the dominions' contribution to victory and were inclined to exaggerate the superiority of their

96. Kemp to Borden, Feb. 24, 1918, P.A.C., M.G. 26, H 1 (a), Vol. 96.
97. Charles E. W. Bean, *Two Men I Knew, Bridges and . . . White* (Sydney: Angus & Robertson, 1957), p. 177.

forces. Borden told the Imperial War Cabinet in June, 1918, that the Canadian Corps was "probably the best organized and most effective unit of its size in the world today." He also said, "Currie [is] . . . the ablest Corps Commander in the British Forces; more than that I believe he is at least as capable as any Army Commander among them." [98] Currie's biographer alleges that Lloyd George told him in 1934 that he had been so impressed with Currie's ability that he had had him in mind as a likely commander in chief if a change in that appointment had had to be made.[99]

The Australians had gained similar prestige, in fact even more with G.H.Q. Shortly before the armistice, Monash sent Pearce full reports of Australian operations and successes in the past six and one-half months. He commented:

This record of the performance of my five Divisions and Corps Troops has not been surpassed in the whole annals of War. . . . We ourselves are under no delusion in entertaining the belief that, speaking both absolutely and relatively, the work of the Corps was the dominating factor, firstly in converting the enemy from an offensive to a defensive attitude; next in compelling him to seek refuge in the Hindenburg Line from which he could attempt to reorganize his resources; and thirdly in forcing him out of the Hindenburg Line and into a situation which is compelling him to sue for peace. I am quite aware that other troops of the Imperial Forces helped materially in all this, but I am able to assert without contradiction that the performance of the Australian Corps, whether measured by the standard of prisoners captured, territory re-occupied, villages conquered, or the number of enemy divisions engaged and defeated, far transcends the performances of any similar body of troops on the Western Front.[100]

In his *War Memoirs*, Lloyd George says Monash would have been a potential commander in chief, with Currie as his Chief of the General Staff, if Haig could have been dismissed.[101]

Nevertheless, dominion leaders believed that these qualities and this military excellence were not widely known in Britain

98. Borden, Memorandum, June 15, 1918, P.A.C., M.G. 26, H 4 (a), Vol. 395.
99. Urquhart, *Arthur Currie*, p. 227.
100. Monash to Pearce, Nov. 5, 1918, A.W.M., Pearce Papers, Bundle 7.
101. Lloyd George, *War Memoirs* . . . , VI, 356. Sir Basil Liddell Hart says that Monash had impressed Lloyd George more favorably than had Currie.

at the time. Monash felt that not enough credit was given where credit was due. He told Pearce, "As you will no doubt learn to realize sooner or later, there has, to a large extent, been a conspiracy of silence on the part of the English Press as to the decisive part played by the Australian troops in the stirring events of the recent past." [102] An Australian historian has claimed that reports of the dominions' achievements were being discounted on the grounds that they were favored by their publicity arrangements. Prime Minister Hughes, discovering that the Australian part in the offensive was not known, and seeking to strengthen his hand to gain political recognition for Australia, invited journalists to visit the battlefield as guests of the Australian government.[103] The root of the matter was probably neither a conspiracy of silence nor skepticism about dominion news reports, but simply the fact that the British press and public, like the British government and soldiers, preferred to think of a single imperial effort. When Canadians complained about the loss of their identity by being called "British," they were asked incredulously, "What objections do Canadians have to being called British?" [104] Some Canadians did, indeed, like to think that they were British as well as Canadian, but most men in the dominion forces had outgrown the anonymity that comes when identity is submerged within the family. They were no longer prepared to be billed in the walk-on parts and crowd scenes offered by British leaders when they knew that they had played leading roles.

What was most important about the growth of dominion military autonomy and competence was the fact that dominion governments now could insist that these developments must be accompanied by a greater share in the running of the war and the making of the peace. The struggle to secure these things led to international recognition of the dominions as independent states and to the unique structure of the future British Commonwealth. Although in common with the other victors the domin-

102. *Ibid.*
103. Scott, *Australia During the War*, pp. 750–751; see also W. J. Sowden, *The Roving Editors* (Adelaide: W. K. Thomas, 1919).
104. Currie to Borden, Nov. 26, 1918, P.A.C., M.G. 27, II D 18, Vol. 21.

ions neglected the sword after the war, and although they looked forward to a world in which peace could be achieved without reliance upon arms, their achievements and their potentialities in war were the basis of their future political claims. Their independent status within the British Commonwealth was born, not in the halls of Versailles, but on the beaches at Gallipoli and in the mud of France and Flanders.

The Dominions and the Imperial Navy

The main case of the protagonists of imperial defense before World War I had rested upon the need for a common naval organization and strategy for the British Empire because "the seas are one." Although the decisive sea battle which they confidently predicted did not occur, the value of control of the seas was demonstrated by the unchallenged movement of colonial troops to the scene of military operations. The importance of sea power appeared to have been vindicated by the Allied blockade, and the belief of its proponents in unity of command in war had clearly been justified by the need for close co-operation in the struggle against the U-boats.

When war began in 1914 and all dominion naval forces were put under the command of the Admiralty, the battle cruiser *H.M.S. New Zealand,* provided by New Zealand, was already part of the Royal Navy; Canada and South Africa had few vessels, and they were old and small; only Australia had very much to contribute. Even though put under Admiralty control, the immediate function of the Australian Squadron was not prewar concentration against the main fleet of the enemy as oversimplified imperial defense theory had postulated, but the destruction of the marauding cruisers in the Pacific that threatened Australasian seaborne trade and might interfere with the sailing of troopships to Europe. On this objective the Australian government and the Admiralty saw eye to eye. Centralization of control therefore raised no conflict of interest. In the preliminary disposition of the ships, the Australian Navy Board suggested to Vice Admiral George E. Patey, commanding the Australian fleet in

H.M.A.S. Australia, that *H.M.A.S. Melbourne* should join him and be replaced at her preliminary war station, Fremantle, by a smaller vessel. Patey accepted this suggestion and acted upon it immediately, subject to future Admiralty confirmation.[105] The possibility of conflicting instructions which this incident suggests was further complicated by the fact that Patey also acted differently from Admiralty instructions when he himself thought the occasion warranted him to do so. However, the destruction of the enemy squadrons, and also of the German cruiser *Emden* when *Sydney* left the Anzac convoy to move to the kill at the Cocos Islands, eliminated the enemy naval threat to the southern dominions for the rest of the war and removed further danger of a conflict of interests between the Admiralty and the Australian Naval Board, and therefore over command of the Royal Australian Navy. Meanwhile, the success of the Australian battle-cruiser had established the prestige of the fledgling Australian navy.

When Canada wished to give naval aid early in the war, Churchill, no doubt relishing the opportunity to point up the lesson that Canada had rejected his advice on imperial defense, said that ships took too long to build and Canada should therefore concentrate her efforts on the army.[106] The First Lord of the Admiralty had apparently neither forgotten Canada's recent refusal to supply battle cruisers nor realized how long it would take to defeat Germany. However, Canada's shipyards were soon hard at work building small naval vessels for Britain; and 1,700 Canadian volunteers were recruited into the Royal Navy Canadian Volunteer Reserve and were sent to Britain for service with the Royal Navy. There was at first no demand for elaborate naval defenses in Canadian waters, but in 1916, when the submarine menace seemed about to reach across the Atlantic, the Admiralty called upon Canada to increase the number of patrol vessels and to supply a commander. After at first reminding the Admiralty that British policy had reduced Canada's naval potential, the government in Ottawa relented and began to increase

105. Australia, *P.P.*, 1914–1915, Vol. 5, 151/1914–1915, 1169.
106. J. E. Masten Smith to Perley, Oct. 9, 1914, P.A.C., M.G. 27, II D 12, Vol. 1.

its flotilla of coastal patrol ships. In 1917, as the submarine menace worsened, the Admiralty ordered ships from Canadian shipyards. It subsequently asked Canada to man some of these new vessels for service in Canadian waters, but this now seemed impossible since all experienced naval men had long ago gone overseas and naval recruits had been sent to England for basic training. However, with British aid, the problems were solved.

By the end of the war the anti-submarine flotilla of the North American coast numbered over a hundred vessels, of which twenty-nine belonged to the Canadian Naval Service. It had nearly two thousand officers and ratings and was commanded by a former Royal Navy officer, Captain Walter Hose of the Canadian Naval Service.[107]

This east coast patrol service was a successful venture in Commonwealth co-operation. As the official historian of the Royal Canadian Navy has said, "The Admiralty prescribed the general policy, which was carried out by officers responsible to the [Canadian] Department of the Naval Service. The Admiralty on the whole acted with restraint and tact, and the Canadian Service cheerfully accepted its subordinate role." Canada knew full well that it had neither the organization nor the experience to do more. But, said Tucker, "the east coast patrols and their organizations now seem like the first run of a play which was to be revived many years later in the same theatre during the Second World War." [108]

The question of the future structure (i.e., design) of the Empire's naval organization was raised at the Imperial War Conference in 1917 by Sir Joseph Ward of New Zealand, who said that there had been no direction on this subject from the Admiralty since 1909 when each dominion had been left to do what it thought best. Ward believed that on the basis of the experience of the war a decision should be made whether there should be one navy or separate navies. In any case, the dominions would want a voice in control. He therefore introduced a resolution recognizing the importance of unity for strategic control and of

107. Foster to Borden, March 21, 1917, P.A.C., M.G. 26, H 1 (a), Vol. 69; Tucker, *Naval Service of Canada*, I, 222, 246–253.
108. Tucker, *Naval Service of Canada*, I, 253–255.

retention of administrative control of its own forces by each of the contributing dominions. The Admiralty was requested to present a plan for future imperial naval organization.

Borden agreed that the navy was especially important in the defense of the Empire but suggested an amendment to omit reference to strategic control. The prime minister of New Zealand, Massey, supported him. He complained that New Zealand's interests had not been sufficiently looked after by the Admiralty without New Zealand's reminders and that "New Zealand deserved better treatment." The Admiralty representative then said that nothing could be done at present, but that it was desirable to know what the dominions would provide in the way of ships. Ward and Massey, however, now agreed in retorting that the plan which the Admiralty was to produce should be based on the strategic needs of the Empire, rather than on what the dominions would provide. The secretary of state for India, Austen Chamberlain, announced that India's great military contribution in the war meant that she could provide nothing for the navy, but that she would still expect protection by the Royal Navy.[109] The resolution, with Borden's amendment, was then carried.

Admiral Sir Rosslyn Erskine Wemyss, First Sea Lord, brought to the Imperial War Cabinet the Admiralty's plan drawn up in accordance with this resolution. The plan proposed a single imperial navy under the control of "an Imperial Naval authority" both in peace and in war, with ships and personnel freely and fully transferable and interchangeable. This imperial naval authority would be responsible for naval strategy, equipment, promotions, appointments, and training. Local naval boards, set up in each dominion to work with the Admiralty, would control local establishments, dockyards, training colleges, construction, and repairs. Each dominion would decide its own share of the cost. The nature of the proposed imperial naval authority was not described but was left for further discussion.[110]

109. Imperial War Cabinet, 1917, Transcript of Proceedings on Naval Defence, March 28, 1917, P.A.C., M.G. 26, H 1 (b), Vol. 136.
110. R. Wemyss, Admiralty Memorandum, May 17, 1918, P.A.C., M.G. 26, H 1 (a), Vol. 119.

When presenting the memorandum, Wemyss had emphasized that the Admiralty, although aware of its political implications, had looked at the matter from the point of view of naval executive officers. The present war had impressed them with the advantages of unity of command, both on sea and on land, and they had followed the lead given by the constitution of the Imperial War Cabinet. There was a need for central naval control in time of peace because naval preparations, owing to the far greater mobility of naval warfare, had to be in closer accordance with war plans than military commitments. If each part of the Empire were to develop a separate strategy in peace, it would be impossible to secure effective co-operation in war. Wemyss claimed that if British naval arrangements had not been completely ready in July, 1914, the war's outcome might have been very different. But unity of naval strategy could only be secured by a central authority; the same need applied to training to strengthen uniformity. Admiral Sims of the United States Navy was reported to have said that the American fleet provided no extra strength, perhaps even the reverse, until it had learned to adopt British methods.[111]

The Admiralty's proposal of an imperial naval authority was a political question. Nevertheless, Lloyd George suggested that the proposal should be discussed straightforwardly by the Admiralty with the dominion prime ministers assembled together. Borden agreed but indicated that Canada might want to discuss some points separately with the Admiralty.[112] He had, however, already come to the conclusion that the Admiralty's suggestions did not sufficiently recognize the status of the dominions and would offend the newly awakened sense of nationhood that pervaded the people of Canada and probably the other dominions as well. At a meeting on August 2 the overseas prime ministers decided that the Admiralty's proposals could not be

111. Imperial War Cabinet, Minutes, No. 21, July 18, 1918, P.A.C., M.G. 27, II D 12, Vol. 14. It may be argued, however, that the Royal Navy's war record does not entirely justify the first lord's confidence in the efficacy of British naval methods. See J. W. Roskill, *The Strategy of Sea Power* (London: Collins, 1962), pp. 134–142.
112. Imperial War Cabinet, Minutes; No. 21, July 18, 1918, P.A.C., M.G. 27, II D 12, Vol. 14.

accepted; this was communicated to Sir Eric Geddes, first lord of the Admiralty, on August 7. Geddes then asked for counter-proposals. Borden was in haste to return to Canada, but by August 15 he had secured the agreement of the prime ministers of all the dominions, except Newfoundland, to a reply to the Admiralty memorandum. The proposal for a single navy and single naval authority in time of peace was declared by the prime ministers to be impracticable. It was said that from a strategic point of view the arguments in favor of it were strong but not unanswerable. It was noticeable, for instance, that the Australian navy had operated with the highest efficiency under the over-all direction and command established after the outbreak of war. Standardization during peacetime was accepted as essential for the various dominion naval forces; to promote it the dominions would welcome a visit from a highly qualified sailor. As dominion naval forces developed, it might be necessary to consider the establishment of an imperial naval authority for conducting naval operations in the event of war. Each of the dominions must be adequately represented.[113]

The dominions were thus not prepared to consider commitment to a central naval authority in peacetime and, in fact, would probably want a voice in the Admiralty in war. The prime ministers had asserted that in naval organization as well as elsewhere the Empire must follow the principle of association rather than of integration, that is to say, of Commonwealth defense cooperation rather than of imperial defense.

It may be noted here that after the war, Admiral of the Fleet Jellicoe in *H.M.S. New Zealand* toured the Empire with an Admiralty mandate to persuade the Empire to accept centralized naval control, but he found that he had to yield something in each dominion that he visited, even in India. He admitted the principle of local navies. New Zealand, however, accepted much of Jellicoe's doctrine and adopted "the more immediate recommendations." An order-in-council on March 14, 1921, set up a New Zealand Naval Board; and a second on June 20, 1921, provided that New Zealand warships should be designated "the

113. Borden, ed., *Robert Laird Borden*, II, 842–843.

New Zealand Division of the Royal Navy." [114] But the other dominions insisted upon the same autonomy in naval matters that
they had long possessed in military affairs. Nevertheless, for a
generation, naval imperialists were to continue to press for unity
in the Empire based on a single imperial navy or a single strategic
doctrine and control. These things were, however, impossible
without a centralized political organization which the dominions
by this time had rejected.

Information and Consultation, 1914–1916

When W. M. Hughes brought journalists to France in 1918 he
appealed over the heads of the British politicians to the British
people to secure Australia's interests. Ever since his first wartime
visit to England in 1916, he had made a practice of delivering
patriotic speeches to play upon British public opinion in order
to achieve his ends.[115] Hughes's objective was always the same:
to obtain a voice for Australia in matters that concerned her. In
1918 he sought support from the British electorate to back Australia's desire for a voice in the peace settlement proportional to
her effort in war. Hughes had told the Imperial War Cabinet
that Australia had "poured its men out into the machine and
had had heavy losses, but had never had a scratch of a pen to
explain what really happened." [116]

In later years Hughes complained that in the first three years
of the war the dominions had never been consulted about a
single military plan.[117] They had begun to demand to be consulted at least as early as the beginning of 1915. In the previous

114. S. D. Waters, *The Royal New Zealand Navy* (Wellington: Department
of Internal Affairs, War History Branch, 1956), pp. 8–9.
115. William M. Hughes, *The Splendid Adventure: A Review of Empire Relations Within and Without the Commonwealth of British Nations* (Toronto:
Doubleday, 1929), p. 39. Hughes was to threaten to do this again at the Peace
Conference in 1919. When Lloyd George said that if Australia continued to hold
New Guinea despite President Wilson's wishes, the Royal Navy would not be
available for its protection, Hughes told him, "You and I will go to England
and ask the people who own the navy what they have to say about the matter."
After cursing Hughes in Welsh, Lloyd George yielded (*Policies and Potentates*
[Sydney: Angus & Robertson, 1950], pp. 237–238).
116. Imperial War Cabinet, Minute No. 19, June 20, 1918, P.A.C., M.G. 27, II
D 12, Vol. 14.
117. Hughes, *Splendid Adventure*, p. 72.

November, when the Cabinet's co-ordination of operations was obviously faltering, Asquith had set up a War Council similar in composition to the core of the prewar Committee of Imperial Defence, with the C.I.D.'s secretary, Maurice Hankey, as its secretary. News of this step leaked out in press reports, which mistakenly said that the Committee of Imperial Defence itself had met. Borden asked Perley, who had been sent as Canada's representative on the C.I.D., for a report. Hankey then told Perley "very secretly" that a "special expert committee" was considering whether "any new move," or "any alteration of tactics," could change the present position which had "become apparently very close to deadlock" on the Western Front. He promised that if any new plan of campaign emerged from the deliberations of the new committee, Perley would be informed. At the same time, he reported that the full Committee of Imperial Defence, which had not sat since the war began, was to meet soon and that Perley would be invited to attend.

Perley soon reported to Borden that the C.I.D. did meet on January 27, 1915, but that it only discussed how to get more recruits in the United Kingdom without bothering the business community any more than was necessary. He was promised, however, that Canada would be consulted when the time came for the discussion of terms of peace. He thought this "a long step in the right direction." [118]

Perley had, in fact, been successfully sidetracked. The War Council organized the attack on Gallipoli for which Australian and New Zealand troops then in Egypt were employed. Canada was not officially or informally apprised in the planning stage. When Australian troops were ordered to Gallipoli, the Australian government was informed, but not consulted. Hughes declared later that if it had been consulted, Australia would have supplied enough troops to make the initial attack a success.[119] But his statement was based on hindsight. Prior consultation would surely have led Hughes to share the general confidence in a successful outcome.

118. Hankey to Perley, Jan. 15, 1915, P.A.C., M.G. 26, Borden Papers, R.L.B. 168; Perley to Borden, Jan. 22, 27, 1915, *ibid.*
119. Hughes, *Splendid Adventure*, p. 76.

The British government was indeed concerned to ward off, rather than to invite, dominion opinions. Before the war began, Australia had been pressing for an imperial conference to discuss unresolved details of the imperial naval arrangements. On April 14, 1915, the secretary of state for the colonies, Lord Harcourt, told the British House of Commons that the British government assumed that an imperial conference "was impossible during the war because everybody was too busy." He said that only Andrew Fisher, the prime minister of Australia (who at the beginning of the war had pledged Australia's support for Britain "to the last man and the last shilling"), continued to want a conference, and that even he had not pressed the matter. Harcourt gave public assurances that the dominions would be consulted about the terms of peace.[120]

When questioned about this statement, Harcourt made it quite clear that he was talking only of a formal conference "with the paraphernalia of miscellaneous resolutions, short-hand reports, and resulting blue books." What he did not reveal was that since January he had been cool to proposals that Borden should visit London separately. Borden had himself suggested the visit, which Perley described as "to talk to the men who are doing the important work at this time and to put before them your views on different matters which will enable you to better understand the situation on this side." If the visit could be arranged, the Canadian government intended to inform the other prime ministers. Harcourt also omitted to tell the House that only a few days before his speech he had reversed his earlier stand against Borden's visit. This affair, however, had now begun to seem likely to develop into something wider. A *Times* article from an Australian correspondent had suggested an informal meeting of all dominion prime ministers in London. Harcourt had yielded to demands of this kind, but only to the extent of agreeing to Borden's first proposal for a separate visit. He said the Canadian would be welcome, "though of course . . . there can

120. Copy of Harcourt's statement, April 14, 1915, P.A.C., M.G. 26, H 1 (c), Vol. 163.

be nothing in the nature of public entertainments . . . ," [121] a reflection of what the British thought about imperial conferences. Before the visit could be arranged, however, the munitions crisis and the resignation of Lord Fisher, First Sea Lord of the Admiralty, caused the fall of the Asquith Liberal government and the establishment of a coalition government under the same prime minister.

In June, 1915, Borden told Perley to inquire of Bonar Law, Canadian-born leader of the Unionist party who had been newly appointed colonial secretary, whether the general conference, for which Australia and New Zealand had been pressing, would now be held. Law replied that there were disadvantages in a formal conference and that he thought the overseas premiers ought to come separately. The premiers of the other dominions were similarly advised. Borden found Law's reply "unsatisfactory and the reasons assigned trivial"; but he agreed to visit England informally during the summer months without any arrangements for a general conference.[122] The new coalition government in Britain, like its predecessor, thus showed itself to be unreceptive not merely to a full-dress imperial conference with its time-consuming ceremony and entertainment, but even to an informal conference of prime ministers.

Borden's visit, first projected in January, 1915, when he had begun to worry about the direction of the war at the top, had now become much more imperative as a consequence of widespread stories about War Office muddle and also about Sam Hughes's behavior which had proved both impulsive and irritating. But an even more important factor was the alarming growth of Canadian casualty lists. In their first major engagement at Ypres, the Canadians had held firm against the first German gas attack and had, as the War Office put it, "undoubtedly saved the situation" in the first three days. But the cost was high: 6,036 lives in the 1st Canadian Division alone. Borden was

121. Perley to Borden, March 30, April 10, 1915, P.A.C., M.G. 27, II D 12, Vol. 13, No. 68.

122. Borden to Perley, June 9, 11, 1915, and Perley to Borden, June 11, 1915, *ibid.*, M.G. 26, H 1 (c), Vol. 163; Perley to Borden, June 10, 1915, *ibid.*, M.G. 27, II D 12, Vol. 4.

strengthened in his resolution to make Canada's voice heard, and he was in a stronger position. He made it perfectly clear that his long-term aim was to obtain a say in the formulation of British policy.[123]

However, in London he found it extremely difficult to get any satisfactory information. He was passed from one department to another and received contradictory conjectures from different Cabinet ministers about the future course of the war. He came to the conclusion that the co-ordination of information and effort in Britain was quite inadequate.[124] Some years afterward he was to recall that his disgust was so great that in order to force the British government to take his request for information seriously, he resorted to threats. Three days before he was due to leave he told Law, "Unless I obtain this reasonable information which is due to me as Prime Minister of Canada, I shall not advise my countrymen to put further effort into the winning of the War." He was then granted a luncheon interview with Lloyd George, who had to come in from the country where he was convalescing from an illness. From what he heard at lunch Borden came to the conclusion that the full strength of the Empire could not be thrown into the war before the fall of 1916, a date which was, of course, to prove much too optimistic.[125]

During the summer of 1915 the war had gone badly for the Allies on the Eastern Front and at Gallipoli. In an attempt to retrieve the situation, the French persuaded the British not to wait until 1916 but to join in a great offensive on the Western Front in Champagne and Artois. This began on September 25, 1915. The newly formed Canadian Corps had a relatively small part in the ensuing Battle of Loos which proved to be another disaster for both French and British arms. Shortly before that battle began, Borden requested that copies of secret dispatches (like those he had been permitted to see when in England) be forwarded to him through Perley by confidential or secret cable

123. Borden, *Robert Laird Borden*, I, 506.
124. Perley to Bonar Law, Nov. 3, 1915, P.A.C., M.G. 26, H 1 (c), Vol. 163.
125. Borden to Beaverbrook, July 5, 1928, *ibid.*, H 1 (a), Vol. 260, Folder 24. In Borden's memoirs the threat to Bonar Law is couched less brusquely, "I shall return to Canada with no definite intention of urging my fellow countrymen to continue in the war work they have already begun." (I, 508).

code. But the only thing arranged was that Aitken would supply him with very confidential information from the front through Perley's secret bag.[126]

The battle of Loos was called off on November 4, 1915. Just before it ended, the Canadian government had again tried to gain access to the inner circle that was directing the war. Perley had reported to Borden on October 28 that he had heard that the military failures had made it likely that a war cabinet of three or four members would be set up. He suggested that if the dominions could agree on one man to represent them all, a seat might be obtained. He said that Borden "could be useful in this position," and that it would be a good opportunity to initiate a change in imperial ideas and relations.[127]

In reply to Perley's report on these exchanges, Borden instructed him to ask for more insight into war planning on which "little or no information was vouchsafed," and to stress that the responsibility of the dominions to their peoples entitled them to fuller information and "consultation respecting general policy in war operations." Referring to the evidence of lack of interdepartmental co-ordination which he had seen in England, he said that he hoped the new council or committee would be able to arrange for information and consultation.[128] Perley gave this information to Bonar Law in writing on November 3, 1915.[129] Bonar Law replied the same day that the British government had been delighted to give Borden secret information when he was in London, but that it was more difficult to do the same thing at a distance. "If there is any way which occurs to him or to yourself in which this can be done I shall be delighted to carry it out." He admitted the right of the Canadian government "to have some share in a war in which Canada is playing so big a part"; but he was "not able to see any way in which this could be practically done." He asked Perley to tell the prime minister

126. Perley to Bonar Law, Sept. 9, 1915, P.A.C., M.G. 27, II D 12, Vol. 4; Perley to Borden, Oct. 7, 1915, *ibid.*
127. Perley to Borden, Oct. 28, 1915, *ibid.*
128. Borden to Perley, Nov. 1, 1915, in Borden, ed., *Robert Laird Borden*, II, 621.
129. Perley to Bonar Law, Nov. 3, 1915, P.A.C., Borden Papers, M.G. 26, H 1 (c), Vol. 163.

that if no scheme was practicable, it was undesirable that the question should be raised.[130]

Perley must have also mentioned to Law his own proposal that Borden should represent the dominions on the new war cabinet, for Law told him verbally that he did not think that the other dominions would accept such an arrangement.[131] In fact, the new reorganization of the British command had not disrupted the Cabinet but had provided a small, dependent War Committee of three to five Cabinet members to take the direction of the war back from the Dardanelles Committee. This War Committee soon grew to five plus the Chief of the General Staff and the First Sea Lord.[132] No consideration was given to the idea of adding dominion members.

Borden found Bonar Law's letter "not especially illuminating" and said that it left the matter exactly where it stood before. He said that since he had left England he had had no information about war planning, except for a few telegrams from Perley and Aitken, to supplement what he could glean from the press. "Steps of the most important and even vital character have been taken, postponed, or rejected without the slightest consultation with the authorities of this Dominion." His government had recently authorized the doubling of the Canadian forces to half a million men, a step which the governor general thought premature when the earlier establishment had not yet been filled. Borden told Perley:

It can hardly be expected we shall put 400,000 or 500,000 men in the field and willingly accept the position of having no more voice and receiving no more consideration than if we were toy automata. Any person cherishing such an expectation harbours an unfortunate and dangerous delusion. Is this war being waged by the United Kingdom alone, or is it a war waged by the whole Empire? If I am correct in supposing that the second hypothesis must be accepted then why do the statesmen of the British Isles arrogate to themselves solely the

130. Bonar Law to Perley, Nov. 3, 1915, in Borden, ed., *Robert Laird Borden*, II, 621.
131. Perley to Borden, Nov. 5, 1915, P.A.C., Borden Papers, M.G. 26, H 1 (c), Vol. 163.
132. Maurice Hankey, *Supreme Command, 1914–1918* (2 vols.; London: Allen & Unwin, 1961), II, 441–442.

methods by which it shall be carried on. . . . It is for them to suggest the method and not for us. If there is no available method and if we are expected to continue in the role of automata the whole situation must be reconsidered.

Borden then went on to criticize the procrastination, inertia, doubt, and hesitation conspicuous in British direction of the war, and he quoted a British Cabinet minister who had said there was "a shortage of brains." He said that knaves and fools who had been pointed out to him by name when he was in England had not yet been turned out of office.[133]

When told of Borden's protest, Law replied that he personally thought Borden should be kept more in touch with what was happening, but he said that it had been difficult to find anything especially interesting to communicate since no special changes had taken place. However, he had collected a number of the most important documents which had been circulated to the War Committee, and he had obtained the prime minister's approval for sending them to Borden. They were for Borden's eyes only and were then to be burned. He said the Foreign Office had protested that no existing means of sending such documents was safe. Nevertheless, he had found an individual going to Canada who could carry the documents personally, an unofficial means of forwarding them which he had approved.[134] The documents reached Ottawa on March 7, 1916, and Borden cabled for permission to show them to the governor general. This was granted. Borden's appreciation for Law's efforts must have been tempered by the fact that this was just a tidbit of information to pacify his hunger for consultation and for a share in the direction of operations in which Canadians were deeply involved. It was obvious that the British had no real belief in the feasibility of sharing either information or control.

For the Australians, wartime representation in England was deemed so important that at the end of 1915 Prime Minister Andrew Fisher had resigned his high office to become high com-

133. Borden to Perley, Jan. 4, 1916, P.A.C., M.G. 27, II D 12, Vol. 5.
134. Bonar Law to Borden, Feb. 11, 1916, in Borden, ed., *Robert Laird Borden*, II, 623–624.

missioner in London.[135] Despite the potential value for Australia of such important representation, his successor, Hughes, decided that he also must visit England. A message, "Prepare for 49% casualties" had, he wrote later, "burnt into my very soul." [136] The Anzac Corps had suffered grievous losses at Gallipoli and evacuation was being considered. Hughes, like Borden, wanted to talk to the men who were running the war. Hughes cabled Borden that he had been invited to London, that he understood that the other prime ministers had also been invited, and that he hoped that those from New Zealand and Canada would accept.[137] Borden promptly wired Perley, "No invitation has come to Canada. Kindly ascertain situation and ask explanation." Bonar Law explained that no special invitation had been sent to Hughes, only the "general intimation" of last spring. The prime ministers of New Zealand and Australia were coming informally, "exactly on the same basis that you made your visit last summer." He invited Borden to join the group. But the Canadian Parliament was in session, and this was impossible. The Australian prime minister was therefore invited to call in at Ottawa on his way to London.[138]

Hughes's proposed visit suggested to Borden the possibility of putting stronger pressure on the British government. He therefore cabled Perley on January 13, 1916, to take no further steps for the present about the consultation requested in the letter sent on January 4.[139] When Hughes called at Ottawa he was most gratified for his reception with "unprecedented honours" including an appointment to the Canadian Privy Council.[140] Borden on his part was much impressed by Hughes's obvious ability, and the two prime ministers quickly came to a general agreement on their position. When Hughes crossed the Atlantic, the British press got wind of the alliance and, to Hughes's embarrassment,

135. London *Times*, Feb. 4, 1916.
136. Hughes, *Splendid Adventure*, p. 76.
137. Hughes to Borden, Nov. 11, 1915, P.A.C., Borden Papers, M.G. 26, H 1 (c), Vol. 163.
138. Borden to Perley, Nov. 13, 1915; Perley to Borden, Nov. 16; Borden to Hughes, Nov. 15, *ibid.*
139. Borden to Perley, Jan. 13, 1916, *ibid.*
140. Governor General of Australia to Pearce, March 25, 1916, A.W.M., Pearce Papers, Bundle No. 1, Folder 2.

hailed him as an ambassador for Canada and New Zealand as well as for his own country.[141] He hastened to assure Borden that no words of his had warranted such a conclusion, and he added his hope that the Canadian session would end soon enough for Borden to join him in London before he had to leave so that they could prosecute their plans together.[142]

Experience showed that although a dominion prime minister could be much more successful than any member of his government or any subordinate official in obtaining access to British government departments and in impressing the British government itself, the prime minister's presence was also required at home to insure the stability of his government, to control factions in his own party, to rebuff the attacks of the opposition, and to maintain the war effort. The impact of Gallipoli on Australia had been so great that Hughes had felt constrained to spend much of 1916 in England. However, in that year it happened that Borden was faced with vigorous Opposition attacks about the sale to the United States of nickel, which it was alleged was going on to Germany, and about problems arising from the irresponsibility of his minister of militia, Sam Hughes. He was also disturbed by the imminent collapse of the Canadian transportation system through the financial failure of railway companies. He was therefore unable to be absent from Canada long enough to go to England.

In consequence, it was W. M. Hughes alone who in 1916 carried on the campaign for dominion representation in the war councils. Hughes continued to insist that he believed the British government had invited the dominion prime ministers for a general conference on the war; but he said he had come to realize that what it had intended was only a briefing on the urgency of the situation and on the "almost superhuman ability of the men in charge." They were then to be sent home to intensify their own dominion's war effort. He claims in his book that he turned the tables on Asquith by making several speeches which,

141. Hughes to Borden, Cable, March 8, 1916, P.A.C., Borden RLB 168; London *Times*, March 8, 1916.
142. Perley to Borden, March 10, 1916, P.A.C., Borden Papers, M.G. 26, H 1 (c), Vol. 163.

he said, led to a demand that he be included in the British Cabinet.[143] Undoubtedly he made a great hit with the British people. And there was a rumor that he would be asked to stay in England as leader of the Opposition, with the prospect of forming a government of his own or of holding a high position in the first postwar government.[144] At length, after an interval to show that the gesture was a favor, he was invited to attend a Cabinet meeting as a visitor, was honored by a seat on the right hand of the prime minister, and was invited to participate in discussions that happened to be about matters which were not of particular concern to the dominions and in which Britain had a preponderant interest. He spoke on two of these, taking the minority point of view. Later invitations to attend the Cabinet came at "spacious intervals" in order, he believed, to make it clear they were an act of courtesy and not a right.[145]

Hughes claimed that he also manipulated public opinion in order to obtain his admission and that of Sir George Foster, the Canadian minister of trade and commerce, to a four-man delegation to represent the British Empire at the Allied Economic Conference in Paris. He said that he was able to secure the withdrawal of Asquith's condition for dominion participation, namely, that the Empire delegation should vote as a unit. As the British government had previously declared itself undecided on the subject under discussion Hughes said he carried the delegation with him in the advocacy of the imposition of a severe blockade of Germany. He said it was ironical that Asquith then had to defend Hughes's proposal in the Commons.[146] During his stay in England in 1916, Hughes thus compelled members of the British government (although they were involved in their own rivalries over politico-strategic questions) to take more seriously dominion pretensions to be heard. He also exercised

143. Hughes, *Splendid Adventure*, p. 40.
144. Keith A. Murdoch to Pearce, April 6, 1916, A.W.M., Pearce Papers, Bundle 7. As there was a coalition government with a powerful majority, this reference to leadership of the Opposition is curious. The chief opposition to the coalition government at this time came from the Northcliffe press which made good use of Hughes's speeches.
145. Hughes, *Splendid Adventure*, p. 41.
146. *Ibid.*, pp. 42–44.

some influence on general policy, and he prepared the way for the adoption of a formal plan for dominion representation in the conduct of war policy.

The Imperial War Cabinet

Despite the proven value of dominion military aid, the British government was slow to attempt to share the task of policy formulation: apparently too many insuperable obstacles presented themselves. Perhaps most important was the fact that the British government was itself ill-organized for conducting a great world war in the circumstances of the twentieth century. Over-all planning and co-ordination of political and military activities were noticeably deficient or lacking. Conflicts over strategic proposals or between departments often proved well-nigh insoluble. The British Cabinet held ultimate responsibility for conducting the war, but it was too unwieldy in size, too diversified in its many interests, and without the agenda paper, minutes, and secretariat necessary for the efficient conduct of business. Cabinet war committees, modeled on the prewar Committee of Imperial Defence, had no real responsibility, tended to grow in size, and lacked continuity and regularity. They could not provide fully for long-term planning and were inadequately prepared to settle the serious differences that inevitably arose between civil and military policy-makers.

Significantly, dominion prime ministers were not invited to the Cabinet committees and war councils where major policy was being decided. But there was no other agency with which a dominion prime minister could co-operate to good purpose. Ministers were occasionally admitted to the Cabinet itself, and while this act of courtesy befitted their status, it produced little good. This was true not merely because their admission was by grace and not by right, and not because of the time-wasting procedure of that body, but because the Cabinet was largely concerned with many general and domestic problems of little interest to the dominion ministers. They were flattered by being asked an opinion about business that concerned the government of the

United Kingdom, and their good will was thereby fostered; but their presence added little or nothing to the efficient conduct of the war and to the recruiting of dominion aid.

Another problem, as we have seen, was that because of his key role in the parliamentary system, a prime minister was usually unable to afford long absences from the seat of his government. Sometimes he could not leave at all. Frequently he had no trusted deputy to act as prime minister in his absence. On the other hand, no substitute could be as effective in London either in gathering information or in influencing British policy. Perley told Borden that the Colonial Office would object to a high commissioner who made direct contacts with British government departments as Borden had done when he visited England.[147] In the face of such formidable obstacles, the British government was unwilling to promote imperial constitutional innovations without compelling reason.

The securing of unanimity among the several British government departments concerned with war policy—or even their mere acceptance of a policy—was fraught with difficulties. British statesmen and soldiers disagreed. British departments came into conflict. Therefore, the idea of deliberately adding four or more dominion vetoes or critical voices was unattractive to British ministers who were already burdened by the day-to-day problems of conducting a world war as well as by the longer-term problems of making policy. It was easy to find reasons for making no change. The safe circulation of military information to distant dominions during the war was difficult if not impossible because of the extent of the security precautions needed. Top-secret information about war plans should be circulated among as few people as possible; but it was information of that kind that dominion governments sought. A compromise (the giving of such plans, under stringent conditions of security, to overseas ministers only) would have left them unable to discuss the most important issues of the war with their Cabinet colleagues. Hence, Cabinet solidarity and stability would have been threatened.

Lloyd George's War Cabinet, set up in December, 1916, went

147. Perley to Borden, May 29, 1916, P.A.C., M.G. 26, H 1 (a), Vol. 33.

a long way toward reducing or removing many of the obstacles to imperial military co-ordination. With only five members, of whom only one had departmental responsibilities, meeting at least once each day, using the business-like techniques of the issuance of agenda papers and the circulation of memoranda, printed minutes, and other papers, being also clothed with unquestioned and unquestionable authority to wage war, the War Cabinet provided what was originally lacking, i.e., efficient governmental control over the total British war effort. By its own eminence, by its willingness to permit the foreign secretary to attend at any time he wished, as well as by its practice of calling in other ministers when questions concerning their departments were under discussion, it was protected against that tendency to grow in numbers and therefore to decline in usefulness that had destroyed the value of its predecessors, the war committees.

The exclusion of the secretary of state for the colonies, Walter Long (among others), from the War Cabinet had had to be explained in special letters to the dominion governments lest they might think that the new system for directing the war would ignore their interests more than ever.[148] But the War Cabinet provided a body with which it seemed the dominion prime ministers could more easily work. Lloyd George's invitation to them to attend the Imperial War Conference, which was issued only nine days after he had assumed the prime ministership and set up the War Cabinet, and his subsequent creation of an Imperial War Cabinet, seemed logical developments to give the dominions a voice. The creation of the Imperial War Cabinet has been described as a deliberate attempt to set up a body that, as Winston Churchill said, "Centred in a single executive the world-spread resources of the British monarchy." [149]

It was not intended to do so. It appears that Lloyd George had been impressed by the success of the Imperial Conference of 1911, when the *in camera* revelations of the dangerous state of world conditions had spurred the dominions to undertake mili-

148. Lloyd George, *War Memoirs* . . . , IV, 7–8.
149. Winston S. Churchill, *The World Crisis, 1916–1919* (London: Thornton Butterworth, 1927), III, Pt. I, 257.

tary preparations which they had hitherto failed to make. He decided therefore to summon the dominions to hear what was now needed to win the war. But there was no provision in the constitution of an imperial conference for secret sessions. In 1911 such sessions had been held at the headquarters of the Committee of Imperial Defence, but that committee did not operate during World War I. Furthermore, it was considered advisable to recognize India's great war effort; but India was not constitutionally a member of an imperial conference. Lloyd George therefore decided to invite the prime ministers and the secretary of state and other representatives of India to a special War Conference. They could attend at the same time "special and continuous meetings of the [British] War Cabinet." [150] The name "Imperial War Cabinet" was not used in the original invitation but was Hankey's inspiration when he was preparing the agenda paper for what was in fact really only a meeting of the British War Cabinet with a few distinguished visitors. [151] The dominion prime ministers were thus simply invited in a body to attend a series of meetings of the British War Cabinet, much in the same way as some of them had previously been invited individually to attend meetings of the earlier British cabinet and of the War Cabinet itself. This was not the revolutionary development which some have thought.

Lloyd George's reorganization had been designed to create a small, vigorous executive to conduct the war. The Imperial War Cabinet, which supplanted it briefly, was much larger than he liked. This was partly because New Zealand's fusion government was a loose alliance of two parties, and it was necessary to invite the leader of the second party, Joseph Ward, as well as W. F. Massey, the prime minister. Canada therefore also asked for two invitations, and the others followed suit. [152] Borden selected Perley to accompany him. The British prime minister thus saw his

150. Long to Governor General of Canada, Dec. 25, 1916, P.A.C., M.G. 26, H 1 (a), Vol. 69.
151. Hankey, *Supreme Command*, II, 657–660.
152. Borden to Perley, March 1, 1917, P.A.C., M.G. 26, H 1 (c), Vol. 163. Other Canadian ministers were to be summoned if questions concerning their departments were to be discussed.

small Imperial War Cabinet swelled by six dominion ministers. As these would have outnumbered the British members of the British War Cabinet, its numbers were increased to eight. In addition, there were present the First Sea Lord of the Admiralty, the director of military operations at the War Office, and representatives of the Colonial Office and of the new War Cabinet Secretariat. Hankey says that Lloyd George became "bored" by this increase of his intended intimate conference by the addition of what he called "the whole caboodle" of dominion ministers.[153]

Any move that had gone further to create closer-knit imperial political organs to centralize the Empire would have been likely to arouse suspicion in many parts of the dominions and this would have not been limited to dominion nationalists. Lionel Curtis's book, *The Problem of the Commonwealth*, published anonymously in 1916, which had resurrected in veiled form the Round Table's aim of imperial federation, was said to have had the effect of arousing opposition in Canada to any form of imperial centralization. Z. A. Lash, a Toronto lawyer and correspondent of Round Tablers Brand, Curtis, and Kerr, therefore sought Borden's opinion about the possible publication of a scheme which he had drafted for a more limited form of centralization, with an imperial council or central authority to control the foreign policy of the Empire and its armies and navies in time of war or during threats of war. Borden had replied that the question of publication must rest with Lash, but that he personally saw no objection.[154]

Borden was sympathetic to some degree of development of imperial governmental machinery; but he was aware that there was division within his Cabinet about the form it should take. An unsigned memorandum from a Cabinet minister about the agenda for the forthcoming Imperial Conference suggested that there ought to be "an Imperial scheme of defence" with Canada represented on a board for that purpose. But the Canadian minister of finance, W. T. White, while recommending the co-

153. Hankey, *Supreme Command*, II, 658.
154. Lash to Borden, Nov. 1, 1916, P.A.C., M.G. 26, H 1 (a), Vol. 66; Borden to Lash, Nov. 3, 1916, *ibid.*

ordination of arms and equipment and consultation in imperial defense said, "all questions as to the forces to be maintained by Canada and as to its military expenditures must devolve upon the Parliament of Canada and not upon some central body in London, no matter how constituted." [155] The creation of a too-powerful imperial defense executive would thus have had powerful opponents, even in circles inclined toward vigorous imperial consolidation.

Meantime, at the Imperial War Conference, which met on different days from the Imperial War Cabinet, in addition to questions concerning the routine problems of day-to-day prosecution of the war, the agenda included the many postwar problems, especially the constitutional reorganization of the Empire. Borden had met Smuts for the first time and had found him "devoted to the unity of the Empire." He therefore drew up with him a resolution about the future constitutional organization of the Empire which, after consulting Australia, New Zealand, and Newfoundland, was presented to the conference. It was to the effect that the subject of imperial organization was too important to be dealt with during the war but should be taken up as soon as possible after the cessation of hostilities. It added that

any such re-adjustment, while thoroughly preserving all existing powers of self-government and complete control of domestic affairs, should be based upon a full recognition of the Dominions as autonomous nations of an Imperial Commonwealth, and of India as an important portion of the same, should recognize the right of the Dominions and India to an adequate voice in foreign policy and in foreign relations, and should provide effective arrangements for continuous consultation in all matters of common Imperial concern, and for such necessary concerted action, founded on consultation, as the several governments may determine. [156]

The only immediate result of this resolution would be to postpone discussion. It therefore passed easily and unanimously. The motion stated officially for the first time the universal desire of the dominions for a voice in foreign policy; but the resolution suggested no machinery for this purpose except consultation,

155. White, Memorandum, Feb. 9, 1917, *ibid.*, Vol. 85.
156. Borden, ed., *Robert Laird Borden*, II, 668.

and it warded off nationalist doubts by speaking of protecting and recognizing the present autonomy of the dominions as "nations." The use of the word "Commonwealth" in an official document was an indication that this was something different from the imperial federation previously demanded by imperialists.

Borden thought that with the constitution of the Imperial War Cabinet, a new day had dawned and a new page of history had been written that would lead to the birth of a new and greater "Imperial Commonwealth." [157] He therefore outlined informally to Walter Long, the secretary of state for the colonies, a proposal for a consultative assembly of the Empire; but he did not say how he thought its members would be chosen, who should preside over it, or what would be the result of its deliberations. Long asked him, "If they are to have no power, how long would they care to meet and do nothing but talk?" The colonial secretary, an old parliamentarian, said that such a plan would command no support whatever in Parliament, and he suggested that the best policy would be to try to make the Imperial War Cabinet permanent, to secure an announcement that any prime minister or any minister sent over by the prime minister of a dominion would be a member of that cabinet, and to get each dominion to work out its ideas in advance about representation after the war.[158] Meanwhile, Smuts, who had no prime ministerial responsibilities and whose wisdom had impressed Lloyd George, was persuaded to stay on in London as a full member of the British War Cabinet. But great care was taken to make it clear that there was no suggestion that he represented the dominions as a group.[159] No single minister from one dominion would have been acceptable to the others.

At the time when Borden wrote to Lloyd George suggesting that if overseas ministers could attend, the policy of holding sessions of the Imperial War Cabinet should be continued for the duration of the war, and that the calling of an imperial

157. Borden's speech to the Empire Parliamentary Association, April 2, 1917, in *ibid.*, II, 691–692.
158. Long to Borden, April 15, 1917, P.A.C., M.G. 26, H 1 (a), Vol. 69.
159. Lloyd George, *War Memoirs* . . . , IV, 93.

constitutional conference at the end of hostilities should be "fore-shadowed," he began to receive urgent messages from Ottawa advising his return. He went back to Canada to find the political scene there more stormy than he had ever known it. It remained that way until December, 1916. The issue was conscription.[160] Meanwhile, Hughes of Australia had not been able to come to the Imperial War Cabinet at all. Rebellion had broken out in Ireland, and this made political trouble in Australia. As Hughes had been one of the leading advocates of a dominion voice in policy, his absence from the Imperial War Cabinet was important.

The Committee of Prime Ministers, 1918

Hughes believed that the Imperial War Cabinet was a significant step toward imperial co-operation, but he was one of the first to point out that it was not, as Churchill was to suggest later, an imperial executive. Every decision that it made had to be submitted to the appropriate cabinets of the Empire for approval. Action was taken by virtue of the authority of those cabinets, and not of the Imperial War Cabinet itself.[161] The latter was, in effect, a session of the British War Cabinet with dominion ministers and other British ministers in attendance. It can best be described as a secret summit conference of the Empire.

However, another lesser-known institution merited this description even more than the Imperial War Cabinet, and at the same time was closer to what was politically possible for the future. This was the subcommittee of prime ministers set up by the Imperial War Cabinet on June 20, 1918, to deal with Hughes and Borden's suggestion that the war was being mismanaged by the generals. Dominion representation on this committee was by prime ministers only, with General Smuts deputizing for Botha. The secretary of state for war was a member, and the C.I.G.S. was available on call.[162] The committee met whenever it could between the sessions of the Imperial War Cabinet and of the

160. Borden, ed., *Robert Laird Borden*, II, 697.
161. Hughes, *Splendid Adventure*, pp. 49–51.
162. Imperial War Cabinet, Minute No. 19, June 20, 1918, P.A.C., M.G. 27, II D 12, Vol. 14.

Imperial War Conference. Lloyd George presided and Hankey was its secretary.

This committee of prime ministers must be distinguished from the occasional informal meetings of dominion prime ministers without Lloyd George and the secretariat which had discussed the stand they would take on issues put to them. The formal Prime Ministers' Committee, from the nature of its original terms of reference to inquire into the conduct of the war, and also as a result of its greater intimacy and informality, became the forum for the discussion of all the important and controversial issues raised at the Imperial War Cabinet. Questions like the transfer of troops from one theater to another were referred directly to it. It also initiated other matters such as the proposed Allied intervention in Siberia. Some of these questions it referred to the Imperial War Cabinet or to the Imperial War Conference.[163] In these ways the committee came to discuss a variety of topics including the competence of generals, the system by which they were appointed, strategy in various theaters of war, and Woodrow Wilson's Fourteen Points. Its report, which was drafted by Hankey, outlined proposals for an offensive in 1919, approved emphasis on the Western Front because the prime ministers thought it inevitable, and declared that the public would accept the necessity of waiting until 1920 for final victory.[164]

Within a short time this report was signed by all the prime ministers except Lloyd George, who thought it smacked too much of the former C.I.G.S., Field Marshal Robertson (he called it "Wully *redivivus*"), and Hughes, who returned it to Hankey with an enigmatic answer. But before it could be discussed further the march of events made it out of date. It remained, therefore, in Hankey's words, "an historical document of considerable interest" which was never circulated or acted upon.[165] Had it had time to become a basis for future policy, as it might well have done had the war not ended, the report would have been the first major war program laid down collectively by the

163. Hankey, *Supreme Command*, II, 816–818.
164. Report of the Committee of Prime Ministers, [Aug., 1918] (Draft), P.A.C., M.G. 26, 1 (a), Vol. 122.
165. Hankey, *Supreme Command*, II, 830, 832.

prime ministers of the Empire. The Prime Ministers' Committee was, in fact, an embryo inner cabinet of the kind that had so frequently developed in the course of past English constitutional history. It came close to being the first executive for the whole Empire.

Hankey realized that, although the committee was nominally and constitutionally merely an *ad hoc* committee of the Imperial War Cabinet, it overshadowed its parent body; but he does not seem to have been aware that it was the committee, and not the parent body, that was the more suitable model for future constitutional development for the obvious reason that in a Commonwealth of parliamentary democracies power rests with the prime ministers.[166]

Future imperial constitutional development was in everybody's mind in 1918. At the Imperial War Cabinet on July 23, Hughes and Borden claimed that the dominions were sister nations of Britain and that this relationship ought to be properly recognized. Leopold Amery, an assistant in the Cabinet Secretariat, suggested to Lloyd George that this claim could best be met by what he called a minor administrative change whereby correspondence from the colonies would go through the Cabinet Secretariat instead of through the Colonial Office.[167] After the question of channels of communication was threshed out in the Imperial War Cabinet, Hankey drafted three resolutions for Lloyd George. The first of these recognized the right of prime ministers to have direct access to the prime minister of the United Kingdom. The second proposed that ministers be nominated to attend meetings of the Imperial War Cabinet to be held regularly between the so-called plenary sessions that were attended by the prime ministers themselves. And the third resolution proposed the establishment of an informal committee of prime ministers to investigate machinery for carrying out the business of the Empire after the war.[168] At the Imperial War Cabinet on July 24, it was found that the first two resolutions were accept-

166. *Ibid.*, II, 816–818, 825–835.
167. L. S. Amery to Lloyd George, July 24, 1918, P.A.C., M.G. 27, II, G–2.
168. Imperial War Cabinet, Minutes Nos. 19, 26, 27, 28, *ibid.*, II D 12, Vol. 14.

able to the dominions; but Borden told Lloyd George and the War Cabinet that the dominion prime ministers had met together in their informal committee and were agreed in opposition to the third. The question of constitutional change had therefore to be left to an imperial conference after the war.

When on August 2 Hankey breakfasted with Borden and obtained from him a promise that a secretary would be left with the Canadian representative who would become an assistant secretary in Hankey's office, it seemed that an important constitutional advance was on the point of being made. Lloyd George had apparently agreed to a proposal that when the full Imperial War Cabinet was not in session, representatives of the dominion prime ministers would be summoned once a week to attend sessions of the British War Cabinet between its ordinary sessions. Borden also seemed to approve the plan, for he said that Loring C. Christie, his private secretary and a former legal adviser to the Canadian Department of External Affairs, would work out the details of the secretariat with Hankey.[169]

Hankey saw all these developments as "in line with the conclusions of 1911 and 1912 which [had] led Borden to send Perley to London as his representative on the Committee of Imperial Defence, and Massey to send Allen to attend meetings of that Committee in 1913, and they prepared the way for the remarkable development of the British Empire Delegation and its joint secretariat at the Peace Conference."[170] In fact, however, the Armistice in November, 1918, came too quickly for interim imperial war cabinets to lead to anything permanent or useful. The Imperial War Cabinet had held its last meeting of the second series on August 2, 1918. Only those prime ministers who still remained in London were invited to its next meeting on August 13. Both Borden and Massey left London in August without naming their representatives to attend the interim sessions.[171] No advance notice was given of the August 13 meeting, and no invitation was sent to other dominion ministers still in London.

169. Hankey, *Supreme Command*, II, 833–834; Borden, ed., *Robert Laird Borden*, II, 836.
170. Hankey, *Supreme Command*, II, 834.
171. *Ibid.*

This meeting was described in its minutes as "Imperial War Cabinet, 30," but also as "War Cabinet (with the Prime Ministers of the Dominions), 457," thus being numbered also in the series of ordinary British war cabinets. Two sets of minutes were prepared showing membership lists appropriate to each of these different titles. This procedure, obviously designed to enmesh the British War Cabinet with the Imperial War Cabinet, was repeated at future weekly sessions of this rump Imperial War Cabinet until signs that the Germans were about to sue for peace brought a call for the resumption of the full Imperial War Cabinet on November 5, 1918.

By that time Sir Joseph Ward had left England in a state of great agitation, claiming that he had been "cut out" of the cabinet. This was reported to Hankey by Colonial Secretary Walter Long's private secretary.[172] Long was already disturbed by the trend toward direct communication between the prime ministers of the dominion and of the United Kingdom which would have the effect of reducing the importance of his portfolio. He must have seen that this interim Imperial War Cabinet, from which he was excluded, was a further step in the same direction. But obviously the root of Ward's trouble was that Massey had not seen fit to appoint him as his representative. The weakness in the proposal for a continuing interim Imperial War Cabinet thus lay in the fact that prime ministers were doubtful about intrusting representatives with vicarious authority to represent them in an imperial cabinet.

The Armistice came too suddenly for this very interesting device of weekly sessions of an Imperial War Cabinet for prime ministers' deputies to get off the ground. If it had been successful, it might have answered the vexing wartime question about information and consultation. Since it was restricted to representatives of prime ministers only, it followed the precedent of the Prime Ministers' Committee rather than of the Imperial War Cabinet. It pointed the way neither to the delegation at the Peace Conference nor to the full-dress imperial conferences of the twenties and thirties, but rather toward the Prime Ministers'

172. H. F. Batterbee to Hankey, Nov. 1, 1918, P.A.C., M.G. 27, II, G–2.

Conference of 1921 and to the prime ministers' conferences after 1945. Had there been more time before the war ended to experiment with the "interim Cabinets," it is possible that the present prime ministers' conference might have developed earlier than it did and even that it might have become a continuous and effective policy-making executive for the Empire. But on the other hand, there is room for doubt whether the prime ministers could have continued to accept it and with it the commitments which it would have imposed or implied.

The machinery which had been built to permit the dominions to share the conducting of the war through the Imperial War Conference, the Imperial War Cabinet, and the Prime Ministers' Committee, led directly to dominion participation in the making of the peace treaty, but only because the dominions demanded it strongly. A share in framing this peace treaty had been promised to them as early as 1915. On October 29, 1918, when the war was obviously coming to an end, Hughes repeated the request. His action was timely, for on that same day the Supreme War Council had met to discuss agreement on Wilson's Fourteen Points as the basis for an armistice; and the dominions had neither been consulted, nor even informed, that the matter was under discussion. Indeed, the Foreign Office was shocked when Borden demanded a seat at the Peace Conference table; yet Canada's losses had been as great as those of small powers like Belgium which would automatically secure a seat. The stand of the British government was that the promise to consult the dominions had been fulfilled by discussions in the Imperial War Cabinet. But the Fourteen Points had been only briefly examined in that body, and without previous information about the various secret treaties the dominions were in no position to make any useful contribution to a discussion of the terms that should be demanded of a defeated foe.

The establishment of the British Empire delegation at Versailles in 1919 was the result of dominion pressure, and particularly of Hughes's success in arousing British public opinion to an awareness of the dominions' war effort. The Treaty of

Versailles was signed both collectively for the Empire and separately by each dominion in its own right as a member of the Empire delegation. These events brought the international recognition that the dominions craved. The first postwar imperial meeting in 1921 was in line with the experiment of the Prime Ministers' Committee and with the proposed interim sessions of the Imperial War Cabinet. It was a Prime Ministers' Conference. It appeared to suggest that the Empire now had a means of working collectively. But this development was short-lived. The Chanak incident in 1922 showed that Canada and South Africa were not ready for the commitments that a common Empire policy might imply. Hence, in future the prewar pattern of full-dress imperial conferences was resumed. With their formality and ceremony, nationalist prime ministers like Mackenzie King could feel more secure.

The Prime Ministers' Conference had failed because without some system of interim cabinets and without their own foreign services, the dominions were ill-informed to keep pace with developing situations and were unable to make their attitudes known in time to prevent the formulation of policies of which they disapproved. Co-operation and a developing practice of consultation and information had been possible in the critical days of the war, but in peacetime the British Commonwealth of Nations was unable to achieve more than a general agreement to inform and discuss formally at relatively long intervals. Nevertheless, the war had seen the development of military co-operation based on the standardization of organization, arms and equipment, and the common policy of military training that had been established shortly before 1914. In the postwar years this form of technical co-operation was slowly re-established.

The Dominions' Section of the Imperial General Staff at the War Office was not revived after the war in its prewar form. In September, 1918, a section of the Directorate of Military Operations (M.O. 5) was created to deal with operations in Russia, Siberia, and the Far East. As Canadian troops were involved, a Canadian officer was attached to it as G.S.O. 2 (General Staff

Officer, 2nd Grade) from November, 1919, until May, 1920. In April, 1922, the Directorate of Military Operations and Military Intelligence were amalgamated. M.O. 1, concerned with strategy, was also responsible for the dominions and the colonies. Several Australian officers and, less frequently, Canadians served in this key section of the War Office which gave them the widest possible insight into British imperial strategic planning. This attachment greatly benefitted dominion officers, and the experience and information they received was advantageous to their governments. As it was an operations section rather than one for organization like the Directorate of Staff Duties, it seemed less likely to be used to exert control. When a new war became imminent, contact between British and dominion military forces was developed through liaison officers attached to the offices of the high commissioners in London rather than through a section of the Imperial General Staff at the War Office.

The Commonwealth military system between the wars provided for technical co-operation that was mutually advantageous. But it could be effective politically as a deterrent to aggression only when there was complete agreement, not merely upon principles but also on the determination that action should be taken. As there was no centralized control or agreement upon foreign policy, there was no full agreement on strategic doctrine. The ideas of the imperial naval defense school which were carried from the old Empire into the postwar Commonwealth by Admiral Sir Herbert Richmond, commandant of the Imperial Defence College, were now challenged, not as earlier by British soldiers, but by some soldiers in the dominions who advocated the strengthening of local dominion defenses.[173] British Commonwealth co-operation for defense found no clear answer to this strategic dilemma.

Naval imperialists and advocates of stronger local defenses in the dominion were, however, also blocked by another phenom-

173. Sir Herbert Richmond, "An Outline of Imperial Defence," *Army Quarterly,* XXIV, (1932), 260–279; Col. J. D. Lavarack, "The Defence of the British Empire with Special Reference to the Far East over Australia," *ibid.,* XXV (1932), 207; Major H. C. H. Robertson, "The Empire and Modern War," *ibid.,* XXVI (1933), 246–253; Anon., "Another Aspect of Imperial Defence," *Canadian Defence Quarterly,* IX (1932), 458–459.

enon, the strength of contemporary dislike for war in all its forms and an accompanying reliance on international programs to keep the peace by less expensive means. When disarmament proved unattainable, and the League of Nations broke down after a disastrous acceptance of appeasement by all members except New Zealand, the Fascist challenge brought a belated closing of British Commonwealth ranks. The system of defense co-operation based on standardized organization and training, and furthered by new arrangements for wartime unity of command, then became effective again and carried the Commonwealth through its greatest trial in World War II.

It was fortunate that the Japanese challenge, which aroused some Australasian tendencies to local instead of imperial defensive measures, was not simultaneous with the initial German onslaught in Europe, and that when Japan attacked in the Pacific the United States was immediately involved. In these circumstances the disruptive concepts of strategy which had threatened Commonwealth unity between the wars had little effect on the main Commonwealth effort. Co-operation between the independent nations of the Commonwealth in World War II proved attainable because there was full agreement on the nature of the common danger and because that danger did not seriously threaten any of the various limbs of the Commonwealth along with the heart.

It has been seen that the basic structure of the Commonwealth providing for the fullest possible decentralization in peace yet fostering the maximum possible co-operation in war had developed in the military and naval spheres before World War I. That principle was confirmed by the successful outcome of that war, chiefly because co-operation on a Commonwealth basis suited the rising national sentiment of the dominions. The experiences of the British Commonwealth in war furnished useful lessons and supplied effective techniques to facilitate the co-operation of the "United Nations" in World War II and also in the Cold War that followed. However, since 1945 the Commonwealth of Nations itself, no longer mainly British or even European in racial composition, and with much less identity of interest than formerly, has obviously found these disruptive tendencies difficult to absorb. It remains to be seen whether sufficient common interest remains to maintain the inherited traditions of military co-operation that would help the Commonwealth to survive.

Selective Bibliography [*]

Bibliographical Guides

Crick, B. R., and Miriam Alman (eds.). *A Guide to Manuscripts Relating to America in Great Britain and Ireland.* Oxford: Oxford University Press, 1961.

Kerr, W. B. "A Survey of the Literature on Canada's Participation in the South African War," *Canadian Historical Review,* XVIII (1937).

Lewin, Percy Evans. *Subject Catalogue of the Library of the Royal Empire Society Formerly Royal Colonial Institute.* London: Royal Commonwealth Society, 1930.

MacLeod, Meryl. "Victorian Defence, 1850–1900: Bibliography Prepared under Direction of the Research Department of the State Library of Victoria." Melbourne: Library Training School, Public Library of Victoria, 1957. (MS copy in State Library of Victoria [formerly Public Library of Victoria].)

Archives

Australia, Commonwealth Archives Office (C.A.O.).

Department of Defence Papers.

Prime Minister's Department Papers.

————, Department of Defence, Victoria Barracks, Melbourne.

Archives of the Navy, *Printed Papers, Naval, 1885–1900.*

————, Department of Defence Library, Canberra.

Department of Defence, *Printed Papers, I, 1862–1901.*

[*] Some references in the text of lesser importance are not included.

————, Mitchell Library, Sydney, New South Wales.

Parkes Correspondence.

Public Men of Australia [Collected Papers].

————, National Library, Canberra (A.N.L.).

Denman Papers.

Jebb Papers.

————, War Memorial, Canberra (A.W.M.).

Monash Papers.

Pearce Papers.

Canada, Douglas Library, Queens University.

Dundonald Papers.

Laurier Papers.

Mackenzie Papers.

————, Public Archives (P.A.C.).

Beaverbrook Papers.

Caron Papers.

Defence Commission (1885) Papers.

Dufferin Papers (Microfilm).

Governor General's Papers.

Hutton Papers.

Laurier Papers (also Microfilm in Douglas Library).

Lloyd George Papers.

Macdonald Papers.

Militia and Defence Department Papers.

Minto Papers.

Perley Papers.

————, Royal Military College.

Bridges Papers.

Great Britain, Admiralty Library.

    Confidential Papers.

————, National Library of Wales, Aberystwyth.

    Lewis Papers.

————, National Maritime Museum, Greenwich.

    Milne Papers.

————, Public Record Office (P.R.O.).

    Admiralty Papers.

    Cabinet Papers.

    Carnarvon Papers.

    Colonial Office Papers.

    War Office Papers.

————, Public Record Office of Northern Ireland, Belfast.

    Dufferin Papers.

————, The Royal Archives, Windsor Castle (R.A.W.)—by gracious permission of Her Majesty the Queen.

    Duke of Cambridge Papers.

————, Royal United Service Institution Library (R.U.S.I.).

    Miscellaneous unpublished pamphlets.

————, War Office, Library.

    Dobell Conference, "Attachment of Officers to Units, 1911."

    [J. Godley]. "Military Expenditures in the Colonies," A 50/1858.

    List of Committees [n.d.].

    Recommendations of Committees on Army Matters.

    Report of the Committee on Colonial Garrisons (A 66/1886).

New Zealand, Public Archives (N.Z.A.).

    Governor, Confidential In-Letters.

    Governor, Confidential Out-Letters.

Government Publications

Australia, Commonwealth. *Official Year Book of the Commonwealth of Australia, 1901–08.* Melbourne: McCarron, Bird, 1909.

―――――, [Department of Defence]. John Forrest. *Memorandum on Naval Defence* (March 15, 1902), in *Printed Papers, Naval, 1885– 1908,* Vol. I. Department of Defence Library, Canberra.

―――――, Department of Defence. *Scheme for a Permanent Force and Naval Reserve of Australia and New Zealand* (1903). Naval Archives, Melbourne.

―――――, Parliament. *Records of Proceedings and the Printed Papers.*

II (1901–1902), 53 (A36). *Military Forces of the Commonwealth. Minute Upon the Defence of Australia, by Major General Sir Edward Hutton, K.C.M.G., C.B., Commanding the Military Forces of the Commonwealth.*

II (1901–1902), 159 (22), Senate. [Rear Adm. Beaumont]. *Naval Defence of the Commonwealth of Australia.*

II (1901–1902), 141 (27), Senate. *Report of the Naval Officers Assembled at Melbourne, Victoria, to Consider the Question of Naval Defence of Australia* (Sept. 11, 1901).

II (1904), 277 (25). Maj. Gen. Sir Edward T. W. Hutton. *Military Forces of the Commonwealth of Australia. Second Annual Report with Appendices.*

II (1905), 311 (66). [Capt. W. R. Creswell]. *Defence of Australia.*

II (1906), 81 (65). *Instruction of the Minister of Defence to Captain W. R. Creswell Relative to His Visit to England to Inquire into the Latest Naval Developments.*

II (1906), 67 (82). *Report by the Director of the Naval Forces [Capt. W. R. Creswell] on a Visit to England in 1906.*

II (1906), 165 (62). *Report of the Committee of Imperial Defence Upon a General Scheme of Defence for Australia.*

II (1906), 83 (98). *Agreement—Naval—Correspondence 28 May 1905 to 23 May 1906.*

II (1906), 45 (44). *Report of the Director of the Naval Forces on the Naval Defence of the Commonwealth of Australia for the Year 1905.*

II (1906), 117 (77). *Military Forces of the Commonwealth, Maj.-Gen. H. Finn, Inspector General, Report* (Sept. 1, 1906).

II (1908), 363 (35). *Articles on the Defence of Australia by Col. H. Foster, Director of Military Studies, Sydney University, Together with Remarks Thereupon by Capt. W. R. Creswell, Naval Director.*

II (1910), 83 (8). Lord Kitchener. *Memorandum on the Defence of Australia.*

II (1911), 87 (7). Adm. Sir Reginald Henderson. *Recommendations* (March 1, 1911).

II (1914), 205 (1). *Memorandum by the Minister of Defence [G. Pearce] Dated 13 April 1914, Together with the Speech of the First Lord of the Admiralty as Reported in Australia.*

V (1914–17), 1167 (231). *The War: Australian Contingents: Correspondence Concerning the Undertaking by the Commonwealth Government to Bear the Whole Cost.*

Australia, New South Wales. *Parliamentary Papers, 1877–78,* III, 295, Sir Hercules Robinson to Carnarvon, Telegram, July 23, 1877.

————, New South Wales, [Secretary's Office]. [Sir William Denison]. *Despatch 14 Aug. 1856 on Military Expenditure in New South Wales. Reply of the Secretary of State for the Colonies [Lord Stanley] 11 March 1858.*

————, Queensland. [Parliamentary Papers]. *Naval Defence of Australasian Colonies, 1891.*

————, [South Australia]. Parliamentary Papers 145 (1889). *Remarks by the Colonial Defence Committee on Major-General Edwards' Report* (May 16, 1890).

————, South Australia. *Parliamentary Papers* 118/1889, 118A/1889 (also Victoria, *Parliamentary Papers* 139/1889). *Report of Major-General Bevan Edwards on the Military Forces of Victoria with a Memorandum Containing Proposals for the Re-organization of the Australian Forces.*

————, Victoria. *Report of Select Committee on National Defences,* July 1865 (A.W.M.).

————, [Victoria]. *Report of Mr. Verdon's Proceedings as the Delegate of Victoria to H. M. Govt. Upon the Subject of the Colonial Defences* (Melbourne, 1867). In Victoria, Department of Defence, *Printed Papers, 1862–1901*, I, No. 3 (Australian Defence Department Library).

————, Victoria. *Votes and Proceedings of the Legislative Assembly, Session 1885.* Melbourne: John Ferres, 1886.

————, Victoria. *Parliamentary Papers*, IV, 605–628, 57/1889. *Correspondence Relating to the Inspection of Colonial Forces by an Imperial General Officer, 1887–1889.*

————, Victoria. *Parliamentary Papers*, IV, 965–974, 139/1889. *Report of Major-General Bevan Edwards on the Military Forces and Defences of Victoria with a Memorandum Concerning Proposals for the Re-organization of the Australian Forces* (found in A.W.M., South Australia, Parliamentary Papers 48/1889, 118A/1889, 145/1889).

[Canada, Province of], [Legislative Assembly]. *Journals of the Legislative Assembly of Canada.*

————, [Legislative Assembly]. *Papers Relating to the Conferences Which Have Taken Place Between Her Majesty's Government and a Deputation from the Executive Council of Canada Appointed to Confer with Her Majesty's Government on the Subject of the Defence of the Province.* Ottawa: n.p., 1865.

————, [Legislative Assembly]. *Public General Orders* (Aug. 16, 1855).

————, [Department of Militia]. Colonel De Rottenburg. *Report on the State of the Militia of the Province [of Canada] 8 Jan., 1857, Appendix No. 3 to the Fifteenth Volume of the Journals of the Legislative Assembly of the Province of Canada.* Toronto: Queen's Printer, 1857.

Canada, Dominion, Department of Militia and Defence.

Regulations and Orders for the Canadian Militia, 1870. Ottawa: Queen's Printer, 1870.

Committee on the Defence of Canada. *The Defences of Canada* (Jan. 1, 1886). Ottawa: Maclean, Robec, 1886.

Defence Committee Report [Leach Committee]. 2 vols. (1898).

Supplementary Report: Organization, Equipment, Despatch, and Service of the Canadian Contingents During the War in

South Africa, 1899–1900. Ottawa: King's Printer, 1901.

General Sir Ian Hamilton. *Report on the Military Institutions of Canada.* Ottawa: King's Printer, 1913.

Colonel A. F. Duguid. *Official History of the Canadian Forces in the Great War, 1914–1919,* Vol. I (2 parts). Ottawa: King's Printer, 1938.

————, Parliament. *Commons Debates.*

————, Parliament. *Sessional Papers.*

Reports of the Department of Militia and Defence.

IV, *1871,* Vol. 5 (146). *Returns to Addresses of the Senate and House of Commons Relative to the Withdrawal of the Troops from the Dominion and in the Defence of the Country and Honourable Mr. Campbell's Report.*

XXXIV, *1900,* Vol. 13 (20). *Correspondence Relating to the Despatch of Colonial Contingents to South Africa.*

XXXIV, *1900.* Vol. 13 (20a). *Supplementary Correspondence Respecting the Despatch of Colonial Military Contingents to South Africa.*

XXXVII, *1903,* Vol. 13 (35a). Department of Militia and Defence. *Further Supplementary Report: Organization, Equipment, Despatch, and Service of the Canadian Contingents During the War in South Africa, 1899–1902.*

XLV, *1911,* Vol. 21 (35a). *Report by General Sir John French . . . Inspector General of the Imperial Forces Upon His Inspection of the Canadian Military Forces.*

XLV, *1911,* Vol. 21 (35b). *Report on the Best Method of Giving Effect to the Recommendations of General Sir John French, G.C.B., G.C.V.O., Regarding the Canadian Militia, by Major General Sir P. H. N. Lake, Inspector General.*

————, Parliament. *Statutes of Canada.*

————, Ministry of Overseas Forces. *Report of the Ministry, Overseas Military Forces of Canada, 1918.* London: Ministry of Overseas Forces of Canada [1919].

Great Britain, Admiralty. Confidential Papers.

"Australian Federal Defence" (Feb. 12, 1896).

R. D. Awdrey. "Local Defence and Protection of Floating Trade on Waters of the Australian Colonies" (Sept. 9, 1885).

H. T. Holland. "Proposed Increase of Australasian Squadron: Remarks on Discussion at the Colonial Office, 5 April 1887" (April 23, 1887).

A. Cooper Key. "Status of Colonial Ships of War" (Feb. 27, 1884).

A. Cooper Key. "The Naval Defence of Our Colonies" (Oct. 28, 1884).

Evan Mcgregor to Undersecretary for Colonies (May 4, 1885).

"The Naval Forces of the Colony of Victoria and the General Question of the Status of Colonial Ships of War" (1884) (Admiralty Library, p. 627).

G. Tryon. "With Reference to Colonial Vessels of War" (Nov. 28, 1884).

————, Colonial Office.

Report of the Commissioners Appointed to Consider the Defences of Canada, 1862. London: n.p., 1862.

Lt. Col. W. F. D. Jervois. *Report on the Defence of Canada . . . February 1864.* London: n.p., 1864.

Lt. Col. W. F. D. Jervois. *Report on the Defence of Canada, 10 November 1864.* London: n.p., 1865.

Miscellaneous No. 111, Confidential, Report of a Conference Between the Right Hon. Joseph Chamberlain and the Premiers of the Self-Governing Colonies of the Empire . . . , June and July, 1897 (Sept., 1897).

Miscellaneous No. 144, Confidential, Colonial Conference, 1902, Conference Between the Secretary of State for the Colonies, and the Premiers of the Self-Governing Colonies, Minutes of Proceedings and Papers laid before the Conference (Oct., 1902).

————, Parliament. *Hansard.*

————, *Parliamentary Papers.*

1834, VI, 1–575 (570). *Report from Select Committee on the Colonial Military Expenditure, 1834.*

1835, VI, 1–475 (473). *Report from Select Committee on Colonial Military Expenditure, 1835.*

1851, XXXVI, 237–372 (1334). *Canada Correspondence Relating to the Civil List and Military Expenditures. . . .*

1852, XXX, 361–697 (1515). *Reports of the Committee Approved by the Treasury Board to Inquire into the Naval, Ordnance, and Commissariat Establishments in the Colonies; with Treasury Minutes and Correspondence Relating Thereto.*

1860, XLI, 573–591 (282). *Report of the Committee on the Expense of Military Defences in the Colonies.*

1861, XIII, 69 (423). *Report from the Select Committee Appointed on Colonial Military Expenditures, to Enquire and Report Whether Any Alterations May Be Advantageously Adopted. . . .*

1884–1885, LII, 569–669 (C. 4324, C. 4437, C. 4494). *Correspondence Regarding Offers by the Colonies of Troops for Service in the Soudan; and Letters of Lord Wolseley on the Service of the Canadian Voyageurs in the Nile Expedition.*

1887, LVI, 892–893 (C. 5901–1). *Proceedings of the Colonial Conferences, 1887, II: Papers Laid Before the Conference.*

1890, XLIII, 175–191 (129). [War Office]. *Copy of Correspondence Between the Secretary of State and the Colonial Office with Regard to the Employment of Major-General Downes.*

1897, LIX, 613–649 (C. 8596). *Proceedings of a Conference Between the Secretary of State for the Colonies and the Premiers of the Self-Governing Colonies . . . 1897.*

1904, XL, 1–870, XLII, 729, XLII, 1–448 (Cd. 1789, Cd. 1790, Cd. 1791, Cd. 1792). *Report of His Majesty's Commissioners Appointed to Inquire into the Military Preparations and Other Matters Connected with the War in South Africa; Minutes of Evidence. . . ; Appendices. . . .*

1904, VIII, 101, (Cd. 1932). *Report of the Committee on the War Office Organization (Reconstitution).*

1904, LXIX, III, (Cd. 2200). *Treasury Minute Dated 4th May 1904 as to Secretariat [of the Committee 'of Imperial Defence].*

1907, LV (Cd. 3404, Cd. 3406, Cd. 3523, Cd. 3524). *Published Proceedings and Précis of the Colonial Conference 15th to 26th April 1907. Published Proceedings and Précis of the Colonial Conference 30th April to 14th May 1907. Minutes of Proceedings of the Colonial Conference, 1907. Papers Laid Before the Colonial Conference, 1907.*

1908, LXXI, 149–208 (Cd. 4325). *Correspondence Relating to the Defence of Australia and New Zealand.*

1909, LI, 627 (Cd. 4475). *Imperial Conference: Correspondence Relating to the Proposed Formation of an Imperial General Staff.*

1909, LIX, 335 (Cd. 4948). *Correspondence and Papers Relating to a Conference with Representatives of the Self-Governing Dominions on the Naval and Military Defence of the Empire.*

1911, LIV (Cd. 5913, Cd. 5741, Cd. 5745, Cd. 57461–1; Cd. 57461–2). *Imperial Conferences, 1911 Correspondence . . . Précis . . . Minutes . . . , Papers Laid Before the Conference.*

1912–1913, LX, 513 (Cd. 5650). *Despatch from the Secretary of State for the Colonies as to the Representation of the Self-Governing Colonies on the Committee of Imperial Defence.*

1914, LX, 637 (Cd. 7347). *Correspondence Relating to Representation of the Self-Governing Dominions on the Committee of Imperial Defence and to a Proposed Naval Conference.*

————, War Office.

J. F. Burgoyne. "Memorandum on Defences for the Foreign Possessions of Great Britain, 28th November, 1856." In *Collected Papers and Memoranda on Foreign Defences, 1856–59.* London: n.p., 1859.

"Memorandum by Sir John Burgoyne on the Defence of Canada" (Feb. 15, 1862). War Office Papers, A 0165.

Duke of Cambridge (Chairman). *Special Committee on Colonial Defence, 1863.* Confidential Papers, 0172.

[Earl of Carnarvon]. *Royal Commission to Enquire into the Defence of British Possessions and Provinces Abroad.* 3 vols. London: War Office, 1880–1883.

War Office List and Administrative Directory. London: H.M.S.O., 1909.

Manual of Military Law. London: War Office, 1914.

Allocation of Rooms with List of Officials (Nov. 30, 1914). *Allocation of Rooms with List of Officials* (March 31, 1915).

New Zealand, General Assembly, *Parliamentary Debates.*

————, General Assembly, House of Representatives, *Journals and Appendix A.*

Newspapers

Advertiser (Adelaide) March 28, 31, April 3, 1902.

Age (Melbourne), Nov. 27, 1886.

Argus (Melbourne), Oct. 30, 1913.

Daily Witness (Montreal), Feb. 12, 1884.

Globe (Toronto), Feb. 18, 1884, Dec. 4, 1896.

[*Canadian*] *Military Gazette* (Ottawa), Jan. 5, 1898, Oct. 3, 1899.

Sydney Morning Herald, Feb. 11, 12, 1885.

Times (London), April 5, 1884, Oct. 17, 1905, May 24, 1909, April 25, 1911, Feb. 20, April 13, April 28, 1914, Feb. 4, 1916.

Vancouver Province, March 18, 1902.

Westminster Gazette, Dec. 9, 1912.

Documentary Collections

Benson, Arthur C., and Viscount Esher (eds.). *The Letters of Queen Victoria: A Selection from Her Majesty's Correspondence Between the Years 1837 and 1861.* 3 vols. London: John Murray, 1907.

Blake, Robert (ed.). *The Private Papers of Douglas Haig, 1914–1919.* London: Eyre and Spottiswoode, 1952.

Brett, Maurice V. (ed.). *Journals and Letters of Reginald Brett, Viscount Esher.* 4 vols. London: Nicholson & Watson, 1934–1938.

Chisholm, Joseph A. (ed.). *The Speeches and Public Letters of Joseph Howe.* 2 vols. Halifax: The Chronicle Publishing Co., 1909.

Clarke, Lt. Col. Sir George Sydenham (ed.). *The Defence of the Empire: A Selection from the Letters and Speeches of Henry*

Howard Molyneux Herbert, Fourth Earl of Carnarvon. London: John Murray, 1897.

de Kiewiet, C. W., and F. H. Underhill (eds.). *The Dufferin-Carnarvon Correspondence, 1874–1878.* Toronto: Champlain Society, 1955.

Douglas, Sir George, Bart., and Sir George Dalhousie Ramsay (eds.). *The Panmure Papers: Being a Selection from the Correspondence of Fox Maule, Second Baron Panmure, Afterwards Eleventh Earl of Dalhousie.* 2 vols. London: Hodder & Stoughton, 1908.

[Duguid, Col. A. Fortescue]. *Official History of the Canadian Forces, in the Great War, 1914–1919: General Series, Vol. I, August 1914–September 1915* [Pt. 2.] *Chronology, Appendices and Maps.* Ottawa: King's Printer, 1938.

Fieldhouse, David (ed.). "British Colonial Policy and New Zealand, 1871–1902." [MS Collection of Unpublished Documents], Canterbury University College, 1956.

Fitzgerald, James Edward (ed.). *A Selection from the Writings and Speeches of John Robert Godley.* Christchurch: Press Office, 1863.

Gladstone, William E. "Confidential Memorandum on the Defence of Canada," July 12, 1864, printed in Paul Knaplund, *Gladstone and Britain's Imperial Policy.* New York: Macmillan, 1927, pp. 228–242.

Kemp, Lt. Commander P. K. *The Papers of Admiral Sir John Fisher,* Vol. I. London: Navy Records Society, 1960.

Marder, Arthur J. *Fear God and Dread Nought: The Correspondence of Admiral of the Fleet Lord Fisher of Kilverstone.* 2 vols. London: Cape, 1952–1956.

Ollivier, Maurice (ed.). *The Colonial and Imperial Conferences from 1887 to 1937.* 3 vols. Ottawa: Queen's Printer, 1954.

Pope, Sir Joseph (ed.). *Correspondence of Sir John Macdonald.* Oxford: Milford, n.d.

Preston, Richard A. *Kingston Before the War of 1812: A Collection of Documents.* . . . Toronto: Champlain Society, 1959.

Skelton, Oscar D. *Life and Letters of Sir Wilfrid Laurier.* 2 vols. Oxford: Oxford University Press, 1922.

Stacey, Charles P. (ed.). *Records of the Nile Voyageurs, 1884–85: The*

Canadian Voyageur Contingent in the Gordon Relief Expedition. Toronto: Champlain Society, 1959.

Studholme, Lt. Col. John. *Record of Personal Services During the War of Officers, Nurses, and First Class Warrant Officers; and Other Facts relating to the N.Z.E.F.: Unofficial but Based on Official Records.* Wellington: Government Printer, 1928.

Contemporary Works

Books

Allen, John A. *A Naval Policy for New Zealand.* Dunedin: Otago Daily Times and Witness, 1912.

Bagehot, Walter. *Count Your Enemies and Economize Your Expenditures.* London: James Ridgway, 1862.

Bignold, H. B. *The Burden of Empire, by an Australian.* [Melbourne]: Imperial Federation Defence League, 1902.

Brassey, Thomas, Lord. *A Colonial Volunteer Force. . . .* London: Longmans, Green, 1878.

Cartwright, Sir Richard John. *Remarks on the Militia of Canada.* Kingston: Daily News Office, 1864.

Clarke, Lt. Col. Sir George S. *Imperial Defence.* London: Imperial Press, 1897.

———— and James R. Thursfield. *The Navy and the Nation, or Naval Warfare and Imperial Defence.* London: John Murray, 1897.

Colomb, John C. R. *The Defence of Great and Greater Britain.* London: Edward Stanford, 1880.

————. *The Protection of Our Commerce and Distribution of Our War Forces Considered.* London: Harrison, 1867.

Cottrell, Lt. Col. R. F. *Imperial Defence After the War.* London: Hugh Rees, 1919.

Dilke, Sir Charles W., and Spenser Wilkinson. *Imperial Defences.* London: Macmillan, 1892.

D'Orsonnens, L. G. D'Odet. *Considérations sur l'Organisation Militaire de la Confédération Canadienne.* Montreal: Duvernay et Dansereau, 1874.

Fletcher, Col. Henry Charles. *Memorandum on the Militia System of Canada.* [Ottawa?]: n.d., n.p., 1873.

Foster, Col. Hubert, R. E. *The Defence of the Empire in Australia.* Melbourne: Rankine, Dobbie & Co., 1908.

―――. *War and the Empire: The Principles of Imperial Defence.* London: Wilkins & Norgate, 1914.

Foxton, J. F. G. *The Evolution and Development of an Australian Naval Policy.* [Brisbane?]: United Service Institute, Queensland, Sept. 3, 1910.

Goodenough, Lt. Gen. W. H., and Lt. Col. J. C. Dalton. *The Army Book for the British Empire: A Record of the Development and Present Composition of the Military Forces and Their Duties in Peace and War.* London: H.M.S.O., 1893.

Grix, Julian J. D. (pseud.). [Cpl. D. Batley, N.Z.A.V.]. *The Defence of New Zealand.* Wellington: Naval and Military Institute, Oct., 1891.

Jebb, Richard. *The Britannic Question.* London: Longmans, Green, 1913.

―――. *The Imperial Conference: A History and Study.* 2 vols. London: Longmans, Green, 1911.

―――. *Studies in Colonial Nationalism.* London: E. A. Arnold, 1905.

Jervois, Maj. Gen. Sir William F. D. *The Defence of Great Britain and Her Dependencies.* Adelaide: Government Printer, 1880.

―――. *The Defence of New Zealand.* Wellington, 1884.

Kia-Ora [pseud.]. *H.M.S. New Zealand.* N.p.: n.p., n.d. [1919?].

Linton, Charles E. T. Stuart. *The Problem of Empire Government.* London: Longmans, Green, 1912.

Macaulay, Capt. D. T. *An Imperial Military System.* London: William Clowes, n.d.

[MacDougall, Gen. Sir Patrick]. *Forts versus Ships: Also Defence of the Canadian Lakes Containing The Defence of the Canadian Lakes and Its Influence on the General Defence of Canada.* London: James Ridgway, 1862.

McHardy, C. McL. *The British Empire: Suggested Bases for the Apportionment of the Expense and Control of the Sea and Land*

Forces and the Representation of the Self-Governing Colonies in an Imperial Council, Parliament, or Congress. London: P. S. King, 1902.

Morrison, Lt. E. W. B. *With the Guns in South Africa.* Hamilton: Spectator, 1901.

Noake, Maillard. *To the Taxpayers of New Zealand: How We May Save £50,000 a Year by Reorganization of Our Forces.* Wanganui: Herald Co., 1887.

Otter, Lt. Col. William D. *The Guide: A Manual for the Canadian Militia, Infantry, etc.* Toronto: Willing and Williamson, 1880.

Peto, Sir S. Morton. *Observations on the Report of the Defence Commissioners.* London: James Ridgway, 1862.

Salmon, Capt. the Hon. C. Carty. *An Australian Navy: A Necessary Part of Imperial Defence.* Melbourne: Imperial Federation League, 1905.

Scoble, Lt. Col. Thomas C. *The Utilization of Colonial Forces in Imperial Defence.* Toronto: Canadian Military Institute, 1879.

Small, J. Stormont. *Suggestions Relating to the Defence of New Zealand and the Re-organization of the Volunteers.* Auckland: John Henry Field, n.d.

Tulloch, Maj. Gen. Sir Alexander Bruce. *Australia's Share in the Empire and Its Defence.* Melbourne: n.p., 1894.

Articles

Armytage, H. "Federation and Defence," *Young Australia,* IV, No. 7 (July, 1890), 141.

Arnold-Forster, H. O. "The New Council of Defence," *National Review,* XXVI (1895–1896), 50–55.

Aston, Maj. Gen. Sir George G. "Empire Defence from the South African Point of View," in *Staff Duties and Other Subjects.* London: Hugh Rees, 1913, pp. 188–203.

Brassey, Lord Thomas. "Imperial Federation for Naval Defence," *Nineteenth Century,* XXXI (Jan., 1892), 90–100.

Carman, Albert R. "Canada and the Navy: A Canadian View," *The Nineteenth Century and After,* LXXI (May, 1912), 821–828.

Clarke, George S. "Australia and the Empire: A Reply to Captain J. Read," *United Service Magazine,* V (1892–1893), 318–323.

Clarke, Sir George S. "Imperial Defence," in Francis P. de Labillière, *Federal Britain: Or Unity and Federation of the Empire.* London: S. Low, Marston & Co., 1894, pp. 125–148.

————. "Imperial Defence," in Clarke and Thursfield, *The Navy and the Nation,* q.v., pp. 12–40.

————. "The Navy and the Colonies," *United Service Magazine* (Nov., 1890); also in Clarke and Thursfield, *The Navy and the Nation,* q.v., pp. 41–50.

Collins, Robert M. "Australian Defence," *United Service Magazine,* V (Aug., 1892), 477–481.

————. "The Colonies and Maritime Defence," *United Service Magazine,* X (Jan., 1895), 329–336.

Colomb, John C. R. "British Defence: Its Popular and Real Aspects," *The New Century Review,* I, No. 4 (April, 1897), 313–320.

————. "The Distribution of Our War Forces," *R.U.S.I Journal,* XIII (1869), 37–74.

————. "Imperial Federation—Naval and Military," *R.U.S.I. Journal,* XXX (1886), 837–872.

————. "Russian Development and Our Naval and Military Position in the North Pacific," *R.U.S.I. Journal,* XXI (1877), 659–707.

————. "Which Way to an Imperial Navy?" *National Review,* XLVII (1906), 684–694.

Cutlack, Frederic M. "Australia and Imperial Defence," *National Review,* LX (1912), 994–1002.

Edwards, Gen. Sir Bevan. "Australasian Defence," *Proceedings of the Royal Colonial Institute,* XXII (1890–1891), 195–224.

Ewart, J. S. "A Revision of War Relations: No Obligation Without Representation," *Kingdom Papers,* No. 9 (Ottawa, 1912), pp. 243–289.

Fletcher, Col. Henry Charles. "A Volunteer Force, British and Colonial, in the Event of War," *R.U.S.I. Journal,* XXI (1877), 631–658.

Gordon, Col. J. M. "The Federal Defence of Australia," *R.U.S.I. Journal,* XLII (1898), 128–158.

Hutton, Maj. Gen. Sir E. T. H. "A Co-operative System for the Defence of the Empire," *Selected Papers of the Canadian Military Institute,* VIII (1896–1897), 97–114; also in *Proceedings of the Royal Colonial Institute,* XIX (1898), 223–258.

————. "Our Comrades of Greater Britain: A Paper Read 24 Nov. 1896," in his *The Defence and Defensive Power of Australia.* Melbourne: Angus & Robertson, 1902, pp. 25–50.

James, Capt. Walter Haweis. "The Necessity for an Army as Well as a Navy for the Maintenance of the Empire," *R.U.S.I. Journal,* XL (1896), 691–718.

Lascelles, A. ff. W. "The Colonies and Imperial Defence: The Question of the Provision of an Imperial Service Army Reserve," *R.U.S.I. Journal,* L, No. 341 (July, 1906), 853–889.

Laurie, Maj. Gen. J. W. "The Protection of Our Naval Base in the North Pacific," *R.U.S.I. Journal,* XXVII (1883), 357–381.

[MacDougall, Gen. Sir Patrick]. "Canada: The Fenian Raid and the Colonial Office," *Blackwood's Edinburgh Magazine,* CVIII (Oct., 1870), 493–508.

Matheson, Sir A. P. "Australia and Naval Defence," *Proceedings of the Royal Colonial Institute,* XXXIX (March 10, 1903), 194–246.

————. "The Military System of the Future in the British Empire," *R.U.S.I. Journal,* LI (1907), 1067–1075, 1183–1189.

Morrison, R. H. "Lessons to Be Derived from the Expedition to South Africa in Regard to the Best Organization of the Land Forces of the Empire," *R.U.S.I. Journal,* XLV (July, 1901), 796–834.

Murray, S. L. "Our Food Supply in Time of War, and Imperial Defence," *R.U.S.I. Journal,* XLV (June, 1901), 656–729.

Otter, Lt. Col. William D. "The Administrative System of a British Regiment (Infantry) and the Adaptations of the Principles of That System to the Actual Militia of Canada," Canadian Military Institute, *Selected Papers from the Transactions . . . ,* II (1892–1893), 32–46.

Owen, Col. J. F. "The Military Defence Forces of the Colonies," *Proceedings of the Royal Colonial Institute,* XXI (1890), 277–326.

Pollock, Sir Frederick. "Imperial Organization: Canadian Opinion," *Nineteenth Century and After,* LVIII (1905), 909–917.

Read, Capt. J. "Australia and the Empire," *United Service Magazine,* VI (1892–1893), 145–149.

Recluse (pseud.). "Australian Defence: A Reply to Collins," *United Service Magazine,* VI (Oct., 1893), 66–71.

Rose, J. Markham. "Lessons to Be Derived from the Expedition to South Africa in Regard to the Best Organization of the Land Forces of the Empire," *R.U.S.I. Journal,* XLV, No. 279 (May, 1901), 541–593.

Thursfield, James R. "The Higher Policy of Defence," *National Review,* XL (1902–1903), 807–830.

Tulloch, Maj. Gen. Alexander B. "Naval and Military Critics on Australian Defences," *United Service Magazine,* VIII (Feb., 1894), 463–476.

Vogel, Sir Julius. "The Naval Defence of the Empire: The Responsibility of the Colonies," *United Service Magazine,* IX (Aug., 1894), 331–342.

Wolseley, Garnet. "England as a Military Power in 1854 and 1878," *Nineteenth Century,* XXII (1878), 433–456.

X (pseud.). "The Committee on Imperial Defence," *United Empire,* III (1912), 727–740.

Unpublished Lectures

José, Arthur W. "The Empire that Found Itself," R.U.S.I. Library Pamphlets 10/21/8, 1901.

Owen, John F. "The Military Forces of Our Colonies," R.U.S.I. Pamphlets 16/214/60, 1900.

Autobiographical Works

Aston, Maj. Gen. Sir George G. *Memories of a Marine: An Amphibiography.* London: John Murray, 1919.

Baker-Carr, Christopher D. B. S., *From Chauffeur to Brigadier.* London: Benn, 1930.

[Clarke, Sir George S.] Lord Sydenham of Combe. *My Working Life.* London: n.p., 1927.

Denison, George T. *Soldiering in Canada: Recollections and Experiences.* Toronto: Macmillan, 1900.

————. *The Struggle for Imperial Unity: Recollections and Experiences.* London: Macmillan, 1909.

Dundonald, Douglas D. M. B. H. Cochrane, Earl of. *My Army Life.* London: Arnold, 1926.

Fisher, John A. *Memories.* London: Hodder & Stoughton, 1919.

[Haldane, R. B.] *Richard Burton Haldane: An Autobiography.* London: Hodder & Stoughton, 1929.

Hankey, Lt. Col. Sir Maurice P. A. *Government Control in War: Lee Knowles Lecture.* Cambridge: Cambridge University Press, 1945.

————. "Origin and Development of the Committee of Imperial Defence," *Army Quarterly,* XIV (1927), 254–273.

————. *The Supreme Command, 1914–1918.* London: Allen and Unwin, 1961.

Hughes, William M. *Policies and Potentates.* Sydney: Angus & Robertson, 1950.

————. *The Splendid Adventure: Or Review of Empire Relations Within and Without the Commonwealth of Britannic Nations.* Toronto: Doubleday, 1929.

Lloyd George, David. *War Memoirs. . . .* 6 vols. Boston: Little, Brown, 1934–1937.

Lyttelton, Sir Neville Gerald. *Eighty Years: Soldiering, Politics, Games.* London: Hodder & Stoughton, 1927.

McHaig, W. H. *From Quebec to Pretoria with the Royal Canadian Regiment.* Toronto: William Briggs, 1902.

Robertson, Field Marshal Sir William Robert. *From Private to Field Marshal.* London: Constable, 1921.

————. *Soldiers and Statesmen, 1914–1918.* 2 vols. London: Cassell, 1926.

Strange, Thomas Bland. *Gunner Jingo's Jubilee.* London: Remington, 1893.

Wolseley, Field Marshal Garnet, Viscount. *The Story of a Soldier's Life.* 2 vols. London: Scribners, 1904.

Secondary Sources

Books

Allen, Harry C. *Great Britain and the United States: A History of Anglo-American Relations, 1783–1952.* London: Odhams, 1954.

Allen, Sir James. *New Zealand and Naval Defence.* Dunedin: n.p., 1929.

Amery, Julian. *Life of Joseph Chamberlain,* Vol. IV. London: Macmillan, 1951.

Bartlett, C. J. *Great Britain and Sea Power 1815–1853.* Oxford: Clarendon Press, 1963.

Bean, Charles E. W. *Anzac to Amiens: A Shorter History of the Australian Fighting Services in the First World War.* Canberra: A.W.M., 1952.

————. *The Official History of Australia in the War of 1914–18,* I, II: *The Story of Anzac.* Sydney: Angus & Robertson, 1921–1924.

————. *The Official History of Australia in the War of 1914–18,* III, IV, V: *The Australian Imperial Force in France . . . 1918.* Sydney: Angus & Robertson, 1929–1937.

————. *Two Men I Knew, Bridges . . . and White.* Sydney: Angus & Robertson, 1957.

Beer, George Louis. *British Colonial Policy, 1754–1765.* New York: Macmillan, 1922.

————. *The Old Colonial System, 1660–1754,* Pt. I. *The Establishment of the System, 1660–1688.* 2 vols. New York: Peter Smith, 1933.

Biddulph, Sir Robert. *Lord Cardwell at the War Office.* London: John Murray, 1904.

Bourne, Ruth. *Queen Anne's Navy in the West Indies.* New Haven: Yale University Press, 1939.

Boyd, John. *Sir George Etienne Cartier: His Life and Times: A Political History of Canada from 1814–1873.* Toronto: Macmillan, 1914.

Brogden, Stanley. *The Sudan Contingent*. Melbourne: Hawthorne, 1943.

Brown, R. Craig. *Canada's National Policy, 1883–1900*. Princeton: Princeton University Press, 1964.

Buchan, John. *Lord Minto*. London: Nelson, 1924.

Buckingham, William and George W. Ross. *The Honourable Alexander Mackenzie: His Life and Times*. Toronto: Rose, 1892.

Burdon, Randal Matthews. *King Dick: A Biography of Richard John Seddon*. Christchurch, N. Z.: Whitcombe and Tombs, 1955.

Burt, Alfred LeRoy. *Imperial Architects: Being an Account of the Proposals in the Direction of a Closer Imperial Union. Made Previous to the Opening of the First Colonial Conference of 1887*. Oxford: Blackwell, 1913.

Callwell, Maj. Gen. Sir C. E. *Field-Marshal Sir Henry Wilson, Bart., G.C.B., His Life and Diaries*. 2 vols. London: Cassell, 1927.

Careless, James Maurice. *Brown of the Globe*, II, *Statesman of Confederation, 1860–1880*. Toronto: Macmillan, 1963.

Charteris, John. *Field-Marshal Earl Haig*. London: Cassell, 1929.

Churchill, Winston L. S. *World Crisis, 1916–1918*. Vol. III, Pt. 1. London: Thornton Butterworth, 1927.

Corbett, Julian S. *History of the Great War, Naval Operations*. 5 vols. London: Longmans, 1920.

Creighton, Donald G. *John A. Macdonald*. 2 vols. Toronto: Macmillan, 1952–1955.

Currie, J. A. *The Red Watch: With the First Canadian Division in Flanders*. Toronto: McClellan, 1916.

Cutlack, Frederic M. *Breaker Morant: A Horseman Who Made History*. Sydney: Ure Smith, 1962.

Dafoe, John W. *Laurier: A Study in Canadian Politics*. Toronto: Allen, 1922.

D'Egville, Howard. *Imperial Defence and Closer Union: A Short Record of the Life-Work of the Late Sir John Colomb. . . .* London: King, 1913.

Dugdale, Blanche E. C. *Arthur James Balfour*. 2 vols. New York: Putnams, 1937.

Duguid, Colonel A. Fortescue. *Official History of the Canadian Forces in the Great War, 1914–1919, General Series*, Vol. I, . . . *August 1914–September 1915* [Pt. 1]. Ottawa: King's Printer, 1938.

Dunlop, Col. John K. *The Development of the British Army, 1899–1914*. London: Methuen, 1938.

Edmonds, Brig. Gen. James E. *History of the Great War . . . : Military Operations, France-Belgium, 1918*. 2 vols. London: Macmillan, 1922–1925.

Ehrman, John. *Cabinet Government and War, 1890–1940*. Cambridge: Cambridge University Press, 1958.

Elliott, William Y. *The New British Empire*. New York: McGraw-Hill, 1932.

Ensor, Robert C. K. *England 1870–1914*. Oxford: Clarendon Press, [1936].

Evans, W. Sanford. *The Canadian Contingents and Canadian Imperialism: A Story and a Study*. Toronto: Publishers' Syndicate, Ltd., 1901.

Farr, David M. L. *The Colonial Office and Canada, 1867–1887*. Toronto: University of Toronto Press, 1955.

Ferraby, H. C. *The Imperial British Navy: How the Colonies Began to Think Imperially Upon the Future of the Navy*. London: Jenkins, 1918.

Fortescue, Sir John William. *A History of the British Army*. 13 vols. in 14. London: Macmillan, 1902–1930.

Gibbs, Norman H. *The Origins of Imperial Defence*. Oxford: Clarendon Press, 1955.

Glover, Richard. *Peninsular Preparation: The Reform of the British Army, 1795–1809*. Cambridge: Cambridge University Press, 1963.

Gordon, Donald C. *The Dominion Partnership in Imperial Defence, 1870–1914*. Baltimore: Johns Hopkins University Press, 1965.

Graham, Gerald S. *Empire of the North Atlantic: The Maritime Struggle for North America*. Toronto: University of Toronto Press, 1958.

Grant, Ruth F. *The Canadian Atlantic Fishery*. Toronto: Ryerson, 1934.

Hall, David O. W. *The New Zealanders in South Africa, 1899–1902.* Wellington: New Zealand Department of Internal Affairs, War History Branch, 1949.

Hall, Henry L. *Australia and England: A Study in Imperial Relations.* London: Longmans, 1934.

Hancock, William Keith. *Survey of British Commonwealth Affairs,* I: *Problems of Nationality, 1918–1936.* London, etc.; Oxford University Press, 1937.

Hankey, Lt. Col. Sir Maurice P. A. *Diplomacy by Conference: Studies in Public Affairs, 1920–1946.* London: Ernest Benn, 1946.

Harlow, Vincent T. *The Founding of the Second British Empire, 1763–1793,* Vol. I. London: Longmans, 1952.

Harrop, Angus John. *England and the Maori Wars.* London: New Zealand News, 1937.

_____. *New Zealand After Five Wars.* London: Jarrolds, n.d.

Harvey, Heather J. *Consultation and Co-operation in the Commonwealth.* London: Royal Institute of International Affairs, 1952.

Hewins, W. A. S. *The Apologies of an Imperialist: Forty Years of Empire Policy.* 2 vols. London: Constable, 1929.

Hitsman, J. Mackay. *Military Inspection Services in Canada, 1855–1950.* Ottawa: Department of National Defence Inspection Services, 1962.

Huyshe, G. L. *The Red River Expedition.* London: Macmillan, 1871.

Johnson, Franklyn. *Defence by Committee: The British Committee of Imperial Defence, 1885–1959.* London: Oxford University Press, 1960.

José, Arthur W. *The Royal Australian Navy, 1914–1918: The Official History of Australia in the War of 1914–1918,* Vol. IX. Sydney: Angus & Robertson, 1928.

Keith, Arthur Berriedale. *Dominion Autonomy in Practice.* Oxford: Oxford University Press, 1929.

_____. *The Governments of the British Empire.* New York: Macmillan, 1935.

_____. *Imperial Unity and the Dominions.* Oxford: Clarendon Press, 1916.

————. *Responsible Government in the Dominions*, Vol. II. 2nd ed. Oxford: Clarendon Press, 1932.

————. *The Sovereignty of the British Dominions*. London: Macmillan, 1929.

————. *War Government of the British Dominions*. Oxford: Clarendon Press, 1921.

Kirkpatrick, Frederick A. *Imperial Defence and Trade*. London: Royal Colonial Institute Monographs, 1914.

Knaplund, Paul. *The British Empire 1815–1939*. New York: Harpers, 1941.

Knight, C. R. B. *Historical Records of the Buffs*. London: Medici Society, 1935.

Laffin, John. *Digger: The Story of the Australian Soldier*. London: Cassell, 1959.

Longstaff, Maj. F. V. *Esquimalt Naval Base: A History of Its Works and Its Defences*. Victoria: Victoria Book & Stationery, 1941.

Lucas, Sir Charles P. (ed.). *The Empire at War*. 5 vols. London: Royal Colonial Institute, 1921–1926.

Lyttelton, Edith. *Alfred Lyttelton: An Account of His Life*. London: Longmans, 1917.

Macandie, G. L. *The Genesis of the Royal Australian Navy*. Sydney: Government Printer, 1949.

MacNutt, W. Stewart. *Days of Lorne: From the Private Papers of the Marquis of Lorne 1878–1883 in the Possession of the Duke of Argyll at Inverary Castle, Scotland*. Frederickton N.B.: Brunswick Press, 1955.

Manning, Helen Taft. *British Colonial Government After the American Revolution, 1782–1820*. New Haven: Yale University Press, 1933.

Marder, Arthur T. *The Anatomy of British Sea Power: A History of British Naval Policy in the Pre-Dreadnought Era, 1880–1905*. New York: Knopf, 1940.

————. *From the Dreadnought to Scapa Flow: The Royal Navy in the Fisher Era, 1904–1919*. London: Oxford University Press, 1961.

Murdoch, Walter. *Alfred Deakin*. London: Constable, 1923.

Neuendorff, Gwen. *Studies in the Evolution of Dominion Status: The*

Governor General of Canada and the Development of Canadian Nationalism. London: Allen and Unwin, 1942.

Nicholson, Col. G. W. L. *Official History of the Canadian Army in the First World War: Canadian Expeditionary Force, 1914–1919*. Ottawa: Queen's Printer, 1962.

Palmer, Gerald E. H. *Consultation and Co-operation in the British Commonwealth*. London: Royal Institute of International Affairs, 1934.

Pares, Richard. *War and Trade in the West Indies, 1739–1763*. Oxford: Clarendon Press, 1936.

Pargellis, Stanley McCrory. *Lord Loudoun in North America*. New Haven: Yale University Press, 1933.

Penlington, Norman. *Canada and Imperialism, 1896–1899*. Toronto: University of Toronto Press, 1965.

Rose, J. Holland, *et al.* (eds.). *Cambridge History of the British Empire*, II: *The Empire 1783–1870*; III: *The Empire-Commonwealth 1870–1909*. Cambridge: Cambridge University Press, 1959.

St. Aubyn, Giles. *The Royal George, 1819–1904: The Life of H.R.H. Prince George, Duke of Cambridge*. London: Constable, 1963.

Schuyler, Robert Livingston. *Parliament and the British Empire: Some Constitutional Controversies Concerning Imperial Legislative Jurisdiction*. New York: Columbia University Press, 1929.

Scott, Ernest. *Official History of Australia in the War of 1914–1918*, IX: *Australia During the War*. Sydney: Angus & Robertson, 1936.

Silburn, F. A. B. *The Colonies and Imperial Defence*. London: Longmans, 1909.

Skelton, Oscar D. *The Day of Sir Wilfrid Laurier: A Chronicle of Our Own Times*. Toronto: Glasgow, Brook, 1920.

Sommer, Dudley. *Haldane of Cloan: His Life and Times, 1856–1928*. London: Allen and Unwin, 1960.

Sowden, W. J. *The Roving Editors*. Adelaide: W. K. Thomas, 1919.

Stacey, Charles P. *Canada and the British Army, 1846–1871: A Study in the Practice of Responsible Government*. London: Longmans, Green, 1936. Rev. ed., Toronto: University of Toronto Press, 1963.

————. *The Military Problems of Canada: A Survey of Defence Poli-*

cies and Strategic Conditions Past and Present. Toronto: Ryerson, [1940].

Stanley, George F. G. *The Birth of Western Canada: A History of the Riel Rebellions.* London: Longmans, 1936. Rev. ed., Toronto: University of Toronto Press, 1961.

————. *Canada's Soldiers: The Military History of an Unmilitary People.* Rev. ed., Toronto: Macmillan, 1960.

Stewart, William Downie. *The Right Honourable Sir Francis Bell.* Wellington: Butterworth, 1937.

Stirling, John. *The Colonials in South Africa 1899–1902: Their Record Based on the Despatches.* Edinburgh: Blackwood, 1907.

Thomson, Dale C. *Alexander Mackenzie: Clear Grit.* Toronto: Macmillan, 1960.

Thornton, Archibald. *The Imperial Idea and Its Enemies: A Study in British Power.* London: St. Martins Press, 1959.

Tucker, Gilbert N. *The Naval Service of Canada: Its Official History.* 2 vols. Ottawa: King's Printer, 1952.

Tyler, John E. *The British Army and the Continent, 1904–14.* London: Arnold, 1938.

————. *The Struggle for Imperial Unity, 1868–1895.* London: Longmans, 1938.

Urquhart, Hugh M. *Arthur Currie.* Toronto: Dent, 1950.

Waters, S. D. *The Royal New Zealand Navy.* Wellington: Department of External Affairs, War History Branch, 1956.

Winks, Robin W. *Canada and the United States: The Civil War Years.* Baltimore: Johns Hopkins University Press, 1960.

Witton, Trent G. R. *Scapegoats of Empire.* Melbourne: D. W. Paterson, 1907.

Woodward, Ernest L. *Great Britain and the German Navy.* Oxford: Clarendon Press, 1935.

Worthington, Larry. *Amid the Guns Below: The Story of the Canadian Corps, 1914–1919.* Toronto: McClellan and Stewart, 1965.

Wrottesley, G. *Life and Correspondence of Field Marshal Sir John Burgoyne, Bart.* 2 vols. London: Bentley, 1873.

Young, Kenneth. *Arthur James Balfour: The Happy Life of the Politician, Prime Minister, Statesman, and Philosopher, 1848–1930.* London: Bell, 1963.

Articles

Adams, George Burton. "The Influence of the American Revolution on England's Government of her Colonies," *Annual Report of the American Historical Association*, I (1896), 373–389.

_____. "The Origin and Results of the Imperial Federation Movement in England," *Proceedings of the State Historical Society of Wisconsin* (1899), pp. 93–116.

Allin, C. D. "Colonial Participation in Imperial Wars in Australia," *Queen's Quarterly* (Jan.–March, 1926), pp. 329–343.

Aston, Maj. Gen. Sir G. "The Committee of Imperial Defence: Its Evolution and Prospects," *R.U.S.I. Journal*, LXXXI (Aug., 1926), 456–463.

Bellairs, Carlyon. "The Standard of Strength for Imperial Defence," *R.U.S.I. Journal*, XLVIII, No. 319 (Sept., 1905), 995–1031.

Bennett, Lt. Col. J. Hyde. "In Retrospect," the Canadian Officers Club and Institute, *Selected Papers*, No. 41. Toronto: Military Publishing Company, 1946.

The Bombardier (pseud.). "The Father of the Canadian Artillery," *Canadian Defence Quarterly*, II, No. 1 (Oct., 1924), 5–9.

Bourne, Kenneth. "British Preparations for War with the North, 1861–1862," *English Historical Review*, LXXVI (1961), 600–632.

Clark, Dora Mae. "The Committee of Imperial Defence: Its Evolution and Prospects," *R.U.S.I. Journal*, LXXI (Aug., 1926), 456–463.

_____. "The Impressment of Seamen in the American Colonies," *Essays in Colonial History Presented to Charles McLean Andrews by His Students* (New Haven: Yale University Press, 1931), pp. 198–224.

Crerar, Lt. Col. Harry D. G. "The Development of Closer Relations Between the Military Forces of the Empire," *R.U.S.I. Journal*, LXXI (1926), 441–445.

Cummins, J. F. "General Sir Edward Selby Smyth, K.C.M.G.," *Canadian Defence Quarterly*, V (July, 1928), 403–411.

_____. "General Sir William Otter," *Canadian Defence Quarterly*, III (1925), 25–28.

Fieldhouse, David. "British Imperialism in the Late Eighteenth Century," in Kenneth Robinson and Frederick Madden (eds.), *Essays in Imperial Government Presented to Margery Perham.* Oxford: Blackwell, 1963, pp. 27–46.

Gordon, Donald C. "The Colonial Defence Committee and Imperial Collaboration 1885–1904," *Political Science Quarterly,* LXXVII (Dec., 1962), 526–545.

Graham, Gerald S. "Imperial Finance, Trade, and Communications, 1895–1914," *Cambridge History of the British Empire,* III, 438–489.

————. "The Naval Defence of British North America, 1739–1763," *Transactions of the Royal Historical Society,* 4th Ser., XXX (1948), 95–125.

Grimshaw, Charles. "Australian Nationalism and the Imperial Connection, 1900–1914," *Australian Journal of Politics and History,* III, No. 2 (May, 1958), 165–180.

Hamilton, Colonel C. F. "The Canadian Militia," *Canadian Defence Quarterly,* V (1927), 288–300, 462–473, VI (1928), 36–48, 199–211, 344–353, 474–483, VII (1929), 78–89, 217–222, 383–389, 537–542, VIII (1930–1931), 94–97, 240–247.

————. "Defence, 1812–1912," in Adam Shortt and A. G. Doughty (eds.), *Canada and its Provinces: A History of the Canadian People and Their Institutions . . . ,* VII (Toronto: Glasgow, Brook, 1914), 379–468.

Harlow, Vincent T. "The New Imperial System, 1783–1815," *Cambridge History of the British Empire,* II, 129–187.

Hitsman, J. Mackay. "Military Defenders of Prince Edward Island, 1775–1864," *Annual Report of the Canadian Historical Association,* 1964, pp. 25–36.

————. "Winter Troop Movements to Canada, 1862," *Canadian Historical Review,* XLIII (1962), 127–135.

Knox, B. A. "Colonial Influence on Imperial Policy, 1858–1866: Victoria and the Colonial Naval Defence Act, 1865," *Historical Studies: Australia and New Zealand,* XI (Nov., 1963), 61–79.

Lavarack, Col. J. D. "The Defence of the British Empire with Special Reference to the Far East and Australia," *The Army Quarterly,* XXV (1932), 207–217.

Luvaas, Jay. "General Sir Patrick MacDougall, the American Civil War, and the Defence of Canada," *Annual Report of the Canadian Historical Association,* 1962, pp. 44–54.

MacCallum, Duncan. "The Alleged Russian Plans for the Invasion of Australia, 1864," *Royal Australian Historical Society, Journal and Proceedings,* XLIV (1958), 301–321.

_____. "Defence in the Eighteen Fifties," *Royal Australian Historical Society, Journal and Proceedings,* XLIV (1958), 71–115.

_____. "The Early 'Volunteer' Associations in New South Wales and the Proposals in the First Quarter of the Nineteenth Century," *Royal Australian Historical Society, Journal and Proceedings,* XLVII (1961), 353–367.

_____. "The Early Volunteer Corps—The Origins of the Modern Australian Army," *Arts: The Proceedings of the Sydney University Arts Association,* I, No. 3 (Sept., 1959), 142–166.

Mackintosh, John P. "The Role of the Committee of Imperial Defence Before 1914," *English Historical Review,* LXXVII (July, 1962), 490–503.

MacLean, Guy R. "The Canadian Offer of Troops for Hong Kong," *Canadian Historical Review,* XXXVIII (1958), 275–283.

Madden, A. F. "Changing Attitudes and Widening Responsibilities, 1895–1914," *Cambridge History of the British Empire,* III, 338–405.

Pares, Richard. "The Manning of the Navy in the West Indies, 1702–1763," *Transactions of the Royal Historical Society,* 4th Ser., XX (1937), 31–60.

Pargellis, Stanley McCrory. "The Four Independent Companies of New York," *Essays in Colonial History Presented to Charles McLean Andrews by His Students.* New Haven: Yale University Press, 1931, pp. 96–123.

Penlington, Norman. "General Hutton and the Problem of Military Imperialism in Canada, 1898–1900," *Canadian Historical Review,* XXIV (1943), 156–176.

Penny, B. R. "The Age of Empire: An Australian Episode," *Historical Studies: Australia and New Zealand,* XI (1963–1965), 33–42.

Perry, Warren. "The General Staff System," *Canadian Army Journal,*

III, No. 5 (1949), 13–15, 30–31; No. 6, 27–30; reprinted from the *Australian Army Journal*.

_____. "The Military Life of Major General Sir John Charles Hoad," *Victoria Historical Magazine*, XXIX (Aug., 1959), 169–204.

_____. "Military Reforms of General Sir Edward Hutton in New South Wales, 1893–96," *The Australian Quarterly*, XXVIII, No. 4 (Dec., 1956), 1–11.

_____. "Military Reforms of General Sir Edward Hutton in the Commonwealth of Australia, 1902–04," *Victoria Historical Magazine*, XXIX, No. 1 (Feb., 1959), 1–26.

Preston, Richard A. "The Military Structure of the Old Commonwealth," *International Journal*, XVII (Spring, 1962), 98–121.

_____. "Sir William Keith's Justification of a Stamp Duty in the Colonies," *Canadian Historical Review*, XXIX (June, 1948), 168–182.

_____. "The Transfer of British Military Institutions to Canada in the Nineteenth Century," in William B. Hamilton (ed.). *The Transfer of Institutions*. Durham, N.C.: Duke University Press, 1964, pp. 81–107.

Quigley, Carroll. "The Round Table Groups in Canada, 1908–1938," *Canadian Historical Review*, XLIII (1962), 206, 219.

Richmond, Adm. Sir Herbert. "An Outline of Imperial Defence," *Army Quarterly*, XXIV, No. 2 (July, 1932), 260–279.

Robertson, Maj. H. C. H. "The Empire and Modern War," *Army Quarterly*, XXVI (1933), 246–253.

Rose, J. Holland. "Conflict with Revolutionary France," *Cambridge History of the British Empire*, II, 36–82.

Schurman, Donald M. "Esquimalt; Defence Problem 1865–1887," *British Columbia Historical Quarterly*, XIX (1955), 57–69.

_____. "King George's Sound and Imperial Defence, 1870–1887," *University Studies in Western Australian History* (Oct., 1959), pp. 85–90.

Schuyler, Robert Livingston. "The Recall of the Legions: A Phase in the Decentralization of the British Empire," *American Historical Review*, XXVI (Oct., 1920), 18–36.

Shakow, Zara. "The Defence Committee: A Forerunner of the Committee of Imperial Defence," *Canadian Historical Review*, XXXVI (1955), 36–44.

Shields, R. A. "Australian Opinion and the Defence of the Empire: A Study in Imperial Relations, 1880–1890," *The Australian Journal of Politics and History*, X (1964), 41–53.

Stacey, Charles P. "Canada and the Nile Expedition," *Canadian Historical Review*, XXIII (Dec., 1952), 319–340.

_____. "The Development of the Canadian Army," in *Introduction to Military History*. Ottawa: Queen's Printer, 1955.

_____. "The Fenian Troubles and Canadian Military Development, 1865–1871," *Canadian Defence Quarterly*, XIII (1936).

_____. "Halifax as an International Strategic Factor, 1749–1909," *Annual Report of the Canadian Historical Association*, 1949, pp. 46–56.

_____. "John A. Macdonald on Raising Troops in Canada for Imperial Service, 1885," *Canadian Historical Review*, XXXVIII (March, 1957), 37–40.

_____. "The North-West Campaign, 1885," *Introduction to the Study of Military History for Canadian Students*. Ottawa: Queen's Printer, 1955, pp. 75–85.

_____. "The Withdrawal of the Imperial Garrison from Newfoundland," *Canadian Historical Review*, XVII (1936), 147–158.

_____ and E. Pye. "Canadian Voyageurs in the Sudan, 1884–5," *Canadian Army Journal*, V (Oct., Nov., Dec., 1951), No. 7, 61–73; No. 8, 58–68; No. 9, 16–26.

Stewart, Alice R. "Sir John A. Macdonald and the Imperial Defence Commission of 1879," *Canadian Historical Review*, XXXV (June, 1954), 119–139.

Stone, Major F. G. "The Canadian Militia System and its Applicability to our Own Requirements at Home," *Selected Papers from the Transactions of the Canadian Military Institute* (1900), 98–108.

Strakhovsky, Leonid Ivan. "Russia's Privateering Projects of 1878," *Journal of Modern History*, VII (March, 1935), 22–40.

[Stuart, General K.]. "Another Aspect of Imperial Defence," *Canadian Defence Quarterly*, IX (1932), 448–450.

————. "Canada and Imperial Defence," *Canadian Defence Quarterly*, XII (1934–1935), 40–46, 183–188.

Talman, James R. "A Secret Military Document," *American Historical Review*, XXXVIII (Jan., 1933), 295–300.

Tapp, E. J. "Australian and New Zealand Defence Relations, 1900–1950," *Australian Outlook*, V (Sept., 1951), 165–175.

Tucker, Gilbert. "The Naval Policy of Sir Robert Borden, 1912–1914," *Canadian Historical Review*, XXVIII (1947), 1–30.

Tunstall, W. C. Brian. "Imperial Defence, 1815–1870," *Cambridge History of the British Empire*, II, 807–842.

————. "Imperial Defence, 1870–97," *Cambridge History of the British Empire*, III, 230–253.

————. "Imperial Defence, 1897–1914," *Cambridge History of the British Empire*, III, 563–604.

Tyler, John E. "The Development of the Imperial Conference, 1887–1914," *Cambridge History of the British Empire*, III, 406–437.

Vince, Donald M. A. R. "The Acting Overseas Sub-Militia Council and the Resignation of Sir Sam Hughes," *Canadian Historical Review*, XXXI (1950), 1–24.

————. "Development in the Legal Status of the Canadian Military Forces, 1914–1919, as Related to Dominion Status," *Canadian Journal of Economics and Political Science*, XX (Aug., 1954), 357–370.

Way, Ronald L. "The Topographical Aspect of Canadian Defence 1783–1871," *Canadian Defence Quarterly*, XIV (1937), 275–287.

Dissertations, Theses, and Manuscripts

Cameron, Capt. L. R. "Constitution of the Army and Militia Councils and the Creation of the Imperial and Canadian General Staffs," Canadian Army Historical Section, March, 1958.

Hensley, Gerald C. "The Withdrawal of British Troops from New Zealand, 1864–1870." M.A. thesis, University of Canterbury, 1957.

Hitsman, J. Mackay. "Canadian Naval Policy." M.A. thesis, Queen's University, 1940.

Lissington, Patricia. "New Zealand and Japan: Relations until December 1941." New Zealand War History Section narrative, [1957?].

Mackinnon, C. S. "The Imperial Fortresses in Canada: Halifax and Esquimalt, 1871–1906." 2 vols. Ph.D. thesis, University of Toronto, 1965.

MacLean, Guy R. "The Imperial Federalism Movement in Canada, 1884–1902." Ph.D. dissertation, Duke University, 1958.

Millar, T. B. "The History of the Defence Forces of the Port Phillip District and Colony of Victoria, 1836–1900." M.A. thesis, University of Melbourne, 1957.

Morton, Desmond P. "The General Officer Commanding in Canada." B.A. Honors thesis, Royal Military College, 1960.

Rooney, Meredith J. "Aspects of Imperial Defence: The Relevance of the 1879 Royal Commission on the Defence of British Possessions and Commerce Abroad." B.Ph. thesis, Oxford University, 1963.

Schurman, Donald M. "Imperial Defence, 1868–1887." Ph.D. thesis, Cambridge University, 1955.

Sellars, Gabrielle J. "Edward Cardwell at the Colonial Office, 1864–66: Some Aspects of his Policy and Ideas." B. Litt. thesis, Oxford University, 1958.

Sissons, D. C. "Attitudes to Japan and Defence." M.A. thesis, University of Melbourne, 1961.

Thomson, Ailsa G. "The Bulletin and Australian Nationalism." M.A. thesis, University of Melbourne, 1953.

Index